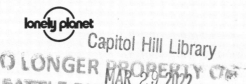

Cambodia

Temples of
Angkor
p137
⊚

⊚
Siem Reap
p103

Northwestern
Cambodia
p233

Eastern Cambodia
p274

✪
Phnom Penh
p48

South Coast
p177

Nick Ray, Greg Bloom, Mark Johanson

PLAN YOUR TRIP

Welcome to Cambodia. . . 4

Cambodia Map 6

Cambodia's Top
Experiences. 8

Need to Know 18

First Time Cambodia . . . 20

What's New 22

Accommodation 24

Month by Month. 26

Itineraries 28

The Great Outdoors. . . . 36

Family Travel 42

Regions at a Glance. . . . 45

TEMPLES OF ANGKOR P137

ANDRE FERREIRA/500PX ©

PHNOM PENH MARKET P89

ALEXANDER MAZURKEVICH/SHUTTERSTOCK ©

ON THE ROAD

PHNOM PENH. 48

Sights. 52

Activities 60

Courses 66

Tours. 67

Festivals & Events 70

Sleeping. 70

Eating. 75

Drinking & Nightlife. 85

Entertainment. 88

Shopping 89

Around Phnom Penh . . . 97

Koh Dach 97

Udong. 98

Tonlé Bati. 99

Phnom Tamao Wildlife
Rescue Centre 100

Phnom Chisor. 101

Kirirom National Park . . . 101

SIEM REAP 103

Sights. 105

Activities 109

Courses 110

Tours. 111

Sleeping. 112

Eating. 117

Drinking & Nightlife. 122

Entertainment. 124

Shopping 125

Around Siem Reap 130

Banteay Srei District 131

Kompong Khleang 134

Prek Toal
Bird Sanctuary 134

Kompong Pluk 135

Me Chrey 135

Floating Village of
Chong Kneas. 135

Ang Trapaeng
Thmor Reserve. 136

TEMPLES OF
ANGKOR 137

Angkor Wat 150

Angkor Thom. 156

Around Angkor Thom. . .161

Small Circuit 161

Big Circuit 165

Roluos Temples. 167

Beyond Angkor 169

Banteay Srei 169

Beng Mealea 170

Phnom Kulen 171

Kbal Spean 172

Banteay Samré. 173

Chau Srei Vibol. 173

Phnom Bok 173

Phnom Krom. 174

Western Baray &
Western Mebon 174

Remote Angkor
Temples 174

Koh Ker 174

SOUTH COAST 177

Koh Kong City. 179

Koh Kong Conservation
Corridor 184

Tatai River
& Waterfall 184

Southern Cardamom
National Park 185

Botum Sakor
National Park 187

Chi Phat. 187

Sihanoukville. 189

Ream National Park. 195

The Southern
Islands 196

Koh Ta Kiev 196

Koh Thmei 197

Koh Rong 197

Koh Rong Sanloem 205

Contents

Koh Sdach
Archipelago 211
Kampot Province 212
Kampot 212
Around Kampot 221
Kep 224
Takeo 230
Around Takeo 231

NORTHWESTERN
CAMBODIA 233
Kompong Chhnang 236
Pursat 237
Kompong Luong 239
**Northern Cardamom
Mountains 240**
**Battambang
Province 241**
Battambang 241
Around Battambang 253
Pailin 254
Poipet 256
Sisophon 258
Banteay Chhmar 258
Anlong Veng 260

**Preah Vihear
Province 262**
Preah Vihear City 262
Prasat Preah Vihear 264
Preah Khan of
Kompong Svay 267
**Kompong Thom
Province 269**
Kompong Thom 269
Around
Kompong Thom 272

EASTERN
CAMBODIA 274
Kompong Cham 276
Kratie 281
Stung Treng 286
Around Stung Treng . . . 289
Preah Rumkel 289
Ratanakiri Province . . . 289
Ban Lung 290
Veun Sai 296
Virachey
National Park 296
Mondulkiri Province . . . 297
Sen Monorom 298

History 308
**Pol Pot & the
Khmer Rouge Trials . . . 325**
People & Culture 328
**The Cambodian
Kitchen 337**
Environment 343

Directory A–Z 350
Transport 359
Health 366
Language 370
Glossary 375
Index 378
Map Legend 383

COVID-19

We have re-checked every business in this book before publication to ensure that it is still open after the COVID-19 outbreak. However, the economic and social impacts of COVID-19 will continue to be felt long after the outbreak has been contained, and many businesses, services and events referenced in this guide may experience ongoing restrictions. Some businesses may be temporarily closed, have changed their opening hours and services, or require bookings; some unfortunately could have closed permanently. We suggest you check with venues before visiting for the latest information.

SPECIAL FEATURES

**Phnom Penh
Image Gallery 58**
**Temples of Angkor
Illustrated Map 144**

Right: Mekong
River, Kratie
(p281)

STEVE BARZE/SHUTTERSTOCK ©

WELCOME TO
Cambodia

I can vividly remember my first trip to Cambodia in 2011. I was lured – as so many others are – by the chance to touch history at the temples of Angkor. Then, I met the Cambodian people, and I think it's their infectious smiles that have kept me coming back. It's also those tangerine sunsets over the Mekong in Kratie, the elephants lumbering across jade green hills in Mondulkiri, that frenetic beat of a night out in Phnom Penh and the hypnotic (though rapidly changing) islands off the South Coast. Come for the temples, sure, but expect the rest of Cambodia to dazzle, too.

By Mark Johanson, Writer
🐦 and 📷 @MarkOnTheMap
For more about our writers, see p384

Cambodia

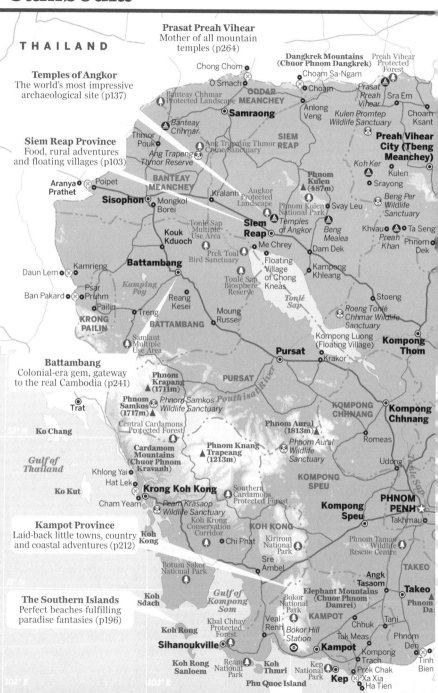

THAILAND

Prasat Preah Vihear
Mother of all mountain
temples (p264)

Temples of Angkor
The world's most impressive
archaeological site (p137)

Siem Reap Province
Food, rural adventures
and floating villages (p103)

Battambang
Colonial-era gem, gateway
to the real Cambodia (p241)

Kampot Province
Laid-back little towns, country
and coastal adventures (p212)

The Southern Islands
Perfect beaches fulfilling
paradise fantasies (p196)

Chong Chom
O Smach
**Dangkrek Mountains
(Chuor Phnom Dangkrek)**
Choam Sa-Ngam
Choam
Preah Vihear
Protected
Forest
Sra Em

Banteay Chhmar
Protected Landscape
**ODDAR
MEANCHEY**
Anlong
Veng
Prasat
Preah
Vihear
Choam
Ksant

Samraong
Banteay
Chhmar
Kulen
Wildlife Sanctuary
Promtep
Sanctuary
**Preah Vihear
City (Tbeng
Meanchey)**

Thmor
Pouk
**SIEM
REAP**
Koh Ker
Kulen

Ang Trapeng
Thmor Reserve
Ang Trapeing Thmor
Crane Sanctuary
**Phnom
Kulen**
▲(487m)
Srayong

**BANTEAY
MEANCHEY**
Kralanh
Angkor
Protected
Landscape
Phnom Kulen
National Park
Svay Leu
Beng Per
Wildlife
Sanctuary

Aranya
Prathet
Poipet

Sisophon
Mongkol
Borei
**Siem
Reap**
Temples
of Angkor
Beng
Mealea
Khvau
Preah
Khan
Ta Seng
Phnom
Dek

Kouk
Kduoch
Tonle Sap
Multiple
Use Area
Me Chrey
Dam Dek

Kamrieng
Prek Toal
Bird Sanctuary
Floating
Village
of Chong
Kneas
Kampong
Khleang

Daun Lem
Battambang
Tonlé Sap
Biosphere
Reserve
*Tonlé
Sap*
Roeng Tonlé
Chhmar Wildlife
Sanctuary

Ban Pakard
Psar
Pruhm
Pailin
*Kamping
Poy*
Reang
Kesei
Moung
Russei

**KRONG
PAILIN**
Treng
BATTAMBANG
Kompong Luong
(Floating Village)
**Kompong
Thom**

Samlaut
Multiple
Use Area
Krakor
Pursat

Trat
**Phnom
Krapang**
▲(1711m)
PURSAT
Pouthisat River

Ko Chang
**Phnom
Samkos**
(1717m)▲
Phnom Samkos
Wildlife Sanctuary
**Phnom
Aural**
(1813m)▲
**KOMPONG
CHHNANG**
**Kompong
Chhnang**

*Gulf of
Thailand*
Central Cardamons
Protected Forest
**Phnom Knang
Trapeang**
▲(1213m)
Phnom Aural
Wildlife
Sanctuary
Romeas

**Cardamom
Mountains
(Chuor Phnom
Kravanh)**
Udong

Khlong Yai
Hat Lek
**KOMPONG
SPEU**

Ko Kut
Krong Koh Kong
Southern
Cardamons
Protected Forest
**PHNOM
PENH**

Cham Yeam
Peam Krasaop
Wildlife Sanctuary
Koh Krong
Conservation
Corridor
**Kompong
Speu**
Takhmau

Koh
Kong
Chi Phat
Kirirom
National
Park
Phnom Tamao
Wildlife
Rescue Centre
TAKEO

Botum Sakor
National Park
Sre
Ambel
Angk
Tasaom
Takeo

Koh
Sdach
*Gulf of
Kompong
Som*
Bokor
National
Park
**Elephant Mountains
(Chuor Phnom
Damrei)**
Phnom
Da

Koh Rong
Kbal Chhay
Protected
Forest
Veal
Renh
Bokor
Hill
Station
KAMPOT
Chhuk
Tani

Sihanoukville
Reaim
National
Park
Koh
Thmri
Tuk Meas
Kampot
Phnom
Den

Koh Rong
Sanloem
Kep
National
Park
Kep
Kompong
Trach
Prek Chak
Xa Xia
Ha Tien
Tinh
Bien

Phu Quoc Island

LAOS

Muang Khong

Anlong Cheuteal ⊗

Siem Pang

Virachey National Park

RATANAKIRI

Voen Sai

PREAH VIHEAR

Stung Treng Ramsar Site

Preah Rumkel ⊗

STUNG TRENG

Ban Lung ⊙

Bokheo

Le Thanh ⊗

Tonlé San

Boeng Yeak Lom

O Yadaw

Thala Boravit ⊗

Tonlé Srepok

Lumphat ⊗

Svay Pak ⊗

Stung Treng

Mondulkiri
Where the wild things are (p297)

Rovieng ⊗

Mekong River

Sen River

Lumphat Wildlife Sanctuary ⊗

KOMPONG THOM

KRATIE

Koh Nhek ⊗

Sambor Prei Kuk ▲

Sambor ⊗

Phnom Prech Wildlife Sanctuary

Sandan ⊗

MONDULKIRI

Mondulkiri Protected Forest

Kratie ⊙

Baray ⊗

Spoe Tbong

Stung Trang ⊗

Sen Monorom ⊙

Nam Lear Wildlife Sanctuary ⊗

Chhlong ⊗

Keo Seima Wildlife Sanctuary ⊗

Skuon ⊗

Kompong Cham

TBONG KHMUM

Snuol ⊗

Trapeang Sre ⊗

Sre Kthum

KOMPONG CHAM

Chup ⊗

Suong ⊗

Trapeang Plong

Memot ⊗

Kratie
Rare dolphins in the Mekong River (p281)

Loc Ninh ⊗

PREY VENG

Xa Mat ⊗

VIETNAM

Prey Veng ⊙

SVAY RIENG

Tay Ninh ⊗

KÂNDAL

Neak Luong ⊗

Ba Phnom ⊗

Phnom Penh
The 'pearl of Asia' is back (p48)

Moc Bai ⊗

Banteay Chakrey

Svay Rieng ⊙

Chiphu ⊗

Bavet ⊗

Kaam Samnor ⊗

Vinh Xuong ⊗

Khanh Binh

Ho Chi Minh City ⊙

Chau Doc ⊗

ELEVATION

	1500m
	1000m
	500m
	250m
	0

SOUTH CHINA SEA

Cambodia's Top Experiences

1 ANCIENT TEMPLES

The ancient Khmers packed the equivalent of all Europe's cathedrals into an area the size of Los Angeles, making the famed temples of Angkor a veritable Disney World for archaeology lovers. Temple-hoppers will find countless more ruins begging to be explored across Cambodia. Channel your inner Lara Croft or Indiana Jones and dive into the fascinating history of one of the world's most illustrious empires. Above: Ta Prohm (p162)

Temples of Angkor

One of the planet's most magnificent sights, the temples of Angkor are even better than the superlatives suggest. Choose from Angkor Wat, the world's largest religious building; Bayon, one of the world's weirdest temples, with its immense stone faces; or Ta Prohm, where nature runs amok. p137

Right: Bayon (p156)

ALEX WILKO/SHUTTERSTOCK ©

NOUN ROTH/SHUTTERSTOCK ©

STEVE BARZE/SHUTTERSTOCK ©

SCENE SNIPER/SHUTTERSTOCK ©

Prasat Preah Vihear

The mother of all mountain temples, Prasat Preah Vihear stands majestically atop the Dangkrek Mountains, forming a border post between Cambodia and Thailand. The foundation stones stretch to the edge of the cliff as it falls precipitously away to the plains below. p264

Above: Prasat Preah Vihear

Banteay Chhmar

Angkor's pre-eminent king, Jayavarman VII, ran riot in this jungle backwater in Northwestern Cambodia, erecting a clutch of temples festooned with his image. Banteay Chhmar and its nine satellite temples boast some of the most intricate bas-reliefs beyond Angkor. p258

Above: Banteay Chhmar

2

SUN, SAND & SEA

Cambodia's up-and-coming southern islands offer your best chance to fulfil those paradise fantasies with swooping hammocks, swaying palms and plenty of sun-kissed solitude. Ever-growing Sihanoukville is your launch pad for most islands, with tranquil white-sand beaches just a quick ferry-ride away. Sleepy Kep (Cambodia's original resort) is a more low-key alternative with a fine array of boutique hotels and seafood restaurants, as well as the backpacker beach of Koh Tonsay (Rabbit Island).

Koh Rong Sanloem

The smaller sibling to Koh Rong, Koh Rong Sanloem is also popular thanks to the cheap lodgings on crescent-shaped Saracen Bay and the legendary Lazy Beach. The mellow island houses tropical hideaway resorts and gentle, shallow bays. p205

Above: Koh Rong Sanloem

Koh Sdach

Koh Sdach is a castaway-cool archipelago just off the southwest tip of Botum Sakor National Park. It's got a handful of authentic restaurants and homestays, plus some vibrant undersea life, but change is on the horizon in the form of new luxury resorts. p211

Top right: Koh Sdach

Koh Rong

Off the coast of Sihanoukville, Koh Rong is the most popular of Cambodia's southern islands. It's home to the backpacker beach of Koh Tuch and its hippie-trippy village. The rest of the island, fringed by silicon sand and clad in dense jungle, is an escape. p197

Above: Koh Rong

3 INTO THE JUNGLE

The endless rice fields and sugar palms that characterise the Cambodian landscape eventually give way to the rolling hills and verdant jungles of the 'wild east' in the little-visited provinces of Mondulkiri and Ratanakiri – both of which house some of the nation's top ecotourism projects. Out west, the Cardamom Mountains rise higher still, offering the kind of dense tropical rainforests where endangered wildlife thrives (at least, for now).

Authentic adventures in Mondulkiri

Wildlife is the big draw to Mondulkiri. Top experiences include the opportunity to 'walk with the herd' at Elephant Valley Project or spot douc langurs and gibbons on a trek through the Keo Seima Wildlife Sanctuary. Add thunderous waterfalls and a jungle zipline to the mix, and you have the perfect ingredients for an authentic adventure. p297

Below: Elephant sanctuary, Mondulkiri (p299)

JM TRAVEL PHOTOGRAPHY/SHUTTERSTOCK ©

DEMAMIEL62/SHUTTERSTOCK ©

TOMAS LESA/SHUTTERSTOCK ©

Red dirt in Ratanakiri

The red dirt roads of Ratanakiri lead to some of Cambodia's wildest nature reserves, including the vast Virachey National Park, home to clouded leopards and sun bears. Closer to the regional hub of Ban Lung you'll find Boeng Yeak Lom, a jungle-clad crater lake that's Cambodia's most inviting natural swimming pool. p289

Above left: Boeng Yeak Lom (p291)

Mountain highs: Koh Kong Conservation Corridor

The Koh Kong Conservation Corridor covers the southern reaches of the fabled Cardamom Mountains, an area of astonishing biodiversity and the jungle-flanked Tatai River, with its eco-adventures and fairy-tale accommodations. p184

Top right: Tatai River (p184)

4

DOWN BY THE RIVER

Cambodia truly bursts to life next to its rivers. The Mighty Mekong may get all the fame and attention as it crashes over from Laos and pours out into Vietnam, but there are plenty of other rivers. The small regional towns and cities that have sprung up alongside them are among the most charming in Cambodia.

Art & charm in Battambang

Unfurling along the banks of the Sangker River, Battambang is one of the country's best-preserved colonial-era towns. Streets of colonial French shop-houses host everything from fair-trade cafes to art galleries. p241.
Below: Colonial architecture in Battambang

ELITE STUDIOS/SHUTTERSTOCK ©

Riverside chill in Kampot

Choose from backpacker hostels, riverside resorts or boutique hotels to take in the French architectural legacy in Kampot, then explore the pretty Kompong Bay River (above) by paddleboard or kayak. p212

Rare dolphins in Kratie

Gateway to the rare freshwater Irrawaddy dolphins, Kratie is a busy crossroads on the overland route with some of the country's best Mekong sunsets. p281
Right: Dolphin-spotting (p284) near Kratie

5 TREASURE HUNTING

PACK-SHOT/SHUTTERSTOCK ©

BTW IMAGES/SHUTTERSTOCK ©

STEVE BARZE/SHUTTERSTOCK ©

Be it fine silks, handwoven cotton, vibrant textiles, miniature statues, shiny lacquerware or intricate carvings; name the craft, and you can probably find it in one of Cambodia's regional markets or more upscale big city boutiques. Cambodia is also a hub for discounted name brand clothing made in regional garment factories. Just be sure to bargain at markets as overcharging is fairly common.

Psar Thmei

Phnom Penh's iconic Psar Thmei (aka Central Market) is a sight to behold. This striking art deco landmark is one of the biggest and best places to browse for souvenirs. p56

Artisans Angkor

Artisans Angkor is a social business that specialises in handmade silks, weavings and other traditional crafts. The main showroom is in Siem Reap, but there's a great boutique in Phnom Penh, too. p105
Above: Artisans Angkor

Russian Market

The jumble of stalls at the Russian Market is a top stop in Phnom Penh for discount factory clothing, shoes, bags and local handicrafts. Browse the surrounding neighbourhood for trendy boutiques and cafes. p89

6 EPICUREAN ADVENTURES

You'll find excellent dishes in both humble markets and upmarket eateries – most based around rice, fish and soup. Siem Reap and Phnom Penh vie for the title of Cambodia's culinary capital, but you'll also find surprising food experiences in regional towns like Kep, Kampot and Battambang.

Dining for a cause

Some of the most renowned restaurants in Siem Reap are run by aid organisations with the money spent on your baked-fish *amok* (top left) helping to fund their important work. p117

Crabs & Kampot pepper

Two of Cambodia's most prized ingredients are its piquant Kampot peppercorns and succulent fresh crabs. Try both at Kep's iconic Crab Market. p228

Take a food tour

Food tours are a great way to make sense of the local cuisine. Phnom Penh offers several tours for an authentic evening of culinary fun. p67

Above: Food stalls at the Russian Market (p89)

7 WILD NIGHTS

Craft Cocktails

Bassac Lane is the epicenter of Cambodia's craft cocktail boom, with Hub Street its reigning king. Few places on earth serve cocktails this good at these prices. p88.

Wine & Beer

Craft breweries are sprouting like bean-stalks across Phnom Penh, but few can match the charm of Botanico. Its leafy beer garden is the perfect setting to cool off with home-brewed Cerevisia beers. p84

Left: Live music at a Phnom Penh bar

Clubbing

Heart of Darkness is a Phnom Penh institution that draws the most diverse crowd in town. Are you gay? Straight? Curious? No matter. Come as you are to this dimly-lit nightclub with frequent drag shows. p87

Phnom Penh has surprisingly vibrant nightlife, with everything from swanky cocktail lounges to Cambodian craft breweries to LGBTQI+-friendly clubs with lavish late-night drag shows. The sleazy hostess bars that once dominated the scene are slowly disappearing as a new wave of young Cambodians showcase what makes this city such a fun place to be after the sun sets.

Need to Know

For more information, see Survival Guide (p349)

Currency
Riel (r), US dollars (US$)

Languages
Khmer, English, Mandarin, French

Visas
A one-month tourist visa costs US$30 on arrival, tourist e-visas cost US$37 and business visas cost US$35.

Money
ATMs are widely available, including in all major tourist centres and provincial capitals. Credit cards are accepted by many hotels and restaurants in larger cities.

Mobile Phones
To prevent excessive roaming charges, buy a local SIM card on arrival.

Time
Indochina Time (GMT/UTC plus seven hours)

When to Go

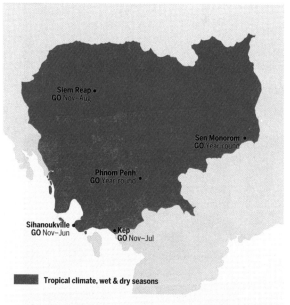

Siem Reap •
GO Nov–Aug

Sen Monorom •
GO Year-round

Phnom Penh
GO Year-round •

Sihanoukville •
GO Nov–Jun

• Kep
GO Nov–Jul

Tropical climate, wet & dry seasons

High Season
(Nov–Feb)

➡ Cooler and windy, with almost Mediterranean temperatures.

➡ Book accommodation in advance during the peak Christmas and New Year period.

Shoulder
(Apr & Oct)

➡ In April and May the mercury hits 40°C and visitors melt.

➡ October and November are excellent for exploration as rains taper off while the dusty dry season has yet to begin.

Low Season
(May–Sep)

➡ Rainy season means emerald landscapes and awesome cloud formations.

➡ Accommodation discounts and protective cloud cover make this a great time to visit the temples.

Useful Websites

Lonely Planet (www.lonely planet.com/cambodia) Destination information, hotel reviews, traveller forum and more.

Phnom Penh Post (www.phnompenhpost.com) Cambodia's newspaper of record.

Travelfish (www.travelfish.org) Opinionated articles and reviews.

Move to Cambodia (www.movetocambodia.com) Insightful guide to living and working in Cambodia.

Cambodia Tribunal Monitor (www.cambodiatribunal.org) Detailed coverage of the Khmer Rouge trials.

Important Numbers

Drop the 0 from a regional (city) code when calling Cambodia from another country.

Ambulance	🕿119
Cambodia's country code	🕿855
Fire	🕿118
International access code	🕿001
Police	🕿117

Exchange Rates

Australia	A$1	3016r
Canada	C$1	3230r
Euro zone	€1	4822r
Japan	¥100	3712r
New Zealand	NZ$1	2856r
Thailand	1B	124r
UK	UK£1	5681r
USA	US$1	4084r

For current exchange rates, see www.xe.com.

Daily Costs

Budget: Less than US$50

➡ Hostel bed or guesthouse room: US$5–10

➡ Local meals and street eats: US$1–4

➡ Local buses (per 100km): US$2–3

Midrange: US$50–200

➡ Air-con hotel room: US$15–50

➡ Decent local restaurant meal: US$5–10

➡ Local tour guide per day: US$25–35

Top End: More than US$200

➡ Boutique hotel or resort: US$50–500

➡ Gastronomic meal with drinks: US$25–50

➡ 4WD rental per day: US$60–120

Opening Hours

Everything shuts down during Khmer New Year, Chinese New Year and P'chum Ben (Festival of the Dead).

Banks 8am–3.30pm Monday to Friday, Saturday mornings

Bars 5pm–late

Government offices 7.30am–11.30am and 2pm–5pm Monday to Friday

Local markets 6.30am–5.30pm

Museums Hours vary, but usually open seven days a week

Restaurants International restaurants 7am–10pm or meal times; local restaurants 6.30am–9pm

Shops 8am–6pm, later in tourist centres

Arriving in Cambodia

Phnom Penh International Airport The airport is 7km west of central Phnom Penh. Official taxis/*remork-motos* to anywhere in the city cost US$12/9 (30 minutes to one hour). The fare on ride-hailing apps is about half that. Options from outside the airport include *moto* (about US$3), public city bus (1500r), shuttle bus (US$2.50) or train (US$2.50).

Siem Reap International Airport The airport is 7km from the town centre; taxis/*remorks* cost US$9/7 (15 to 30 minutes), or about half that with a ride-hailing app. Many hotels and guesthouses offer free airport pickup with advance bookings.

Land borders Shared with Laos, Thailand and Vietnam; Cambodian visas are available on arrival. Most borders are open 7am to 5pm.

Getting Around

Bus The most popular form of transport for most travellers, connecting all major destinations.

Car Private car or 4WD is an affordable option for those who value time above money.

Motorbike An amazing way to travel for experienced riders.

Air Domestic flights link Phnom Penh, Siem Reap and Sihanoukville with each other.

Boat Less common than in the old days, but Siem Reap to either Battambang or Phnom Penh remain popular routes.

Train Newly resumed service has sporadic and slow services linking Phnom Penh with Takeo, Kampot and Sihanoukville.

For much more on **getting around**, see p362.

First Time Cambodia

For more information, see Survival Guide (p349)

Checklist

➡ Make sure your passport is valid for at least six months beyond the date of arrival.

➡ Arrange any recommended inoculations at a travel-health clinic.

➡ Arrange for appropriate travel insurance.

➡ Check the airline baggage restrictions.

➡ Inform your debit-/credit-card company that you're heading away.

➡ Check to make sure you can obtain a visa-on-arrival in Cambodia.

What to Pack

➡ Lightweight, light-coloured clothing to reflect the sun

➡ Comfortable sandals or shoes

➡ Refillable water bottle

➡ Powerful sunscreen and long-lasting deodorant

➡ Earplugs

➡ Universal travel adaptor

➡ Unlocked mobile phone for use with a Cambodian SIM card

➡ Raincoat if travelling in wet season

Top Tips for Your Trip

➡ Do your homework on land-border crossings before you cross to ensure you don't great stranded in a remote location after dark.

➡ Overnight sleeper buses are generally pretty comfortable in Cambodia and will save the cost of a night's accommodation.

➡ If time is more important than money, consider domestic flights between Siem Reap and Sihanoukville, as the road is long.

➡ Buy a *krama*, a checked traditional scarf, for your travels, as it is a multipurpose travel towel that the locals use in a multitude of ways.

What to Wear

Lightweight and loose-fitting clothes are the best all-round option in Cambodia, including cottons and linens to combat the humidity. Cambodia is not a very dressy place unless you are living the high life in Phnom Penh or Siem Reap, so smart clothes are not really a necessity. If heading to the upland northeast in November to March, then pack a jacket and/or sweater for the cool nights. While shorts are acceptable throughout the country, have something to cover elbows and knees for temple visits. On the South Coast, it's not considered appropriate to walk around in swimwear when not on the beach; cover up with a sarong or something similar.

Sleeping

It's worth booking accommodation in advance in popular destinations during peak-season months of November to February and major holidays.

➡ **Guesthouses** Usually family-run, locally owned places that offer good-value rooms.

➡ **Hotels** Everything from cheap business pads to luxury hotels.

➡ **Hostels** Hostels are popular with backpackers and offer a mix of dorm beds and private rooms, sometimes with a pool, but are concentrated in Phnom Penh, Siem Reap and the South Coast.

➡ **Homestays** These usually involve staying with a family in a village where there is a basic sleeping set-up and rustic facilities.

Bargaining

It's important to haggle in markets in Cambodia, otherwise the stallholder may 'shave your head' (local vernacular for 'rip you off'). As well as in markets, bargaining is the rule when arranging share taxis and pickups, and in some guesthouses. The Khmers are not ruthless hagglers, so a persuasive smile and a little friendly quibbling is usually enough to get a price that's acceptable to both you and the seller.

Tipping

➡ **Hotels** 2000r to US$1 per bag; leave a small tip for the cleaner at fancy hotels.

➡ **Restaurants** A few thousand riel, up to 5% or 10% at fancier restaurants.

➡ **Remorks and moto drivers** Not expected for short trips.

➡ **Temples** Leave a few thousand riel in the contribution box, especially if a monk has shown you around.

Temples of Angkor (p137)

Etiquette

Cambodian people are very gracious hosts, but there are some important spiritual and social conventions to observe.

➡ **Buddhism** When visiting temples, cover up to the knees and elbows, and remove your shoes and any head covering when entering temple buildings. Sit with your feet tucked behind you to avoid pointing them at Buddha images. It's also good to leave a small donation. Women should never touch a monk or his belongings.

➡ **Meet and greet** Called the *sompiah,* the local greeting in Cambodia involves putting your hands together in a prayer-like manner. Use this when introduced to new Khmer friends. When beckoning someone over, always wave towards yourself with the palm down.

➡ **Modesty** Avoid wearing swimsuits or scanty clothing around towns in Cambodia, even in beach destinations.

➡ **Saving face** Never get into an argument with a Khmer person. It's better to smile through any conflict.

Language

English is widely spoken in Cambodia and many visitors are pleasantly surprised by the general level of English after travelling through neigbouring Thailand or Vietnam where English speakers are often confined to the tourism industry. It is worth learning a few basic words in Khmer as a matter of courtesy to the locals and they are usually very pleased if you can use phrases such as hello and thank you. The script is derived from the Indian alphabet of Sanskrit and is very difficult to learn during a short visit.

What's New

COVID-19 dealt a big punch to Cambodia's travel industry, but it won't alter the rise of sustainable tourism, which arrived in a big way with the 'Refill Not Landfill' water bottle campaign and several new ecolodges in far-flung outposts. The arts scene continues to experience a renaissance, although, sadly, the same cannot be said for the political scene.

Siem Reap Cuisine Scene

Siem Reap has long boasted a world-class dining scene, but now some of the younger Cambodian chefs are coming through and making a name for themselves with innovative flavours in homegrown restaurants such as Mahob (p121), Pou Kitchen (p119) and Jomno Street Food (p119).

Refill Not Landfill

Refill Not Landfill is a homegrown campaign working with hotels, restaurants and shops to provide refillable water bottles and drinking-water refill stations to help battle the ever-present plastic water bottles.

The Factory in Phnom Penh

This impressive new creative space, located in a former Levi's factory (p56) on the southern outskirts of Phnom Penh, is home to a massive contemporary-art gallery – Kbach Arts (p56) – a microbrewery, coworking space, trampoline park, skate park, cinema room, stage, cafes and more.

Sihanoukville on the Slide, Southern Islands on the Rise

Well documented in the international press, Sihanoukville is a development disaster with chaotic construction, terrible traffic and numerous casinos, but

LOCAL KNOWLEDGE

WHAT'S HAPPENING IN CAMBODIA

Nick Ray and Mark Johanson, Lonely Planet writers

Democracy is on trial in Cambodia with opposition leader Kem Sokha facing politically motivated 'treason' charges. The banning of the opposition Cambodia National Rescue Party (CNRP) has created an international fault line, with China supporting the governing Cambodian People's Party (CPP) of Prime Minister Hun Sen and the Western donors threatening sanctions and trade restrictions if the political climate does not improve.

China sees Cambodia as a close ally in its 'Belt and Road Initiative' to spread trade across the globe, and the kingdom has taken some controversial stances against its Asean partners on key issues. Chinese investment is changing the face of modern Cambodia and not always for the better, as Sihanoukville tragically demonstrates.

Tourism, meanwhile, had been a blossoming industry up until the pandemic. Despite reporting some of the world's lowest Covid-19 infection rates, the sector fell off a cliff in 2020 and failed to pick up again in 2021 due to both slow vaccination rates and a late-arriving first wave. Yet, thanks to agriculture and manufacturing, the country's economy continues to chug along. Meanwhile, its cities are being reimagined by a young population unencumbered by the country's dark history.

the islands are taking up the slack thanks to beautiful beaches and a great range of accommodation.

Craft Distilleries in the Capital

First came craft beer and now it's time to get into the spirit of Phnom Penh with the new Seekers (p84) gin distillery and the longer-running Samai (p84) rum distillery, both of which offer weekly tasting sessions.

Cool Kampot

Once-sleepy Kampot has woken up and is now a lively riverside hub boasting hip cafes, affordable epicurean experiences, some late-night bars and a thriving little arts community.

Art & Crafts in Siem Reap

Several art galleries have opened their doors in Siem Reap, adding to the creative community in temple town. Browse high-end pieces from local and international artists.

Prumsodun Ok & Natyarasa

Cambodia's first gay dance company, it infuses Khmer classics with a contemporary (and LGBTIQ+) spirit at its shows each weekend in the Counterspace Theater (p88).

An Outbreak of Peace

Two 'peace'-themed museums have opened recently, including the CMAC Peace Museum of Mine Action (p168) in Bakong District, Siem Reap, and the Cambodia Peace Gallery (p244) in Battambang, both telling a poignant tale of Cambodia's long journey from war to peace.

Trains from Phnom Penh to Battambang and Poipet

There are now infrequent trains from Phnom Penh to the Thai border at Poipet via the city of Battambang. Look out for international trains in the not-too-distant future.

Irrawaddy Dolphins

Some rare good news in Cambodian conservation: a dolphin census found that, for

LISTEN, WATCH & FOLLOW

For inspiration and travel stories from Cambodia, visit https://www.lonelyplanet.com/cambodia/articles.

First They Killed My Father (2017) Director Angelina Jolie's adaptation of the bestselling Loung Ung book, which tells the story of her childhood surviving the Khmer Rouge regime.

Blue Lady Blog (https://blueladyblog.com/) Popular blog from Kounila Keo, one of Cambodia's rising digital stars.

Beautiful Cambodia (https://www.instagram.com/beautifulcambodia/) Cambodia's best travel photography.

Best Cambodia Podcasts (https://player.fm/podcasts/cambodia) From the Khmer Rouge to the China factor today.

Tweet Cambodia (https://twitter.com/tweetcambodia) All things Cambodia.

FAST FACTS

Food trend Deep-fried tarantulas, known as *a-ping* in Cambodia, are one of the most popular snacks with the Khmer people.

Flag fact Cambodia is the only country to feature a building on its flag, the one and only Angkor Wat.

Guinness World Records Cambodia holds several obscure records: the biggest line dance, the longest *krama* (checked scarf) and longest dragon boat.

Pop 16.5 million

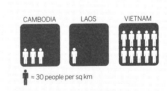

CAMBODIA　　LAOS　　VIETNAM

≈ 30 people per sq km

the first time since counting began in 1997, the population actually increased in 2017 to 92, up from 80 in 2015.

Accommodation

Find more accommodation reviews throughout the On the Road chapters (from p48)

Accommodation Types

Guesthouses Usually family-run, locally owned places that offer good-value rooms.

Hotels In Phnom Penh, Siem Reap and the South Coast, hotels improve significantly once you start spending more than US$20 a night. If you spend between US$30 and US$50, it is possible to arrange something extremely comfortable with the potential bonus of a swimming pool. There has been an explosion of boutique hotels in Phnom Penh, Siem Reap, Kep and Battambang. These atmospheric places are usually in the US$50 to US$100 range.

Homestays There are several organised homestays around the country in provinces including Kompong Cham and Kompong Thom, as well as lots of informal homestays in out-of-the-way places such as Preah Vihear. The Mekong Discovery Trail includes a slew of homestays between Kratie and the Lao border. There are also plenty of easily accessible homestays in Siem Reap Province.

Hostels Backpacker hostels are abundant in Cambodia, particularly in popular destinations such as Phnom Penh, Siem Reap and Kampot. These are lively and well run, but the dorms are not always the best value and are often the same price as

a private room in a locally owned guesthouse. However, most hostels also offer private rooms and some have bonus draws such as a swimming pool. Booking is generally cheaper if you just show up, rather than pay online through a third-party website.

Best Places to Stay

Best on a Budget

Budget guesthouses can be found in nearly all provincial capitals. Costs hover around US$5 to US$10 for a bed, usually with fan, bathroom and satellite TV. Most guesthouses in this range do not have hot water, but may offer a few more expensive rooms where it is available. Basic thatched bungalows with a mattress and fan can be found in some coastal destinations and in the hills of Mondulkiri and Ratanakiri.

➡ Onederz Hostel (p113)
➡ Lonely Beach (p203)
➡ Mad Monkey (p207)
➡ Tree Top Ecolodge (p293)
➡ Eighty8 Backpackers (p72)

Best for Families

Families are well catered to at several midrange-to-high-end hotels in Siem Reap and Phnom Penh, as well as resorts on the South Coast. More remote areas of the provinces are, in general, less accustomed to visitors with kids. However, there are often family-friendly (and budget-friendly) rooms at local guesthouses with several beds all crammed together within four walls.

➡ Navutu Dreams (p116)
➡ Sambor Village Hotel (p270)

- ⇒ Mayura Hill Hotel & Resort (p304)
- ⇒ Kabiki (p74)
- ⇒ Les Manguiers (p218)
- ⇒ Lazy Beach (p209)

Best for Solo Travellers

Hotels rarely offer a single rate, though there are a few notable exceptions in Siem Reap and Phnom Penh. Local guesthouses offer a more affordable way to sleep comfortably without breaking the bank. Solo travellers looking to make new friends should consider sleeping in Cambodia's excellent hostels, which range from social party pads to serene and ecofriendly 'poshpackers'. Most include private rooms alongside the dorms for those who prefer privacy.

- ⇒ Funky Flashpacker (p113)
- ⇒ Nest Beach Club (p202)
- ⇒ Patio Hotel & Urban Resort (p75)
- ⇒ Here Be Dragons (p247)
- ⇒ SLA Boutique Hostel (p72)
- ⇒ High Tide Kampot (p216)

Best for Boutique Hotels

Cambodia offers a masterclass in the art of boutique hotels with some of the most beautiful properties in the region. Siem Reap is the epicentre of boutique beds and offers insane value in the green season months. Phnom Penh has a superb selection of boutique hotels with garden oases to escape the bustle beyond. Upcountry, most popular towns have a boutique hotel in which to indulge, including Battambang, Kampot, Kep, Kratie, Sen Monorom and Ban Lung.

- ⇒ Le Relais de Chhlong (p283)
- ⇒ Plantation (p73)
- ⇒ Maisons Wat Kor (p248)
- ⇒ Viroth's Hotel (p115)

Four Rivers Floating Lodge (p185), Tatai River

Booking

Cambodia Impact Explorer (https://impact explorer.asia/) Book local homestays online.

Lonely Planet (lonelyplanet.com/cambodia/) Accommodation recommendations and independent reviews.

Month by Month

TOP EVENTS

Chinese New Year,
January/February

Khmer New Year, April

Festival of the Dead,
September/October

Water Festival,
October/November

Angkor Wat International Half Marathon,
December

January

This is peak tourist season in Cambodia with Phnom Penh, Siem Reap and the South Coast heaving. Chinese and Vietnamese New Years sometimes fall in this month, too.

✨ Chaul Chnam Chen (Chinese New Year)

The Chinese inhabitants of Cambodia celebrate their New Year somewhere between late January and mid-February – for the Vietnamese, this is Tet. As many of Phnom Penh's businesses are run by Chinese-Khmers, commerce grinds to a halt around this time and there are dragon dances all over town.

February

One of the busiest times of year for tourist arrivals, February is also often the month for Chinese and Vietnamese New Years, which see regional tourist numbers peak.

✨ Giant Puppet Parade

This colourful annual fundraising event (www.facebook.com/giantpuppetproject) takes place in Siem Reap. Local organisations, orphanages and businesses come together to create giant puppets in the shape of animals, deities and contemporary characters, and the whole ensemble winds its way along the Siem Reap River.

March

As the cool season draws to a close, the temperatures begin to rise, but it remains a popular month to travel.

April

This is the most important month in the calendar for Khmers, as the New Year comes in the middle of April. Be warned that the mercury regularly hits 40°C (104°F).

✨ Chaul Chnam Khmer (Khmer New Year)

This is a three-day celebration of the Khmer New Year. Cambodians make offerings at wats, clean out their homes and exchange gifts. It is a lively time to visit the country as the Khmers go wild with water in the countryside.

May

This is the beginning of the low season for visitors as the monsoon arrives (and lasts till October), but there may be a last blast of hot weather to welcome mango season and some delicious ripe fruits.

✨ Chat Preah Nengkal (Royal Ploughing Ceremony)

Led by the royal family, the Royal Ploughing Ceremony is a ritual agricultural festival held to mark the traditional beginning of the rice-growing season. It takes place in early May and rotates around different provincial capitals.

✲ Visakha Puja (Buddha Day)

A celebration of Buddha's birth, enlightenment and *parinibbana* (passing). Activities are centred on wats. The festival falls on the eighth day of the fourth moon (May or June) and is best observed at Angkor Wat, where you can see candlelit processions of monks.

June

The start of the wet season, young rice is planted and the landscape begins to come to life once more in a blaze of greens.

July

Tourism numbers experience a bounce in July thanks to school holidays in Europe, with French, Italians and Spanish tourists often travelling to Cambodia in summer.

August

Another busy summer month, as a number of backpackers descend on Cambodia and the Mekong region to take advantage of university and college holidays.

September

Traditionally the wettest month in Cambodia, September is usually a time of sporadic flooding along the Mekong. The calendar's second-most-important festival, P'chum Ben, usually falls in this month.

✲ P'chum Ben (Festival of the Dead)

This festival resembles All Souls' Day, when respects are paid to the dead through offerings made at wats. P'chum Ben lasts for several days and devout Buddhists are expected to visit seven wats during the festival. Local wats are a blaze of colour, ceremony and chanting.

October

The rains often extend into October and this has led to some late flooding in recent years. However, the countryside is extraordinarily green, and it's a rewarding time for boat travel between Siem Reap and Battambang.

✲ Bon Om Tuk (Water Festival)

Celebrating the victory of Jayavarman VII over the Chams, this important festival also marks the extraordinary natural phenomenon of the reversal of the current of Tonlé Sap River. It's a wonderful, chaotic time to be in Phnom Penh or Siem Reap.

November

November brings the dry, windy season and signals the start of the best period to be in the country (which extends through until January or February). Bon Om Tuk (Water Festival) often takes place in November.

✲ Angkor Photo Festival

In Siem Reap, resident and regional photographers descend on the temples and team up with local youths to teach them the tricks of the trade (https://angkor-photo.com). Photography exhibitions are staged all over town and some famous Vietnam War–era photographers are sometimes in attendance.

✲ Kampot Writers & Readers Festival

Launched in 2015, this festival (www.kampotwritersfestival.com) brings four days of literary discussions, poetry readings, art exhibitions, concerts and creative workshops to Kampot. Events are held in town and at selected guesthouses and lodges upriver on the banks of the Kompong Bay.

December

Christmas and New Year are peak season at Angkor and leading beach resorts; book a long way ahead. Sign up for a half marathon or bicycle ride if you fancy doing something for charity.

🏃 Angkor Wat International Half Marathon

This half marathon (www.facebook.com/angkorwathalfmarathon) has been a fixture for more than 15 years. Choose from a 21km half marathon, a 10km fun run or various bicycle races. It's hard to imagine better backdrops than the incredible temples of Angkor.

Plan Your Trip
Itineraries

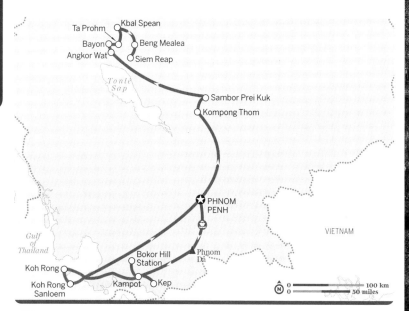

The Best of Cambodia

This is the ultimate journey, via temples, beaches and the capital. It can be run in any direction, but it is best followed to the letter, starting in the capital, exploring the coastline and winding up at the world's most impressive collection of temples, Angkor.

Hit **Phnom Penh** for its impressive National Museum and stunning Silver Pagoda. It's home to the most eclectic dining scene in Cambodia, with fine-dining Khmer restaurants, an international array of eateries and some safe street-food eating. There's also superb shopping at Russian Market, and a night shift that never sleeps.

Take a fast boat to the hilltop temple of **Phnom Da**, dating from the pre-Angkorian time, and then continue south to the colonial-era town of **Kampot**, which makes a good base for this area. From here, visit the seaside town of **Kep**, then head to Rabbit Island, just off the coast, and nearby cave pagodas. It's also possible to make a side trip to **Bokor Hill Station** or visit a pepper plantation.

Angkor Wat (p150)

Go west to the mess of construction and casinos that is now Sihanoukville, which is the best jumping-off point to explore Cambodia's idyllic islands, **Koh Rong** and **Koh Rong Sanloem**, where you can feast on seafood, dive or snorkel the nearby waters, or just relax in a hammock. Then backtrack via Phnom Penh to **Kompong Thom** and visit the pre-Angkorian brick temples of **Sambor Prei Kuk**.

Finish the trip at Angkor, a mindblowing experience with which few sights can compare. See **Angkor Wat**, perfection in stone; **Bayon**, weirdness in stone; and **Ta Prohm**, nature triumphing over stone – before venturing further afield to **Kbal Spean** or jungle-clad **Beng Mealea**.

Save some time for soaking up **Siem Reap**, one of the most diverse destinations in Cambodia, with a host of activities on tap. Everything from cooking classes to Vespa tours is on offer, and some of these activities are a great way to punctuate the temple tours.

This trip can take two weeks at a steady pace or three weeks at a slow pace. Public transport serves most of this route, although some of the side trips will require chartered transport or a motorbike trip.

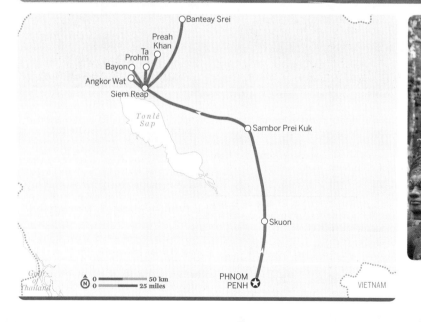

A Tale of Two Cities

If time is tight, focus on the big hitters of Phnom Penh and Siem Reap. With two nights in the capital and three or four nights in temple town, discover the best of modern and ancient Cambodia.

Start out in **Phnom Penh** to encounter Cambodia's contrasting history. Relive the glories of the past at the National Museum and the Royal Palace, then discover a darker past with a visit to the Tuol Sleng Genocide Museum and the Killing Fields of Choeung Ek. Explore the excellent wining-and-dining scene by night.

From the capital, travel through the Cambodian countryside to Siem Reap via the improved overland route. Along the way, stop off briefly in **Skuon**, also known affectionately as 'Spiderville' thanks to being the home of the deep-fried tarantula, and the pre-Angkorian temples of **Sambor Prei Kuk**, now officially Cambodia's third Unesco World Heritage site. If you decide to travel overland between these two cities, the months from July to December are best time to do so, as the landscape is lush and green.

Once in **Siem Reap**, spend a couple of days touring the nearby temples of Angkor, including headline names such as **Angkor Wat**, **Bayon** and **Ta Prohm**. Allow some time to catch the support acts, like beautiful **Banteay Srei** and immense **Preah Khan**. Add some activities to the mix with a zipline experience, a quad-bike adventure or some pampering at a sumptuous spa. If you decide to travel overland between these two cities, the months from July to December are best for this, as the landscape is lush and green.

Top: Royal Palace (p53)
Bottom: Angkor Thom (p156)

The Big One

4 WEEKS

Cambodia is a small country and even though the roads are sometimes bad and travel can be slow, most of the highlights can be visited in a month.

Setting out from the hip capital that is **Phnom Penh**, pass through the bustling Mekong town of **Kompong Cham** before heading on to **Kratie** for an encounter with the elusive Irrawaddy river dolphins. Then it is time to make a tricky choice to experience the beauty of the northeast. To ensure maximum time elsewhere, choose between **Ratanakiri Province** and the volcanic crater lake of Boeng Yeak Lom, or **Mondulkiri Province** and the original Elephant Valley Project. Both offer primate experiences for those who fancy a bit of monkey business along the way. If you have a bit of extra time up your sleeve, you could combine the two in a grand loop, now that the road between Sen Monorom and Ban Lung is in good shape.

Next up, head to the South Coast. Take your time and consider a few nights in relaxing **Kep** or laid-back **Kampot**, and a boat trip from Sihanoukville to explore the up-and-coming **southern islands** off the coast. Turning back inland, check out **Kirirom National Park**, home to pine trees, black bears and some spectacular views of the Cardamom Mountains.

Then it's time to go northwest to charming **Battambang**, one of Cambodia's best-preserved colonial-era towns and a base from which to discover rural life. Take the proverbial slow boat to **Siem Reap**, passing through stunning scenery along the snaking Sangker River, and turn your attention to the **temples of Angkor**.

Visit all the greatest hits in and around Angkor, but set aside some extra time to venture further afield to the rival capital of **Koh Ker**, which is cloaked in thick jungle, or **Prasat Preah Vihear**, a mountain temple perched precariously atop a cliff on the Thai border.

Overlanders can run this route in reverse, setting out from Siem Reap and exiting Cambodia by river into Vietnam or Laos. Entering from Laos, divert east to Ratanakiri before heading south. Getting around is generally easy, as there are buses on the big roads, taxis on the small roads and buzzing boats on the many rivers.

Top: Koh Rong island (p197)
Bottom: Catholic Church (p223), Bokor Hill Station

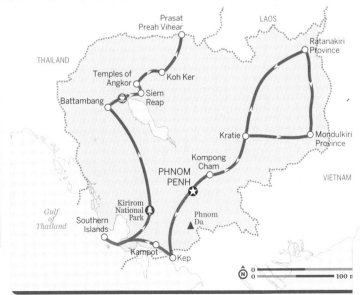

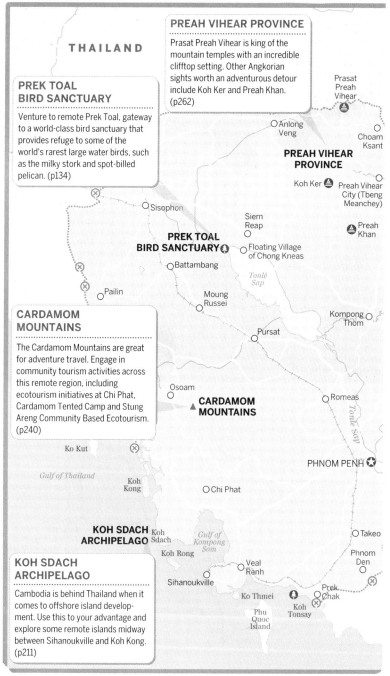

PREAH VIHEAR PROVINCE

Prasat Preah Vihear is king of the mountain temples with an incredible clifftop setting. Other Angkorian sights worth an adventurous detour include Koh Ker and Preah Khan. (p262)

PREK TOAL BIRD SANCTUARY

Venture to remote Prek Toal, gateway to a world-class bird sanctuary that provides refuge to some of the world's rarest large water birds, such as the milky stork and spot-billed pelican. (p134)

CARDAMOM MOUNTAINS

The Cardamom Mountains are great for adventure travel. Engage in community tourism activities across this remote region, including ecotourism initiatives at Chi Phat, Cardamom Tented Camp and Stung Areng Community Based Ecotourism. (p240)

KOH SDACH ARCHIPELAGO

Cambodia is behind Thailand when it comes to offshore island development. Use this to your advantage and explore some remote islands midway between Sihanoukville and Koh Kong. (p211)

THAILAND

Prasat Preah Vihear

Anlong Veng

Choam Ksant

PREAH VIHEAR PROVINCE

Koh Ker · Preah Vihear City (Tbeng Meanchey)

Sisophon

Siem Reap

Preah Khan

PREK TOAL BIRD SANCTUARY

Floating Village of Chong Kneas

Battambang

Tonlé Sap

Pailin

Moung Russei

Kompong Thom

Pursat

Osoam

CARDAMOM MOUNTAINS

Romeas

Tonle Sap

Ko Kut

PHNOM PENH

Gulf of Thailand

Koh Kong

Chi Phat

KOH SDACH ARCHIPELAGO · Koh Sdach

Gulf of Kompong Som

Koh Rong

Takeo

Phnom Den

Veal Renh

Sihanoukville

Ko Thmei

Prek Chak

Koh Tonsay

Phu Quoc Island

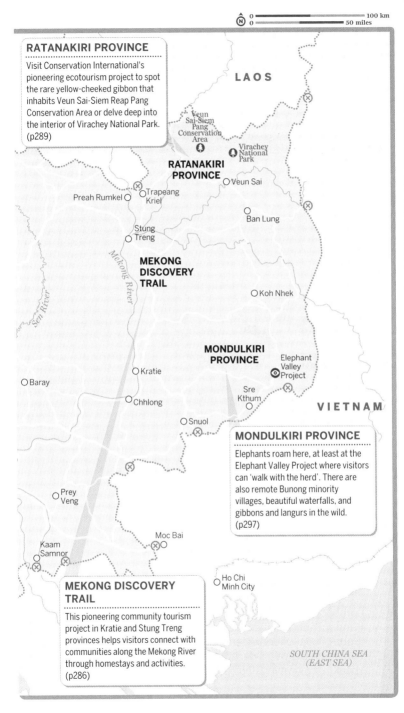

0 — 100 km
0 — 50 miles

RATANAKIRI PROVINCE

Visit Conservation International's pioneering ecotourism project to spot the rare yellow-cheeked gibbon that inhabits Veun Sai-Siem Reap Pang Conservation Area or delve deep into the interior of Virachey National Park. (p289)

LAOS

Veun Sai-Siem Pang Conservation Area

Virachey National Park

RATANAKIRI PROVINCE

Veun Sai

Preah Rumkel ○   ○ Trapeang Kriel

Stung Treng

Ban Lung

MEKONG DISCOVERY TRAIL

Mekong River

Sen River

Koh Nhek ○

MONDULKIRI PROVINCE

Elephant Valley Project

○ Kratie

Sre Kthum ○

VIETNAM

○ Baray

○ Chhlong

○ Snuol

MONDULKIRI PROVINCE

Elephants roam here, at least at the Elephant Valley Project where visitors can 'walk with the herd'. There are also remote Bunong minority villages, beautiful waterfalls, and gibbons and langurs in the wild. (p297)

○ Prey Veng

Moc Bai ○

Kaam Samnor ○

○ Ho Chi Minh City

MEKONG DISCOVERY TRAIL

This pioneering community tourism project in Kratie and Stung Treng provinces helps visitors connect with communities along the Mekong River through homestays and activities. (p286)

SOUTH CHINA SEA (EAST SEA)

Koh Rong (p197)

Plan Your Trip

The Great Outdoors

Cambodia is catching up with its more-developed neighbours: Phnom Penh and Siem Reap have plenty of activities, while the South Coast offers water sports and the northeast is the place for a walk on the wild side. Whether you are hiking, biking, ascending peaks or plumbing depths, Cambodia delivers the action.

BLUEORANGE STUDIO/SHUTTERSTOCK ©

When to Go

November to February

This is the cooler dry season and the best time for strenuous activities such as trekking and cycling. Higher-altitude places, including Mondulkiri and Ratanakiri, are worth considering any time of year because they're always cooler, although they can get chilly at night.

March to May

The mercury regularly hits 40°C during the hot season, so this is the perfect time to cool off with some water sports such as scuba diving, stand-up paddleboarding or sailing, all on the South Coast.

June to October

The wet season is not ideal for hiking or biking due to torrential downpours and the presence of leeches in many jungle areas. However, it's a great time for boat trips and kayaking on Cambodia's extensive network of rivers.

Boat Trips

With so much water around the country, it's hardly surprising that boat trips are popular with visitors. Some of these are functional, such as travelling up the Tonlé Sap River from Phnom Penh to Siem Reap, or along the Sangker River from Siem Reap to Battambang. Particularly in the wet season, when the Mekong is in full flow and the Tonlé Sap at its maximum extent, do as the locals do and travel by boat.

Where to Go

Southern islands Travellers can hop on boats from various launching points to explore underwater environs and islands near and far such as Koh Rong (p197), Koh Rong Sanloem (p205) and Koh Sdach (p211).

Kampot The riverside town of Kampot (p212) offers boat trips upriver to mangroves and downriver to isolated beaches and the open sea.

Mekong River The mother river flows through the heart of Cambodia and offers some rewarding opportunities for discovering tranquil islands and quiet homestays along the Mekong Discovery Trail (p286).

Tonlé Sap lake Explore floating villages (p135), flooded forests (p135) and bird sanctuaries (p134) with a boat trip on the Great Lake.

Cycling

Cambodia is a great country for adventurous cyclists to explore. Given the country's legendary potholes, a mountain bike is the best bet. Some roads remain in poor condition, but there is usually a flat unpaved trail along the side. Travelling at such a gentle speed allows for much more interaction with the locals. Bicycles can be transported on the roof of minibuses.

Cycling around Angkor is a rewarding experience, as it really helps to get a measure of the size and scale of the temple complex. Mountain biking is likely to take off in Mondulkiri and Ratanakiri Provinces over the coming years, as there are some great trails. Guesthouses and hotels throughout Cambodia rent out bicycles for as little as US$2 per day, or US$7 to US$15 for an imported brand.

Where to Go

Battambang The beautiful countryside around Battambang (p241) is perfect for exploring.

Kampot Pedal along rivers, through rural landscapes and out to organic pepper farms that dot Kampot Province (p212).

Koh Dach Silk Island (p97) is the perfect place to escape the hustle and bustle of Phnom Penh on two wheels.

Mondulkiri Province The meeting of the hills is an appropriate name for this mountainous province, and there are some great biking trails to Bunong villages (p299) and jungle waterfalls (p298).

Temples of Angkor The temples (p137) can get very busy in peak season, so leave the crowds behind and follow local jungle trails. Organised tours are available (p111).

Dirt Biking

For experienced riders, Cambodia is one of the most rewarding off-road biking destinations in the world. The roads are generally considered some of the worst in Asia (or best in Asia for die-hard biking enthusiasts!). There are incredible rides all over the country, particularly in the provinces of Preah Vihear, Mondulkiri, Ratanakiri and the Cardamom Mountains, but it is best to stay away from the main highways as traffic and dust make them a choking experience.

The advantage of motorcycle travel is that it allows for complete freedom of movement and you can stop in small villages that Westerners rarely visit. It is possible to take motorcycles upcountry for tours, but only experienced off-road bikers should take to these roads with a dirt bike. Motorcycles are available for hire in most popular tourist destinations. Costs are US$7 to US$10 per day for a 100cc motorcycle and around US$10 to US$25 for a 250cc dirt bike.

Where to Go

Cardamom Mountains Not for the fainthearted, the Cardamom Mountains offer some tough jungle trails north to Pailin or Pursat. Seek an experienced operator such as Jungle Cross (p186).

Kampot The landscapes around Kampot (p212) include rice fields, salt pans, pepper farms, karst peaks and Bokor Hill Station (p222).

Mondulkiri Province The rolling hills of Mondulkiri are perfect for dirt biking, and include the stunning road that follows the Keo Seima Wildlife Sanctuary (p304) to Sen Monorom (p298).

Preah Vihear Province Get your kicks on Cambodia's Route 66 (NH66), which runs from Beng Mealea (p170) to the remote temple of Preah Khan (p268). Or ascend to the realm of the gods at Prasat Preah Vihear (p264).

Ratanakiri Province Red-earth Ratanakiri offers some rewarding biking for experienced riders, including elements of the old 'Sihanouk Trail' that was a Cambodian continuation of the Ho Chi Minh Trail back in the 1960s.

Silvered langur, Battambang (p241)

Water Sports

Snorkelling and diving are available off the islands of Koh Rong and Koh Rong Sanloem, and while the underwater scenery may not be as spectacular as in Indonesia or the Philippines, there is still plenty out there in the deep blue yonder. It's best to venture to the more remote dive sites, such as Koh Tang and Koh Prins, staying overnight on a boat. There are many unexplored areas off the coast between Koh Kong and Sihanoukville that could one day put Cambodia on the dive map of Asia. Other water sports available along the South Coast include kayaking, stand-up paddleboarding and sailing.

Where to Go

Kep Hit the waterfront Sailing Club (p224) to rent a Hobie Cat sailing boat or kayak to explore the calm waters off the coast.

Kampot Explore the river and mangrove channels on a stand-up paddleboard with SUP Asia (p214), or if that sounds like too much hard work, laze around in an inner tube.

Cycling near Siem Reap (p103)

Southern islands Koh Rong (p197) and Koh Rong Sanloem (p205) provide an up-and-coming base for serious divers wanting some big-fish action.

Koh Kong Conservation Corridor Explore the bird- and wildlife-laden rivers of the Cardamoms and Botum Sakur National Park by kayak out of Rainbow Lodge (p185) or Cardamom Tented Camp (p187).

Trekking

Trekking is not the first activity most people would associate with Cambodia, due to the ongoing presence of landmines, but there are plenty of safe areas in the country – including the nascent national parks – where walking can be enjoyed. The northeastern provinces of Mondulkiri and Ratanakiri, with their wild, natural scenery, abundant waterfalls and ethnic-minority populations, are emerging as the country's leading trekking destinations.

Cambodia has an established network of national parks with visitor facilities; Bokor National Park, Kirirom National Park and Ream National Park all offer day trekking potential, while Virachey National Park in

Ratanakiri has multiday treks. Chi Phat and the Cardamom Mountains also offer the possibility of a walk on the wild side.

Angkor is a good place for gentle walks between the temples; as visitor numbers skyrocket, this is one way to experience peace and solitude.

Where to Go

Koh Kong Province Coastal gateway to the Cardamoms, Koh Kong has several trekking companies offering jungle treks around Tatai (p184).

Mondulkiri Province One of Cambodia's most rewarding trekking destinations thanks to cooler climes and the Bunong minority encounters offered by operators such as WEHH (p299), not to mention tracking elephants at Elephant Valley Project (p299) or gibbons at Keo Seima Wildlife Sanctuary (p304).

Ratanakiri Province Choose from gentle treks to ethnic-minority villages or hardcore treks into the heart of Virachey National Park (p296).

Temples of Angkor From a base in Siem Reap, explore Angkor Thom (p156) on foot or ascend to the stunning River of a Thousand Lingas at Kbal Spean (p172).

Angkor Zipline (p154)

such as the spot-billed pelican, black-headed ibis and painted stork.

Ratanakiri Province This remote jungle province is home to a pioneering gibbon-spotting project, Cambodian Gibbon Ecotours (p292).

Siem Reap Visit the Angkor Centre for Conservation of Biodiversity (p131), where rare animals, including the giant ibis, pangolin, silvery langur and leopard cat, can be seen.

Ziplining

Ziplining has recently taken off in Cambodia. Angkor Zipline (p154) offers the longest zipline course in the country, with 10 lines and the chance to spot some gibbons in the wild. Mayura Zipline (p299) is a newer adrenaline-fuelled adventure above the Bou Sraa Waterfall in Mondulkiri Province. There is also the High Point Rope Adventure (p199) zipline on Koh Rong if you need more than a beach buzz, and a super-scenic and affordable canopy tour at BeTreed Adventures (p268) near Preah Khan of Kompong Svay. Ziplining doesn't come cheap though – Angkor Zipline charges around US$100 per person.

Wildlife Spotting

Cambodia is home to rich and varied wildlife that has somehow survived the dramatic events that engulfed the country in the past decades. Big cats, small cats, elephants, primates and some curious critters all call the Cambodian jungle their home, and it's possible to see them across the country. Birdwatching is a big draw, as the country is home to some of the region's rarest waterbirds, including pelicans, adjutants and other storks.

Where to Go

Kratie Province Extremely rare freshwater river dolphins inhabit stretches of the Mekong River between Kratie (p281) and the Lao border.

Mondulkiri Province Walk with the herd at Elephant Valley Project (p299) or spot gibbons and doucs in the Keo Seima Wildlife Sanctuary (p304).

Phnom Tamao Wildlife Rescue Centre So much more than a zoo, this wildlife sanctuary (p100) offers behind-the-scenes tours to meet the animals.

Prek Toal Bird Sanctuary Cambodia's world-class bird sanctuary (p134); see rare waterbirds

Quad Biking

Quad bikes or ATVs are growing in popularity in Cambodia thanks to the prevalence of dirt roads across the country. Siem Reap has three operators (p108) offering countryside tours around temple town. Phnom Penh has one quad-bike outfit, Village Quad Bike Trails (p65), which offers a very different experience to city life. Prices for quad biking range from US$25 per hour to more than US$125 for a full-day adventure.

Rock Climbing

Rock climbing is very much in its infancy compared with neighbouring Laos, Thailand and Vietnam, but there is a climbing outfit down in Kampot Province, where the landscape is peppered with karst outcrops. Climbodia (p213) offers cabled routes up Phnom Kbal Romeas, about 5km south of Kampot town, from US$40 for a half day.

Top: Phnom Kulen
waterfall (p172)

Bottom: Red garden
lizard, Kep National
Park (p224)

Plan Your Trip
Family Travel

Like many places in Southeast Asia, travelling with children in Cambodia can be a lot of fun as long as you have the right attitude. The Khmer people adore children and will shower attention on your offspring, who will find playmates and a temporary babysitter at practically every stop.

Need to Know

Car travel Most vehicles have seat belts, but child seats are not common. Request one in advance via a tour operator.

Pushchairs City footpaths can be overcrowded, making it tricky to navigate a large pushchair. In rural areas, there won't be a pavement (sidewalk), so prepare to walk along the roadside and consider a durable pushchair with sturdy wheels.

Health Regular handwashing is important to head off potential medical problems. Children should not play with animals, as rabies is common in Cambodia.

Safety Do not let children stray from the path in remote areas, as Cambodia remains one of the most landmine-affected countries in the world.

Nappy changing Facilities in public restrooms are rare, limited to a few tourist-friendly establishments in the big cities.

Baby products Bring along a sufficient supply of baby products if travelling in rural areas.

Restaurants Children's menus and high chairs are rare beyond the main tourist centres, but most restaurants are welcoming to children of all ages.

Supermarkets There are some good supermarkets in the main centres, but options thin out in the provinces.

Children Will Love...

Beaches

Long Beach This 7km-long beach on the west coast of Koh Rong (p197) has fine white sand and clear turquoise waters.

Lazy Beach Long home to just one eponymous resort, Lazy Beach (p209) on Koh Rong Samloem is a beautiful spot for families to kick back and let time stand still for a while.

Koh Ta Kiev While Sihanoukville turns into a concrete jungle and Koh Russei is populated with high-end resorts, Koh Ta Kiev (p196) remains a relatively deserted island close to the mainland.

Koh Tonsay Rabbit Island or Koh Tonsay (p224) is a short boat ride from Kep and offers a real beach and delicious fresh seafood, including the legendary Kep crab.

Wildlife Encounters

Phnom Tamao Wildlife Rescue Centre Learn how to be a 'bear keeper' or 'elephant keeper' for a day at this world-class wildlife rescue centre (p100) outside Phnom Penh.

Elephant Valley Project Walk with the herd at this elephant retirement home (p299) in the jungle-clad hills of Mondulkiri Province in northeast Cambodia.

Angkor Zipline Fly through ancient jungles around the temples on the Angkor Zipline (p154) near Siem Reap and listen for the calls of the resident family of gibbons.

Freshwater dolphins Encounter small groups of the extremely rare Irrawaddy dolphins (p284) living in the Mekong River at Kampi, just north of Kratie.

Temples

Ta Prohm The original jungle temple (p162) was used as a backdrop for *Lara Croft: Tomb Raider*, starring Angelina Jolie, so should earn kudos with *Maleficent* fans.

Bayon This temple (p156) is just plain weird thanks to all the massive faces staring out into the jungle. Children will relish the photo opportunities.

Beng Mealea Kids can clamber about wooden walkways and staircases in this immense jungle temple (p170), which is like an ancient sacred playground.

Phnom Kulen Not strictly a temple but a holy mountain (p171) that was the location of one of the first Angkorian capitals. It has an iconic waterfall, a pretty riverbed carved with *lingas* (phallic symbols) and a giant reclining Buddha carved from a massive boulder.

Tropical Fruits

Durian This might not be the most popular fruit for visiting children thanks to the noxious smell, but they won't forget it in a hurry.

Lychee Known as *kulen* in Khmer, as in the holy mountain of Phnom Kulen near Siem Reap, lychee season falls around May to July.

Mango Year-round mangoes are available in Cambodia, but it is the Khmer New Year fruits that are turbocharged by the heatwave of April and May that are simply out of this world.

Mangosteen It is rumoured that Queen Victoria offered 100 pounds to anyone who could deliver her a ripe mangosteen, so it is now known as the queen of fruit.

Rambutan It may be hard to persuade the children to eat this fruit due to its curious appearance, but it is a great travel snack and available year-round.

Region by Region

Phnom Penh & Around

The capital is getting busier all the time, but still offers some good accommodation with swimming pools, plus home comforts like cinemas, bowling and shopping malls. Out of town highlights include Phnom Tamao Wildlife Rescue Centre (p100) and the gentle back roads of Koh Dach (Silk Island; p97).

Siem Reap

Siem Reap has a whole range of activities beyond the temples, including mountain biking, ziplining, escape rooms, crazy golf, cooking and pottery classes, and sumptuous spas offering family pampering. There are some excellent dining spots, and many are child-friendly. Accommodation is also impressive and offers incredible value for money from April to October. Most hostels, guesthouses and hotels have inviting swimming pools.

Temples of Angkor

The temples of Angkor are the headline act for parents, but children may tire of exploring after one or two, so it pays to plan ahead. Breaking up temple visits into bite-sized half-day chunks is a winning formula and ensures some time for nontemple activities like ziplining. The jungle temple of Ta Prohm (p162) is always a favourite for budding Indiana Joneses or Lara Crofts. The enigmatic faces of Bayon (p156) are also a winner, although note that the upper levels will be closed until at least 2022. The massive face gates of Angkor Thom (p156) are an epic alternative, particularly the jungle-clad east gate.

South Coast

Down on the coast, islands such as Koh Rong (p197) and Koh Rong Sanloem (p205) are proving popular with families thanks to their beautiful beaches and gentle seas. There are also plenty of other beaches around Kep and Koh Kong, and some river estuaries that offer water-based activities like boat trips, kayaking and firefly spotting.

Northwestern Cambodia

This is arguably the least compelling region for families thanks to some long road journeys to remote temples and niche wildlife activities like birdwatching. The best place in the region is Battambang, which offers the novelty of the Bamboo Train (p248) and is a charming place to hunker down in a bargain boutique hotel with a pool.

Eastern Cambodia

Mondulkiri is home to the Elephant Valley Project (p299), where you can walk with the herd; a flagship gibbon-spotting project in Keo Seima Wildlife Sanctuary (p304); and the impressive Bou Sraa Waterfall (p298), one of the highest in Cambodia. It is also possible to view rare freshwater-river dolphins near Kratie or swim in the crystal-clear waters of Yeak Lom lake in Ratanakiri.

Good to Know

Look out for the 👪 icon for family-friendly suggestions throughout this guide.

Useful Resources

Lonely Planet Kids (www.lonelyplanetkids.com) Lots of activities and family-oriented blog articles.

ChildSafe (www.thinkchildsafe.org) ChildSafe is a global movement to protect children and certifies hotels, restaurants and other businesses as child-safe, in the fight against human trafficking and sex tourism.

Move to Cambodia (www.movetocambodia.com) Leading resource for foreigners planning a move to Cambodia, which includes useful recommendations for families.

Kids' Corner

Say What?

Hello.	ជំរាបសួរ. johm riab sua
Goodbye.	លាសិនហើយ. lia suhn hao-y
Thank you.	អរគុណ. aw kohn
My name is ...	ខ្ញុំឈ្មោះ... kh"nyohm ch'muah ...

Did You Know?

- Around 40% of Cambodians are under 18.

- Angkor Wat appears on the Cambodian flag.

Have You Tried?

Deep-fried tarantula
A Cambodian favourite.

Regions at a Glance

Phnom Penh, Cambodia's resurgent capital, is the place to check the pulse of contemporary life. Siem Reap, gateway to the majestic temples of Angkor, is starting to give the capital a run for its money with sophisticated restaurants, funky bars and chic boutiques. World Heritage Site Angkor houses some of the most spectacular temples on earth.

Down on the South Coast are several up-and-coming beach resorts and a smattering of tropical islands that are just beginning to take off, unlike those of neighbouring countries. Northwestern Cambodia is home to Battambang, a slice of more traditional life, and several remote jungle temples. The country's wild east is where elephants roam, waterfalls thunder and freshwater dolphins can be found.

Phnom Penh

Shopping
Dining
Bars

Chic Boutiques

Choose from colourful local markets where bargains abound or check out the impressive collections of local designers. There are plenty of good-cause shops where your spending assists Cambodia.

Creative Cuisine

French bistros abound, and outstanding fusion restaurants blend the best of Cambodian and European flavours. Ubiquitous Cambodian barbecues offer a local experience, or try gourmet Khmer cuisine in a designer restaurant.

Happy Hour

Get started early in a breezy establishment overlooking the Mekong, move on to a live-music bar, and dance till dawn in a club. Phnom Penh is 24/7, one of the liveliest capitals in Asia.

p48

Siem Reap

Activities
Temples
Dining

Adventures Beyond Angkor

Take to the skies by helicopter to see Angkor from a different angle. Zipline through the jungle or quad bike through rice fields. Experience a cooking class or unwind with a massage.

Divine Inspiration

It's not just all about Angkor Wat. True, it's one of the world's most iconic buildings, but down the road are the enigmatic faces of Bayon and the jungle temple of Ta Prohm.

Eclectic Epicurean Experiences

Contemporary Khmer cuisine, spiced-up street food, fine French dining and more: Siem Reap is a dining destination in itself. Continue the night along Pub St and the gentrified lanes beyond.

p103

South Coast

Activities
Dining
Beaches

Land or Sea

National parks and protected areas dot the region, offering trekking, mountain biking, kayaking, rock climbing and stand-up paddleboarding. Water sports abound or venture underwater to experience snorkelling or scuba diving.

Seafood Specialities

Each coastal town has its speciality. In Kep, it's delectable crab. In Takeo, it's river lobster. In Kampot, it's anything cooked with the region's famous pepper. The southern islands offer a seafood banquet.

Tropical Bliss

Claim a strip of sand all to yourself or relax in a beachfront bar. Choose life in the fast lane in Kampot, the slow lane in Kep or forget the roads altogether and escape to the islands.

p177

Northwestern Cambodia

Temples
Boat Trips
Towns

Beyond the Crowds

Heard enough about Angkor Wat? Don't forget the pre-Angkorian capital of Sambor Prei Kuk, the jungle temples of Preah Vihear Province and atmospheric Banteay Chhmar.

Floating Villages

One of the best boat rides in Cambodia links Battambang to Siem Reap following the Sangker River. Explore the largest floating village on the Tonlé Sap lake, Kompong Luong.

The Real Cambodia

Riverside Battambang has some of the country's best-preserved French architecture, while Kompong Chhnang and Kompong Thom are off the tourist trail and offer a slice of real Cambodia.

p233

Eastern Cambodia

Culture
River Life
Wildlife

A World Apart

Northeast Cambodia is home to a mosaic of ethnic minorities. Encounter the Bunong people of Mondulkiri or venture up jungle rivers to visit the remote tribal cemeteries in Ratanakiri.

The Mighty Mekong

The Mekong cuts through the region's heart and includes the Mekong Discovery Trail, a community-based tourism initiative. Beyond the Mekong is the Tonlé Srepok tributary, as depicted in *Apocalypse Now*.

The Wild Things

View rare freshwater dolphins around Kratie, walk with a herd of elephants in Mondulkiri, or spot primates on forest treks around Mondulkiri or Ratanakiri.

p274

On the Road

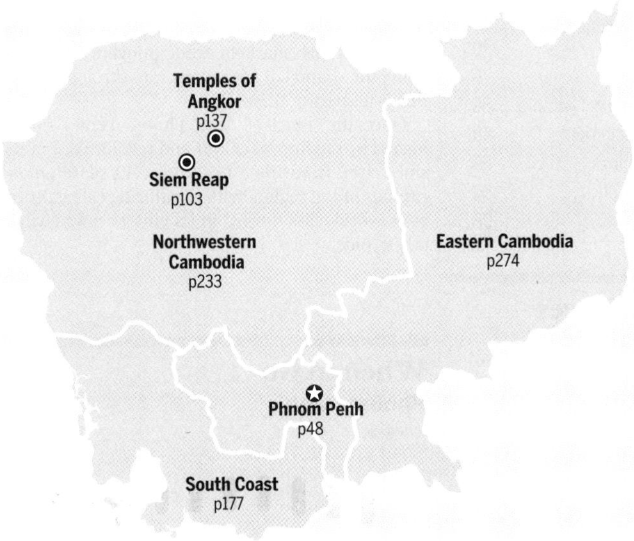

Temples of Angkor p137

Siem Reap p103

Northwestern Cambodia p233

Eastern Cambodia p274

Phnom Penh p48

South Coast p177

Phnom Penh

Includes ➡

Sights 52
Activities 60
Courses 66
Tours 67
Festivals & Events 70
Sleeping 70
Eating 75
Drinking & Nightlife . . . 85
Entertainment 88
Shopping 89
Koh Dach 97
Udong 98

Best Places to Eat

➡ Nesat Seafood House (p83)

➡ Vibe Cafe (p76)

➡ House of Scott (p76)

➡ Malis (p81)

Best Places to Stay

➡ Eighty8 Backpackers (p72)

➡ Manor House (p74)

➡ SLA Boutique Hostel (p72)

➡ Patio Hotel & Urban Resort (p75)

Why Go?

With the glimmering spires of the Royal Palace, the fluttering saffron of the monks' robes and the luscious location on the banks of the mighty Mekong – Phnom Penh (ភ្នំពេញ) is the Asia many daydream about from afar.

Cambodia's fast-growing capital can be an assault on the senses. Motorbikes whiz down lanes without a thought for pedestrians; markets exude pungent scents; and all the while the sounds of life reverberate through the streets. But this is all part of the enigma.

Once the 'Pearl of Asia', Phnom Penh's shine was tarnished by the impact of war and revolution. But the city has since risen from the ashes to take its place among the hip capitals of the region, with an alluring cafe culture, bustling bars, world-class dining and a glittery new skyline growing on steroids.

When to Go
Phnom Penh

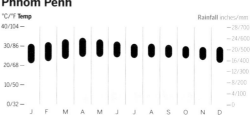

Jan & Feb The holiday crush is over and pleasant northeasterly breezes massage the riverfront.

Sep & Oct Heavy rains provide relief from searing sun; many hotels offer steep discounts.

Oct & Nov Bon Om Tuk water festival is one giant street party on the riverbanks.

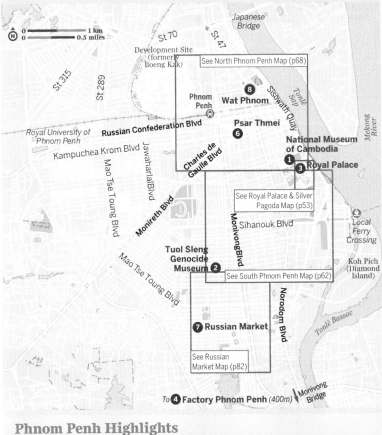

Phnom Penh Highlights

1 National Museum of Cambodia (p54) Discovering the world's finest collection of Khmer sculpture.

2 Tuol Sleng Genocide Museum (p54) Delving into the dark side of Cambodian history here and at the Killing Fields of Choeung Ek.

3 Royal Palace (p53) Exploring King Sihamoni's striking official residence.

4 Factory Phnom Penh (p56) Checking the pulse of Cambodia's contemporary art scene at this one-time Levi's factory turned cultural centre.

5 Nightlife (p85) Diving into Phnom Penh's frenzied nightlife with a happy-hour cocktail at Sundown Social Club, a Bassac Lane bar crawl and a late-night drag show at Heart of Darkness.

6 Psar Thmei (p56) Browsing the iconic domed Central Market, a striking building designed like a Babylonian ziggurat.

7 Russian Market (p89) Shopping till you drop (of heat exhaustion) at this bounteous market.

8 Wat Phnom (p56) Praying for luck during your trip at this historic hilltop temple.

History

Legend has it that the city of Phnom Penh was founded when an old woman named Penh found four Buddha images that had come to rest on the banks of the Mekong River. She housed them on a nearby hill, and the town that grew up here came to be known as Phnom Penh (Hill of Penh).

In the 1430s, Angkor was abandoned and Phnom Penh chosen as the site of the new Cambodian capital. Angkor was poorly situated for trade and subject to attacks from

Greater Phnom Penh

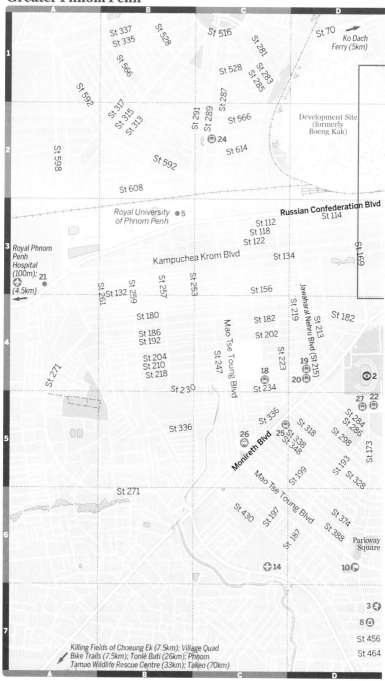

St 337
St 335
St 528
St 516
St 281
St 70
Ko Dach Ferry (5km)
St 566
St 528
St 283
St 285
St 592
St 287
St 317
St 315
St 313
St 291
St 289
St 566
St 598
● 24
St 614
St 592
St 608

Development Site (formerly Boeng Kak)

Royal University of Phnom Penh ● 5
Russian Confederation Blvd
St 114
St 112
St 118
St 122
St 169
Royal Phnom Penh Hospital (100m); 21
(4.5km)
Kampuchea Krom Blvd
St 134
St 261
St 132
St 259
St 257
St 253
St 156
St 180
St 219
St 182
St 182
St 186
St 192
St 182
St 202
St 213
St 204
St 210
St 218
St 223
St 271
St 230
18
St 234
19
20
◉ 2
27 22
Mao Tse Toung Blvd
St 247
St 336
St 336
St 318
St 284
St 286
26
25
St 338
St 298
St 173
Monireth Blvd
St 348
St 199
St 193
St 328
St 271
Mao Tse Toung Blvd
St 430
St 197
St 374
St 388
St 187
Parkway Square
14
10
3
8
St 456
St 464

Killing Fields of Choeung Ek (7.5km); Village Quad Bike Trails (7.5km); Tonlé Bati (26km); Phnom Tamao Wildlife Rescue Centre (33km); Takeo (70km)

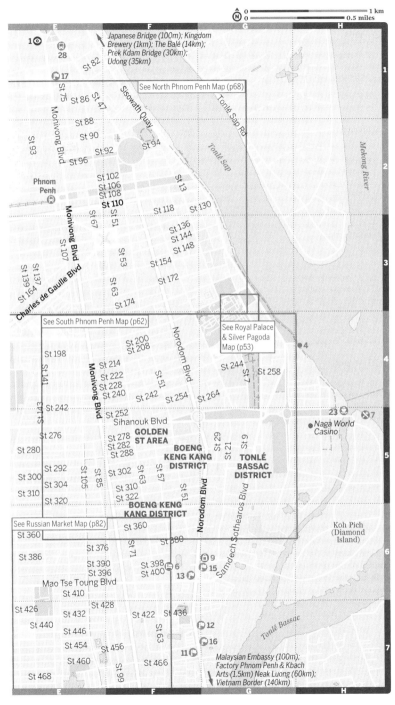

0 1 km
0 0.5 miles

Japanese Bridge (100m); Kingdom Brewery (1km); The Balé (14km); Prek Kdam Bridge (30km); Udong (35km)

See North Phnom Penh Map (p68)

See South Phnom Penh Map (p62)

See Royal Palace & Silver Pagoda Map (p53)

See Russian Market Map (p82)

Mekong River

Tonlé Sap

Tonlé Sap Rd

Sisowath Quay

Monivong Blvd

Charles de Gaulle Blvd

Phnom Penh

St 82
St 75
St 86
St 47
St 88
St 90
St 92
St 94
St 96
St 93
St 102
St 106
St 108
St 110
St 67
St 51
St 53
St 63
St 107
St 137
St 139
St 164
St 13
St 118
St 130
St 136
St 144
St 148
St 154
St 172
St 174

St 198
St 200
St 208
St 214
St 222
St 228
St 240
St 242
St 51
St 254
St 264
St 244
St 7
St 258
St 141
St 143
St 242
St 252
Sihanouk Blvd
GOLDEN ST AREA
St 278
St 282
St 288
St 276
St 280
St 292
St 300
St 304
St 310
St 105
St 85
St 302
St 63
St 57
St 310
St 322
St 320
St 51
Norodom Blvd
Norodom Blvd
St 29
St 21
St 9
Samdech Sothearos Blvd

BOENG KENG KANG DISTRICT
BOENG KENG KANG DISTRICT
TONLÉ BASSAC DISTRICT

Naga World Casino

23
7

Koh Pich (Diamond Island)

St 360
St 360
St 386
St 376
St 390
St 396
St 71
St 380
St 398
St 400
6
9
15
13
Mao Tse Toung Blvd
St 410
St 426
St 428
St 432
St 422
St 436
St 440
St 446
St 454
St 456
St 63
St 460
St 99
St 466
St 468
12
16
11

Tonlé Bassac

Malaysian Embassy (100m); Factory Phnom Penh & Kbach Arts (1.5km) Neak Luong (60km); Vietnam Border (140km)

1
28
17
4

Greater Phnom Penh

◉ Sights
1 French Embassy......................................E1
2 Olympic Stadium...................................D4

◆ Activities, Courses & Tours
3 C4 Adventures...D7
4 Kanika Boat Tour......................................H4
5 Royal University of Phnom Penh B3

🛏 Sleeping
6 House Boutique......................................F6

✕ Eating
7 Koh Pich Barbecues H5

🛍 Shopping
8 Rajana...D7
9 Watthan Artisans G6

ℹ Information
10 Chinese Embassy................................D6
   French Embassy...........................(see 1)
11 Indonesian Embassy............................F7
12 Japanese Embassy G7
13 Myanmar Embassy F6
14 National Blood Transfusion
    Centre..C6
15 Philippine Embassy...........................G6
16 Thai Embassy G7
17 UK Embassy..E1

ℹ Transport
   Cambodia Angkor Air ....(see 15)
18 Ekareach Express................................C4
19 Kampot Express....................................D4
20 Kim Seng Express D4
21 Lanmei Airlines....................................A3
22 Long Phuong...D5
23 Mekong Ferry..H5
24 Mey Hong Transport...........................C2
25 Olongpich Express C5
26 Psar Dang Kor Taxi Park C5
27 Sapaco...D5
28 Seila Angkor...E1

the Siamese (Thai) kingdom of Ayuthaya. Phnom Penh commanded a more central position in the Khmer territories and was perfectly located for riverine trade with Laos and China via the Mekong Delta.

By the mid-16th century, trade had turned Phnom Penh into a regional power. Indonesian and Chinese traders were drawn to the city in large numbers. A century later, however, the landlocked and increasingly isolated kingdom had become little more than a buffer between the ascendant Thais and Vietnamese, until the French took over in 1863.

The French protectorate in Cambodia gave Phnom Penh the layout we know today. They divided the city into districts or *quartiers* – the French and European traders inhabited the area north of Wat Phnom between Monivong Blvd and Tonlé Sap. By the time the French departed in 1953, they had left many important landmarks, including the Royal Palace, the National Museum, Psar Thmei (Central Market) and many impressive government ministries.

The city grew fast in the post-independence peacetime years of Norodom Sihanouk's rule: by the time he was overthrown in 1970, the population of Phnom Penh was approximately 500,000. As the Vietnam War spread into Cambodian territory, the city's population swelled with refugees and reached nearly three million in early 1975. The Khmer Rouge took the city on 17 April 1975, and as part of its radical revolution immediately forced the entire population into the countryside. Whole families were split up on those first fateful days of 'liberation'.

During the time of Democratic Kampuchea, many tens of thousands of former Phnom Penhois – including the vast majority of the capital's educated residents – were killed. The population of Phnom Penh during the Khmer Rouge regime was never more than about 50,000, a figure made up of senior party members, factory workers and trusted military leaders.

Repopulation of the city began when the Vietnamese arrived in 1979, although at first it was strictly controlled by the new government. During much of the 1980s, cows were more common than cars on the streets of the capital. The 1990s were boom years for some: along with the arrival of the UN Transitional Authority in Cambodia (UNTAC) came US$2 billion (much of it in salaries for expats).

Phnom Penh has really begun to change in the last two decades, with roads being repaired, sewage pipes laid, parks inaugurated and riverbanks reclaimed. Business is booming in many parts of the city, where skyscrapers are sprouting like beanstalks and investors rubbing their hands with the sort of glee once reserved for Bangkok or Hanoi. Phnom Penh is back, and bigger changes are set to come.

◉ Sights

Phnom Penh, a relatively small city, is easy to navigate as it is laid out in a numbered grid. The most important cultural sights can be visited on foot and are located near the riverfront. Most other sights are also fairly central, just a short *remork-moto (tuk tuk)* ride from the riverfront.

★ **Royal Palace** PALACE

(ព្រះបរមរាជវាំង; Map p53; Samdech Sothearos Blvd; admission incl camera 40,000r, guide per hour US$10; ⊙8-11am & 2-5pm) With its classic Khmer roofs and ornate gilding, the Royal Palace once dominated the skyline of Phnom Penh. It's a striking structure near the riverfront, bearing a remarkable likeness to its counterpart in Bangkok. Being the official residence of King Sihamoni, parts of the massive palace compound are closed to the public. The adjacent Silver Pagoda is open to visitors.

Tourists are allowed to visit only the Throne Hall and a clutch of buildings surrounding it. All visitors need to wear shorts that reach to the knees, and a T-shirt or blouse that reaches to the elbows; otherwise you will have to buy an appropriate sarong as a covering at the ticket booth. The palace gets very busy on Sundays, when countryside Khmers come to pay their respects, but being among crowds of locals can be a fun way to experience the place.

Visitors enter into the eastern portion of the palace compound, not far from the Chan Chaya Pavilion (ព្រះទីនាំង ប្រាសាទ ចន្ទឆាយា). Performances of classical Cambodian dance were once staged in this pavilion, which is still sometimes lit up at night to commemorate festivals or anniversaries.

The main attraction in the palace compound is the Throne Hall, topped by a 59m-high tower inspired by the Bayon at Angkor. The hall is used for coronations and ceremonies such as the presentation of credentials by diplomats. Many of the items once displayed here were destroyed by the Khmer Rouge.

South of the Throne Hall, check out the curious iron Napoleon III Pavilion (វិមានស្ដេចណាប៉ូឡេអុងទី៣). Given to King Norodom by Napoleon III of France, it was hardly designed with the Cambodian climate in mind. In fact, it was originally built for the inauguration of the Suez Canal in 1869, before being shipped to Cambodia in pieces.

★ **Silver Pagoda** BUDDHIST TEMPLE

(ព្រះវិហារព្រះកែវមរកត; Map p53; Royal Palace compound; incl in admission to Royal Palace; ⊙7.30-11am & 2-5pm) Within the Royal Palace compound is this extravagant temple, also

Royal Palace & Silver Pagoda

Royal Palace & Silver Pagoda

◎ **Top Sights**
1 Royal Palace..A2
2 Silver Pagoda.......................................B3

◎ **Sights**
3 Chan Chaya Pavilion............................A1
4 Napoleon III Pavilion...........................A2
5 Ramayana Mural.................................B2
6 Throne Hall...A2

known as Wat Preah Keo or Temple of the Emerald Buddha. The Silver Pagoda is so named for its floor, which is covered with 5 tonnes of gleaming silver. You can sneak a peek at some of the 5000 tiles near the entrance, but most are covered for protection. Inside is a series of lavish Buddha statues made of precious metals.

The staircase leading to the Silver Pagoda is made of Italian marble. Rivalling the silver floor is the Emerald Buddha, an extraordinary Baccarat-crystal sculpture sitting atop an impressive gilded pedestal. Adding to the lavish mix is a life-sized solid-gold Buddha adorned with 2086 diamonds, the largest weighing in at 25 carats. Created in the palace workshops during 1906 and 1907, the gold Buddha weighs 90kg. Directly in front of it, in a Formica case, is a miniature silver-and-gold stupa containing a relic of Buddha brought from Sri Lanka. To the left is an 80kg bronze Buddha, and to the right a silver Buddha. On the far right, figurines of solid gold tell the story of the Buddha.

The pagoda was originally constructed of wood in 1892 during the rule of King Norodom, who was apparently inspired by Bangkok's Wat Phra Kaew, and was rebuilt in 1962. It was preserved by the Khmer Rouge to demonstrate to the outside world its concern for the conservation of Cambodia's cultural riches. Although more than half of the pagoda's contents were lost, stolen or destroyed in the turmoil that followed the Vietnamese invasion, what remains is spectacular. This is one of the few places in Cambodia where bejewelled objects embodying some of the brilliance and richness of Khmer civilisation can still be seen.

Along the walls of the pagoda are examples of extraordinary Khmer artisanship, including intricate masks used in classical dance and dozens of gold Buddhas. The many precious gifts given to Cambodia's monarchs by foreign heads of state appear rather spiritless when displayed next to such diverse and exuberant Khmer art. (Note that photography is not permitted inside the Silver Pagoda.)

Ramayana Mural   PUBLIC ART
(Map p53; Royal Palace compound) The Silver Pagoda complex is enclosed by walls plastered with an extensive and, in parts, spectacular mural depicting the classic Indian epic of the *Ramayana* (known as the *Reamker* in Cambodia). The story begins just south of the east gate and includes vivid images of the Battle of Lanka. The mural was created around 1900 and parts of it have recently undergone restoration.

★ National Museum
of Cambodia   MUSEUM
(សារមន្ទីរជាតិ; Map p68; www.cambodia museum.info; cnr Sts 13 & 178; US$10; ⊙ 8am-5pm) The National Museum of Cambodia is home to the world's finest collection of Khmer sculpture: a millennium's worth and more of masterful Khmer design. It's housed in a graceful terracotta structure of traditional design (built from 1917 to 1920) with an inviting courtyard garden, just north of the Royal Palace.

Most visitors start left and continue in a clockwise, chronological direction. One of the first significant sculptures to greet visitors is a large fragment – including the relatively intact head, shoulders and two arms – of an immense bronze reclining Vishnu statue, which was recovered from the Western Mebon temple near Angkor Wat in 1936. Continue into the southern pavilion, where the pre-Angkorian collection begins, illustrating the journey from the human form of Indian sculpture to the more divine form of Khmer sculpture from the 5th to 8th centuries. Highlights include an imposing, eight-armed Vishnu statue from the 6th century, found at Phnom Da, and a staring Harihara, combining the attributes of Shiva and Vishnu, from Prasat Andet in Kompong Thom Province. The Angkor collection includes several striking statues of Shiva from the 9th, 10th and 11th centuries; a giant pair of wrestling monkeys (Koh Ker, 10th century); a beautiful 12th-century stele (stone) from Oddar Meanchey Province inscribed with scenes from the life of Shiva; and the sublime statue of a seated Jayavarman VII (r 1181–1219), his head bowed slightly in a meditative pose (Angkor Thom, late 12th century).

The museum also contains displays of pottery and bronzes dating from the pre-Angkorian periods of Funan and Chenla (4th to 9th centuries), the Indravarman period (9th and 10th centuries) and the classical Angkorian period (10th to 14th centuries), as well as more recent works, such as a beautiful wooden royal barge.

Note that visitors are not allowed to photograph the collection, only the central courtyard. English-, French-, Spanish- and Japanese-speaking guides are available for tours (US$6). A comprehensive booklet, *The New Guide to the National Museum* (US$15), is available at the front desk, while the smaller *Khmer Art in Stone* (US$2) covers some signature pieces. There are also audio guides available in eight languages (US$5).

★ Tuol Sleng
Genocide Museum   MUSEUM
(សារមន្ទីរឧក្រិដ្ឋកម្មប្រល័យពូជសាសន៍ទួលស្លែង; Map p82; www.tuolsleng.gov.kh; cnr Sts 113 & 350; adult/child US$5/3, audio tour US$3, guide by donation; ⊙ 8am-5pm) In 1975 Tuol Svay Prey High School was taken over by Pol Pot's security forces and turned into a prison known as Security Prison 21 (S-21); it soon became the largest centre of detention and torture in the country. S-21 has been turned into the

Tuol Sleng museum, which serves as a testament to the crimes of the Khmer Rouge.

Between 1975 and 1978, some 20,000 people held at S-21 were taken to the Killing Fields of Choeung Ek. Like the Nazis, the Khmer Rouge leaders were meticulous in keeping records of their barbarism. Each prisoner who passed through S-21 was photographed, sometimes before and after torture. The museum displays include room after room of harrowing B&W photographs; virtually all of the men, women and children pictured were later killed. You can tell which year a picture was taken by the style of number-board that appears on the prisoner's chest. Several foreigners from Australia, New Zealand and the USA were also held at S-21 before being murdered. It's worth hiring a guide, as they can tell you the stories behind some of the people in the photographs. An audio tour is also available, and recommended for greater insight for visitors without a guide.

As the Khmer Rouge 'revolution' reached ever greater heights of insanity, it began devouring its own. Generations of torturers and executioners who worked here were in turn killed by those who took their places. During early 1977, when the party purges of Eastern Zone cadres were getting under way, S-21 claimed an average of 100 victims a day.

When the Vietnamese army liberated Phnom Penh in early 1979, there were only seven prisoners alive at S-21, all of whom had used their skills, such as painting or photography, to stay alive. Fourteen others had been tortured to death as Vietnamese forces were closing in on the city. Photographs of their gruesome deaths are on display in the rooms where their decomposing corpses were found. Their graves are nearby in the courtyard. Two of the survivors, Chum Mey and Bou Meng, are still alive, and often spend their time at S-21 promoting their first-hand accounts of their time in the prison.

A visit to Tuol Sleng is a profoundly depressing experience. The sheer ordinariness of the place makes it even more horrific: the suburban setting, the plain school buildings and the grassy playing area where children kick around balls, juxtaposed with rusted beds, instruments of torture and wall after wall of disturbing portraits. It demonstrates the darkest side of the human spirit that lurks within us all. Tuol Sleng is not for the squeamish.

Behind many of the displays at Tuol Sleng is the Documentation Center of Cambodia (www.dccam.org). DC-Cam was established in 1995 through Yale University's Cambodian Genocide Program to research and document the crimes of the Khmer Rouge. It became an independent organisation in 1997 and researchers have spent years translating confessions and paperwork from Tuol Sleng, mapping mass graves, and preserving evidence of Khmer Rouge crimes.

French-Cambodian director Rithy Panh's film *The Khmer Rouge Killing Machine* includes interviews with former prison guards, including chief interrogator Him Huy, and is shown daily at 9am. Another Khmer Rouge documentary, *Behind the Wall*, screens at 3.45pm daily.

★**Killing Fields of Choeung Ek** MEMORIAL

(វាលពិឃាតជើងឯក; admission incl audio tour US$6; ⏱7.30am-5.30pm) Between 1975 and 1978, about 20,000 men, women, children and infants who had been detained and tortured at S-21 prison were transported to the extermination camp of Choeung Ek. It is a peaceful place today, where visitors can learn of the horrors that unfolded here decades ago. Admission includes an excellent audio tour, available in several languages.

The remains of 8985 people, many of whom were bound and blindfolded, were exhumed in 1980 from mass graves in this one-time longan orchard; 43 of the 129 communal graves here have been left untouched. Fragments of human bone and bits of cloth are scattered around the disinterred pits. More than 8000 skulls, arranged by sex and age, are visible behind the clear glass panels of the Memorial Stupa, which was erected in 1988.

The audio tour includes stories by those who survived the Khmer Rouge, plus a chilling account by Him Huy, a Choeung Ek guard and executioner, about some of the techniques they used to kill innocent and defenceless prisoners, including women and children. There's also a museum here with some interesting information on the Khmer Rouge leadership and the ongoing trial. A memorial ceremony is held annually at Choeung Ek on 20 May.

The site is well signposted in English about 7.5km south of the city limits. Figure on about US$10 for a *remork* (drivers may ask for more) for a half day. A shuttle-bus tour is available with Phnom Penh Hop On Hop Off (p96), which includes hotel pickup from 8am in the morning or 1.30pm in the afternoon.

★**Psar Thmei** MARKET
(ផ្សារធំថ្មី, Central Market; Map p68; St 130; ⊙6.30am-5.30pm) A landmark building in the capital, the art deco Psar Thmei (literally 'New Market') is often called the Central Market, a reference to its location and size. The huge domed hall resembles a Babylonian ziggurat and some claim it ranks as one of the 10 largest domes in the world.

The design allows for maximum ventilation, and even on a sweltering day the central hall is cool and airy. The market was recently renovated with French government assistance and is in good shape. It has four wings filled with stalls selling gold and silver jewellery, antique coins, dodgy watches, clothing and other such items. For photographers, the fresh-food section affords many opportunities. For a local lunch, there are a host of food stalls located on the western side, which faces Monivong Blvd.

Psar Thmei is undoubtedly the best market for browsing. However, it has a reputation among Cambodians for overcharging on most products.

★**Factory Phnom Penh** CULTURAL CENTRE
(ហ្វេកធើរីភ្នំពេញ; http://factoryphnompenh. com; 1159 NH2; ⊙7am-9pm Mon-Fri, to 7pm Sat & Sun) FREE This 3.4-hectare Levi's garment factory, 2km south of town, was completely transformed in 2018 into a graffiti-covered hub for entrepreneurs, artists and creative thinkers. On a ride through the sprawling campus (there are 50 free-to-use bikes) you'll encounter four art galleries, most run by Kbach Arts, as well as a skate park, trampoline park, craft brewery, stage, cinema,

market and the **Workspace 1** (WS1; ☑017 999547; http://factoryphnompenh.com/work space-1; day pass US$8; ⊙7am-8pm Mon-Sat) coworking space. It's virtually impossible to visit this aspirational complex and leave uninspired.

★**Kbach Arts** ARTS CENTRE
(ក្បាចំអាគ; ☑031 3871444; http://kbachgallery. com; 1159 NH2; ⊙10am-6pm) FREE Cambodia finally got a sizable contemporary arts space in 2019, when Kbach moved into three galleries covering 400 sq metres of Factory Phnom Penh. The mission is to provide a platform for young Khmer artists to showcase their work, while also inviting resident artists from abroad to serve as mentors. Dazzling murals cover the exterior, and the interior houses urban and mixed-medium art. A small art market with original works and limited edition prints was set to open by 2020.

Futures Factory CULTURAL CENTRE
(ហ្វ៊ូជើរហ្វេកធើរី; Map p68; 215 St 13; ⊙8.30am-10pm) Helmed by the ever-popular Friends (p76) restaurant, this new community space aims to become the cultural heart of central Phnom Penh with a regular lineup of live music, family activities and gallery exhibitions, plus a market with indie shops, a bar and plenty of pallet furniture to lounge around in.

Wat Phnom BUDDHIST TEMPLE
(វត្តភ្នំ; Map p68; Norodom Blvd; entry US$1; ⊙7am-6pm) Set on top of a 27m-high tree-covered knoll, Wat Phnom is on the only 'hill' in town. According to legend, the first pagoda on this site was erected in 1372 to house four statues of Buddha deposited here by the waters of the Mekong River and discovered by Lady Penh. Hence the city name Phnom Penh or 'hill of Penh'.

The main entrance to Wat Phnom is via the grand eastern staircase, which is guarded by lions and naga (mythical serpent-being) balustrades. Today, many people come here to pray for good luck and success in school exams or business affairs. When a wish is granted, the faithful return to deliver on the offering promised, such as a garland of jasmine flowers or a bunch of bananas (of which the spirits are said to be especially fond).

The *vihara* (temple sanctuary) was rebuilt in 1434, 1806, 1894 and 1926. West of the *vihara* is a huge stupa containing the

---

GIVE BLOOD!
• •

Cambodia has a critical shortage of blood, as there's a local stigma against donating blood and a high rate of thalassaemia. If you want to help, donate at the **National Blood Transfusion Centre** (Map p50; ☑023-217524; Khmer-Soviet Friendship Hospital, St 271; ⊙8am-5pm). It's perfectly safe and you get a T-shirt, although only 18- to 60-year-olds can donate.

LOCAL KNOWLEDGE

WARNING: BAG & PHONE SNATCHING

Bag snatching has become a real problem in Phnom Penh, with foreigners often targeted. Hotspots include the riverfront and busy areas around popular markets, but there is no real pattern; the speeding motorbike thieves, usually operating in pairs, can strike any time, any place. Countless expats and tourists have been injured falling off their bikes in the process of being robbed, and in 2007 a young French woman was killed after being dragged from a speeding *moto* (motorcycle taxi) into the path of a vehicle. Wear close-fitting bags (such as backpacks) that don't dangle from the body temptingly. Don't hang expensive cameras around the neck and keep mobile phones close to the body or out of sight, particularly when walking along the road, crossing the road or travelling by *remork-moto* or especially by *moto*. These people are real pros and only need one chance.

ashes of King Ponhea Yat (r 1405–67). In a pavilion on the southern side of the passage between the *vihara* and the stupa is a statue of a smiling Lady Penh.

A bit to the north of and below the *vihara* is an eclectic shrine dedicated to the genie Preah Chau, who is especially revered by the Vietnamese. On either side of the entrance to the central altar are guardian spirits bearing iron bats. In the chamber to the right of the statue are drawings of Confucius, as well as two Chinese-style figures of the sages Thang Cheng (on the right) and Thang Thay (on the left).

Down the hill from the *vihara,* in the northwest corner of the complex, is a worthwhile arts and crafts centre, where women and disabled people sell sculptures, silks, jewellery, ceramics and more.

Independence Monument   MONUMENT
(វិមានឯករាជ្យ; Map p62; cnr Norodom & Sihanouk Blvds) Modelled on the central tower of Angkor Wat, Independence Monument was built in 1958 to commemorate the country's independence from France in 1953. It also serves as a memorial to Cambodia's war dead. Wreaths are laid here on national holidays.

Norodom
Sihanouk Statue   MEMORIAL
(រូបសំណាកព្រះបរមរតនកោដ្ឋ; Map p62; Sihanouk Blvd) This impressive statue shows the legendary former king/prime minister/statesman King Father Norodom Sihanouk, who died a national hero in 2012.

It's in the park just east of Independence Monument.

Wat Ounalom   BUDDHIST TEMPLE
(វត្តឧណ្ណាលោម; Map p68; Samdech Sothearos Blvd; ⊙6am-6pm) FREE This wat is the headquarters of Cambodian Buddhism. It was founded in 1443 and comprises 44 struc-

tures. The wat received a battering during the Pol Pot era, but today it has come back to life. The head of the country's Buddhist brotherhood lives here, along with a large number of monks.

On the 2nd floor of the main building, to the left of the dais, is a statue of Huot Tat, fourth patriarch of Cambodian Buddhism, who was killed by Pol Pot. The statue, made in 1971 when the patriarch was 80 years old, was thrown in the Mekong by the Khmer Rouge to show that Buddhism was no longer the driving force in Cambodia. It was retrieved after 1979. To the right of the dais is a statue of a former patriarch of the Thummayuth sect, to which the royal family belongs.

Seek out the stairway to the left behind the dais. It leads up to the 3rd floor, where a glass case houses a small marble Buddha of Burmese origin that was broken into pieces by the Khmer Rouge and later reassembled. There are some good views of the Mekong from up here, though the door at the top of the stairs is often locked.

Behind the main building is a stupa containing an eyebrow hair of Buddha with an inscription in Pali (an ancient Indian language) over the entrance.

Olympic Stadium   LANDMARK
(ពហុកីឡដ្ឋានជាតិអូឡាំពិក; Map p50; Monireth Blvd; ⊙6am-10pm) FREE Despite the lofty name, this multipurpose sports complex has never hosted an Olympic Games. Nevertheless, it's a striking example of 1960s 'New Khmer' architecture, with an arena and facilities for boxing, gymnastics, volleyball and other sports. Turn up after 5pm to see countless football matches, *pétanque* duels or badminton games. It's also a popular spot for sunrise or sunset mass musical aerobics.

Phnom Penh

Cambodia's capital casts its spell over all who enter. It might be the gleaming spires
of the Royal Palace, or the graceful French architecture, a waft of lemongrass from
a street stall, or the infectious buzz of the cafe-lined riverfront. Somehow, some way,
Phnom Penh will grab you.

MATHIJS VAN DEN BOSCH/500PX ©

MARK READ/LONELY PLANET ©

1. Traditional Dance Show (p88)

Cambodian Living Arts (p67) puts on dance shows in the grounds of the National Museum of Cambodia (p54).

2. Royal Palace (p53)

Built between 1866 and 1870, the Royal Palace has been the home of generations of Cambodian kings.

3. Tuol Sleng Genocide Museum (p54)

This former prison complex is a solemn testament to the brutality of the Khmer Rouge regime.

4. Ramayana Mural (p54)

Artists working to restore the mural of the classic Indian epic, the *Ramayana* (known to Cambodians as *Reamker*).

XPACIFICA/GETTY IMAGES ©

French Embassy LANDMARK

(Map p50; 1 Monivong Blvd) Located at the northern end of Monivong Blvd, the French embassy played a significant role in the dramas that unfolded after the fall of Phnom Penh on 17 April 1975. About 800 foreigners and 600 Cambodians took refuge in the embassy. Within 48 hours, the Khmer Rouge informed the French vice-consul that they did not recognise diplomatic privileges – and if the Cambodians in the compound were not handed over, the lives of the foreigners inside would also be forfeited.

National Library LIBRARY

(បណ្ណាល័យជាតិ, Bibliothèque Nationale; Map p68; St 92; ⊙ 7.30-11.30am & 2-5pm Mon-Fri) The National Library is in a graceful old building constructed in 1924, near Wat Phnom. During its rule, the Khmer Rouge turned the building into a stable and destroyed most of the books. Many were thrown out into the streets, where they were picked up by people, some of whom donated them back to the library after 1979; others used them as food wrappings. Today it houses, among other things, a time-worn collection of English and French titles.

🏃 Activities

C4 Adventures OUTDOORS

(Map p50; www.c4-adventures.com; 12C St 444) Founded by former French legionnaire David Minetti, this adventure outfit specialises in taking thrill seekers far off the beaten path in Cambodia for kayaking, biking, canyoning and trekking. The jungles, mountains and remote islands where they lead tours are places few other agencies operate.

Hash House Harriers RUNNING

(Map p68; www.p2h3.com; Phnom Penh Railway Station; US$5-8; ⊙ 2.15pm Sun) A good opportunity to meet local expatriates is via the Hash House Harriers, usually referred to simply as 'the Hash'. A run/walk takes place every Sunday. Participants meet in front of the train station at 2.15pm. The fee includes refreshments – mainly a lot of beer – at the end.

Aerobics (Line Dancing)

Every morning at the crack of dawn, and again at dusk, Cambodians gather in several pockets throughout the city to participate in quirky and colourful aerobics sessions. This quintessential Cambodian phenomenon sees a ringleader, equipped with boom box and microphone, whip protégés into shape with a mix of 1980s, Soviet-style calisthenics and *Thriller*-inspired line-dancing moves. It's favoured by middle-aged Khmer women, but you'll see both sexes and all ages participating, and tourists are more than welcome.

There are many places to join the fun or just observe. Olympic Stadium (p57) is probably the best spot for the sheer volume of participants; several instructors compete for clients and the upper level of the grandstand becomes a cacophony of competing boom boxes.

The riverfront usually sees some action: the space at the terminus of St 144 is a good bet. Another popular place that usually sees several groups in action is Wat Botum Park, along Samdech Sothearos Blvd.

Boat Cruises

Boat trips on the Tonlé Sap and Mekong Rivers are very popular with visitors. Sunset cruises are ideal, the burning sun sinking slowly behind the glistening spires of the Royal Palace. A slew of cruising boats are available for hire on the riverfront about 500m north of the tourist-boat dock. Just rock up and arrange one on the spot for around US$20 an hour, depending on negotiations and numbers. You can bring your own drinks or buy beer and soft drinks on the boat.

Public river cruises are another option. They leave every 30 minutes or so from 5pm to 7.30pm from the tourist-boat dock (p93) and last about 45 minutes (US$5 per head).

Kanika Boat Tour BOATING

(Map p50; ☑ 089 848959; www.kanika-boat. com; sunset/dinner cruise US$8/22) The *Kanika* is a striking white catamaran that sails the waters of the Tonlé Sap and Mekong nightly. Book in advance and choose from a sunset cruise at 5pm or a longer dinner cruise from 7pm.

Memorable Cambodia BOATING

(Map p68; ☑ 069 555433; www.memorablecam bodia.com; off Sisowath Quay) Half-day cruises to Koh Dach (Silk Island, US$30) and full-day excursions to Udong (US$65) run by enthusiastic Cambodian students from a local hospitality school. Also operates popular evening sunset cruises (US$15).

Koh Dach Boat Trips BOATING

(Map p68; ☑ 012 860182; rimvuth@gmail.com; Sisowath Quay; per person US$15) Daily boat

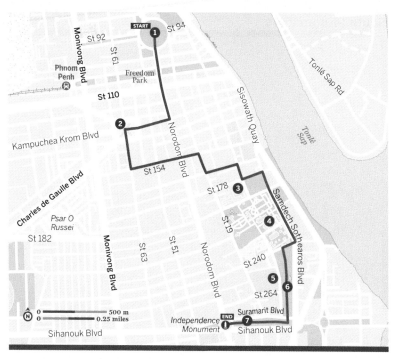

🏃 Walking Tour
Architecture of Cambodia's Capital

START WAT PHNOM
END INDEPENDENCE MONUMENT
LENGTH 4.5KM; FIVE HOURS

With erratic traffic, overflow parking on the pavement and little deference for pedestrians, Phnom Penh may not seem like the best city for walking. Yet, if you can build up some confidence (and patience), you'll find it's the most rewarding way to explore the city's varied architecture. Start your walking tour in the very spot where the city began: ❶ **Wat Phnom** (p54). Legend has it that the first pagoda was built on an artificial hill here in 1372 to house four statues of Buddha discovered nearby in the Mekong by the widow Lady Penh. Hence the city name Phnom Penh or 'hill of Penh'.

Heading south on Norodom Blvd, you'll pass several examples of French colonial architecture, including a former Peugeot car factory (today a Chinese bank) and an old art-nouveau-inspired customs office. Then, let the looming art-deco market ❷ **Psar Thmei** (p54), its huge domed hall resembling a Babylonian ziggurat, lure you west on St 130.

Depart Psar Thmei onto St 63 and turn east on St 154 for more colonial architecture. Next, zigzag over to the ❸ **National Museum of Cambodia** (p54). French architect George Groslier is said to have been inspired by temple prototypes seen on ancient bas-reliefs when he built this between 1917 and 1920. Nearby is the ❹ **Royal Palace** (p53) compound, a treasure trove of traditional Khmer architecture with gilded halls, lavish pavilions and honorary shrines. It's also the official residence of King Sihamoni.

Continue south into ❺ **Wat Botum Park**, where you'll find the Cambodia–Vietnam Friendship Monument, which was built in 1979. Turning west at Sihanouk Blvd, you'll encounter an imposing 27m-high shrine holding a bronze ❻ **statue of King Father Norodom Sihanouk** (p57), who died a national hero in 2012. Your walking tour ends nearby at the ❼ **Independence Monument** (p57), which is modelled on the central tower of Angkor Wat. It was built in 1958 to commemorate the country's independence from France. It also serves as a memorial to Cambodia's war dead.

South Phnom Penh

Psar
O Russei
🔒86

St 178

St 107

St 182

Capitol
Tour

Lucky!
Lucky!

St 198

St 184

St 200

St 51

⭐75

St 208

St 214

Indian
Embassy

German
Embassy

Moniyong Blvd

St 222

St 228

St 240

St 242

St 141
St 125
St 115
St 111
St 107
St 105

67

St 63

Ph 232

●6

27

🔒

St 242

48
⊗
69
🔗Raffles
Medical

St 55

41
⊗

18

54⊗

46⊗

29

28

St 252

🔒81

20

Sihanouk Blvd

11
8
66

St 276

St 278

87
72
59⊗

St 282

GOLDEN
ST AREA

St 280

⊗49

50⊗

St 292

St 113

St 95

St 294

65
19

St 57

St 300

St 302

7

55⊗

St 304

St 306

BOENG
KENG
KANG
DISTRICT

St 310

Moniyong Blvd

St 310

St 57

St 310

73

St 322

14

St 320

89

St 330

77⭐

St 334

St 334

80

St 348

St 352

See Russian Market Map (p82)

St 350

St 360

St 113

St 71

St 360

St 360

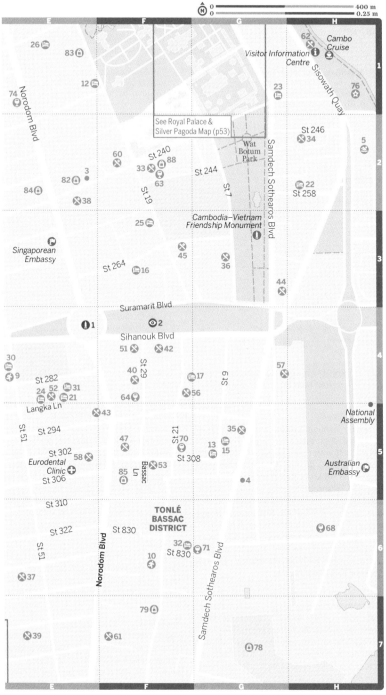

0   400 m
0   0.25 m

26
83
12
74
Norodom Blvd

62
Cambo
Cruise
Visitor Information
Centre
Sisowath Quay
23
76
5
St 246
34
60
St 240
88
33   63
82   3
84   38
St 19
St 244
St 7
Wat
Botum
Park
Samdech Sothearos Blvd
22
St 258
25
Cambodia–Vietnam
Friendship Monument
Singaporean
Embassy
St 264   16
45
36
44

Suramarit Blvd
1   2
Sihanouk Blvd
51   42
St 29
30
9
St 282
24 52   31
21
Langka Ln
43
40
64
17
St 9
57
56

St 51   St 294
47
St 21
St 70
St 308
13
15
35
National
Assembly
Eurodental
Clinic
St 302   58
85
Bassac
Ln
53
4
Australian
Embassy
St 306
St 310
St 322
Norodom Blvd
St 830
St 51
37
TONLÉ
BASSAC
DISTRICT
10
32
St 830
71
68
79
39
61
Samdech Sothearos Blvd
78

South Phnom Penh

◉ Sights
1 Independence Monument.....................E4
2 Norodom Sihanouk Statue..................F4

⊕ Activities, Courses & Tours
3 Cambodia Cooking Class.....................E2
4 Cambodian Living Arts.......................G5
5 FitnessOne Himawari Hotel.................H2
6 Maison Apsara...................................A3
7 NataRāj Yoga.....................................C5
8 Samantha Spa....................................D4
9 The Place...E4
10 Yoga Phnom Penh..............................F6

⊜ Sleeping
11 Anise...D4
12 Aura Thematic Hostel.........................E1
13 Corner 9 Bassac.................................G5
14 Envoy Hostel......................................D6
15 Hotel Corduroy...................................G5
16 Kabiki..F3
17 La Rose Suites....................................F4
18 Lumiere Hotel.....................................D3
19 Mad Monkey.......................................D5
20 Manor House......................................D4
21 Mini Banana Guesthouse.....................E4
22 Number 9 Guesthouse.........................H2
23 Palace Gate Hotel...............................G1
24 Patio Hotel & Urban Resort..................E4
25 Pavilion...F3

26 Plantation..E1
27 Tat Guesthouse..................................A3
28 Tattoo Guesthouse..............................A4
29 Teahouse...D3
30 Top Banana Guesthouse.....................E4
31 Villa Langka..E4
32 You Khin Art House..............................F6

⊗ Eating
Aeon Mall Food Court...................(see 78)
33 ARTillery..F2
34 Backyard Cafe....................................H2
Bistrot Langka.............................(see 21)
35 Boat Noodle Restaurant......................G5
36 Curry Noodle Stalls.............................G3
37 Eleven One Kitchen.............................E6
38 Enso Cafe...E2
39 Farm to Table.....................................E7
40 Feel Good Cafe II................................F4
41 House of Scott....................................C2
42 Java Creative Café..............................F4
43 JoMa Bakery Cafe...............................E5
44 Kravanh...G3
45 Limoncello...F3
46 Magnolia..D3
47 Malis...F5
Mama Wong's..............................(see 53)
Meat & Drink...............................(see 53)
48 Mercy House Restaurant......................D2
49 Mexicano Restaurant..........................D5

tours to Koh Dach depart at 9am and 11am from the tourist-boat dock (minimum three people).

Cycling

It is easy enough to hire a bike and go it alone, although take some time to familiarise yourself with traffic conditions first. Koh Dach (p97) is a doable DIY trip, or venture across the Mekong River on a local ferry (Map p50; Sihanouk Blvd; incl bike 1000r), which departs from the riverfront just north of the eastern end of Sihanouk Blvd, and pick up bucolic back roads on the other side. Alternatively, opt for something more organised (with or without a guide). Grasshopper Adventures runs daily group tours to Udong (p98) or Koh Dach.

★**Grasshopper**
Adventures   MOUNTAIN BIKING
(Map p68; ☑ 012 430622; www.grasshopper
adventures.com; 59 St 174; tours from US$45) This recommended bike company runs half-day tours around Phnom Penh or Koh Dach, as well as a full-day cycle along back roads and an abandoned railway line out to Udong. Also rents well-maintained bikes (US$12 for 24 hours).

Fitness Centres & Swimming

The fanciest hotels in Phnom Penh will let nonguests use their gyms and pools for a fee. A few of the boutique hotels will let you swim if you buy a few bucks' worth of food or cocktails. Most other midrange boutiques charge US$5 for pool rights. Keep in mind that the pools at most boutique hotels are pretty small, more for dipping and cooling off than for doing laps.

The Place   GYM
(Map p62; ☑ 023-999799; 11 St 51; walk-in US$15; ⊙ 6am-9.30pm Mon-Fri, to 9pm Sat & Sun) This is absolutely state of the art, with myriad machines, a big pool and a range of cardio classes.

FitnessOne
Himawari Hotel   SWIMMING
(Map p62; ☑ 023-214555; 313 Sisowath Quay; weekday/weekend US$9/10; ⊙ 6am-10pm) The Himawari has one of the best hotel pools

50 Mok Mony...D5
51 Ngon...F4
52 No Style...E4
53 Piccola Italia Da Luigi............................F5
54 Sleuk Chhouk..D3
55 Sonoma Oyster Bar D5
56 Sovanna II...F4
57 Super Duper...G4
58 Sushi Bar..E5
59 Taste Budz..D4
   Terrazza ....(see 59)
60 The Shop..F2
61 Topaz...F7
62 Yi Sang Riverside....................................H1

Drinking & Nightlife
   Battbong...(see 21)
63 Bong Bong Bong F2
64 Botanico Wine & Beer Garden...............F4
   Box Office...(see 63)
65 Brown Coffee...D5
66 Duplex...D4
67 Eclipse Sky Bar.......................................B3
   Embargo...(see 21)
68 Epic...H6
   Hangar 44..(see 53)
   Harry's Bar ....(see 53)
69 Hops Brewery..D2
70 Hub Street Cocktails...............................F5
   Le Boutier..(see 53)

Library ....(see 53)
   Red Bar..(see 53)
71 Samai Distillery G6
72 Score D4
   Seibur...(see 53)
73 Treehouse..A6
74 Vito...E1
   Zeppelin Bar.....................................(see 11)

Entertainment
75 Bophana Centre......................................C2
76 Chatomuk Theatre H1
77 Flicks..B7

Shopping
78 Aeon Mall...G7
79 Amboh...F7
80 Cambodian Handicraft
   Association..A7
81 DAH Export...C4
82 D's Books..E2
83 Estampe..E1
84 Monument Books.....................................E2
85 Paperdolls...F5
86 Psar O Russei A1
87 Smateria D4
88 Space Four Zero F2
89 Villageworks A6

in town. It's located near the banks of the Mekong. Admission includes use of the FitnessOne gym.

Golf

If you can't survive without a swing, Phnom Penh has several 18-hole courses, but most of them lie about 30km or more out of town.

Grand Phnom Penh Golf Club　　GOLF

(☑012 502491; www.grandphnompenhgolf.com; Hanoi Rd; weekdays/weekends US$95/115, plus caddy & cart US$45) The most convenient of the 18-hole golf courses around the capital, this was designed by none other than Jack Nicklaus. Turn north off the Airport Rd and follow Hanoi Rd for 5km until you spot the imposing entrance on the right.

Massage & Spa

There is no shortage of massage parlours in Phnom Penh. Some are purveying 'naughty' massages, but there are also scores of legitimate massage centres and some superb spas for that pampering palace experience.

★Bodia Spa　　SPA

(Map p68; ☑023-226199; www.bodia-spa.com; cnr Samdech Sothearos Blvd & St 178; massages from US$35; ⊙10am-11pm) Arguably the best massages and spa treatments in town, and in a Zen-like setting just off the riverfront. All products are locally sourced and produced by the Bodia Nature team.

Samantha Spa　　SPA

(Map p62; ☑023-210278; http://samathaspa.com; 7CD St 278; massage from US$25; ⊙10am-11pm) One of the city's top spas, with a curvaceous design, air-con and highly professional staff. Choose your own massage oil before being led into a private room with either a bath or shower (to clean up after the treatment). Facials, scrubs and body wraps round out the menu of soothing treatments.

Daughters Spa　　SPA

(Map p68; ☑077 657678; www.daughtersofcambodia.org; 321 Sisowath Quay; 1hr foot spa US$10; ⊙9am-5.30pm Mon-Sat) 🕊 Hand and foot massages are administered by participants in this NGO's vocational training program for at-risk women. Shorter (15- to 30-minute) treatments are also available.

Seeing Hands Massage MASSAGE
(Map p68; 016 856188; 12 St 13; 1hr massage US$7; ⊙7am-10pm) The original Seeing Hands establishment, this place helps you ease those aches and pains and also helps blind masseurs stay self-sufficient. One of the best-value massages in the capital.

Nail Workshop SPA
(Map p68; www.facebook.com/nailworkshop. kh; Futures Factory, 215 St 13; manicure/pedicure US$5.50/6; ⊙11am-7.30pm) Provides cheap manicures, pedicures and nail painting, all to help the Mith Samlanh organisation train street children in a new vocation.

Yoga

Yoga studios are found mostly in the southern neighbourhoods where expats live. Check their websites for schedules. Some offer discounts for multiple classes.

NaṭaRāj Yoga YOGA
(Map p62; 012 250817; www.yogacambodia.com; 52 St 302; classes from US$9) Phnom Penh's longest running yoga studio with a range of daily classes.

Yoga Phnom Penh YOGA
(Map p62; 077 541975; www.yogaphnompenh. com; 39 St 21; classes from US$7) Yoga sessions from 6am to 8pm daily, including weekends. This small studio also offers classes in reiki healing, meditation and *bokator* (a Khmer martial art).

🎓 Courses

Cambodia Cooking Class COOKING
(Map p62; 023-220953; www.frizz-restaurant. com; booking office 67 St 240; half-/full day US$25/35) Learn the art of Khmer cuisine through Frizz Restaurant on St 240. Classes involve a trip to the market and lots of pestle and mortar action. Reserve one day ahead.

Maison Apsara HEALTH & WELLBEING
(Map p62; 088 2128002; http://byapsara.com; 23A St 232; workshops US$20-25; ⊙10am-6pm) Sign up for a workshop to make your own

---

THE SCOURGE OF CHILD PROSTITUTION

The sexual abuse of children by foreign paedophiles is a serious problem in Cambodia. Paedophilia is a crime in Cambodia and several foreigners have served or are serving jail sentences. There is no such thing as an isolation unit for sex offenders in Cambodia. Countries such as Australia, France, Germany, the UK and the USA have also introduced much-needed legislation that sees nationals prosecuted in their home country for committing sex crimes abroad.

Child abuse is slowly but surely being combated here, although in a country as poor as Cambodia, money can tempt people into selling babies for adoption and children for sex. The trafficking of innocent children has many shapes and forms, and the sex trade is just the thin end of the wedge. Poor parents have been known to rent out their children as beggars, labourers or sellers; many child prostitutes in Cambodia are Vietnamese and have been sold into the business by family back in Vietnam. Once in the trade, it is difficult to escape a life of violence and abuse. Drugs are also being used to keep children dependent on their pimps, with bosses giving out *yama* (a dirty methamphetamine) or heroin to dull their senses.

Paedophilia is not unique to Western societies and it is a big problem with Asian tourists as well. The problem is that some of the home governments don't treat it as seriously as some of their Western counterparts. Even more problematic is the domestic industry of virgin-buying in Cambodia, founded on the superstition that taking a girl's virginity will enhance one's power.

Visitors can do their bit by keeping an eye out for any suspicious behaviour. Don't ignore it – pass on any relevant information, such as the name and nationality of the individual, to the embassy concerned. To report abuse, there is a Cambodian hotline (023-997919) and ChildSafe (p93) maintains confidential hotlines in Phnom Penh (012 311112), Siem Reap (017 358758) and Sihanoukville (012 478100). When booking into a hotel or jumping on transport, look out for the ChildSafe logo, as each establishment or driver who earns this logo is trained to identify and respond to child abuse. End Child Prostitution and Trafficking (www.ecpat.net) is a global network aimed at stopping child prostitution, child pornography and the trafficking of children for sexual purposes, and has affiliates in most Western countries.

skincare products using essential oils and local ingredients. The shop is hidden on the 2nd floor of a generic yellow office building.

Pras Khan Chey
Bokator School
MARTIAL ARTS

(Map p68; ☑087 752998; www.facebook.com/lbokator; 10 St 109; ⊙6-7.30am & 6-8pm) Offers martial-arts lessons (per hour US$10) or full brown-belt courses (US$2000). Call ahead to ensure you get an English-speaking instructor.

Royal University of Phnom Penh
LANGUAGE

(Map p50; ☑023-885419; www.rupp.edu.kh/ifl; Russian Confederation Blvd) The Institute of Foreign Languages at the Royal University of Phnom Penh offers some of the only official language courses available in Cambodia.

👉 Tours

There are some interesting niche tours in and around Phnom Penh. If you want an organised city tour, most of the leading guesthouses and travel agencies can arrange one.

★Lost Plate
FOOD & DRINK

(☑011 646801; http://lostplate.com; food/bar tour from US$60/50; ⊙food tour 6pm, bar tour 8pm Fri) Explore the history of Cambodia through its food on these excellent culinary tours, which take in four off-the-beaten-path restaurants and one craft beer and cocktail bar. Just want to drink? There's a tour for that, too, where you'll visit the city's lesser-known bars and toss back unlimited craft beverages.

★Khmer Architecture Tours
ARCHITECTURE

(www.ka-tours.org; 3hr tour US$15) Those interested in cycling past the colonial buildings of central Phnom Penh, diving into Cambodia's four main religions at local holy sites, or walking a circuit of new-wave Khmer architecture from the Sangkum era (1953–70) should look no further. One of these three signature tours runs each Sunday. Check the website for dates and times.

Cambodian Living Arts
CULTURAL

(CLA; Map p62; ☑023-986032; www.cambodianlivingarts.org; 128 Samdech Sothearos Blvd) Cambodian Living Arts supports talented Cambodian musicians, actors and dancers through scholarships, fellowships and the mentorship of local troupes and individuals. Visitors can participate in CLA's 'Living Arts Tours', dance workshops and other cultural experiences; see the website for details.

Urban Tales
HISTORY

(Map p68; ☑078 911899; www.urbantales-phnompenh.com; National Library; 3hr tour adult/child US$38/28; ⊙departures 8:15am & 9:15am) City tour meets treasure hunt in this interactive adventure, where you'll follow in the footsteps of a mysterious French explorer in search of a lost Khmer antique. Tours depart from the National Library (p60) and traverse about 3km of the historic centre. Bookings must be made at least 48 hours in advance.

Phnom Penh Food Tours
FOOD & DRINK

(www.phnompenhfoodtours.com; 3½hr tour adult/child US$65/35; ⊙tours 8am & 5.45pm) The team behind the popular Siem Reap Food Tours have opened a branch in Phnom Penh, where you can sample the capital's bustling markets, street-food stands and hole-in-the-wall eateries with a knowledgeable English-speaking guide. Groups are intimate at four to six people and dietary restrictions are no problem if you inform them in advance.

Village Quad Bike Trails
ADVENTURE

(☑099 952255; www.villagequadbiketrails.com; tours 90min/half-day/full day US$30/65/135) Offers quad biking in the countryside around Phnom Penh. The quads are automatic, and so are easy to handle for beginners (maximum two passengers per bike). Full-day tours take in Tonlé Bati (p99) and Phnom Tamao (p100); despite the area's proximity to the capital, this is rural Cambodia and very beautiful. Longer trips are also available.

Follow signs to the Killing Fields of Choeung Ek (p55); it's about 300m before the entrance. Call ahead as numbers are limited.

Dancing Roads
TOURS

(☑012 822803; www.dancingroads.com) This operator offers motorbike tours around the capital and gentle tours further afield to the South Coast. Based in Phnom Penh, the driver-guides are fun and friendly.

Kingdom Brewery
BREWERY

(☑023-430180; www.kingdombreweries.com; 1748 NH5; tours US$15; ⊙1-7pm Mon-Fri) Tours include unlimited free-flow drinks on tap, and you don't even have to book ahead: just show up. It's exactly 1km north of the Japanese Bridge on NH5.

Cyclo Conservation & Careers Association
TOURS

(Map p68; ☑097 7009762; cyclocca@gmail.com; 9 St 158; per hour/day from US$3/12) 🖋 Dedicated

North Phnom Penh

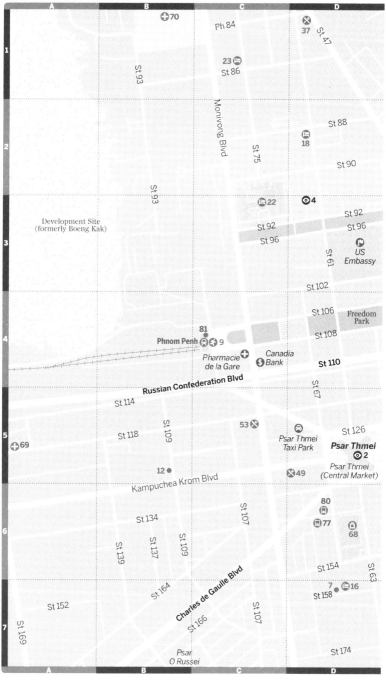

Ph 84

70

23
St 86

St 93

Monivong Blvd

37
St 47

St 88
18

St 75

St 90

St 93

22

4

Development Site
(formerly Boeng Kak)

St 92
St 96

St 92
St 96

St 92
St 96

US
Embassy

St 61

St 102

St 106

St 108

Freedom
Park

81
Phnom Penh 9

Pharmacie
de la Gare

Canadia
Bank

St 110

St 67

Russian Confederation Blvd

St 114

St 118

St 109

53

Psar Thmei
Taxi Park

St 126

Psar Thmei
2

Psar Thmei
(Central Market)

69

12

Kampuchea Krom Blvd

49

St 134

St 107

80
77

68

St 139

St 137

St 109

St 154

St 63

St 164

Charles de Gaulle Blvd

7   16
St 158

St 152

St 166

St 107

St 169

Psar
O Russei

St 174

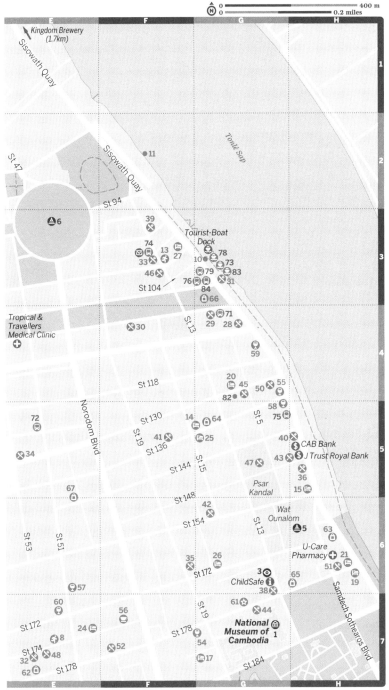

Kingdom Brewery
(1.7km)

Sisowath Quay

St 47

Sisowath Quay

St 94

11

Tonle Sap

6

39

Tourist-Boat
Dock

74
13
33 27
46
St 104

10 78
73
79 83
76 31
84
66

71
30   29 28

59

St 13

St 118

20 45 50 55
82   58 75

72

St 130
14 64
St 19 41 25
St 136

34

40
CAB Bank
43   J Trust Royal Bank
47   36
Psar   15
Kandal

St 5

St 144 St 15

St 148

67

42
St 154

Wat
Ounalom   5
63
U-Care
Pharmacy   21
35   26   51
St 172   65   19
3
ChildSafe
38

St 13

St 53   St 51

57

60
56
24   52
St 172   8
32 48
62 St 178

61   44

National
Museum of
Cambodia
St 178   1
54
17
St 184

Tropical &
Travellers
Medical Clinic

North Phnom Penh

⊚ **Top Sights**
1 National Museum of Cambodia G7
2 Psar Thmei D5

⊚ **Sights**
3 Futures Factory G6
4 National Library D3
5 Wat Ounalom H6
6 Wat Phnom E3

⊕ **Activities, Courses & Tours**
Bodia Spa .... (see 51)
7 Cyclo Conservation & Careers
   Association D7
Daughters Spa .... (see 63)
8 Grasshopper Adventures E7
9 Hash House Harriers C4
10 Koh Dach Boat Trips G3
11 Memorable Cambodia F2
Nail Workshop .... (see 3)
12 Pras Khan Chey Bokator School B5
13 Seeing Hands Massage F3
Urban Tales .... (see 4)

🛏 **Sleeping**
14 11 Happy Backpacker G5
15 Amanjaya Pancam Hotel H5
16 Billabong D7
17 Blue Lime G7
18 Eighty8 Backpackers D2

19 Foreign Correspondents' Club H6
20 Monsoon Boutique Hotel G4
21 Panorama Mekong Hostel H6
22 Raffles Hotel Le Royal C3
23 Sangkum C1
24 SLA Boutique Hostel E7
25 Sun & Moon Urban Hotel G5
26 Sundance Inn & Saloon G6
27 Sundance Riverside F3

🍴 **Eating**
28 iViva! G4
29 18 Rik Reay BBQ G4
30 Armand's The Bistro F4
31 Bopha Phnom Penh Restaurant G3
32 Bouchon Wine Bar E7
33 Cam Cup Cafe F3
Daughters Cafe .... (see 63)
34 Dim Sum Emperors E5
35 Dine in the Dark F6
36 Eric Kayser H5
37 Exchange D1
Flavours of Cambodia .... (see 68)
38 Friends G6
Grand River .... (see 21)
Happy Herb Pizza .... (see 21)
39 Khema La Poste F3
40 La Croisette H5
41 Le Saint Georges F5
Lemongrass .... (see 50)

to supporting *cyclo* (bicycle rickshaw) drivers in Phnom Penh, these tours are a great way to see the sights. Themed trips such as pub crawls or cultural tours are also available.

★ Festivals & Events

As the Cambodian capital and largest city in the country, Phnom Penh can be an interesting place to join in some local festivities. The city tends to empty out on big holidays such as Khmer New Year (April) and P'chum Ben (September/October), as residents return to their home provinces to visit families. However, the Water Festival (Bon Om Tuk; October/November) sees the opposite phenomenon, as hundreds of thousands of rural residents flood the city to watch the boat races on the Tonlé Sap. The festival doesn't always go ahead and has been cancelled several times in the past decade.

🛏 Sleeping

Accommodation in Phnom Penh, as in the rest of the country, is great value no matter your budget, with quite literally hundreds of guesthouses and hotels to choose from. There are some great boutique hotels around the city if you want to treat yourself after an upcountry adventure.

North Central (Riverfront)

While the idea of resting up on the riverfront has obvious appeal, you'll find better value elsewhere. Also keep in mind that hotels along the river tend to be noisy, and most budget rooms are windowless or face away from the river. A few superb options exist at the top end, but worthwhile pickings are much slimmer in the budget and midrange categories.

Panorama Mekong Hostel HOSTEL **$**
(Map p68; ☑093 389336; www.facebook.com/panoramamekong178; 357 Sisowath Quay; dm US$3.50-6; ☞) There's good news and bad news here. The good news is this place has panoramic views of the Mekong and you can even look down on the iconic Foreign Correspondents' Club (FCC), something that is unique for a backpacker pad. The bad news is there is no lift and four flights of stairs.

42 Majorelle	G6
43 Metro Hassakan	G5
44 Museum Cafe	G7
45 Noodle House	G4
46 Palais de la Poste	F3
Pepe Bistro	(see 38)
47 Psar Kandal	G5
48 Romdeng	E7
49 Sam Too Restaurant	D5
50 Sher-e-Punjab	G4
51 Special Pho	H6
52 Sugar Palm	F7
53 Thai Huot	C5

Drinking & Nightlife
54 Blue Chilli	G7
55 Cheers	G4
Elephant Bar	(see 22)
FCC	(see 19)
56 Happy Damrei	F7
57 Heart of Darkness	E6
Le Moon	(see 15)
58 Olala	G5
Orphic	(see 36)
59 Oskar Bistro	G4
60 Pontoon	E7

Entertainment
| 61 Meta House | G7 |
| Traditional Dance Show | (see 1) |

Shopping
62 Ambre	E7
Artisans Angkor	(see 13)
63 Daughters of Cambodia	H6
64 DinArt Gallery	G5
65 Mekong Arts	H6
66 Night Market	G3
67 Sobbhana	E5
68 Sorya Shopping Centre	D6

Information
| 69 Cabinet Medical Francais | A5 |
| 70 Calmette Hospital | B1 |

Transport
71 Angkor Express	G4
72 Bayon VIP	E5
73 Blue Cruiser	G3
74 Cambodia Post Van	F3
75 CTT Transport & Tours	G5
76 Giant Ibis	G3
77 GTF Express	D6
78 Hang Chau	G3
79 Mekong Express	G3
80 Phnom Penh Sorya	D6
81 Royal Railways	C4
82 Vannak Motorcycle Shop	G4
83 Victoria Chau Doc Hotel Boat	G3
84 Virak Buntham	G3

Foreign Correspondents' Club BOUTIQUE HOTEL $$

(FCC; Map p68; 023-210142; www.fcccollection.com; 363 Sisowath Quay; r incl breakfast from US$50; ✳️ 🛜) This landmark location is a fine place to recapture the heady days of the war correspondents. The rooms are exquisitely finished in polished wood and include fine art, top-of-the-line furniture and vintage *Phnom Penh Post* covers on the wall. The deluxe rooms have breezy balconies with prime river views.

Renovations were underway through 2020 and 2021 to make the place as great as it was in its heyday.

⭐ **Palace Gate Hotel** BOUTIQUE HOTEL $$$

(Map p62; 023-900011; www.palacegatepp.com; 44B Samdech Sothearos Blvd; r incl breakfast US$125-257; ✳️ @ 🛜 ☒) Close to the riverfront, the Palace Gate has an unrivalled location overlooking the walls of, well obviously, the Royal Palace. The hotel is built around an old French colonial villa and the majority of rooms are set in a modern building behind. All are beautifully appointed with contemporary furnishings.

Amanjaya Pancam Hotel BOUTIQUE HOTEL $$$

(Map p68; 023-214747; www.amanjaya-suites-phnom-penh.com; 1 St 154; r incl breakfast US$130-180; ✳️ @ 🛜) Amanjaya boasts a superb riverfront location and spacious rooms finished with luxuriant dark-wood floors, elegant Khmer drapes and tropical furnishings. Luscious Le Moon (p85) bar is on the roof, trendy K West cafe at ground level.

The Balé LUXURY HOTEL $$$

(023-900425; www.thebalephnompenh.com; NH6A; ste from US$140; ✳️ @ 🛜 ☒) The 18 suites in this luxury resort, opened in 2018, are situated around a courtyard or at the edge of the Mekong, 15km north of town. Huge rooms pair minimalist dark-wood furnishings with Cambodian artefacts. You'll enjoy views across the river to Koh Dach (Silk Island) from the blue-tiled swimming pool, and dine by candlelight under the palms.

North Central (Inland)

If you want to be near the riverfront but not pay riverfront prices, this area is a happy hunting ground. Be aware, though, that the blocks running west off the river from St 104 to about St 144 are gritty and have sleazy areas; a handful of delectable new boutique hotels point to the slow gentrification of this prime real estate. Meanwhile, St 172 between St 19 and St 13 has become Phnom Penh's most popular backpacker area, though discerning budgeteers will find nicer options elsewhere.

★Eighty8 Backpackers
HOSTEL $

(Map p68; ☑023-500 2440; www.88backpackers.com; 98 St 88; incl breakfast dm US$5-7, r US$22-28; ❋ 🕏 🛎) A hostel with a swimming pool means party time, and this place hosts a big one each Saturday. The extensive property has a variety of private rooms, mixed or female-only dorms and Japanese-style sleeping pods. The courtyard boasts a central bar with a pool table, and there are plenty of spots to lounge around the swimming pool.

★SLA Boutique Hostel
HOSTEL $

(Map p68; ☑023-997515; www.slahostel.com; 15 St 174; dm/r from US$6.50/20; ❋ 🕏) 🏊 This shoes-off 'poshpacker' is the cleanest hostel in the city, with hoop-like dorm beds and sleek privates – all with crisp white sheets. It's also environmentally conscious, featuring solar-powered showers, energy-saving air-con and green cleaning products. The community kitchen and stylish patio make this a no-brainer for discerning budgeteers.

Sundance Inn & Saloon
GUESTHOUSE $

(Map p68; ☑016 802090; www.sundancecambodia.com; 61 St 172; r from US$20; ❋ @ 🕏 🛎) A step above the guesthouse pack on St 172, Sundance has oversize beds, designer bathrooms, kitchenettes and computers that hook up to flat-screens in every room. With open-mic Tuesdays, frequent live music, all-day US$1 beers and a pool out back, it is quite the party pad. Free airport pickup with 24 hours' notice.

Billabong
BOUTIQUE HOTEL $

(Map p68; ☑023-223703; www.thebillabonghotel.com; 5 St 158; r US$19-30, dm US$5-7; ❋ 🕏 🛎) Great-value Billabong may be near Psar Thmei, but it's an oasis of calm by comparison. Stylish rooms surround an open courtyard with a large swimming pool in the middle. Aim for the ground-level pool-view rooms, which have private verandahs and more space compared with rooms at the back. The newer dorms make for some bargain boutique beds.

11 Happy Backpacker
HOSTEL $

(Map p68; ☑088 7777421; 87-89 St 136; dm US$5, r US$8-15; ❋ 🕏) This is one of the original backpacker pads in Phnom Penh, with a sprawling rooftop bar-restaurant for chilling out or shooting pool. Cleanliness, however, doesn't seem to be much of a priority these days; nor does customer service.

Blue Lime
BOUTIQUE HOTEL $$

(Map p68; ☑023-222260; www.bluelime.asia; 42 St 19z; r incl breakfast US$50-115; ❋ @ 🕏 🛎) The Blue Lime offers smart, minimalist rooms and a leafy pool area that invites relaxation. The pricier rooms have private plunge pools, four-poster beds and concrete love seats. The cheaper rooms upstairs in the main building are similarly appealing. No children.

Sangkum
BOUTIQUE HOTEL $$

(Map p68; ☑096 2860106; www.thesangkum.com; 35A St 75; r US$55-85; ❋ 🕏) Set in a 1960s-inspired villa to the north of Wat Phnom, the hotel's name pays homage to Cambodia's so-called golden years, under the rule of Sihanouk and his Sangkum political party. The 12 rooms are decorated with a contemporary flourish and there's a small swimming pool for cooling off.

Monsoon Boutique Hotel
BOUTIQUE HOTEL $$

(Map p68; ☑023-989856; www.monsoonhotel.com; 53-55 St 130; r incl breakfast US$30-45; ❋ @ 🕏) Blink and you'll miss this little oasis on chaotic St 130, which is otherwise swarming with hostess bars. Hidden inside are attractive rooms with polished concrete walls and pleasing murals. It's a real deal considering the sophistication of the design and proximity to the river.

★Raffles Hotel Le Royal
HOTEL $$$

(Map p68; ☑023-981888; www.raffles.com/phnompenh; cnr Monivong Blvd & St 92; r from US$235; ❋ @ 🕏 🛎) From the golden age of travel, this is one of Asia's grand old dames, in the illustrious company of the Oriental in Bangkok and Raffles in Singapore. This classic colonial-era property is Phnom Penh's leading address, with a heritage to match its service and style. Indulgent diversions include two swimming pools, a gym, a spa and lavish bars and restaurants.

Between 1970 and 1975, many famous journalists working in Phnom Penh stayed here. More recent celebrated guests have included Barack Obama and Angelina Jolie.

★ **Plantation**　　　BOUTIQUE HOTEL **$$**
(Map p62; ☎ 023-215151; www.theplantation.asia; 28 St 184; r incl breakfast US$80-400; ❈ @ 🛜 🞷) The largest and most ambitious hotel in the MAADS group of properties, Plantation ticks all the boxes with its high ceilings, stylish fixtures and fittings, open-plan bathrooms and balconies. There are two swimming pools here and a beautiful courtyard reception that hosts regular art exhibitions.

Sun & Moon Urban Hotel　DESIGN HOTEL **$$$**
(Map p68; ☎ 023-961888; www.sunandmoonhotel.com; 68 St 136; r US$69-129; @ 🛜 🞷) This is one of the most stylish high-rises in the Cambodian capital, offering designer rooms with geometric patterns, pop art on the walls and splashes of saffron in the furnishings. One of the most impressive features is the rooftop infinity pool with expansive views across the city and the attached Cloud 9 Sky Bar.

South Central (Norodom East)

The hotels in this zone are ideally positioned: they're located on or within walking distance of the river and are close to the Royal Palace. Cosy boutique hotels set around a pool are in abundance here. Walk-in backpackers can target St 258, which has a clutch of cheap guesthouses.

Aura Thematic Hostel　　HOSTEL **$**
(Map p62; ☎ 023-986211; www.aurahostel.com; 205A St 19; dm US$5-12; ❈ @ 🛜) A funky hostel behind the Royal Palace, the rooms here are themed along the lines of 'Desert', 'Jungle' and 'Sea'. In reality this is more about a large image on the wall, but the rooms are spotless and include boutique bathrooms. Head to the rooftop to wind down at the stylish Eluvium Lounge.

Number 9 Guesthouse　　HOSTEL **$**
(Map p62; ☎ 023-984999; www.number9hotel.com; 7C St 258; r US$17-35; ❈ 🛜 🞷) The first of Phnom Penh's old-school backpacker pads to be transformed into a flashpacker hotel, Number 9 is still going strong thanks to great rates, a rooftop pool and a lively bar-restaurant with generous happy hours (4pm to 8pm). It's not fancy, but well run and worth a splash for backpackers who have been exploring rural Cambodia.

Corner 9 Bassac　　BOUTIQUE HOTEL **$$**
(Map p62; ☎ 023-210169; www.corner9boutique.com; 19 St 9; r US$30-40; ❈ 🛜 🞷) This tranquil oasis is stumbling distance from the bars of Bassac Lane, yet a world away. It's a handsome midrange option with modern rooms oriented around a leafy courtyard and pool. Large flat-screen TVs, rain showers and attractive bed runners take it up a notch.

Hotel Corduroy　　BOUTIQUE HOTEL **$$**
(Map p62; ☎ 085 981818; http://hotelcorduroy.asia; 30 St 9; r US$60-80; ❈ 🛜 🞷) Tucked away in the Bassac district of town, this chic hotel (formerly the Teav Bassac and now under Japanese ownership) has a quiet location in a central area. Rooms are minimalist-cool and include all the three-star amenities you might expect. There is also a small swimming pool to escape the heat of the city.

You Khin Art House　　GUESTHOUSE **$$**
(Map p62; ☎ 061 828577; ykarthouse@gmail.com; 13A St 830; r US$20-45; ❈ 🛜 🞷) Tucked away down discreet St 830, this has the feel of a large private home and, Tardis-like, is considerably bigger on the inside. As the name implies, there's a great display of artwork on the walls, while the on-site restaurant specialises in vegan food. 'Kitchen' rooms are suite-like, great value and a good choice for families.

★ **Pavilion**　　BOUTIQUE HOTEL **$$$**
(Map p62; ☎ 023-222280; www.thepavilion.asia; 227 St 19; r incl breakfast US$60-100, apt US$120-164; ❈ @ 🛜 🞷) Housed in an elegant French villa, this immensely popular and atmospheric place kick-started Phnom Penh's boutique-hotel obsession. All rooms have inviting four-poster beds, stunning furniture and Bluetooth-enabled speakers, and some of the newer rooms include a private plunge pool. Guests can use bikes for free. Also free is a 25-minute welcome massage. No children allowed.

La Rose Suites　　BOUTIQUE HOTEL **$$$**
(Map p62; ☎ 023-222254; www.larose.com.kh; 4B St 21; ste US$175-380; ❈ @ 🛜 🞷) A stylish contemporary all-suite boutique hotel in lively little St 21, La Rose offers smart and spacious rooms, including some two-bedroom apartments for families. The elegant bathrooms include ample terrazzo bathtubs and rain showers.

Kabiki
BOUTIQUE HOTEL **$$$**

(Map p62; ☑ 023-222290; www.thekabiki.com; 22 St 264; r incl breakfast US$60-125; ❄@🞱🞲) The most family-friendly place in town, the Kabiki offers a large, lush garden and an inviting swimming pool with a kiddie pool. Family rooms include bunks and most rooms have a private garden terrace.

South Central (Norodom West & Psar O Russei)

With the downfall of the Boeng Kak area, the zone south of Psar O Russei has emerged as a popular alternative for budget travellers. It's a mix of high-rise hotels and backpacker-oriented guesthouses. Closer to Norodom Blvd you'll find more atmospheric boutique hotels and flashpacker pads.

★ Manor House
HOSTEL **$**

(Map p62; ☑ 023-992566; www.manorhouse cambodia.com; 21 St 262; dm US$5-7, r from US$25; ❄🞱🞲) A villa that had a second life as a boutique hotel has transformed again into a chic hostel with some of the most luxurious dorms in town. The pool (and pool table) give it a fun atmosphere without tipping into full-on party hostel territory. A great choice for backpacking couples!

Tat Guesthouse
GUESTHOUSE **$**

(Map p62; ☑ 012 921211; tatcambodia@yahoo. com; 52 St 125; s without bathroom US$5, r US$7-15; ❄🞱) A super-friendly spot with a breezy rooftop hang-out that's perfect for chilling. The rooms aren't going to wow you, but they are functional. For US$12 you get air-con.

They also own nearby **Tattoo Guesthouse** (Map p62; ☑ 012 921211; 62A St 125; r US$10-20; ❄🞱), which has a great name and smarter rooms.

House Boutique
HOTEL **$$**

(Map p50; ☑ 023-220884; http://houseboutique hotel.com; 76 St 57; r from US$30; ❄🞱🞲) 🞲 The best feature of this solid midrange hotel is its bamboo-shaded pool (and attendant bar). Rooms come with tiled floors, sunken beds and furnishings made from upcycled timber. Other sustainable features include solar power, while the staff are hired from a local hospitality NGO.

Double Leaf
BOUTIQUE HOTEL **$$**

(Map p82; ☑ 023-226288; www.doubleleaf hotel.com; 32 St 123; r incl breakfast US$40-80; ❄@🞱🞲) There are precious few hotels in the newly hip Russian Market area, but this stylish boutique makes up for it with its luscious L-shaped pool, curio-packed central lobby and soothing art-filled rooms. We particularly like the hand-painted drawings and hanging light fixtures above the beds, as well as the foot-massaging stones in the bathrooms.

Teahouse
BOUTIQUE HOTEL **$$**

(Map p62; ☑ 023-212789; www.theteahouse.asia; 32 St 242; r incl breakfast US$35-85; ❄@🞱🞲) A smaller, cheaper version of sister hotel Plantation (p73), the rooms here are exceptional value given the chic look. The open-air reception area under a Chinese-style pavilion has relaxing seating, free internet and daily tea tastings.

Lumiere Hotel
HOTEL **$$$**

(Map p62; ☑ 023-971168; www.thelumierehotel. com; 26 St 55; r from US$85; ❄@🞱) A stylish and dizzyingly geometric high-rise hotel in the heart of the city, Lumiere is mainly aimed at business travellers, but will surely end up catering to some enlightened tourists drawn to its slick, contemporary rooms and cityscape views. Perks include Bose speakers, 16th-floor Jacuzzis and a 14th-floor bar.

South Central (BKK Area)

Popular among NGO workers and expats, the Boeng Keng Kang (BKK) and Tonlé Bassac districts, south of Independence Monument, comprise the hipster zone, with an expanding selection of artsy midrange hotels to go with the wealth of trendy bars and restaurants (plus a few top hostels). Most accommodation options are found near St 278, dubbed 'Golden St' for the preponderance of hotels that feature 'Golden' in their name. The area around Bassac Lane has also seen a boom in chic midrange hotels.

★ Mad Monkey
HOSTEL **$**

(Map p62; ☑ 023-987091; www.madmonkey hostels.com; 26 St 302; dm US$5-9, r US$18-32; ❄@🞱) This colourful and vibrant hostel is justifiably popular. The spacious dorms have air-con and sleep six to 22; the smaller ones have double-width bunk beds that can sleep two. The private rooms are swish for the price, but lack TVs and, often, windows. The rooftop bar above quiet St 302 serves free beer and punch daily from 7.30pm to 8pm.

There's also a restaurant and tour desk on-site, while nightly events keep guests wholly entertained.

Top Banana Guesthouse
HOSTEL $

(Map p62; 012 885572; www.topbanana.biz; 9 St 278; dm from US$5, r US$16-18; ❈ ❀) The rooms are in good shape by hostel standards, and there are some dorms available, including a four-bed female dorm. The main draw is the strategic location overlooking Wat Langka and St 278, plus the open-air chill-out area. It can get noisy, as the rooftop bar is raucous most nights. Book way ahead.

Mini Banana Guesthouse
GUESTHOUSE $

(Map p62; 089 390379; www.facebook.com/minibananaguesthouse; Langka Lane; dm US$2.50-6, r US$8-20; ❈ ❀) It's almost a banana republic in this part of town, with three guesthouses playing on the name. Renovated dorms with sturdy bunks, comfortable rooms with fan or air-con and a lively little bar-restaurant make this one of the most likeable of the bunch.

Envoy Hostel
HOSTEL $

(Map p62; 023-220840; www.envoyhostel.com; 32 St 322; dm US$5.50-7.50, r from US$25; ❈ ❀) This shoes-off urban oasis is one of the most serene hostels in the city, located in a lovely villa with artistic flourishes. All dorms – including one for females only – are air-conditioned and in spectacular shape. There's also a useful on-site tour desk.

★ Patio Hotel
& Urban Resort
BOUTIQUE HOTEL $$

(Map p62; 023-997900; www.patio-hotel.com; Langka Lane; s/d from US$35/60; ❈ ❀ ❅) If you hate high-design rooms with ultra-comfy beds, rooftop bars with twinkling fairy lights, hallways lined in contemporary art and 8th-floor infinity pools with sweeping city views, then definitely steer clear of this place. It's right in the heart of the action on one of the city's hippest alleyways.

★ Rambutan Resort
BOUTIQUE HOTEL $$

(Map p82; 017 992240; www.rambutanresort.com; 29 St 71; r incl breakfast US$75-170; ❈ ❀ ❅) Sixties-groovy, gay-friendly and extremely well run, this striking villa once belonged to the US embassy. The soaring original structure and a newer wing shade a boot-shaped swimming pool. Concrete floors set an industrial tone in the smart rooms, which are outfitted with top-quality furnishings.

Villa Langka
BOUTIQUE HOTEL $$

(Map p62; 023-726771; www.villalangka.com; 14 St 282; r incl breakfast US$55-125; ❈ ❀ ❅) Villa Langka was one of the first players in the poolside-boutique game and has long been a Phnom Penh favourite, even as the competition heats up. The rooms ooze postmodern panache, although there are big differences in size and style. The leafy pool area is perfect.

Anise
HOTEL $$

(Map p62; 023-222522; www.anisehotel.com.kh; 2C St 278; r incl breakfast US$35-95; ❈ @ ❀) If a leafy boutique hotel with a pool isn't the thing for you, Anise is one of the better midrange high-rises in town (though it lacks an elevator). Indigenous textiles and hand-some wood trim add character to rooms that boast extras including DVD players. Pricier rooms are gargantuan; all rooms include free laundry.

✕ Eating

For foodies, Phnom Penh is the real deal, and visitors are spoilt for choice. There's a superb selection of restaurants that showcase the best in Khmer cooking and the greatest hits from world cuisines, such as Chinese, Vietnamese, Thai, Indian, French, Italian, Mexican and more.

North Central (Riverfront)

18 Rik Reay BBQ
BARBECUE $

(Map p68; 095 361818; 3 St 108; US$2-8; 24hr; ❀) One of the best local barbecue restaurants near the riverfront, the Rik Reay is packed with locals every night, partly thanks to its convenient location near the Night Market, but also as a testament to the quality of its food. Choose from grilled beef, ribs, chicken, squid, shrimp and much more, all with signature dipping sauces.

Eric Kayser
BAKERY $

(Map p68; 085 691333; http://maison-kayser-cambodia.asia; 277 Sisowath Quay; pastries from US$2; 6.30am-10.30pm; ❀) The flagship branch of this impressive French bakery chain in Phnom Penh, Eric Kayser offers designer breads, delectable pastries and a range of gourmet sandwiches. Set lunches are available, offering a sandwich, pastry and drink for US$10. Weekend brunches are also a popular draw.

Special Pho
VIETNAMESE $

(Map p68; 012 538904; 11 St 178; mains US$3-5; 8am-9pm) A great location near the riverfront for good pho – the noodle soup that keeps Vietnam driving forward – plus cheap fried rice and fried noodles.

DON'T MISS

DINING FOR A CAUSE

There are several restaurants around town that are run by aid organisations to help fund their social programs in Cambodia. The proceeds of a hearty meal go towards helping Cambodia's development and allow restaurant staff to gain valuable work experience.

North Central

Daughters Cafe (Map p68; www.daughtersofcambodia.org; 321 Sisowath Quay; mains US$4-7; ⊙9am-5.30pm Mon-Sat; 🛜) 🍃 This fantastic air-conditioned cafe on the top floor of the Daughters of Cambodia visitors centre features soups, smoothies, original coffee drinks, cupcakes and Western mains, served by former victims of trafficking.

Dine in the Dark (DID; Map p68; ☑077 589458; www.didexperience.com; 126 St 19; set menu US$22; ⊙6-11pm, last orders 9.30pm) 🍃 It's the Tea Garden by day, with a verdant hidden courtyard and speciality loose-leaf teas, but by night the lights go out and the upstairs is transformed into Dine in the Dark. Choose from a set menu of Khmer, Western or vegan dishes, eaten in darkness with the help of a sight-impaired guide.

Friends (Map p68; ☑012 802072; www.tree-alliance.org; 215 St 13; tapas US$4-7, mains US$6-10; ⊙11am-10.30pm; 🛜) 🍃 One of Phnom Penh's best-loved restaurants, with tasty tapas bites, heavenly smoothies and creative cocktails. It offers former street children a head start in the hospitality industry. Book ahead.

Romdeng (Map p68; ☑092 219565; www.romdeng-restaurant.org; 74 St 174; mains US$5-9; ⊙11am-11pm; 🛜) 🍃 Set in a gorgeous colonial villa, Romdeng specialises in Cambodian country fare, including a famous baked-fish *amok*, two-toned pomelo salad and tiger-prawn curry. Sample deep-fried tarantulas or stir-fried tree ants with beef and holy basil if you dare. Staffed by former street youths and their teachers.

House of Scott (Map p62; ☑023-966895; www.houseofscott-kh.com; 29 St 228; share plates US$4-9, mains US$10-25; ⊙11am-11pm Tue-Sun; 🛜) 🍃 Chic and art-lined House of Scott works with the Cambodian Children's Fund by donating all proceeds towards education and job creation for Cambodian youth. The menu includes delicious shared plates, such as homemade pork and shrimp sausages or Kampot pepper beef sashimi.

South Central

Vibe Cafe (Map p82; ☑061 764937; www.vibecafeasia.com; 26A St 446; mains US$4.50-7; ⊙7.30am-9pm Tue-Sun, to 4.30pm Mon; 🛜🖉) 🍃 This three-storey air-conditioned cafe by the Russian Market sets itself out as the capital's first 100% vegan restaurant and creates original homemade superfood recipes in its laboratory-like kitchen. Ten per cent of profits go towards providing 10,000 Cambodian schoolchildren with healthy daily meals.

Feel Good Cafe II (Map p62; ☑078 866651; www.feelgoodcoffee.com.kh; 11B St 29; dishes US$2-6; ⊙7.30am-4.30pm; 🛜) 🍃 One of the only cafes in town to roast and grind its own coffee, with responsibly sourced blends that are a fusion of Cambodian, Lao and Thai coffee beans.

Jars of Clay (Map p82; http://jarsofclay.asia; 39B St 155; cakes US$2, mains US$4-6; ⊙7.30am-9pm Mon-Sat; 🛜) 🍃 More than just a bakery, with authentic Khmer mains including their patented *lok lak* (a Cambodian beef dish), plus drinks and welcome air-con. Ten per cent of profits go to those in need.

Lot 369 (Map p82; www.lot369.com; 13C St 454; mains US$3.50-8.50; ⊙7.30am-6.30pm Mon-Sat, 8am-6pm Sun; 🛜🖉) 🍃 Kids, vegetarians, vegans and gluten avoiders will all find plenty of options at this crowd-pleasing cafe, which whips up healthy bowls, all-day breakfasts and heat-beating smoothies in a breezy open-air setting. The cafe is involved in a host of hospitality and sustainability initiatives, too.

¡Viva! MEXICAN **$**
(Map p68; 139 Sisowath Quay; dishes US$2-8; ⊙11am-10pm; 🛜) It doesn't look like much, but this riverfront place offers some bargain-basement dining and drinking, including a bucket of margarita for US$5. The

Mexican food is not the most authentic in town, but then nor are the prices.

Metro Hassakan
FUSION $$

(Map p68; ☑ 023-222275; 271 Sisowath Quay; small plates US$4-10, large plates US$8-26; ⊙ 9.30am-1am; 🛜) Metro is one of the hottest spots on the riverfront strip thanks to a striking design and an adventurous menu. Small plates are for sampling and include beef with red ants and tequila black-pepper prawns; large plates include steaks and honey-soy roasted chicken. It also does a mean eggs Benedict.

La Croisette
INTERNATIONAL $$

(Map p68; ☑ 023-220554; 241 Sisowath Quay; mains US$5-18; ⊙7am-1am; 🛜) The stylish La Croisette is a popular riverfront spot with homemade pasta and gnocchi, plus hearty steaks, lamb chops and some Cambodian offerings.

Grand River
INTERNATIONAL $$

(Map p68; ☑ 023-220244; 357 Sisowath Quay; mains US$6-12; ⊙8am-11pm; 🛜) One of the more lively riverfront restaurants, this is a great spot for watching the world go by. The menu includes moderately priced Cambodian and international dishes, plus a quaffable drinks selection.

Yi Sang Riverside
CHINESE $$

(Map p62; ☑ 016 320808; Sisowath Quay; dim sum US$3-5; ⊙7am-10pm; 🛜) This is one of the few places in the city where you can dine right on the riverside – perfect for a relaxing sunset cocktail. The menu includes a mix of well-presented Cambodian street flavours such as *naom banchok* (rice noodles with curry), plus plenty of dim sum.

Bopha Phnom
Penh Restaurant
CAMBODIAN $$

(Map p68; ☑ 023-427209; www.bopha-phnom penh.com; Sisowath Quay; mains US$4-20; ⊙6am-10.30pm; 🛜) Also known as Titanic, Bopha is right on the river and designed to impress, with Angkorian-style carvings and elegant wicker furniture. The menu is punctuated with exotic flavours – especially water buffalo – but there's a European menu for the less adventurous. Regular traditional music and dance performances take place here.

Happy Herb Pizza
PIZZA $$

(Happy Paradise Pizza; Map p68; ☑ 010 722924; 345 Sisowath Quay; medium pizzas US$6-9; ⊙11am-11pm; 🛜) A Phnom Penh institution. No, happy doesn't mean it comes with free toppings, it means pizza à la ganja. The non-marijuana pizzas are also pretty good, but don't involve the free trip. It's a nice place to sip a cheap beer and watch the riverfront action unfold.

North Central (Inland)

Cam Cup Cafe
CAFE $

(Map p68; ☑ 093 771577; Central Post Office, St 13; mains US$2-4; ⊙6.30am-8.30pm; 🛜) This elegant little cafe is the perfect way to make the iconic main post office relevant once more for a new generation of travellers. It offers fresh brews, herbal teas and some of the best-value Khmer dishes you can hope to find in this sort of setting.

Decoration includes old postage stamps and outmoded machinery from the bygone days of the postal system.

Museum Cafe
CAFE $

(Map p68; ☑ 023-722275; National Museum, St 178; mains US$4-6; ⊙7am-8pm; 🛜) Set in the spacious grounds of the National Museum, this is a cultured place for a cuppa, but the menu includes a good selection of well-priced Khmer classics and some international wraps and salads as well.

Try lunch before or after browsing the museum or combine dinner with the excellent nightly traditional dance show (p88).

Noodle House
ASIAN $

(Map p68; ☑ 077 919110; 32A St 130; dishes US$3-5; ⊙11am-11pm; 🛜) Set in a lovingly restored French-era gem of a building, this place looks more expensive than it actually is. The menu offers a global noodle tour with stops everywhere from Cambodian *kyteow* soup to pad thai and pasta carbonara.

Flavours of Cambodia
CAMBODIAN $

(Map p68; www.soryacenterpoint.com; 11 St 63, Sorya Shopping Centre; 5000-10,000r; ⊙9am-9pm; 🛜) The 4th-floor food court at Sorya Shopping Centre is a sanitised, air-cooled way to experience a variety of local fare, with stalls arranged by province serving affordable regional dishes. You can take a culinary tour of the entire country without ever leaving this Phnom Penh mall. Note: the stalls operate on a prepaid card system.

★ Bouchon Wine Bar
INTERNATIONAL $$

(Map p68; ☑ 077 881103; 82 St 174; mains $7-25; ⊙11am-2pm & 4pm-midnight Mon-Fri, 4pm-midnight Sat; 🛜) Rehoused in a stunning French-colonial villa on St 174, Bouchon is now as much a classy restaurant as an elegant wine bar. The menu includes confit duck legs and some calorific homemade desserts. It also has a great selection of French wines by the glass, plus some of the more potent cocktails around town.

Sugar Palm
CAMBODIAN **$$**

(Map p68; ☑085 646373; www.thesugarpalm.com; 13 St 178; mains US$5-8; ⊙11am-3pm & 6-10pm Mon-Sat) Set in an attractive French villa, the Sugar Palm is the place to sample traditional flavours infused with herbs and spices, including delicious *char kreung* (curried lemongrass) dishes. Owner Kethana showed celebrity chef Gordon Ramsay how to prepare *amok* (baked fish dish).

Le Saint Georges
FRENCH **$$**

(Map p68; ☑081 688020; 111 St 136; US$5-20; ⊙10am-2pm & 6-10pm Tue-Sun; 🛜) Le Saint Georges specialises in the cuisine of southwest France, featuring a number of dishes that don't often turn up on other menus around town, including a signature *cassoulet* (chicken and sausage casserole) and a *confit de canard* made from whole fresh duck. A genuine dining experience thanks to the passionate host from Toulouse.

Majorelle
FUSION **$$**

(Map p68; ☑096 9990278; 169 St 154; mains US$9-15; ⊙11am-2pm & 6-10pm Mon-Sat; 🛜) The amiable French owner of this intimate royal blue eatery prepares fusion food inspired by far-off lands such as Tunisia, Madagascar and Tahiti. You won't find the kind of dishes featured on the chalkboard menu here anywhere else in Cambodia.

Khema La Poste
FRENCH **$$**

(Map p68; ☑015 841888; www.khema-restaurant.com; cnr Sts 13 & 98; US$5-15; ⊙6.30am-10.30pm; 🛜) This delicatessen-restaurant is winning plaudits for its good-value French food, including boeuf bourguignon, Toulouse sausages and lamb shank. There are also competitively priced pastas and delicious desserts, adding up to a great-value meal in sophisticated surrounds.

Sam Too Restaurant
CHINESE **$$**

(Map p68; ☑081 778227; 42-44 Kampuchea Krom Blvd; mains US$2.50-7.50; ⊙7am-2am; 🛜) Many Chinese Khmers swear that this eatery near Central Market (formerly known as Sam Doo and located four doors over) has the best Middle Kingdom food in town. This bright new outlet still has the signature Sam Doo fried rice, *trey chamhoy* (steamed fish

with soy sauce and ginger), fresh seafood, hotpots and dim sum.

Exchange
INTERNATIONAL **$$**

(Map p68; ☑023-992865; http://theexchange-cambodia.com; 28 St 47; mains US$5-19; ⊙10am-midnight) One of the grandest old French houses in the city is home to this stylish bistro and bar. The menu takes diners on a global tour and includes some excellent sharing platters with Mediterranean and ocean themes, plus some top imported steaks.

Dim Sum Emperors
CHINESE **$$**

(Map p68; ☑023-690 7452; 48 St 130; dim sum US$2-3, mains US$5-15; ⊙6am-10pm; 🛜) Wildly popular for both its dim sum and its powerful air-con, which comes as welcome relief after a shopping session at nearby Psar Thmei.

Lemongrass
THAI **$$**

(Map p68; ☑012 996707; 14 St 130; mains US$4.50-9; ⊙10am-11pm; 🛜) A higher-class Thai restaurant with a fair selection of Khmer classics. The prices are pretty reasonable given the look of the place. Splurge for the *choo chee goong* (ocean tiger prawns in red curry).

Sher-e-Punjab
INDIAN **$$**

(Map p68; ☑023-216360; www.sherepunjabindian food.com; 16 St 130; mains US$3-8; ⊙10am-11pm; ☑) This is the top spot for a curry fix according to many members of Phnom Penh's Indian community. The tandoori dishes here are particularly good, as are the excellent-value prawn curries.

Armand's The Bistro
FRENCH **$$$**

(Map p68; ☑015 548966; 33 St 108; meals US$15-30; ⊙6pm-midnight Tue-Sun) The best steaks in town are served in Cognac flambé-style by the eponymous owner of this French bistro. The meat is simply superb, but every item on the chalkboard menu shines. Space is tight, so this is one place to book ahead.

Palais de la Poste
FRENCH **$$$**

(Map p68; ☑023-722282; www.palais-restaurant.com; 5 St 102; mains US$15-145; ⊙11.30am-2pm & 6.30-10pm) Located in one of the city's grandest buildings, the former Banque Indochine, Palais de la Poste features old vault doors en route to the refined dining room upstairs. Dishes are presented with a decorative flourish; menu highlights include langoustine ravioli, beef carpaccio and grilled scallops with Kampot pepper.

GOING LOCAL

Khmer Barbecues & Soup Restaurants

After dark, Khmer eateries scattered across town illuminate their neon signs, calling locals in for fine food and generous jugs of draught beer. Don't be shy – the food is great and the atmosphere lively. The speciality at most of these places is grilled strips of meat or seafood, but they also serve fried noodles and rice, curries and other pan-fried favourites, along with some veggie options.

Many of these places also offer *phnom pleung* (hill of fire), which amounts to cook-your-own meat over a personal barbecue. Another speciality is *soup chhnang dei* (cook-your-own soup in a clay pot), which is great fun if you go in a group. Other diners will often help with protocol, as it is important to cook things in the right order so as not to overcook half the ingredients and eat the rest raw.

Khmer barbecues are all over the place, so it won't be hard to find one. **Koh Pich** (Diamond Island; Map p50; US$2-6; ⊙ hours vary), east of the hulking Naga World Casino, has a cluster of well-reputed barbecues.

Street Fare & Markets

Street food is not quite as familiar or user-friendly here as in, say, Bangkok. But if you're a little adventurous and want to save boatloads of money, look no further. The street-side eateries really get hopping during breakfast, when many Cambodians eat out. Look for filled seats and you can't go wrong.

Phnom Penh's many markets all have large central eating areas, where stalls serve up local favourites such as noodle soup and fried noodles. Most dishes cost a reasonable US$1 to US$2. The best market for eating is the Russian Market (p89), with an interior food zone that's easy to find and has a good variety of Cambodian specialities; the large car park on the west side converts to seafood barbecues and more from around 4pm. Psar Thmei (p56) and **Psar O Russei** (Map p62; St 182; ⊙ 6.30am-5.30pm) are also great choices. **Psar Kandal** (Map p68; St 13 btwn Sts 144 & 154; meals 4000-6000r; ⊙ market 6am-8pm), just off the riverfront, gets going a little later and is an early-evening option where Cambodians come for takeaway food.

If the markets are too hot or claustrophobic for your taste, look out for the mobile street sellers carrying their wares on their shoulders or wheeling them around in small carts. Another popular all-day option is a row of **curry noodle stalls** (Map p62; St 7; mains US$1-2) opposite Wat Botum Park.

Pepe Bistro FRENCH $$$
(Map p68; ☏ 087 605688; 223 St 13; mains US$10-25; ⊙ noon-2pm Mon, noon-2pm & 7-9.30pm Tue-Sat; ☎) This swanky French bistro oozes class with evocative paintings on royal blue walls, fresh flowers on curvaceous wooden tables and house-infused rums on a zig-zagging bar. Monthly wine specials and an ever-changing menu of homemade pâté, foie gras and truffled everything only add to the fun.

Thai Huot SUPERMARKET $
(Map p68; 103 Monivong Blvd; ⊙ 7am-8.30pm) This is the place for French travellers who are missing home, as it stocks many French products, including Bonne Maman jam and the city's best cheese selection. There are several branches around town.

South Central

★ **Sovanna II** BARBECUE $
(Map p62; ☏ 011 840055; 2C St 21; mains US$2-8; ⊙ 4-11pm; ☎) Sovanna II is always jumping with locals and a smattering of expats, who have made this their barbecue of choice thanks to the huge menu and cheap local beer. **Sovanna I**, on the same street, opens from 6.30am and is as good a place as any to sample the national breakfast, *bei sait chrouk* (pork and rice).

Mercy House Restaurant ASIAN $
(Map p62; 157 St 51; mains 5000-15,000r; ⊙ 8am-7pm; ☏) This outdoor vegetarian eatery serves Japanese dishes with a Cambodian twist. Go for the teppanyaki hot plates – sizzling fake meat topped with an egg and served over rice – or the sweet-and-sour 'pork ribs'.

Sleuk Chhouk
CAMBODIAN $$

(Map p62; ☑012 208222; 165 St 51; mains US$5-10; ⊙10am-10pm; ☎) This place's picture-board menu may not look too appealing from the street, but venture inside for a stylish and authentic dining experience. Dishes include fish-egg soup or clay pots with zesty frogs' legs and quails' eggs in sugar palm and black pepper.

The Shop
CAFE $$

(Map p62; ☑092 955963; www.theshop-cambodia.com; 39 St 240; mains US$3.50-12; ⊙7am-7pm; ☎🍴) If you are craving the local deli back home, make for this haven, which has a changing selection of sandwiches and salads with healthy and creative ingredients such as wild lentils, forest mushrooms and lamb. The pastries, cakes and chocolates are delectable and well worth the indulgence.

Java Creative Café
CAFE $$

(Map p62; ☑012 833512; www.javacreativecafe.com; 56 Sihanouk Blvd; mains US$3-8; ⊙7am-10pm; ☎) Consistently popular thanks to a breezy balcony, air-conditioned interior and a creative menu that includes crisp salads, delicious homemade sandwiches, burgers and excellent coffee from several continents. The upstairs doubles as an art gallery, the downstairs as a bakery.

Kravanh
CAMBODIAN $$

(Map p62; ☑012 539977; www.kravanhrestaurant.com; 112 Samdech Sothearos Blvd; mains US$3-8; ⊙11am-2.30pm & 5.30-9.30pm; ☎) A stylish Khmer restaurant under the stewardship of a Franco-Khmer, the chic decor sets this place apart from its neighbours. The menu includes traditional salads, scented soups and regional specialities.

Enso Cafe
CAFE $$

(Map p62; ☑078 626240; http://enso-cafe.com; 50B St 240; US$4-9.50; ⊙7am-8pm; ☎🍴) A mod Australian cafe that started out with a top breakfast and brunch, Enso now offers a dinner menu too. Brunch options include leek, Gruyère cheese and salmon tart and a hangover-tastic *chakchouka* (poached eggs in a tomato, pepper and onion sauce). The vegan menu includes shepherdless pie.

Head upstairs to the 'healing space', where you'll find daily meditation sessions, aromatherapy, yoga and more.

Backyard Cafe
VEGAN $$

(Map p62; ☑078 751715; www.backyardeats.com; 11B St 246; dishes US$4-7; ⊙7.30am-4.30pm Mon, to 9pm Tue-Sun; ☎🍴) A cool and contemporary superfoods cafe, this is the place to check the pulse(s) of the vegetarian dining scene in the capital. Come for raw smoothies, gluten-free protein bowls and vegan burgers. The mouth-watering desserts are vegan, too.

ARTillery
CAFE $$

(Map p62; ☑078 985530; http://artillerycafe. ☎🍴) Healthy salads, sandwiches, shakes and snacks such as hummus and falafel are served in this creative space on an artsy alley off St 240, imaginatively named St 240½. The menu is mostly vegetarian, though there are some meat and gluten-free options as well. The daily specials are worth a sample.

Magnolia
VIETNAMESE $$

(Map p62; ☑012 529977; 55 St 51; mains US$3-9; ⊙7am-10pm Mon-Sat; ☎) Set in a gracefully restored old French villa, this place's affordable menu features wafer-thin *ban xeo* (Vietnamese savoury pancakes) and an array of other classics from Hanoi to Saigon. Great value for those seeking an authentic Vietnamese meal.

Limoncello
ITALIAN $$

(☑081 800210; 14B St 264; pizzas US$6-10; ⊙11.30am-2pm & 5.30-10pm; ☎) The pizza here is simply outstanding – some of the best in town. Also great desserts that can be washed down with an eponymous limoncello shot.

Super Duper
SUPERMARKET $

(Map p62; www.super-duper.biz; 3 Samdech Sothearos Blvd; ⊙24hr) One of Phnom Penh's few 24-hour supermarkets, this could be handy if the midnight munchies strike. It has one of the best product ranges in town, as the owners import containers direct from the US and Australia.

BKK & Tonlé Bassac Area

Boat Noodle Restaurant
THAI $

(Map p62; ☑012 774287; 57 Samdech Sothearos Blvd; mains US$3-7; ⊙6.30am-10pm; ☎) This long-running Thai-Khmer restaurant has some of the best-value regional dishes in town. Choose from the contemporary but traditionally decorated space at the front or a traditional wooden house behind. There are delicious noodle soups and lots of local specialities, ranging from fish cakes to spicy curries.

Eleven One Kitchen
CAMBODIAN $

(Map p62; ☑086 619111; www.elevenonekitchen.
com; 37 St 334; US$3.50-6; ☺7am-9.30pm; ☏)
Eleven One Kitchen specialises in healthy
Cambodian cuisine, using pesticide-free
vegetables and no MSG in their flavour-
some food. A standout dish is the stir-fried
chicken with mango and cashew nut. Set
lunch options start from just US$3.75 and
the menu includes some Western dishes to
round things out.

JoMa Bakery Cafe
CAFE $

(Map p62; www.joma.biz; cnr Norodom Blvd & St
294; dishes US$3-5; ☺7am-9pm; ☏) Originat-
ing in Laos, JoMa Bakery Cafe has used a
winning formula to expand rapidly in the
Cambodian capital. Salads and sandwiches
in various combinations make up the menu,
but the coffee, cakes and shakes are not to
be missed.

No Style
JAPANESE $

(Map p62; ☑096 3973318; Langka Lane; mains
US$2-4; ☺6pm-midnight Tue-Sun; ☏) This hole-
in-the-wall 12-seat 'skewer counter' ticks all
the right boxes. Beyond the US$1 skewers,
you'll also find US$3 rice and noodle tapas,
cheap Japanese whisky and ultra-friendly
staff.

Aeon Mall Food Court
ASIAN $

(Map p62; 132 Samdech Sothearos Blvd; mains
US$1-6; ☺9am-10pm; ☏) It may be surprising
to venture into the country's swankiest mall
to find cheap eats, but there are two food
courts here covering the best of Asia and
beyond. The more local option has noodle
soups, fried rice and fresh sushi. The nearby
World Dining Food Court has fancier furnishings and live music some evenings.

Taste Budz
SOUTH INDIAN $

(Map p62; ☑092 961554; 13E St 282; mains
US$2-8; ☺10am-2.30pm & 5-10pm) This pint-
sized outfit with the curious moniker is
one of the best of Phnom Penh's many Indian restaurants. The speciality is Kerala
(South Indian) cuisine, including spicy *ke-
dai* dishes, which are divine. Order *porotta*
(flat bread) on the side and dig in with your
hands.

★ Malis
CAMBODIAN $$

(Map p62; ☑015 814888; www.malis-restaurant.
com; 136 Norodom Blvd; mains US$6-25; ☺7am-
10.30pm) The leading Khmer restaurant in
the Cambodian capital, Malis is a chic place
to dine al fresco. The original menu includes

beef steamed in lotus leaf, goby with Kampot
peppercorns, and traditional soups and sal-
ads. It's popular for a boutique breakfast: the
breakfast sets are a good deal at US$8. Book
ahead for dinner or you won't get a seat.

★ Bistrot Langka
FRENCH $$

(Map p62; ☑070 727233; Langka Lane; US$8-
12; ☺6-10pm; ☏) Bistrot Langka offers fine
French dining in an intimate atmosphere
at an affordable price. Tuna tataki and an
original beef tartare are some standout moments. Book ahead, as this slick spot will
only a handful of tables and is one of the
city's busiest dinner destinations.

Terrazza
ITALIAN $$

(Map p62; ☑018 9474272; www.terrazza.asia; 1C
St 282; mains US$8-30; ☺11.30am-2pm & 5.30-
10pm; ☏) Plenty of places in Cambodia at-
tempt Italian cuisine, but prim and proper
Terrazza nails it, offering a fantastic Italian
wine list, bulging antipasto platters and am-
bitious pastas such as tagliolini with crab-
meat and Kampot pepper. Oh, and did we
mention the Neapolitan pizza available by
the metre? Raise up a negroni. *Saluti!*

Piccola Italia Da Luigi
PIZZA $$

(Map p62; ☑017 323273; 36 St 308; pizzas
US$3-9; ☺11.30am-2pm & 6.30-10.30pm Tue-Sun;
☏) This is the place where the Bassac Lane
renaissance began, and it's hard to believe
this was just a quiet residential street a few
years ago. A bustling kerbside eatery just
like you'd find in Italy, Luigi's certainly has
a claim to making some of the best pizza in
Phnom Penh. After dark, reservations are
recommended.

Ngon
STREET FOOD $$

(Map p62; ☑023-987151; www.ngonpnh.com; 60
Sihanouk Blvd; dishes US$3-9; ☺6.30am-10pm;
☏) A Cambodian outpost of the popular
Quan An Ngon in Saigon, this place brings
street food to a sophisticated setting. The
concept is simple: just wander around the
hawkers with their wares and choose the
tastiest-looking dishes, although it's also fine
to order straight from the menu.

Mama Wong's
CHINESE $$

(Map p62; ☑097 8508383; 41 St 308; mains US$3-
7; ☺11am-11pm; ☏) This red-lit hang-out
brings a contemporary touch to the city's
Chinese dining scene, serving up inventive
dumplings, noodle bowls and Asian tapas
such as duck pancakes or chilli and garlic
prawns. Good value, good fun.

Russian Market

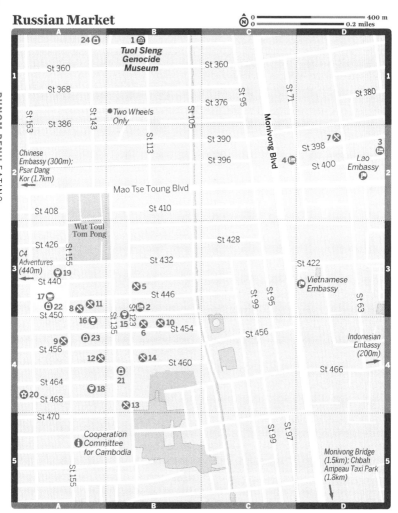

Ⓝ N 0 0 400 m 0.2 miles

St 360

St 368

St 163

St 386

St 143

Chinese
Embassy (300m);
Psar Dang
Kor (1.7km)

St 408

Wat Toul
Tom Pong

St 426

St 155

C4
Adventures
(440m)

Ⓖ19
St 440

17Ⓖ
Ⓖ22 8Ⓧ Ⓧ11
St 450

16Ⓖ
St 135 Ⓖ15 Ⓧ Ⓧ10
Ⓖ23 Ⓖ2
9Ⓧ
St 456 6 St 454

12Ⓧ Ⓧ14 St 460

Ⓖ21
Ⓧ20
St 468 Ⓖ18

St 470 Ⓧ13

St 155

Cooperation
ⓘ Committee
for Cambodia

24 Ⓖ 1 Ⓖ

Tuol Sleng
Genocide
Museum

●Two Wheels
Only

St 113

St 105

Mao Tse Toung Blvd

St 410

St 428

St 432

St 446

Ⓧ5

St 360

St 376

St 390

St 396

St 95

St 71

St 380

Monivong Blvd

St 398 7Ⓧ
4Ⓖ St 400

St 422

Vietnamese
Ⓖ Embassy

St 95

St 99

St 456

St 466

St 99

St 97

3
Ⓖ

Lao
Embassy
Ⓖ

Indonesian
Embassy
(200m)

St 63

Monivong Bridge
(1.5km); Chbah
Ampeau Taxi Park
(1.8km)

Farm to Table
CAFE **$$**

(Map p62; ☐ 078 899722; www.farm2table.life; 16
St 360; mains US$4-9; ⊙ 8am-10pm; ⓢⓙ) ✿
Aiming to promote organic farming meth-
ods in Cambodia, Farm to Table offers a
healthy menu of all-day breakfasts, salads,
sandwiches and shakes. It has a lush garden
laden with jackfruit trees and an old tractor
for kids to clamber around on. Live music
from 6.30pm on Fridays.

D's
JAPANESE **$$**

(Map p82; ☐ 023-666 1602; 65 St 63; US$7-15;
⊙11.30am-2.30pm & 5-10pm; ⓢ) Widely acknowledged as Phnom Penh's best Japanese
restaurant by the growing Japanese community, D's offers one of the city's best set-lunch
deals, with a selection of mains from US$7
to US$10 accompanied by an array of sides.

Mok Mony
CAMBODIAN **$$**

(Map p62; ☐ 093 696799; www.mokmony.com;
63C St 294; mains US$4-12; ⊙11am-10pm; ⓢⓙ)
A cutesy little Khmer restaurant with indoor
and outdoor tables that often demand a
wait. Lots of vegetarian and vegan options
are available, as well as more exotic choices
such as lemongrass frogs' legs. Feel free to go

Russian Market

◎ Top Sights
1 Tuol Sleng Genocide Museum B1

◎ Sleeping
2 Double Leaf B3
3 House Boutique D2
4 Rambutan Resort C2

◎ Eating
5 Brooklyn Bistro B3
6 Buffalo Sister B4
7 D's D2
8 Intégrité A3
9 Jars of Clay..A4
10 Lot 369 ....B4
11 Nesat Seafood House..........................A3
12 Sesame Noodle Bar A4
13 Sumatra..B4
14 Trattoria Bello......................................B4
   Vibe Cafe ....(see 11)

◎ Drinking & Nightlife
15 Alchemy GastroPub.............................B3
16 Long After Dark A4
17 Mr Bounnareth A3
18 Riel Brewing Taproom A4
19 Sundown Social Club...........................A3

◎ Entertainment
20 Counterspace Theater A4
   Prumsodun Ok & Natyarasa.....(see 20)

◎ Shopping
21 For Someone I Like B4
22 Russian Market.....................................A3
23 Seekers Independent Spirits A4
24 Tuol Sleng Shoes.................................A1

out of your comfort zone; if you don't like it, send it back for a different plate under the 'no question ask return' policy.

Mexicano Restaurant   MEXICAN $$
(Map p62; ☑ 096 8612353; 29 St 288; US$6-15; ☺ noon-2.30pm & 6-11pm; 🛜) One of the leaders in Phnom Penh's new wave of Mexican restaurants, Mexicano offers some delicious tacos, including pulled pork or succulent river fish. Frozen margaritas and Corona beer complete the picture. Step inside and you'll swear you've been transported to the backstreets of the Mexican capital.

Sushi Bar   JAPANESE $$
(Map p62; ☑ 023-726438; 2D St 302; sushi rolls from US$3; ☺ 11am-10pm; 🛜) Purists may scoff at the low sushi prices, but it's always packed and is definitely one of the better places in town for quick-and-easy raw fish. Sit down-

stairs at the bar, outside on the patio or in private rooms upstairs.

Sonoma Oyster Bar   SEAFOOD $$
(Map p62; ☑ 077 723911; 22 St 306; 6-oyster platters US$7.50-9; ☺ 10am-10pm; 🛜) The owner of this low-key restaurant sells premium imported oysters wholesale to top-end hotels and, luckily for us, offers them here to drop-in diners at bargain prices. A must for raw oyster lovers. Scallops and steaks are among other tempting options.

Topaz   FRENCH $$$
(Map p62; ☑ 015 821888; www.topaz-restaurant.com; 162 Norodom Blvd; dishes US$20-100; ☺ 11am-2pm & 6-10.30pm; 🛜) Topaz was one of Phnom Penh's original designer restaurants, but, as the competition increases around town, it's starting to feel a bit stale. The menu is classic Paris, including delicate Burgundy snails drizzled in garlic, and steak tartare for those with rare tastes.

✕ Russian Market Area

There is nothing better than an iced coffee or fresh fruit shake after surviving the scrum that is the Russian Market (p89). In the market's central food-stall area, look out for the charismatic **Mr Bounnareth** (Map p82; Shop 547; ☺ 7am-5pm), whose patented 'best iced coffee in Phnom Penh' has been living up to its name for more than three decades. Other stalls sell fried noodles and *banh chev* (meat or seafood and veggies wrapped inside a thin egg pancake and lettuce leaf) for US$1 to US$2.

The streets emanating east and south from the Russian Market are home to some of the city's hippest new restaurants and bars, most of which offer great value for money.

★**Nesat Seafood House**   SEAFOOD $
(Map p82; ☑ 077 683003; St 446; mains US$3-7; ☺ 11am-11.30pm Mon-Sat; 🛜) Incredibly cheap seafood cooked to perfection and served in trendy, sea-inspired surrounds. What more could you ask for? All the critters arrive fresh each day from Kampot and Kep, so you can be sure they haven't been squirming around under the sun in the nearby Russian Market. Reserve ahead; a deal this good doesn't go unnoticed.

Trattoria Bello   ITALIAN $
(Map p82; ☑ 096 3410936; 17C St 460; medium pizzas US$3.25-8.80; ☺ noon-2.30pm & 5.30-

PHNOM PENH EATING

LOCAL KNOWLEDGE

CRAFT BREWERIES AND HOMETOWN SPIRITS

Cambodia is now home to more than a dozen microbreweries, all but three of which are found in Phnom Penh. Restrictive rules for craft brewing in neighbouring Thailand have helped fuel growth, as Cambodian upstarts ramp up production to meet the demand of bars both at home and abroad. Coinciding with the beer boom is a boomlet in craft alcohol, with boutique brands distilling the flavours of Cambodia into quaffable spirits. Below are some of Phnom Penh's top artisanal drinking experiences.

Botanico (Map p62; ☑ 077 943135; www.facebook.com/botanicowineandbeergarden; 9B St 29; ⊙ 9am-10pm Sun-Thu, to midnight Fri & Sat; ☎) Bringing US-style craft brewing to Phnom Penh, this great little hideaway stocks Irish Red, IPA and other home-brewed beers. It is set in a verdant garden tucked down a winding alley. Live music on weekends and Tuesday trivia nights keep expats coming back for more.

Riel Brewing Taproom (Map p82; ☑ 017 635592; www.rielbrewing.com; 8F St 464; ⊙ 5-10pm Fri, 2-10pm Sat) This upstart craft brewery from a pair of Aussie and American expats makes nine of the tastiest beers in town. The tiny taproom is only open twice a week, though that will change soon. A new brewery, 36 times the size of the original, is scheduled to open near Tuol Sleng in 2020, signalling big things to come.

Hops Brewery (Map p62; ☑ 023-217039; www.hops-brewery.com; 17 St 228; ⊙ 11am-1am; ☎) Hops has claimed a big slice of the craft-beer action in Phnom Penh thanks to its flashy beer garden with casino-style lighting and snazzy pool tables. German-run, it follows the 500-year-old purity law of brewing, though hardcore beer buffs say the place is more style than substance. Tipples include wheat beer Amber Witch and Hops IPA, while the menu is predominantly Mitteleuropa.

Seekers Independent Spirits (Map p82; ☑ 093 998850; www.seekersspirits.com; 80 St 454; ⊙ 10am-5pm Mon-Fri, to 7pm Sat) Cambodia's only gin distillery makes a sippable Mekong Dry Gin, which is distilled with 13 botanicals, including pandan leaves, galangal, kaffir lime and lemongrass. An on-site bar operates on Saturdays, when there are distillery tours at 4pm and 5.30pm (US$12.50, including two drinks). There are also after-hours parties with signature cocktails on the first Friday of each month (5pm to 11pm).

Samai Distillery (Map p62; http://samaidistillery.com; 9B St 830; ⊙ 6pm-midnight Thu) The origins of sugar cane are in Southeast Asia, so the Venezuelan owners of this beloved rum distillery see themselves as bringing the tradition full circle. Samai opens to visitors on Thursday nights for lavish parties, typically with guest bartenders and live music. Private tours can also be arranged by appointment. The artisan rums here, including one with Kampot pepper, taste far superior to mass-market spirits.

10.30pm; ☎) Hidden away near the Russian Market, Bello turns out some of the most delicious pizzas in town at good prices. The Japanese owner also offers pasta, gnocchi and *polpettine* (meatballs).

Sesame Noodle Bar NOODLES $
(Map p82; ☑ 089 750212; www.sesamenoodle bar.com; 9 St 460; mains US$3.50-5.75; ⊙ 11.30am-2.30pm & 5-9.30pm Tue-Sun; ☎) A Japanese-American duo is behind one of the Russian Market's longest-running little diners. Cold noodles arrive in vegetarian or egg varieties and come heaped with an egg and caramelised pork or grilled tofu. Simply delicious.

Sumatra INDONESIAN $
(Map p82; www.sumatracuisines.com; 67 St 123; mains US$2.50-5; ⊙ 11am-9pm Mon-Sat; ☎ ✏) The vegetarian dishes, which average around US$3, are fantastic value, although hearty eaters may want to order two. The spicy *balado* (tomato and chilli sauce) plates are a good bet, too. Dining is on a garden patio under a tin roof or in an air-conditioned interior.

Brooklyn Bistro AMERICAN $$
(Map p82; ☑ 011 871504; 20 St 123; dishes US$6-17; ⊙ 11am-10pm; ☎) A stylish American diner, this is incredibly popular with Phnom Penh expats in the know. The 16in pizzas are

the largest in town, plus there's a dedicated menu of wings, as well as great deli sandwiches and the best New York cheesecake we've tasted in this part of the world. Weekend roasts draw huge crowds.

Buffalo Sister SANDWICHES **$$**
(Map p82; ☑ 017 879403; 15 St 454; sandwiches from US$5; ⊙ 11am-7.30pm Sun-Fri; 🛜) The extensive sandwich list is ever growing at this self-described carvery. Dig into a roast pork with apple sauce sandwich or go healthy with a grilled veggie or falafel wrap. Famous for its Sunday roast.

Intégrité ASIAN **$$**
(Map p82; ☑ 012 982184; http://integrite phnompenh.com; 67 St 450; mains US$5-6; ⊙ 11.30am-midnight; 🛜) This cafe-cum-restaurant-cum-bar is a bite-sized slice of sophistication next to the chaos of the Russian Market. Come in the morning for fair-trade coffee or a detox juice and return at sunset for Bruneian curries, Shanghai dumplings and global craft cocktails.

Drinking & Nightlife

Phnom Penh has an ever-more sophisticated bar scene, so it's definitely worth one big night out here. There are lots of late-night spots clustered around the intersection of Sts 51 and 172, nicknamed 'Area 51'. 'Golden St' (St 278) is also popular, and the riverfront has its share of bars. Bassac Lane and the Russian Market area have emerged as the hipster parts of town.

Bars

Happy hours are a big thing in Phnom Penh, so it pays to get started early, when even such storied watering holes as the Foreign Correspondents' Club and Raffles offer two-for-one specials. Wednesday is 'Ladies' Night' at some of the smarter bars around town, with two-for-one deals all night or even free drinks.

Most bars are open until at least midnight, which is about the time that Phnom Penh's clubs swing into action.

There are some great hostel bars in Phnom Penh, so keep these in mind if you want to meet other travellers on a night out. Top Banana (p75) is one of the liveliest rooftop bars. Mad Monkey (p74), in the same part of town, offers free beer and punch nightly from 7.30pm to 8pm at its rooftop

bar. Eighty8 Backpackers (p72) throws wild pool parties each Saturday. Sundance Inn has lively bars at its two locations on St 172 (p72) and the **riverside** (Map p68; ☑ 096 2436300; www.sundanceriverside.com; 79 Sisowath Quay; r US$15-30; ❈ 🛜).

North Central (Riverfront)

Oskar Bistro BAR
(Map p68; www.oskar-bistro.com; 159 Sisowath Quay; ⊙ 5pm-2am; 🛜) This upscale gastro-pub blends the bar and restaurant to perfection. Choose from creative cocktails and a huge wine list of nearly 60 tipples, while relaxing to subtle DJ beats. A top spot for a late-night feed, as the kitchen stays open until 11pm.

FCC BAR
(Foreign Correspondents' Club; Map p68; 363 Sisowath Quay; ⊙ 6am-midnight; 🛜) A Phnom Penh institution, the 'F' is housed in a colonial gem with great views and cool breezes. It's one of those Cambodian classics that's still holding onto its charm, though some needed renovations were planned through 2020. FCC also offers an excellent food menu both day and night.

Le Moon ROOFTOP BAR
(Map p68; www.facebook.com/lemoonphnompenh; 1 St 154; ⊙ 5pm-1am) The Amanjaya Pancam Hotel's rooftop number scores points for atmosphere and views over the river, though service is spotty. Bring patience.

Orphic BAR
(Map p68; ☑ 086 887787; 227 Sisowath Quay; ⊙ 5pm-2am; 🛜) Suspended bartenders whip up craft cocktails and deliver them to guests seated at plush leather couches in this slick riverfront bar, which hides behind giant porthole windows and dons a sexy amber glow. There's also a tempting menu of tapas, such as crab cakes or beef satay, if you want to make a night of it.

Olala BAR
(Map p68; ☑ 023-223193; 219 Sisowath Quay; ⊙ 7am-3am; 🛜) Probably the cheapest beer on the riverfront, thanks to a generous happy hour that starts at 7am and rumbles on until closing (yea, that's all day!). The US$0.75 draught beer and US$2 cocktails make it hard to pass up. A restaurant as much as a bar, it's a good place to watch the world go by.

Cheers SPORTS BAR
(Map p68; 209 Sisowath Quay; ☺7am-midnight; 🛜) A real jack of all trades with good pub grub, cheap beer, big screens for sports viewing, and occasional live music. All this in a perfect riverside location.

North Central (Inland)

Elephant Bar BAR
(Map p68; Raffles Hotel Le Royal, St 92; ☺noon-midnight; 🛜) Few places are more atmospheric than this sophisticated bar at the Raffles. It has been drawing journalists, politicos, and the rich and famous for more than 90 years. Singapore slings and many more drinks are half-price during the generous happy hour (4pm to 9pm). The bar also boasts world-class G&Ts.

Eclipse Sky Bar ROOFTOP BAR
(Map p62; http://eclipseskybar.business.site; Phnom Penh Tower, 455 Monivong Blvd; ☺5pm-2am) Located on the 24th floor, this open-air venue is the dry-season venue of choice for big breezes and bigger views. The menu includes cocktails, wine by the glass and beers, but you pay a premium for the dramatic location.

Box Office BAR
(Map p62; 76 St 244; ☺2-11pm Mon-Sat, noon-8pm Sun; 🛜) This little bar is a popular watering hole for local expats, including a thespian crowd thanks to its role as a rehearsal space for theatre and arts productions. It has craft beer from Fuzzy Logic Brewing (in Ho Chi Minh City) on tap and lots of events such as Sunday roasts.

Blue Chilli GAY
(Map p68; www.facebook.com/newbluechilli; 36 St 178; ☺5pm-2am; 🛜) The owner of this long-running gay bar stages popular drag shows from Wednesday to Saturday nights at 11pm. Sunday and Monday are karaoke nights from 8pm. The drag shows, in particular, draw a mixed crowd of gay and straight visitors.

Bong Bong Bong BAR
(Map p62; ☏010 281702; St 240½; ☺5-11pm; 🛜) Secondhand clothes and first-rate cocktails join forces at this tiny vintage shop on an up-and-coming alleyway that masquerades as an urban street bar. The French-Khmer owner ensures that strangers become new friends.

BKK & Tonlé Bassac Area

★**Hub Street**
Cocktails COCKTAIL BAR
(Map p62; ☏017 369594; 20 St 21; ☺6pm-1am) Cheap craft cocktails and killer street cuisine collide to great effect at this marvellous bamboo bar, beloved by expats and Cambodians alike. Arriving here feels like stumbling upon a familiar yet exotic block party, where strangers are quick friends.

★**Battbong** BAR
(Map p62; ☏069 291643; Langka Lane; ☺6pm-late; 🛜) An always-packed speakeasy, Battbong is tricky to locate. Look out for the Coca-Cola machine at the end of Langka Lane and locate the hidden button. Inside is a decadent beatnik-style bar with signature craft cocktails, plush sofas and the kind of low lighting that makes everyone look gorgeous. Down-tempo beats set the mood when there are no live bands.

Duplex BAR
(Map p62; 3 St 278; ☺11am-3am; 🛜) A self-styled Belgian *taverne* with an extensive beer selection, Duplex is also a cool contemporary space that hosts regular salsa and bachata evenings. Great cocktails and a good range of light meals are available. Upstairs it morphs into Club Love, a popular late-night spot for travellers and expats alike.

Le Boutier COCKTAIL BAR
(Map p62; www.leboutier.com; 32 St 308; ☺5pm-late Mon-Sat; 🛜) One of the coolest cocktail bars in Phnom Penh, Le Boutier has an original menu of concoctions that pay homage to Cambodia's golden era of the 1960s, including 'Sinn Sisamouth in the Second City' with bourbon, honey, Averna, coffee and cinnamon. Golden hour kicks off at 5pm with discounted cocktails and two-for-one beers.

Score SPORTS BAR
(Map p62; ☏078 621702; www.scorekh.com; 5 St 282; ☺8am-2am; 🛜) With its cinema-sized screen and television banks on every wall, this cavernous bar is the best place to watch a big game. It's not just the usual footy and rugby, as almost all sports are catered for here. Several pool tables tempt those who would rather play than watch.

Red Bar BAR
(Map p62; www.facebook.com/redbbarcambodia; cnr Sts 308 & 29; ☺5pm-1am; 🛜) A friendly

little local bar in the popular St 308. The drinks here are so cheap that drinkers find themselves lingering long into the night...or maybe that's just us?

Embargo
CRAFT BEER

(Map p62; ☑099 868046; www.facebook.com/embargophnompenh; Langka Lane; ⏱5pm-midnight Tue-Sun) Check the pulse of the local craft-beer scene at this intimate beer bar, where the friendly bartenders pour from eight taps of Cambodia's best. There are also 30 craft beers by the bottle and video games waiting to be played on the upstairs deck.

Zeppelin Bar
BAR

(Map p62; 13 St 278; ⏱5pm-late) Who says vinyl is dead? It lives on here, thanks to the owner of this old-school rock bar spinning the turntables every night. The mainstay on the menu is '70s big rock. There is also a pool table. Zeppelin has a breezy upstairs location on popular 'Golden St'.

Russian Market Area

★ Long After Dark
BAR

(Map p82; ☑093 768354; http://longafterdarkcambodia.com; St 450; ⏱noon-midnight Sun-Thu, to 2am Fri & Sat; 🛜) This place keeps visitors hanging around the Russian Market area long after dark with its combination of rare single-malt whiskies, Cambodian craft beers and a vinyl collection that starts a-spinnin' at weekends. Brief happy hour at 5pm on Friday and some interesting whisky flights available with Highlands or global themes. Cool and cosy all at once.

★ Sundown Social Club
ROOFTOP BAR

(Map p82; ☑015 526373; 86 St 440; ⏱noon-11pm; 🛜) Look at the Russian Market from a different angle in this funky rooftop bar on St 440. Head here for sundowners, including Club Tropicana–inspired cocktails and craft beers, and a menu of innovative pub grub and bar snacks.

Alchemy GastroPub
BAR

(Map p82; ☑031 2346845; 36 St 123; ⏱10am-2pm & 5pm-2am; 🛜) This is one of the capital's more stylish brewpubs, offering a selection of local and regional craft brews and some high-octane cocktails, with two-for-one offers on at least one cocktail every night. Weekend events include live music and there is an impressive menu to help ensure the drinking stays on track.

Cafes

Brown Coffee
CAFE

(Map p62; www.browncoffee.com.kh; cnr Sts 294 & 57; ⏱6.30am-9pm; 🛜) The flagship outlet of a homegrown coffee chain that has outperformed all the expensive imports to produce some of Phnom Penh's most refined spaces and best coffee. There are lots of branches around town, as the company has set its sights on cracking Cambodia and, possibly, Asia.

Happy Damrei
CAFE

(Map p68; ☑010 227149; 1 St 174; ⏱7am-11pm; 🛜) This cool little cafe is the epicentre of board games in Phnom Penh and has everything from classics such as Risk and Cluedo to contemporary offerings including Cards Against Humanity. It's US$1.50 per hour to play. Food and drinks accompany the games.

Treehouse
CAFE

(Map p62; 44 St 113; ⏱8am-6pm Mon-Sat) The perfect place to decompress from the horrors of the nearby Tuol Sleng Genocide Museum over a caramelly cold brew, bubbly kombucha or earthy matcha latte. Come in the afternoon and you can also swig some craft beer at a table below hanging plants and (empty) birdcages.

Nightclubs

For the low-down on club nights, check out Phnom Penh Underground (www.phnom-penh-underground.com), an online guide to the club scene in Cambodia's capital.

★ Pontoon
CLUB

(Map p68; www.pontoonclub.com; 80 St 172; ⏱10pm-late; 🛜) After floating around from pier to pier for a few years (hence the name), the city's premier nightclub found a permanent home on terra firma. It draws top local DJs and occasional big foreign acts. Admission is US$3 to US$8 at weekends; free on weeknights. Thursday is ladies night. Adjacent Pontoon Pulse is more of a lounge club, with electronica and ambient music.

★ Heart of Darkness
CLUB

(Map p68; http://heartofdarknessclub.com.kh; 38 St 51; ⏱9pm-late) This Phnom Penh institution with an alluring Angkor theme has evolved into more of a nightclub than a bar over the years, with drag shows that drop jaws Wednesday to Saturday nights. The place attracts all – and we mean *all* – sorts. Everybody should stop in at least once just

DON'T MISS

BASSAC LANE BARS

Bassac Lane is the moniker given to an alley that leads south off St 308. The brainchild of Kiwi brothers the Norbert-Munns, who have a flair for drinks and design, there are half a dozen or more hole-in-the-wall boozers in this eclectic spot. Choose from fusion wraps and burgers at the original **Meat & Drink** (Map p62; ✆089 666414; www. facebook.com/meatanddrink; mains US$4-8; ⊙5pm-midnight), tiny and intimate **Seibur** (www.facebook.com/seibur.pp; ⊙5pm-midnight Tue-Sun), the refined and book-filled **Library** (www.facebook.com/ thelibrarydaiquiribar; ⊙4.30pm-midnight; �🛜), rooftop cocktail bar **Harry's** (✆010 275273; ⊙4.30pm-midnight) or custom-bike tribute bar, **Hangar 44** (⊙5pm-midnight).

Bassac Lane has cemented its reputation as the new bohemian district of Phnom Penh and is well worth a visit.

to bask in the aura and atmosphere of the place.

Vito
CLUB

(Map p62; 8 St 208; ⊙8pm-3am) A popular retro club spinning some older dance tunes, from the '90s to the '00s, and even back to the '80s. Popular with a slightly older crowd who want to have a conversation as well as a dance.

Epic
CLUB

(Map p62; ✆010 600608; www.epic.com.kh; 122B Tonlé Bassac; ⊙9pm-3am) The superclub comes to Phnom Penh with the emergence of Epic. A huge warehouse space, its decor and design are anything but 'warehouse' with 3D mapping and a top-tier sound system. It's primarily aimed at Cambodia's rich young things.

☆ Entertainment

Classical Dance & Arts

★ **Traditional Dance Show** PERFORMING ARTS

(Map p68; ✆017 998570; http://experience.cam bodianlivingarts.org; National Museum, St 178; adult/child from US$15/9; ⊙7pm) 🏵 For this must-see performance, put on daily by Cambodian Living Arts (p67), artists come from CLA's incubator program and work on specific shows for up to two years. Each is set in

the attractive grounds of the National Museum. There's an optional dinner-show combo ticket (from US$30) that includes a meal at nearby Friends (p76).

Prumsodun Ok & Natyarasa
DANCE

(Map p82; www.prumsodun.com; 53 St 468; 1hr show US$25; ⊙6.30pm Sat & Sun) Cambodia's first gay dance company infuses Khmer classics with a contemporary (and LGBTQI+) spirit at its evocative performances in the **Counterspace Theater** (http://javacreative cafe.com/events) each weekend. The works displayed here aim for high art and are more along the lines of what you'd find on the international festival circuit than the tourist-pleasing affairs elsewhere in town.

Chatomuk Theatre
THEATRE

(Map p62; Sisowath Quay) Check the flyer out front for information on performances at the landmark Chatomuk Theatre, located in the heart of Phnom Penh's popular riverfront. Officially, it has been turned into a government conference centre, but it regularly plays host to cultural performances.

Cinema

★ **Meta House**
ARTS CENTRE

(Map p68; www.meta-house.com; 47 St 178; ⊙9am-11pm Tue-Sun; 🛜) This German-run cultural centre screens art-house films, documentaries and shorts from Cambodia and around the world at its rooftop cinema. Films are sometimes followed by Q&As with those involved. There's also a large art gallery and on-site Art Cafe, while dance, theatre and music events round out the busy cultural calendar.

Bophana Centre
CINEMA

(Map p62; ✆023-992174; www.bophana.org; 64 St 200; ⊙8am-noon & 2-6pm Mon-Fri, 2-6pm Sat) Established by Cambodian-French filmmaker Rithy Panh, this is a free audiovisual resource for filmmakers and researchers. Visitors can explore its archive of old photographs and films, and attend free film screenings on Saturdays at 5pm. There are also regular lectures and photo exhibitions.

Major Cineplex
CINEMA

(Map p62; ✆023-901111; www.majorcineplex.com. kh; Aeon Mall, 132 Samdech Sothearos Blvd; US$3-12; ⊙9am-midnight) The smartest cinema in town, with seven screens, including a business-class-like VIP screen and a 4DX screen for interactive viewing (complete with moving seats and surprise effects).

Flicks   CINEMA
(Map p62; www.theflicks.asia; 39B St 95; tickets US$4; 🛜) Flicks shows at least three movies a day (more on weekends) in an uber-comfortable, air-conditioned screening room. As a bonus, you can watch all films on one ticket.

🛍 Shopping

There is some great shopping to be had in Phnom Penh, but don't forget to bargain in the markets or you'll have your 'head shaved' – local slang for being ripped off.

Markets & Malls

As well as the traditional markets, there are now several shopping malls in Phnom Penh. While they are not quite as glamorous as the likes of the Siam Paragon in Bangkok, they are good places to browse (especially thanks to the air-conditioning) and offer some reliable food courts and restaurants.

★Russian Market   MARKET
(Psar Tuol Tom Pong; Map p82; St 155; ⊙6am-5pm) This sweltering bazaar is the one market all visitors should come to at least once during a trip to Phnom Penh. It is *the* place to shop for souvenirs and discounted name-brand clothing. We can't vouch for the authenticity of everything, but, along with plenty of knock-offs, you'll find genuine articles stitched in local factories.

Brands you're likely to see include Banana Republic, Billabong, Calvin Klein, Colombia Sportswear, Gap and Next. The Russian Market, so-called by foreigners because the predominantly Russian expat population shopped here in the 1980s, also has a large range of handicrafts and antiquities (many

fake), including miniature Buddhas, woodcarvings, betel-nut boxes, silks, silver jewellery, musical instruments and so on. Bargain hard, as hundreds of tourists pass through here every day. There are also some good food stalls in the Russian Market.

Night Market   MARKET
(Psar Reatrey; Map p68; cnr St 108 & Sisowath Quay; ⊙5-11pm) A cooler, al fresco version of the Russian Market, this night market takes place every evening if it's not raining. Bargain vigorously, as prices can be on the high side. Surprisingly, it's probably more popular with Khmers than foreigners.

Aeon Mall   MALL
(Map p62; www.aeonmallphnompenh.com; 132 Samdech Sothearos Blvd; ⊙9am-10pm; 🛜) The swankiest mall in Phnom Penh, this Japanese-run establishment has international boutiques, several food courts and extensive dining outlets, plus a seven-screen multiplex cinema and a bowling alley.

Sorya Shopping Centre   MALL
(Map p68; www.soryacenterpoint.com; cnr Sts 63 & 154; ⊙9am-9pm) Still a popular mall, this long-running place has a good range of shops, a food court, a cinema, a central location and superb views from the top-floor viewing gallery over the more traditional Psar Thmei (p56).

Silks, Clothing & Accessories

While the markets are best known for international clothing from the local garment factories, a multiplying number of stores surrounding the Russian Market sell authentic brand-name gear, made locally and in neighbouring Vietnam. There are also several boutiques around town specialising

---

THE BAREFOOT DIVA OF THE CAMBODIAN RICE FIELDS

Singer **Kak Channthy** overcame an impoverished childhood in Prey Veng Province to become one of the most recognisable singers in Phnom Penh as the frontwoman for Cambodian Space Project (www.cambodianspaceproject.org), a mixed expat and Khmer band that helped rejuvenate the Cambodian rock 'n' roll sound of the 1960s.

Her career began in a small-town karaoke bar, but within a few years she was gracing prestigious global stages, such as the Kennedy Center in Washington, DC, as the so-called 'barefoot diva of the Cambodian rice fields'. The rising star had performed gigs with Australian music icon Paul Kelly and American Motown legend Dennis Coffey by the time she met her untimely death at age 38 in a 2018 Phnom Penh accident.

Not Easy Rock 'n' Roll is a 2015 documentary that traces Channthy's rise from an illiterate farm girl to a renowned chanteuse credited with reviving the spirit of Cambodia's 'golden era'. Space Four Zero (p91) in Phnom Penh was the unofficial HQ of Cambodian Space Project and remains a vital resource on golden era music.

SHOPPING TO MAKE A DIFFERENCE

There is a host of tasteful shops selling handicrafts and textiles to raise money for projects that assist disadvantaged Cambodians. These are good places to spend some dollars, as they help to put a little bit back into the country.

Artisans Angkor (Map p68; www.artisansdangkor.com; 12 St 13; ⊙9am-6pm) ✐ Classy Phnom Penh branch of the venerable Siem Reap sculpture and silk specialist, which supports some 800 craftspeople across the country.

Cambodian Handicraft Association (CHA; Map p62; www.cha-cambodia.org; 28 St 330; ⊙7.30am-5.30pm) ✐ Sells fine, handmade silk clothing, scarves, toys and bags produced by victims of landmines and polio.

Daughters of Cambodia (Map p68; www.daughtersofcambodia.org; 321 Sisowath Quay; ⊙9am-5.30pm Mon-Sat) ✐ An NGO that runs a range of programs to train and assist former prostitutes and victims of sex trafficking. The clothes, bags and accessories here are made with ecofriendly cotton and natural dyes.

Rajana (Map p50; ☑023-993642; www.rajanacrafts.org; 61C St 450; ⊙8am-5pm Mon-Sat) ✐ One of the best all-round handicraft stores, Rajana aims to promote fair wages and training. It has a beautiful selection of cards, some quirky metalware products, jewellery, bamboo crafts, lovely shirts, gorgeous wall hangings and more.

Sobbhana (Map p68; 23 St 144; ⊙8am-5pm Mon-Sat) ✐ A not-for-profit organisation training women in traditional weaving. Beautiful silks in a stylish boutique.

Villageworks (Map p62; www.villageworks.biz; 118 St 113; ⊙8am-5pm Mon-Sat) ✐ Opposite the Tuol Sleng museum, this shop has the inevitable silk scarves, as well as signature items such as accessories made from recycled cement bags by poor and disadvantaged artisans in Kompong Thom Province.

Watthan Artisans (Map p50; www.watthanartisans.com; 180 Norodom Blvd; ⊙8am-5pm) ✐ At the entrance to Wat Than, selling silk and other products, including contemporary handbags, made by a cooperative of landmine and polio victims. Also has on-site woodworking and weaving workshops.

---

in silk furnishings and stylish original clothing, as well as glam accessories. Many are conveniently located on St 240.

★ **Ambre** CLOTHING
(Map p68; ☑023-217935; www.romydaketh.net; 37 St 178; ⊙10am-6pm) Leading Cambodian fashion designer Romyda Keth has turned this striking French-era mansion into the perfect showcase for her stunning silk collection. There is also a wide array of homewares.

Amboh SHOES
(Map p62; ☑088 9059509; www.amboh espadrilles.com; 45 St 21; ⊙9am-7pm Mon-Fri, 2-5.30pm Sat) A small shoe shop near Aeon Mall where you can craft your own custom-made espadrilles (US$35) or choose from the attractive handmade collection (US$30), most of which feature Cambodian *krama* patterns.

Smateria FASHION & ACCESSORIES
(Map p62; 8 St 57; ⊙8am-9pm) Smateria's speciality is bags, including a line of quirky kids'

backpacks, made from fishing net and other recycled materials.

Paperdolls CLOTHING
(Map p62; Bassac Lane; ⊙2-10pm Tue-Sun) Great stuff for women, including sundresses, shoes, movie-star shades, handbags, jewellery – you name it.

Tuol Sleng Shoes SHOES
(Map p82; 138 St 143; ⊙8am-7pm) Scary name, but there's nothing scary about the price of these custom-fit, handmade shoes. It is surrounded by a sea of newer competitors, so shop around before you commit.

DAH Export CLOTHING
(Map p62; 87 Sihanouk Blvd; ⊙9am-9pm) This is the biggest and best of the factory overrun outlets, with an impressive winter collection (North Face Gore-Tex ski jackets for US$99, anyone?), plenty of kiddie clothing and a prominent location.

Art & Books

Plenty of shops sell locally produced paintings along St 178, opposite the Royal University of Fine Arts between Sts 13 and 19. With a new generation of artists coming up, the selection is much stronger than it once was. Lots of reproduction busts of famous Angkorian sculptures are available along this stretch, great for the mantelpiece back home. Make sure to bargain.

You'll find the largest concentration of bookstores near the intersection of Norodom Blvd and St 240.

Mekong Arts ART
(Map p68; ☎012 928005; 33 St 178; ⊙8am-8pm) A refined store near the National Museum with a great collection of local art, antiquities, jewellery, silks and more.

DinArt Gallery ART
(Map p68; ☎017 931900; dinart30@gmail.com; 79 St 136; ⊙10am-6pm Mon-Fri, from noon Sat & Sun) The Kampot-born painter Din (Teang Borin) displays his ethereal Khmer modern art in a small gallery space above the Feel Good Cafe.

For Someone I Like ARTS & CRAFTS
(Map p82; ☎076 2226897; http://for-someone-i-like.business.site; 66A St 135; ⊙10.30am-7.30pm Tue-Sun) Some 98% of all the products in this stylish boutique are made in Cambodia, and you won't find the typical menagerie sold in every other store in town. Instead, there are one-of-a-kind ceramics, homewares, textiles and jewellery.

Space Four Zero MUSIC
(http://spacefourzero.com; St 240½; ⊙9am-7pm) This cool pop-art gallery pays tribute to the lost artists of Cambodia's golden years, many of whom perished under the Khmer Rouge regime, in an original series of 'sticky fingers' art prints. Rare vinyl is also on sale.

Estampe VINTAGE
(Map p62; 197A St 19; ⊙9.30am-6.30pm Mon-Sat) Reproduction images, posters, journals and more, plus original collectibles from old Indochine, including books, maps and postcards.

Monument Books BOOKS
(Map p62; www.monument-books.com; 111 Norodom Blvd; ⊙7am-8pm) The best-stocked bookshop in town, with almost every Cambodia-related book available and a superb maps-and-travel section.

D's Books BOOKS
(Map p62; 79 St 240; ⊙9am-9pm) The largest chain of secondhand bookshops in the capital, with a good range of titles.

ℹ Information

EMERGENCY
In the event of a medical emergency, it may be necessary to be evacuated to Bangkok.

Ambulance (☎119 in emergency; ☎023-724891)
Fire (☎118 in emergency; ☎023-723555)
Police (☎117 in emergency; ☎023-726158)

INTERNET
Pretty much all hotels, guesthouses, cafes and restaurants offer free wi-fi connections. Local SIM cards are widely available with cheap data packages, so if you are travelling with an unlocked mobile phone or tablet, sign up soon after arrival and stay connected.

Internet cafes are less common since the wi-fi explosion, but the main backpacker strips – St 258, St 278 and St 172 – have a few places. Most internet cafes are set up for Skype or similar services. Digital nomads passing through Cambodia should set up shop at Workspace 1 (p56) in Factory Phnom Penh.

MEDIA
The *Phnom Penh Post* and the *Khmer Times* are widely available. They mix original local-news content with international stories pulled from wire services.

MEDICAL SERVICES
It is important to be aware of the difference between a clinic and a hospital in Phnom Penh. Clinics are good for most situations, but in a genuine emergency, it is best to go to a hospital.

Cabinet Medical Francais (Map p68; ☎012 634115; 18 St 118; ⊙7.30am-7pm Mon-Fri, to noon Sat) International-standard care from English- and French-speaking doctors.

Calmette Hospital (Map p68; ☎012 772789; www.calmette.gov.kh; cnr Monivong Blvd & St 80; ⊙24hr) The best of the local hospitals, with the most comprehensive services and an intensive-care unit, but it really helps to go with a Khmer speaker.

Eurodental Clinic (Map p62; ☎012 893174; www.facebook.com/eurodentalclinichcm; 9 St 306; ⊙8am-1pm & 2-7pm Mon-Fri, 8am-1pm Sat) Has international-standard dental services and a good reputation.

Pharmacie de la Gare (Map p68; www.pharmacie-delagare.com; 124 Monivong Blvd; ⊙7.30am-7pm Mon-Sat, to noon Sun) A pharmacy with English- and French-speaking consultants.

Raffles Medical (Map p62; ☎023-216911; www.rafflesmedicalgroup.com; 161 St 51; ⊙8am-

5.30pm Mon-Fri, to noon Sat, emergency 24hr) Formerly International SOS Medical Centre, this is a top clinic with a host of international doctors and dentists, and prices to match.

Royal Phnom Penh Hospital (☑ 023-991000; www.royalphnompenhhospital.com; 888 Russian Confederation Blvd; ☾24hr) International hospital affiliated with Bangkok Hospital. Boasts top facilities. Expensive.

Tropical & Travellers Medical Clinic (Map p68; ☑ 023-306802; www.travellers medicalclinic.com; 88 St 108; ☾9.30-11.30am & 2.30-5pm Mon-Fri, to 11.30am Sat) Well-regarded clinic run for more than two decades by a rather brash British general practitioner.

U-Care Pharmacy (Map p68; 26 Samdech Sothearos Blvd; ☾8am-10pm) International-style pharmacy with a convenient location near the river.

MONEY

Visa and MasterCard are the most widely accept-ed cards. Cash only for street vendors. There's little need to turn US dollars into riel; greenbacks are universally accepted.

You can change a wide variety of currencies into dollars or riel in the jewellery stalls around Psar Thmei and the Russian Market. Many upmarket hotels offer 24-hour money-changing services, although this is usually reserved for their guests.

Banks with ATMs and money-changing facili-ties are ubiquitous. Malls and supermarkets are good bets, and there are dozens of ATMs along the riverfront. Note that most ATMs dispense US$50 and US$100 notes by default, yet few businesses accept such large bills. Requesting an odd amount (US$180, for example) will give you some smaller US$20 bills to work with.

CAB Bank (Map p68; 263 Sisowath Quay; ☾8am-9pm) Convenient hours and location, plus there's also a Western Union office here (one of several in the city).

Canadia Bank (Map p68; cnr St 110 & Monivong Blvd; ☾8am-3.30pm Mon-Fri, to 11.30am Sat) Has ATMs around town, with a US$5 charge. At its flagship branch you can also get cash advances on MasterCard and Visa. Also represents MoneyGram.

J Trust Royal Bank (Map p68; 265 Sisowath Quay; ☾8.30am-4pm Mon-Fri, to noon Sat) J Trust has ATMs galore all over town, including at supermarkets and petrol stations, but there is a US$5 charge per transaction.

POST

Central Post Office (Map p68; www.cambodia post.post/en; St 13; ☾8am-5pm) A landmark, it is housed in a French-colonial classic just east of Wat Phnom.

SAFE TRAVEL

Phnom Penh is not as dangerous as people im-agine, but it is important to take care.

➡ Armed robberies do sometimes occur, but statistically you would be very unlucky to be a victim.

➡ Should you become the victim, do not panic and do not struggle. Calmly raise your hands and let your attacker take what they want. *Do not* reach for your pockets, as the assailant may think you are reaching for a gun.

➡ Flooding is a major problem in the wet season (June to October), when downpours turn some streets into canals for a few hours.

➡ Scammers also work the city streets.

There are fewer con artists in Phnom Penh than there used to be, but it still pays to be aware of these common scams.

➡ The riverfront area of Phnom Penh attracts many beggars, as do Psar Thmei and the Rus-sian Market. Generally, however, there is little in the way of push and shove. Watch out for fake monks from China or Taiwan begging as a scam. They usually have grey or brown robes instead of the saffron robes of Khmer monks.

➡ Another common racket is the blackjack scam, where friendly-seeming locals (usually from elsewhere in Southeast Asia) invite you to their home for a betting game that is rigged from the start. The jig typically ends with the unsuspecting tourist made to withdraw 'owed' funds from an ATM under the threat of violence.

➡ If you ride your own motorbike during the day, some police may try to fine you for the most trivial of offences. They will most likely demand US$5 and threaten to take you to the police

---

ⓘ GETTING TO VIETNAM: PHNOM PENH TO HO CHI MINH CITY

Getting to the border The original Bavet/Moc Bai land crossing between Vietnam and Cambodia (open 8am to 8pm) has seen steady traffic for more than two decades. The easiest way to get to Ho Chi Minh City (HCMC; Saigon) is to catch an international bus (US$9 to US$15, six hours) from Phnom Penh. Several companies making this trip.

At the border Long lines entering either country are not uncommon, but otherwise it's straightforward provided you prepurchase a Vietnamese visa (should you require one).

Moving on If you are not on the international bus, it's not hard to find onward transport to HCMC or elsewhere.

GETTING TO VIETNAM: PHNOM PENH TO CHAU DOC

The most scenic way to end your travels in Cambodia is to sail the Mekong to Kaam Samnor (about 100km south-southeast of Phnom Penh), cross the border to Vinh Xuong in Vietnam, and proceed to Chau Doc overland or on the Tonlé Bassac River via a small channel. Chau Doc has onward land and river connections to points in the Mekong Delta and elsewhere in Vietnam.

Various companies do trips all the way through to Chau Doc using a single boat or some combination of bus and boat; prices vary according to speed and level of service, but all boats depart from Phnom Penh's tourist-boat dock. Both Capitol Tour (p95) and **Hang Chau** (Map p68; ☏088 8787871; http://hangchautourist.vn) have services departing at 12.30pm, charging US$29 and US$25 respectively. The entire journey is by boat and lasts about five hours.

The more upmarket and slightly faster **Blue Cruiser** (Map p68; ☏016 824343; www.blue cruiser.com; US$35) departs at 1pm; **Victoria Chau Doc Hotel** (Map p68; www.victoriahotels. asia; US$95) also has a boat making several runs a week between Phnom Penh and its Chau Doc hotel. These companies take about four hours, including a slow border check, and use a single boat to Chau Doc. Backpacker guesthouses and tour companies sometimes offer cheaper bus/boat combo trips, though these are becoming increasingly less common.

Some nationalities require a Vietnam visa in advance and some do not require a visa. Check with the Vietnamese embassy (p351) in Phnom Penh to see if you need a visa or not, as visas are not available on arrival. If arriving from Vietnam, Cambodia visas are available on arrival.

station for an official US$20 fine if you do not pay. If you are patient and smile, you can usually get away with handing over a few dollars.

➧ Don't accept drinks from strangers or leave drinks unattended at bars. Reports of drinks being drugged for theft or sexual assault aren't super common, but do occur.

ChildSafe (Map p68; ☏ hotline 012 311112; www.thinkchildsafe.org; Futures Factory) Helps tourists to learn about best behaviour relating to child begging, the dangers of orphanage tours, exploitation and other risks to children (see www.thinkchildsafe.org for tips). You can also look out for the ChildSafe logo on *remorks* and hotels: this network of people is trained to protect children in Cambodia.

Visitor Information Centre (Map p62; Sisowath Quay; ⏰8am-5pm Mon-Sat; 🛜) Located on the riverfront near the Chatomuk Theatre in the Yi Sang Riverside restaurant. It doesn't carry a whole lot of information. On the other hand, it does offer free internet access, free wi-fi, air-con and clean public toilets.

❶ Getting There & Away

AIR

Phnom Penh International Airport (PNH; ☏023-862800; http://pnh.cambodia-airports. aero) is 7km west of central Phnom Penh, via Russian Confederation Blvd. Facilities include free wi-fi, a host of internationally recognisable cafes and restaurants, and some decent

handicraft outlets for last-minute purchases. There are also ATMs for US dollars withdrawals on arrival or departure.

Phnom Penh International Airport was the world's fastest growing major airport in 2019, with most of the new demand coming from China. It receives direct flights from across East and Southeast Asia, as well as the Middle East.

Domestically, there are now several airlines connecting Phnom Penh and Siem Reap. **Cambodia Angkor Air** (Map p50; ☏023-666 6786; www.cambodiaangkorair.com; 206A Norodom Blvd) flies three to six times daily to Siem Reap (from US$45 to US$110 one way, 30 minutes), while **Cambodia Airways** (☏096 8525555; www.cambodia-airways.com), **JC International Airlines** (☏018 5666888; www.jcairlines.com) and **Lanmei Airlines** (Map p50; ☏023-981363; www.lanmeiairlines.com; 575 Russian Confederation Blvd) have a few flights each week from US$35 to US$75 one way. Healthy competition has driven down prices, though crowded skies have led to a rapid turnover, with new airlines rising as others fall. It pays to do some research and book ahead for special promotions.

BOAT

Fast boats up the Tonlé Sap to Siem Reap and down the Mekong to Chau Doc in Vietnam operate from the **tourist-boat dock** (Map p68; 93 Sisowath Quay) at the eastern end of St 104. There are no public boat services up the Mekong to Kompong Cham and Kratie.

The fast boats to Siem Reap (US$35, five to six hours) aren't as popular as they used to be. When it costs from as little as US$6 for an air-conditioned bus or US$35 to be bundled on the roof of a boat, it's not hard to see why. It is better to save your boat experience for elsewhere in Cambodia. Several companies have daily services departing at 7am and usually take it in turns to make the run. The first stretch of the journey along the river is scenic, but once the boat hits the lake, the fun is over: it's a vast inland sea with not a village in sight. The boats to Siem Reap run from roughly July through March (water levels are too low at other times), but do not necessarily depart daily, so plan ahead.

BUS

All major towns in Cambodia are accessible by air-conditioned bus from Phnom Penh. Most buses leave from company offices, which are generally clustered around Psar Thmei or located near the corner of St 106 and Sisowath Quay. Buying tickets in advance is a good idea for peace of mind, although it's not always necessary.

Not all buses are created equal, or priced the same. Buses run by Capitol Tour and Phnom Penh Sorya are usually among the cheapest, while Giant Ibis and Mekong Express buses are better and pricier.

Most of the long-distance buses drop off and pick up in major towns along the way, such as Kompong Thom en route to Siem Reap, Pursat on the way to Battambang, or Kompong Cham en route to Kratie. However, full fare is usually charged anyway.

Express minivans are generally faster than buses on most routes, but some travellers prefer the size and space of a large bus.

To book bus tickets online, visit www.cambo ticket.com.

Capitol Tour (Map p62; ☑ 023-404645; www. capitoltourscambodia.com; 14 St 182) Cheap buses to popular destinations such as Siem Reap, Sihanoukville and Battambang.

Giant Ibis (Map p68; ☑ 096 9993333; www. giantibis.com; 3 St 106; 🛜) 'VIP' specialist with big buses to Siem Reap, Ho Chi Minh City (Vietnam) and Kampot. All have plenty of legroom and wi-fi. A portion of profits goes towards giant ibis conservation.

GTF Express (GST; Map p68; ☑ 012 434373; 13 St 142) Sleeper bus specialist with trips to secondary regional destinations.

Long Phuong (Map p50; ☑ 097 3110999; 315 Sihanouk Blvd) Buses to Ho Chi Minh City.

BUS CONNECTIONS FROM PHNOM PENH

DESTINATION	DURATION (HR)	COST (US$)	COMPANIES	FREQUENCY
Bangkok	13-17	18-25	Mekong Express, Virak Buntham	early morning & late evening
Battambang (day)	6	9-11	PP Sorya, Capitol Tour	frequent
Battambang (night)	6	10-15	Virak Buntham, Capitol Tour	4 per night
Ho Chi Minh City	6-7	9-18	most companies	frequent
Kampot (direct)	4	7-10	Capitol Tour, Giant Ibis	morning & afternoon
Kampot (via Kep)	5	8	PP Sorya	frequent
Kep	4	8-10	PP Sorya, Giant Ibis	frequent to 3pm
Koh Kong	8-9	11	Virak Buntham	7.45am
Kompong Cham	3	7	PP Sorya, Capitol Tour	hourly to 3pm
Kratie	6-7	8	PP Sorya	regularly in the morning
Poipet (day)	8	9-11	Capitol Tour, PP Sorya	hourly to 2.30pm
Poipet (night)	8	13-18	Virak Buntham, Capitol Tour	at least 1 daily
Preah Vihear City	6½	8	GTF	8.30am
Siem Reap (day)	6	7-12	most companies	frequent
Siem Reap (VIP)	6	10-15	Giant Ibis, Mekong Express	regular
Siem Reap (night)	6	12-17	Virak Buntham, Giant Ibis, Mekong Express, PP Sorya	frequent 6pm to midnight
Sihanoukville	5½	9-13	most companies	frequent
Stung Treng	9	10	PP Sorya	6.45am, 7.15am, 9.45am

Mekong Express (Map p68; ☑ 098 833399; www.catmekongexpress.com; Sisowath Quay) VIP buses to Ho Chi Minh City and Bangkok, plus Siem Reap.

Phnom Penh Sorya (PP Sorya; Map p68; www. ppsoryatransport.com.kh; cnr Charles de Gaulle Blvd & St 67) Bus services all over the country.

Sapaco (Map p50; ☑ 023-218341; www. sapaco.net.vn; 341 Sihanouk Blvd) Buses to Ho Chi Minh City.

Virak Buntham (Map p68; ☑ 092 666821; www.virakbuntham.com; 1 St 106) Night-bus specialist with services to Siem Reap, Sihanoukville and Koh Kong.

EXPRESS MINIVAN

Speedy express minivans (minibuses) with 12 to 14 seats serve popular destinations such as Siem Reap, Sihanoukville and Sen Monorom. These cut travel times significantly, but they tend to be cramped and often travel at very high speeds, so are not for the faint of heart. Several of the big bus companies also run vans, most notably Mekong Express and Virak Buntham. It's a good idea to book express vans in advance.

Angkor Express (Map p68; ☑ 092 966669; 5 St 108)

Bayon VIP (Map p68; ☑ 023-966968; www. bayonvip.com; 3 St 126)

Cambodia Post (Map p68; ☑ 012 931255; www. cambodiapost.post; Main Post Office, St 13)

CTT Transport & Tours (Map p68; ☑ 023-217217; 223 Sisowath Quay)

Ekareach Express (Map p50; ☑ 017 910333; 98A St 230)

Kampot Express (Map p50; ☑ 012 555123; 2 St 215)

Kim Seng Express (Map p50; ☑ 012 786000; cnr Sts 336 & 230)

Mey Hong Transport (Map p50; ☑ 095 777966; www.meyhongbus.com; 46 St 289)

Olongpich Express (Map p50; ☑ 092 868782; 70 Monireth Blvd)

Seila Angkor (Map p50; ☑ 012 766976; www. seilaangkorexpress.com; 13B St 47)

SHARE TAXI

Share taxis and local minibuses leave Phnom Penh for destinations all over the country. Taxis to Kampot, Kep and Takeo leave from **Psar Dang Kor** (Map p50; Mao Tse Toung Blvd), while packed local minibuses and taxis for most other places leave from the northwest corner of **Psar Thmei** (Map p68; cnr Sts 120 & 126). Vehicles for the Vietnam border leave from **Chbah Am-peau** taxi park, on the eastern side of Monivong Bridge in the south of town. You may have to wait awhile (possibly until the next day if you arrive in the afternoon) before your vehicle fills up, or pay for the vacant seats yourself.

Share Taxi Charter Fares

DESTINATION	COST (US$)	DURATION (HR)
Battambang	55	4½
Kampot	35	3
Kep	40	3
Koh Kong	65	4½
Kompong Cham	25	2½
Kompong Thom	45	3
Kratie	50	5
Pursat	45	3
Siem Reap	70	5
Sihanoukville	50	4
Takeo	20	2
Vietnam border	50	3

TRAIN

Phnom Penh's train station is located at the western end of St 106 and St 108, in a grand old

EXPRESS MINIVAN CONNECTIONS FROM PHNOM PENH

DESTINATION	DURATION (HR)	COST (US$)	COMPANIES	FREQUENCY
Ban Lung	9-10	10-14	Virak Buntham	2-3 daily
Battambang	5	8-12	Mekong Express, Virak Buntham, Bayon VIP, Cambodia Post	regular
Kampot	3½	7-8	Kampot Express, Ekareach Express, Mekong Express, Kim Seng Express, Cambodia Post	regular
Kep	3½	6-8	Olongpich Express, Cambodia Post	7.45am
Sen Monorom	6-7	11-12	Kim Seng Express, Virak Buntham	regular
Siem Reap	5-6	8-12	Angkor Express, Bayon VIP, Mekong Express, Mey Hong, Seila Angkor, Virak Buntham	frequent
Sihanoukville	4	7-12	CTT Transport, Bayon VIP, Olongpich Express, Cambodia Post, Mekong Express, Virak Buntham	frequent

colonial-era building. Passenger train services returned to Cambodia in 2016 with weekend trains from Phnom Penh to Kampot and Sihanoukville. Royal Railways (p365) runs trains in either direction, departing Phnom Penh or Sihanoukville at 7am on Saturday and Sunday, with an additional afternoon train on Sunday at 4pm. There are also morning trains departing from Phnom Penh at 7am on Friday and from Sihanoukville at 7am on Monday. Phnom Penh to Sihanoukville is US$8, taking seven hours. Phnom Penh to Kampot is US$7, taking five hours.

Trains to Poipet, on the border with Thailand, hit the rails in 2018, with hopes of creating a seamless service from Phnom Penh to Bangkok in the near future. The trip takes 12 hours all the way to Poipet (US$7) and nine to Battambang (US$5), with departures from Phnom Penh on Friday and Sunday and departures from Poipet on Saturday and Monday. All trains leave at 7am.

Getting Around

Being such a small city, Phnom Penh is quite easy to get around, although traffic is getting worse by the year. Traffic jams can be expected during the morning and evening rush hours, particularly around the two main north–south boulevards, Monivong and Norodom, as well as Russian Confederation Blvd heading out to the airport.

GETTING TO/FROM THE AIRPORT

When arriving by air at Phnom Penh International Airport, there is an official booth outside the airport arrivals area to arrange taxis to the centre for US$12; a *remork* costs a flat US$9. You can get a *remork* for US$5 to US$7 and a *moto* (motorcycle taxi) for about US$3 if you exit the airport and arrange one on the street.

Even cheaper is Line 3 on the city's bus system, which passes by the airport and will take you into town, with stops at Psar Thmei and Wat Phnom (1500r, 5am to 8.30pm). It can be slow with 20 or more stops along the way, but then so can taxis with all the traffic.

The **KKStar Shuttle Bus** (☏023-688 5858; www.facebook.com/KKStarBus; US$5) is another option. It departs from the airport every 30 to 60 minutes from 9am to 7.45pm, making seven stops before terminating at the Sofitel near Aeon Mall. Royal Railways (p365) also operates a shuttle train from the airport to downtown Phnom Penh (US$2.50, 30 minutes, every 30 minutes).

Heading to the airport from central Phnom Penh, a taxi/*remork moto* will cost about US$10/6/3. The journey usually takes between 30 minutes and one hour depending on the traffic, but can take up to 90 minutes during rush hour.

BICYCLE

It's possible to hire bicycles at some of the guesthouses around town for about US$1 to US$2 a day,

but take a look at the chaotic traffic conditions before venturing forth. Once you get used to the anarchy, it can be a fun way to get around.

BUS

Phnom Penh has a few local bus lines running north to south and east to west, but they are not widely used by visitors, as the routes are very limited. Most useful is bus no 3, which links the city centre with the airport.

There is a popular sightseeing bus, the **Phnom Penh Hop On Hop Off** (☏016 745880; www. phnompenhhoponhopoff.com; half-day/full day from US$15/25, excl entry fees), which connects leading sights around the city.

CAR & MOTORCYCLE

Car hire is available through travel agencies, guesthouses and hotels in Phnom Penh. Everything from cars (from US$30) to 4WDs (from US$60) is available for travelling around the city, but prices rise fast once you venture beyond. Most visitors who are not used to driving in Southeast Asia opt to hire a car and driver as it's not that much more expensive. **Mr Seng Vannak** (☏012 799552; vannakseng36@gmail.com) is an impeccably mannered English-speaking driver with some of the most competitive rates in town (from US$50 per day within Phnom Penh or US$70 to US$80 further afield). He does frequent full-day sightseeing runs between Phnom Penh and Siem Reap, as well as day trips out to Kirirom National Park or anywhere else in Cambodia you want to go, in a comfy Toyota Highlander seating four.

Exploring Phnom Penh and the surrounding areas on a motorbike is a very liberating experience if you are used to chaotic traffic conditions.

There are numerous motorbike-hire places around town. A 100cc Honda costs US$4 to US$7 per day and 250cc dirt bikes run from US$13 to US$30 per day. You'll have to leave your passport – a driver's licence or other form of ID isn't enough. Remember, you usually get what you pay for when choosing a bike.

A Cambodia licence isn't a bad idea if you'll be doing extensive riding. Motorbike rental shops can get you one for about US$40. Otherwise you technically need an international licence to drive in Cambodia (although it is not unusual for police to take small bribes from drivers who don't have one). If you want to purchase insurance (available at motorbike rental shops for about US$22 per month), you'll need an international or Cambodian licence. Remember to lock your bike, as motorbike theft is common.

Lucky! Lucky! (Map p62; ☏023-212788; lucky motorcyclerental@yahoo.com; 413 Monivong Blvd) Motorbikes are US$4 to US$7 per day, less for multiple days. Trail bikes from US$13.

Two Wheels Only (Map p82; ☏012 200513; www.facebook.com/motorbikehire; 34C St

376) Has well-maintained bikes available to rent (motorbike/trail bike per day US$6/25), but call or email first as the entry gate is often closed.

Vannak Bikes Rental (Map p68; ✆012 220970; 46 St 130) Has high-performance trail bikes up to 1500cc for US$15 to US$50 per day, and smaller motorbikes for US$5 to US$7.

CYCLO

Travelling by *cyclo* (bicycle rickshaw) is less common these days. It's certainly a more relaxing way to see the sights in the centre of town, but this option doesn't work well for long distances. For a day of sightseeing, expect to pay around US$12 – find one on your own or negotiate a tour through the Cyclo Conservation & Careers Association (p67). For short, one-way jaunts, costs are similar to *moto* fares. You won't see many *cyclos* on the road late at night.

MOTO

In areas frequented by foreigners, *moto* drivers generally speak English and sometimes a little French. Elsewhere around town, it can be difficult to find anyone who understands where you want to go. Most short trips are about 2000r to 3000r, although if you want to get from one end of the city to the other, you have to pay US$1 or more. There are fewer *motodups* (*moto* drivers) than in the past, as many have upgraded to *remork-motos* or auto-rickshaws.

Cambodians never negotiate when taking rides (they just pay what they think is fair), but foreigners should always work out the price in advance, especially with *motodups* who hang out in touristy areas such as the riverside or outside luxury hotels. Likewise, night owls taking a *moto* home from popular drinking holes should definitely negotiate to avoid an expensive surprise.

The remaining *moto* drivers who wait outside the popular guesthouses and hotels have reasonable English and are able to act as guides for a daily rate of about US$10 and up, depending on the destinations.

TAXI

At 4000r per kilometre, taxis are cheap, but don't expect to flag one down on the street. Call **Global Meter Taxi** (✆011 311888), **Choice Taxi** (✆010 888010, 023-888023) or **Taxi Vantha** (✆012 855000) for a pickup.

Ride-hailing apps are now widely used in Phnom Penh and can often be simpler to manage for tourists. Among the best are **PassApp** (www.passapptaxis.com) and **Grab** (www.grab.com/kh). Both can link you up with standard taxis, while PassApp also has an SUV option.

TUK TUK

Tuk tuks come in two forms in Phnom Penh. The more traditional *remork-motos* are motorbikes with carriages. These have historically been the main way of getting around for tourists. Average fares are about double those of *motos*: US$2 for short rides around the centre, US$3 and up for longer trips. *Remork* drivers will try to charge more for multiple passengers, but don't let them – generally pay per ride, not per person (groups of four or more should pay an extra US$1 or so).

Newer, partly electric-powered Indian-style auto-rickshaws are now widely used on the streets of Phnom Penh. Most work for Uber-like ride-hailing apps, including PassApp and Grab. These apps tend to offer cheaper rates.

AROUND PHNOM PENH

Exploring the sights beyond the capital is a rewarding experience. The beautiful Mekong island of Koh Dach is the easiest trip to undertake and is best done by mountain bike or local transport. Udong, once the stupa-studded capital of Cambodia, is a half-day trip and can be combined with a visit to Kompong Chhnang.

The Angkorian temple of Tonlé Bati and the hilltop pagoda of Phnom Chisor, located near NH2 towards Takeo, can be combined with the excellent Phnom Tamao Wildlife Rescue Centre, where behind-the-scenes tours get visitors up close with endangered animals. En route to Sihanoukville, Kirirom National Park is the closest protected area to Phnom Penh, offering cool climes amid the pines.

Koh Dach

Known as 'Silk Island' by foreigners, Koh Dach (កោះដាច់) is actually a pair of islands lying in the Mekong River about 5km north-east of the Japanese Friendship Bridge. They make an easy, half-day DIY excursion for those who want to experience the 'real Cambodia'. The hustle-bustle of Phnom Penh feels light years away here.

The name derives from the preponderance of silk weavers who inhabit the islands. When you arrive by ferry, you may be approached by one or more smiling women who speak a bit of English and will invite you to their house to observe weavers in action and – they hope – buy a *krama* (checked scarf), sarongs or other silk items. If you are in the market for silk, you might follow them and have a look. Otherwise, feel free to smile back and politely decline their offer. You'll see plenty of weavers as you journey around the islands.

Most visitors to Koh Dach overnight in Phnom Penh for the stark contrast between urban and rural life. However, there is now a handful of homestays and guesthouses on Koh Dach, where you can experience life with a local family. Conveniently, most of them are within walking distance of each other in the northern part of the island.

There are some food stalls and local restaurants on Koh Dach, but they are fairly rustic. The best restaurants are located at the guesthouses and homestays. Fresh fruit is available on the island, including coconut juice or sugar-cane juice, useful for an energy boost if you are pedalling on two wheels. The best option is the dry-season picnic stalls on the northern tip of the island.

★ **Bonnivoit Garden Homestay**   HOMESTAY $

(🖉 012 222583; www.homestay-cambodia.com; dm US$10, r US$16-22, with air-con US$25; 🅮 🛜) The leading homestay on Koh Dach, run by an English- and German-speaking tour guide who really understands what guests want from the experience. Set in an extensive old wooden house, rooms come in a variety of shapes and sizes. The lush gardens include a large restaurant where day trippers can have a set meal for US$8.

Bicycles for guests to explore the island are available for US$2 per day.

Le Kroma Villa   BOUTIQUE HOTEL $$

(🖉 012 933939; http://lekromavilla.com; r US$35-75; 🅮 🛜 🏊) Boutique accommodation has come to Koh Dach in the shape of Le Kroma Villa, an attractive French-run establishment with its own swimming pool. Rooms are clean and contemporary and decorated with the ubiquitous *krama* (checked scarf) that gives the place its name. There is also a great little restaurant.

❶ Getting There & Away

Remork drivers offer half-day tours to Koh Dach; US$20 should cover it (less if you just want to be dropped off at the ferry), but they have been known to charge as much as US$40. The daily boat tours (p60), departing at 9am and 11am from the tourist-boat dock, are another option (minimum three people). **Cambo Cruise** (Map p62; 🖉 092 290077; www.cambocruise.com; Sisowath Quay; with lunch from US$28) offers a daily trip to Koh Dach at noon with lunch included, plus a free pickup in town. Cyclists can ride over with guides from Grasshopper Adventures (p64).

Otherwise, hire a mountain bike or motorbike and go it alone. Ferries cross the Mekong in three places and cost 500r per person, plus 500r per bike. The southernmost ferry crossing is the most convenient. To get there, cross the Japanese Bridge and follow NH6 for 4km, then turn right just after the Medical Supply Pharmaceutical Enterprise. You immediately hit a small dirt road that parallels the Mekong. Turn left and follow it north for about 500m until you see the ferry crossing.

Udong

Udong (ឧដុង្គ; literally, 'victorious') served as the capital of Cambodia under several sovereigns between 1618 and 1866, during which time 'victorious' was an optimistic epithet, as Cambodia was in terminal decline. A number of kings, including King Norodom, were crowned here. The main attractions today are the twin humps of **Phnom Udong** (ភ្នំឧដុង្គ), which have several stupas on them. Both ends of the ridge have good views of the Cambodian countryside, dotted with innumerable sugar-palm trees.

The larger main ridge – the one you'll hit first if approaching from NH5 – is known as **Phnom Preah Reach Throap** (ភ្នំព្រះរាជទ្រព្យ, Hill of the Royal Fortune). It is so named because a 16th-century Khmer king is said to have hidden the national treasury here during a war with the Thais.

Phnom Udong really fills up with locals at weekends, but is quiet during the week. Admission is US$1 for foreigners.

◎ Sights

Ascend the 509 steps of the main, monkey-lined north stairway from the parking area and the first structure you come to at the top of the ridge is a modern temple containing 5334 small Buddhas. There's also a relic of the Buddha, believed to be an eyebrow hair and fragments of teeth and bones. The relics were brazenly stolen in 2013 (though later recovered). Follow the path behind this stupa along the ridge and you'll come to a line of three large stupas. The first (northwesternmost) is **Damrei Sam Poan** (ចេតិយសាមពាន់), built by King Chey Chetha II (r 1618–26) to hold the ashes of his predecessor, King Soriyopor. The second stupa, **Ang Doung** (ចេតិយព្រះបាទអង្គដួង), is decorated with coloured tiles; it was built in 1891 by King Norodom to house the ashes of his father, King Ang Duong (r 1845–59), although some say King Ang Duong was in fact buried next to the Silver Pagoda in Phnom Penh. The last stupa is **Mak Proum** (ចេតិយមុខព្រហ្ម), the final resting place of King Monivong (r 1927–41). Decorated with *garudas* (mythical half-man, half-bird creatures), floral designs and elephants, it has four faces on top.

Continuing along the path beyond Mak Proum, you'll pass a stone *vihara* with a cement roof and a revered five-star general seated inside, then arrive at a clearing dotted by a gaggle of structures, including three small *vihara* and a stupa. The first *vihara* you come to is **Vihear Prak Neak**, its cracked walls topped with a tin roof. Inside is a seated Buddha, who is guarded by a mythical naga serpent-being (*prak neak* means 'protected by a naga'). The second structure also has a seated Buddha inside, which was made from a single stone. The third structure is **Vihear Preah Keo**, a cement-roofed *vihara* that contains a statue of Preah Ko, the sacred bull; the original statue was carried away by the Thais long ago. Beyond this, near the stupa, red and black mountain lions guard the entrance to a modern brick-walled *vihara*.

Continue southeast along a lotus-flower-lined concrete path to the most impressive structure on Phnom Preah Reach Throap, **Vihear Preah Ath Roes** (វិហារព្រះអដ្ឋរ៉ស្ស). The *vihara* and an enormous seated Buddha, dedicated in 1911 by King Sisowath, were blown up by the Khmer Rouge in 1977. The *vihara,* supported by eight enormous columns and topped by a soaring tin roof, has since been rebuilt, as was the 20m-high Buddha.

At the base of the main (northern) staircase leading up to Phnom Preah Reach Throap, near the restaurants, is a **memorial** (ទីសំរាប់រំឭកវិញ្ញាណក្ខន្ធដងរងគ្រោះសម័យខ្មែរក្រហម) to the victims of Pol Pot. It contains the bones of some of the people who were buried in approximately 100 mass graves, each containing about a dozen bodies. Instruments of torture were unearthed along with the bones when a number of the pits were disinterred in 1981 and 1982.

Southeast of Phnom Preah Reach Throap, the smaller ridge has two structures and several stupas on top. **Ta San Mosque** faces westward towards Mecca. Across the plains to the south of the mosque, you can see **Phnom Vihear Leu**, a small hill on which a *vihara* stands between two white poles. To the right of the *vihara* is a building that was used as a prison under Pol Pot's rule. To the left of the *vihara* and below it is a pagoda known as **Arey Ka Sap** (អរិយក្សត្រ).

A guide will be able to offer more context on everything. If you don't bring one from Phnom Penh, ask for Oy at the small booth where you pay your entrance fee (US$1). He has no phone or email, but was born in Udong, speaks pretty good English and knows a lot about the history of the place.

🛌 Sleeping & Eating

Most day trippers to Udong base themselves in Phnom Penh or stop en route from the capital to Battambang. The renowned **Cambodia Vipassana Dhura Buddhist Meditation Center** (📞contact Mr Um Sovann 016 883090; www.cambodiavipassanacenter.com; donation per person incl breakfast & lunch US$25) is at Udong if you want to work on a deeper sleep.

There are scores of food stalls around the bustling main parking area at the base of the northern staircase.

ℹ Getting There & Away

Udong is around 37km from the capital. Take a Phnom Penh Sorya bus bound for Kompong Chhnang (10,000r, one hour to Udong). It will drop you off at the access road to Phnom Udong, and from there it's 3km (4000r by *moto*). Other bus companies also make the trip to Udong. To return to Phnom Penh, flag down a bus on NH5.

If going it alone, head north out of Phnom Penh on NH5 and turn left (south) at a prominent archway between the 36km and 37km markers.

A taxi for the day trip from Phnom Penh will cost around US$45. *Remork* drivers also run people to Udong for about US$20 or so for the day. Several hostels promote half-day tours here, which typically include a stop in the silversmith village of Kompong Luong to see local craftsmen at work.

Tonlé Bati

The collective name for a pair of old Angkorian-era temples, Ta Prohm and Yeay Peau, and a popular lakeside picnic area, **Tonlé Bati** (ទន្លេបាទី; incl lake & temples US$3) is worth a detour if you are on the way from the capital to Phnom Tamao and Phnom Chisor.

Ta Prohm   HINDU TEMPLE
(តាព្រហ្ម; US$3) The laterite temple of Ta Prohm was built by King Jayavarman VII (r 1181–1219) on the site of a 6th-century Khmer shrine. The main sanctuary consists of five chambers, each containing a modern

Buddha. The facades of the chambers contain intricate and well-preserved bas-reliefs. In the central chamber is a *linga* (phallic symbol) that shows signs of the destruction wrought by the Khmer Rouge.

Yeay Peau   HINDU TEMPLE
(ប្រាសាទយាយពៅ; US$3) What little remains of Yeay Peau temple, named after King Prohm's mother, can be found 150m north of Ta Prohm in the grounds of a modern pagoda.

Legend has it that Peau gave birth to a son, Prohm. When Prohm discovered his father was King Preah Ket Mealea, he set off to live with the king. After a few years, he returned to his mother but did not recognise her; taken by her beauty, he asked her to become his wife. He refused to believe Peau's protests that she was his mother. To put off his advances and avoid the impending marriage, Peau suggested a temple-building contest whereby the winner would get their wish. When Yeay Peau was completed first, Prohm was forced to acknowledge Peau as his mother.

Phnom Tamao Wildlife Rescue Centre

This wonderful wildlife sanctuary (មជ្ឈមណ្ឌលសង្គ្រោះសត្វព្រៃភ្នំតាម៉ៅ; adult/child US$5/2; ⊙8.30am-4.30pm; 🚻) 🅿 for rescued animals is home to gibbons, sun bears, elephants, tigers, lions, deer, enormous pythons and a massive bird enclosure. They were all taken from poachers or abusive owners and receive care and shelter here as part of a sustainable breeding program. Wherever possible, animals are released back into the wild once they have recovered.

The sanctuary occupies a vast site south of the capital and its animals are kept in excellent conditions by Southeast Asian standards, with plenty of room to roam in enclosures that have been improved and expanded over the years with help from Wildlife Alliance, Free the Bears and other international wildlife NGOs. Spread out as it is, it feels like a zoo crossed with a safari park.

The centre operates breeding and release programs for a number of globally threatened species, including pileated gibbons, smooth-coated otters and Siamese crocodiles, and provides a safe home to other iconic species, such as tigers and the gentle giants – Asian elephants. The centre is also home to the world's largest captive collection of Malayan sun bears, and you'll find a walk-through area with macaques, deer and a huge aviary.

Cambodia's wildlife is usually very difficult to spot, as larger mammals inhabit remote areas of the country, so Phnom Tamao is the perfect place to discover more about the country's incredible variety of animals. If you don't like zoos, you might not like this wildlife sanctuary, but remember that these animals have been rescued from traffickers and poachers and need a home. Visitors who come here will be doing their own small bit to help in the protection and survival of Cambodia's varied wildlife.

Both Wildlife Alliance and Free the Bears offer more-exclusive experiences at Phnom Tamao for fixed donations. Wildlife Alliance offers a behind-the-scenes tour, which includes access to feeding areas and the nursery area. Free the Bears has a 'Bear Care Tour', which allows guests to help out the on-site team for the day. These tours include transport from Phnom Penh. Otherwise, the easiest option is a rental motorbike or car from Phnom Penh in combination with Tonlé Bati or Phnom Chisor.

Wildlife Alliance   WILDLIFE
(☑095 970175; www.wildlifealliance.org; minimum donation US$150) Wildlife Alliance has created an exciting, full-day interactive tour to raise funds for Phnom Tamao Wildlife Rescue Centre. Donors get to interact with a variety of rescued animals, including elephants and macaques, and get up close with tigers, leopards, gibbons and what is possibly the world's only captive hairy-nosed otter. All proceeds go towards the rescue and care of wildlife at Phnom Tamao.

Tours include a visit to the sanctuary's nursery, which is normally off-limits to the public, for a rare look at the baby animals.

Free the Bears   WILDLIFE
(☑092 434597; www.freethebears.org; per person US$90) Operates a 'Bear Care' program to give students and adults with a genuine interest in wildlife a better understanding of the moon bear (Asian black bear) and sun bear. Participants have no contact with the animals, but spend the day behind the

scenes of the Phnom Tamao Wildlife Rescue Centre, learning the ins and outs of caring for the 120-plus bears here.

Volunteer positions are also available, with a minimum commitment of four days and a maximum of eight weeks.

Phnom Chisor

A temple from the Angkorian era, Phnom Chisor (ភ្នំជីសូរ; US$2; ☺ 7.30am-5pm) is set upon a solitary hill in Takeo Province, offering superb views of the countryside. Try to get here early in the morning or late in the afternoon, as it is an uncomfortable climb in the heat of the midday sun. Phnom Chisor lies about 55km south of Phnom Penh.

The main temple stands on the eastern side of the hilltop. Constructed of laterite and brick with carved sandstone lintels, the complex is surrounded by the partially ruined walls of a 2.5m-wide gallery with windows. Inscriptions found here date from the 11th century, when this site was known as Suryagiri.

On the plain to the west of Phnom Chisor are the sanctuaries of Sen Thmol (just below Phnom Chisor), Sen Ravang and the former sacred pond of Tonlé Om. All three of these features form a straight line from Phnom Chisor in the direction of Angkor. During rituals held here 900 years ago, the king, his Brahmans and their entourage would climb a monumental 400 steps to Suryagiri from this direction.

If you haven't got the stamina for an overland adventure to Preah Vihear or Phnom Bayong (near Takeo), this is the next best thing for a temple with a view. Near the main temple is a modern Buddhist *vihara*, which is used by resident monks.

Renting a motorbike in Phnom Penh is one of the most enjoyable ways to get here in combination with Tonlé Bati or Phnom Tamao Wildlife Rescue Centre. Booking a share taxi is a comfortable option in the wet or hot seasons or you can take a Takeo-bound bus to the access road, about 49km south of Phnom Penh, and arrange a *moto* from there.

Kirirom National Park

You can really get away from it all at this lush, elevated park (ឧទ្យានជាតិគីរីរម្យ; US$5) a three-hour drive southwest of Phnom Penh.

Winding trails lead through pine forests to cascading wet-season waterfalls and cliffs with amazing views of the Cardamom Mountains, and there's some great mountain biking to be done if you're feeling adventurous.

From NH4, it's 10km on a sealed road to a small village near the park entrance. From the village you have two choices: the left fork takes you 50m to the park entrance and then 17km up a fairly steep sealed road to the unstaffed Kirirom Information Centre inside the national park; the right fork takes you 10km along the perimeter of the park on a dirt road to Chambok commune, the site of an excellent community-based ecotourism (CBET; ☑ 012 698529; touchmorn@gmail.com; adult/child US$3/1) program. These are two vastly different experiences, and they are nowhere near each other, so it's recommended to devote a day to each.

 Activities

National Park

Up in the actual national park, you'll find myriad walking trails and dirt roads (apt for mountain biking) that lead to small wet-season waterfalls, lakes, wats and abandoned 1960s-era mansions, including one built for former King Norodom Sihanouk. You'll need a map or a guide to navigate them. vKirirom Pine Resort can provide both at its excellent activities centre, which also offers kayaking, ziplines, mountain bikes and cooking classes, among an array of tours, courses and rentals.

One of the best hikes is the 14km trail up to Phnom Dat Chivit (End of Life Mountain), where an abrupt cliff face offers an unbroken view of the Elephant Mountains and Cardamom Mountains to the west. VKirirom calls this trek the 'Kirirom Heaven Climb' and provides a guide and transportation to the trailhead for US$30.

Chambok

The main attraction at the Chambok community-based ecotourism site is a 4km hike to a series of five waterfalls (no guide required). The second waterfall has a swimming hole; the third one is an impressive 40m high. Bikes are available for US$2, but won't get you very far as the trail deteriorates fairly quickly after the first kilometre.

Other activities include traditional ox-cart rides (US$5), basic cooking or handicraft classes (US$2) and guided nature walks to a bat cave (guides cost US$15 to US$20 per day, depending on the activity).

To reach the ecotourism office, turn left at Wat Chambok and drive 1km. Ask for Mr Morn or Mr Cham, who both speak English.

🛏 Sleeping & Eating

There are two hotels located within the boundaries of Kirirom National Park, as well as cheaper homestays located near Chambok as part of the long-running community tourism initiative.

Chambok Homestays   HOMESTAY $

(☏012 938920; http://chambok.org; per person US$4, home-cooked meals each US$3-4) An astounding 63 homestays are available in Chambok commune as part of the well-run community-based ecotourism program.

★vKirirom Pine Resort   RESORT $$

(☏078 777384; www.vkirirom.com; camping US$22, r US$45-85, ste US$145-300; 🛜🐾) A sprawling Japanese-run resort, vKirirom has a dizzying array of rooms, including slightly surreal circular-pipe rooms, some impressively simple, open-plan Khmer cottages made of rattan, and luxurious bungalows with all the trimmings. The attractive open-plan restaurant is the best lunch stop for day trippers to the park. There are also loads of activities on offer that will keep you busy.

ℹ Getting There & Away

Kirirom National Park is accessed from the village of Treng Trayern, which straddles NH4, 87km southwest of Phnom Penh and 139km northeast of Sihanoukville. A taxi from either city is about US$80; or have a bus drop you at the turn-off in Treng Trayern, where a *moto* will want US$5 per person to get you to the entrance (a bit more to Chambok commune, and still more to ascend into the national park itself). Travelling under your own steam is highly recommended.

Siem Reap

☏ 063 / POP 195.000 (CITY)

Includes ➡

Sights 105
Activities 109
Sleeping 112
Eating 117
Drinking & Nightlife . . .122
Shopping 125
Banteay
Srei District 131
Prek Toal
Bird Sanctuary 134
Kompong Pluk 135
Me Chrey 135
Floating Village
of Chong Kneas 135

Best Places to Eat

➡ Cuisine Wat Damnak (p119)

➡ Marum (p121)

➡ Pou Kitchen (p119)

➡ Spoons Cafe (p119)

Best Places to Stay

➡ Hideout Hostel (p116)

➡ Montra Nivesha (p116)

➡ Phum Baitang (p116)

➡ Pomme (p116)

Why Go?

The gateway for the temples of Angkor, Siem Reap (*see*-em ree-*ep*; សៀមរាប) was always destined for great things. Visitors come here to see the temples, of course, but there is plenty to do in and around the city when you're templed out. Siem Reap has reinvented itself as the epicentre of chic Cambodia, with everything from backpacker party pads to hip hotels, world-class wining and dining across a range of cuisines, sumptuous spas, great shopping, local tours to suit both foodies and adventurers, and a creative cultural scene that includes Cambodia's leading contemporary circus.

Angkor is a place to be savoured, not rushed, and this is the base from which to plan your adventures. Still think three days at the temples is enough? Think again with Siem Reap on the doorstep.

When to Go
Siem Reap

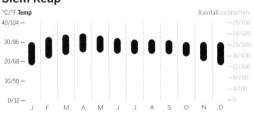

Nov–Mar Peak season at Siem Reap and the temples, so explore further afield.

Apr & May Intense heat equals sweaty touring amid dry and barren landscape.

Jun–Oct Wet season; the floating villages of Tonlé Sap are at their most colourful.

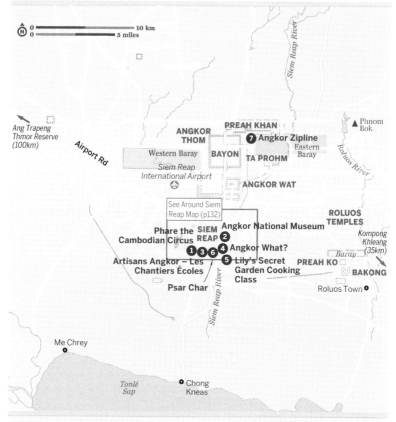

Siem Reap Highlights

❶ Phare the Cambodian Circus (p124) Seeing a unique performance of the fabulous Cambodian Circus.

❷ Angkor National Museum Discovering the Khmer civilisation and the majesty of Angkor.

❸ Artisans Angkor – Les Chantiers Écoles Taking a tour of a school where students learn traditional

artisanal skills and browsing the attached shop.

❹ Angkor What? (p123) Diving into Pub St, the drinking capital of Siem Reap, after lining your stomach at nearby restaurants.

❺ Lily's Secret Garden Cooking Class (p110) Learning the secrets of Khmer cuisine with a cooking

course, the perfect way to impress friends back home.

❻ Psar Chaa (p125) Browsing, bargaining and buying at Psar Chaa (Old Market) then following up with the Angkor Night Market.

❼ Angkor Zipline (p154) Ziplining through the treetops in the Angkor protected area.

History

Siem Reap was little more than a village when French explorers came across Angkor in the 19th century. With the return of Angkor to Cambodian – or should that be French – control in 1907, Siem Reap began to grow, absorbing the first wave of tour-

ists. The Grand Hotel d'Angkor opened its doors in 1932 and the temples of Angkor remained one of Asia's leading draws until the late 1960s, luring luminaries such as Charlie Chaplin and Jackie Kennedy. With the advent of war and the Khmer Rouge, Siem Reap entered a long slumber from which it only began to awaken in the mid-1990s.

◎ Sights

The sights in and around the town pale in comparison to Angkor, but they are a good diversion if you happen to get templed out after a few days. That said, some of the best sights are...yet more temples. The modern pagodas around Siem Reap offer an interesting contrast to the ancient sandstone structures of Angkor.

Outside town attractions include the up-and-coming Banteay Srei District and the stilted and floating villages of the Tonlé Sap lake, such as Kompong Khleang and Kompong Pluk. And don't forget to include a visit to the Angkor Centre for Conservation of Biodiversity (p131) out near Kbal Spean, one of the more remote Angkorian sites.

★ **Angkor National Museum**   MUSEUM
(សារមន្ទីរអង្គរ; Map p106; ☎ 063-966601; www. angkornationalmuseum.com; 968 Charles de Gaulle Blvd; adult/child under 1.2m US$12/6; ☺ 8.30am-6pm May-Sep, to 6.30pm Oct-Apr) Looming large on the road to Angkor is the Angkor National Museum, a state-of-the-art showpiece on the Khmer civilisation and the majesty of Angkor. Displays are themed by era, religion and royalty as visitors move through the impressive galleries. After a short presentation, visitors enter the Zen-like Gallery of a Thousand Buddhas, which has a fine collection of images. Other exhibits include the pre-Angkorian periods of Funan and Chenla; the great Khmer kings; Angkor Wat; Angkor Thom; and the inscriptions.

Exhibits include touch-screen videos, epic commentary and the chance to experience a panoramic sunrise at Angkor Wat. Although there appears to be less sculpture on display than in the National Museum in Phnom Penh, the presentation of the artefacts here is cutting edge.

Some of the standout pieces in the collection include a late-12th-/early-13th-century seated Buddha sheltered by a naga (mythical serpent-being); a 7th-century standing Vishnu from Sambor Prei Kuk in Kompong Thom; and a stunning 10th-century lintel from the beautiful temple of Banteay Srei.

As the museum is entirely air-conditioned, plan a visit during the middle of the day to avoid the sweltering midday temperatures at the temples of Angkor. Audio tours are available for US$5 and are useful for those who want a more comprehensive under-standing of the exhibits on display. Wheelchairs are available free of charge for visitors with mobility impairment.

Allow about two hours to visit the museum in depth and to stop by the shop and small cafe at the end of your visit.

★ **Apopo Visitor Centre**   VISITOR CENTRE
(មជ្ឈមណ្ឌលទស្សនាអាប៉ូប៉ូ; Map p132; ☎ 081 599237; www.apopo.org; Koumai Rd; US$5; ☺ 8.30am-5.30pm Mon-Sat) ✆ Meet the hero rats that are helping to clear landmines in Cambodia. Apopo has trained the highly sensitive, almost-blind Gambian pouched rat to sniff explosives, which dramatically speeds up the detection of mines in the countryside. The visitor centre gives background on the work of Apopo, with a short video and the chance to meet the rats themselves.

★ **Artisans Angkor –
Les Chantiers Écoles**   ARTS CENTRE
(អាទីសង់អង្គរ; Map p106; www.artisansdangkor. com; ☺ 7.30am-6.30pm) ✆ **FREE** Siem Reap is the epicentre of the drive to revitalise Cambodian traditional culture, which was dealt a harsh blow by the Khmer Rouge and the years of instability that followed its rule. Les Chantiers Écoles teaches wood- and stone-carving techniques, traditional silk painting, lacquerware and other artisan skills to impoverished young Cambodians. Free guided tours explaining traditional techniques are available daily from 7.30am to 6.30pm. Tucked down a side road, the school is well signposted from Sivatha St.

On the premises the school runs a beautiful shop called Artisans Angkor (p127), and Les Chantiers Écoles also maintains Angkor Silk Farm (p108), which produces clothing, decor and accessories.

War Museum   MUSEUM
(សារមន្ទីរប្រវត្តិសាស្ត្រសង្គ្រាម; Map p132; ☎ 097 457 8666; www.warmuseumcambodia.com; Kaksekam village; incl guide US$5; ☺ 8am-5.30pm) The unique selling point here is that the museum encourages visitors to handle the old weapons, from an AK-47 right through to a rocket launcher. We're not sure what health and safety think about it, but it makes for a good photo op. Other war junk includes Soviet-era T-54 tanks and MiG-19 fighters. Former soldiers act as tour guides.

**Preah Ang Chek
Preah Ang Chorm**   BUDDHIST SHRINE
(ព្រះអង្គចេក ព្រះអង្គចម; Map p106; Royal Gardens; ☺ 6am-10pm) **FREE** Located just west

Siem Reap

N

0 — 400 m
0 — 0.2 miles

NH6

Airport Rd (NH6 West)

Angkor National Museum 1

68

Charles de Gaulle Blvd

See North Siem Reap Map (p110)

46

Sivatha St

23

Siem Reap Tourism Office

Royal Gardens

Airport Rd (NH6 West)

3

Royal Residence

Taphul St

30

Oum Chhay St

St 3

37

NH6

28

Oum Khun St

34

19

Angkor Hospital for Children

52

St 14

Pokambor Ave

Siem Reap River Rd

St 20

71

15

25

59

20

38

69

Tep Vong St

Hup Guan St

31

St 21

9

13

74

7

55

16

72

73

45

66   11   41

21

70

Central Market St

18

63

Sivatha St

See Psar Chaa Map (p114)

32

56

39

St 22

47

26

St 24

St 23

27

Tep Vong St

4

43   St 25

48

8

St 26

36   29

61

Sok San Rd

Siem Reap River Rd East

57

14   St 26

12

2

Artisans Angkor – Les Chantiers Écoles

49

75

65

67

58

44

Wat Bo Rd

Pokambor Ave

Siem Reap River

42

5

54

Psar Krohm St

60

50

24

17

7 Makara St

51

Tonle Sap Rd

62

53

10

6

35

40

64

22

33

Siem Reap

◉ Top Sights
1 Angkor National Museum C1
2 Artisans Angkor – Les Chantiers
  Écoles A6

◉ Sights
3 Preah Ang Chek Preah Ang Chorm C3
4 Wat Bo D5
5 Wat Dam Nak B6

◎ Activities, Courses & Tours
6 Cambodia Bird Guide Association........C7
7 Frangipani Spa.................................B4
8 Grasshopper Adventures......................C5
9 Off Track Tours A4
10 Osmose C7
11 PURE! Countryside Bicycle Tour B4
12 Sam Veasna Center D6
13 Seeing Hands Massage 4......................A4

◎ Sleeping
14 Angkor Village..................................C6
15 Babel Guesthouse D3
16 Bemond La Résidence d'Angkor.........C4
17 Downtown Siem Reap Villa.................B6
18 Ivy Guesthouse 2.............................B4
19 Mad Monkey B3
20 Mulberry Boutique Hotel.......................A4
21 Onederz Hostel................................A4
22 Pomme C7
23 Raffles Grand Hotel d'Angkor...............C2
24 Rambutan Resort.............................B6
25 Seven Candles Guesthouse.................D4
26 Treeline Urban Resort C5
27 Viroth's Hotel...................................C5

◎ Eating
28 Angkor Market.................................B3
29 Banllé Vegetarian Restaurant C5
30 Bayon Pastry School Coffee Shop........A2
31 Cafe .9...B4
32 Chanrey Tree C5
33 Cuisine Wat Damnak D7
34 Curry Walla......................................B3
35 Dine in the Dark D7
36 Embassy...C5
37 FCC Angkor......................................C3
   Footprints Cafe...........................(see 43)
38 Glasshouse.......................................A4
39 Hashi...C5
40 Haven..D7
41 Hive Siem Reap B4
42 Jomno Street Food B6
43 Jungle Burger C5

44 King's Road......................................B6
45 Mamma Shop...................................B4
46 Marum...D2
47 Moloppor Cafe C5
48 Pages Cafe.......................................C5
49 Pot & Pan Restaurant............................A6
50 Pou Kitchen B6
51 Rice Thai D6
52 Siem Reap Brewpub............................C4
53 Spoons Cafe B7
54 Sugar Palm D6
   Svay Chek Organic Farm
     Shop ....(see 41)
55 Vibe Cafe...B4
   Village Cafe.................................(see 31)

◎ Drinking & Nightlife
56 Barcode...B5
57 Dialogue C6
58 Hard Rock Cafe B6
59 Local Brewpub D4
60 Wild B6

✿ Entertainment
61 Apsara Theatre C5
62 Bambu Stage....................................B7

◎ Shopping
63 Angkor Night Market............................A5
   Artisans Angkor ....(see 2)
64 IKTT..A7
   Louise Labatieres ....(see 11)
   Made in Cambodia Market ....(see 44)
65 Monument Books B6
   Sirivan ....(see 31)
66 Soieries du Mekong..........................B4
   Sra May ....(see 11)
67 Susu..B6
68 T Galleria C1
   Tribe ....(see 11)
   trunkh...(see 11)

ⓘ Information
69 ABA Bank...B4
70 Canadia Bank...................................A4
   J Trust Royal Bank.......................(see 31)

ⓘ Transport
   Asia Van Transfer ....(see 31)
71 Bayon VIP..D3
72 Giant Ibis..A4
73 Green e-bikes B4
74 Mekong Express B4
75 Virak Buntham A6

SIEM REAP SIGHTS

of the royal residence is this shrine. Said to represent two Angkorian princesses, these sacred statues were originally housed at the Preah Poan gallery in Angkor Wat, but were moved all over Siem Reap to protect them from invaders, eventually settling here in 1990. Locals throng here to pray for luck, especially newlyweds, and it is an atmospheric place to visit around dusk, as the incense smoke swirls around.

Next to the shrine are the tall trees of the Royal Gardens, home to a resident colony of fruit bats (also known as flying foxes), which takes off to feed on insects around dusk.

Angkor Silk Farm
FARM

(កសិដ្ឋានសូត្រ; www.artisansdangkor.com; ☺ 7.30am-5.30pm) 🖈 FREE Les Chantiers Écoles (p105) maintains the Angkor Silk Farm, which produces some of the best work in the country, including clothing, interior-design products and accessories. All stages of the production process can be seen here, from the cultivation of mulberry trees to the nurturing of silkworms to the dyeing and weaving of silk. Free tours are available daily. A free shuttle bus departs from Les Chantiers Écoles in Siem Reap at 9.30am and 1.30pm.

The farm is about 16km west of Siem Reap, just off the road to Sisophon in the village of Puok.

Cambolac
ARTS CENTRE

(កាំបូឡាក់; Map p132; ☎ 088 355 6078; http://cambolac.com; 196 Slorkram village; ☺ 8-11.30am & 1-5pm Mon-Sat) FREE Cambodia has a long tradition of producing beautiful lacquerware, although the years of upheaval resulted in some of the skills being lost. Cambolac is a social enterprise helping to restore Cambodia's lacquer tradition and create a new contemporary scene. You can tour the workshop to learn more about the perfectionism required to produce a piece. Most of the guides are hearing-impaired and a tour allows some great interaction and the opportunity to learn some basic sign language.

Senteurs d'Angkor Botanic Garden
GARDENS

(ស្ងួនរុក្ខសាស្ត្រសិនសង់ទ័រអង្គរ; Map p132; Airport Rd; ☺ 7.30am-5.30pm) The botanic garden of Senteurs d'Angkor (p127) is a sort of Willy Wonka's for the senses, where you can sample infused teas and speciality coffees in the on-site cafe. More a laboratory than a garden, the operators also make soaps, oils and perfumes here. It recently relocated to a stunning new centre near the Angkor Golf Resort.

Wat Bo
BUDDHIST TEMPLE

(វត្តបូ; Map p106; Tep Vong St; ☺ 6am-6pm) FREE This is one of the town's oldest temples and has a collection of well-preserved wall paintings from the late 19th century depicting the *Reamker*, Cambodia's interpretation of the *Ramayana*. The monks here regularly chant sometime between 4.30pm and 6pm, and this can be a spellbinding and spiritual moment if you happen to be visiting.

Wat Preah Inkosei
BUDDHIST TEMPLE

(វត្តព្រះឥន្ទកោសីយ៍; Map p110; Siem Reap River Rd; ☺ 6am-6pm) FREE This wat north of town is built on the site of an early Angkorian brick temple, which still stands today at the rear of the compound.

Wat Athvea
BUDDHIST TEMPLE

(វត្តអធ្វា; Map p140; incl in Angkor admission 1/3/7 days US$37/62/72; ☺ 6am-6pm) South of the city centre, Wat Athvea is an attractive pagoda on the site of an ancient temple. The old temple is still in very good condition and sees far fewer visitors than the main temples in the Angkor area, making it a peaceful spot in the late afternoon.

SIEM REAP FOR CHILDREN

Siem Reap is a great city for children thanks to the range of activities on offer beyond the temples. A temple visit may appeal to older children, particularly the Indiana Jones atmosphere found at Ta Prohm and Beng Mealea, the sheer size and scale of Angkor Wat, and the weird faces at the Bayon.

Other activities include boat trips on the Tonlé Sap to visit otherworldly villages, swimming at a hotel or resort, ziplining in the jungle, exploring the countryside on horseback or quad bike (p110), goofing around at the Cambodian Cultural Village, playing minigolf at Angkor Wat Putt, exploring the Banteay Srei Butterfly Centre (p131), or just enjoying the cafes and restaurants of Siem Reap at a leisurely pace. Ice-cream shops will be popular, while the local barbecue restaurants are always enjoyably interactive for older children.

Siem Reap is not necessarily that well geared for travelling with infants and small children, but it's fine for parents willing to improvise. Dedicated baby-change facilities are rare, but many bathrooms are single sex, single cubicle. Child seats are not generally available unless requested through a travel agent. Supermarkets are well stocked with nappies (diapers), milk formula and more should you need supplies.

Wat Dam Nak
BUDDHIST TEMPLE

(វត្តដំណាក់; Map p106; ⊙6am-6pm) FREE
Formerly a royal palace during the reign of
King Sisowath, hence the name *dam nak*
(palace), today Wat Dam Nak is home to the
Center for Khmer Studies (www.khmerstud
ies.org), an independent institution promot
ing a greater understanding of Khmer cul
ture with a drop-in research library on-site.

Wat Thmei
BUDDHIST TEMPLE

(វត្តថ្មី; Map p132; ⊙6am-6pm) FREE Wat Thmei
has a small memorial stupa containing the
skulls and bones of victims of the Khmer
Rouge. It also has plenty of young monks
eager to practise their English.

Cambodian Cultural Village
CULTURAL CENTRE

(ភូមិវប្បធម៌កម្ពុជា; Map p132; ☏063-963836;
www.cambodianculturalvillage.com; Airport Rd;
adult/child under 1.1m US$9/free; ⊙8am-7pm; ☺)
It may be kitsch, it may be kooky, but it's very
popular with Cambodians and provides a di
version for families travelling with children.
This is the Cambodian Cultural Village, which
tries to represent all of Cambodia in a whirl
wind tour of recreated houses and villages.
The visit begins with a wax museum and in
cludes homes of the Cham, Chinese, Kreung
and Khmer people, as well as miniature repli
cas of landmark buildings in Cambodia.

🏃 Activities

There is an incredible array of activities on
offer in Siem Reap, ranging from predicta
ble swimming pools, spa centres and golf
courses right through to less predictable
ziplining, horse riding, quad biking and an
Angkor-themed minigolf course.

It's hot work clambering about the tem
ples, and there's no better way to wind down
than with a dip in a swimming pool. You
can pay by the day for use of the pool and/
or gym at most hotels; prices range from
just US$5 to US$20 at the five-star palaces. More and
more of the cheaper hotels and resorts are
putting in pools, and this can be a worth
while splash for weary travellers. Locals like
to swim in the waters of the Western Baray
at the weekend.

Cambo Beach Club
SWIMMING

(Map p132; ☏087 466616; www.cambobeach
club.com; Steung Thmey village; per person US$3;
⊙9am-10pm; ☺) Boasting the only beach in
Siem Reap, Cambo Beach Club is a great
spot to hang out day or night. The centre
piece is a huge swimming pool complete
with floating beanies and a high dive pool.
Dining options include lip-smackin' ribs at
The Dancing Pig and there is the late-night
Underdog Sports Bar for big games.

There are regular DJs for weekend parties
and a whole host of special offer combina
tions involve booze and entry such as VIP
Bubbles and Chillin & Sipping.

Great Escape
LIVE CHALLENGE

(Map p132; ☏063-506 9777; http://greatescape
cambodia.com; C-39 Angkor Shopping Arcade, Airport
Rd; per person US$18, under-16s US$10; ⊙10am-
10pm) Escape the room in 60 minutes using
only your wits. That's the premise of the Great
Escape, Siem Reap's answer to the Crystal
Maze. Try the Lost Room, an Angkor-themed
mystery. Prices include round-trip transport
by *remork-moto (tuk tuk)*.

Peace Cafe Yoga
YOGA

(Map p110; ☏063-965210; www.peacecafeangkor.
org; Siem Reap River Rd East; per session US$6)
This popular community centre and cafe has
daily morning and evening yoga sessions, in
cluding ashtanga and hatha sessions.

Happy Ranch
HORSE RIDING

(Map p132; ☏012 920002; www.thehappyranch.
com; trail rides US$38-95; ⊙11am-10pm) For
get the Wild West – try your hand at horse
riding in the Wild East. Happy Ranch of
fers the chance to explore Siem Reap on
horseback, taking in surrounding villages
and secluded temples. This is a calm way
to experience the countryside, far from the
traffic and crowds.

Popular rides take in Wat Athvea, a mod
ern pagoda with an ancient temple on its
grounds, and Wat Chedi, a temple set on a
flood plain near the Tonlé Sap lake. Riding
lessons are available for children and begin
ners. Book directly for the best prices.

Golf

Angkor Wat Putt
GOLF

(Map p140; ☏012 302330; www.angkorwatputt.
com; Chreav District; adult/child US$5/4; ⊙8am-
8pm) Crazy golf to the Brits among us, this
home-grown minigolf course contrasts with
the big golf courses out of town. Navigate
minitemples and creative obstacles for 14
holes and win a beer for a hole-in-one. Re
cently relocated to a more remote location,
it is well worth seeking out.

North Siem Reap

North Siem Reap

◉ Sights
1 Angkor Conservation B2
2 Wat Preah Inkosei B2

➕ Activities, Courses & Tours
3 Hidden Cambodia B1
4 Khmer Ceramics Fine Arts Centre B2
Peace Cafe Yoga .... (see 8)
Vegetarian Cooking Class .... (see 8)

🛏 Sleeping
5 Montra Nivesha A2

🍴 Eating
6 Mahob A2
7 Mie Cafe A2
8 Peace Cafe A3

🎭 Entertainment
9 Angkor Dynasty A1
10 Sacred Dancers of Angkor B3

Angkor Golf Resort GOLF
(Map p132; ☎ 063-761139; www.angkor-golf.com; green fees US$115; ⏱ 6.30am-5.30pm) This world-class course was designed by British golfer Nick Faldo. Fees rise to US$175 with clubs, caddies, carts and all.

Massage & Spas
Frangipani Spa SPA
(Map p106; ☎ 063-964391; www.frangipanisiem reap.com; 615 Hup Guan St; US$20-75; ⏱ 10am-10pm) This delightful hideaway offers massages and a whole range of spa treatments.

Seeing Hands Massage 4 MASSAGE
(Map p106; ☎ 012 836487; 324 Sivatha St; fan/air-con room US$5/7) 🖐 Seeing Hands trains blind people in the art of massage. Watch out for copycats, as some of them are just exploiting the blind for profit.

Quad Biking
Cambodia Quad Bike ADVENTURE SPORTS
(Map p140; ☎ 012 893447; www.cambodia quadbike.com; Salakamreuk Rd; 1hr/half day US$30/100) Quad-bike tours around the Siem Reap countryside, including sunrise and sunset options.

Quad Adventure Cambodia ADVENTURE SPORTS
(Map p132; ☎ 092 787216; www.quad-adventure-cambodia.com; Country Rd Laurent; sunset ride US$32, full day US$175) The original quad-bike operator in town. Rides around Siem Reap involve rice fields at sunset, pretty temples and back roads through traditional villages.

Siem Reap Quad Bike Adventure ADVENTURE SPORTS
(Map p132; ☎ 012 324009; www.srquadbikead venture.com; Salakamreuk Rd; 1hr US$30, with 1 child US$40) A locally owned ATV company with fully automatic quad bikes.

🎓 Courses
Khmer Ceramics Fine Arts Centre ARTS & CRAFTS
(សិរ្បៈម៉ិច; Map p110; ☎ 017 843014; www.khmer ceramics.com; 207 Siem Reap River Rd; pottery course US$25; ⏱ 8am-8pm) 🏺 Located on the banks of the Siem Reap River in the north of town, this ceramics centre is dedicated to reviving the Khmer tradition of pottery, which was an intricate art during the time of Angkor. It's possible to visit and try your hand at the potter's wheel, and courses in traditional techniques, including pottery and ceramic painting, are available.

Lily's Secret Garden Cooking Class COOKING
(☎ 016 353621; www.lilysecretgarden.com; off Sombai Rd; per person US$25; ⏱ 9am-1pm & 3-7pm) This immersive cooking class takes

place in a traditional Cambodian house on the outskirts of Siem Reap. Morning and afternoon sessions end in a three-course lunch or dinner. The price includes pickup and drop-off in town at the Hard Rock Cafe (p123), as the 'secret garden' cannot be revealed online. Closed at the time of writing but expected to reopen by end of 2021.

Vegetarian Cooking Class COOKING
(Map p110; ☑092 177127; http://peacecafeangkor. org; Siem Reap River Rd East; per person US$20) A vegetarian cooking class with tofu *amok*, papaya salad and vegie spring rolls on the menu, daily at 1pm.

Tours

Most visitors are in Siem Reap to tour the temples of Angkor, but not all operators are created equal. Be sure to ask around before booking. Nontemple tours include two-wheeled adventures on bicycles or motorbikes, as well as some foodie tours.

Siem Reap Art Tours TOURS
(www.siemreaparttours.com; per person incl transport US$90) Siem Reap Art Tours offers an educational experience for visitors with a deeper interest in the ever-evolving local art scene. The tours include four leading galleries and boutiques around town, but can be tailor-made to suit guest interest in anything from fashion to photography. Tours run morning or afternoon and usually last about four hours.

Terre Cambodge TOURS
(☑077 448255; www.terrecambodge.com) Francophone operator offering tours to remote sites around Angkor, bicycle tours, and boat trips on the Tonlé Sap lake.

Indochine Exploration TOURS
(☑092 650096; www.indochineex.com) Me Chrey kayaking, trekking adventures, remote temple tours and more.

Birding

★**Sam Veasna Center** BIRDWATCHING
(SVC; Map p106; ☑092 554473; www.samveasna.org; St 26; per person from US$100) Sam Veasna Center, in the Wat Bo area of Siem Reap, is the authority on birdwatching in Cambodia, with professionally trained English-speaking guides, powerful spotting scopes and a network of camps and bird hides scattered throughout north Cambodia. It uses ecotourism to provide an income for local communities in return for a ban on hunting and cutting down the forest.

Osmose BIRDWATCHING
(Map p106; ☑063-765506; www.osmosetonlesap.net; Salakamreuk Rd; per person in group of 5/2 US$95/165) Osmose runs organised day trips to see rare waterbirds in Prek Toal and visit one of the local communities. The price include transport, entrance fees, guides, breakfast, lunch and water, and binoculars are available on request. Hotel pickup is at around 6am and drop-off is by nightfall. Overnight trips for serious enthusiasts can be arranged.

Boeng Pearaing BIRDWATCHING
(☑085 303050; www.pearaing.org; entry US$10, plus boat fees; ⊙6am-6pm) This is an up-and-coming birding site based around a natural reservoir just south of the Tonlé Sap where it's possible to spot large numbers of rare pelicans, storks and ibis. It is an affordable and accessible birdwatching alternative to Prek Toal as it lies just half an hour south of downtown Siem Reap. Entry fees go towards conservation and community support.

Cambodia Bird Guide Association BIRDWATCHING
(CBGA; Map p106; ☑092-657656; www.birdguideasso.org; 203 Salakamreuk Rd; ⊙8.30am-5.30pm Mon-Fri) Formed by experienced staffers from the award-winning Sam Veasna Center, the CBGA is a very professional birding outfit offering birdwatching tours to Prek Toal, Ang Trapaeng Thmor and beyond.

SIEM REAP TOURS

FIGHT CLUB

If the martial-arts action on the bas-reliefs of the Bayon makes you want to learn some of the moves, contact the **Angkor Fight Club** (Map p132; ☑095 839725; www.facebook.com/angkorfightclub; Bakheng Rd; private/group class US$15/5) for very reasonably priced kickboxing or MMA classes with international instructors. There are also *bokator* classes, an ancient Khmer martial art that translates as 'strike like a lion', with Grand Master San Kimsean at his **Cambodia Bokator Academy** (Map p132; ☑012 651845; http://sankimsean.com; Dragon Bridge, Sangkat Slokram) school, including residential courses to pass the belts.

Cycling

The beautiful countryside around Siem Reap is perfect for two-wheeled adventures. Specialist tour operators will get you on the back roads and away from tourist traffic.

★ Off Track Tours CYCLING

(Map p106; ☑093 903024; www.kko-cambodia.org; Taphul Rd; tours US$35-60) ☝ Cycling and *moto* (motorcycle taxi) tours around the paths of Angkor or into the countryside beyond the Western Baray. Proceeds go towards Khmer for Khmer Organisation, which supports education and vocational training.

PURE! Countryside Bicycle Tour CYCLING

(Map p106; ☑097 235 6862; Hup Guan St; per person US$25-35) ☝ Based out of the Sra May gift shop (p127), this outfit organises half-day tours that take in local life around Siem Reap, including lunch with a local family. All proceeds go towards supporting Pure's educational and vocational training projects. Book a few days ahead so operators can notify the families.

Grasshopper Adventures CYCLING

(Map p106; ☑012 462165; www.grasshopperadventures.com; 586 St 26; per person from US$39; ⊙7am-8pm) Rides around the Siem Reap countryside, plus a dedicated temple tour on two wheels and a long-distance trip to Beng Mealea. Bicycle hire too.

Food

Cambodian food is now on the map and there are some cracking culinary tours to give you an insight into the food scene in Siem Reap. The night-time Vespa tours are a good option for those who want to combine a Vespa ride with a culinary adventure.

★ Siem Reap Food Tours FOOD & DRINK

(☑012 505542; www.siemreapfoodtours.com; per person US$75) Established by an American food writer and an experienced Scottish chef, these tours continue to be a recipe for engaging food encounters despite the founders having moved on. Choose from a morning tour that takes in local markets and the *naom banchok* (thick rice noodles) stalls of Preah Dak or an evening tour that takes in street stalls and local barbecue restaurants.

Taste Siem Reap FOOD

(☑017 479162; www.tastesiemreap.com; per person incl transport US$55-72; ⊙evenings only) Taste Siem Reap offers private evening dine-arounds in leading restaurants and bars in Temple Town, which is a great way to discover the vibrant culinary scene developing here. Themes include fine dining, art and cocktails, hidden gems and good cause.

Motorbiking

Most Cambodians still use motorbikes to get around the countryside. 'When in Rome' also applies to 'When in Siem Reap', so consider taking a motorbike adventure deep into the countryside. There are also a couple of tours on modern Vespas. You can also customise a motorbike tour with any of the English-speaking *moto* drivers in Siem Reap, which will work out a lot cheaper than taking an organised tour.

Siem Reap
Vespa Adventures TOURS

(☑012 861610; www.vespaadventures-sr.com; tours per person US$75-126) The modern Vespa is a cut above the average *moto* and is a comfortable way to explore the temples, learn about local life in the countryside or check out some street food after dark, all in the company of excellent and knowledgeable local guides.

Vespa Adventures TOURS

(☑017 881384; http://vespaadventures.com/siem-reap-bike-tours; tours US$70-115) The original Vespa tour operator in Vietnam offers a popular combination of countryside experiences and temple tours, and Siem Reap by night.

Hidden Cambodia TOURS

(Map p110; ☑012 655201; www.hiddencambodia.com; 1 Slokram Commune) A Siem Reap–based company specialising in motorcycle trips throughout the country, including to the remote temples of northern Cambodia and beyond.

Khmer Ways TOURS

(☑088 606 3374; www.khmerways.com; tours US$60-95) Live the dream with Khmer Ways...or at least ride the Honda Dream. Choose from a countryside tour, a longer ride to Beng Mealea or an adventure on the jungle roads of Phnom Kulen.

🛏 Sleeping

Siem Reap has the best range of accommodation in Cambodia. A vast number of family-run guesthouses (US$5 to US$20 per room) and a growing number of hostels cater for budget travellers. In the midrange, there's a dizzying array of good-value pool-equipped boutiques (US$30 to US$70), with something of a price war breaking out in low season. High-end options abound but don't always offer more than you'd get at the midrange.

During the low season (May to early October), there are lots of special offers available, ranging from stay three/pay two deals to big discounts in the range of 30% to 50%. Top-end hotels usually publish high- and low-season rates.

It's advisable to book ahead from November to March, particularly if you're eyeing one of the glamorous spots, but with more than 600 guesthouses and hotels in town, you won't be without a bed if you just show up.

Commission scams abound in Siem Reap, so keep your antennae up. Touts for budget guesthouses wait at the taxi park and at the airport. Even if you've not yet decided where to stay in Siem Reap, don't be surprised to see a noticeboard displaying your name, as most guesthouses in Phnom Penh either have partners up here or sell your name on to another guesthouse. This system usually involves a free ride into town. There's no obligation to stay at the guesthouse if you don't like the look of it, but the 'free lift' might suddenly cost a few dollars.

Most hotels will include a free transfer from the airport, bus station or boat dock if you ask, and breakfast is almost always included at midrange and top-end establishments.

Many top-end hotels levy an additional 10% government tax, a 2% tourist tax, and sometimes an extra 10% for service.

Psar Chaa Area

Psar Chaa is the liveliest part of town, brimming with restaurants, bars and boutiques. Staying here can be a lot of fun, but it's not the quietest area.

Downtown Siem Reap Villa HOSTEL **$**
(Map p106; ☎012 675881; www.downtownsiem reaphostel.hostel.com; Wat Dam Nak area; r incl breakfast US$15-35; ❋❂▨) The hostel has been reborn as a villa and the dorms have been reinvented as rooms, but the rates here are still inviting when you factor in the swimming pool in the garden. There is also the lively little garden drinking hole called Star Bar, which pulls in an outside crowd.

★**1920 Hotel** BOUTIQUE HOTEL **$$**
(Map p114; ☎063-969920; www.1920hotel.com; St 9; r US$50-80; ❋@❂) Set in a grand old building near Psar Chaa dating from, well, we'd hazard a guess at 1920, this is a

thoughtfully presented budget boutique hotel with modernist touches in the rooms. The location is great for dining and drinking options in the gentrified alleys nearby.

Shadow of Angkor Residence GUESTHOUSE **$$**
(Map p114; ☎063-964774; www.shadowangkor residence.com; 353 Pokambor Ave; r US$25-55; ❋@❂▨) In a grand old French-era building overlooking the river, this friendly place offers stylish air-conditioned rooms in a superb setting close to Psar Chaa.

Rambutan Resort RESORT **$$**
(Map p106; ☎063-766655; www.rambutans.info; Wat Dam Nak area; r incl breakfast US$75-100; ❋@❂▨) This atmospheric, gay-friendly resort is spread over two stunning villas, each with spacious and stylish rooms and an inviting courtyard swimming pool. It also operates two chic off-site penthouses, which are like having a private apartment.

Sivatha Street Area

The area to the west of Sivatha St has a good selection of budget guesthouses and midrange boutique hotels. Off the southern end of Sivatha St is Sok San Rd, fast becoming Siem Reap's travellers' mecca as high rents force many budget and midrange properties out of the centre.

★**Onederz Hostel** HOSTEL **$**
(Map p106; ☎063-963525; https://onederz.com; Angkor Night Market St; dm US$5.50-9.50, r US$20-33; ❋@❂▨) Winner of several 'Hoscars' (Hostelworld's Oscars), this is one of the smartest hostels in Siem Reap. Facilities include a huge cafe-bar downstairs, which acts as a giant waiting room for all those coming and going from Siem Reap. Dorms are a little higher-priced than some crashpads, but don't forget this is because prices include access to the rooftop swimming pool.

Mad Monkey HOSTEL **$**
(Map p106; www.madmonkeyhostels.com; Sivatha St; dm US$6.50-9, r US$16-26; ❋@❂) The Siem Reap outpost of an expanding Monkey business, this classic backpacker has deluxe dorms with air-con and extra-wide bunk beds, good-value rooms for those wanting privacy and the obligatory rooftop bar, only this one's a beach bar!

Funky Flashpacker HOSTEL **$**
(Map p132; ☎070 221524; www.funkyflashpacker. com; Funky Lane; dm US$4-8, r US$12-40;

Psar Chaa

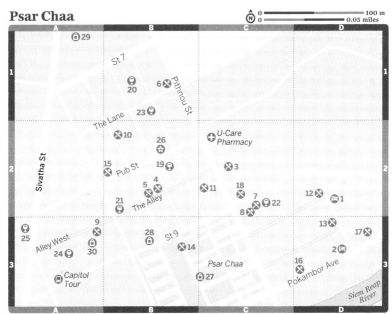

Psar Chaa

🛏 Sleeping
1 1920 Hotel..D2
2 Shadow of Angkor Residence D3

🍴 Eating
3 Blue Pumpkin...C2
4 Cambodian BBQ.....................................B2
5 Chamkar...B2
6 Dakshin's...B1
7 Elia Greek Kitchen.................................C2
8 Fifty5 Kitchen & Bar..............................C2
9 Gelato Lab A3
10 Il Forno..B2
11 Khmer Kitchen Restaurant..................C2
12 New Leaf Book Cafe.............................D2
13 Olive..D3
14 Psar Chaa..B3
15 Red Piano..B2
16 Sister Srey Cafe....................................D3
17 Swenson's Ice Cream D3
18 Viva..C2

🍸 Drinking & Nightlife
19 Angkor What?..B2
20 Asana Wooden House...........................B1
21 Beatnik Bar..B2
22 Laundry Bar C2
23 Miss Wong B1
24 Picasso..A3
25 X Bar A3

🎭 Entertainment
26 Temple Club B2

🛍 Shopping
27 Psar Chaa..C3
28 Saomao..B3
29 Senteurs d'Angkor................................A1
30 Smateria A3

✳@🛜🖳) Siem Reap's number-one party address among backpackers. The entire downstairs courtyard is taken up with a swimming pool where regular bouts of water polo take place, while the rooftop bar sizzles with inebriated youth hopped up on cheap shooters. It also offers free rooms to genuine influencers, but no, sorry, that is not the same as being under the influence.

Mulberry Boutique Hotel BOUTIQUE HOTEL **$$**
(Map p106; 📞063-621 2168; www.mulberry-boutiquehotel.com; Tep Vong St; r incl breakfast US$80-130; ✳🛜🖳) Set amid lush gardens in

a sophisticated villa down a side street near the centre, Mulberry scores points for its generously proportioned rooms decked out with love seats, Jacuzzi-like baths and balconies. The well-furnished suites, many with pool views, are a worthy splurge.

For the best rates, book directly on the website. Free airport transfers included.

Riverfront & Royal Gardens

The smart end of town, this is where the royal residence is to be found, along with many of the luxury hotels and boutique resorts.

Ivy Guesthouse 2 — GUESTHOUSE $
(Map p106; ☑012 800860; www.ivy-guesthouse. com; Central Market St; r with fan US$6-8, with aircon US$15; ✳@☞) An inviting guesthouse with a chill-out area and bar, the Ivy is a lively place to stay. The restaurant is as good as it gets among the guesthouses in town, with a huge vegetarian selection and US$1.25 'Tapas Fridays'.

★Treeline Urban Resort — BOUTIQUE HOTEL $$$
(Map p106; ☑063-961234; www.treelinehotels. com; Siem Reap River Rd East; d US$100-250; ✳@☞☎) A beautiful contemporary space from the team behind the uber-successful Brown Coffee group in Cambodia, the rooms are creatively decorated with a mix of modernity and traditional items from nature. The rooftop pool above reception offers great views across the Siem Reap River. Attached is Hok, a superb, and superbly affordable, noodle bar offering Asian fusion flavours.

Raffles Grand Hotel d'Angkor — HOTEL $$$
(Map p106; ☑063-963888; www.raffles.com; 1 Charles de Gaulle Blvd; r incl breakfast from US$250; ✳@☞☎) This historic hotel has been welcoming guests such as Charlie Chaplin, Charles de Gaulle, Jackie Kennedy and Bill Clinton since 1932. Ensconced in opulent surroundings, you can imagine what it was like to be a tourist in colonial days. Rooms include classic touches and a dizzying array of bathroom gifts. It recently underwent a major refurbishment.

Belmond La Résidence d'Angkor — RESORT $$$
(Map p106; ☑063-963390; www.residencedangkor. com; Siem Reap River Rd East; d incl breakfast from US$440; ✳@☞☎) The original woodfinished rooms, among the most tasteful and inviting in town, come with verandahs

or small gardens. The gorgeous swimming pool is perfect for laps. The newer wing is ultra-contemporary, as is the sumptuous Kong Kea Spa, but rates are some of the highest in town. Prices significantly lower from April to November (from US$280).

Wat Bo Area

This popular area on the east bank of the Siem Reap River features socially responsible guesthouses as well as some hip boutique hotels. There is a great guesthouse ghetto in a backstreet running parallel to the northern end of Wat Bo Rd, which is a good option for browsers without a booking.

Seven Candles Guesthouse — GUESTHOUSE $
(Map p106; ☑063-963380; www.sevencandles guesthouse.com; 307 Wat Bo Rd; r US$20-38; ✳@☞) ✐ Seven Candles uses profits to help a local foundation that seeks to promote education in rural communities. Rooms include hot water, TV and fridge, plus some decorative flourishes.

Babel Guesthouse — GUESTHOUSE $$
(Map p106; ☑063-965474; www.babelsiemreap. com; 738 Wat Bo village; r US$22.50-35; ✳@☞) ✐ This Norwegian-run guesthouse set in a relaxing tropical garden offers service and presentation that are a cut above the nearby budget places. The Babel owners are keen supporters of responsible tourism, and leaf and tree motifs feature prominently in all the rooms.

Angkor Village — BOUTIQUE HOTEL $$$
(Map p106; ☑063-963561; www.angkorvillage. com; St 26; r US$75-350; ✳@☞☎) The original boutique hotel in Siem Reap (when boutique was still an upmarket shopping experience to most), Angkor Village remains one of the most atmospheric places in Temple Town. Rooms are set in beautiful wooden bungalows around a stunning pond with a central restaurant. Sister hotel, Angkor Village Resort, is even more opulent.

Viroth's Hotel — BOUTIQUE HOTEL $$$
(Map p106; ☑063-766107; www.viroth-hotel.com; St 24; r incl breakfast US$100-195; ✳@☞☎) Viroth's is an ultra-stylish, retro-chic property with 30 rooms fitted out with classy contemporary furnishings. Behind the impressive facade lies a 20m swimming pool, a gym and a spa. The original seven-bedroom hotel is still operating as Viroth's Villa.

Further Afield

Don't shy away from staying out of town, as some of the most memorable boutique hotels lie hidden there and are usually only a short *remork-moto* ride from the centre. Homestays are starting to take off around more distant temples like Banteay Srei, Bakong and Beng Mealea.

★**Hideout Hostel**   HOSTEL $
(Map p132; ☏ 086 418606; www.hideouthostels. asia/siem-reap; Rose Apple Rd; dm US$3-6, r per person US$10-20; ❄ @ 🛜 ☏) One of the many 'super' hostels that have recently opened in Siem Reap in an alternative universe it might have been a boutique hotel. Dorms are super cheap and include free access to the pool. Rooms are pretty swish for the money and some include free-standing bathtubs. Add two free beers from 7pm and it's the real deal.

★**Pomme**   HOSTEL $
(Map p106; www.facebook.com/pommesiemreap; Salakamreuk Rd; dm US$5-8; ❄ 🛜) Set in a spacious Cambodian wooden house with a lush tropical garden, this is one of the most welcoming hostels in town. Air-con dorms are set behind the main building and include lockers and reading lights. The restaurant and bar attract guests and residents alike, as there is comfort food and nightly specials.

Green Home I   HOMESTAY $
(Map p140; ☏ 012 221790; www.thegreenhome.org; Chreav Commune; d with fan/air-con from US$8/10; ❄ 🛜) Setting the standard for the homestay experience around Siem Reap, the Green Home is set up like a family guesthouse and offers beautiful garden views over the surrounding rice fields. Bathrooms are shared but meticulously clean and the downstairs rooms include air-con. Cooking classes are available, as well as village walks, farm visits and birding trips.

It is located about 4km south of town in Chreav District.

Pavillon Indochine   BOUTIQUE HOTEL $$
(Map p132; ☏ 012 849681; www.pavillon-indochine. com; r US$50-125; ❄ @ 🛜 ☏) The Pavillon offers charming colonial-chic rooms set around a small swimming pool. The trim includes Asian antiques, billowing mosquito nets and a safe. Also included in the higher rates is a *remork* driver for the day to tour the temples, making it very good value.

Baby Elephant Boutique Hotel   HOTEL $$
(Map p132; ☏ 063-621 2168; www.babyelephant. asia; St 53; r US$45-125; ❄ 🛜 ☏) Run by a friendly and helpful Australian clan, this place is a short walk south of Sok San Rd. It has great beds and bathrooms and a fine pool area, plus a lovely rooftop where yoga sessions happen at 9.30am on Sunday. Topwhack rooms have more design flourishes and easy rooftop access.

The towel origami in the shape of – what else? – a baby elephant is some of the most impressive we've seen.

Navutu Dreams   BOUTIQUE HOTEL $$$
(Map p140; ☏ 063-688 0607; www.navutudreams. com; r US$80-230; ❄ 🛜 ☏) Set in the semi-rural suburbs of Siem Reap, Navutu Dreams offers a selection of open-plan villas set around lush gardens and three swimming pools. There is also a highly regarded yoga and wellness centre here.

★**Phum Baitang**   RESORT $$$
(Map p132; ☏ 063-961111; www.zannierhotels. com; Neelka Way; villas US$500-720; ❄ @ 🛜 ☏) This beautiful resort feels like a boutique Cambodian village. Rooms are set in spacious, elegantly furnished wooden villas, some with private pools, and all connected by extensive wooden walkways over the rice fields. The decor is very designer driftwood. Angelina Jolie stayed here for three months while shooting *First They Killed My Father,* and it's not hard to see what attracted her to the place.

★**Montra Nivesha**   BOUTIQUE HOTEL $$$
(Map p110; ☏ 063-760582; www.montranivesha. com; 5 Krom 2; r US$60-150; ❄ @ 🛜 ☏) 🕮 A beautiful boutique hotel that gives guests a real sense of Cambodia, Montra Nivesha is set around lush gardens and offers two swimming pools, one suited to laps and one for families. Rooms are decorated with collectables but include modern touches such as smart TV, minibar and safe. The property boasts an in-house drinking water system to cut the use of plastic.

★**Maison Polanka**   BOUTIQUE HOTEL $$$
(Map p132; ☏ 012 499810; www.maisonpolanka. com; Wat Polanka; r from US$210, ste US$485; ❄ 🛜 ☏) Imagine a luxurious homestay that caters to your every need and Maison Polanka comes to mind, a lush private estate near Wat Polanka that offers a small number of traditional Khmer houses and artfully decorated rooms. The gardens are extensive and

include a swimming pool and al fresco garden restaurant. It is a zenlike escape from the bustle of downtown.

★ **Sala Lodges** BOUTIQUE HOTEL **$$$**
(Map p140; ✉ 063-766699; www.salalodges.com; 498 Salakamreuk Rd; r US$190-600; ▦ 🖥 🖼) An original concept, Sala Lodges offers 11 traditional Khmer houses that have been retro-fitted inside to bring them up to the standard of a rustic boutique hotel. Enter the resort and you'll think you have stumbled upon an idyllic Cambodian village, but the pool and restaurant will soon confirm you have stumbled upon a gem.

✕ Eating

Siem Reap's dining scene is something to savour, offering a superb selection of street food, Asian eateries and sophisticated international restaurants. The range encompasses something from every continent, with new temptations regularly opening up. Sample the subtleties of Khmer cuisine in town, or indulge in home comforts prior to – or after – hitting the remote provinces. Some of the very best restaurants also put something back into community projects or offer vocational training.

Tourist numbers mean many top restaurants are heaving during from November to March. But with so many places to choose from, keep walking and you'll find somewhere more tranquil. Quite a lot of restaurants work with tour groups to some degree. If you prefer to avoid places with tour groups, stick to the Psar Chaa area and explore on foot.

Some budget guesthouses have good menus offering a selection of local dishes and Western meals. Several of the midrange hotels and all of the top-end places have restaurants, some of them excellent. Several hotels and restaurants around town feature dinner and a performance of classical dance.

Pub Street & Around

Pub St may not seem to be the most relaxing dining area, particularly at night, but the criss-crossing alleys are wall-to-wall with good restaurants. Take a stroll and see what takes your fancy.

Psar Chaa and other markets are well stocked with fruit and fresh bread. Eating locally usually works out cheaper than self-catering, but some folks like to make up a picnic for longer days on the road.

Pot & Pan Restaurant CAMBODIAN **$**
(Map p106; ✉ 017 970780; www.thepotandpanrestaurant.com; Stung Thmei St; meals US$2-5; ⊙10am-10pm; 🖥) One of the best-value Khmer restaurants in the downtown area, Pot & Pan specialises in well-presented, authentic dishes at affordable prices. The menu includes spicy soups and subtle salads, and rice is beautifully served in a lotus leaf. Some of the cheapest pizzas in town are, somewhat surprisingly, available here.

Sister Srey Cafe CAFE **$**
(Map p114; www.sistersreycafe.com; 200 Pokambor Ave; mains US$3-6; ⊙7am-6pm Tue-Sun; 🖉) Sister Srey, a funky and fun cafe on the riverfront near Psar Chaa, offers an ambitious breakfast menu, including eggs benedelicious, which is perfect after a sunrise at the temples. Lunch is Western food with a creative twist, including burgers, wraps and salads. Profits go towards supporting the 'Hero Rats' of Apopo (p105) and demining in Cambodia.

CRAVING ICE CREAM?

....

After a hot day exploring the temples, there's nothing quite like an ice-cream fix and Siem Reap delivers some superb surprises:

Gelato Lab (Map p114; www.facebook.com/gelatolabsiemreap; 109 Alley West; 1/2 scoops US$1.50/2.50; ⊙9am-11pm; 🖥) State-of-the-art equipment, all-natural ingredients and, most importantly, plenty of passion courtesy of the Italian owner add up to great ice cream.

Blue Pumpkin (Map p114; www.bluepumpkin.asia; Pithnou St; mains US$3-8; ⊙6am-10pm; ▦🖥) Homemade ice cream in original tropical flavours from ginger to passion fruit.

Glasshouse (Map p106; www.facebook.com/theglasshousedelipatisserie; Park Hyatt, Sivatha St; cones US$2; ⊙6am-10pm; 🖥) Velvety ice creams, including chocolate and tangy sorbets.

Swenson's Ice Cream (Map p114; Pokambor Ave; cones US$1.25; ⊙9am-9pm) One of America's favourites has become a Siem Reap favourite. Located in the Angkor Trade Centre.

Psar Chaa
CAMBODIAN $

(Map p114; mains US$1.50-5; ⊙7am-9pm) When it comes to cheap Khmer eats, Psar Chaa market has plenty of food stalls on the north-western side, all with signs and menus in English. These are atmospheric places for a local meal at local-ish prices. Some dishes are on display, others are freshly wok-fried to order, but most are wholesome and filling.

New Leaf Book Cafe
CAFE $

(Map p114; http://newleafeatery.com; near Psar Chaa; mains US$3-6.75; ⊙7.30am-10pm; 🎅) 🍴 The profits from this cafe and secondhand bookshop go towards supporting NGOs working in Siem Reap Province, as well as a forward-thinking profit share with their staff. The menu includes some home favourites, an Italian twist and some Cambodian specials.

Khmer Kitchen Restaurant
CAMBODIAN $

(Map p114; ☎012 763468; www.khmerkitchens. com; The Alley; mains US$3-7; ⊙11am-10pm; 🎅) Can't get no (culinary) satisfaction? Then follow in the footsteps of Sir Mick Jagger and try this popular place, which offers an affordable selection of Khmer and Thai favourites, including zesty curries. It now covers a whole block of classic colonial-era buildings.

Il Forno
ITALIAN $$

(Map p114; ☎063-763380; http://ilforno.restaurant; The Lane; mains US$7-19; ⊙11am-11pm; 🎅) Aficionados of fine Italian cuisine will be delighted to know that there is, as the name suggests, a full-blown brick oven in this cosy little trattoria. The menu includes fresh antipasti, authentic pizzas and some home-cooked Italian dishes.

Elia Greek Kitchen
GREEK $$

(Map p114; ☎089 325245; https://elia-greek-kitchen.business.site; St 9; mains US$4.50-15; ⊙11am-11pm; 🎅) This little taverna near Psar Chaa looks like it comes straight out of the Med, and the food tastes pretty authentic too. Choose from all the Greek favourites like souvlaki, skewers and moussaka, plus some immense seafood and meat platters that could feed a family. Very atmospheric.

Fifty5 Kitchen & Bar
INTERNATIONAL $$

(Map p114; ☎010 271548; cnr Sts Pithnou & 9; mains US$5-12; ⊙7am-11pm; 🎅) An inviting bistro with a prime location opposite Psar Chaa, Fifty5 is the place to come for a range of Asian and international flavours. Break-fast includes a much-heralded eggs Benedict, or try fresh salads, homemade burgers or a vegan bowl later in the day. Premium Illy coffee and tempting gelato complete the picture.

Cambodian BBQ
BARBECUE $$

(Map p114; ☎063-966052; https://cambodian bbq-restaurant.com; The Alley; 7 meat BBQ sets US$13.50; ⊙3-11pm; 🎅) Crocodile, snake, ostrich and kangaroo meat add an exotic twist to the traditional *phnom pleung* (hill of fire) grills. Cambodian BBQ has spawned half a dozen or more copycats in the surrounding streets, many of which offer discount specials.

Chamkar
VEGETARIAN $$

(Map p114; ☎092 733150; The Alley; mains US$4-8; ⊙11am-10.30pm Mon-Sat, 5-10.30pm Sun; 🎅🍴) The name translates as 'farm', and the ingredients must be coming from a pretty impressive organic vegetable supplier given the creative dishes on the menu here. Asian flavours dominate and include dishes such as vegetable kebabs in black-pepper sauce and stuffed pumpkin.

Red Piano
INTERNATIONAL $$

(Map p114; ☎063-963240; www.redpianocambodia.com; Pub St; mains US$3-10; ⊙9.30am-12.30am; 🎅) Strikingly set in a restored colonial-era gem, Red Piano has a big balcony for watching the action unfold below. The menu has a reliable selection of Asian and international food, all at decent prices. Former celebrity guest Angelina Jolie has the Tomb Raider cocktail named in her honour.

Viva
MEXICAN $$

(Map p114; ☎092 209154; www.ivivasiemreap.com; Pithnou St; mains US$2.50-12.50; ⊙7am-11.30pm; 🎅) Spice up your life with Mexican food and margaritas at this long-running place, strategically situated opposite Psar Chaa for great people-watching. It also offers a range of other dishes, including Khmer and Italian, plus there's a budget guesthouse located above.

Dakshin's
INDIAN $$

(Map p114; ☎012 808011; Pithnou St; mains US$4-9; ⊙11am-3pm & 5-11pm; 🎅) Arguably the best of Siem Reap's numerous Indian restaurants, Dakshin's serves up a delicious butter chicken alongside the highlights of northern and southern Indian cuisine. Such is their confidence in their subcontinental skills that they have an open-plan kitchen.

Olive FRENCH $$$
(Map p114; 📞012 244196; www.facebook.com/
olivecuisinedesaison; off Pokambor Ave; mains
US$7.50-24; ⏰10am-10pm; ❄️🛜) The crisp
white linens and air-con beckon diners into
this French restaurant hidden away down
a side street near Psar Chaa. The menu in-
cludes a good range of Gallic classics, includ-
ing rack of lamb and pork tenderloin. Save
space for the desserts or a cheese platter.

Wat Dam Nak Area

Jomno Street Food CAMBODIAN $
(Map p106; 📞092 762539; https://jomnostreet
food.business.site; Wat Dam Nak village; dishes
US$3-7.50; ⏰11am-10pm; 🛜) Earning rave re-
views for its original flavour combinations,
Jomno promotes its signature platters (from
US$7.50) offering a bite-size taste of a range
of dishes from the Cambodian street such
as *naom banchok* noodles and Battam-
bang sausage. Twists on the classic *amok*
(baked fish) include a crispy chicken *amok*
salad and a vegan mushroom *amok*. Highly
recommended.

★**Pou Kitchen** CAMBODIAN $$
(Map p106; 📞092 262688; www.poukitchen.com;
opposite Wat Dam Nak; US$3-6.50; ⏰11am-11pm,
closed Wed; 🛜) Under the direction of homegrown chef Mengly, Pou Kitchen has taken
off as one of the most popular and innovative Cambodian restaurants in town. Choose
from grilled beehive salad or chicken with
red ant for starters, and move on to Phnom
Kulen pork-belly sausage or spicy vegetable-
cake curry. Simple surrounds, but far from
simple flavours.

★**Spoons Cafe** CAMBODIAN $$
(Map p106; 📞076 277 6667; www.spoonscambodia.
org; Bambu Rd; mains US$6.25-12; ⏰11.30am-
10pm Mon-Sat; 🛜) 🍴 This excellent contem-
porary-Cambodian restaurant supports local
community EGBOK (Everything's Gonna Be
OK), which offers education, training and
employment opportunities in the hospitali-
ty sector. The menu includes some original
flavours such as *trey saba* (whole macker-
el) with coconut-turmeric rice, tiger-prawn
curry and *tuk kroeung*, a pungent local fish-
based broth. Original cocktails are shaken,
not stirred.

★**Cuisine Wat Damnak** CAMBODIAN $$$
(Map p106; 📞077 347762; www.cuisinewatdam
nak.com; Wat Dam Nak area; 5-/6-course set menu

US$29/34; ⏰6.30-10.30pm Tue-Sat, last orders
9.30pm) Set in a traditional wooden house is
this highly regarded restaurant from Siem
Reap celeb chef Joannès Rivière. The menu
delivers the ultimate contemporary Khmer
dining experience. Seasonal set menus focus
on market-fresh ingredients and change
weekly; vegetarian options are available
with advance notice.

Sivatha Street Area

Curry Walla INDIAN $
(Map p106; Sivatha St; mains US$3-8; ⏰10.30am-
11pm) For good-value Indian food, this place
is hard to beat. The *thalis* (set meals) are a
bargain, and the owner, long-time resident
Ranjit, knows his share of spicy specials
from the subcontinent.

Angkor Market SUPERMARKET $
(Map p106; Sivatha St; ⏰8am-9pm) The best all-
round supermarket in town, this place has a
steady supply of international treats.

Kandal Village

Hive Siem Reap CAFE $
(Map p106; www.facebook.com/thehive.siemreap;
Psar Kandal St; dishes US$2-6; ⏰7am-6pm; ❄️🛜)
This place generates a real buzz among foreign residents in Siem Reap thanks to its
creative coffees, jam-jar juices and healthy
open sandwiches, such as smashed avocado or smoked salmon on rye. Try an espresso martini if you like your coffee with
a kick, provided by Rumble Fish Coffee of
Kampot fame.

Svay Chek Organic Farm Shop CAFE $
(Map p106; 📞099 277477; www.svaychekorganic
farm.com; Central Market St; US$2-6; ⏰10am-
7pm; ❄️🛜) Located out in Angkor Thom District, the Svay Chek Organic Farm produces
delicious organic fruits and veggies, and it
is now possible for everyone to sample their
wares in this shop and cafe. Salads feature
prominently as well as delicious fruit shakes
made with freshly picked produce.

★**Mamma Shop** ITALIAN $$
(Map p106; www.facebook.com/mammashop.
italian.restaurant; Hup Guan St; mains US$5-10;
⏰11.30am-10.30pm Mon-Sat; ❄️🛜) A compact
menu of terrific homemade pasta is the sig-
nature of this bright, friendly Italian corner
bistro in the bohemian Kandal village dis-
trict. Add a selection of *piadina romagnola*

(stuffed flatbread) pizza, a nice wine list and delicious desserts, and this place is highly recommended.

★ Village Cafe FRENCH $$

(Map p106; ☑092 305401; www.facebook.com/villagecafecambodia; 586 Tep Vong St; mains US$5-15; ☺5pm-late Mon-Sat; ✷☎) Bar, Bites, Beats is the motto at Village Cafe, a happening little bistro that delivers on its promise. Drop in for tapas, wholesome gastropub grub and a glass of wine or four to wash it all down. Features one of the longest bars in Siem Reap. Regular DJ events at weekends draw a crowd.

Cafe .9 CAFE $$

(Map p106; ☑095 269900; 577 Hup Guan St; mains US$4-7; ☺8.30am-6pm; ✷☎) This Australian-run cafe is generating a real reputation among expats in Siem Reap thanks to a great range of cafe-bistro comfort food like homemade burgers and wraps and some of the best cakes in town. Friday is curry night, and the weekend roasts are becoming a sell-out event.

Vibe Cafe VEGAN $$

(Map p106; ☑069 937900; www.vibecafeasia.com; 715 St 14; mains US$3-7; ☺7.30am-9pm Tue-Sun, to 4.30pm Mon; ✷☎✐) This vegan spot serves up raw organically sourced superfood bowls and cleansing juices such as the cash-ew, date, Himalayan salt, vanilla bean and Ayurvedic spices concoction. If that sounds too healthy for you after partying on Pub St, try the excellent vegan desserts such as raspberry cheesecake and chocolate-ganache truffle.

Riverfront & Royal Gardens

Moloppor Cafe INTERNATIONAL $

(Map p106; www.facebook.com/molopporcafeofficial; Siem Reap River Rd East; mains US$1.50-5; ☺10am-11pm; ☎) One of the cheapest deals in Siem Reap, Moloppor Cafe serves up Japanese, Asian and Italian dishes at almost giveaway prices for what is a real restaurant. Nice location offering river views.

Chanrey Tree CAMBODIAN $$

(Map p106; ☑063-767997; www.chanreytree.com; Pokambor Ave; mains US$5-15; ☺11am-2pm & 5.30-10pm; ✷☎) Chanrey Tree is all about contemporary Khmer cuisine, combining a stylish setting with expressive presentation, while retaining the essentials of traditional

Cambodian cooking. Try the eggplant with pork ribs or grilled stuffed frog.

Siem Reap Brewpub INTERNATIONAL $$

(Map p106; ☑080 888555; www.siemreapbrewpub.asia; St 5; meals US$4-15; ☺11am-11pm) Designer dining meets designer brewing. Set in an open-plan villa, the menu is international fusion, including everything from light bites and tapas to gourmet meals. The beer comes in several flavours, including blonde, golden, amber and dark, and a sampling platter is available.

King's Road INTERNATIONAL $$

(Map p106; https://kingsroadangkor.com; Siem Reap River Rd East; ☺7am-midnight; ☎) King's Road is an upmarket dining destination on the east bank of the Siem Reap River. You can browse the daily Made in Cambodia (p127) community market of craft stalls, then choose from about half a dozen restaurants set in beautiful traditional Cambodian wooden buildings.

Dining choices include Cambodian, Asian, fusion and international.

Embassy CAMBODIAN $$$

(Map p106; ☑089 282911; www.embassy-restaurant.com; St 27, King's Road; set menus US$36; ☺6-11pm) Part of the King's Road village, Embassy is all about Khmer gastronomy, offering an evolving menu that changes with the seasons. Under the supervision of the Kimsan twins, who studied with Michelin-starred chef Régis Marcon, this is Khmer cuisine prepared at its most creative.

FCC Angkor INTERNATIONAL $$$

(Map p106; ☑063-760280; www.fcccambodia.com; Pokambor Ave; mains US$7-20; ☺7am-midnight; ☎) This landmark building draws people in from the riverside thanks to a reflective pool, torchlit dining and a garden bar. Inside, the colonial-chic atmosphere continues with lounge chairs and an open kitchen turning out a range of Asian and international food.

Wat Bo Area

Banllé Vegetarian Restaurant VEGETARIAN $

(Map p106; www.banlle-vegetarian.com; St 26; dishes US$2.50-5; ☺11am-9.30pm Wed-Mon; ☎✐) Set in a traditional wooden house with its own organic vegetable garden, this is a great place for a healthy bite. The menu offers a blend of international and Cambodian dishes, including a vegetable *amok* and zesty fruit and vegetable shakes.

Footprints Cafe
CAFE $

(Map p106; ☑092 800308; https://footprintcafes. org; St 26; mains US$3-6; ⊗7am-10pm; 🛜) 🍴 This popular not-for-profit cafe on lively St 26 supports education projects and community initiatives in Siem Reap. The menu includes an eclectic range of all-day breakfast offerings, a good selection of Cambodian favourites and some familiar flavours from home. Save space for dessert to try the Eton Mess Siem Reap Style.

Pages Cafe
CAFE $

(Map p106; ☑092 966812; www.pages-siemreap. com; St 24; dishes US$3-6; ⊗6.30am-9.30pm; 🛜) This hip little hideaway is no longer as hidden as it once was with popular Viroth's Hotel opposite. Exposed brickwork and designer decor make it a good place to linger over the excellent breakfasts or tapas. On Saturday it offers an outdoor grill with wine and pool access. Rooms also available.

★ Sugar Palm
CAMBODIAN $$

(Map p106; ☑012 818143; www.thesugarpalm. com; St 27; mains US$6-9; ⊗11.30am-3pm & 5.30-10.30pm Mon-Sat; 🛜) The Sugar Palm is a beautiful space and a popular place to sample traditional flavours infused with herbs and spices, including delicious *char kreung* (curried lemongrass) dishes.

Jungle Burger
INTERNATIONAL $$

(Map p106; ☑098 293400; www.facebook.com/ jungleburgersiemreap; St 26; burgers US$2.50-10; ⊗11am-11pm; 🛜) There are more than 10 types of burger on offer here, including the towering Burg Kalifa burger, plus pizzas, foot-long subs and Kiwi comfort food such as homemade pies, thanks to the NZ owner. It doubles as a small but super-friendly sports bar with a popular pool table.

Hashi
JAPANESE $$$

(Map p106; www.thehashi.com; Wat Bo Rd; meals US$10-50; ⊗11am-3pm & 6-11pm; ⊞🛜) A big, bright and boisterous sushi parlour. Navigate through the SUVs parked outside, waddle up to the fish-shaped sushi bar and order the likes of spicy tuna rolls, *chirashi* sushi bowls or, for the fish averse, wagyu beef tenderloin.

Further Afield

Road 60 Night Market
MARKET $

(Map p132; Rd 60; snacks US$1-4; ⊗4-11pm) For a slice of local life, head to the Road 60 Night Market located on the side of the road near the main Angkor ticket checkpoint. Stallholders set up each night, and it's a great place to sample local Cambodian snacks, including the full range of deep-fried insects and barbecue dishes such as quail. Plenty of cheap beer too.

Peace Cafe
VEGETARIAN $

(Map p110; www.peacecafeangkor.org; Siem Reap River Rd East; mains US$2.50-4.50; ⊗7am-9pm; 🛜🍴) 🍴 This popular garden cafe serves affordable vegetarian meals, while healthy drinks include a tempting selection of vegetable juices. A focal point for community activities, it hosts twice-daily yoga sessions and twice-weekly Khmer classes and monk chanting.

Bayon Pastry School Coffee Shop
BAKERY $

(Map p106; ☑012 604170; http://ecoledubayon. org; off Taphul St; US$1.50-4; ⊗8am-5.30pm) 🍴 The Bayon Pastry School has played host to British celebrity chef Nadiya Hussein on her journey of self-discovery in Cambodia, and the coffee shop is the place to sample their fluffy croissant or pain au chocolate and their delightful cakes, all in the good cause of training disadvantaged youths in the art of hospitality.

★ Marum
INTERNATIONAL $$

(Map p106; ☑017 363284; www.marum-restau rant.org; Wat Polanka area; mains US$4-9.75; ⊗11am-10.30pm; 🛜🍴👶) 🍴 Set in a delightful wooden house with a spacious garden, Marum serves up lots of vegetarian and seafood dishes, plus some mouth-watering desserts. Menu highlights include beef with red ants and chilli stir-fry, and mini crocodile burgers. Marum is part of the Tree Alliance group of training restaurants; the experience is a must.

There's a great shop here too, and the whole place is extremely kid-friendly.

★ Mahob
CAMBODIAN $$

(Map p110; ☑063-966986; www.mahobkhmer. com; near Angkor Conservation; dishes US$3.50-15; ⊗11am-11pm) The Cambodian word for food is *mahob*, and at this restaurant it is delicious. Set in a traditional wooden house with a contemporary twist, this place takes the same approach to cuisine as it does to decor, serving up dishes such as caramelised pork shank with ginger and black pepper, or wok-fried local beef with red tree ants. Cooking classes available.

The owners have also opened the first farm-to-table restaurant in Siem Reap called Lum Orng (www.lumorngrestaurant.com), located out in Thlok Andong village, but it is only open for dinners and it is essential to book.

⭐ Haven   FUSION $$
(Map p106; ☑ 078 342404; www.haven-cambodia. com; Chocolate Rd; mains US$4.50-8; ⊘ 11.30am-2.30pm & 5.30-9.30pm Mon-Sat, closed Aug; 🛜) 🍴 A culinary haven indeed. Dine here for the best of East meets West; the fish fillet with green mango is particularly zesty. Proceeds go towards helping young adult orphans make the step from institution to employment.

Mie Cafe   CAMBODIAN $$
(Map p110; ☑ 069 999096; www.miecafe-siem reap.com; near Angkor Conservation; mains US$5-14; ⊘ 11am-2pm & 5.30-10pm Wed-Mon; 🛜) An impressive Cambodian eatery offering a fusion take on traditional flavours. It is set in a wooden house just off the road to Angkor and offers a gourmet set menu for US$24. Dishes include everything from succulent marinated pork ribs to squid-ink ravioli.

Rice Thai   THAI $$
(Map p106; ☑ 088 890 3953; www.ricethai.restau rant; St 27; mains US$5-9; ⊘ 5-9.30pm Tue-Sat; 🌿) Arguably the best Thai restaurant in Siem Reap, this little eatery specialises in succulent duck dishes, but has a whole range of vegetarian options available to boot. The khao soy noodles are an unexpected treat this far from home, and the Bangkok Bad Boy stir-fry will spice up your life.

Dine in the Dark   INTERNATIONAL $$
(Map p106; ☑ 012 558714; https://did-siemreap. com; 7 Makara St; set menu US$18; ⊘ 7-9.30pm) 🍴 Set in a handsome Khmer villa on the edge of town, Dine in the Dark brings a uniquely sensory dining experience to Temple Town. Set in a grand old wooden house, the lights go out at night and diners are served a set menu by sight-impaired staff. Be prepared to eat with your hands.

🍷 Drinking & Nightlife

The transformation from sleepy overgrown village to an international destination for the jet set has been dramatic and Siem Reap is now firmly on the nightlife map of Southeast Asia. For the morning after, there are lots of cafes and coffee shops, several of which operate as social enterprises to help local causes.

The heaving 'Pub St' area near Psar Chaa makes Siem Reap feel more like a beach town than a cultural capital. Pub St is closed to traffic every evening as food carts, drink carts and scores of party people take over. If this is your thing, just stroll around and see what's happening. The action spills into the street as the night wears on.

Great spots running parallel to Pub St include The Alley, to the south, where the volume control is just a little lower, plus a series of smaller lanes to the north. Late night, the crowd wanders on to Wat Preah Prohm Roth St and, eventually, to Sok San Rd, where there are a number of 'late-night' bars – although 'early morning' might be more apt, as they stay open until daybreak.

Most bars have happy hours, as do some of the fancier hotels. The FCC Angkor (p120) and Grand Hotel d'Angkor (p115) hotels both have legendary bars with happy hours.

Hostels bars are a big thing, drawing backpackers who guzzle shooters and play drinking games until the wee hours. The 'beach bar' at Mad Monkey (p113) is one of the best, although it closes before midnight. The no-holds-barred party at Funky Flashpacker (p113) near Sok San Rd, on the other hand, can go all night long. One of our favourites is the mellow Pomme (p116), set in the verdant gardens of a wooden house. Several hostels also organise their own pub crawls, which take in the most popular spots around Pub St.

⭐ Asana Wooden House   BAR
(Map p114; www.asana-cambodia.com; St 7; ⊘ 6pm-1am; 🛜) This is a traditional Cambodian countryside home dropped into the backstreets of Siem Reap, which makes for an atmospheric place to drink. Lounge on kapok-filled rice sacks while sipping a classic cocktail made with infused rice wine. Khmer cocktail classes (US$15 per person) with Sombai spirits are available at 6pm.

⭐ Miss Wong   BAR
(Map p114; www.misswong.net; The Lane; ⊘ 6pm-1am; 🛜) Miss Wong carries you back to chic

1920s Shanghai. The cocktails are a draw here, making it a cool place to while away an evening, and there's a menu offering dim sum. Gay-friendly and extremely popular with the well-heeled expat crowd.

★ Laundry Bar   BAR
(Map p114; www.facebook.com/laundry.bar.3; St 9; ⏰4pm-late; 📶) One of the most chilled, chic bars in town thanks to low lighting and discerning decor. Laundry is the place to come for electronica and ambient sounds; it heaves on weekends or when guest DJs crank up the volume. Happy hour until 9pm.

Beatnik Bar   BAR
(Map p114; www.facebook.com/beatniksiemreap; The Alley; ⏰9.30am-1.30am; 📶) A hip little bar on the corner of The Alley, it's just far enough away from Pub St not to be drowned out by the nightly battle of the bars. Cheap drinks, friendly staff and a convivial crowd add up to a great pit stop.

Picasso   BAR
(Map p114; www.facebook.com/picassobarsiem reap; Alley West; ⏰5pm-late; 📶) This tiny tapas bar in the Alley West area is a convivial spot for a bit of over-the-counter banter. With only a dozen or so stools, expect spillover into the street – especially once the cheap sangria, worldly wines and cheap Tiger bottles start flowing.

Wild   BAR
(Map p106; www.wild-siemreap.com; Wat Dam Nak area; ⏰5-10.30pm, closed Tue; 📶) 🍃 Hidden away down a small side alley near Wat Dam Nak, Wild is an unprepossessing door from the front, but enter the threshold to discover a secret garden and an old wooden house. Cocktails with local infusions are a popular choice for locals, and the light menu is blissfully simple as all items are a fusion interpretation of spring rolls.

Harbour   BAR
(Map p132; www.theharboursiemreap.com; Stung Thmei St; ⏰10am-1am; 📶) Shiver me timbers, this self-styled 'pirate tavern' is a lovable bar housed in an atmospheric wooden house in Stung Thmei. Upstairs are cocktails, booze aplenty and regular open mic, comedy and other events.

Angkor What?   BAR
(Map p114; www.facebook.com/theangkorwhatbar; Pub St; ⏰5pm-late; 📶) Siem Reap's original bar claims to have been promoting irresponsible drinking since 1998. The happy hour

(to 9pm) lightens the mood for later when everyone's bouncing along to dance anthems, sometimes on the tables, sometimes under them. Regular DJs and live music add to the party mood.

X Bar   BAR
(Map p114; www.xbarsiemreap.com; Sivatha St; ⏰4pm-sunrise; 📶) One of the late-night spots in town, X Bar draws revellers for the witching hour when other places are closing up. It offers early-evening movies on the big screen, pool tables and even a skateboard pipe – take a breath test first!

Barcode   GAY
(Map p106; www.barcodesiemreap.com; Wat Preah Prohm Roth St; ⏰5pm-late; 📶) A superstylin' gay bar that's metrosexual-friendly. The cocktails here are worth the stop, as is the regular drag show at 9.30pm. Happy hour runs from 5pm to 7pm daily.

Dialogue   BAR
(Map p106; www.facebook.com/dialoguesiemreap; St 27; mains US$3-6; ⏰7am-midnight; 📶) Cool coffee shop by day and hip little bar by night, this place has a split personality: one all about coffee and the other all about craft beer. And it works thanks to the coffee being hand roasted and supervised by a former Cambodian barista of the year and the craft ales being sourced from across the region.

Local Brewpub   BAR
(Map p106; https://thelocalsiemreap.com; St 20; ⏰6am-late; 📶) Sitting pretty at the end of a popular guesthouse lane, Local Brewpub draws a local and visiting crowd thanks to its impressive range of craft and homebrew beers. Signature IPA Apology Juice is popular, but it also offers regular wheat beers, amber ales and stouts.

Hard Rock Cafe   BAR
(Map p106; 📞063-963964; www.hardrock.com/cafes/angkor; Siem Reap River Rd East; ⏰11am-midnight; 📶) While you might not head to the Hard Rock Cafe in London or New York, it is well worth making the diversion across the bridge from the Old Market to catch the live band here. They bang out music from the 1960s to the '90s, ranging from the Rolling Stones to the Red Hot Chili Peppers.

Sombai   DISTILLERY
(Map p140; 📞095 810890; www.sombai.com; Salakamreuk Rd; ⏰4-11pm) Is it drinking or is it shopping? A bit of both, actually, as this rice-wine distillery sells beautiful hand-painted

bottles of infused spirits and also offers free tastings. Set in the beautiful house of the renowned artist Leang Seckon, choose from around eight flavours, including ginger and chilli or anise coffee.

Sombai spirits are also on sale in bars around Siem Reap and it also has a stall at the Made in Cambodia Market in King's Road.

☆ Entertainment

Several restaurants and hotels offer cultural performances during the evening, and for many visitors such shows offer the only opportunity to see Cambodian classical dance or traditional shadow puppetry. While they may be aimed at tourists and are nowhere near as sophisticated as a performance of the Royal Ballet in Phnom Penh, to the untrained eye they are nonetheless graceful and alluring. Prices usually include a buffet meal.

★Phare the Cambodian Circus   CIRCUS
(Map p132; ☎ 015 499480; www.pharecircus.org; cnr Ring & Sok San Rds; adult/child US$18/10, premium seats US$38/18; ☺8pm) Cambodia's answer to Cirque du Soleil, Phare the Cambodian Circus is so much more than a conventional circus, with an emphasis on performance art and a subtle yet striking social message behind each production. Cambodia's leading circus, theatre and performing-arts organisation, Phare Ponleu Selpak opened its big top for nightly shows in 2013, and the results are unique, must-see entertainment.

Several generations of performers have graduated through Phare's original Battambang campus and have gone on to perform in international shows around the world. Many of the performers have deeply moving personal stories of abuse and hardship, making their talents a triumph against the odds. An inspiring night out for adults and children alike, all proceeds are reinvested into Phare Ponleu Selpak activities. Animal lovers will be pleased to note that no animals are used in any performance.

There are additional 5pm performances from November through March and special standard tickets plus dinner are available for US$30.

Sacred Dancers of Angkor   DANCE
(Map p110; ☎ 012 772641; www.nkfc.org/sacred-dancers-of-angkor; Siem Reap River Rd East; US$30; ☺7pm Wed & Sun) There are countless Apsara dance shows around Siem Reap, but only the Sacred Dancers of Angkor can claim royal patronage from HRH Princess Norodom Bopha Devi, one of the most accomplished classical dancers in the kingdom. The mesmerising performance takes place in the garden of the Nginn Karet Foundation, which supports the dancers' extensive training.

Bambu Stage   THEATRE
(Map p106; ☎ 097 726 1110; https://bambustage.com; Bambu Rd; show US$24, incl dinner US$38; ☺shows from 7pm Mon-Sat; 🐾) Bambu Stage offers an eclectic variety of traditional entertainment, including a nightly shadow puppet show that weaves a historical tale of the Cambodian civil war. Other shows include Temples Decoded (Tuesday) and Snap (Friday), a history of Cambodian photography. The venue also hosts Cambodia Living Arts' all-female drum performance, The Call, on Wednesday, Friday and Sunday at 8pm.

New Cambodian Artists   DANCE
(Map p132; ☎ 077 283804; www.facebook.com/newcambodianartists; Men's Rd; US$12; ☺6.30pm Sat) This small contemporary-dance theatre is set in a black box on the east side of the river and has been making a name for itself thanks to the innovative fusion of contemporary dance and classical Apsara dance created by the three young all-female performers. One show a week for now, but look out for updates on the Facebook page.

Angkor Dynasty   LIVE PERFORMANCE
(Map p110; ☎ 070 888900; www.angkordynasty.cn; Charles de Gaulle Blvd; US$39-49; ☺7.30-8.45pm) Move over Macau (and Las Vegas), as the Angkor Dynasty show has come to town. This is an epic multimedia performance that tells the story of Angkor through dance, song and acrobatics, involving tens if not hundreds of Cambodian and Chinese performers. Choreographed by Chinese, it is not classical Khmer dance by any means, but it is entertainment.

Apsara Theatre   DANCE
(Map p106; ☎ 063-963561; www.angkorvillagehotel.asia/apsara-theatre; St 26; show US$27; ☺7.30pm) The setting for this Cambodian classical-dance show is a striking wooden pavilion finished in the style of a wat. The price includes dinner. It tends to be packed to the rafters with tour groups.

Temple Club   DANCE
(Map p114; www.facebook.com/templeclubpubstreet; Pub St; ☺from 7.30pm; 🐾) Temple Club

stages a free traditional-dance show upstairs nightly, providing punters order some food and drink from the reasonably priced menu.

🔒 Shopping

Siem Reap is a hub for handicrafts with stone and wood carvings, lacquerware, silk and cotton weaving and a whole lot more. Be sure to bargain at the markets, as overcharging is pretty common. Kandal village is an up-and-coming shopping destination with boutiques, galleries, cafes and restaurants.

Much of what you see on sale in the markets of Siem Reap can also be purchased from children and vendors throughout the temple area. Some visitors get fed up with the endless sales pitches as they navigate the ancient wonders, while others enjoy the banter and a chance to interact with Cambodian people. It's often children out selling, and some visitors will argue that they should be at school instead. However, most do attend school at least half of the time, joining for morning or afternoon classes, alternating with siblings.

Cheap books on Angkor and Cambodia are hawked by kids around the temples and Pub St. Be aware that many are illegal photocopies and the print quality is poor.

★Angkor Night Market   MARKET
(Map p106; https://angkornightmarket.com; Angkor Night Market St; ⊗4pm-midnight) Siem Reap's original night market near Sivatha St has sprung countless copycats, but it remains the best and is well worth a browse. It's packed with stalls selling a variety of handicrafts, souvenirs and silks. Island Bar offers regular live music and Sombai offers infused organic rice wines for those that want to make a night of it.

★Theam's House   ART
(Map p132; www.theamshouse.com; 25 Veal St; ⊗8am-7pm) After years spent working with Artisans Angkor (p105) to revitalise Khmer handicrafts, Cambodian artist and designer Theam operates his own studio of lacquer creations and artwork. Highly original, this beautiful and creative space can be tricky to find, so make sure you find a driver who knows where it is.

★Eric Raisina Couture House   FASHION & ACCESSORIES
(Map p132; ☑063-963207; www.ericraisina.com; 75-81 Charles de Gaulle Blvd; ⊗store 8am-7pm, workshop 8-11am & 1-5pm) Renowned designer Eric Raisina brings a unique cocktail of influences to his couture. Born in Madagascar, partly educated in France and resident in Cambodia, he offers a striking collection of clothing and accessories. Ask one of the staff for a tour of the workshop upstairs and see where his striking, original designs are created.

trunkh   GIFTS & SOUVENIRS
(Map p106; www.trunkh.com; Hup Guan St; ⊗10am-6pm) The owner here has a great eye for the quirky, stylish and original, including beautiful shirts, throw pillows, jewellery, poster art and T-shirts, plus some offbeat items such as genuine Cambodian water-buffalo bells.

Psar Chaa   MARKET
(Old Market; Map p114; ⊗6am-9pm) When it comes to shopping in town, Psar Chaa is well stocked with anything you may want, and lots that you don't. Silverware, silk, wood carvings, stone carvings, Buddhas, paintings, rubbings, notes and coins, T-shirts, table mats...the list goes on. There are bargains to be had if you haggle patiently and humorously.

Sirivan   FASHION & ACCESSORIES
(Map p106; www.sirivan.asia; 10 Hup Guan St; ⊗8am-7pm) Established by French-Cambodian fashion designer Sirivan Chak Dumas, this shop has an elegant collection of women's and men's clothing in light linens and cottons, perfect for exploring the temples in high humidity. It also stocks high-tech travel accessories from Biniky (www.biniky.com).

Louise Labatieres   HOMEWARES
(Map p106; http://louiseloubatieres.com; 632 Hup Guan St; ⊗10am-7pm Mon-Sat) This little lifestyle boutique was the first to open on this strip, and it still offers a treasure trove of designer homewares in silk, cotton, lacquer and ceramics.

Jayav Art   ART
(Map p132; ☑089 787345; www.facebook.com/JayavArt; A25 Charles de Gaulle Blvd; ⊗7am-6pm) Have you been inspired by the beautiful Angkorian sculpture around the temples,

but lack the excess baggage space to transport replica statues home? Talk to Jayav Art, which specialises in exquisite papier-mâché replica sculptures in various sizes.

Samatoa FASHION & ACCESSORIES
(Map p140; www.samatoa.com; 11 Rd 63; ☺9am-5pm Mon-Sat) Samatoa experiments in organic fibres, blending silk and cotton with lotus to create 'the most spiritual fabric in the world'. Plants such as lotus and banana have natural fibres that create a softness and texture not found in pure silk or cotton. Order tailor-made clothes to measure or visit the lotus farm to learn about the process.

Tribe ART
(Map p106; Central Market St; ☺10am-6pm; ☞) This urban art gallery exhibits new collections from up-and-coming Cambodian artists and other collectables from here and there. It also has an on-site cafe and bar, so it's a good place to escape the heat, enjoy a cool drink and appreciate the art. Part of the Kandal village scene.

T Galleria FASHION & ACCESSORIES
(Map p106; ☎063-962511; www.dfs.com/en/siem-reap; 968 Charles de Gaulle Blvd; ☺9am-10pm; ☞) Located next to the Angkor National Museum, this is a flagship DFS duty-free shop that stocks everything from Paul Smith to Prada. It is extremely popular with Chinese visitors who flock here for discounted luxury items, but prices aren't particularly low compared with discount outlets back home.

Monument Books BOOKS
(Map p106; www.monument-books.com/bookshop; Pokambor Ave; ☺9am-9pm) Well-stocked bookstore near Psar Chaa, with an additional branch at the airport.

❶ Orientation

Siem Reap is still a small town at heart and is easy enough to navigate. The centre is around Psar Chaa (Old Market) and nearby Pub St, but accommodation is spread throughout town. National Hwy 6 (NH6) cuts across the northern part of town, passing Psar Leu (Main Market) in the east of town and the Royal Residence and the Grand Hotel d'Angkor in the centre, and then heads to the airport and beyond to the Thai border. The Siem Reap River (Stung Siem Reap) flows north–south through the centre of town, and has enough bridges that you won't have to worry too much about being on the wrong side. Street numbering is haphazard to say the least, so take care when hunting down specific addresses.

Angkor Wat and Angkor Thom are only 6km and 8km north of town respectively.

❶ Information

EMERGENCY
Fire (☎012 784464)
Hospital (☎063-761888)
Tourist police (☎012 402424)

INTERNET
Almost all accommodation providers, restaurants, cafes and bars offer free wi-fi now, so internet cafes have mostly disappeared, other than for the 24-hour use of local online gamers.

MEDICAL SERVICES
Siem Reap now has an international-standard hospital for emergencies. However, any serious complications will still require relocation to Bangkok.

Angkor Hospital for Children (AHC; Map p106; ☎063-963409; www.angkorhospital.org; cnr Oum Chhay & Tep Vong Sts; ☺24hr) This international-standard paediatric hospital is the place to take your children if they fall sick. It will also assist adults in an emergency for up to 24 hours. Donations accepted.

Royal Angkor International Hospital (Map p132; ☎063-761888; www.royalangkorhospital. com; Airport Rd) This international facility affiliated with the Bangkok Hospital is on the expensive side as it's used to dealing with insurance companies.

U-Care Pharmacy (Map p114; ☎063-965396; Pithnou St; ☺8am-10pm) Smart pharmacy and shop similar to Boots in Thailand (and the UK). English spoken.

MONEY
For cash exchanges, markets (usually at jewellery stalls or dedicated money-changing stalls) are faster and less bureaucratic than the banks.

ABA Bank (Map p106; Tep Vong St; ☺8.30am-3.30pm Mon-Fri, to 11.30am Sat) Withdrawals are limited to US$100 per transaction, and there is a US$4 transaction fee per withdrawal.

Canadia Bank (Map p106; Sivatha St; ☺8.30am-3.30pm Mon-Fri, to 11.30am Sat) Offers credit-card cash advances (US$4) and changes travellers cheques in most major currencies at a 2% commission.

J Trust Royal Bank (Map p106; Tep Vong St; ☺8.30am-3.30pm Mon-Fri, to 11.30am Sat) Does credit-card advances. Several branches and many ATMs (US$5 per withdrawal) around town.

POST
Main Post Office (Map p106; Pokambor Ave; ☺7am-5.30pm) Services are more reliable these days, but it doesn't hurt to see your

SHOPPING FOR A CAUSE

Several shops support Cambodia's disabled and disenfranchised through their production process or their profits. The shop at Peace Cafe (p121) sells a range of products produced by other do-good brands.

Artisans Angkor (Map p106; www.artisansdangkor.com; ⏱ 7.30am-6.30pm; 📞) On the premises of Les Chantiers Écoles (p105) is this beautiful shop, which sells everything from stone and wood reproductions of Angkorian-era statues to household furnishings. It also has a second shop opposite Angkor Wat in the Angkor Cafe building, and outlets at Phnom Penh and Siem Reap international airports.

All profits from sales go back into funding the school and bringing more young Cambodians into the training program, which is 20% owned by the artisans themselves.

AHA Fair Trade Village (Map p132; 🗐 078 341454; www.aha-kh.com; Rd 60, Trang village; ⏱ 10am-7pm) For locally produced souvenirs (unlike much of the imported stuff that turns up in Psar Chaa), drop in on this handicraft market. It's a little out of the way, but there are more than 20 stalls selling a wide range of traditional items. There's a Khmer cultural show every second and fourth Saturday of the month, with extra stalls, traditional music and dancing. Two-hour pottery classes are offered here through Mordock Ceramics, one of the stalls.

Soieries du Mekong (Map p106; www.soieriesdumekong.com; 668 Hup Guan St; ⏱ 10am-7pm) Soieries du Mekong is the Siem Reap gallery for a leading handwoven silk project based in remote Banteay Chhmar, which seeks to stem the tide of rural migration by creating employment opportunities in the village. Beautiful silk scarves and other delicate items are for sale.

Made in Cambodia Market (Map p106; www.facebook.com/madeincambodiamarket; Siem Reap River Rd East; ⏱ noon-10pm) King's Road hosts the daily Made in Cambodia community market, bringing together many of the best local craftsfolk and creators in Siem Reap, many promoting good causes.

Smateria (Map p114; www.smateria.com; Alley West; ⏱ 10am-10pm) Smateria makes recycling cool, with funky bags made from construction nets, plastic bags, motorbike seat covers and more. It's a fair-trade enterprise employing some disabled Cambodians.

Senteurs d'Angkor (Map p114; 🗐 063-964801; https://senteursdangkor.com; Sivatha St; ⏱ 7.30am-10.30pm) Relocated to Sivatha St, this shop has an eclectic collection of silk and carvings, as well as a superb range of traditional beauty products and spices, all made locally. It targets rural poor and disadvantaged Cambodians for jobs and training, and sources local products from farmers. Visit its Botanic Garden (p108) near the Angkor Golf Resort to sample infused teas and speciality coffees.

Susu (Map p106; www.susucambodia.com; Psar Chaa; ⏱ 1-10pm Mon-Fri, 2-10pm Sat & Sun) Good-cause store Susu sells handmade handicrafts, including tasteful cotton *krama* (checked scarves), leather sandals and handbags, to help women's training and employment in rural Cambodia.

Sra May (Map p106; 🗐 086 975425; 640 Hup Guan St; ⏱ 10am-6pm Mon-Sat) Sra May is a social enterprise that uses traditional local materials such as palm leaves to create boxes and artworks. It also specialises in handwoven *krama*. This is also the drop-in office to book the PURE! Countryside Bicycle Tour (p112).

Saomao (Map p114; 🗐 012 818130; http://saomao.com; St 9; ⏱ 8am-10pm Mon-Sat) A social enterprise selling wonderful jeweller. It also has a wide variety of additional gifts, including coconut art, original *krama* and silks, pepper, and elegant runners and wall hangings. Now part of the Made in Cambodia Market at King's Road.

IKTT (Institute for Khmer Traditional Textiles; Map p106; www.ikttearth.org; Tonlé Sap Rd; ⏱ 9am-5pm) This traditional wooden house is home to the Japanese-run Institute for Khmer Traditional Textiles, which sells fine *krama*, throws and more. It also operates a homestay out at its silk farm in Angkor Thom District.

stamps franked. Includes a branch of EMS express mail.

SAFE TRAVEL

Siem Reap is a pretty safe city, even at night, although it pays to stay in small groups if you are planning a drunken night out.

➡ If you rent a bike, don't keep your bag in the basket as it will be easy pickings.

➡ Children sell souvenirs around the temples; have patience and give a thought to their circumstances.

➡ Out at the remote temple sites beyond Angkor, stick to clearly marked trails. There are still landmines at locations such as Phnom Kulen and Koh Ker.

TOURIST INFORMATION

ConCERT (www.concertcambodia.org) Works to build bridges between tourists and good-cause projects in the Siem Reap/Angkor area, with information offices at Sister Srey Cafe (p117) and New Leaf Book Cafe (p118). It offers information on anything from ecotourism initiatives to volunteering opportunities.

Siem Reap Tourism Office (Map p106; ☑ 063-959600; Royal Gardens; ☺ 7am-5pm) Check out the swanky office in the Royal Gardens, which includes a branch of popular Thai coffee chain Inthanin.

ℹ️ Getting There & Away

AIR

All international flights arrive at the **Siem Reap International Airport** (Map p140; ☑ 063-962400; www.cambodia-airports.com), 7km west of the town centre. Facilities at the airport include cafes, restaurants, bookshops, international ATMs and money-changing services.

There are no direct flights between Cambodia and the West, so all visitors will end up transiting through an Asian hub. International flight links include Bangkok in Thailand; Vientiane, Luang Prabang and Pakse in Laos; Ho Chi Minh City (Saigon), Hanoi and Danang in Vietnam; Hong Kong; Kuala Lumpur in Malaysia; Beijing, Guangzhou, Kunming and Shanghai in China; Busan and Seoul in South Korea; Singapore; Taipei in Taiwan; and Manila in the Philippines.

Domestic links are currently limited to Phnom Penh and Sihanoukville. Airlines operating domestic flights include **Cambodia Angkor Air** (www.cambodiaangkorair.com), **Lanmei Airlines** (www.lanmeiairlines.com) and **JC International Airlines** (www.jcairlines.com). Demand for seats is high during peak season, so book as far in advance as possible.

BOAT

There are daily express boat services between Siem Reap and Phnom Penh (US$35, five to six hours) or Battambang (US$20, four to eight hours or more, depending on the season). The boat to Phnom Penh is rather overpriced these days, given it is just as fast by road and so much cheaper. The Battambang trip is seriously scenic, but breakdowns are *very* common.

Boats from Siem Reap leave from the floating village of Chong Kneas near Phnom Krom, about 11km south of Siem Reap. The boats dock in different places at different times of the year; when the lake recedes in the dry season, both the port and floating village move with it. An all-weather road has improved access around the lake area, but the main road out to the lake takes a pummelling in the annual monsoon.

Most of the guesthouses in town sell boat tickets. Buying the ticket from a guesthouse usually includes a *moto* or minibus ride to the port. Otherwise, a *moto* out there costs about US$3, a *remork* about US$7 and a taxi about US$15.

BUS

All buses officially depart from the **bus station and taxi park** (Map p132), which is 3km east of town and nearly 1km south of NH6. However, tickets are available at bus offices in town, guesthouses, hotels, travel agencies and ticket kiosks. Most bus companies depart from their in-town offices or send a minibus around to pick up passengers at their place of lodging. Upon arrival in Siem Reap, be prepared for a rugby scrum of eager *moto* drivers when getting off the bus at the main bus station.

Bus companies in Siem Reap:

Asia Van Transfer (AVT; Map p106; ☑ 063-963853; www.asiavantransfer.com; Hup Guan St) A daily express minivan departs at 8am to Stung Treng via Preah Vihear City (Tbeng Meanchey), with onward services from Stung Treng to Don Det (Laos), Ban Lung and Kratie.

Bayon VIP (Map p106; ☑ 063-966968; www.bayonvip.com; Wat Bo Rd) Express minivan services to Phnom Penh.

Capitol Tour (Map p114; ☑ 012 830170; www.capitoltourscambodia.com; St 9) Buses to destinations across Cambodia.

Giant Ibis (Map p106; ☑095 777809; www.giantibis.com; Sivatha St) Has free wi-fi on board.

Larryta Express (Map p132; ☑ 016 202020; http://larryta.com; 752 NH6) Smart Ford Transit minibuses to Phnom Penh hourly throughout the day.

Liang US Express (Map p132; ☑ 081 954546; Borey Seang Nam Rd) Has some direct buses to Kompong Cham.

Mekong Express (Map p106; ☑063-963662; www.catmekongexpress.com; 14 Sivatha St) Upmarket bus company with hostesses and drinks.

Mey Hong (Map p132; ☑ 095 777933; NH6) Express minivans to Phnom Penh.

Nattakan (Map p132; ☎ 070 877727; nattakan.sr@gmail.com; Concrete Drain Rd) The first operator, and still one of the most reliable, to do direct trips to Bangkok. It's out of the way, so request a free pickup.

Phnom Penh Sorya (PP Sorya; Map p132; ☎ 063-969097; https://ppsoryatransport.com.kh; Psar Krom Rd) Most extensive bus network in Cambodia.

Virak Buntham (Map p106; ☎ 017 790440; www.virakbuntham.com) The night-bus specialist to Phnom Penh and Sihanoukville.

Night buses are an option between Siem Reap and Phnom Penh, but leave as late as possible to avoid a middle-of-the-night arrival. Giant Ibis is the smartest operator servicing Phnom Penh (US$15, five hours), with four daytime and two overnight express services and free wi-fi on board.

Express minibus services to Phnom Penh (from US$10, four hours), such as those offered by Mey Hong, are popular as they can save considerable time compared with much slower buses. These services do have a reputation for speeding, however, and we strongly advise against using them at night. Larryta Express runs Ford Transit minivans hourly to Phnom Penh throughout the day.

Many companies advertise trips to Sihanoukville. These almost all involve a change of bus in Phnom Penh. This can work out well if you're taking a night bus, as the stop in Phnom Penh can help towards a more reasonable hour of arrival, but if you're travelling to Sihanoukville by day be prepared for a long journey. The Virak Buntham sleeper buses to Sihanoukville do not usually involve a bus change, for what it's worth. Advertised services to Kep and Kampot are even less reliable, and may involve a huge detour and a second change of bus in Sihanoukville. Ask about the routing and timing when making a booking.

For Ratanakiri, take the Asia Van Transfer minivan across Preah Vihear Province to Stung Treng and change there. For Mondulkiri, change in Kompong Cham; Liang US Express advertises this trip, with the transfer, or Virak Buntham has a service via Phnom Penh. Be aware that you are not guaranteed a comfortable or efficient onward trip after your transfer: we've heard plenty of horror stories.

CAR & SHARE TAXI

The road linking Siem Reap to Phnom Penh is in excellent shape and private cars can now do the journey in four hours, much of that on a divided four-lane highway. The roads west to Sisophon and north to Anlong Veng are also in great condition.

Share taxis and other vehicles operate along some of the main routes and these can be a little quicker than buses. Destinations include Phnom Penh (US$10, five hours), Kompong Thom (US$5, two hours), Sisophon (US$5, two hours) and Poipet (US$7, three hours). To get to the temple of Banteay Chhmar, head to Sisophon and arrange onward transport there (leave very early).

🛈 Getting Around

GETTING TO/FROM THE AIRPORT

Many hotels and guesthouses in Siem Reap offer a free airport pickup service with advance bookings. Official taxis/*remork-motos* are available next to the terminal for US$9/7. Book using a taxi app like Grab or PassApp and the price drops to US$5.25/3.50.

BICYCLE

Some guesthouses around town hire out bicycles, as do a few shops around Psar Chaa, usually for US$1 to US$2 a day.

The **White Bicycles** (www.thewhitebicycles.org; per day US$2) project rents bikes through over 50 guesthouses and hotels in Siem Reap, with all proceeds going towards supporting local development projects around town. Imported mountain bikes are available from cycling operators for around US$8 to US$10 per day.

Another option are the wonderful **Green e-bikes** (Map p106; ☎ 095 700130; www.greene-bike.com; Central Market; per 24hr US$11; ⊙ 7.30am-7pm), an environmentally sound compromise between bicycle and motorbike, with three charge points out at the temples and several more in the city. Several additional shops in the centre hire out electric bikes.

TRANSPORT CONNECTIONS TO SIEM REAP

DESTINATION	CAR & MOTORCYCLE	BUS	BOAT	AIR
Bangkok, Thailand	8hr	US$15-28, 10hr, frequent	N/A	US$50-150, 1hr, 8 daily
Battambang	3hr	US$5-8, 4hr, frequent	US$20, 6-8hr, 7am	N/A
Kompong Thom	2hr	US$5, 2hr, frequent	N/A	N/A
Phnom Penh	4-5hr	US$6-15, 5-6hr, frequent	US$35, 5hr, 7am	US$30-120, 30min, frequent
Poipet	3hr	US$5-8, 3hr, frequent	N/A	N/A

CAR & MOTORCYCLE

Most hotels and guesthouses can organise car hire for the day, with a going rate of US$35 and up. Upmarket hotels will charge more. Foreigners are technically forbidden to rent motorcycles in and around Siem Reap, but the rules have relaxed and motorbike hire is now widely available for about US$10. You can now even rent self-drive *remorks* through **Angkor e-Tuk Hostel** (Map p140; ☑088 770 7733; www.facebook.com/angkoretuk; Siem Reap River Rd East), which has a fleet of powerful, oversized electric *remorks* (per day US$24). You can easily drive these to outlying temples and back on a single charge.

MOTO

A *moto* (unmarked motorcycle taxi) with a driver will cost from US$10 per day depending on the destination. Far-flung temples will involve a higher fee. The average cost for a short trip within town is 2000r or so, and around US$1 or more to places strung out along the roads to Angkor or the airport. It is probably best to negotiate in advance as some drivers may otherwise overcharge.

TUK TUK

Remork-motos are sweet little motorcycles with carriages (commonly called *tuk tuks* around town), and are a nice way for couples to get about Siem Reap, although drivers like to inflate the prices. Trips around town start from US$2, but you'll need to pay more to reach the edge of town at night. Prices rise when you add three or more people. Another type of *tuk tuk* is the auto-rickshaw, and these tend to be a bit cheaper, but a lot more cramped and less breezy, as the driver has a protective windshield.

AROUND SIEM REAP

Let's be honest, most people are in Siem Reap to explore the majestic temples of Angkor, rightly regarded as the most spectacular collection of temples on earth. But there is more to this province than the awe-inspiring remnants of the Khmer empire. Siem Reap is emerging as a destination in itself, with a slew of stylish restaurants and an ever-growing bar scene centred on the infamous Pub St. Beyond Temple Town are a handful of impressive attractions, including the otherworldly floating and stilted villages of the Tonlé Sap and some high-profile bird sanctuaries that are home to rare large waterbirds. The province is also emerging as an accessible place to experience a homestay and a slice of local life in a traditional village. Throw in a hatful of remote jungle temples and sacred mountains, and it's best to extend your stay by a few days.

BUS CONNECTIONS FROM SIEM REAP

DESTINATION	DURATION (HR)	PRICE (US$)	COMPANIES	FREQUENCY
Bangkok (direct)	9	15-28	Mekong Express, Nattakan, Virak Buntham	morning only
Bangkok (with bus transfer)	10	10	Capitol Tour	8am
Battambang	3-4	4-6	Capitol Tour, Mekong Express, PP Sorya	frequent in the morning
Kompong Cham	5-6	6.50	Liang US Express	6.45am & 7.30am
Phnom Penh (bus)	6-7	6-15	Capitol Tour, Giant Ibis, Liang US Express, Mekong Express, PP Sorya, Virak Buntham (sleeper only)	frequent
Phnom Penh (minivan)	4-5	10-12	Capitol Tour, Bayon VIP Express, Larryta Express, Virak Buntham	frequent
Poipet	3	5-8	Capitol Tour	frequent in the morning
Preah Vihear City (via Kompong Thom)	5½	10	Liang US Express	2 daily
Sihanoukville	10-11	13-17	Capitol Tour, Virak Buntham	mostly night buses
Stung Treng	5	20	Asia Van Transfer	8am

ℹ INTERNATIONAL BUSES TO BANGKOK

There are a few direct services to Bangkok that do not involve a change of bus at the border, but most require a change. There are some 'night' buses to Bangkok advertised, but these are pretty pointless given the Poipet border does not open until 7am!

Nattakan (p129) is the original and still one of the most reliable operators servicing Bangkok. It has direct buses to Bangkok (US$28, 7½ hours, 8am and 9am), which include fast-track immigration at the border – potentially a big advantage during peak periods to bypass long lines.

Any advertised services to Ho Chi Minh City or Pakse or the Four Thousand Islands in southern Laos invariably involve a time-consuming transfer or two. For Pakse, you're best off taking a minivan to Stung Treng and changing there – Asia Van Transfer (p128) can sort you out with this. Note that any advertised *bus* trip to Laos will invariably take a six-hour detour through Kompong Cham, with a possible overnight in Kratie. You've been warned.

Banteay Srei District

Famous for its petite pink-coloured temple, there is more to Banteay Srei than its iconic Angkor sites, such as the 'River of a Thousand Lingas' at Kbal Spean and the 12th-century temple of Banteay Samré. New destinations and experiences, including homestays, village walks, ox-cart rides, fruit farms and handicraft workshops, are under development to encourage visitors to stay longer and explore further. It's a good area to explore on two wheels, either by motorbike from Siem Reap or by a bicycle rented via a local homestay.

◉ Sights

While the temples of the Banteay Srei District are the main attraction, make sure you also check out the Angkor Centre for Conservation of Biodiversity when visiting River of a Thousand Lingas at Kbal Spean (p172). Other activities include walks in the Kbal Teuk Community Forest, home to rare carnivorous pitcher plants.

★ Cambodia Landmine Museum   MUSEUM
(www.cambodialandminemuseum.org; NH67; US$5; ◷7.30am-5pm) 🖉 Established by DIY deminer Aki Ra, this museum has eye-opening displays on the curse of landmines in Cambodia. The collection includes mines, mortars, guns and weaponry, and there is a mock minefield where visitors can attempt to locate the deactivated mines. Proceeds from the museum are ploughed into mine-awareness campaigns. The museum is about 25km from Siem Reap, near Banteay Srei.

Angkor Centre for Conservation
of Biodiversity   WILDLIFE RESERVE
(ACCB; 🗷099 604017; www.accb-cambodia.org; donation US$3; ◷tours 9am & 1pm Mon-Sat; 🖈) donation US$3; ◷tours 9am & 1pm Mon-Sat; 🖈) Conveniently located at the base of the trail to Kbal Spean is the Angkor Centre for Conservation of Biodiversity, which is committed to rescuing, rehabilitating and releasing threatened wildlife into Cambodian forests. It also operates conservation breeding programs for selected threatened species in an attempt to preserve them from extinction. Daily tours (in English) are available at 9am and 1pm (except Sunday), taking about 1½ hours.

The centre takes care of about 45 species totalling more than 550 animals. It is possible to see pileated gibbon, Indochinese silvered langur, several turtle and tortoise species, green peafowl, small carnivores and a variety of birds of prey. There are also several large wading birds, including the impressive sarus crane and one of the largest collections of threatened storks in the world.

A minimum donation of US$3 per person is requested. Tours outside core hours and special private tours are available upon request at variable costs. It is recommended to book tours in advance by phone or email. Note that you don't need an Angkor pass to visit ACCB, only to visit Kbal Spean.

Banteay Srei
Butterfly Centre   WILDLIFE RESERVE
(ស្ទូនមេអំបៅបន្លាយស្រី; www.angkorbutterfly.com; NH67; adult/child US$5/2; ◷9am-5pm) 🖉 The Banteay Srei Butterfly Centre is one of the largest fully enclosed butterfly centres in Southeast Asia, with more than 30 species of Cambodian butterflies fluttering about. It is a good experience for children, as they can see the whole life cycle from egg to caterpillar to cocoon to butterfly.

Around Siem Reap

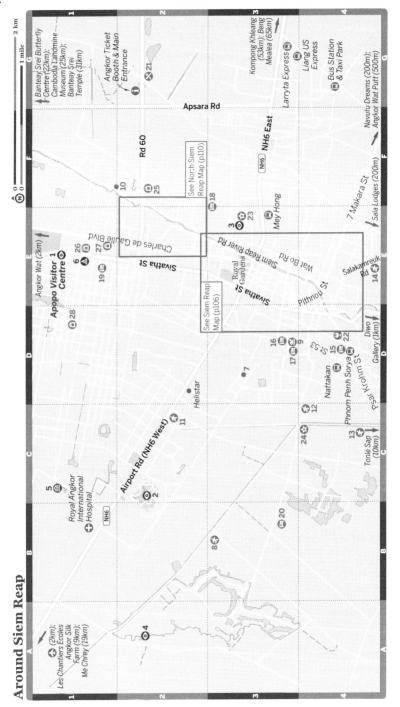

Banteay Srei Butterfly Centre (22km); Cambodia Landmine Museum (25km); Banteay Srei Temple (31km)

Angkor Ticket Booth & Main Entrance

Apsara Rd

Rd 60

NH6 East

NH6

Kompong Khleang (53km); Beng Mealea (65km)

Larryta Express

Liang US Express

Bus Station & Taxi Park

Navutu Dreams (200m); Angkor Wat Putt (500m)

7 Makara St

Sala Lodges (200m)

See North Siem Reap Map (p110)

Mey Hong

Salakamreuk Rd

Charles de Gaulle Blvd

Angkor Wat (2km)

Apopo Visitor Centre

Siem Reap River Rd

Wat Bo Rd

See Siem Reap Map (p106)

Royal Gardens

Sivatha St

Pithnou St

Diwo Gallery (1km)

Nattakan

Phnom Penh Sorya

Psar Krohm St

St 53

Helistar

Airport Rd (NH6 West)

Royal Angkor International Hospital

NH6

Tonlé Sap (10km)

Les Chantiers Écoles (2km); Angkor Silk Farm (9km); Me Chrey (19km)

N

0   1 mile
0   2 km

Around Siem Reap

◎ **Top Sights**
1 Apopo Visitor Centre E1

◎ **Sights**
2 Cambodian Cultural Village C2
3 Cambolac E3
4 Senteurs d'Angkor Botanic
   Garden A2
5 War Museum C1
6 Wat Thmei E1

◉ **Activities, Courses & Tours**
7 Angkor Fight Club D3
8 Angkor Golf Resort B3
9 Cambo Beach Club D3
10 Cambodia Bokator Academy F1
11 Great Escape C2
12 Happy Ranch C4
   Helistar .... (see 11)
13 Quad Adventure Cambodia C4
14 Siem Reap Quad Bike Adventure E4

⬢ **Sleeping**
15 Baby Elephant Boutique Hotel D4
16 Funky Flashpacker D3
17 Hideout Hostel D3
18 Maison Polanka E3
19 Pavillon Indochine E1
20 Phum Baitang B3

⊗ **Eating**
21 Road 60 Night Market G2

◉ **Drinking & Nightlife**
22 Harbour D4

◉ **Entertainment**
23 New Cambodian Artists E3
24 Phare the Cambodian Circus C4

◉ **Shopping**
25 AHA Fair Trade Village F2
26 Eric Raisina Couture House E1
27 Jayav Art E1
28 Theam's House D1

The centre aims to provide a sustainable living for the rural poor and most of the butterflies are farmed around Phnom Kulen. It's about 7km before Banteay Srei temple on the left side of the road.

⫶ Sleeping

Tbeng Village Homestays HOMESTAY **$**
(☎ 092 966047; Tbeng village; house US$15) Tbeng is a pretty little village in the east of Banteay Srei where local schoolteacher Mr

Khuon has set up a homestay project with around a dozen houses. Try for a house with a tiled roof, as it's cooler than corrugated metal. Mattresses and bedding are provided together with a mosquito net.

Bayon Smile Homestay HOMESTAY **$**
(☎ 011 985069; sarouensean@gmail.com; Banteay Srei village; s/d US$10/15) Run by the enthusiastic Mr Sarouen, this group of spacious and attractive village homes is set just north of Banteay Srei temple. Guests sleep on mattresses under mosquito nets upstairs. Lots of activities are promoted here, including woodcarving, village tours, cycling and some more adventurous treks to remote sites such as Phnom Cheur and Phnom Hop.

Bong Thom Home Stay HOMESTAY **$$$**
(☎ 012 520092; www.thebongthomhomestay.com; NH67; r US$70-170; ⊛⊠) Very much a boutique homestay, Bong Thom offers some beautiful wooden houses in the countryside complete with four-poster beds and tasteful decor. Lots of activities are available, including cooking classes, cycling and ox-cart rides. The restaurant here is well regarded and open to nonguests with an advance booking. An infinity pool with views over the rice fields was recently added.

✗ Eating

★**Naom Banchok Noodle Stalls** NOODLES **$**
(Preah Dak village; noodles 4000r; ⊗ 6am-6pm) Preah Dak village is renowned for its *naom banchok* stalls, which hug the main road to Banteay Srei. These homemade noodles come with a mild fish broth or chicken curry, plus an assortment of vegetables.

Borey Sovann Restaurant CAMBODIAN **$**
(☎ 012 224115; NH67; meals US$3-8; ⊗ 11am-6pm; ⊛) The inviting Borey Sovann Restaurant, located near the entrance to Kbal Spean, is a great place to wind down before or after an ascent to the River of a Thousand Lingas. The menu includes a full range of Cambodian dishes, plus a smattering of Chinese, Thai and international options.

Devatas CAMBODIAN **$$**
(☎ 011 292142; www.devatas-restaurant.com; NH67; mains US$4.50-9; ⊗ 10.30am-4pm; ⊛) From the team behind Sugar Palm in Siem Reap, Devatas is set in an idyllic country garden by a pretty lake and is the perfect

place to unwind before or after a visit to Banteay Srei temple. The menu includes many Sugar Palm favourites such as Khmer curry and *lok lak* (traditional beef dish).

ℹ Information

For more on community-based tourism in Banteay Srei District, head to www.visitbanteaysrei.org.

ℹ Getting There & Away

Banteay Srei is about 32km northeast of Siem Reap on good roads. It should take about 45 minutes to reach by car or one hour by *remork-moto;* agree to a price before setting off. As a rough guide, it will cost US$10/20/40 by *moto/remork/*car, but it really depends on the exact destinations on your itinerary.

Kompong Khleang

One of the largest communities on the Tonlé Sap, Kompong Khleang (កំពង់ឃ្លាំង) is more of a town than the other villages, and comes complete with several ornate pagodas. Most of the houses here are built on towering stilts to allow for a dramatic change in water level. There is only a small floating community on the lake, but the stilted town is an interesting place to browse for an hour or two. Fewer tourists visit here compared with the floating villages closer to Siem Reap, so that might be a reason to visit in itself.

St 63 Homestay   HOMESTAY $$
(☏012 241966; www.facebook.com/kampong khleanghomestay; per night incl meals US$45; ☁) This boutique homestay is rented out in its entirety. It is an attractive wooden house on stilts with some extra love and care put into the furnishings, with a wooden swing bed and an international-standard bathroom.

ℹ Getting There & Away

Kompong Khleang is about 50km from Siem Reap and not difficult to reach thanks to an all-weather road via the junction town of Dam Dek. The trip takes around an hour and costs about US$60 return by taxi; it's a longer ride by *remork-moto,* but should be around US$25 to US$30.

Prek Toal Bird Sanctuary

Prek Toal is one of three biospheres on the Tonlé Sap lake, and this stunning **bird sanctuary** (ជម្រកសត្វស្លាបបឹកព្រែកទាល់; US$20; ☉6am-6pm) 🕊 makes it the most

worthwhile and straightforward of the three to visit. It's an ornithologist's fantasy, with a significant number of rare breeds gathered in one small area, including the huge lesser and greater adjutant storks, the milky stork and the spot-billed pelican. Even the uninitiated will be impressed, as these birds have a huge wingspan and build enormous nests.

During the peak season (December to early February), visitors will find the concentration of birds like something out of a Hitchcock film. As water starts to dry up elsewhere, the birds congregate here. The birds remain beyond February but the sanctuary becomes virtually inaccessible due to low water levels. It is also possible to visit from September, but the bird numbers may be lower. Serious twitchers know that the best time to see birds is early morning or late afternoon and this means an early start or an overnight at Prek Toal's environment office, where there is very basic accommodation (single/double bed US$15/20).

Several ecotourism companies in Siem Reap arrange trips out to Prek Toal including the Sam Veasna Center (p111), Cambodia Bird Guide Association (p111), Osmose (p111) and **Prek Toal Tours & Travel** (☏077 797112; www.prektoal-tours.com; birdwatching per person in group of 5/2 US$65/128), which is run by Prek Toal villagers. Tours include transport, entrance fees, guides, breakfast, lunch and water. Binoculars are available on request, plus the Sam Veasna Center has spotting scopes that they set up at observation towers within the park. All outfits can arrange overnight trips for serious enthusiasts. Day trips include a hotel pickup at around 6am and a return by nightfall.

Getting to the sanctuary under your own steam requires you to take a 20-minute *moto* (US$3 or so) or taxi (US$15 one way) ride to the floating village of Chong Kneas (depending on the time of day additional fees may have to be paid at the new port), and then a boat to the environment office (around US$60 return, one hour each way). From here, a small boat (US$30 including a park guide) will take you into the sanctuary, which is about one hour beyond. The park guides are equipped with booklets with the bird names in English, but they speak little English themselves, hence the advantage of visiting with a tour company that provides English-speaking guides.

Trips to the sanctuary also bring you up close and personal with the fascinating floating village of Prek Toal, a much more rewarding destination than over-touristed, scam-ridden Chong Kneas closer to Siem Reap. Part of your entrance to the sanctuary goes towards educating children and villagers about the importance of the birds and the unique flooded-forest environment.

Always bring sunscreen and head protection to Prek Toal, as it's a long day in boats and the sun can be relentless.

Kompong Pluk

The village of Kompong Pluk (ភូមិលិចទឹកកំពង់ភ្លុក; boat trip per person US$20, community fee US$2) is a friendly, otherworldly place where houses are built on soaring stilts about 6m high. Nearby is a flooded forest, inundated every year when the lake rises to take the Mekong's overflow. As the lake drops, the petrified trees are revealed like something out of Grimm's Tales. Exploring this area by wooden dugout in the wet season is very atmospheric.

Best visited from July to December when there is high water in the lake, it is a very different scene in the dry season months of January to June, although it is very rewarding to explore the dry flooded forest on foot as it looks like something out of a fairy tale.

Prices to visit have been fixed rather high, and when you add up all the separate costs, it may work out cheaper to sign up to a budget tour out of Siem Reap. If you are unlucky enough to come alone, you may be charged US$30, but have the option to link up with other independent travellers. There are a couple of basic homestays in Kompong Pluk and lots of good floating restaurants for lunch or a snack. There is also the incredible Kompong Pluk Riverside Restaurant built on stilts over the flooded forest with an extensive wooden walkway passing through the treetops, but it is looking somewhat dilapidated these days.

The most popular way to get here is via the small town of Roluos by a combination of road (about US$10/15/30 by moto/remork/taxi) and then boat. All said, the road-and-boat route will take up to two hours, but it depends on the season – sometimes it's more by road, sometimes more by boat. The new road brings the dry season access time to around one hour. Tara Boat

(☎ 092 957765; www.taraboat.com; per person incl lunch/dinner US$29/36) also offers day trips here from US$38 per person. The other option is to come via the floating village of Chong Kneas, where a boat (1¼ hours, from US$55 return) can be arranged.

Me Chrey

One of the more recently 'discovered' floating villages, Me Chrey (មេជ្រៃ; boat trip per person from US$18, entrance fee US$1) lies midway between Siem Reap and Prek Toal. It is one of the smaller villages in the area but sees far fewer tourists than busy Chong Kneas. Arrange transport by road (moto/remork/taxi around US$10/20/30) before switching to a boat to explore the area.

Me Chrey moves with the water level and is prettier during the wet season, when houses are anchored around an island pagoda. It is located to the south of Puok District, about 25km from Siem Reap, on a pretty dirt road through lush rice fields if you are travelling between July and November.

Unique Kayak Cambodia   KAYAKING
(☎ 012 766971; http://uniquekayakcambodia.com; half day US$70-115, full day US$100-150) Unique Kayak Cambodia offers kayaking trips to explore the flooded forest near Me Chrey and paddle around the village. The flooded forest is really beautiful and it's possible to spot some waterbirds. A half day is probably enough unless you are an Olympic paddler. Tours include all car and boat transfers (so they're reasonably priced if you have a group), and stop at the Artisans Angkor Silk Farm in Puok District.

Floating Village of Chong Kneas

The famous floating village of Chong Kneas (ចុងឃ្នាស; boat trip per person US$20, entrance fee US$3) has become somewhat of a circus in recent years. Tour groups have taken over and there are countless scams to separate tourists from their money. In-the-know travellers opt for harder-to-reach but more memorable spots such as Kompong Khleang (p134) or Prek Toal (p134).

For all its flaws, Chong Kneas is very scenic in the warm light of late afternoon and can be combined with a sunset from the nearby hilltop temple of Phnom Krom.

KHNAR PO HOMESTAYS

There are 12 **homestays** (☏061 947105; khnarpocommunity@gmail.com; Khnar Po village; per person US$5) in Khnar Po village, and they have received support from a local tour operator to help improve standards. The community includes a best practice 'model' homestay, and the host families are known for the quality of their home-cooking (breakfast/meals US$3/6). Guests sleep on mattresses under a mosquito net. Activities include village walks and ox-cart rides.

Avoid the crowds by asking your boat driver to take you down some back channels. Boat prices are fixed at US$20 per person, plus a US$3 entrance fee (although in practice it may be possible to pay just US$20 for the boat shared between several people). Your boat driver will invariably try to take you to an overpriced floating restaurant and souvenir shop, but there is no obligation to buy anything.

One of the best ways to visit the floating village of Chong Kneas is to hook up with the Tara Boat, which offers all-inclusive trips with a meal aboard its converted cargo boat. Prices include transfers, entry fees, local boats, a tour guide and a two-course meal.

To get to Chong Kneas from Siem Reap costs US$3 by *moto* each way (more if the driver waits), or US$15 or so by taxi. The round trip, including the village visit, takes two to three hours. Alternatively, rent a bicycle in town and just pedal out here, as it is a leisurely 11km through pretty villages and rice fields.

Visitors arriving by boat from Phnom Penh or Battambang get a sneak preview, as the floating village is near Phnom Krom, where the boat docks.

Ang Trapaeng Thmor Reserve

This **bird sanctuary** (អាងត្រពាំងថ្ម; US$10) 🐾 is one of only a handful of places in the world where it's possible to see the extremely rare sarus crane, as depicted on bas-reliefs at Bayon. Reputedly the tallest bird in the world, these grey-feathered birds have immensely long legs and striking red heads. Sam Veasna Center (p111) arranges birdwatching excursions (from US$130 per person with a group of five) out here, which is probably the easiest way to undertake the trip.

The sanctuary is based around a reservoir created by forced labour during the Khmer Rouge regime, and facilities are very basic, but it is an incredibly beautiful place. Bring your own binoculars, as none are available.

The bird sanctuary is just across the border in the Phnom Srok region of Banteay Meanchey Province, about 100km from Siem Reap. To reach here, follow the road to Sisophon for about 72km before turning north at Prey Mon. It's 22km to the site, passing through some famous silk-weaving villages.

Temples of Angkor

Includes ➡

Angkor Wat 150
Angkor Thom 156
Small Circuit 161
Big Circuit 165
Roluos Temples 167
Banteay Srei 169
Beng Mealea 170
Phnom Kulen 171
Kbal Spean 172
Banteay Samré 173
Koh Ker 174

Best Places to Eat

➡ Angkor Cafe (p155)

➡ Devatas (p133)

➡ Naom Banchok Noodle Stalls (p133)

➡ Natural Vegetable Food Place (p169)

Best Places to Stay

➡ Angkor Rural Boutique Hotel (p169)

➡ Bong Thom Home Stay (p133)

➡ Khnar Po Homestays (p136)

Why Go?

Welcome to heaven on earth. Angkor (ប្រាសាទអង្គរ) is the earthly representation of Mt Meru, the Mt Olympus of the Hindu faith and the abode of ancient gods. The temples are the perfect fusion of creative ambition and spiritual devotion. The Cambodian 'god-kings' of old each strove to better their ancestors in size, scale and symmetry, culminating in the world's largest religious building, Angkor Wat.

The temples of Angkor are a source of inspiration and national pride to all Khmers as they struggle to rebuild their lives after the years of terror and trauma. Today, the temples are a point of pilgrimage for all Cambodians, and no traveller to the region will want to miss their extravagant beauty. Angkor is one of the world's foremost ancient sites, with the epic proportions of the Great Wall of China, the detail and intricacy of the Taj Mahal, and the symbolism and symmetry of the pyramids, all rolled into one.

Don't Miss

➡ Angkor Wat (p150) Watching the sun rise over the holiest of holies, Angkor Wat, the world's largest religious building.

➡ Bayon (p156) Contemplating the serenity and splendour of Bayon, its 216 enigmatic faces staring out into the jungle.

➡ Ta Prohm (p162) Witnessing nature reclaiming the stones at this mysterious ruin, the *Tomb Raider* temple.

➡ Banteay Srei (p169) Staring in wonder at the delicate carvings adorning Banteay Srei, the finest seen at Angkor.

➡ Kbal Spean (p172) Trekking deep into the jungle to discover the 'River of a Thousand Lingas'.

➡ Beng Mealea (p170) Exploring the tangled vines, crumbling corridors and jumbled sandstone blocks.

History

The Angkorian period spans more than 600 years from CE 802 to 1432. This incredible age saw the construction of the temples of Angkor and the consolidation of the Khmer empire's position as one of the great powers in Southeast Asia. This era encompassed periods of decline and revival, and wars with rival powers in Vietnam, Thailand and Myanmar.

The hundreds of temples surviving today are but the sacred skeleton of the vast political, religious and social centre of Cambodia's ancient Khmer empire, a city that, at its zenith, boasted a population of one million when London was a small town of 50,000. The houses, public buildings and palaces of Angkor were constructed of wood – now long decayed – because the right to dwell in structures of brick or stone was reserved for the gods.

An Empire is Born

The Angkorian period began with the rule of Jayavarman II (r 802–50). He was the first to unify Cambodia's competing kingdoms before the birth of Angkor. His court was situated at various locations, including Phnom Kulen, 40km northeast of Angkor Wat, and Roluos (known then as Hariharalaya), 13km east of Siem Reap.

Jayavarman II proclaimed himself a *devaraja* (god-king), the earthly representative of the Hindu god Shiva, and built a 'temple-mountain' at Phnom Kulen, symbolising

VISITOR CODE OF CONDUCT

While the temples of Angkor are not a million miles away from the beaches of the South Coast, it is important to remember that the temples of Angkor represent a sacred religious site to the Khmer people, and the authorities have begun cracking down on inappropriate dress at the temples. Expect to be sent back to your guesthouse to change if you are wearing sleeveless tops, hot pants or short skirts. Local authorities have recently released visitor 'code of conduct' guidelines and a video to encourage dressing appropriately, as well as reminding tourists not to touch or sit on the ancient structures, to pay attention to restricted areas, and to be respectful of monks.

Shiva's dwelling place of Mt Meru, the holy mountain at the centre of the universe. This set a precedent that became a dominant feature of the Angkorian period and accounts for the staggering architectural productivity of the Khmers at this time.

Indravarman I (r 877–89) is believed to have been a usurper, and probably inherited the mantle of *devaraja* through conquest. He built a 6.5-sq-km *baray* (reservoir) at Roluos and established Preah Ko. The *baray* was the first stage of an irrigation system that created a hydraulic city, the ancient Khmers mastering the cycle of nature to water their lands. Form and function worked together in harmony, as the *baray* also had religious significance, representing the oceans surrounding Mt Meru. Indravarman's final work was Bakong, a pyramidal representation of Mt Meru.

Indravarman I's son Yasovarman I (r 889–910) looked further afield to celebrate his divinity and glory in a temple-mountain of his own. He first built Lolei on an artificial island in the *baray* established by his father, before beginning work on the Bakheng. Today this hill is known as Phnom Bakheng, a favoured spot for viewing the sunset over Angkor Wat. A raised highway was constructed to connect Phnom Bakheng with Roluos, 16km to the southeast, and a large *baray* was constructed to the east of Phnom Bakheng. Today it is known as the Eastern Baray but has entirely silted up. Yasovarman I also established the temple-mountains of Phnom Krom and Phnom Bok.

After the death of Yasovarman I, power briefly shifted from the Angkor region to Koh Ker, around 80km to the northeast, under another usurper king, Jayavarman IV (r 924–42). In CE 944 power returned again to Angkor under the leadership of Rajendravarman II (r 944–68), who built the Eastern Mebon and Pre Rup. The reign of his son Jayavarman V (r 968–1001) produced the temples Ta Keo and Banteay Srei, the latter built by a Brahman rather than the king.

The Golden Age of Angkor

The temples that are now the highlight of a visit to Angkor – Angkor Wat and those in and around the walled city of Angkor Thom – were built during the golden age or classical period. While this period is marked by fits of remarkable productivity, it was also a time of turmoil, conquests and setbacks. The great city of Angkor Thom owes its existence to the fact that the old city of Angkor, which stood on the same site, was destroyed during the Cham invasion of 1177.

Suryavarman I (r 1002–49) was a usurper to the throne who rose to power through strategic alliances and military conquests. Although he adopted the Hindu cult of the god-king, he is thought to have come from a Mahayana Buddhist tradition and may even have sponsored the growth of Buddhism in Cambodia. Buddhist sculpture certainly became more commonplace in the Angkor region during his time.

Little physical evidence of Suryavarman I's reign remains at Angkor, but his military exploits brought much of central Thailand and southern-central Laos under the control of Angkor. His son Udayadityavarman II (r 1049–65) embarked on further military expeditions, extending the empire once more, and building Baphuon and the Western Mebon. Many major cities in the Mekong region were important Khmer settlements in the 11th and 12th centuries, including the Lao capital of Vientiane and the Thai city of Lopburi.

From 1066 until the end of the century, Angkor was again divided as rival factions contested the throne. The first important monarch of this new era was Suryavarman II (r 1112–52), who unified Cambodia and extended Khmer influence to Malaya and Burma (Myanmar). He also set himself apart religiously from earlier kings through his devotion to the Hindu deity Vishnu, to whom he consecrated the largest and arguably most magnificent of all the Angkorian temples, Angkor Wat.

The reign of Suryavarman II and the construction of Angkor Wat signifies one of the high-water marks of Khmer civilisation. However, there were signs that decline was lurking. It is thought that the hydraulic system of reservoirs and canals that supported the agriculture of Angkor had by this time been pushed beyond its limits, and was slowly starting to silt up due to overpopulation and deforestation. The construction of Angkor Wat was a major strain on resources, and, on top of this, Suryavarman II led a disastrous campaign against the Dai Viet (Vietnamese) late in his reign, during the course of which he was killed in battle.

Enter Jayavarman VII

In 1177 the Chams of southern Vietnam, then the Kingdom of Champa and long annexed by the Khmer empire, rose up and sacked Angkor. This attack caught the Khmers com-

TEMPLE ADDICTS

The god-kings of Angkor were dedicated builders. Each king was expected to dedicate a temple to his patron god, most commonly Shiva or Vishnu, during the time of Angkor. Then there were the ancestors, including mother, father and grandparents (both maternal and paternal), which meant another half dozen temples or more. Finally there was the mausoleum or king's temple, intended to deify the monarch and project his power, and each of these had to be bigger and better than one's predecessor. This accounts for the staggering architectural productivity of the Khmers at this time and the epic evolution of temple architecture.

pletely unawares, as it came via sea, river and lake rather than the traditional land routes. The Chams burnt the wooden city and plundered its wealth. Four years later Jayavarman VII (r 1181–1219) struck back, emphatically driving the Chams out of Cambodia and reclaiming Angkor.

Jayavarman VII's reign has given scholars much to debate. It represents a radical departure from the reigns of his predecessors. For centuries the fount of royal divinity had reposed in the Hindu deity Shiva (and, occasionally, Vishnu). Jayavarman VII adopted Mahayana Buddhism and looked to Avalokiteshvara, the Bodhisattva of Compassion, for patronage during his reign. In doing so he may well have been converting to a religion that already enjoyed wide popular support among his subjects. It may also be that the destruction of Angkor was such a blow to royal divinity that a new religious foundation was thought to be needed.

During his reign, Jayavarman VII embarked on a dizzying array of temple projects that centred on Baphuon, which was the site of the capital city destroyed by the Chams. Angkor Thom, Jayavarman VII's new city, was surrounded by walls and a moat, which became another component of Angkor's complex irrigation system. The centrepiece of Angkor Thom was Bayon, the temple-mountain studded with faces that, along with Angkor Wat, is the most famous of Cambodia's temples. Other temples built during his reign include Ta Prohm, Banteay Kdei and Preah Khan. Further away, he

Temples of Angkor

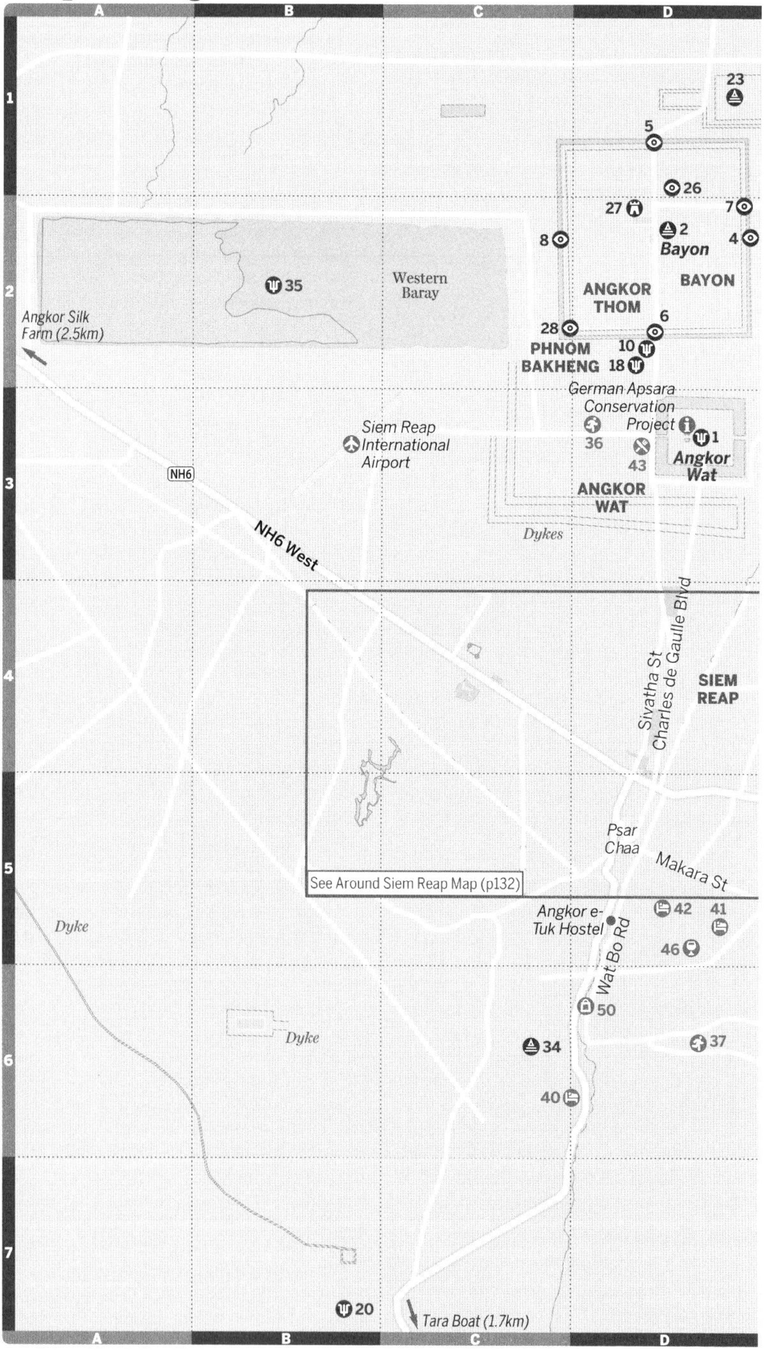

23

5

26

27 7

8 2 4
Bayon BAYON

ANGKOR THOM

35 Western Baray

Angkor Silk Farm (2.5km)

28 6

10

PHNOM BAKHENG 18

German Apsara Conservation Project

36 1

Siem Reap International Airport

43 *Angkor Wat*

ANGKOR WAT

NH6

NH6 West

Dykes

Charles de Gaulle Blvd

Sivatha St

SIEM REAP

Psar Chaa Makara St

See Around Siem Reap Map (p132)

Angkor e-Tuk Hostel 42 41

46

Wat Bo Rd

50

Dyke

34

Dyke

37

40

20 Tara Boat (1.7km)

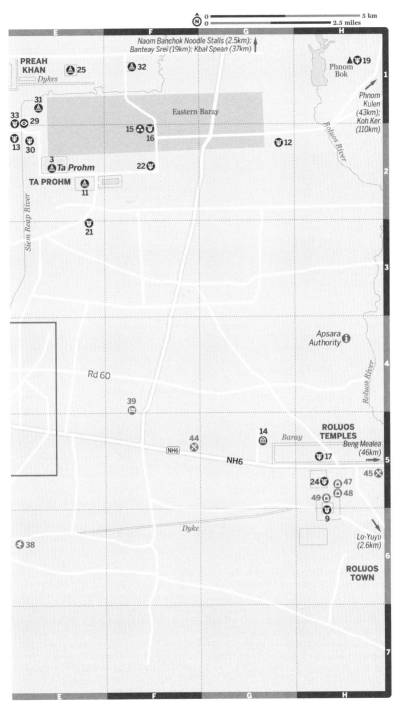

Temples of Angkor

◎ Top Sights
1 Angkor Wat D3
2 Bayon...D2
3 Ta Prohm...E2

◎ Sights
4 Angkor Thom East Gate...................D2
5 Angkor Thom North Gate.................. D1
6 Angkor Thom South Gate D2
7 Angkor Thom Victory Gate D2
8 Angkor Thom West Gate...................C2
  Army of Suryavarman II ....(see 1)
9 Bakong..H6
10 Baksei Chamkrong............................D2
11 Banteay Kdei & Sra Srang E2
12 Banteay Samré..................................G2
  Baphuon .... (see 27)
  Battle of Kurukshetra ....(see 1)
  Battle of Lanka ....(see 1)
  Battle of the Gods & the
    Demons ....(see 1)
13 Chau Say Tevoda E2
  Churning of the Ocean of Milk........(see 1)
14 CMAC Peace Museum of Mine
  Action..G5
15 Eastern Baray F2
16 Eastern Mebon F2
  Heaven & Hell ....(see 1)
  Kleangs & Prasat Suor Prat .... (see 26)
  Krishna & the Demon King..............(see 1)
17 Lolei..H5
18 Phnom Bakheng.................................D2
19 Phnom Bok..H1
20 Phnom Krom..B7
  Prasat Chrung ....(see 28)
21 Prasat Kravan E3
22 Pre Rup...F2
23 Preah Khan.. D1
24 Preah Ko...H5
25 Preah Neak Poan................................E1
  Preah Palilay .... (see 27)

26 Preah Pithu...D1
27 Royal Enclosure & Phimeanakas..........D2
28 Run Ta Dev...C2
29 Spean Thmor...................................... E1
30 Ta Keo E2
31 Ta Nei E1
32 Ta Som... F1
  Terrace of Elephants...................(see 27)
  Terrace of the Leper King............(see 27)
33 Thommanon.. E1
  Vishnu Conquers the Demons........(see 1)
34 Wat Athvea C6
35 Western Baray & Western Mebon........ B2

◎ Activities, Courses & Tours
36 Angkor Balloon..................................D3
37 Angkor Wat Putt D6
  Angkor Zipline .... (see 31)
38 Cambodia Quad Bike E6

◎ Sleeping
39 Angkor Rural Boutique Hotel F4
40 Green Home I D6
41 Navutu Dreams D5
42 Sala Lodges D5

◎ Eating
43 Angkor Cafe D3
  Angkor Reach Restaurant ....(see 43)
  Khmer Angkor Restaurant ....(see 43)
44 Natural Vegetable Food Place F5
45 Stoeng Trorcheak Restaurant H5

◎ Drinking & Nightlife
46 Sombai...D5

◎ Shopping
47 Dy Proeung Master Sculptor...............H5
48 Khmer Group Art of Weaving...............H5
49 Prolung Khmer....................................H5
50 Samatoa...D6

rebuilt vast temple complexes, such as Banteay Chhmar and Preah Khan in Preah Vihear Province, making him by far the most prolific builder of Angkor's many kings.

Jayavarman VII also embarked on a major public-works program, building roads, schools and hospitals across the empire. Remains of many of these roads and their magnificent bridges can be seen across Cambodia. Spean Praptos at Kompong Kdei, 65km southeast of Siem Reap on National Hwy 6 (NH6), is the most famous, but there are many more lost in the forest on the old Angkorian road to the great Preah Khan, including the now accessible Spean Ta Ong, about 28km east of Beng Mealea near the village of Khvau.

After the death of Jayavarman VII around 1219, the Khmer empire went into decline. The state religion reverted to Hinduism for a century or more and outbreaks of iconoclasm saw Buddhist sculpture adorning Hindu temples vandalised or altered. The Thais sacked Angkor in 1351, and again with devastating efficiency in 1431. The glorious Siamese capital of Ayuthaya, which enjoyed a golden age from the 14th to the 18th centuries, was in many ways a recreation of the glories of Angkor from which the Thai conquerors drew inspiration. The Khmer court moved to Phnom Penh, only to return fleetingly to Angkor in the 16th century; in the meantime, it was abandoned to pilgrims, holy men and the elements.

Angkor 'Rediscovered'

The French 'discovery' of Angkor in the 1860s made an international splash and created a great deal of outside interest in Cambodia. But 'discovery', with all the romance it implied, was something of a misnomer. When French explorer Henri Mouhot first stumbled across Angkor Wat on his Royal Geographic Society expedition, it included a wealthy, working monastery with monks and slaves. Moreover, Portuguese travellers in the 16th century encountered Angkor, referring to it as the Walled City. Diego do Couto produced an accurate description of Angkor in 1614, but it was not published until 1958. A 17th-century Japanese pilgrim drew a detailed plan of Angkor Wat, though he mistakenly recalled that he had seen it in India.

Still, it was the publication of *Voyage à Siam et dans le Cambodge* by Mouhot, posthumously released in 1868, that first brought Angkor to the public eye. Although the explorer himself made no such claims, by the 1870s he was being celebrated as the discoverer of the lost temple-city of Cambodia. In fact, a French missionary known as Charles-Emile Bouillevaux had visited Angkor 10 years before Mouhot and had published an account of his own findings. However, the Bouillevaux account was roundly ignored and it was Mouhot's account, with its rich descriptions and tantalising pen-and-ink colour sketches of the temples, that turned the ruins into an international obsession.

Soon after Mouhot, other adventurers and explorers began to arrive. Scottish photographer John Thomson took the first photographs of the temples in 1866. He was the first Westerner to posit the idea that they were symbolic representations of the mythical Mt Meru. French architect Lucien Fournereau travelled to Angkor in 1887 and produced plans and meticulously executed cross-sections that were to stand as the best available until the 1960s.

From this time Angkor became the target of French-financed expeditions, and in 1901 the École Française d'Extrême-Orient (EFEO; www.efeo.fr) began a long association with Angkor by funding an expedition to Bayon. In 1907 Angkor was returned to Cambodia, having been under Thai control for more than a century, and the EFEO took responsibility for clearing and restoring the whole site. In the same year, the first foreign tourists arrived in Angkor – an unprecedented 200 of them in three months. Angkor had been 'rescued' from the jungle and was assuming its place in the modern world.

Restoring Angkor

With the exception of Angkor Wat, which was restored for use as a Buddhist shrine in the 16th century by the Khmer royalty, the temples of Angkor were left to the jungle for many centuries. The majority of temples are made of sandstone, which tends to dissolve when in prolonged contact with dampness. Bat droppings took their toll, as did sporadic pilfering of sculptures and cut stones. At some monuments, such as Ta Prohm, the jungle had stealthily waged an all-out invasion, and plant life could only be removed at great risk to the structures it now supported in its web of roots.

Initial attempts to clear Angkor under the aegis of the EFEO were fraught with technical difficulties and theoretical disputes. On a technical front, the jungle tended to grow back as soon as it was cleared; on a theoretical front, scholars debated the extent to which temples should be restored and whether later additions, such as Buddha images in Hindu temples, should be removed.

It was not until the 1920s that a solution was found, known as anastylosis. This was the method the Dutch had used to restore Borobudur in Java. Put simply, it was a way of reconstructing monuments using the original materials and in keeping with the original form of the structure. New materials were permitted only where the originals could not be found, and were to be used discreetly. An example of this method can be seen on the causeway leading to the entrance of Angkor Wat, as the right-hand side was originally restored by the French.

The first major restoration job was carried out on Banteay Srei in 1930. It was deemed such a success that many more extensive restoration projects were undertaken elsewhere around Angkor, culminating in the massive Angkor Wat restoration in the 1960s. Large cranes and earth-moving machines were brought in, and the operation was backed by a veritable army of surveying equipment.

The Khmer Rouge victory and Cambodia's subsequent slide into an intractable civil war resulted in far less damage to Angkor than many had assumed, as EFEO and Ministry of Culture teams had removed many of the statues from the temple sites

Temples of Angkor

THREE-DAY EXPLORATION

The temple complex at Angkor is simply enormous and the superlatives don't do it justice. This is the site of the world's largest religious building, a multitude of temples and a vast, long-abandoned walled city that was arguably Southeast Asia's first metropolis, long before Bangkok and Singapore got in on the action.

Starting at the Roluos group of temples, one of the earliest capitals of Angkor, move on to the big circuit, which includes the Buddhist-Hindu fusion temple of **① Preah Khan** and the ornate water temple of **② Preah Neak Poan**.

On the second day downsize to the small circuit, starting with an early visit to **③ Ta Prohm**, before continuing to the temple pyramid of Ta Keo, the Buddhist monastery of Banteay Kdei and the immense royal bathing pond of **④ Sra Srang**.

Next venture further afield to Banteay Srei temple, the jewel in the crown of Angkorian art, and Beng Mealea, a remote jungle temple.

Saving the biggest and best until last, experience sunrise at **⑤ Angkor Wat** and stick around for breakfast in the temple to discover its amazing architecture without the crowds. In the afternoon, explore **⑥ Angkor Thom**, an immense complex that is home to the enigmatic **⑦ Bayon**.

Three days around Angkor? That's just for starters.

Bayon
The surreal state temple of legendary king Jayavarman VII, where 216 faces bear down on pilgrims, asserting religious and regal authority.

Angkor Wat
The world's largest religious building. Experience sunrise at the holiest of holies, then explore the beautiful bas-reliefs – devotion etched in stone.

TOP TIPS

➡ To avoid the crowds, try dawn at Sra Srang, post-sunrise at Angkor Wat and lunchtime at Banteay Srei.

➡ Three-day passes can be used on non-consecutive days over the course of a week, but be sure to request this.

Angkor Thom
The last great capital of the Khmer empire conceals a wealth of temples and its epic proportions would have inspired and terrified in equal measure.

Preah Khan
A fusion temple dedicated to Buddha, Brahma, Shiva and Vishnu; the immense corridors are like an unending hall of mirrors.

Preah Neak Poan
If Vegas ever adopts the Angkor theme, this will be the swimming pool; a petite tower set in a lake, surrounded by four smaller ponds.

North Gate, Angkor Thom

Preah Pithu

Thommanon Temple

Prasat Suor Prat

Victory Gate Angkor Thom

East Gate Angkor Thom

Ta Nei Temple

Chau Say Tevoda

Ta Keo Temple

Banteay Srei

Banteay Kdei Temple

Roluos, Beng Mealea

Bat Chum Temple

Prasat Kravan

Ta Prohm
Nicknamed the *Tomb Raider* temple; *Indiana Jones* would be equally apt. Nature has run riot, leaving iconic tree roots strangling the surviving stones.

Sra Srang
Once the royal bathing pond, this is the ablutions pool to beat all ablutions pools and makes a good stop for sunrise or sunset.

THE TOP 10 KINGS OF ANGKOR

A mind-numbing array of kings ruled the Khmer empire from the 9th to the 14th centuries CE. All of their names include the word '*varman*', which means 'armour' or 'protector'. Forget the small fry and focus on the big fish in our Top 10:

Jayavarman II (r 802–50) Founder of the Khmer empire in CE 802.

Indravarman I (r 877–89) Builder of the first *baray* (reservoir), Preah Ko and Bakong.

Yasovarman I (r 889–910) Moved the capital to Angkor and built Lolei and Phnom Bakheng.

Jayavarman IV (r 924–42) Usurper king who moved the capital to Koh Ker.

Rajendravarman II (r 944–68) Builder of Eastern Mebon, Pre Rup and Phimeanakas.

Jayavarman V (r 968–1001) Oversaw construction of Ta Keo and Banteay Srei.

Suryavarman I (r 1002–49) Expanded the empire into much of Laos and Thailand.

Udayadityavarman II (r 1049–65) Builder of the pyramidal Baphuon and the Western Mebon.

Suryavarman II (r 1112–52) Legendary builder of Angkor Wat and Beng Mealea.

Jayavarman VII (r 1181–1219) The king of the god-kings, building Angkor Thom, Preah Khan and Ta Prohm.

for protection. Nevertheless, turmoil in Cambodia resulted in a long interruption of restoration work, allowing the jungle to resume its assault on the monuments. The illegal trade of *objets d'art* on the world art market has also been a major threat to Angkor, although it is the more remote sites that have been targeted recently. Angkor has been under the jurisdiction of the UN Educational Scientific and Cultural Organisation (Unesco) since 1992 as a World Heritage Site, and international and local efforts continue to preserve and reconstruct the monuments. In a sign of real progress, Angkor was removed from Unesco's endangered list in 2003.

Many of Angkor's secrets remain to be discovered, as most of the work at the temples has concentrated on restoration efforts above ground rather than archaeological digs and surveys below. Underground is where the real story of Angkor and its people lies – the inscriptions on the temples give us only a partial picture of the gods to whom each structure was dedicated, and the kings who built them.

Architectural Styles

From the time of the earliest Angkorian monuments at Roluos, Khmer architecture was continually evolving, often from the rule of one king to the next. Archaeologists therefore divide the monuments of Angkor into nine periods, named after the foremost example of each period's architectural style.

The evolution of Khmer architecture was based on a central theme of the temple-mountain, preferably set on a real hill (but an artificial hill was allowed if there weren't any mountains to hand). The earlier a temple was constructed, the more closely it adheres to this fundamental idea. Essentially, the mountain was represented by a tower mounted on a tiered base. At the summit was the central sanctuary, usually with an open door to the east, and three false doors at the remaining cardinal points of the compass. For Indian Hindus, the Himalayas represent Mt Meru, the home of the gods, while the Khmer kings of old adopted Phnom Kulen as their symbolic Mt Meru.

By the time of the Bakheng period, this layout was being embellished. The summit of the central tower was crowned with five 'peaks' – four at the points of the compass and one in the centre. Even Angkor Wat features this layout, though on a grandiose scale. Other features that came to be favoured include an entry tower and a causeway lined with naga (mythical serpent) balustrades leading up to the temple.

As the temples grew in ambition, the central tower became a less prominent feature, although it remained the focus of the temple. Later temples saw the central tower flanked by courtyards and richly decorated galleries. Smaller towers were placed on gates and on the corners of walls, their over-all number often of religious or astrological significance.

These refinements and additions eventually culminated in Angkor Wat, which effectively showcases the evolution of Angkorian architecture. The architecture of the Bayon period breaks with tradition in temples such as Ta Prohm and Preah Khan. In these temples, the horizontal layout of the galleries, corridors and courtyards seems to completely eclipse the central tower.

The curious narrowness of the corridors and doorways in these structures can be explained by the fact that Angkorian architects never mastered the flying buttress to build a full arch. They engineered arches by laying blocks on top of each other, until they met at a central point; known as false arches, they can only support very short spans.

Most of the major sandstone blocks around Angkor include small circular holes. These originally held wooden stakes that were used to lift and position the stones during construction before being sawn off.

When to Go

➡ Avoid the sweltering temperatures of March to May.

➡ November to February is the best time of year to travel, but this is no secret, so it coincides with peak season. And peak season really is mountainous in this day and age, with more than two million visitors a year descending on Angkor.

➡ The summer months of July and August can be a surprisingly rewarding time, as the landscape is emerald green, the moats overflowing with water, and the moss and lichen in bright contrast to the grey sandstone.

➡ The Angkor Wat International Half Marathon takes place annually in December, including the option of bicycle rides for those not into running.

Itineraries

Back in the early days of tourism, the decision of what to see and in what order came down to a choice between two basic temple itineraries: the Small (Petit) Circuit and the Big (Grand) Circuit. It's difficult to imagine anyone following these to the letter any more, but in their time they were an essential component of the Angkor experience

and were often undertaken on the back of an elephant.

Today, most budget and midrange travellers prefer to take in the temples at their own pace, and tend to use a combination of transport options, such as car, *remork-moto*, bicycle or minivan. Plan a dawn-to-dusk itinerary with a long, leisurely lunch to avoid the heat of the midday sun. Alternatively, explore the temples through lunch, when it can be considerably quieter than during the peak morning and afternoon visit times. However, it will be searingly hot and the light is not conducive to photography.

Angkor in One Day

If you have only one day to visit Angkor, arrive at Angkor Wat (p150) in time for sunrise and then stick around to explore the mighty temple while it's quieter. From there continue to the tree roots of Ta Prohm (p162) before breaking for lunch. In the afternoon, explore the temples within the walled city of Angkor Thom (p156) and the beauty of the Bayon (p156) in the late-afternoon light.

Angkor in Two Days

A second day allows you to include some of the big hitters around Angkor. Spend the first morning visiting petite Banteay Srei (p169), with its fabulous carvings; stop at Banteay Samré (p173) on the return leg. In the afternoon, visit immense Preah Khan (p165), delicate Preah Neak Poan (p166) and the tree roots of Ta Som (p166), before taking in a sunset at Pre Rup (p166).

Angkor in Three to Five Days

If you have three to five days to explore Angkor, it's possible to see most of the important sites. One approach is to see as much as possible on the first day or two and then spend the final days combining visits

ⓘ **WHERE TO STAY AROUND ANGKOR**

For most people nearby Siem Reap is the base for exploring the temples of Angkor, with an incredible array of accommodation (p112) on offer ranging from budget hostels to opulent hotels. There is no accommodation around Angkor as such, although for those seeking a local experience there are some rustic options in the rural surrounds such Banteay Srei District (p131).

to other sites such as the Roluos temples (p167) and Banteay Kdei (p163). Better still is a gradual build-up to the most spectacular monuments. After all, if you see Angkor Wat (p150) on the first day, then a temple like Ta Keo (p164) just won't cut it. Another option is a chronological approach, starting with the earliest Angkorian temples and working steadily forwards in time to Angkor Thom (p156), taking stock of the evolution of Khmer architecture and artistry.

It is well worth making the trip to the 'River of a Thousand Lingas' at Kbal Spean (p172) for the chance to stretch your legs amid natural and human-made splendour, or the remote, vast and overgrown temple of Beng Mealea (p170). Both can be combined with Banteay Srei (p169) in one long day.

Angkor in One Week

Those with the time to spend a week at Angkor will be richly rewarded. Not only is it possible to visit all the temples of the region, but a longer stay also allows for nontemple activities, such as relaxing by a pool, indulging in a spa treatment or shopping around Siem Reap. You may also want to throw in some of the more remote sites such as Koh

ℹ️ DODGING THE CROWDS

Angkor is well and truly on the tourist trail and it is only getting busier, with over two million visitors annually, but – with a little planning – it is still possible to escape the crowds. One important thing to remember, particularly when it comes to sunrise and sunset, is that places are popular for a reason, and it is worth going with the flow at least once.

It is received wisdom that as Angkor Wat faces west, one should be there for late afternoon, and in the case of the Bayon, which faces east, in the morning. Ta Prohm, most people seem to agree, can be visited in the middle of the day because of its umbrella of foliage. This is all well and good, but if you reverse the order, the temples will still look good – and you can avoid some of the crowds.

Only four temples are open at 5am for sunrise: Angkor Wat, Phnom Bakheng, Sra Srang and Pre Rup. The most popular place is Angkor Wat. Most tour groups head back to town for breakfast, so stick around and explore the temple while it's cool and quiet between 7am and 9am. Sra Srang is usually pretty quiet, and sunrise here can be spectacular thanks to reflections in the extensive waters. Phnom Bakheng could be an attractive option, because the sun comes up behind Angkor Wat and you are far from the madding crowd that gathers here at sunset, but there are now strict limitations on visitor numbers each day.

The hilltop temple of Phnom Bakheng is the definitive sunset spot. This was getting well out of control, with as many as 1000 tourists clambering around the small structure. However, new restrictions limit visitors to no more than 300 at any one time. It is generally better to check it out for sunrise or early morning and miss the crowds. Staying within the confines of Angkor Wat for sunset is a rewarding option, but it is quite busy at this time. Pre Rup is popular with some for an authentic rural sunset over the countryside, but this is also crowded these days. Better is the hilltop temple of Phnom Krom, which offers commanding views across Tonlé Sap lake, but involves a long drive back to town in the dark. The Western Baray takes in the sunset from the eastern end, across its vast waters, or from Western Mebon island, and is generally a quiet option.

When it comes to the most popular temples, the middle of the day is generally the quietest time. This is because the majority of the large tour groups head back to Siem Reap for lunch. It is also the hottest part of the day, which makes it tough going around relatively open temples such as Banteay Srei and the Bayon, but fine at well-covered temples such as Ta Prohm, Preah Khan and Beng Mealea, or even the bas-reliefs at Angkor Wat. The busiest times at Angkor Wat are from 6am to 7am and 3pm to 5pm; at the Bayon, from 8am to 10am; and at Banteay Srei, mid-morning and mid-afternoon. However, at other popular temples, such as Ta Prohm and Preah Khan, the crowds are harder to predict, and at most other temples in the Angkor region it's just a case of pot luck. If you pull up outside and see a car park full of tour buses, you may want to move on to somewhere quieter. The wonderful thing about Angkor is that there is always another temple to explore.

Ker (p174), Prasat Preah Vihear (p265) or Banteay Chhmar (p259).

Tours

Visitors who have only a day or two at this incredible site may prefer something organised locally. It is possible to link up with an official tour guide in Siem Reap (p111), where a number of operators run tours ranging from simple day trips to cycling tours to excursions to more remote temple sites. The Khmer Angkor Tour Guide Association (☎ 095 828248; www.khmerangkortourguide. com) represents some of Angkor's authorised guides. English- or French-speaking guides can be booked from US$30 per day; guides speaking other languages, such as Italian, German, Spanish, Japanese and Chinese, are available at a higher rate as there are fewer of them.

Orientation

Heading north from Siem Reap, Angkor Wat is the first major temple, followed by the walled city of Angkor Thom. To the east and west of this city are two vast former reservoirs, which once helped to feed the huge population; the eastern reservoir is now completely dried up. Further east are temples including Ta Prohm, Banteay Kdei and Pre Rup. North of Angkor Thom is Preah Khan, and way beyond in the northeast, Banteay Srei, Kbal Spean, Phnom Kulen and Beng Mealea. To the southeast of Siem Reap is the early Angkorian Roluos group of temples.

Information

ADMISSION FEES

Visitors have the choice of a one-day pass (US$37), a three-day pass (US$62) or a one-week pass (US$72). The three-day passes can be used over three nonconsecutive days in a one-week period, while one-week passes can be used on seven nonconsecutive days over a month.

The Angkor **ticket booth & main entrance** (Map p134; Rd 60; ☺ 5am-6pm) is out by the Siem Reap Convention Centre, about 2km east of the old checkpoint. It's part of a gleaming new complex that also includes the ambitious Angkor Panorama Museum. Tickets are not sold at the old ticket checkpoint.

Passes include a digital photo snapped at the entrance booth, so queues can be slow at peak times. The fee includes access to all the monuments in the Siem Reap area but not the sacred mountain of Phnom Kulen (US$20) or the remote complexes of Beng Mealea (US$5) and Koh Ker (US$10).

All the major temples now have uniformed staff to check the tickets, which has reduced the opportunity for scams. These days all roads into the central temples (including Angkor Wat, Angkor Thom and Ta Prohm) have checkpoints as well; foreigners who can't produce a pass will be turned away and asked to detour around the temples between 7am and 5pm. Visitors found inside any of the main temples without a ticket will be fined a whopping US$100.

USEFUL WEBSITES

Angkor – Unesco World Heritage Site (http://whc.unesco.org/en/list/668) Information, images and videos on the world's top temples.

Angkor Ruins (www.angkor-ruins.com) For a great online photographic resource on the temples of Angkor, look no further than this Japanese website with an English version.

Lonely Planet (www.lonelyplanet.com/cambodia/temples-of-angkor) Destination information, bookings and more.

National Geographic (www.nationalgeographic.com/magazine/2009/07/diving-angkor) In-depth feature on the rise and fall of Angkor.

Getting There & Around

Visitors heading to the temples of Angkor – in other words, pretty much everybody coming to Cambodia – need to consider the most suitable way to travel between the temples. The central temple area is just 8km from Siem Reap, and can be visited using anything from a car or motorcycle to a sturdy pair of walking shoes. For the independent traveller, there will be many alternatives to consider.

For the ultimate Angkor experience, try a pick-and-mix approach, with a *moto* (motorcycle taxi), *remork* or car for one day to cover the remote sites, a bicycle to experience the central temples, and an exploration on foot for a spot of peace and serenity.

Transport will be more expensive to remote temples such as Banteay Srei or Beng Mealea, due to extra fuel costs.

BICYCLE

Bicycles are a great way to get around the temples, and they are used by many locals in the villages around Angkor. There are few hills and the roads are good, so there's no need for much cycling experience. Moving about at a slower speed, you soon find that you take in more than from out of a car window or on the back of a speeding *moto*.

White Bicycles (p130) is supported by some guesthouses around Siem Reap, with proceeds from the hire fee going towards community projects. Many guesthouses and hotels in town rent bikes for around US$1 to US$2 per day.

Some rental places offer better mountain bikes, such as Trek or Giant, for US$7 to US$10 per day. Try Grasshopper Adventures (p112), which offers mountain bikes and helmets for US$8 per day. Electric bicycles hired out by Green e-bikes (p130) and others are also a very popular way to tour the temples.

When exploring by bicycle, always use a sturdy lock and leave your bike at a guarded parking area or with a stallholder outside each temple.

CAR & MOTORCYCLE

Cars are a popular choice for getting about the temples. The obvious advantage is protection from the elements, be it heavy downpours or the punishing sun. Shared between several travellers, they can also be an economical way to explore. The downside is that visitors are a little more isolated from the sights, sounds and smells as they travel between temples. A car for the day around the central temples is US$25 to US$35 and can be arranged with hotels, guesthouses and agencies in Siem Reap. It costs more to outlying temples like Banteay Srei and Beng Mealea.

Motorcycle rental in Siem Reap was prohibited for more than a decade, but recently the rules seem to have been unofficially relaxed and a number of travellers are renting small motorbikes for around US$10 per day. When exploring by motorbike, leave it at a guarded parking area or with a stallholder outside each temple; otherwise it might be stolen.

HELICOPTER & HOT-AIR BALLOON

For those with a flexible budget, there are helicopter flights around Angkor Wat (US$90) and the temples outside Angkor Thom (US$150). **Helicopters Cambodia** (☏ 012 814500; www.helicopterscambodia.com) or **Helistar** (Map p134; www.helistarcambodia.com; NH6 West; Angkor Wat/Angkor Thom flights US$90/150; ⊙ 7am-5.30pm), which operate out of Siem Reap Airport, also offer expensive charters to remote temples such as Prasat Preah Vihear and Preah Khan.

Angkor Balloon (☏ 092 765386; www.angkorballoon.com; daytime per person US$15, sunrise or sunset US$25; ⊙ 5am-7pm) offers a bird's-eye view of Angkor Wat. The balloon carries up to 20 people, is on a fixed line and rises 200m above the landscape. It doesn't drift across the temples like balloons over Bagan in Myanmar, so it's best to manage expectations.

MINIVAN

Minivans are available from various hotels and travel agents around town. A 12-seat minivan costs from US$50 per day.

MOTO

Some independent travellers visit the temples by *moto. Moto* drivers accost visitors from the moment they set foot in Siem Reap, but they often end up being knowledgeable and friendly, and good companions for a tour around the temples. Prices start at around US$10 per day. They can drop you off and pick you up at allotted times and places, and even tell you a bit of background about the temples as you zip around. Many of the better drivers go on to become official tour guides, although most have upgraded their *motos* to *remorks* these days.

TUK TUK

Remork-motos, motorcycles with hooded carriages towed behind, are more commonly known as *tuk tuks.* They are a popular way to get around Angkor as fellow travellers can talk to each other as they explore (unlike on the back of a *moto*). They also offer some protection from the rain. Some *remork* drivers are very good companions for a tour of the temples. Prices run from US$15 to US$25 for the day, depending on the destination and number of passengers. Slightly cheaper are the smaller auto-rickshaws, but they offer a little less breeze than *remorks*.

WALKING

From Siem Reap, it's easy enough to walk to Angkor Wat and the temples of Angkor Thom, and this is a great way to meet up with villagers in the area. Those who want to get away from the roads should try the peaceful walk along the walls of Angkor Thom. It is about 13km in total, and offers access to several small, remote temples and some birdlife. One way to save more time at the temples is to negotiate a drop-off and pickup by *moto* or *remork* at Angkor Thom and explore on foot. Another rewarding walk is from Ta Keo to Ta Nei through the forest, but the best all-round jungle hike is to the River of a Thousand Lingas at Kbal Spean.

ANGKOR WAT

The traveller's first glimpse of Angkor Wat (អង្គរវត្ត; incl in Angkor admission 1/3/7 days US$37/62/72; ⊙ 5am-5.30pm), the ultimate expression of Khmer genius, is matched by only a few select spots on earth. Built by Suryavarman II (r 1112–52) and surrounded by a vast moat, the temple is one of the most inspired monuments ever conceived by the human mind.

Angkor Wat is the heart and soul of Cambodia: it is the national symbol, the epicentre of Khmer civilisation and a source of fierce national pride. It was never aban-

MOTIFS, SYMBOLS & CHARACTERS AROUND ANGKOR

The temples of Angkor are intricately carved with myths and legends, symbols and signs, and a cast of characters in the thousands. Deciphering them can be quite a challenge, so we've highlighted some of the most commonly seen around the majestic temples. For more help understanding the carvings of Angkor, pick up a copy of *Images of the Gods* by Vittorio Roveda.

Apsaras Heavenly nymphs or goddesses, also known as *devadas;* these beautiful female forms decorate the walls of many temples.

Asuras These devils feature extensively in representations of the Churning of the Ocean of Milk, such as at Angkor Wat.

Devas The 'good gods' in the creation myth of the Churning of the Ocean of Milk.

Flame The flame motif is found flanking steps and doorways and is intended to purify pilgrims as they enter the temple.

Garuda Vehicle of Vishnu; this half-man, half-bird creature features in some temples and was combined with his old enemy, the nagas, to promote religious unity under Jayavarman VII.

Kala The temple guardian appointed by Shiva; he had such an appetite that he devoured his own body and appears only as a giant head above doorways. Also known as Rehu.

Linga A phallic symbol of fertility, *lingas* would have originally been located within the towers of most Hindu temples.

Lotus A symbol of purity, the lotus features extensively in the shape of towers, the shape of steps to entrances and in decoration.

Makara A giant sea serpent with a reticulated jaw; features on the corner of pediments, spewing forth a naga or some other creature.

Naga The multiheaded serpent, half-brother and enemy of *garudas*. Controls the rains and, therefore, the prosperity of the kingdom; seen on causeways, doorways and roofs. The seven-headed naga, a feature at many temples, represents the rainbow, which acts as a bridge between heaven and earth.

Nandi The mount of Shiva; there are several statues of Nandi dotted about the temples, although many have been damaged or stolen by looters.

Rishi A Hindu wise man or ascetic, also known as *essai;* these bearded characters are often seen sitting cross-legged at the base of pillars or flanking walls.

Vine Another symbol of purity, the vine graces doorways and lintels and is meant to help cleanse visitors on their journey to this heaven on earth, the abode of the gods.

Yama God of death who presides over the underworld and passes judgement on whether people continue to heaven or hell.

Yoni Female fertility symbol that is combined with the *linga* to produce holy water infused with the essence of life.

doned to the elements and has been in virtually continuous use since it was built.

Simply unique, it is a stunning blend of spirituality and symmetry, an enduring example of humanity's devotion to its gods. Relish the very first approach, as that spine-tingling moment when you emerge on the inner causeway will rarely be felt again. It is the best-preserved temple at Angkor, and repeat visits are rewarded with previously unnoticed details.

Symbolism

There is much about Angkor Wat that is unique among the temples of Angkor. The most significant fact is that the temple is oriented towards the west. Symbolically, west is the direction of death, which once led many scholars to conclude that Angkor Wat must have existed primarily as a tomb. This idea was supported by the fact that the magnificent bas-reliefs of the temple were

Angkor Wat

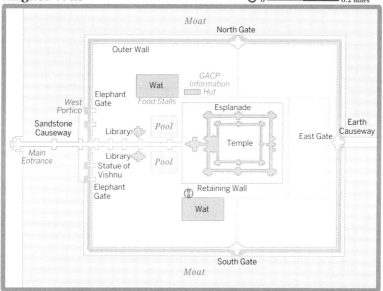

designed to be viewed in an anticlockwise direction, a practice that has precedents in ancient Hindu funerary rites. Vishnu, however, is also frequently associated with the west, and it is now commonly accepted that Angkor Wat most likely served both as a temple and as a mausoleum for Suryavarman II.

Visitors to Angkor Wat are struck by its imposing grandeur and, at close quarters, its fascinating decorative flourishes and extensive bas-reliefs. Holy men at the time of Angkor must have revelled in its multilayered levels of meaning in much the same way a contemporary literary scholar might delight in James Joyce's *Ulysses*.

Eleanor Mannikka explains in her book *Angkor Wat: Time, Space and Kingship* that the spatial dimensions of Angkor Wat parallel the lengths of the four ages (Yuga) of classical Hindu thought. Thus the visitor to Angkor Wat who walks the causeway to the main entrance and through the courtyards to the final main tower, which once contained a statue of Vishnu, is metaphorically travelling back to the first age of the creation of the universe.

Like the other temple-mountains of Angkor, Angkor Wat also replicates the spatial universe in miniature. The central tower is Mt Meru, with its surrounding smaller peaks, bounded in turn by continents (the lower courtyards) and the oceans (the moat). The seven-headed naga becomes a symbolic rainbow bridge for humanity to reach the abode of the gods.

While Suryavarman II may have planned Angkor Wat as his funerary temple or mausoleum, he was never buried there as he died in battle during a failed expedition to subdue the Dai Viet (Vietnamese).

Layout

Angkor Wat is surrounded by a 190m-wide moat, which forms a giant rectangle measuring 1.5km by 1.3km. From the west, a sandstone causeway crosses the moat. The sandstone blocks from which Angkor Wat was built were quarried more than 50km away (from the holy mountain of Phnom Kulen) and floated down the Siem Reap River on rafts. The logistics of such an operation are mind-blowing, consuming the labour of thousands – an unbelievable feat given the machinery we take for granted in contemporary construction projects. According to inscriptions, the construction of Angkor Wat involved 300,000 workers and 6000 elephants, yet it was still not fully completed.

The rectangular outer wall, which measures 1025m by 800m, has a gate on each side, but the main entrance, a 235m-wide portico richly decorated with carvings and sculptures, is on the western side. There is a statue of Vishnu, 3.25m in height and hewn from a single block of sandstone, located in the southeast tower (it was originally housed in the central tower of the temple). Vishnu's eight arms hold a mace, a spear, a disc, a conch and other items. You may also see locks of hair lying about. These are offerings both from young people preparing to get married and from pilgrims giving thanks for their good fortune.

An avenue, 475m long and 9.5m wide and lined with naga balustrades, leads from the main entrance to the central temple, passing between two graceful libraries (restored by a Japanese team) and then two pools, the northern one a popular spot from which to watch the sun rise.

The central temple complex consists of three storeys, each made of laterite, which enclose a square surrounded by intricately interlinked galleries. The Gallery of a Thousand Buddhas (Preah Poan) used to house hundreds of Buddha images before the war, but many of these were removed or stolen, leaving just the handful we see today.

The corners of the second and third storeys are marked by towers, each topped with symbolic lotus-bud towers. The stairs to the upper level are immensely steep, because reaching the kingdom of the gods was no easy task. Also known as Bakan, the upper level of Angkor Wat was closed to visitors for several years, but it is once again open (8am to 5pm daily, except religious holidays) to a limited number per day with a timed queuing system. This means it is once again possible to complete the pilgrimage with an ascent to the 55m summit: savour the cooling breeze, take in the extensive views and then find a quiet corner in which to contemplate the symmetry and symbolism of this Everest of temples. Clothing that covers to the elbows and knees is required to visit this upper level of Angkor Wat.

At the time of research, the western causeway was closed to visitors for an extensive renovation and access is via a floating pontoon, which has become something of a local tourist attraction in itself.

Bas-Reliefs

Stretching around the outside of the central temple complex is an 800m-long series of intricate and astonishing bas-reliefs. The majority were completed in the 12th century, but in the 16th century several new reliefs were added to unfinished panels.

The bas-reliefs at Angkor Wat were once sheltered by the cloister's wooden roof, which long ago rotted away except for one original beam in the western half of the north gallery. The other roofed sections are reconstructions.

Churning of the Ocean of Milk
ARCHAEOLOGICAL SITE

(ការកូរសមុទ្រទឹកដោះ) The southern section of the east gallery is decorated by the most famous of the bas-relief scenes at Angkor Wat, the Churning of the Ocean of Milk. This brilliantly executed carving depicts 88 *asuras* on the left, and 92 *devas,* with crested helmets, churning up the sea to extract from it the elixir of immortality.

The demons hold the head of the serpent Vasuki and the gods hold its tail. At the centre of the sea, Vasuki is coiled around Mt Mandala, which turns and churns up the water in the tug of war between the demons and the gods. Vishnu, incarnated as a huge turtle, lends his shell to serve as the base and pivot of Mt Mandala. Brahma, Shiva, Hanuman (the monkey god) and Lakshmi (the goddess of wealth and prosperity) all make appearances, while overhead a host

THE APSARAS OF ANGKOR WAT

Angkor Wat is famous for its beguiling *apsaras* (heavenly nymphs). Almost 2000 *apsaras* are carved into the walls of Angkor Wat, each of them unique, and there are 37 different hairstyles for budding stylists to check out. Many of these exquisite *apsaras* have been damaged by centuries of bat droppings and urine, but they are now being restored by the **German Apsara Conservation Project** (GACP; www.gacp-angkor.de; ☺ 7am-5pm). The organisation operates a small information booth in the northwestern corner of Angkor Wat, near the modern wat, where beautiful B&W postcards and images of Angkor are available.

DON'T MISS

ANGKOR ZIPLINE

Angkor provides the ultimate backdrop for this **zipline experience** (📞 096 999 9100; www.angkorzipline.com; short/full course US$60/100; ⊘ 6am-5pm), although you won't actually see the temples while navigating the course, despite it being located inside the Angkor protected area. The course includes 10 ziplines, 21 treetop platforms, four skybridges and an abseil finish. There is a panoramic rest stop halfway, and highlights include a tandem line for couples.

Safety is a priority and high-flyers are permanently clipped to lines via karabiners, with clear English instruction throughout. There is also a conservation element to the project, with a resident gibbon family living in the forest here. The price includes a minivan transfer to/from town, plus lunch before or after the zipline. It is located near Ta Nei temple, so those with a temple pass might want to build in a visit. You do not require a temple pass to enjoy the zipline experience.

of heavenly female spirits sing and dance in encouragement. Luckily for us, the gods won through, as the *apsaras* above were too much for the hot-blooded devils to take. Restoration work on this incredible panel by the World Monuments Fund (WMF) was completed in 2012.

Army of Suryavarman II ARCHAEOLOGICAL SITE

(ទ័ពព្រះបាទសូរ្យវរ្ម័នទី២) The remarkable western section of the south gallery depicts a triumphal battle march of Suryavarman II's army. In the southwestern corner about 2m from the floor is Suryavarman II on an elephant, wearing the royal tiara and armed with a battleaxe; he is shaded by 15 parasols and fanned by legions of servants.

Compare this image of the king with the image of Rama in the northern gallery and you'll notice an uncanny likeness that helped reinforce the aura of the god-king.

Further on is a procession of well-armed soldiers and officers on horseback; among them are bold and warlike chiefs on elephants. Just before the end of this panel is the rather disorderly Siamese mercenary army, with their long headdresses and ragged marching, at that time allied with the Khmers in their conflict with the Chams. The Khmer troops have square breastplates and are armed with spears; the Thais wear skirts and carry tridents.

The rectangular holes seen in the Army of Suryavarman II relief were created when, so the story goes, Thai soldiers removed pieces of the scene containing inscriptions that reportedly gave clues to the location of the golden treasures of Suryavarman II, later buried during the reign of Jayavarman VII.

Battle of Kurukshetra ARCHAEOLOGICAL SITE

(ចម្បាំងនៅកុរុក្ស្រេត្រ) The southern portion of the west gallery depicts a battle scene from the Hindu *Mahabharata* epic, in which the Kauravas (coming from the north) and the Pandavas (coming from the south) advance upon each other, meeting in furious battle. Infantry are shown on the lowest tier, with officers on elephants, and chiefs on the second and third tiers.

Some of the more interesting details (from left to right): a dead chief lying on a pile of arrows, surrounded by his grieving parents and troops; a warrior on an elephant who, by putting down his weapon, has accepted defeat; and a mortally wounded officer, falling from his carriage into the arms of his soldiers. Over the centuries, some sections have been polished (by the millions of hands that have fallen upon them) to look like black marble. The portico at the southwestern corner is decorated with sculptures representing characters from the *Ramayana*.

Heaven & Hell ARCHAEOLOGICAL SITE

(នរកទាំ២ និងស្ថានសួគ៌ាំ៣៧) The punishments and rewards of the 37 heavens and 32 hells are depicted in the eastern half of the south gallery. On the left, the upper and middle tiers show fine gentlemen and ladies proceeding towards 18-armed Yama (the judge of the dead) seated on a bull; below him are his assistants, Dharma and Sitragupta. On the lower tier, devils drag the wicked along the road to hell.

To Yama's right, the tableau is divided into two parts by a horizontal line of *garudas*: above, the elect dwell in beautiful mansions, served by women and attendants; below, the condemned suffer horrible tortures that might have inspired the Khmer Rouge. The ceiling in this section was restored by the French in the 1930s.

Battle of Lanka ARCHAEOLOGICAL SITE

(សមរភូមិលង្កា) The northern half of the west gallery shows scenes from the *Ramayana*. In the Battle of Lanka, Rama (on the shoulders of Hanuman), along with his army of monkeys, battles 10-headed, 20-armed Ravana, captor of Rama's beautiful wife Sita. Ravana rides a chariot drawn by monsters and commands an army of giants.

Battle of the Gods & the Demons ARCHAEOLOGICAL SITE

(ចម្បាំងវាងទេវតា និងពួកអសុរៈ) The western section of the north gallery depicts the battle between the 21 gods of the Brahmanic pantheon and various demons. The gods are featured with their traditional attributes and mounts. Vishnu has four arms and is seated on a *garuda*, while Shiva rides a sacred goose.

Krishna & the Demon King ARCHAEOLOGICAL SITE

(ក្រិស្ណៈ និងបាបាណ្ឌ:) The eastern section of the north gallery shows Vishnu incarnated as Krishna riding a *garuda*. He confronts a burning walled city, the residence of Bana,

the demon king. The *garuda* puts out the fire and Bana is captured. In the final scene Krishna kneels before Shiva and asks that Bana's life be spared.

Vishnu Conquers the Demons ARCHAEOLOGICAL SITE

(ជ័យជម្នៈរបស់ព្រះវិស្ណុ លើពួកអសុរៈ) The northern section of the east gallery shows a furious and desperate encounter between Vishnu, riding on a *garuda,* and innumerable devils. Needless to say, he slays all comers. This gallery was most likely completed in the 16th century, and the later carving is notably inferior to the original work from the 12th century.

✖ Eating

There is an extensive selection of restaurants lined up opposite the entrance to Angkor Wat that includes several local eateries such as **Khmer Angkor Restaurant** (mains US$3-8; ◷6am-6pm; 🛜) and **Angkor Reach Restaurant** (mains US$3-8; ◷6am-6pm; 🛜). There is also a handy branch of Blue Pumpkin, called the **Angkor Cafe** (Blue Pumpkin; www.bluepumpkin.asia; dishes US$2-8; ◷7am-7pm; ❄🛜), churning out sandwiches, salads and ice creams, as well as divine fruit shakes, all to take away if required.

TEMPLES OF ANGKOR ANGKOR WAT

Angkor Wat – Central Structure

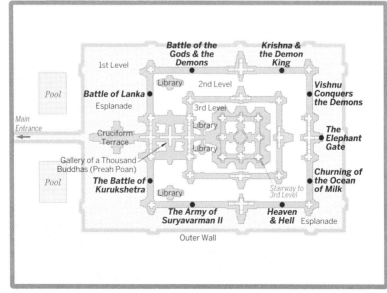

Central Area of Angkor Thom

N 0 _____ 400 m
  0 _____ 0.2 miles

North Gate of
Angkor Thom (500m);
Preah Khan (2.5km)

Preah
Palilay

Tep Pranam   Food
              Stalls

Terrace of
the Leper King

Preah Pithu

Northern Ave

Gate   Gate

Royal
Enclosure

Prasat
Suor Prat

North
Kleang

Victory Gate (1km);
Ta Prohm (3.5km)

Central
Square   Ave of Victory

Phimeanakas

Terrace
of Elephants

Gate   Gate

South
Kleang

Baphuon

Main
Entrance

Bayon

Main
Entrance

West Gate of
Angkor Thom (1km)

East Gate of
Angkor Thom (1km)

South Gate of Angkor Thom
(1.2km); Angkor Wat (3.3km)

❶ Getting There & Away

Angkor Wat lies at the heart of the Angkor Archaeological Park, just 6km north of central Siem Reap. Even if you only visit it once, you'll likely pass by the iconic temple several times while visiting other temples within the main area of the park.

There are a range of transport options from Siem Reap including *moto, remork* and car. Cycling and walking are also possible.

ANGKOR THOM

It's hard to imagine any building bigger or more beautiful than Angkor Wat, but in Angkor Thom (អង្គរធំ, Great City; incl in Angkor admission) the sum of the parts add up to a greater whole. Set over 10 sq km, the aptly named last great capital of the Khmer empire took monumental to a whole new level.

Centred on Bayon, the surreal state temple of Jayavarman VII, Angkor Thom is enclosed by a formidable *jayagiri* (square wall), 8m high and 13km in length, and encircled by a 100m-wide *jayasindhu* (moat) that would have stopped all but the hardiest invaders in their tracks. This architectural layout is an expression of Mt Meru surrounded by the oceans.

In the centre of the walled enclosure are the city's most important monuments, including Bayon, Baphuon, the Royal Enclosure, Phimeanakas and the Terrace of Elephants. Visitors should set aside a half-day to explore Angkor Thom in depth.

⊙ Sights

★ Bayon   BUDDHIST TEMPLE
(បាយ័ន; ⊙7.30am-5.30pm) At the heart of Angkor Thom is the 12th-century Bayon, the mesmerising, if slightly mind-bending, state temple of Jayavarman VII. It epitomises the

creative genius and inflated ego of Cambodia's most celebrated king. Its 54 Gothic towers are decorated with 216 gargantuan smiling faces of Avalokiteshvara, and it is adorned with 1.2km of extraordinary bas-reliefs incorporating more than 11,000 figures.

The upper level of Bayon was closed for restoration in December 2019 and is not scheduled to reopen until 2022.

However, the lower levels, including the epic bas-reliefs, will remain open throughout the restoration. The temple's eastward orientation leads most people to visit in the morning, though, Bayon looks equally good around late afternoon.

Unique, even among its cherished contemporaries, the architectural audacity was a definitive political statement about the change from Hinduism to Mahayana Buddhism. Known as the 'face temple' thanks to its iconic visages, these huge heads glare down from every angle, exuding power and control with a hint of humanity. This was precisely the blend required to hold sway over such a vast empire, ensuring the disparate and far-flung population yielded to Jayavarman VII's magnanimous will. As you walk around, a dozen or more of the heads are visible at any one time, full face or in profile, sometimes level with your eyes, sometimes staring down from on high.

Though Bayon is now known to have been built by Jayavarman VII, for many years its origins were unknown. Shrouded in dense jungle, it also took researchers some time to realise that it stands in the exact centre of the city of Angkor Thom. There is still much mystery associated with Bayon – such as its exact function and symbolism – and this seems only appropriate for a monument whose signature is an enigmatic smiling face.

Unlike Angkor Wat, which looks impressive from all angles, Bayon looks rather like a glorified pile of rubble from a distance. It's only when you enter the temple and make your way up to the third level that its magic becomes apparent.

The basic structure of Bayon comprises a simple three levels, which correspond more or less to three distinct phases of building. This is because Jayavarman VII began construction of this temple at an advanced age, so he was never confident it would be completed. Each time one phase was completed, he moved on to the next. The first two levels are square and adorned with bas-reliefs. They lead up to a third, circular level, with the towers and their faces.

Some say that the Khmer empire was divided into 54 provinces at the time of Bayon's construction, hence the 54 pairs of all-seeing eyes keeping watch on the kingdom's outlying subjects.

The famous carvings on the outer wall of the first level depict vivid scenes of everyday life in 12th-century Cambodia. The bas-reliefs on the second level do not have the epic proportions of those on the first level and tend to be fragmented. The reliefs described are those on the first level. The sequence assumes that you enter the Bayon from the east and view the reliefs in a clockwise direction.

TEMPLES OF ANGKOR ANGKOR THOM

THE GATES OF ANGKOR THOM

It is the gates that grab you first, flanked by a vast representation of the Churning of the Ocean of Milk, 54 demons and 54 gods engaged in an epic tug of war on the causeway. Each gate towers above the visitor, the magnanimous faces of the Bodhisattva Avalokiteshvara staring out over the kingdom. Imagine being a peasant in the 13th century approaching the forbidding capital for the first time. It would have been an awe-inspiring, yet unsettling, experience to enter such a gateway and come face to face with the divine power of the god-kings.

The **south gate** (ខ្លោងទ្វារទ្នើ្ងអ្ន) is most popular with visitors, as it has been fully restored and many of the heads (mostly copies) remain in place. The gate is on the main road into Angkor Thom from Angkor Wat, and it gets very busy. More peaceful are the east and west gates, found at the end of dirt trails. The **east gate** (ខ្លោងទ្វារខ្លោច) was used as a location in *Lara Croft: Tomb Raider,* where the bad guys broke into the 'tomb' by pulling down a giant polystyrene *apsara*. The causeway at the **west gate** (ខ្លោងទ្វារតាកៅ) of Angkor Thom has completely collapsed, leaving a jumble of ancient stones sticking out of the soil, like victims of a terrible historical pile-up.

Bayon

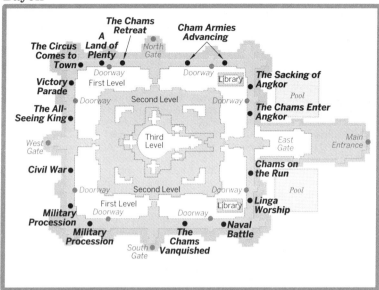

Moving in a clockwise direction from just south of the east gate you'll encounter your first bas-relief, **Chams on the Run**, a three-level panorama. On the first tier, Khmer soldiers march off to battle – check out the elephants and the ox-carts, which are almost exactly like those still used in Cambodia today. The second tier depicts coffins being carried back from the battlefield. In the centre of the third tier, Jayavarman VII, shaded by parasols, is shown on horseback followed by legions of concubines (to the left).

Moving on, the first panel north of the southeastern corner shows **Hindus praying to a linga** (phallic symbol). This image was probably originally a Buddha, later modified by a Hindu king.

The **Naval Battle** panel has some of the best-carved reliefs. The scenes depict a naval battle between the Khmers and the Chams (the latter with head coverings), and everyday life around the Tonlé Sap lake, where the battle was fought. Look for images of people picking lice from each other's hair, of hunters and, towards the western end of the panel, a woman giving birth.

In the **Chams Vanquished**, scenes from daily life are featured while the battle between the Khmers and the Chams takes place on the shore of Tonlé Sap lake, where

the Chams are soundly thrashed. Scenes include two people playing chess, a cockfight and women selling fish in the market. The scenes of meals being prepared and served are in celebration of the Khmer victory.

The most western relief of the south gallery, depicting a **Military Procession**, is unfinished, as is the panel showing elephants being led down from the mountains. Brahmans have been chased up two trees by tigers.

The next panel depicts scenes that some scholars maintain is a **Civil War**. Groups of people, some armed, confront each other, and the violence escalates until elephants and warriors join the melee.

Just north of the Civil War panel, the fighting continues on a smaller scale in the **All-Seeing King**. An antelope is being swallowed by a gargantuan fish; among the smaller fish is a prawn, under which an inscription proclaims that the king will seek out those in hiding.

The next panel depicts a procession that includes the king (carrying a bow). Presumably it is a **Victory Parade**.

At the western corner of the northern wall is a **Khmer circus**. A strongman holds three dwarfs, and a man on his back is spinning a wheel with his feet; above is a group of tightrope walkers. To the right of the circus, the royal court watches from a terrace, below which is a procession of animals. Some of the reliefs in this section remain unfinished.

In A Land of Plenty, two rivers – one next to the doorpost and the other a few metres to the right – are teeming with fish.

On the lowest level of the unfinished three-tiered Chams Defeat, the Cham armies are being defeated and expelled from the Khmer kingdom. The next two panels depict the Cham Armies Advancing, and the badly deteriorated panel shows the Chams (on the left) chasing the Khmers.

The Sacking of Angkor shows the war of 1177, when the Khmers were defeated by the Chams, and Angkor was pillaged. The wounded Khmer king is being lowered from the back of an elephant and a wounded Khmer general is being carried on a hammock suspended from a pole. Directly above, despairing Khmers are getting drunk. The Chams (on the right) are in hot pursuit of their vanquished enemy.

The next panel, the Chams Enter Angkor, depicts a meeting of the Khmer and Cham armies. Notice the flag bearers among the Cham troops (on the right). The Chams were defeated in the war, which ended in 1181, as depicted on the first panel in the sequence.

Baphuon
HINDU TEMPLE

(ប្រាសាទបាពួន; ⊙ 7.30am-5.30pm) Some have called Baphuon the 'world's largest jigsaw puzzle'. Before the civil war the Baphuon was painstakingly taken apart piece-by-piece by a team of archaeologists, but their meticulous records were destroyed during the Khmer Rouge regime, leaving experts with 300,000 stones to put back into place. After years of excruciating research, this temple has been partially restored. In the 16th century, the retaining wall on the western side of the second level was fashioned into a 60m reclining Buddha.

In its heyday, Baphuon would have been one of the most spectacular of Angkor's temples. Located 200m northwest of Bayon, it's a pyramidal representation of mythical Mt Meru. Construction probably began under Suryavarman I and was later completed by Udayadityavarman II. It marked the centre of the capital that existed before the construction of Angkor Thom.

The site is approached by a 200m elevated walkway made of sandstone, and the central structure is 43m high. Clamber under the elevated causeway for an incredible view of the hundreds of pillars supporting it.

It takes around one hour to fully explore Baphuon, although it is possible to have a faster visit if you skip the upper levels.

Terrace of the Leper King
ARCHAEOLOGICAL SITE

(ទីលានព្រះគម្លង់; ⊙ 7.30am-5.30pm) The Terrace of the Leper King is just north of the Terrace of Elephants. Dating from the late 12th century, it is a 7m-high platform, on top of which stands a nude, though sexless, statue. The front retaining walls of the terrace are decorated with at least five tiers of meticulously executed carvings. On the southern side of the Terrace of the Leper King, there is access to a hidden terrace with exquisitely preserved carvings.

The aforementioned statue is yet another of Angkor's mysteries. The original of the statue is held at Phnom Penh's National Museum, and various theories have been advanced to explain its meaning. Legend has it that at least two of the Angkor kings had leprosy, and the statue may represent one of them. Another theory – a more likely explanation – is that the statue is of Yama, the god of death, and that the Terrace of the Leper King housed the royal crematorium.

The carved walls include seated *apsaras* and kings wearing pointed diadems, armed with short double-edged swords and accompanied by the court and princesses, the latter adorned with beautiful rows of pearls.

On the southern side of the Terrace of the Leper King (facing the Terrace of Elephants), there is access to the front wall of a hidden terrace that was covered up when the outer structure was built, a sort of terrace within a terrace. The four tiers of *apsaras* and other figures, including nagas, look as fresh as if they had been carved yesterday, thanks to being covered up for centuries. Some of the figures carry fearsome expressions. As you follow the inner wall of the Terrace of the Leper King, notice the increasingly rough chisel marks on the figures, an indication that this wall was never completed, like many of the temples at Angkor.

Terrace of Elephants
ARCHAEOLOGICAL SITE

(ទីលានដំរី; ⊙ 7.30am-5pm) The 350m-long Terrace of Elephants was used as a giant viewing stand for public ceremonies and served as a base for the king's grand audience hall. Try to imagine the pomp and grandeur of the Khmer empire at its height,

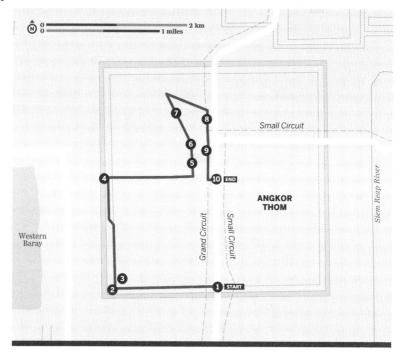

🏃 Walking Tour
Angkor Thom

START SOUTH GATE
END BAYON
LENGTH 6KM; FOUR HOURS

Angkor Thom is the top trekking spot thanks to its manageable size and rewarding temples.

Start at the spectacular **1 south gate** (p157), admiring the immense representation of the Churning of the Ocean of Milk before ascending the wall of this ancient city and heading west, enjoying views of the vast moat to the left and the thick jungle to the right. Reaching the southwestern corner, admire **2 Prasat Chrung** (ប្រាសាទ ជ្រុង), one of four identical temples marking the corners of the city. Head down below to see the water outlet of **3 Run Ta Dev** (រន្ធ កា ដែវ). In its heyday this once powerful city was criss-crossed by canals.

Back on the gargantuan wall, continue to the west gate, looking out for a view to the immense Western Baray on your left. Descend at the **4 west gate** (p157) and admire the artistry of the central tower. Wander east along the path into the heart of Angkor Thom, but don't be diverted by the beauty of Bayon, as this

is best saved until last. If you are with a tour guide, you will have to travel this first and follow the designated running order, but independent travellers can plot their own course.

Veer north into **5 Baphuon** (p159) and wander to the back of what some have called the 'world's largest jigsaw puzzle'. Pass the small temple of **6 Phimeanakas** and the former royal palace compound, an area of towering trees, tumbling walls and atmospheric foliage. Continue further north to petite but pretty **7 Preah Palilay**.

It's time to make for the mainstream with a walk through the **8 Terrace of the Leper King** (p159) and along the front of the royal viewing gallery, the **9 Terrace of Elephants** (p159). If there's time, you may want to zigzag east to visit the laterite towers of Prasat Suor Prat and the atmospheric Buddhist temple of Preah Pithu. Otherwise, continue to the top billing of **10 Bayon** (p156): weird yet wonderful, this is one of the most enigmatic of the temples at Angkor. Take your time to decipher the bas-reliefs before venturing up to the legendary faces of the upper level.

with infantry, cavalry, horse-drawn chariots and elephants parading across Central Square in a colourful procession, pennants and standards aloft. Looking on is the god-king, shaded by multitiered parasols and attended by mandarins and handmaidens bearing gold and silver utensils.

The Terrace of Elephants has five piers extending towards the Central Square – three in the centre and one at each end. The middle section of the retaining wall is decorated with life-size *garudas* and lions; towards either end are the two parts of the famous parade of elephants, complete with their Khmer mahouts.

Preah Palilay   BUDDHIST TEMPLE

(ព្រះបាលិឡៃ្យ; ⊘7.30am-5.30pm) Preah Palilay is located about 200m north of the Royal Enclosure's northern wall. It was erected during the rule of Jayavarman VII and originally housed a Buddha, which has long since vanished. There are several huge tree roots looming large over the central tower, making for a memorable photo opportunity of a classic 'jungle temple'.

Royal Enclosure & Phimeanakas   PALACE

(ភិមានអាកាស; ⊘7.30am-5pm) Phimeanakas stands close to the centre of a walled area that once housed the royal palace. There's very little left of the palace today except for two sandstone pools near the northern wall. Phimeanakas means 'Celestial Palace', and some scholars say that it was once topped by a golden spire. It is currently undergoing restoration and the upper level is off-limits to visitors.

Construction of the palace began under Rajendravarman II, although it was used by Jayavarman V and Udayadityavarman I. It was later added to and embellished by Jayavarman VII and his successors. The royal enclosure is fronted to the east by the Terrace of Elephants. The northwestern wall of the Royal Enclosure is very atmospheric, with immense trees and jungle vines cloaking the outer side, easily visible on a forest walk from Preah Palilay to Phimeanakas.

The temple is another pyramidal representation of Mt Meru, with three levels. Most of the decorative features are broken or have disappeared.

Preah Pithu   TEMPLE

(ព្រះពិធូរ; ⊘7.30am-5.30pm) Preah Pithu, located across Northern Ave from Tep Pranam, is a group of 12th-century Hindu and Buddhist temples enclosed by a wall. It includes some beautifully decorated terraces and guardian animals in the form of elephants and lions. It sees few tourists, and so is a good place to explore at a leisurely pace, taking in the impressive jungle backdrop.

Kleangs & Prasat Suor Prat   ARCHAEOLOGICAL SITE

(ប្រាសាទឡ្បុង និងប្រាសាទសួរប្រិត; ⊘7.30am-5pm) Along the eastern side of Central Square are two groups of buildings, called Kleangs. The North Kleang, dated from the period of Jayavarman V, and the South Kleang may at one time have been palaces. Along Central Square in front of the two Kleangs are 12 laterite towers – 10 in a row and two more at right angles facing the Ave of Victory – known as the Prasat Suor Prat, meaning 'Temple of the Tightrope Dancers'.

Archaeologists believe the towers, which form an honour guard, were constructed by Jayavarman VII. It is likely that each one originally contained either a *linga* or a statue. It is said artists performed for the king on tightropes or rope bridges strung between these towers, hence the name.

According to 13th-century Chinese emissary Chou Ta-Kuan, the towers of Prasat Suor Prat were also used for public trials of sorts. During a dispute the two parties would be made to sit inside two towers, one party eventually succumbing to illness and proven guilty.

ℹ Getting There & Away

If coming from Angkor Wat, you'll enter Angkor Thom through the south gate (p157). From Ta Prohm, you'll enter through the **Victory Gate** (ខ្លោងទ្វារជ័យ) on the eastern side. The immense **north gate** (ខ្លោងទ្វារជើង) of Angkor Thom connects the walled city with Preah Khan and the temples of the Grand Circuit. The west gate (p157) leads to the Western Baray.

There are a range of transport options from Siem Reap including bicycle, *moto, remork* and car.

AROUND ANGKOR THOM

Small Circuit

The 17km Small Circuit begins at Angkor Wat (p150) and heads north to Phnom Bakheng (p163), **Baksei Chamkrong** (បក្សីចាំក្រុង; ⊘7.30am-5.30pm) and Angkor

Thom (p156), including the city wall and gates, the Bayon (p156), the Baphuon, the Royal Enclosure, Phimeanakas, Preah Palilay, the Terrace of the Leper King, the Terrace of Elephants, the Kleangs and Prasat Suor Prat. It exits from Angkor Thom via the Victory Gate in the eastern wall, and continues to Chau Say Tevoda (p164), Thommanon (p164), Spean Thmor (p164) and Ta Keo (p164). It then heads northeast of the road to Ta Nei (p164), turns south to Ta Prohm, continues east to Banteay Kdei and Sra Srang, and finally returns to Angkor Wat via Prasat Kravan (p167).

★ Ta Prohm   BUDDHIST TEMPLE

(តាព្រហ្ម; ⊘7.30am-5.30pm) The so-called 'Tomb Raider Temple', Ta Prohm is cloaked in dappled shadow, its crumbling towers and walls locked in the slow muscular embrace of vast root systems. Undoubtedly the most atmospheric ruin at Angkor, Ta Prohm should be high on the hit list of every visitor. Its appeal lies in the fact that, unlike the other monuments of Angkor, it has been swallowed by the jungle, and looks very much the way most of the monuments of Angkor appeared when European explorers first stumbled upon them.

Well, that's the theory, but in fact the jungle is pegged back and only the largest trees are left in place, making it manicured rather than raw like Beng Mealea. Still, a visit to Ta Prohm is a unique, other-worldly experience. There is a poetic cycle to this venerable ruin, with humanity first conquering nature to rapidly create, and nature once again conquering humanity to slowly destroy. If Angkor Wat is testimony to the genius of the ancient Khmers, Ta Prohm reminds us equally of the awesome fecundity and power of the jungle.

Built from 1186 and originally known as Rajavihara (Monastery of the King), Ta Prohm was a Buddhist temple dedicated to the mother of Jayavarman VII. It is one of the few temples in the Angkor region where an inscription provides information about the temple's dependents and inhabitants. Almost 80,000 people were required to maintain or attend at the temple, among them more than 2700 officials and 615 dancers.

Ta Prohm is a temple of towers, closed courtyards and narrow corridors. Many of the corridors are impassable, clogged with jumbled piles of delicately carved stone blocks dislodged by the roots of long-decayed trees. Bas-reliefs on bulging walls are carpeted with lichen, moss and creeping plants, and shrubs sprout from the roofs of monumental porches. Trees, hundreds of years old, tower overhead, their leaves filter-

Ta Prohm

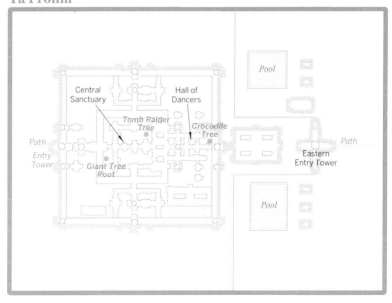

ON LOCATION WITH TOMB RAIDER

Several sequences for the film *Lara Croft: Tomb Raider* (2001), starring Angelina Jolie as Lara Croft, were shot around the temples of Angkor. The Cambodia shoot opened at Phnom Bakheng, with Lara looking through binoculars for the mysterious temple. The baddies were already trying to break in through the east gate of Angkor Thom by pulling down a giant (polystyrene!) *apsara*. Reunited with her custom Land Rover, Lara made a few laps around Bayon before discovering a back way into the temple from Ta Prohm. After battling a living statue and dodging Daniel Craig (aka 007) by diving off the water-fall at Phnom Kulen, she emerged in a floating market in front of Angkor Wat, as you do. She came ashore here before borrowing a mobile phone from a local monk and venturing into the Gallery of a Thousand Buddhas, where she was healed by the abbot.

ing the sunlight and casting a greenish pall over the whole scene.

The most popular of the many strangulating root formations is the one on the inside of the easternmost *gopura* (entrance pavilion) of the central enclosure, nicknamed the Crocodile Tree. One of the most famous spots in Ta Prohm is the so-called Tomb Raider tree, where Angelina Jolie's Lara Croft picked a jasmine flower before falling through the earth into...Pinewood Studios.

It used to be possible to climb onto the damaged galleries, but this is now prohibited, to protect both temple and visitor. Many of these precariously balanced stones weigh a tonne or more and would do some serious damage if they came down. Ta Prohm is currently under stabilisation and restoration by an Indian team of archaeologists working with their Cambodian counterparts.

The temple is at its most impressive early in the day. Allow as much as two hours to visit, especially if you want to explore the maze-like corridors and iconic tree roots.

Banteay Kdei & Sra Srang

BUDDHIST TEMPLE

(បន្ទាយក្តី និងស្រះស្រង់; ⊘7.30am-5.30pm) Banteay Kdei, a massive Buddhist monastery from the latter part of the 12th century, is surrounded by four concentric walls. Each of its four entrances is decorated with *garudas,* which hold aloft one of Jayavarman VII's favourite themes: the four faces of Avalokiteshvara. East of Banteay Kdei is a vast pool of water, Sra Srang, measuring 800m by 400m, reserved as a bathing pool for the king and his consorts.

The outer wall of Banteay Kdei measures 500m by 700m. The inside of the central tower was never finished and much of the temple is in a ruinous state due to hasty construction. It is considerably less busy than

nearby Ta Prohm and this alone can justify a visit.

A tiny island in the middle of Sra Srang once bore a wooden temple, of which only the stone base remains. This is a beautiful body of water from which to take in a quiet sunrise.

Allow about one hour to visit Banteay Kdei and admire the view over nearby Sra Srang.

Phnom Bakheng

HINDU TEMPLE

(ភ្នំបាខែង; ⊘5am-7pm) Located around 400m south of Angkor Thom, the main attraction at Phnom Bakheng is the sunset view over Angkor Wat. For many years, the whole affair turned into a circus, with crowds of tourists ascending the slopes of the hill and jockeying for space. Numbers are now restricted to just 300 visitors at any one time, so get here early (4pm) to guarantee a sunset spot. The temple, built by Yasovarman I (r 889–910), has five tiers, with seven levels.

Phnom Bakheng lays claim to being home to the first of the temple-mountains built in the vicinity of Angkor. Yasovarman I chose Phnom Bakheng over the Roluos area, where the earlier capital (and temple-mountains) had been located.

At the base are – or were – 44 towers. Each of the five tiers had 12 towers. The summit of the temple has four towers at the cardinal points of the compass as well as a central sanctuary. All of these numbers are of symbolic significance. The seven levels represent the seven Hindu heavens, while the total number of towers, excluding the central sanctuary, is 108, a particularly auspicious number and one that correlates to the lunar calendar.

Some prefer to visit in the early morning, when it's cool (and crowds are light), to climb the hill. That said, the sunset over the Western Baray is very impressive from

Phnom Bakheng

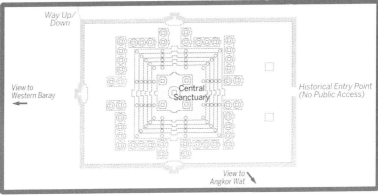

Way Up/ Down

View to Western Baray ←

Central Sanctuary

Historical Entry Point (No Public Access)

View to Angkor Wat ↘

here. Allow about two hours for the sunset experience.

To get a decent picture of Angkor Wat in the warm glow of the late-afternoon sun from the summit of Phnom Bakheng, you will need at least a 300mm lens, as the temple is 1.3km away.

Ta Keo
HINDU TEMPLE

(តាកែវ; ⊙ 7.30am-5.30pm) Ta Keo is a stark, undecorated temple that undoubtedly would have been one of the finest of Angkor's structures, had it been finished. Built by Jayavarman V, it was dedicated to Shiva and was the first Angkorian monument built entirely of sandstone. The summit of the central tower, which is surrounded by four lower towers, is almost 50m high. The four towers at the corners of a square and a fifth tower in the centre is typical of many Angkorian temple-mountains.

No one is certain why work was never completed, but a likely cause may have been the death of Jayavarman V. Others contend that the hard sandstone was impossible to carve and that explains the lack of decoration. According to inscriptions, Ta Keo was struck by lightning during construction, which may have been seen as a bad omen and led to its abandonment. Allow about 30 minutes to visit Ta Keo.

Ta Nei
BUDDHIST TEMPLE

(តានី; ⊙ 7.30am-5.30pm) Ta Nei, 800m north of Ta Keo, was built by Jayavarman VII (r 1181–1219). There is something of the spirit of Ta Prohm here, albeit on a lesser scale, with moss and tentacle-like roots covering many outer areas of this small temple. However, the number of visitors is also on a lesser scale, making it very atmospheric.

It can be accessed via a jungle road from Ta Keo through the forest, a guaranteed way to leave the crowds behind. Including the access, allow about one hour to visit Ta Nei.

Chau Say Tevoda
HINDU TEMPLE

(ចៅសាយទេវតា; ⊙ 7.30am-5.30pm) Just east of Angkor Thom's Victory Gate is Chau Say Tevoda. It was probably built during the second quarter of the 12th century, under the reign of Suryavarman II, and dedicated to Shiva and Vishnu. It has been renovated by the Chinese to bring it up to the condition of its twin temple, Thommanon.

Thommanon
HINDU TEMPLE

(ធម្មនន្ទ; ⊙ 7.30am-5.30pm) Just north of Chau Say Tevoda, Thommanon borrows many features from Angkor Wat and was dedicated to Shiva and Vishnu. The small temple is in good condition thanks to extensive work undertaken by the EFEO in the 1960s. It is regularly used for high-end gala dinners by VIP visitors.

Spean Thmor
BRIDGE

(ស្ពានថ្ម, Stone Bridge) Spean Thmor, of which an arch and several piers remain, is 200m east of Thommanon. Jayavarman VII constructed many roads with these immense stone bridges spanning watercourses. This is the only large bridge remaining in the immediate vicinity of Angkor. It vividly highlights how the water level has changed over the centuries and may offer another clue to the collapse of Angkor's extensive irrigation system. Just north of Spean Thmor is a large water wheel.

Big Circuit

The 26km Big Circuit is an extension of the Small Circuit: instead of exiting the walled city of Angkor Thom at the east gate, the Grand Circuit exits at the north gate and continues to Preah Khan and Preah Neak Poan (p166), east to Ta Som (p166), then south via the Eastern Mebon (p166) to Pre Rup (p166). From there it heads west and then southwest on its return to Angkor Wat (p150).

Preah Khan   BUDDHIST TEMPLE

(ព្រះខ័ន, Sacred Sword) The temple of Preah Khan is one of the largest complexes at Angkor, a maze of vaulted corridors, fine carvings and lichen-clad stonework. It is a good counterpoint to Ta Prohm and generally sees slightly fewer visitors. Like Ta Prohm it is a place of towered enclosures and shoulder-hugging corridors. Unlike Ta Prohm, however, the temple of Preah Khan is in a reasonable state of preservation thanks to the ongoing restoration efforts of the WMF.

Preah Khan was built by Jayavarman VII and probably served as his temporary residence while Angkor Thom was being built. The central sanctuary of the temple was dedicated in CE 1191.

A large stone stela tells us much about Preah Khan's role as a centre for worship and learning. Originally located within the first eastern enclosure, this stela is now housed safely at **Angkor Conservation** (អភិរក្សអង្គរ; Map p108; Angkor Conservation St; US$5; ⊘unofficially 8am-5pm) in Siem Reap. The temple was dedicated to 515 divinities, and during the course of a year 18 major festivals took place here, requiring a team of thousands just to maintain the place.

Preah Khan covers a very large area, but the temple itself is within a rectangular enclosing wall of around 700m by 800m. Four processional walkways approach the gates of the temple, and these are bordered by another stunning depiction of the Churning of the Ocean of Milk, as in the approach to Angkor Thom, although most of the heads have disappeared. From the central sanctuary, vaulted galleries extend in the cardinal directions. Many of the interior walls were once coated with plaster that was held in place by holes in the stone. Today many delicate reliefs remain, including *rishi* and *apsara* carvings.

A genuine fusion temple, the eastern entrance is dedicated to Mahayana Buddhism with equal-sized doors, and the other cardinal directions dedicated to Shiva, Vishnu and Brahma with successively smaller

Preah Khan

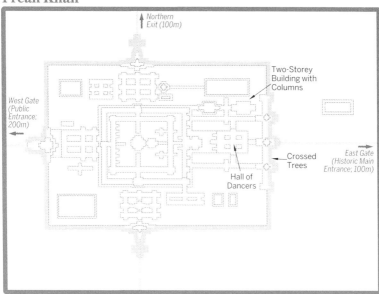

doors, emphasising the unequal nature of Hinduism.

The main entrance to Preah Khan is in the east, but most tourists enter at the west gate near the main road, walk the length of the temple to the east gate before doubling back to the central sanctuary and exiting at the north gate. Approaching from the west, there is little clue to nature's genius, but on the outer retaining wall of the east gate is a pair of trees with monstrous roots embracing, one still reaching for the sky. There is also a curious Grecian-style two-storey structure in the temple grounds, the purpose of which is unknown, but it looks like an exile from Athens. Nearby is the Hall of Dancers, a former performance space that has some impressive *apsara* carvings.

Another option is to enter from the north and exit from the east. Given its vast size, it is sensible to set aside at least 1½ to two hours to explore this temple.

Preah Neak Poan   BUDDHIST TEMPLE
(នាគព័ន្ធ, Temple of the Intertwined Nagas; ☉7.30am-5.30pm) The Buddhist temple of Preah Neak Poan is a petite yet perfect temple constructed by Jayavarman VII in the late 12th century. It has a large square pool surrounded by four smaller square pools. In the middle of the central pool is a circular 'island' encircled by the two nagas whose intertwined tails give the temple its name.

It's a safe bet that if an 'Encore Angkor' casino is eventually developed in Las Vegas or Macau, Preah Neak Poan will provide the blueprint for the ultimate swimming complex.

THE LONG STRIDER

One of Vishnu's best-loved incarnations was when he appeared as the dwarf Vamana, and proceeded to reclaim the world from the evil demon king Bali. The dwarf politely asked the demon king for a comfortable patch of ground upon which to meditate, saying that the patch need only be big enough so that he could easily walk across it in three paces. The demon agreed, only to see the dwarf swell into a mighty giant who strode across the universe in three enormous steps. From this legend, depicted at Prasat Kravan, Vishnu is sometimes known as the 'long strider'.

In the pool around the central island there were once four statues, but only one remains, reconstructed from the debris by the French archaeologists who cleared the site. The curious figure has the body of a horse supported by a tangle of human legs. It relates to a legend that Avalokiteshvara once saved a group of shipwrecked followers from an island of ghouls by transforming into a flying horse. A beautiful replica of this statue decorates the main roundabout at Siem Reap International Airport.

Water once flowed from the central pool into the four peripheral pools via ornamental spouts, which can still be seen in the pavilions at each axis of the pool. The spouts are in the form of an elephant head, a horse head, a lion head and a human head. The pool was used for ritual purification rites.

Preah Neak Poan was once in the centre of a huge 3km-by-900m *baray* serving Preah Khan, known as Jayatataka, once again partially filled with water. Access is restricted to the edge of the complex via a wooden causeway, so a visit takes only 30 minutes.

Ta Som   BUDDHIST TEMPLE
(តាសោម; ☉7.30am-5.30pm) Standing to the east of Preah Neak Poan, Ta Som is one of the late-12th-century Buddhist temples of prolific builder Jayavarman VII. The most impressive feature at Ta Som is the huge tree completely overwhelming the eastern *gopura,* which provides one of the most popular photo opportunities in the Angkor area.

Eastern Mebon   HINDU TEMPLE
(ប្រាសាទមេបុណ្យខាងកើត; ☉7.30am-5.30pm) This Hindu temple, erected by Rajendravarman II, would once have been situated on an islet in the centre of the Eastern Baray (បារាយណ៍ខាងកើត), it is now very much on dry land. Its temple-mountain form is topped off by a quintet of towers. The elaborate brick shrines are dotted with neatly arranged holes, which attached the original plasterwork. The base of the temple is guarded at its corners by perfectly carved stone figures of elephants.

Pre Rup   HINDU TEMPLE
(ប្រែរូប; ☉5am-7pm) Pre Rup, built by Rajendravarman II, is about 1km south of the Eastern Mebon and is a popular spot for sunset. The temple consists of a pyramid-shaped temple-mountain with the uppermost of the three tiers carrying five lotus towers. Pre Rup means 'Turning the Body'

Preah Neak Poan

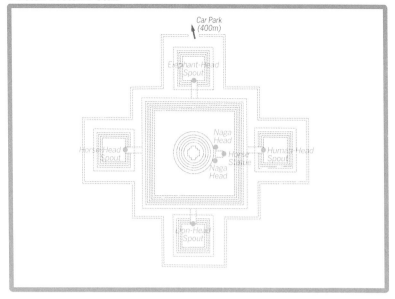

and refers to a traditional method of cremation in which a corpse's outline is traced in the cinders: this suggests that the temple may have served as an early royal crematorium.

The brick sanctuaries here were once decorated with a plaster coating, fragments of which remain on the southwestern tower; there are some amazingly detailed lintel carvings here. Several of the outermost eastern towers are perilously close to collapse and are propped up by an army of wooden supports.

Pre Rup is one of the most popular sunset spots around Angkor, as the view over the surrounding rice fields of the Eastern Baray is beautiful, although some lofty trees have rather obscured it these days. It gets pretty crowded.

Prasat Kravan   HINDU TEMPLE
(ប្រាសាទក្រវ៉ាន់; ⊙ 7.30am-5.30pm) Uninspiring from the outside, the interior brick carvings concealed within its towers are the hidden treasure of Prasat Kravan. The five brick towers, arranged in a north–south line and oriented to the east, were built for Hindu worship in CE 921. The structure is unusual in that it was not constructed by royalty; this accounts for its slightly distant location, away from the other temples. Pra-

sat Kravan is just south of the road between Angkor Wat and Banteay Kdei.

ROLUOS TEMPLES

The monuments of Roluos (រលួស), which served as Indravarman I's capital, Hariharalaya, are among the earliest large, permanent temples built by the Khmers and mark the dawn of Khmer classical art. Before the construction of Bakong temple, generally only lighter (and less durable) construction materials such as brick were employed. As well as the imposing pyramid temple of Bakong, the Roluos group also includes Preah Ko and Lolei.

Plan a half-day visit together with the stilted village of Kompong Pluk or allow three hours or so to explore the three temples and nearby handicraft projects.

☉ Sights

Bakong   HINDU TEMPLE
(បាគង; ⊙ 7.30am-5.30pm) Bakong is the largest and most interesting of the Roluos group of temples. Built and dedicated to Shiva by Indravarman I, it's a representation of Mt Meru, and it served as the city's central temple. The east-facing complex consists

GOOD CAUSE SHOPPING AROUND ROLUOS

Several good-cause initiatives have sprung up around the Roluos area. Look out for **Prolung Khmer** (www.prolung khmer.blogspot.com; ◷8am-5pm) 🍴 on the road between Preah Ko and Bakong. It's a weaving centre producing stylish cotton *krama* (checked scarves), set up as a training collaboration between Cambodia and Japan.

Right opposite Preah Ko is the **Khmer Group Art of Weaving** (Preah Ko; ◷7am-5pm), turning out silk and cotton scarves on traditional looms. Also here is **Dy Proeung Master Sculptor** (donations accepted; ◷6am-6pm), who has created scale replicas of Preah Ko, Bakong and Lolei, plus Angkor Wat, Preah Vihear and Banteay Srei for good measure.

Not far from here on NH66 is the **Lo-Yuyu** (www.loyuyuceramics.com; NH66; ◷8am-6pm) ceramics workshop, producing traditional Angkorian-style pottery.

of a five-tier central pyramid of sandstone, 60m square at the base, flanked by eight towers of brick and sandstone, and by other minor sanctuaries. A number of the lower towers are still partly covered by their original plasterwork.

The complex is enclosed by three concentric walls and a moat. There are well-preserved statues of stone elephants on each corner of the first three levels of the central temple. There are 12 stupas – three to each side – on the third tier. The sanctuary on the fifth level of Bakong temple was a later addition during the reign of Suryavarman II, in the style of Angkor Wat's central tower. There is an active Buddhist monastery here, dating back a century or more, which has recently been restored.

Preah Ko   HINDU TEMPLE

(ប្រះគោ; ◷7.30am-5.30pm) Preah Ko was erected by Indravarman I in the late 9th century and dedicated to Shiva. In CE 880 the temple was also dedicated to his deified ancestors: the front towers relate to male ancestors or gods, the rear towers to female ancestors or goddesses. Lions guard the steps up to the temple. Preah Ko (Sacred

Ox) features three *nandis* (sacred oxen), all of whom look like a few steaks have been sliced off over the years.

The six *prasat* (stone halls), aligned in two rows and decorated with carved sandstone and plaster reliefs, face east; the central tower of the front row is a great deal larger than the other towers. Some of the best surviving examples of plasterwork in Angkor can be seen here, restored by the German Apsara Conservation Project (p153). There are elaborate inscriptions in the ancient Hindu language of Sanskrit on the doorposts of each tower.

Lolei   HINDU TEMPLE

(លលៃ; ◷7.30am-5.30pm) The four brick towers of Lolei, an almost exact replica of the towers of Preah Ko (although in much worse shape), were built on an islet in the centre of a large reservoir – now rice fields – by Yasovarman I, the founder of the first city at Angkor. The sandstone carvings in the niches of the temples are worth a look, and there are Sanskrit inscriptions on the doorposts.

CMAC Peace Museum of Mine Action   MUSEUM

(សារមន្ទីរសន្តិភាពសកម្មភាពកំចាត់មីន; www. cmac.gov.kh; Prasat Bakong District; donations accepted; ◷7.30am-5pm) 🍴 FREE Located in the Roluos HQ of CMAC (Cambodian Mine Action Centre), this museum gets very few visitors due to its out-of-the-way location, but it is an educational and sobering experience to learn about the legacy of landmines in the country. Exhibits include numerous bombs and landmines, all thankfully decommissioned. A local guide will show you around.

🛏 Sleeping & Eating

The vast majority of travellers who visit the Roluos temples stay in Siem Reap, although there are some homestays and a boutique hotel located in Prasat Bakong District.

Lom Lam Homestay   HOMESTAY $$

(☏012 656662; http://lomlameco.weebly.com; s/d/tr US$40/45/50; 🛜) This traditional village homestay has support from a Japanese benefactor, ensuring that comfort and quality are a cut above the average homestay around Siem Reap. Set in a large Cambodian house, the furnishing and bedding are more like that of an upscale guesthouse than a homestay. Airport transfers and activities such as a *remork* tour and village experience are included.

Angkor Rural Boutique Hotel
BOUTIQUE HOTEL $$$

(☑012 817616; www.angkorruralboutique.com; Chrey Thom village; r US$130-180; ☻✳🛜🏊) This charming boutique hotel offers a slice of the countryside in comfort. Rooms are in traditional houses set around a lush garden with a small swimming pool and a natural pond. Furnishings are elegant and in keeping with the surrounds. The sophisticated owner is involved in community tourism initiatives, including recycled jewellery and offering ox-cart rides. Airport transfers included.

Natural Vegetable Food Place
CAMBODIAN $

(☑012 674670; meals US$3-7; ☉9am-9pm) Set amid extensive farmland on the road between Siem Reap and Roluos, this restaurant specialises in organic vegetables grown in its very own gardens. Fish and meat dishes are also available, but all come with a variety of freshly grown vegetables such as okra, long bean and cucumber with a pungent *prahoc ktis* dip (crushed, salted and fermented fish with herbs).

Stoeng Trorcheak Restaurant
CAMBODIAN $$

(☑012 717815; meals US$3-12; ☉7am-10pm; ✳🛜) The shady gardens at this sprawling restaurant set by the Roluos River are a good place to cool off during the heat of the day. The extensive menu includes Cambodian classics, Chinese favourites, Thai tasters and some international appearances. Many of the tables are set up underneath pretty thatched pavilions, but some indoor air-conditioned dining is also available.

ⓘ Getting There & Away

The temples can be found 13km east of Siem Reap along NH6 near the modern-day town of Roluos. A half-day trip from Siem Reap to the Roluos temples by *remork* costs about US$20, or you can add the temples to an existing *remork* tour of the main temples around Siem Reap for an extra US$5 or so (US$20 to US$25 total for the day). You can also reach the temples easily enough on your own by bicycle or electric bike.

BEYOND ANGKOR

Banteay Srei

Considered by many to be the jewel in the crown of Angkorian art, **Banteay Srei** (បន្ទាយស្រី; incl in Angkor admission; ☉7.30am-5.30pm) is cut from stone of a pinkish hue and includes some of the finest stone carving anywhere on earth. Begun in CE 967, it is one of the smallest sites at Angkor, but what it lacks in size it makes up for in stature. The art gallery of Angkor, this Hindu temple dedicated to Shiva is wonderfully well preserved, and many of its carvings are three-dimensional.

Banteay Srei means 'Citadel of the Women', and it is said that it must have been built by a woman, as the elaborate carvings are supposedly too fine for the hand of a man.

Banteay Srei is one of the few temples around Angkor to be commissioned not by a king but by a Brahman, who may have been a tutor to Jayavarman V. The temple is square and has entrances at the east and west, with the east approached by a causeway. Of interest are the lavishly decorated libraries and the three central towers, which are decorated with male and female divinities and beautiful filigree relief work.

Classic carvings at Banteay Srei include delicate women with lotus flowers in hand and traditional skirts clearly visible, as well as breathtaking recreations of scenes from the epic *Ramayana* adorning the library pediments (carved inlays above a lintel). However, the sum of the parts is no greater than the whole – almost every inch of these interior buildings is covered in decoration. Standing watch over such perfect creations are the mythical guardians, all of which are copies of originals stored in the National Museum.

Banteay Srei was the first major temple restoration undertaken by the EFEO in 1930 using the anastylosis method. The project, as evidenced today, was a major success and soon led to other larger projects such as the restoration of Bayon. Banteay Srei is also the first to have been given a full makeover in terms of facilities, with a large car park, a designated dining and shopping area, clear visitor information and a state-of-the-art exhibition on the history of the temple and its restoration. There is also a small *baray* behind the temple where local boat trips

(US$7 per boat) are possible through the lotus pond.

When Banteay Srei was first rediscovered, it was assumed to be from the 13th or 14th centuries, as it was thought that the refined carving must have come at the end of the Angkor period. It was later dated to CE 967, from inscriptions found at the site.

Banteay Srei is about 32km northeast of Siem Reap and 21km northeast of Bayon. It is well signposted and the road is surfaced all the way, so a trip from Siem Reap should take about 45 minutes by car or one hour by *remork*. Moto and *remork* drivers will want a bit of extra cash to come out here, so agree on a sum first. You can eat at one of several small restaurants, complete with ornate wood furnishings cut from Cambodia's forests, near the entrance to the temple.

There's plenty to do in Banteay Srei District as well as several homestays should you wish to stay and explore the area. It is possible to combine a visit to Banteay Srei as part of a long day trip to the River of a Thousand Lingas at Kbal Spean and Beng Mealea. A half-day itinerary might include Banteay Srei, the Cambodia Landmine Museum and Banteay Samre. It takes 45 minutes to explore Banteay Srei temple, but allow 1½ hours to visit the information centre and explore the area.

Beng Mealea

A spectacular sight to behold, Beng Mealea (បឹងមាលា; US$5; ⊙7.30am-5.30pm), located about 68km northeast of Siem Reap, is one of the most mysterious temples at Angkor, as nature has well and truly run riot. Exploring this *Titanic* of temples, built to the same floor plan as Angkor Wat, is the ultimate Indiana Jones experience. Built in the 12th century under Suryavarman II, Beng Mealea is enclosed by a massive moat measuring 1.2km by 900m.

The temple used to be utterly consumed by jungle, but some of the dense foliage has been cut back and cleaned up in recent years. Entering from the south, visitors wend their way over piles of finely chiselled sandstone blocks, through long, dark chambers and between hanging vines. The central tower has completely collapsed, but hidden away among the rubble and foliage are several impressive carvings, including a small but striking rendition of the Churning of the Ocean of Milk, as well as a well-preserved library in the northeastern quadrant. The temple is a special place and it is worth taking the time to explore it thoroughly. The large wooden walkway to and around the centre was originally construct-

Beng Mealea

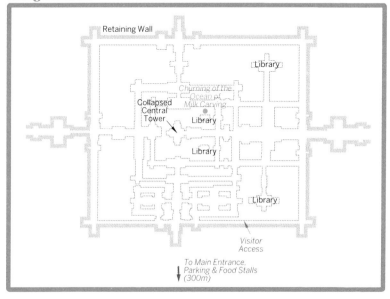

THE LOST CITY OF MAHENDRAPARVATA

Phnom Kulen hit the headlines in 2013 thanks to the 'discovery' of a lost city known in Angkorian times as Mahendraparvata. Using jungle-piercing LIDAR radar technology, the structures of a more extensive archaeological site have been unveiled beneath the jungle canopy. However, it wasn't quite as dramatic a discovery as initially reported, as Phnom Kulen had long been known as an important archaeological site. The LIDAR research confirmed the size and scale of the ancient city, complete with canals and *barays*, in the same way NASA satellite imagery had helped identify the size and scale of the greater Angkor hydraulic water system more than a decade earlier. Some new temples and features were identified beneath the jungle, but they remain remote and inaccessible due to terrain and the possibility of landmines. An additional LIDAR survey of the entire Kulen plateau was conducted in 2015.

ed for the filming of Jean-Jacques Annaud's *Two Brothers* (2004), set in 1920s French Indochina and starring two tiger cubs.

Beng Mealea has a large *baray* to the east and some atmospheric satellite temples such as Prasat Chrey. Apsara Authority (Authority for Protection & Management of Angkor & the Region of Siem Reap; www.apsara authority.gov.kh; Prasat Bakong District; ⏱8am-4pm Mon-Fri) has plans to reflood the ancient *baray,* as they did earlier with Jayatataka (Northern Baray), surrounding Neak Poan temple.

There are several stop-and-dip food stalls (dishes US$2 to US$4) opposite the temple entrance. Run by friendly, English-speaking Sreymom, the Sreymom Beng Mealea Homestay (✆087 555229; Beng Mealea village; r incl meals US$25) is just a short walk away from Beng Mealea. The overnight rates include all home-cooked meals. It is also possible to prearrange lunch here, even if you don't stay overnight.

It costs US$5 to visit Beng Mealea and there are additional small charges for transport, so make sure you work out in advance with the driver or guide who is paying for these. Beng Mealea is about 40km east of Bayon (as the crow flies) and 6.5km southeast of Phnom Kulen. By road it is about 68km (one hour by car, longer by *moto* or *remork*) from Siem Reap. The shortest route is via the junction town of Dam Dek, located on NH6 about 37km from Siem Reap in the direction of Phnom Penh. Turn north immediately after the market and continue on this road for 31km. The entrance to the temple lies just beyond the left-hand turn to Koh Ker. Allow a half day to visit, including the journey time from Siem Reap or combine it with Koh Ker in a long day trip best undertaken by car or 4WD.

Beng Mealea is at the centre of an ancient Angkorian road connecting Angkor Thom and Preah Khan (Prasat Bakan) in Preah Vihear Province, now evocatively numbered Rte 66. A small Angkorian bridge just west of Chau Srei Vibol temple is the only remaining trace of the old Angkorian road between Beng Mealea and Angkor Thom; between Beng Mealea and Preah Khan there are at least 10 bridges abandoned in the forest. This is a way for extreme adventurers to get to Preah Khan temple, but do not undertake this journey lightly.

Phnom Kulen

Considered by Khmers to be the most sacred mountain in Cambodia, Phnom Kulen (ភ្នំគូលែន; www.adfkulen.org; US$20; ⏱6-11am to ascend, noon-5pm to descend) is a popular place of pilgrimage on weekends and during festivals. It played a significant role in the history of the Khmer empire, as it was from here in CE 802 that Jayavarman II proclaimed himself a *devaraja*, giving birth to the Cambodian kingdom. Attractions include a giant reclining Buddha, hundreds of *lingas* carved in the riverbed, an impressive waterfall and some remote temples.

From the entrance a sealed road winds its way through some spectacular jungle scenery, emerging on the plateau after a 12km ascent. The road eventually splits: the left fork leads to the picnic spot, waterfall and ruins of a 9th-century temple; the right fork continues over a bridge (you'll find the riverbed carvings around here) to the base of Wat Preah Ang Thom, which sits at the summit of the mountain and houses the large reclining Buddha carved into the sandstone boulder upon which it is built. This is the focal

LINGER AMONG THE LINGAS

Fertility symbols are prominent around the temples of Angkor. The *linga* is a phallic symbol and would have originally been located within the towers of most Hindu temples. It sits inside a *yoni*, the female fertility symbol, combining to produce holy water, charged with the sexual energy of creation. Brahmans poured the water over the *linga* and it drained through the *yoni* and out of the temples through elaborate gutters to anoint the pilgrims outside.

point of a pilgrimage for Khmer people, so it is important to take off your shoes and any head covering before climbing the stairs to the sanctuary. These days the views from the 487m peak are partially obstructed by foliage run amok.

The **waterfall** is an attractive spot and was featured in *Lara Croft: Tomb Raider*. However, it could be much more beautiful were it not for all the litter left here by families picnicking at the weekend. Near the top of the waterfall is a jungle-clad temple known as **Prasat Krau Romeas**, dating from the 9th century.

There are plenty of other Angkorian sites on Phnom Kulen, including as many as 20 minor temples around the plateau, the most important of which is **Prasat Rong Chen**, the first pyramid or temple-mountain to be constructed in the Angkor area. Most impressive of all are the giant stone animals or guardians of the mountain, known as **Sra Damrei** (Elephant Pond). These are quite difficult to reach, particularly during the wet season. The few people who make it, however, are rewarded with a life-size replica of a stone elephant – a full 4m long and 3m tall – and smaller statues of lions, a frog and a cow. These were constructed on the southern face of the mountain and from here there are spectacular views across the plains below. Getting to Sra Damrei requires taking a *moto* from Wat Preah Ang Thom for about 12km on very rough trails. Don't try to find it on your own; expect to pay the *moto* driver about US$10 for a two-hour trip to explore this area and carry plenty of water.

Other impressive sites that could be included in an adventurous day trip around Phnom Kulen include the ancient rock carvings of **Poeung Tbal,** an atmospheric site of enormous boulders, and the partially restored temple of **Damrei Krap**. Add these to the mix and it will cost more like US$15 to explore for three hours or more.

Phnom Kulen is a huge plateau around 50km from Siem Reap and about 15km from Banteay Srei. To get here on the toll road, take the well-signposted right fork just before Banteay Srei village and go straight ahead at the crossroads. Just before the road starts to climb the mountain, there is a barrier and it is here that the admission charge is levied. It is only possible to go up Phnom Kulen before 11am and only possible to come down after midday, to avoid vehicles meeting on the narrow road. There is a new road under construction that links Phnom Kulen to Svay Leu, a small town to the east of the holy mountain, so a one-way system may eventually be introduced: ascending the mountain by the old road and descending via the new road. There are plenty of small restaurants and food stalls located around the parking area at the base of Wat Preah Ang Thom.

Moto drivers are likely to want about US$20 or more to bring you out here, and rented cars will hit passengers with a surcharge, more than double the going rate for Angkor; forget coming by *remork* as the hill climb is just too tough. With the long journey here, it is best to plan on spending the best part of a day exploring, although it can be combined with either Banteay Srei or Beng Mealea.

Kbal Spean

A spectacularly carved riverbed, **Kbal Spean** (ក្បាលស្ពាន, River of a Thousand Lingas; incl in Angkor admission; ⊙ 7.30am-5.30pm) is set deep in the jungle to the northeast of Angkor. More commonly referred to in English as the 'River of a Thousand Lingas', the name actually means 'bridgehead', a reference to the natural rock bridge here. Lingas have been elaborately carved into the riverbed, and images of Hindu deities are dotted about the area. It was 'discovered' in 1969, when ethnologist Jean Boulbet was shown the area by a hermit.

It is a 2km uphill walk to the carvings, along a pretty path that winds its way up into the jungle, passing some interesting boulder formations along the way. Carry plenty of water up the hill, as there is none available beyond the parking area. The path eventually splits to the waterfall or the river carvings. There is an impressive carving of Vishnu on the upper section of the river, followed by a series of carvings at the bridgehead itself, some of which were hacked off in the past few years, but have since been replaced by excellent replicas. This area is now roped off to protect the carvings from further damage.

Following the river down, there are several more impressive carvings of Vishnu, and Shiva with his consort Uma, and further downstream hundreds of *lingas* appear on the riverbed. At the top of the waterfall are many animal images, including a cow and a frog, and a path winds around the boulders to a wooden staircase leading down to the base of the falls. Visitors between January and June will be disappointed to see very little water here. The best time to visit is between July and December. When exploring Kbal Spean, it's best to start with the river carvings and work back down to the waterfall to cool off. From the car park, the visit takes about two hours including the walk, nearer three hours with a natural shower or a picnic. A day trip here can be combined with Angkor Centre for Conservation of Biodiversity (p131), Banteay Srei temple (p169) and the Cambodia Landmine Museum (p131).

Kbal Spean is about 50km northeast of Siem Reap or about 18km beyond the temple of Banteay Srei. The road is in great shape, as it forms part of the main road north to Anlong Veng and the Thai border, so it takes just one hour or so from town. There are food stalls at the bottom of the hill that can cook up fried rice or a noodle soup, or the fancier, excellent Borey Sovann Restaurant (p133), located near the entrance.

Moto drivers will no doubt want a bit of extra money to take you here; figure on US$15 or so for the day, including a trip to Banteay Srei. Likewise, *remork* drivers will probably up the price to US$25 or so. A surcharge is also levied to come out here by car. Admission to Kbal Spean is included in the general Angkor pass; the last entry to the site is at 3.30pm.

Banteay Samré

Banteay Samré (បន្ទាយសំរែ; ⊘7.30am-5.30pm) dates from the same period as Angkor Wat and was built by Suryavarman II.

The temple is in a fairly healthy state of preservation due to some extensive renovation work, although its isolation has resulted in some looting during the past few decades. The area consists of a central temple with four wings, preceded by a hall and also accompanied by two libraries, the southern one remarkably well preserved.

The whole ensemble is enclosed by two large concentric walls around what would have been the unique feature of an inner moat, now dry.

Banteay Samré is 400m east of the Eastern Baray. A visit here can be combined with a trip to Banteay Srei and/or Phnom Bok.

Chau Srei Vibol

This petite **hilltop temple** (ចៅស្រីវិបុល; ⊘7.30am-5.30pm) is actually part of a larger complex that spanned the entire hill. It is relatively under-visited compared with more centrally located temples, making it an atmospheric option for sunset. The central sanctuary is in a ruined state but is nicely complemented by the construction of an early-20th-century wat nearby.

Surrounding the base of the hill are laterite walls, each with a small entrance hall in reasonable condition, outlining the dimensions of what was once a significant temple.

To get here, turn east off the Bakong to Anlong Veng highway at a point about 8km north of NH6, or 5km south of Phnom Bok. There is a small sign (easy to miss) that marks the turn. Locals are friendly and helpful should you find yourself lost.

Phnom Bok

One of three temple-mountains built by Yasovarman I in the late 9th or early 10th century, this peaceful but remote location (about 25km from Siem Reap) sees few visitors. The small **temple** (ភ្នំបូក; ⊘7.30am-5.30pm) is in reasonable shape, but it is the views of Phnom Kulen to the north and the plains of Angkor to the south from this 212m hill that make it worth the trip.

The remains of a 5m *linga* are visible at the opposite end of the hill, and it's believed there were similar *linga* at Phnom Bakheng and Phnom Krom.

There is a long, winding trail snaking up the hill at Phnom Bok, which takes about 20 minutes to climb, plus a faster cement staircase, but the latter is fairly exposed. Avoid the heat in the middle of the day and carry plenty of water, which can be purchased locally.

Phnom Bok is clearly visible from the road to Banteay Srei. It is accessed by continuing east on the road to Banteay Samré for another 6km. It is possible to loop back to Siem Reap via the temples of Roluos by heading south instead of west on the return journey, and gain some rewarding glimpses of the countryside. Unfortunately, it is not a sensible place to see the sun rise or sun set, as it would require a long journey in the dark.

Phnom Krom

The temple of Phnom Krom (ភ្នំក្រោម; incl in Angkor admission; ⊗7.30am-5.30pm), 12km south of Siem Reap on a hill overlooking Tonlé Sap lake, dates from the reign of Yasovarman I in the late 9th or early 10th century. The name means 'Lower Hill' and is a reference to its geographic location in relation to its sister temples of Phnom Bakheng and Phnom Bok. Phnom Krom remains one of the more tranquil spots from which to view the sunset, complete with an active wat.

The three towers, dedicated (from north to south) to Vishnu, Shiva and Brahma, are in a ruined state. It is necessary to have an Angkor pass to visit the temple at the summit of Phnom Krom, so don't come all the way out here without one, as the guards won't allow you access to the summit of the hill. If coming here by *moto* or car, try to get the driver to take you to the summit, as it is a long, hot climb otherwise. Consider a half-day visit in tandem with exploring the floating village of Chong Kneas.

Western Baray & Western Mebon

The Western Baray (បារាយណ៍ខាងលិច; ⊗7.30am-5.30pm), measuring an incredible 8km by 2.3km, was constructed by hand to provide water for the intensive cultivation of lands around Angkor. These enormous *barays* weren't dug out, but had huge dykes built up around the edges. In the centre of the Western Baray is the ruin of the Western Mebon (ប្រាសាទមេបុណ្យខាងលិច)

temple, where the giant bronze statue of Vishnu, now in the National Museum (p54) in Phnom Penh, was found. The Western Mebon is accessible by boat.

The Western Baray is the main local swimming pool around Siem Reap. There is a small beach of sorts at the western extreme, complete with picnic huts and inner tubes for rent, which attracts plenty of Khmers at weekends.

REMOTE ANGKOR TEMPLES

Koh Ker

Abandoned to the forests of the north, Koh Ker (កោះកេរ៍; US$10; ⊗7.30am-5.30pm), capital of the Angkorian empire from CE 928 to 944, is one of the most remote temple complexes around Angkor. Most visitors start at Prasat Krahom, where impressive stone carvings grace lintels, doorposts and slender window columns. The principal monument is Mayan-looking Prasat Thom, a 55m-wide, 40m-high sandstone-faced pyramid whose seven tiers offer spectacular views across the forest.

Long one of Cambodia's most remote and inaccessible temple complexes, the toll road from Dam Dek (via Beng Mealea) has placed Koh Ker (pronounced ko-kayer) within day-tripping distance of Siem Reap. To really appreciate the temples – the ensemble has 42 major structures in an area that measures 9km by 4km – some visitors prefer to spend a night here.

A usurper capital established under Jayavarman IV around CE 928, Koh Ker is one of the least-studied temple areas from the Angkorian period. Louis Delaporte visited in 1880 during his extensive investigations into Angkorian temples. It was surveyed in 1921 by the great Henri Parmentier for an article in the *Bulletin de l'École d'Extrême Orient*, but no restoration work was ever undertaken here. Archaeological surveys were carried out by Cambodian teams in the 1950s and 1960s. But all records vanished during the destruction of the 1970s, helping to preserve this complex as something of an enigma.

Several of the most impressive pieces in the National Museum (p54) in Phnom Penh

Koh Ker

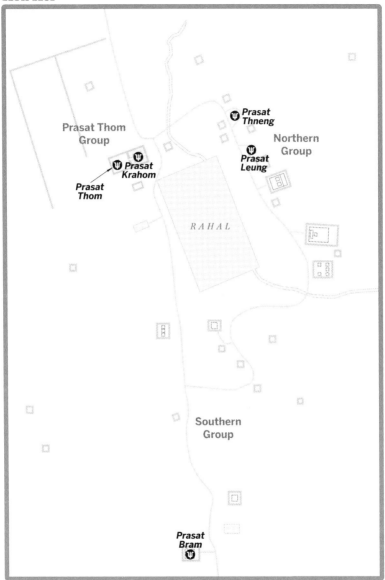

come from Koh Ker, including the huge *garuda* that greets visitors in the entrance hall and a unique carving depicting a pair of wrestling monkey-kings.

◉ Sights

Prasat Thom   HINDU TEMPLE

(ប្រាសាទធំ, Prasat Kompeng; ☉ 7.30am-5.30pm) The principal monument at Koh Ker is Prasat Thom. The staircase to the top is open

LANDMINE ALERT!

Many of the Koh Ker temples were mined during the war, but by 2008 most had been cleared: demining teams reported removing from the area a total of 1382 mines and 1,447,212 pieces of exploded and unexploded ordnance. However, considering what's at stake, it's best to err on the side of caution. Do not stray from previously trodden paths or wander off into the forest, as there may be landmines within a few hundred metres of the temples.

to a limited number of visitors and the views are spectacular if you can stomach the heights. Some 40 inscriptions, dating from 932 to 1010, have been found here.

Prasat Krahom   HINDU TEMPLE

(ប្រាសាទក្រហម, Red Temple; ⊘ 7.30am-5.30pm) Prasat Krahom, the second-largest structure at Koh Ker, is so named for the red bricks from which it is constructed. Sadly, none of the carved lions for which this temple was once known remain, though there's still plenty to see, with stone archways and galleries leaning hither and thither. A naga-flanked causeway and a series of sanctuaries, libraries and gates lead past trees and vegetation-covered ponds.

Just west of Prasat Krahom, at the far western end of a half-fallen colonnade, are the remains (most of the head) of a statue of Nandin.

Prasat Bram   HINDU TEMPLE

(ប្រាសាទប្រាំ; ⊘ 7.30am-5.30pm) Among the many smaller temples found around Koh Ker, Prasat Bram is a real highlight. It consists of a collection of brick towers, at least two of which have been completely smothered by voracious strangler figs; the probing roots cut through the brickwork like liquid mercury.

Prasat Leung   HINDU TEMPLE

(ប្រាសាទលិង្គ; ⊘ 7.30am-5.30pm) Some of the largest *linga* (phallic symbols) in Cambodia can still be seen in a cluster of four temples about 1km northeast of Prasat Thom, collectively known as the *linga* temples. The largest is found in **Prasat Thneng**, while Prasat Leung is similarly well endowed.

🛏 Sleeping & Eating

The only place to stay in the immediate vicinity of Koh Ker's temples is the Koh Ker Jungle Lodge, plus there are a couple of guesthouses in nearby Srayong, about 10km away.

Near the main temple of Prasat Thom there are a few small food stalls (open during daylight hours) run by the wives of the heritage police stationed here. The nearby village of Srayong also has a few eateries.

Mom Morokod Koh Ker
Guesthouse   GUESTHOUSE $

(☑ 011 935114; r US$12) About 200m south of the Koh Ker toll plaza, 8km south of Prasat Krahom, this quiet guesthouse has 11 clean, spacious rooms with elaborately carved wooden doors and bathrooms. There's no restaurant on-site, but the host family can cook up meals on request.

Koh Ker Jungle Lodge   LODGE $$

(☑ 012 655201; www.facebook.com/kohkerjungle lodge; Koh Ker village; based on private booking per r US$65) Located in the small village of Koh Ker about 1km from the main temple of Prasat Thom, most tourists don't even realise this place exists. Set in a striking old wooden house with two private bedrooms, this is a great option to experience local life within walking distance of the temples.

Dinner is available for US$9, but you will need to sort out breakfast and lunch at temple stalls. Guests need to book three days in advance, so plan ahead.

ℹ Getting There & Away

Koh Ker is 127km northeast of Siem Reap (two hours by car) and 72km west of Preah Vihear City (1½ hours). The toll road from Dam Dek, paved only as far as the Preah Vihear Province line, passes by Beng Mealea, 61km southwest of Koh Ker; one-day excursions from Siem Reap often visit both temple complexes. Admission fees are collected at the toll barrier near Beng Mealea if travelling from Siem Reap.

From Siem Reap, hiring a private car for a day trip to Koh Ker costs about US$80. There's no public transport to Koh Ker, although a few minibuses (10,000r) link Srayong, 10km south of Prasat Krahom, with Siem Reap. It might also be possible to take one of the shared taxis that link Siem Reap with Preah Vihear City (Tbeng Meanchey) and get off at Srayong.

South Coast

POP 2 MILLION

Includes ➡

Koh Kong City 179

Koh Kong Conservation
Corridor 184

Sihanoukville 189

Koh Ta Kiev 196

Koh Rong 197

Koh Rong
Sanloem 205

Koh Sdach
Archipelago 211

Kampot 212

Kep 224

Takeo 230

Best Places to Eat

➡ Twenty Three Bistro (p219)

➡ Crab Market (p229)

➡ Sandan (p192)

➡ Tertúlia (p220)

Best Places to Stay

➡ Cardamom Tented Camp (p187)

➡ Lonely Beach (p203)

➡ Rainbow Lodge (p185)

➡ Huba-Huba (p209)

Why Go?

Cambodia's South Coast (ផ្នែរខាងត្បូង) provides the antidote to temple-hopping tick lists. The beaches draw most folk here, but stick around and you'll see this region is more than its sandy bits.

The Koh Kong Conservation Corridor's emerald-green vistas offer trekking potential that is only now being tapped into, providing a host of nature-filled adventures. Down south, travellers can dig into history, admiring Kampot's preserved architecture, then dig into plates piled with crab in Kep, before exploring the surrounding countryside, patchworked with rice fields and studded with caves.

Just here to answer the call of the beach? The islands off Sihanoukville have something for everyone, from die-hard partiers to those seeking sun-kissed solitude. Pick your beach, sprawl on the sand, make friends with your hammock. There's a reason many visitors never leave.

When to Go
Sihanoukville

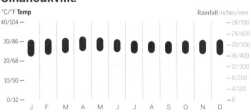

°C/°F **Temp**   Rainfall inches/mm

40/104 —   — 28/700

    — 24/600

30/86 —   — 20/500

    — 16/400

20/68 —   — 12/300

    — 8/200

10/50 —   — 4/100

0/32 —   — 0

J   F   M   A   M   J   J   A   S   O   N   D

Nov–Jan Prime hiking time. Hit the Cardamom Mountains while comfortable temperatures reign.

Feb Peak season finishes on the islands. The crowds fizzle out but the weather's still glorious.

Jun–Oct Hotel prices nosedive across the coast with bargains galore – but pack an umbrella.

South Coast Highlights

1 Koh Rong (p197)
Extending your stay indefinitely on this glorious island, where there's a beach to suit every agenda.

2 Kampot (p212) Ambling the alleys of Cambodia's best-preserved old town, then heading out for river and cave adventures in the countryside.

3 Koh Kong Conservation Corridor (p184) Penetrating the Cardamom Mountains on a groundbreaking ecotour, then booking a boutique stay on the jungle-fringed Tatai River.

4 Koh Rong Sanloem (p205) Basking on the photogenic white sands of Saracen Bay or castaway-cool Sunset Beach.

5 Kep (p224) Feasting on the famous Kampot pepper crab then working off the calories in Kep National Park.

6 Koh Ta Kiev (p196) Soaking up the bohemian vibe and getting into electricity-free living at this bird-laden beauty.

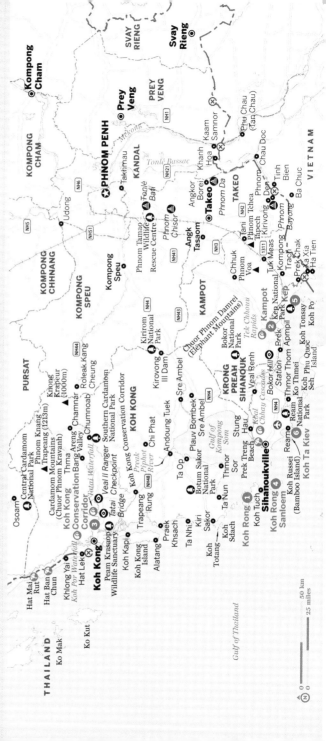

① Getting There & Away

Depending on your destination, getting to and from the South Coast isn't always straightforward, particularly in the low season. So while it may be easy enough to hop a bus to Sihanoukville, Kampot or Koh Kong, the far-flung islands and Central Cardamoms destinations often require a combination of *moto*, taxis, boats, bicycles and your own two feet.

Taking the train, which runs between Phnom Penh, Takeo, Kampot and Sihanoukville, is good fun, and a lovely, if sluggish, way to see the countryside. And flying into or out of Sihanoukville Airport (p193) can be a timesaver, if you don't mind spending a few extra dollars.

KOH KONG CITY

☑ 035 / POP 36,053

Sleepy Koh Kong (ក្រុងកោះកុង) was once Cambodia's Wild West with its isolated frontier economy dominated by smuggling and gambling. Although remnants of its less-salubrious past still cling on, today this low-slung town is striding towards respectability as ecotourists, aiming to explore the Cardamom Mountains and coastline, bring in alternative sources of revenue..

Motorboats from Koh Kong can whisk you to rushing waterfalls, secluded islands, sandy coves and Venice-like fishing villages on stilts. The city's still-dusty sprawl of streets sits on the banks of the Koh Poi River, which spills into the Gulf of Thailand a few kilometres south of the centre.

◉ Sights

Koh Kong's main appeal is as a launching pad for adventures in and around the Cardamom Mountains and the Koh Kong Conservation Corridor, but there are a few diversions around town as well. If you want to take a dip, the pool at Oasis Bungalow Resort (p182) is open to nonguests (US$4) from 9am to 6pm.

Sun-worshippers will discover additional beaches further north on the Gulf of Thailand near the Thai border.

Peam Krasaop
Wildlife Sanctuary   NATURE RESERVE
(ជម្រកសត្វព្រៃបឹងក្រព៊ើក នៅពាមក្រសោប; 5000r; ⏲7am-5pm) Anchored to alluvial islands – some no larger than a house – this 260-sq-km sanctuary's magnificent mangroves protect the coast from erosion, offer vital breeding and feeding grounds for fish, shrimp and shellfish, and are home to myriad birds. To get a feel for the delicate mangrove ecosystem, head to the park entrance, 5.5km east of Koh Kong, where a **mangrove walk** wends its way above the briny waters to a 15m observation tower. A *moto/tuk tuk* ride costs US$5/8 return.

Travellers with little ones in tow should keep a vigilant eye on children as the walkway is not well maintained. If you're lucky, you'll come across cavorting monkeys with a fondness for fizzy drinks. Also here are a restaurant and the **Mangrove Sanctuary Resort** (☑097 411 0808; www.mangrovesanctuaryresort.com; Peam Krasaop Wildlife Sanctuary entrance; bungalow incl breakfast US$50; ✳☎).

You can hire a motorboat to take you through the sanctuary; wooden boats are available for hire from the dock at the sanctuary entrance. Short tours cost US$25 for up to eight people. Half-day trips (US$60) head deeper into the sanctuary's interior, while full-day tours (US$90) include Koh Kong Island (high season only). Fishing is possible. Tour companies in town arrange cheaper half-day and full-day group tours of the sanctuary, with departures from the city boat dock (p181).

On a boat tour you'll have a chance to visit **fishing hamlets** where residents use spindly traps to catch fish, which they keep alive till market time in partly submerged nets attached to floating wooden frames. Further out, on some of the more remote mangrove islands, you pass isolated little beaches where you can land and lounge alongside ambling hermit crabs.

Much of Peam Krasaop is on the prestigious **Ramsar List of Wetlands of International Importance** (www.ramsar.org). The area, which is part of the Koh Kong Conservation Corridor, is all the more valuable from an ecological standpoint because similar forests in Thailand have been trashed by short-sighted development.

Unfortunately Peam Krasaop's habitats and fisheries are threatened by large-scale sand-dredging operations controlled by Cambodian tycoon Ly Yong Phat. Kalyanee Mam's 'short film *A Lost World* brought attention to the issue, which saw more than 72 million tons of sand exported to Singapore from 2007 to 2017, according to the UN. In 2017 the Cambodian government halted sand exports to Singapore. But the equipment remains ominously in place and residents fear

Koh Kong City

Koh Kong City

🟢 Activities, Courses & Tours
1 Paddy's Bamboo Tours B3
2 Ritthy Koh Kong Eco Adventure
  Tours A2

🔵 Sleeping
3 99 Guesthouse B2
  Paddy's Bamboo
  Guesthouse .... (see 1)
  Ritthy's Retreat .... (see 2)

⊗ Eating
4 Fat Sam's B3
5 Food Carts A2
6 Psar Leu A3
7 Wood House A3

🟡 Drinking & Nightlife
8 Pisey's Bar A2
9 Stevie C's A3

ⓘ Information
10 Koh Kong Provincial Hospital B2
11 Tourist Information Centre A1

ⓘ Transport
12 Emerald Express B2
13 Olongpich Express B3
  Rith Mony .... (see 12)
14 Vibol Express B1
15 Virak Buntham B2

that large-scale dredging will resume to serve domestic needs – if it hasn't already.

Koh Kong Island ISLAND

(កោះកុង) Cambodia's largest island towers over seas so crystal-clear you can make out individual grains of sand in a couple of metres of water. A strong military presence on the island means access is tightly controlled. You must visit on a guided boat tour out of Koh Kong or Tatai. These cost US$21 per person, including lunch and snorkelling equipment, or US$55 for overnight trips with beach camping or homestay accommodation. The island is only accessible from October to May.

During the June to September rainy season, strong onshore (southwesterly) breezes make access impossible. It's forbidden to explore the island's thickly forested interior at any time of year.

The island has seven **beaches**, all of them along the western coast. Several of the beaches – lined with coconut palms and lush vegetation, just as you'd expect in a tropical paradise – are at the mouths of little streams. At the sixth beach from the north, a narrow channel leads to a hidden lagoon.

Unfortunately the beaches are becoming increasingly polluted as irresponsible tour operators fail to properly dispose of waste. Hopefully the situation can be reversed, as the island is a real gem. Rampant sand fleas are also notoriously bad during certain times of the year.

On Koh Kong Island's eastern side, half a dozen forested hills – the highest towering 407m above the sea – drop steeply to the mangrove-lined coast. The Venice-like fishing village of **Alatang**, with its stilted houses and colourful fishing boats, is on the southeast coast facing the northwest corner of Botum Sakor National Park.

Koh Yor Beach BEACH

(ឆ្នេរកោះយ៉ នៅបាក់ខ្លង) This long windswept beach is on the far (western) side of the peninsula that forms the west bank of Koh Poi River opposite Koh Kong City. Although it's not the world's prettiest beach, it offers good shell-collecting and you're nearly guaranteed to have it to yourself. To get there, cross the bridge that spans the river north of the town centre and go left at the roundabout about 2km beyond the bridge. The beach is about 6km from the roundabout.

Wat Neang Kok BUDDHIST TEMPLE

(វត្តនាងកុក) This rocky promontory on the right (western) bank of the Koh Poi River is decorated with life-size statues demonstrating the violent punishments that await sinners in the Buddhist hell. This graphic tableau belongs to Wat Neang Kok, a Buddhist temple. To get here, cross the bridge, turn right after 800m, and proceed to the statues, which are 150m beyond a modern temple.

🏃 Activities & Tours

Koh Kong has two competing tour companies – **Ritthy Koh Kong Eco Adventure Tours** (☏ 016 555885; www.kohkongeco adventure.com; St 1) and **Paddy's Bamboo Tours** (☏ 015 533223; ppkohkong@ gmail.com) – offering a mix of **jungle treks** and **boat trips**, both public and private. Their offerings are similar, albeit they use different base camps and their routes vary slightly. Guesthouses in town arrange tours through one of these two companies.

Boat tours are an excellent way to view Koh Kong's many coastal attractions. Tours depart from the city **boat dock** (cnr St 1 & St 9) to **Koh Kong Island**, taking in some of the mangroves of Peam Krasaop Wildlife Sanctuary (p179) (full day per person including lunch and snorkelling equipment from US$21, or overnight for US$55). Overnight trips involve beach camping or a homestay on the island. There's a good chance of spotting Irrawaddy river dolphins early in the morning on these trips.

Note that trips to Koh Kong Island do not take place in rainy season (June to September) because of strong onshore (southwesterly) breezes, although half-day excursions to Peam Krasaop are possible year-round. Also possible year-round are trips upriver into the Cardamoms. These river trips often have a trekking component – either short walks to waterfalls from the riverbank, or overnight or even multiday treks into the jungle.

Single-day or multiday trekking trips into the Cardamoms begin with a boat ride up-river or an approximately 30-minute *tuk tuk* ride east out of town to the trailhead. Multiday trips involve sleeping in homestays or in hammocks in the jungle, and can be tailored to include birdwatching, waterfalls or wildlife-spotting.

Wild KK Project   OUTDOORS
(☏ 097 438 3772; www.wildkkproject.com) 🖉 Get in touch with these guys for tours of the Areng Valley. They are a green social enterprise that is closely involved in the CBET project (p186) there, and all profits go back into protecting the forest. They also organise tours to mangrove-lined Koh Pao Island in Peam Krasaop National Park.

🛏 Sleeping

Koh Kong is a popular holiday destination for Khmer families; hotels fill up and raise their rates during Cambodian holidays. If staying in town doesn't appeal, check out Tatai River (18km east), with its handful of fabulous eco-accommodation options.

Hula Hula Bungalows   BUNGALOW $
(☏ 071 210 7405, 016 616056; Koh Yor Beach; bungalow US$6-10; 🖙) Escapists rejoice! This place was recently taken over by a Polish couple who have created a real sanctuary for vagabonds, many of whom extend their stay indefinitely. Delightfully simple, airy bungalows sit on a windswept, sunset-facing sprawl of empty sand. The restaurant leans Asian but with some Western (including Polish) options. It usually closes during July.

Ritthy's Retreat   GUESTHOUSE $
(☏ 012 707719; www.kohkongecoadventure.com; St 1; dm US$4, r US$6-15; ❄ 🖙) Long-time tour operator Ritthy has opened a welcoming guesthouse and restaurant on the riverfront. It features spacious en-suite dorms with double-wide beds and basic but roomy doubles. The fancier air-con rooms upstairs

SWIFT KNOWLEDGE

You could be forgiven for feeling like you've arrived on the set of a Hitchcock movie when you get to Koh Kong. From the wee morning hours until well into the evening the air is filled with a deafening cacophony of bird calls. The high-pitched chirping is artificially pumped through rooftop megaphones to coax swifts into building nests out of saliva in the drab-looking concrete structures you'll see around town. The nests are a key ingredient in bird's-nest soup and are worth a lot of money.

This phenomenon happens across South Cambodia, but in Koh Kong it's on another level. Light sleepers are advised to choose a hotel with some distance from the din – the riverside hotels are generally a bit quieter in this respect than hotels in the centre.

ℹ GETTING TO THAILAND: KOH KONG TO TRAT

Getting to the border The Cham Yeam/Hat Lek border crossing (open 6am to 10pm) links the beaches of Cambodia and Thailand. Leaving Cambodia, take a taxi (US$10), *tuk tuk* (US$6) or *moto* (US$3) from Koh Kong to the border (about 8km).

At the border Departing Cambodia is pretty straightforward. Coming in the other direction and arriving in Cambodia is another story, as Cambodian authorities are notorious for visa overcharging – anywhere from US$5 (standard) to US$20 extra, depending on how gullible you look. Hold your ground and pay no more than the standard surcharge here. Paying the prescribed US$30 is doable but may cost you some time. This is one border where e-visas (US$36) are not a bad idea as they are fairly scam-proof.

Moving on From the Hat Lek border, take a silver minibus straight to Trat (120B, 1½ hours, every 40 minutes from 7.10am to 5.10pm). From there the company Cherdchai runs regular buses to Bangkok's Ekami bus terminal (230B, five hours). Buses depart hourly from 6am until 11.30pm. Anyone heading to the nearby island of Koh Chang can arrange onward transport in Trat.

Coming into Cambodia, there's a parking lot right over the border with plenty of taxis (400 baht or US$10), *motos* (200 baht or US$5) and the occasional *tuk tuk* waiting (note that the dollar rate is cheaper).

have semiprivate balcony with river views, while the downstairs bar-restaurant, with a pool table, is a top hang-out.

Paddy's Bamboo Guesthouse HOSTEL $
(☑ 015 533223; ppkohkong@gmail.com; dm with/without fan US$3/2, r US$5-10; ❉ ⓢ) Paddy's targets backpackers with basic rooms, a bustling bar with pool table and a balcony for chilling out. The wood-floored, fan-cooled rooms upstairs over the bar are preferred to the cramped dorms and musty concrete aircon rooms at the back.

Oasis Bungalow Resort BUNGALOW $$
(☑ 092 228342; http://oasisresort.netkhmer.com; d/tr US$35/40; ❉ ⓢ ◪) Nestled in a lush garden 2km north of Koh Kong centre, Oasis really lives up to its name. Five large, beautifully designed bungalows set around a gorgeous infinity pool with views of the Cardamom Mountains provide a tranquil base in which to chill out and reset your travel batteries. To get here, follow the blue signs from Acleda Bank.

Outsiders may use the pool from 9am to 6pm for US$4. Booking directly through the resort saves you US$5.

✕ Eating

Koh Kong's dining scene is surprisingly appealing, with local restaurants that are cheap, authentic and delicious. The riverfront food carts are also worth checking out. There are also food stalls in the southeast corner of the market, Psar Leu (ផ្សារលើ; St 3; mains from US$1.50; ⊙ 8am-11pm).

Wood House INTERNATIONAL $
(☑ 096 864 3254; St 8; US$2.75-6.75; ⊙ 9am-10pm; ⓢ) A French–Khmer couple have retired to this little corner of Cambodia to cook the town's best Euro–Asian fusion food in a charming mint-green-and-yellow house marked by long wood floorboards and whirring fans. Plenty of cocktails available and French wine by the glass (US$3.50).

Happy Beach CAMBODIAN $
(Mlub Kov Su Restaurant; ☑ 097 744 4454; mains US$2.50-7; ⊙ 7am-9pm) Northeast of town, this place offers a unique slice of Cambodian life with seaside, covered decks on stilts where families and friends laze about with their shoes off, taking down heaping portions of Khmer food served off a wooden block on the ground.

It's hard to find – go right when the road forks and continue another 150m.

Crab Shack SEAFOOD $
(Koh Yor Beach; mains US$3-10; ⊙ 10am-10pm) A family-run place on Koh Yor Beach (p180), this spot is known for perfect sunsets and heaping portions of fried crab with pepper. Several restaurants have sprung up around it, including one with the same name just south of this original.

Fat Sam's INTERNATIONAL $
(☑ 097 737 0707; off St 3; mains US$3.50-7; ⊙ 8am-1pm & 4-9.30pm Mon-Sat; ⓢ ◪) The menu at this informal bar-restaurant runs the gamut from fish and chips and chilli con carne to authentic Khmer and Thai favour-

ites. There's also a decent beer selection and a small wine list. The English owner (*not* named Fat Sam) is a long-time Koh Kong resident and fount of information about the area. Motorbike hire is available.

Food Carts
STREET FOOD $

(St 1; US$2-10; ☺5-11pm) Riverfront food carts can fire up a seafood barbecue for US$5 to US$10, combining crab, shrimp, squid, clams and/or fish. They also serve fried rice, fried noodles and sell cans of beer for a few thousand riel, making this a good sunset drinking spot.

Drinking & Nightlife

Pisey's Bar
BAR

(St 7; ☺5pm-late) Hostess Pisey is the Cleopatra of Koh Kong, and her dive bar is where pretty much everybody ends up after everything else in town has closed (about 9.30pm). There's a pool table and guests are welcome to take control of the tunes selection. Good fun all around.

Stevie C's
SPORTS BAR

(☑097 969 9845; St 8; ☺noon-late; ☎) Dyed-in-the-wool Chelsea fan Stevie has turned his home into a sports bar complete with satellite dish and an Italian chef preparing the best pizzas in town for US$5 to US$8.

ⓘ Information

Thai baht are widely used so there's no urgent need to change baht into dollars or riel. To do so, use one of the many mobile-phone shops around Psar Leu.

Acleda Bank (St 3; ☺8am-3.30pm Mon-Fri, to 11.30am Sat, ATM 24hr)

Canadia Bank (St 1; ☺8am-3.30pm Mon-Fri, to 11.30am Sat, ATM 24hr)

There's a **Tourist Information Centre** (☑015 333778; St 1; ☺7-11.30am & 2-5.30pm) but it's often closed. Tour companies and guesthouses are the best places to get the local low-down.

Koh Kong Provincial Hospital (☑016 854824, 016 300119, snake bites 016 922223; St 3; ☺24hr) is the main hospital and has antivenoms and a snake-bite expert, Dr Meng. For anything serious, evacuation to Thailand via the Cham Yeam–Hat Lek border crossing is possible 24 hours a day. In Thailand, the closest decent hospital (66 39 552555) is in Trat, 92km from the border.

ⓘ Getting There & Away

Koh Kong City is on NH48, 220km northwest of Sihanoukville, 290km west of Phnom Penh and 8km southeast of the Thai border. It's linked to the Thai border by a surfaced road that begins on the other side of the 2km bridge over the Koh Poi River.

BUS

The three main bus companies in town are **Olongpich Express** (☑097 505 0226; St 3), **Rith Mony** (☑012 640344; St 3) and **Virak Buntham** (☑089 998760; St 3), while **Vibol Express** (St 3) and **Emerald Express** (☑012 829852; St 3) run speedy minivans to Phnom Penh.

Buses drop passengers at their offices in town, or sometimes at Koh Kong's **bus station** (St 4), on the northeast edge of town, where *moto* and *tuk tuk* drivers await, eager to overcharge tourists. Don't pay more than US$1.50/3 for the five-minute *moto/tuk tuk* ride into the centre. Departures are from the company offices in town, with a stop at the bus station on the way out.

Advertised trips to Battambang, Kampot, Kep or Siem Reap will involve a change of bus or two (or even three).

If heading to Thailand, note that Bangkok-bound buses can also get you to Ko Chang (US$15 to US$18, including ferry to the island), with a change of bus or minivan at the border.

TAXI

From the bus station, share taxis head to Phnom Penh (US$15 to US$20, five hours), Kiri Sakor (for Koh Sdach; US$10, 2½ hours, 10am), Andoung Tuek (US$5, two hours), Osoam (US$12, 2½ hours, 3.30pm) and Kampot (US$20, one morning trip). Share taxis are rare to Sihanoukville so hire a private taxi (an inflated US$100 because of poor roads into Sihanoukville), or

BUSES FROM KOH KONG

DESTINATION	FARE (US$)	DURATION (HR)	FREQUENCY	COMPANY	TYPE
Bangkok	20-22	8	3 daily	Rith Mony, Virak Buntham	bus/minivan
Phnom Penh	8-12	6-8	several daily	Emerald Express, Olongpich Express, Rith Mony, Vibol Express, Virak Buntham	bus/minivan
Sihanoukville	9	5-6	8am	Virak Buntham	bus

take a packed local minivan from the same lot. Guesthouses can set you up with a private taxi to Phnom Penh (US$75) or Kampot (US$75).

ℹ️ Getting Around

Short *moto* rides within the centre are 2000r; *tuk tuk* rides are double that, but overcharging is common. To hire a *moto* for the day costs about US$18.

English speaking *remork-moto* (*tuk tuk*) drivers in town can whisk you to Tatai Waterfall (US$18 return), the Peam Krasaop mangrove walk (US$12) or Koh Yor Beach (US$15 return). All-day rental is US$35. 'Harry' (016 629941) is a recommended driver. Non-English speaking drivers will cost less.

Motorbike hire (US$4 or US$5 per day) is available from most guesthouses as well as Ritthy Koh Kong Eco Adventure Tours (p181), Wood House (p182) and Fat Sam's (p182).

Ritthy Koh Kong Eco Adventure Tours (p181), **99 Guesthouse** (📋 035-660 0999; 99guesthouse@gmail.com; St 6; s/d with fan US$8/10, air-con US$13/15; ❄️ 📶) and Paddy's Bamboo Guesthouse (p182) rent bicycles for about US$1 per day.

KOH KONG CONSERVATION CORRIDOR

Stretching along both sides of NH48 from Koh Kong to the Gulf of Kompong Som (the bay northwest of Sihanoukville), the Koh Kong Conservation Corridor encompasses the southern reaches of the fabled Cardamom Mountains, an area of breathtaking beauty and astonishing biodiversity. Many of Cambodia's most outstanding natural sites and protected areas lie within the corridor, including Southern Cardamom National Park, Botum Sakor National Park and the Tatai Wildlife Sanctuary.

Part of the greater 20,746-sq-km Cardamom Rainforest Landscape (p186), the corridor is the site of several groundbreaking ecotourism projects, as well as the jungle-flanked Tatai River, with its myriad eco-adventures and fairy-tale accommodation. If you want to spot wildlife, this is a good place to do it, although as always you'll need luck on your side.

Tatai River & Waterfall

The Phun Daung (Tatai) Bridge, about 18km east of Koh Kong on NH48, is your gateway to jungle living. The main sight here is the Tatai Waterfall.

However, the real attraction of the Tatai River (ស្ទឹងតាតៃ) is its isolated setting with dense forest plunging down to the riverbank. Spending a few days here, either exploring the lush and tranquil natural environment or swinging in a hammock while contemplating river life, is a pure get-away-from-it-all experience that offers extra kudos for sustainability.

💿 Sights

Tatai Waterfall   WATERFALL

(ទឹកធ្លាក់តាតៃ; NH48, Km 134; US$1) Tatai Waterfall is a thundering set of rapids during the wet season, plunging over a 4m rock shelf. Water levels drop in the dry season, but you can swim year-round in the surrounding refreshing pools. The water is fairly pure as it comes down from the isolated high Cardamom Mountains. Access to the

SOUTH COAST TATAI RIVER & WATERFALL

END OF THE LINE FOR THE PANGOLIN?

In China and Vietnam the meat of the Malayan (Sunda) pangolin – a kind of nocturnal anteater whose only food is ants and termites – is considered a delicacy, while the creature's blood and scales are believed to have healing powers. As a result, the pangolin is believed to be the most trafficked mammal in the world, according to the International Union for Conservation of Nature, which estimates that more than a million of the scaly animals have been illegally taken across international borders since 2000.

In Cambodia's Cardamom Mountains, villagers often hunt pangolin with dogs and are paid a whopping US$100 per kilo for live animals (the price rises to US$175 in Vietnam and as much as US$7000 in China). As a result, pangolin populations have been in free fall. But in 2016, the pangolin was granted the highest level of protection by the Convention on International Trade in Endangered Species (CITES). Cambodia is a member of the group, and the country's enforcement personnel are doing their best to crack down on poaching before it's too late.

In the first half of 2017, three pangolins were confiscated from poachers in the Cardamom Mountains.

waterfall is by car or motorbike. The clearly marked turn-off is on NH48 about 15km southeast of Koh Kong and exactly 3km northwest of the Tatai Bridge.

From the highway it's about 2km to the falls along a rough access road. There's a stream crossing about halfway – at the height of the wet season you may have to cross it on foot and walk the last kilometre. From Koh Kong, a half-day *remork-moto* excursion to Tatai Waterfall costs US$15 to US$18, or less to go one way to the bridge.

🛏 Sleeping

Donut Guesthouse GUESTHOUSE $
(☎016 724290; cheaoudom999@gmail.com; off NH48; cottages US$10) This is your budget accommodation option in Tatai, with four cute, stilted faux-wood cottages shaded by a grove of fruit trees about 300m off the river on the Phnom Penh side of the bridge. They have king-sized beds and private bathroom and balcony. It's on a farm and therefore prone to malodorous wafts of fertiliser.

Neptune River Bungalows ECOLODGE $$
(☎088 777 0576; www.neptuneadventure-cambodia.com; Tatai River; bungalow incl breakfast US$30-50) 🌿 Want to play Robinson Crusoe? You're in the right place. German proprietor Thomas has created a jungle getaway with bags of rustic charm. The four stilted wood-and-bamboo bungalows are set amid fruit trees and have lovely bathrooms, albeit with scoop showers. Meals (US$3 to US$7), using produce from the on-site gardens, are taken right on the river.

★ Rainbow Lodge ECOLODGE $$$
(☎012 160 2585; www.rainbowlodgecambodia.com; Tatai River; s/d/f incl all meals US$89/106/140; 🗇) 🌿 A slice of jungle-chic, Rainbow Lodge proves being sustainable doesn't mean having to sacrifice creature comforts. Powered by solar panels and biofuel, the bungalows here are set back from the river. They are reached by elevated walkways hugged by foliage and centred on a sleek open-air lounge with an impressive bar.

Rainbow Lodge is located about 10 minutes upstream from Tatai Bridge by long-tail boat (free transfer), and is just a short kayak away from Tatai Waterfall. Activities include kayaking, day treks, river cruises, local village visits and overnight camping, while a riverfront spa pavilion provides pampering massages.

Rainbow Lodge is a partner in several trend-setting national sustainability initiatives and is involved in projects to support local communities to protect the Cardamoms. You'll save 10% booking directly on its website.

Four Rivers Floating Lodge RESORT $$$
(☎097 643032; www.ecolodges.asia; Tatai River; d incl breakfast US$180-395; 🗇) 🌿 Glamping with extra wow-factor. The 21 canvas tent-villas here, some floating on pontoons, are on Koh Andet, an island in the Tatai River 6km downstream from Tatai Bridge. The use of wicker and dark wood provides a colonial-cool ambience, topped off by the most sumptuous bathrooms you'll see under canvas anywhere. Boat transfers to/from Tatai Bridge are included (20 minutes).

❶ Getting There & Away

All buses travelling to or from Koh Kong pass through Tatai. If heading to one of the resorts, ask the driver to let you off at the bridge and arrange onward transport through your resort.

A *tuk tuk* trip from Koh Kong to the bridge will cost US$15 to US$18 return, or about half that for a *moto*.

Southern Cardamom National Park

Cambodia's newest national park (2016) and also its largest at 4104 sq km, Southern Cardamom National Park (ឧទ្យានជាតិជួរភ្នំក្រវាញកណ្ដាល, SCNP) is home to more than 50 species listed on the IUCN Red List of Threatened Species, including Asian elephants, Siamese crocodiles, sun bears, gibbons and pangolins.

The rangers and military police who patrol this vast area are engaged in an uphill battle to save it from illegal hunting and logging, operating out of remote ranger stations spread across four provinces: Koh Kong, Pursat, Kampong Speu and Kompong Som (Sihanoukville). Ecotourism is playing a major role too, with Koh Kong city serving as the main jumping-off point for excursions to community-based programmes in the Areng Valley and Osoam (p240).

Crocodile Protection Sanctuary ANIMAL SANCTUARY
(ដែនជម្រកការពារសត្វក្រពើអែរសោម) Some 13km south of Osoam village lies this protected crocodile habit, where about 40 to 60 Siamese crocodiles reside. Visitors have

CARDAMOM RAINFOREST LANDSCAPE – A CAMBODIAN TREASURE

Spread over seven provinces in southwestern Cambodia, the vast Cardamom Rainforest Landscape represents the largest mainland forest watershed in Southeast Asia. The remote peaks here – up to 1800m high – and 18 major waterways are home to at least 54 globally threatened animal species including Asian elephants, tigers, bears, Siamese crocodiles, pangolins and eight species of tortoise and turtle. The area receives a staggering amount of rainfall – some 3500mm to 4500mm per year – and its rivers provide drinking water for more than 30,000 people and support rice and fish production in the lowlands.

While forests elsewhere in Cambodia were being ravaged by developers and well-connected logging companies, the Cardamom Mountains and the adjacent mangrove forests were protected from the worst ecological outrages by their sheer remoteness. As a result, much of the area is still in pretty good shape, ecologically speaking, so the potential for ecotourism is huge – akin, some say, to that of Kenya's game reserves or Costa Rica's national parks.

Conservationists have been working diligently with the Cambodian government to preserve this vital national treasure, and in 2016 the entire 20,746-sq-km Cardamom Rainforest Landscape became officially protected with the formation of Southern Cardamom National Park. Comprising 11 national parks, biodiversity corridors and wildlife sanctuaries, the Cardamom Rainforest Landscape is now thought to be the largest contiguous protected area in all Southeast Asia.

The next few years will be critical in determining the future of the Cardamom Mountains. NGOs such as Conservation International (www.conservation.org), Fauna & Flora International (www.fauna-flora.org), Wildlife Alliance (www.wildlifealliance.org) and homegrown Mother Nature Cambodia (www.mothernaturecambodia.org), along with teams of armed enforcement rangers, are working round the clock to help protect the area's 16 distinct ecosystems from loggers and poachers. Ecotourism, too, is playing a major role in providing local people with sustainable alternatives to logging and poaching.

the best chance of spotting the mostly fish-eating (never human-eating) reptiles from December to May, but the area has other attractions, too: namely a spirit house built by the Choung indigenous group, and wildlife.

Stung Areng Community Based Ecotourism   OUTDOORS
(☑097 355 5638; www.areng-valley.org) Yet another promising Wildlife Alliance community-based ecotourism (CBET) initiative in the Cardamoms, this UK-funded programme offers trekking, boat trips, kayaking and homestays in the wildlife-rich Areng Valley. The area is home to Asian elephants and the last remaining wild population of Siamese crocodiles. The best way to experience the site is on a tour with Wild KK Project (p181).

Jungle Cross   ADVENTURE
(☑097 939 8012, 015 601 633; www.junglecross.com; dirt-bike rental per day US$28) Fantastic, expat-run dirt-bike and 4WD operation based deep in the Cardamoms. The knowledgeable and entertaining owner also leads trekking tours to more remote parts, with transport by 4WD

to the start point. The office is in a blue house east of the main bridge in Osoam.

🛏 Sleeping & Eating

There is accommodation in Osoam and homestay available through Stung Areng CBET. Bring warm clothes, as the temperature can drop as low as 10°C.

Delicious meals using plenty of local ingredients are part of the equation at the CBET programmes in Osoam and Stung Areng, and Osoam has some basic restaurants.

ℹ Getting There & Away

From Koh Kong, a share taxi heading north to Osoam departs daily at 3.30pm and returns to Koh Kong the next morning (US$12, 2½ hours). A private taxi costs US$60 one-way to/from Osoam. The mostly unsealed road, which cuts through the heart of Southern Cardamom National Park, is in good shape and passable year-round (the occasional landslide notwithstanding).

Share taxis and pickups also link Osoam with Pursat via Pramoay (the main town in the Phnom Samkos Wildlife Sanctuary), but note that the 60km from Osoam to Pramoay is notoriously rough and barely passable (pickups only) in the rainy season (June to mid-October).

You'll need private transport to reach Thma Bang and Areng Valley. Thma Bang is also linked to Chi Phat by a difficult trail that can be handled by motorbike, but just barely and only in dry season. We don't recommend it. Only attempt it in a large group of experienced bikers who can help navigate bikes over the more difficult river crossings.

Botum Sakor National Park

Occupying the 35km-wide peninsula northwest across the Gulf of Kompong Som from Sihanoukville, this is one of Cambodia's largest and most biodiverse national parks. Alas, some 75% of the park (ឧទ្យានជាតិបុមសាគរ) has been sold off. Developments include a US$3.5 billion Chinese-run tourism project that has swallowed up roughly the park's western third. Hope has arrived in the form of Wildlife Alliance, which has a concession to manage 10% of the park and has set up the Cardamom Tented Camp.

Encircled by mangroves and beaches, Botum Sakor National Park is home to a profusion of wildlife, including Asian elephants, fishing cats, pangolins, slow loris, sun bears, hog badgers and hog deer. But their habitat is fast disappearing because of the rampant development in the park.

Hundreds of people were evicted from the area to build the Chinese tourism project, dubbed Dara Sakor. The project includes the giant Dara Sakor Airport and a four-lane highway through the national park that provides access to the Koh Sdach Archipelago (p211). Meanwhile, Cambodian businessman Ly Yong Phat has established a rubber plantation on a large central swathe of the park.

Trail-bikers and intrepid *moto* riders can bypass the newer highway and take the rugged road around the park's east coast via the scenic fishing village of Thmor Sor, which is largely built on stilts over the alluvial bay, stretching almost 1km out to sea.

Also on the largely undeveloped eastern side, boats hired in Andoung Tuek can take you up into four mangrove-lined streams that are rich with wildlife, including the pileated gibbon, long-tailed macaque and black-shanked douc langur. The streams are Ta Op (the largest), Ta Nun, Ta Nhi and Preak Khsach. Kiem (☑088 795 8585) is a boat driver in Andoung Tuek, although you'll need a translator.

★**Cardamom Tented Camp**   TENTED CAMP **$$$**
(☑090 312196; www.cardamomtentedcamp.com; Botum Sakor National Park; tent from US$190; ✳🛜) 🏊 Nestled deep in Botum Sakor National Park on the banks of the wildlife-laden Prek Tachan River, Cardamom Tented Camp is both a model ecotourism success story and one of the most unique and enchanting overnight stays you'll find anywhere. Luxurious safari tents allow guests to live in style while participating in real conservation activities like forest patrols and tree planting.

Trekking and kayaking trips are de rigueur, offering the chance to spot pileated gibbons, river otters, and countless species of bird. More elusive critters in the vicinity include the sunda pangolin, the Bengal slow loris and the fishing cat.

The camp is located within a Wildlife Alliance concession comprising about 10% of Botum Sakor National Park, about half of which has been developed after being sold off to business interests. The project represents a milestone in the struggle of Wildlife Alliance and other conservation groups to save Cambodia's wild spaces from extinction. Here you'll feel every bit like you are making a positive contribution to that struggle.

There's a two-night minimum stay at the camp and all meals are included in the price. A state-of-the-art solar-power system supplies most of the electricity. The boat ride here from Trapaeng Rung takes about one hour and gets progressively more beautiful the deeper you get into the park. Trapaeng Rung is 40km southeast of Tatai on the NH48.

Chi Phat

Once notorious for land-grabbing, illegal logging and poaching, the river village of Chi Phat is now home to a popular community-based ecotourism project (CBET) launched by Wildlife Alliance (www.wildlifealliance.org) in 2002 to transform the Cardamoms into a source of jobs and income for local people. Chi Phat offers travellers an opportunity to explore the Cardamoms' ecosystems while contributing to their conservation and providing an alternative livelihood to the former poachers who now act as the landscape's protectors and guides.

🏃 Activities & Tours

All activities and tours in Chi Phat must be booked by 5pm the day before through the CBET Community Visitor Centre, a five-minute walk from the river pier. Head straight there when you arrive to meet the guides and other guests returning from treks. Some guests report excellent experiences, though management can be disorganised. There's not always a lot of English spoken.

Prices for tours range from US$25 to US$35 per person per day including lunch, transport and equipment. All-inclusive multiday trips (three nights maximum) cost a bit more per day. On these you sleep in hammocks in the jungle. Most tours require guides.

Trekking

CBET treks range from one to seven days, with shorter trips exploring the bat caves, waterfalls, mountain communities and mysterious burial-jar sites in the nearby surroundings.

On overnight trips you either sleep in hammocks or at one of five campsites set up by Wildlife Alliance, equipped with eco-toilets, field kitchens and comfortable hammocks with mosquito-proof nets. Wildlife-spotting isn't guaranteed but there are usually plenty of opportunities to shoot (with a camera) monkeys and hornbills. Although the guides wear flip-flops, it's recommended to bring walking shoes for the treks. Also, bring bug spray.

Boat Tours

CBET's sunrise birdwatching boat trips and sunset stargazing cruises (per person US$12 to US$35) are a great way to experience the languid beauty of the Preak Piphot River. The former involves a 1½-hour long tailboat ride before jumping in a traditional stand-up-rowing boat (with rower) and silently paddling along the placid Proat River, an unlogged tributary.

Mountain Biking

CBET's one- to two-day mountain-biking tours (per person per day US$20 to US$25) follow trails to waterholes, burial-jar sites, waterfalls and rural communities in the surrounding forest. If you want to explore the countryside around Chi Phat village solo, you can also hire mountain bikes at the CBET visitor centre.

Wildlife Tours

Wildlife Alliance Release
Station Tours   TOURS
(☏010 690864; www.wildlifealliance.org/wildlife-release-koh-kong; 1 night adult/child US$120/50, 2 nights US$200/75) 🏃 Wildlife Alliance operates tours to its release station (about 45 minutes from Chi Phat), where animals such as sun bears, binturongs, pangolins and a great many hornbills are released into the wild after being rescued from illegal trafficking. Accommodation, food and activities – jungle trekking, wildlife tracking, and river swims – are included. Advance bookings essential.

Transport (by motorbike) is provided from either Andoung Tuek or Chi Phat, and it's one thrilling ride through forests, over streams and across grasslands.

🛏 Sleeping & Eating

All accommodation is routed through the CBET visitor centre, with three types of lodging offered: homestay, guesthouse and more private bungalow. Express your preference to the visitor centre, which will assign you a place to stay. Bungalows and some guesthouse rooms are en suite. All rooms have fans, mosquito nets, cotton sheets and towels. The village has 24-hour electricity but bring a torch (flashlight) because brownouts are frequent.

Visitor Centre Restaurant   CAMBODIAN $
(breakfasts/mains US$2.50/3.50; ⊙6-8.30am, 11am-1pm & 6-7.30pm; 🍴) 🏃 The best restaurant in town is at the visitor centre. Everybody enjoys the same selection of three dishes for lunch, and three dishes for dinner, and the menu changes daily. Vegetarians are catered for and packed lunches are available. All the food is sourced locally, and much is locally grown or raised.

ℹ Information

For information on all activities, tours, accommodation and getting to Chi Phat, visit the **CBET Community Visitor Centre** (☏035-675 6444, 092 720925; www.chi-phat.org; ⊙7-11am & 2-5pm; 📶). The visitor centre has free wi-fi, solar-powered electricity and a good restaurant serving both meat and vegetarian Khmer food.

Book your stay by emailing Chi Phat rather than filling out the form on the website, which frequently malfunctions.

Chi Phat has no bank or ATM, but it does have a credit-card machine. Bring a decent amount of cash just in case, though.

ℹ Getting There & Away

Chi Phat is on the scenic Preak Piphot River, 21km upriver from Andoung Tuek, which is on NH48, 98km from Koh Kong. All buses travelling between Koh Kong and Phnom Penh or Sihanoukville pass through here.

Arriving in Andoung Tuek, buses usually stop outside **Kim Chhoun Guesthouse** (the restaurant with blue pillars), where the management works in conjunction with CBET to help organise onward transport to Chi Phat. This is the place to organise a *moto* or ask about the CBET boat if you haven't already booked through the CBET website (www.chi-phat.org).

CBET's long-tail boat (US$30), which makes the two-hour trip from Andoung Tuek when reserved in advance, is the most atmospheric way to get to Chi Phat. The latest the boat can pick you up at Andoung Tuek is 4.30pm. If you miss the CBET boat, you can usually hire a local to take you upstream to Chi Phat for US$30 for up to five people.

A *moto* is faster (45 minutes) and costs US$7 for the 17km trip. A CBET-partnered *moto* that supplies passenger helmets can be booked in advance through the CBET site, although this is also easily organised upon arrival in Andoung Tuek. *Moto* drivers drop passengers off across the river from Chi Phat and a tiny raft-ferry (1000r) takes passengers to the village itself.

Travelling from Chi Phat, a boat or *moto* can be booked the night before to return to Andoung Tuek in the morning, in time to catch onward buses. The CBET office can also book bus tickets.

SIHANOUKVILLE

♫ 034 / POP 91.000

The sad story of Sihanoukville (p193; ក្រុងព្រះសីហនុ), Cambodia's main port, is well documented. Travellers are advised to spend as little time as possible in this quagmire of construction. If you do end up here for a night, it won't be easy to find budget accommodation, as almost all the town's hostels have closed.

Of course if you are headed to the popular islands of Koh Rong or Koh Rong Sanloem, a trip through Sihanoukville is a necessary evil. The best plan is to shoot for an early arrival, then get out of Dodge on a morning or afternoon ferry. If you get stuck in town for a night, the Serendipity area near the main ferry pier has plenty of overpriced accommodation, while some cheaper, Western-run guesthouses are holding out on once-popular Otres Beach.

◉ Sights

Kbal Chhay Cascades   WATERFALL

(ទឹកធ្លាក់កប្បាលឆាយ; US$1, picnicking platforms per day 5000r) Thanks to their appearance in *Pous Keng Kong* (*The Giant Snake;* 2000), one of the most successful Cambodian films

of the post-civil-war era, these cascades on the Prek Toeuk Sap River draw numerous domestic tourists. Hence all the picnicking platforms, drink stands and food stalls. Not much water flows here in dry season (November to May). Take the well-marked turn-off from the NH4 about 5.5km southeast of the Cambrew junction, then follow the road about 10km to the falls.

Wat Leu   BUDDHIST TEMPLE

(វត្តលើ, Wat Chhnothean; Wat Leu Rd) Spectacular views of almost every casino (finished and unfinished) in Sihanoukville and gorgeous sunset panoramas await at Wat Leu, situated on a peaceful, forested hilltop 1.5km northwest of the city centre.

Beaches

Otres Beach   BEACH

(ឆ្នេរអូរត្រៈ) Past the southern end of Ochheuteal Beach, beyond the **Phnom Som Nak Sdach** (Hill of the King's Palace) headland, lies stunning Otres Beach, a seemingly infinite strip of casuarinas and blinding white sand. In Sihanoukville's glory days it could give southern Thailand a run for its money, but in recent years it has largely been defaced by wanton development. That said, the beach itself is still gorgeous, and the 2km stretch between **Otres 1** and **Otres 2** remains empty.

Inland from Otres Beach, **Otres Village** was an easy-going backpacker zone before being swallowed up in 2019 by a megacity rising to the east of Otres. A few guesthouses remain but most are just riding out their leases.

Otres Beach is about 5km south of the Serendipity area. The road is in disastrous shape and prone to huge traffic jams because of all the trucks heading out here to build the megacity. A *tuk tuk* from Sihanoukville centre or Serendipity costs US$6 to US$10, depending on your negotiation skills (about half that for a *moto*).

Ochheuteal Beach   BEACH

(ឆ្នេរអូរឈើទាល) This 4km-long beach qualifies as Sihanoukville's main beach, but it's no place to swim these days as the rapid development of high-rise casinos along its length has had drastic consequences on the water quality (which was questionable at the best of times). The laid-back bars and barbecue shacks that once lined the beach have all been cleared out. Tune back in around 2021, when some of the casinos might be complete.

Sihanoukville

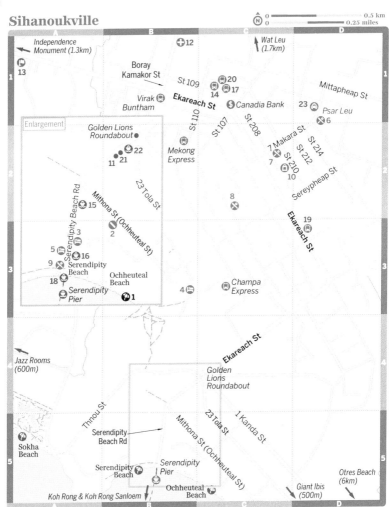

🛏 Sleeping

★ **Sunset Lounge Guesthouse**   RESORT **$$**

(☎097 734 0486; www.sunsetlounge-guesthou se.com; South Ochheuteal; r/bungalow from US$40/55; ❄️🛜🏊) Surrounded by developments at the far-south end of Ochheuteal Beach, this German-run boutique-quality resort has thick mattresses, dreamy shaded balconies, appealing bathrooms and a well-reputed restaurant. Splurge for the bungalows. The location, while a bit far from the ferry terminal, is more practical than Otres Beach as it saves you an uncomfortable and expensive *tuk tuk* ride.

★ **Patchouly Chili House**   RESORT **$$**

(☎098 832230; patchouly.chillhouse@gmail.com; St 1033; r from US$40; ❄️🛜🏊) With elegantly designed rooms, attentive service, fine food and a leafy pool, this French–Khmer-run boutique is a throwback to happier times in Sihanoukville. It is also about the only affordable sleeping option left in the casino-laden Golden Lions area. That it remains open is a minor miracle; let's hope it stays that way.

Dara Independence Beach Resort   HOTEL **$$$**

(☎034-934300; www.independencehotel.net; 2 Thnou St; r from US$105; ❄️@🛜🏊) Original-

Sihanoukville

⊙ **Sights**
1 Ochheuteal Beach.................................B3

⊙ **Activities, Courses & Tours**
2 Dive Shop B3

⊜ **Sleeping**
3 Benny's City Hotel...............................A3
4 Patchouly Chili House B3
5 Serendipity Beach Resort A3

⊗ **Eating**
6 Psar Leu...D1
7 Samudera Supermarket C2
8 Sandan...C2
Starfish Bakery & Cafe ....(see 10)
9 Yasmin A3

⊜ **Shopping**
10 Starfish C2
Tapang..(see 8)

ⓘ **Information**
11 Ana Travel B2
12 CT Polyclinic B1
13 Vietnamese Consulate A1

ⓘ **Transport**
14 Bus Station...C1
15 Buva Sea..A2
16 Cambodia Island Speed Ferry A3
17 Capitol Tours & Transport C1
18 GTVC Speedboat A3
19 Larryta D3
20 Olongpich Express C1
Phnom Penh Sorya ....(see 14)
Rith Mony ....(see 14)
21 Samnang Mini-Mart B2
22 Speed Ferry Cambodia B2
23 Taxi Park..D1

ly opened in 1963, this seven-storey hotel retains the jet-set feel of Sihanoukville's movie-star heyday. Following years of neglect it was reopened in 2007 and features fresh, contemporary rooms, some with sea panoramas. It was a top option when Sihanoukville was a destination unto itself; these days it's more of a fancy option for a stopover before hitting the islands.

Serendipity Area

Serendipity Beach Rd, which runs up the hill from Serendipity Beach to the Golden Lions Roundabout, went from backpacker-ville to casino-ville almost overnight. The ferry companies and the main pier are still here, along with a few restaurants and travel agents, so

it's a logical choice for a one-night stay if you can afford it.

Benny's City Hotel HOTEL $$
(☎016 864043; bennycityhotel@hotmail.com; Serendipity Beach Rd; r US$60-70; ❋☎) If you need to catch a ferry the next morning, you can't do much better in terms of location than this colourful high-rise near the ferry offices and the pier. Rooms are a bit small for the price and lack natural light, but are well appointed. In the new Sihanoukville this counts as a deal.

Serendipity Beach Resort HOTEL $$$
(☎034-938888; Serendipity Beach Rd; r US$80-100; ❋☎☒) Rooms at this high-rise are large and stylish, with 4-star amenities, although the service and maintenance standards lag. Room rates have doubled in recent years, removing it from 'good value' territory. Still, the location is perfect for the ferries.

Otres Beach

With a few guesthouses holding out, the Otres area – consisting of Otres Beach I, Otres Beach II and Otres Village – is still a decent choice but note that it's a bumpy and expensive *tuk tuk* ride from the centre. It's probably only worth slogging out here if you are staying for a couple of nights. Most budget lodging is in Otres Village, which also has a few bars and restaurants hanging on. Resorts give discounts of about 30% to 40% during low season (roughly May to October).

Sok Sabay BOUTIQUE HOTEL $$
(☎016 406080; Otres Village; r from US$55; ❋☎☒) One of few viable accommodation options left in Otres Village, the rooms here are set around an elegant pool, with inlaid-bamboo walls and balconies strewn with well-cushioned furniture. The restaurant – best in the village – serves upscale Khmer and Western food and overlooks what was once the village lake (now filled in with dirt).

★**Naia Resort** RESORT $$$
(☎069 337900; www.naiacambodia.com; Otres 2; r incl breakfast from US$100; ❋☎☒) One of few Otres 2 boutique resorts to have retained both its Western management and its charm, style-conscious Naia is all about white-washed minimalism. With marvellous beds, well-furnished room terraces, a long

swimming pool and a playground, it's family friendly too. The beach at Otres 2 (p189) is nice, even if the neighbourhood isn't.

Sahaa Beach Resort
RESORT $$$

(☎ 095 808075; www.sahaabeach.com; Otres 1; r incl breakfast US$90-160; ❄ 🛜 🌊) This poolside boutique has elected to remain on Otres Beach even as everything has crumbled around it. The standards have not suffered a bit. The beautiful bathrooms are flooded with natural light, and the reading lights and other furniture are gallery-quality. The restaurant, in a gorgeous bamboo structure, is tops in the Otres area.

✖ Eating & Drinking

Once known for raucous bars, Sihanoukville has – almost unthinkably – seen most of the watering holes dry up. The Western-oriented eating establishments have mostly shut down, but cheap eats can still be found around the main market, **Psar Leu** (7 Makara St; mains from US$1; ⊙ 7am-9pm). Once known for raucous bars, Sihanoukville has – almost unthinkably – seen most of its watering holes dry up. That said, fans of smoky casino bars are well served.

Starfish Bakery & Cafe
CAFE $

(☎ 012 952011; www.facebook.com/thestarfish bakerysihanoukville; St 208; sandwiches US$3.50-4.75; ⊙ 7am-5.30pm; 🛜 🍴) 🍴 This NGO-run cafe in the heart of the downtown area specialises in filling Western breakfasts, baked cakes and tarts, and healthy, innovative sandwiches heavy on Mexican and Middle Eastern flavours. Income goes to sustainable development projects. It is having trouble surviving in the new Sihanoukville, so it may be forced to move – check its Facebook page.

Gelato Italiano
ICE CREAM $

(Mittapheap St; mains US$3-6, gelati US$1; ⊙ 7.30am-9pm; ❄ 🛜) 🍴 Run by students from **Don Bosco Hotel School** (☎ 016 919834; www.donboscoguesthouse.com; Ou Phram St; r US$10-25; ❄ 🛜 🌊) 🍴, this cafe specialises in gelato (Italian-style ice cream) but offers so much more, including coffee, pizza and full-blown Asian-fusion meals in a bright, airy space. Wonderful value.

Samudera Supermarket
SUPERMARKET $

(7 Makara St; ⊙ 6.30am-9pm) Samudera has rows of imported goods including surprises like Vegemite, Ritz crackers, European cheeses and wine.

★ Sandan
CAMBODIAN $$

(☎ 098 454400; www.mloptapang.org; St 10311; mains US$4-10; ⊙ 11.30am-11pm; 🛜 🍴) 🍴 Loosely modelled on the beloved Phnom Penh institution Romdeng (p76), this superb restaurant is an extension of the vocational-training programmes for at-risk Cambodians run by local NGO M'lop Tapang. The menu features creative Cambodian cuisine targeted at a slightly upmarket clientele. The place is brimming with potted plants and hosts the wonderful gift shop and clothing boutique Tapang.

Yasmin
INTERNATIONAL $$

(Serendipity Beach Rd; mains US$5-11; ⊙ 24hr; 🛜) This is where pretty much everybody gathers before catching their ferry at Serendipity Pier. Good luck getting a table in high season, but if you do you'll be treated to a global menu that includes Thai, Chinese and Khmer tastes along with burgers and pizzas. Service can be jaded, however.

Jazz Rooms
BAR

(2 Thnou St; ⊙ 5pm-2am) Jazz Rooms has embraced the changes happening in Sihanoukville by catering to the universally loved diversions of music and sports. Easily the best bet for a night out.

🛍 Shopping

Starfish
ARTS & CRAFTS

(www.starfishcambodia.org; St 208; ⊙ 7am-5.30pm) 🍴 Beside the bakery & cafe of the same name; it sells silks and other gifts produced by good-cause NGO the Handicraft People.

Tapang
ARTS & CRAFTS

(www.mloptapang.org; St 10311; ⊙ 11am-9pm) 🍴 Run by a local NGO that works with at-risk children, this shop within Sanda restaurant sells good-quality bags, scarves, T-shirts and children's clothes made by street kids (and their families) so that they can attend school instead of peddling on the beach.

ℹ Information

Sihanoukville's banks – all with ATMs – are in the city centre along Ekareach St. There are plentiful standalone ATMs along Serendipity Beach Rd and a couple in the Otres area.

Canadia Bank (197 Ekareach St; ⊙ 8am-3.30pm Mon-Fri, to 11.30am Sat)

Vietnamese Consulate (p351) Exceedingly speedy at issuing tourist visas.

CT Polyclinic (☎ 034-936888, 081 886666; www.ctpolyclinic.com; 47 Boray Kamakor St;

emergency 24hr) The best medical clinic in town. Can administer rabies shots, and anti-venin in the event of a snake bite.

Getting There & Away

National Hwy 4 (NH4), which links Sihanoukville to Phnom Penh (230km), is in miserable condition, especially the 45km from Sihanoukville to the junction town of Prey Nob (where the highway splits off to Kampot). This stretch alone takes two to three hours because of heavy truck traffic and appalling road conditions. Chinese investors are building a new divided four-lane highway between Phnom Penh and Sihanoukville, but it's unclear when this might open.

The prevalence of trucks and high-speed overtaking on blind corners makes NH4 one of Cambodia's most dangerous highways; it's doubly dicey around dusk and at night. There have been scores of fatalities on this road over the years, including the wife of Prince Norodom Ranariddh in 2018 (the prince himself was seriously injured in the same crash). It's safer if not faster to drive via Kampot (105km) along NH3, which was also in pretty rough condition at the time of research. By contrast, NH48 to Koh Kong and the Thailand border was in great shape.

AIR

Sihanoukville International Airport (012-333524; https://kos.cambodia-airports.aero; off Hwy 4) is 15km east of town, just off NH4. A taxi to town costs a fixed US$20.

Airlines serving Siem Reap and/or Phnom Penh include the following:

Cambodia Airways (www.cambodia-airways.com)

Cambodia Angkor Air (www.cambodiaangkorair.com)

Lanmei Airlines (www.lanmeiairlines.com)

Sky Angkor Airlines (www.skyangkorair.com)

Internationally, the handiest flights are Air Asia (www.airasia.com) and JC International (www.jcinternational.com) direct to Bangkok, and Cambodia Angkor Air direct to Ho Chi Minh City. In addition, a dizzying array of Chinese airlines serve several mainland China cities plus Hong Kong.

BOAT

Sihanoukville is the gateway to Cambodia's southern islands, with four main companies

SOUTH COAST SIHANOUKVILLE

THE DEMISE OF SIHANOUKVILLE

Back in the day, Sihanoukville was a fixture on the Southeast Asia backpacker party circuit. Nicknamed 'Sinville', it was a town full of lovable (and some less lovable) expat rogues, B-list Russian mobsters and high-rollin' Khmers. Cheap beds and cheap vice ruled the day. It was nobody's favourite tourist town, but it was *fun*.

Sihanoukville had beaches in its favour, in particular dreamy Otres Beach. Over about a decade, Otres went from practically deserted beach to easy-going flashpacker magnet, complete with its own homegrown traveller ghetto, dubbed Otres Village. Otres played yin to Sinville's yang, attracting a more respectable crowd.

When islands like Koh Rong emerged on the tourist radar shortly after Otres, Sihanoukville's status as nerve centre of tourism in South Cambodia was cemented. Pretty much everybody passed through and plenty of them stayed for a few days to party or lie on Otres Beach.

Around 2017, everything changed. Cambodian and Chinese politicians made deals, then suddenly the entire city was turned over to Chinese business interests, who proceeded to embark on a casino-building frenzy. Today the city is a construction zone. Cranes dominate the skyline. A gargantuan new 'city' is rising behind Otres Beach. Cement mixers and heavy machinery clog roads pockmarked by bathtub-sized potholes. And sidewalks are nonexistent. It all adds up to one giant mess – indeed just getting from point A to point B in Sihanoukville has become almost unbearable.

Perhaps the best that can be hoped for at this point is that the developers carry through with the project and make the city liveable again – and that they do so without eviscerating the coastal environment. No guarantees there. Already there have been allegations of casinos improperly disposing of sewage in and around Sihanoukville.

Meanwhile, a 2019 ban on online gambling, which had driven much of Sihanoukville's development, could result in half-built projects. That would be devastating for locals, who have not exactly warmed to the Chinese embrace. Tens of thousands of locals have picked up and left. Moving forward, the city will need help from lady luck for its great development gamble to pay off.

operating speedboats between Sihanoukville and various stops on Koh Rong and Koh Rong Sanloem.

Tickets cost US$22 and include an open-ended return. Confirm the return trip with your ferry company a day before you plan to depart from the islands. Hopping between Koh Rong Sanloem and Koh Rong (with any of the speedboats) costs an additional US$7. Schedules are unpredictable. See Sihanoukville Ferry Tips (p204) for tricks and advice on minimising the pain of navigating these notoriously unreliable ferries.

Most boats leave from **Serendipity Pier** in high season (October to May). During the rainy months (June to September), departures generally move to the **Sihanoukville Port Ferry Dock**. Boat companies deliver you there free of charge from the Serendipity area, but this adds at least an hour to the trip.

You can purchase tickets online via www.book mebus.com, through your guesthouse, through a travel agent, or at ferry company offices in Sihanoukville. Ferry companies have additional ticket-sales booths at Serendipity Pier.

The four main companies, each with two to five departures daily to both Koh Rong (about one hour) and Koh Rong Sanloem (about 45 minutes), include the following:

Speed Ferry Cambodia (081 466880; www.speedferrycambodia.com; Golden Lions Roundabout; return ticket US$20) The original Koh Rong ferry company. Its distinctive yellow boats serve Koh Rong Sanloem and Koh Rong, including (on request) secondary beaches on Koh Rong like Sok San Village, Love Resort, Treehouse Bungalows and Pagoda Beach.

Buva Sea (097 888 8950; www.buvasea. com; Serendipity Beach Rd) Runs compact and zippy speedboats to Koh Rong Sanloem and Koh Rong, including regular stops at secondary Koh Rong beaches such as Coconut Beach, Long Set Beach and Sok San Beach.

Cambodia Island Speed Ferry (TBC; 087 811711; www.islandspeedferry.com; Serendipity Beach Rd; return ticket US$20) Its blue-and-white speedboats link Sihanoukville with Koh Rong Sanloem and Koh Rong (Koh Tuch village).

GTVC Speedboat (070 221234; www.gtvc speedboatcambodia.com; Serendipity Pier). With a booth at the Serendipity Pier, it runs fast boats to Koh Rong (Koh Tuch only) and Koh Rong Sanloem (Saracen Bay and M'pai Bay).

A cheaper option to Koh Rong and Koh Rong Sanloem is the cargo 'slow boat' run by Speed Ferry Cambodia from the port area (US$5 each way). The boat leaves Sihanoukville daily at about 9am and the usual loop is to Koh Rong Sanloem and then Koh Rong before returning to port. Life jackets aren't guaranteed on these, and they take two to three hours to the islands.

BUS

All the major bus companies have frequent connections to Phnom Penh. **Capitol Tours & Transport** (034-934042; St 109, bus station) and **Rith Mony** (081 785858; St 109, bus station) are the cheapest. The more expensive **Giant Ibis** (096 999 3333; www.giantibis.com; Ochheuteal St;) 'deluxe' bus to Phnom Penh, complete with hostess and wi-fi, is well worth the splurge. It departs daily at 3.30pm. There are sleeper options to Phnom Penh but they tend to leave on the early side (around 7.30pm) and arrive in the capital at an obscenely early hour.

For minivans to Kampot (US$5) and Kep (US$7), try **Champa Express** (069 698282; Mithona St), with four daily departures, or go through **Ana Travel** (034-933929; info@ anainternet.com; Serendipity Beach Rd; 8.30am-8.30pm). Some of these trips continue to Ha Tien, Vietnam (US$13, four hours).

Other companies include the following:
Larryta (016 202020; www.larrytacarrental. com.kh; Ekareach St)

BUSES FROM SIHANOUKVILLE

DESTINATION	PRICE	DURATION (HR)	FREQUENCY	COMPANIES
Bangkok	US$25-28	14-16	several daily	Rith Mony
Kampot (minivan)	US$5-6	4-5	several daily	Champa Express
Kep (minivan)	US$7-8	5-6	several daily	Champa Express
Koh Kong	US$9	5-6	8.15am	Virak Buntham
Phnom Penh (bus)	US$5-12	7-10	frequent	Capitol Tour, Giant Ibis, Olongpich, Phnom Penh Sorya, Rith Mony
Phnom Penh (minivan)	US$10-12	6-8	frequent	Mekong Express, Larryta
Siem Reap	US$15-17	15-20	6 daily (change in Phnom Penh)	Capital Tour, Phnom Penh Sorya, Rith Mony

Mekong Express ([icon] 012 257599; www.cat mekongexpress.com; St 110)

Olongpich Express (Olympic Express; [icon] 015 540240; St 109, bus station)

Phnom Penh Sorya ([icon] 034-933888; St 109, bus station)

Virak Buntham ([icon] 092 222423; Ekareach St)

SHARE TAXI

Cramped share taxis (US$9 per person or US$45 per car) depart throughout the day (mornings best) while minibuses (15,000r) to Phnom Penh depart from the **bus station** (St 109) until about 8pm. Avoid the minibuses if you value things like comfort and your life.

Hotels can arrange taxis to Phnom Penh for US$50 to US$60 (about four hours). Share taxis to Kampot (US$8, four to five hours) leave mornings only from a **taxi park** (7 Makara St) opposite Psar Leu. This taxi park and the bus station are good places to look for share taxis to Koh Kong or the Thai border. If nobody's sharing, expect to pay US$75 for Koh Kong and US$80 to the Thai border.

TRAIN

Trains are a fine option to Kampot and Phnom Penh given the poor state of the road network in the south these days. Royal Railways (p365) operates trains from the **train station** (Pher St) to Phnom Penh (US$8, seven hours) via Kampot (US$6, two hours) and Takeo (US$7, five hours) at 7am on Saturday, Sunday and Monday, with an additional trip at 4pm on Sunday.

ⓘ Getting Around

Sihanoukville's *moto* drivers are notorious for aggressively hassling passers-by and, more than anywhere else in Cambodia, shamelessly trying to overcharge. The situation has only gotten worse in the new Sihanoukville, which has seen inflation spike, so haggle hard (with a smile) over the price before setting out.

A *moto* should cost about US$2 from the centre to Serendipity; a *tuk tuk* ride around US$4. A *tuk tuk* on the disastrous road from Serendipity to Otres Beach costs at least US$6, but even that will take some haggling.

Several guesthouses and travel agents in Otres Beach still rent motorbikes for US$5 to US$7 a day. Motorbike hire in Sihanoukville cente is hard to come by – try **Samnang Mini-Mart** (Serendipity Beach Rd; per day US$6; ⊙7am-9pm) near the Golden Lions Roundabout.

Ream National Park

Just 15km east of Sihanoukville, Ream National Park (ឧទ្យានជាតិរាម) has sadly not been spared the onslaught of development that has affected most of the Sihanoukville region. Those who make the effort to get here can still take invigorating boat trips through coastal mangroves and along long stretches of unspoilt beach. Trekking in the park is no longer allowed, however, and Chinese resort cities have taken over large portions of the coast, including the best beaches.

The park is home to breeding populations of several regionally and globally endangered birds of prey, including the Brahminy kite, grey-headed fish eagle and white-bellied sea eagle: look for them soaring over Prek Toeuk Sap Estuary. Endangered birds that feed on the mudflats include the lesser adjutant, milky stork and painted stork.

Long-tail boat rides through the mangrove channels of the **Prek Toeuk Sap Estuary** can be arranged at the **Prek Toeuk Sap Ranger Station** ([icon] 016 328882; www.ream nationalpark.com; NH4; ⊙7am-5pm), which is about 3km east of the Sihanoukville airport turn-off, on the right side of the NH4, just before a major bridge. Trips last about two hours (US$35 return for one to five people). The boat disgorges passengers midtrip at a **mangrove walk**, where you stand a chance of spotting rare birds, monkeys, squirrels and other wildlife. You might also see both Irrawaddy and bottle-nosed **dolphins** near the mouth of the estuary around Koh Thmei – January to April are the best months.

Ream Beach   BEACH

(ឆ្នេររាម; Ream National Park) Lined with barbecue shacks, this is not Ream's prettiest beach but this is the main jumping-off point for boats to Koh Ta Kiev. It's the first beach you hit when coming from the airport, north of the Naval base.

ⓘ Getting There & Away

To get to Ream Beach, follow NH4 east from Sihanoukville to the airport turn-off, which is 15km from the Cambrew brewery at the junction of NH4 and Wat Leu Rd. Turn right and proceed straight, past the airport entrance, for about 10km. A return trip to Ream Beach from Sihanoukville by *moto/tuk tuk/taxi* should cost about US$10/15/25. If coming from the east, whatever you do don't drive into Sihanoukville or you will have to backtrack through hell. Jump off at the airport, where taxis wait near the exit.

THE SOUTHERN ISLANDS

Cambodia's southern islands are the tropical Shangri-La many travellers have been seeking – as yet untouched by the megaresorts that have sprouted across southern Thailand. Many of the islands have been tagged for major development, but developers have been slow to press go, paving the way for rustic bungalow resorts and chic Western-run boutiques to move in.

The much ballyhooed overhaul of Sihanoukville (p193) could portend darker times ahead, but for now Cambodia's islands are still paradise the way you imagined it: endless crescents of powdered-sugary-soft sand, hammocks swaying in the breeze, photogenic fishing villages on stilts, technicolor sunsets and the patter of raindrops on thatch as you slumber. It seems too good to last, so enjoy it while it does.

Koh Ta Kiev

If your beach-break perfection is about logging off and slothing out, this little island off Ream National Park ticks all the right boxes. Despite the fact that much of the island has been leased to developers – and a rudimentary road has recently been sliced through the jungle interior, signalling major development may not be far off – for the moment the southern tip of Koh Ta Kiev (កោះតាគៀវ) still has a clutch of delightfully bohemian and ecofriendly budget digs.

The best beach is **Long Beach**, which extends north from Ten103 Treehouse Bay. Various tracks branch off through the forest for those who want to explore. It's about a 25-minute walk from Ten103 Treehouse Bay to Last Point and Kactus Eco Village on the south tip of the island. The forest teems with wildlife and the entire island is a birdwatching mecca – we saw dozens of hornbills on our last visit.

🛏 Sleeping & Eating

There's no wi-fi on Koh Ta Kiev, although Smart's 4G network has relatively comprehensive coverage. Most places only have limited solar-powered electricity (bring a torch/flashlight) and rudimentary shared bathrooms (bucket showers and squat toilets).

The lodgings are the main option for food, with a handful of beach vendors around selling the occasionally odd snack (fried frogs on a stick, anyone?).

★ Ten103 Treehouse Bay   BUNGALOW $

(☏097 943 7587; www.ten103-cambodia.com; hammocks US$4, dm US$6, huts with shared bathroom US$25-35, private bathroom US$40) Unplug, unwind, destress – Ten103 is a beachfront backpacker bolthole that dishes up simple beach living the way it used to be. Stilted open-air 'tree houses' have sea views, while the towering open-air dorm and palm-thatch hammock shelters provide more basic back-to-nature options. Excellent food and drink, boat trips and kayaks available. The only place on the island open year-round.

Solar power runs from about 6pm to 11pm. Ten103 is a reference to Sihanoukville's GPS coordinates. Owner Joel is an area legend who has had a hand in launching most Koh Ta Kiev resorts over the years.

Kactus Eco Village   BUNGALOW $

(☏098 292381; www.kactusktk.com; dm US$8, bungalow US$25-45; 📶) 🍴 Under new French management, Kactus is a labyrinthine backpacker estate that hosts new-agey stuff like meditation, tantra yoga and creative art workshops using objects found on the beach. It's all part of its sustainable-living mantra, which also includes solar power, a vegan menu, detox drinks and horse riding (discovery rides US$25). A handsome beach extends 1km or so northwest.

Kayaks, stand-up paddleboards and snorkelling gear are available and it has 24-hour electricity.

Sea Garden   BUNGALOW $

(☏096 802 3648; www.facebook.com/seagarden island; dm US$3-5, bungalow from US$30) Once part of Treehouse Bay next door, the formula is similar here: cobble together a few bamboo bungalows and chuck them on an isolated cove. Add a rickety beach bar and a flush-with-the-sea, open-air dorm to create that perfect pirate vibe. A trail into the jungle starts just beyond here, leading to the resorts on the other side.

Last Point   BUNGALOW $

(☏088 502 6930; www.lastpointisland.com; hammocks US$3-5, dm US$5-8, d/q in bungalow US$25/40; 🕑Oct-May) The Last Point sits in splendid isolation on a sandy stretch of Koh Ta Kiev's south coast. There's a variety of small, sweet palm-thatch bungalows

ISLAND KNOW-HOW

➡ There are no banks or ATMs on any of the islands. Bring enough cash.

➡ Don't forget to pack insect repellent. The sand flies can be ferocious.

➡ It's not a bad idea to come equipped with a decent topical antiseptic. Insect bites can quickly turn into tropical ulcers if scratched.

➡ A torch (flashlight) or headlamp is also useful.

➡ When leaving, if you have an onward transport connection booked from Sihanoukville, don't take the last possible ferry/boat. Sailing times can be delayed or cancelled at short notice due to sea conditions.

where you can play out your Robinson Crusoe dreams, as well as a magnificent beach bar and breezy, 24-bed open-front dorm. No fans but the property catches the prevailing winds in the high season.

❶ Getting There & Away

Resorts have their own boats, and will connect you with a return trip for US$15 to US$20 (about 45 minutes). These traditionally depart from Otres Beach in the high season and from Ream Beach in Ream National Park in the rainy season.

However, as travellers vacate Otres Beach, expect high-season departures to move to Ream Beach as well. Ream Beach is just 15 minutes from the airport by taxi. If you are arriving from the north, jumping off from Ream allows you to bypass Sihanoukville altogether – a huge relief given the sorry state of the NH4 highway between the airport and the city centre.

There is also talk of a regular ferry service from Ream Beach being launched. Watch this space.

Koh Thmei

The large island of Koh Thmei (កោះថ្មី) is part of Ream National Park. It was once slated for a major development, including a bridge to the mainland, but as projects elsewhere have taken priority, this bird-laden island has remained miraculously pristine.

The only accommodation here, **Koh Thmei Resort** (www.koh-thmei-resort.com; d/f bungalow US$50/75) 🌿 is a gem, with tidy bungalows that use solar panels and biofuel for electricity. The resort sits on a private beach, and you can easily walk to more. Or go sea-kayaking, snorkelling or hiking. It's open year-round, with table football and board games to keep you entertained when it rains.

Excellent Khmer meals (US$6) and a full bar. The resort is right on the maritime bor-

der with Vietnam, with prime views to nearby Phu Quoc Island. The only available cell signal is Vietnamese. Electricity runs from 6.30am to 11pm.

It's an extremely atmospheric one-hour boat ride from the mainland fishing village of Koh Kchhang in the resort's private boat (US$8.50 per person one-way). We spotted Irrawaddy dolphins on our most recent trip. Management can arrange transport to Koh Kchhang from Sihanoukville, Kampot or the Sihanoukville airport.

❶ Getting There & Away

To get to Koh Thmei, make your way to Bat Kokir (Ou Chamnar), on NH4 about 12km east of Sihanoukville airport. All buses heading to or from Sihanoukville pass by Bat Kokir. Next, hire a *moto* (US$2) to take you 10km to the fishing village of Koh Kchhang. From here, Koh Thmei Resort can arrange private transport to the island, or negotiate in the village if you want to explore the island on your own.

Koh Rong

Ten years ago Koh Rong (កោះរ៉ុង) was a jungle-clad wilderness rimmed by swathes of sugary-white sand, with a few beach-hut resorts speckling the shore around tiny Koh Tuch village. Today the Koh Tuch village street-strip is a bottleneck of back-to-back backpacker crash pads, restaurants and hole-in-the-wall bars. You'll either love it or hate it, but for young travellers who descend off the ferry in droves, Koh Tuch is a vital stop on any Southeast Asia party itinerary.

As roads are built and ferry companies expand their services to beaches and villages around the island, many travellers are bypassing Koh Tuch for more sedate locales. In places like Long Set Beach, Sok San village and Prek Svay, the evening frog chorus

KOH RONG DEVELOPMENT

Koh Rong is a gigantic island clad in jungle and ringed by dozens of isolated beaches. For now it has been spared the Chinese-led development that has affected Sihanoukville and is beginning to affect neighbouring Koh Rong Sanloem. That could change quickly – check the situation on the ground before arriving. Cambodian developers have long planned to develop Koh Rong into a Cambodian version of Thailand's Koh Samui, complete with sealed ring roads and an airport. Those plans have stalled, save for a couple of large developments at the south end of Sok San Beach. A few roads have been built, but they remain unsealed and often impassable in the wet season. For now Koh Rong as we know it – sleepy, dreamy, impossibly gorgeous, relatively pristine – lives on.s.

overpowers the drifting bass from the late-night raves, phosphorescence shimmers in the sea and the island's natural charms of head-turning beaches backed by lush forest interior are clear to see.

◉ Sights

Long Set Beach BEACH
(ឆ្នេរទ្រូវង់សិន, 4K Beach) Past the Koh Tuch Beach headland (near Treehouse Bungalows) is beautiful Long Set Beach. Walk another half-hour along the sand and encounter little more than hermit crabs. A handful of hostels and boutique resorts are here, but it's still very peaceful. At the extreme east end of Long Set Beach, behind Koh Rong Hill Beach Resort, a short path leads to Nature Beach. From Nature Beach, it's a 30-minute walk through the forest to Coconut Beach (the trailhead is behind Romduol Resort).

Sok San Beach BEACH
(ឆ្នេរសុខសាន្ត, Long Beach) On the west side of the island is Koh Rong's finest beach, a 7km, almost empty stretch of drop-dead-gorgeous white sand. Sok San village at the northern end has a cluster of local eating spots and simple guesthouses. Unfortunately the beach around the village is quite dirty; walk south for cleaner waters. Two ferry companies service Sok San village in high season (November to May). You can walk from Koh Tuch to Sok San's south end via the jungle trail.

You can also reach the village fairly easily by *moto* from Kuh Tuch (US$15). Developers, not surprisingly, have their eye on this sensational sunset-facing strip. A luxury resort has opened on the beach's south end and there's another one in the works.

Coconut Beach BEACH
(ឆ្នេរដូង) At the easternmost point of the island, this jungle-clad, white-sand cove is roughly two hours from Koh Tuch on foot along the coast or 30 minutes by *moto* on a rugged road that dissolves into mud in the rainy season (June to mid-October). A lone speedboat company (Buva Sea) drops guests off at the pier a couple of times a day. Island-hopping boats from Koh Tuch anchor here late in the afternoon during rainy season.

A long-tail water taxi to Koh Tuch costs US$10 per person – order one from the counter at the foot of the pier. Coconut Beach was once popular with raucous groups of island-hoppers from Sihanoukville, but these trips have closed down and may or may not resume for Sihanoukville's now almost exclusively Chinese customer base.

Police Beach BEACH
(ឆ្នេរប៉ូលិស) Named because the island's police station is located here, Police Beach, just south of Koh Tuch, hosts wild all-night parties on Wednesdays and Saturdays, and during full moons. These get pretty quiet in low season. During the day sunbathing, cocktails and chill-out music are the name of the game.

Koh Tuch Beach BEACH
(ឆ្នេរកោះតូច) The wide sweep of Koh Tuch Beach extends for about 1km northeast from Koh Tuch village pier and gets lovelier the further out you go. We do not recommend swimming here because of questionable sewage practices. Walk towards the headland (near Treehouse Bungalows) for white sand, cleaner water and a more mellow scene.

🏃 Activities

Boat trips around the island are the main activity. **Sea Kayaking** is popular (US$5/8 per hour for a single/tandem kayak). From Koh Tuch or Long Set Beach, it's a 30-minute paddle out to **Pagoda Island** just offshore. Back on terra firma, you can take a jungle walk, spot birds and other wildlife, or go ziplining. Sky Bar (p205) hosts high-season yoga sessions.

Long-tail island-hopping day trips (with snorkelling, fishing and swimming thrown in) are the main Koh Rong activity and can be organised from any of the main beaches for about US$10 per person including lunch. For US$20 you can stay out longer and add dinner and an evening plankton (bioluminescence) run. Dinner includes whatever fish you catch.

From Koh Tuch, these group boat trips head to Sok San Beach in the high season (mid-October to mid-May), and to Coconut Beach in the low season. Three Brothers is a recommended operator in Koh Tuch, while popular tour guide Adventure Adam can tailor private trips.

★**Adventure Adam**   ADVENTURE SPORTS
(☑ 010 354002; www.adventureadam.org; Long Set Beach) 🏄 If lazing about by day and partying all night on Koh Rong seems like a missed opportunity to, you know, actually experience the island, consider booking a trip with Adventure Adam. His private day and overnight tours around Koh Rong include stops at fishing villages, remote beaches and deep jungle and earn high marks for cultural immersion and adventure.

Three Brothers   BOATING
(☑ 016 775110; South Pier, Koh Tuch; group tours per person US$10-20) These guys specialise in public group island-hopping trips, but can also organise private fishing trips, plus land-based tours around the island. High-season boat trips run daily to Sok San Beach, while less-frequent low-season journeys head the other way, to Coconut Beach. You'll cook and eat whatever fish you catch on board as part of the complimentary dinner.

High Point
Rope Adventure   ADVENTURE SPORTS
(☑ 016 839993; www.high-point.asia; Koh Tuch; per person US$35; ⊙ 9am-6pm; 🚸) A collection of ziplines, swing bridges and walking cables takes thrillseekers on an adrenaline-packed, 400m-long journey through the forest canopy above Koh Tuch village. Your ticket gets you unlimited access to the course for the entire day. From April to October, tickets are US$5 cheaper.

Koh Rong Dive Center   DIVING
(☑ 096 560 7362; www.kohrongdivecenter.com; Centre Pier, Koh Tuch; ⊙ 9am-6pm) Koh Rong's main dive centre organises trips in the waters around Koh Rong, Koh Rong Sanloem and a few other islands nearby. Also offers boat trips to other islands, snorkelling excursions and diving courses.

Jungle Trail   HIKING
FREE A beautiful jungle trail, rigorous in parts, links Koh Tuch village with the south end of Sok San Beach. The walk takes 45 minutes to one hour and can be done year-round. Starting at **White Rose Guesthouse** (Koh Tuch), walk up the hill about five minutes to the trailhead, where crude signs point the way to Sok San Beach.

Be aware that the hike involves some serious scrambling and is definitely not flip-flops territory. Don't do this at night or alone. The steep, rope-assisted descent to Sok San Beach is particularly perilous as some of the ropes have disintegrated. These days the trail ends abruptly at an unfinished road being hacked out of the forest behind Sok San Beach; once you hit this road, feel your way to the beach following the sound of the waves.

🛏 Sleeping

During high season (particularly December and January), Koh Rong's accommodation fills up fast. Travellers with no bed for the night during busy periods usually end up renting a hammock. Nearly all accommodation on Koh Rong has 24-hour electricity and wi-fi. Rates drop precipitously – by 50% or more across the board – during the rainy season (June to early October).

Koh Tuch

It wasn't too long ago that Koh Rong's bustling main village was the only choice for accommodation on the island. It's still the main port of entry for visitors, and remains firmly cemented as party central for the backpacker crowd. The scene mellows as you walk north along Koh Tuch Beach, where a string of wonderful flashpacker resorts awaits.

White Beach Bungalows   BUNGALOW $$
(☑ 069 320556; www.whitebeachkohrong.com; Koh Tuch; d/q in bungalow with fan US$60/90, air-con US$90/120; ❄ 🛜) Down at the more preferable far end of Koh Tuch Beach, the 17 polished-wood bungalows here are roomy and attractive, with well-furnished private

Koh Rong

0 ────── 1 km
0 ────── 0.5 mile

17
22

2
Koh Tuch
Beach

Koh Tuch
Village
25
26
27
7
23
9
8
12
6

Police
Beach

0 ────── 200 m
0 ────── 0.1 miles

4

Lonely
Beach
13

Prek Svay
11

16
Palm Beach
Song Saa
Island

14

Sok San
Village
18
19

20
Pagoda
Beach

Daem
Thkov

5

15 24 **3**
28
Koh Tuch
Beach
Police
Beach
21
4km
Beach

Pagoda
Island

Nature
Beach

1
10

See Enlargement

↓ *Koh Rong*
  Sanloem

← *Sihanoukville*

Koh Rong

⊙ Sights
1 Coconut Beach D6
2 Koh Tuch Beach B1
3 Long Set Beach B6
4 Police Beach A2
5 Sok San Beach..A6

⊙ Activities, Courses & Tours
Adventure Adam .... (see 3)
6 High Point Rope Adventure A2
7 Jungle Trail..A2
8 Koh Rong Dive Center A2
9 Three Brothers A2

⊙ Sleeping
Bunnan Bungalows ....(see 1)
10 Coconutbeach Bungalows....................D6
11 Firefly Guest House D2
12 Green Ocean Guesthouse.....................A2
Happy Elephant Bungalows............(see 7)
13 Lonely Beach C2
Long Set Resort............................. (see 3)
14 Love Resort...C4
15 Nest Beach Club......................................B6
16 Palm Beach Bungalow Resort D3
17 Paradise Bungalows B1
Reef on the Beach .... (see 3)

18 Sok San Beach Bungalows....................B4
19 Sok San Beach Resort B4
Sunrise Resort ....(see 1)
20 Tamu Koh Rong D5
21 Treehouse Bungalows B7
22 White Beach Bungalows B1

⊙ Eating
Coco Hut ....(see 10)
23 Koh Lanta...A2
Moon...(see 18)
24 White Pearl Beach B6

⊙ Drinking & Nightlife
25 Runaways A1
26 Sky Bar A1

⊙ Information
White Rose Guesthouse ....(see 9)

⊙ Transport
Buva Sea ....(see 9)
Cambodia Island Speed
Ferry ....(see 27)
27 GTVC Speedboat A1
28 Long Set Pier C6
Speed Ferry Cambodia ....(see 8)

balconies facing the sea. Hot water in the pricier air-con cottages only.

Paradise Bungalows BUNGALOW **$$**
(☑ 093 407825; www.paradise-bungalows.com; Koh Tuch Beach; bungalows US$35-100; 🛜) The delightfully rustic bungalows at Koh Rong's original resort come in all shapes and sizes, and climb up a hill amid rambling jungle foliage. The US$35 rooms are way up the slope while more expensive options are practically lapped by waves at high tide. The loungey restaurant, with its soaring palm-leaf panel roof and shoreline panorama, is a real highlight.

Treehouse Bungalows BUNGALOW **$$**
(☑ 015 755594; www.treehousebungalows.com; Koh Tuch; bungalows US$30-55, tree houses US$80-85; ❄🛜) Nestled on a secluded cove about a 15-minute beach walk from Koh Tuch pier, Treehouse has more than a touch of the fairy tale about it. The glass-doored bungalows have balconies strung with sea-shells, high-raised bungalow 'tree houses' have prime vistas, and the restaurant (specialising in wood-fired pizza) is set beside a natural reservoir with an organic garden out back.

Happy Elephant Bungalows GUESTHOUSE **$$**
(☑ 069 371897; happyelephantkohrong@gmail. com; Koh Tuch; bungalow from US$45; 🛜) You'll be happy about the hot water and the roomy, glass-doored bungalows made of solid wood at this place up the hill (it's on the right of the path – not to be confused with Happy Elephant *Guesthouse* opposite). Great place to swing in your porch hammock and listen to the rainfall on the forest canopy behind the property.

Green Ocean Guesthouse GUESTHOUSE **$$**
(☑ 097 272 7866; greenoceankohrong@gmail. com; Koh Tuch; d from US$50; ❄🛜) With air-conditioning and hot water – rarities in Koh Tuch – this is a fine option during the rainy season, when prices drop by about 60%. At other times the rooms, while comfortable, are too small to justify the price. It adds a dorm room in the high season and there's a communal balcony with sea views upstairs from reception.

Long Set & Coconut Beaches

A clutch of groovy beach hostels fronts the gleaming white sand and turquoise waters of Long Set Beach (p198). There's plenty of separation between the resorts on Long Set and the party scene tends to be confined to your hostel. Long Set's eastern half is flashpacker territory. Beyond Long Set Beach is agreeable Coconut Beach (p198), with several guesthouses along its relatively protected shoreline.

Bunnan Bungalows
BUNGALOW $

(☏096 963221; Coconut Beach; tent/bungalow US$6.50/32; 🛜) Bunnan is a steady if unspectacular option near the middle of Coconut Beach, with a mix of wood and concrete bungalows slinking up a hillside, plus a few spacious fan-cooled tents on platforms. There is a small beachfront restaurant on the premises. Walk in or book direct by phone to save 20%.

★ Nest Beach Club
HOSTEL $

(☏096 634 2320; www.nestcambodia.com; Long Set Beach; dm for 1/2 persons US$15/22.50; ❄🛜) This poshtel at the southern end of Long Set Beach is a step up from anything in Koh Tuch. The well-designed dorms are air-conditioned and feature double-wide bunks divided by walls and curtains. The restaurant has a stunner of an open-air, oceanfront terrace with delicious sesame-battered chicken, veggie wraps and chilli-cheese fries. The all-day 'Nestival' takes place every Monday.

Coconutbeach Bungalows
BUNGALOW $

(☏010 351248; www.coconutbeachbungalows.com; Coconut Beach; tent/r/bungalow US$5/25/40; 🛜) Coconut Beach's original guesthouse sprawls up a hillside overlooking cerulean water and powdery white sand. The owners go above and beyond for guests and have a huge library of books and games. The small semiprivate rooms have shared bathrooms, as do the basic tents atop platforms down by the ocean, or pay up for the comfortable en-suite bungalows.

Reef on the Beach
RESORT $

(☏096 759 8583; www.facebook.com/reefonthe beach; Long Set Beach; dm US$12-15, tent US$21-35, bungalow US$55-80) Reef's formula is best described as beach games all day, drinking games all night. Dorms feature individually fan-cooled, couples-ready double beds, while the raised private bungalows are spacious and sturdy with drying areas and big balconies – great value. It also has 50 to 60 electricity-enabled glamping tents spread across three 'tent cities'; the pricier ones are safari-standard.

Sunrise Resort
RESORT $$

(☏012 645369; Coconut Beach; r from US$60) This is easily the fanciest place on Coconut Beach, with a 25m pool and 4-star-quality rooms, but it's a work in progress. For now there's no air-con, no wi-fi and no cable TV. The Khmer owner assured us that these perks were on the way (air-con would be a game-changer). Walk-ins can use the pool for US$5.

Tamu Koh Rong
BOUTIQUE HOTEL $$$

(☏096 326 9025; www.tamucambodia.com; Pagoda Beach; r & tent incl breakfast from US$95; ❄🛜❄) Near the pier on up-and-coming Pagoda Beach, 15 minutes west of Coconut Beach by *moto*, this sleek little boutique offers a mix of luxury safari tents and concrete bungalows, all well appointed with air-con, designer furniture, private terrace and marvellous open-plan bathroom (no TV). The beach out front is exquisite, or do laps in the charcoal-toned pool.

One ferry company – Speed Ferry Cambodia (p205) – does drop-offs at Pagoda Beach pier on request, or arrange a private transfer (US$40 per person round trip) through the resort.

Long Set Resort
RESORT $$$

(☏086 796666; www.longsetresort.com; d from US$168; ❄🛜❄) In the middle of the eponymous beach, these represent by far the classiest digs on Long Set Beach, with stylish bathrooms, minifridges, bathrobes, spa tubs and glorious beds. Active sorts will find three lap pools, a fleet of kayaks, and off-road motorbikes for rent. Two restaurants, including one with air-con.

Rates are 35% lower in the low season.

Northeast Coast & Prek Svay

North/northwest of Long Set and Coconut beaches, the main road takes you to Pagoda Beach then on to Palm Beach and the delightful local fishing village of Prek Svay at the island's northern tip. Several upscale boutique resorts have colonised Pagoda Beach. Otherwise this coastline is mostly about isolated resorts geared at backpackers.

Love Resort
TENTED CAMP $

(☏016 963198; www.kohronkloveresort.com; Prek Svay; tent US$20-25; 🛜) Set amid mangroves with a small but pleasant beach out front, Love Resort has several dozen midsized tents equipped with big beds, fans and power out-

DIVING IN THE SOUTHERN ISLANDS

Cambodia might not be as famous for diving as neighbouring Thailand, but heading below the water's surface here still offers up some serious highlights. Though fish stocks may indeed be lower than in other Asian dive destinations (a consequence of years of irresponsible fishing practices, now being reversed by marine conservation organisations), the waters surrounding the southern islands off Sihanoukville are famed for their biodiverse, multicoloured corals and unique array of tiny sea creatures.

The best of Cambodia's diving is among the fringing reefs of Koh Rong Sanloem and Koh Koun, which are home to a mind-boggling collection of weird and wacky nudibranchs, starfish and seahorses. Commonly spotted fish include angelfish, damselfish and scorpionfish. Further afield, the island of Koh Sdach is a great base for exploring nearby reefs where cuttlefish and massive cobias are often spotted, and the islands of Koh Tang and Koh Prins are famous for bamboo sharks, blue-spotted ribbontail rays, wrasse and batfish. Whale sharks have also been sighted by divers.

Most dive operators are concentrated on Koh Rong Sanloem, with Saracen Bay, Sunset Beach and M'Pai Bay all represented. Koh Rong also has a dive shop, although dive trips out of Koh Rong tend to head towards Koh Rong Sanloem. Koh Sdach now has two dive centres serving the Koh Sdach Archipelago.

lets. Activities – all free for guests – include snorkelling, archery and kayaking on the adjacent river. The restaurant sits under a soaring pavilion – this would be a great place for a budget-friendly retreat or party.

Love Resort is on Koh Rong's northeast coast, just 15 minutes by motorbike from either Sok San or Prek Svay village.

Firefly Guest House GUESTHOUSE $
(☏010 418567; hunoukk@gmail.com; Prek Svay; dm/d/q US$10/25/45) For rustic living in an authentic Khmer fishing village, look no further than this riverside delight. A half-dozen rooms and a delicious Khmer restaurant share an over-water veranda with views that never get old, albeit the rooms are overpriced, especially given the lack of fans. The entire place is well cared for and the hosts are super friendly.

★**Lonely Beach** BUNGALOW $$
(www.lonely-beach.net; Prek Svay; dm US$12, bungalow with shared/private bathroom from US$45/60) ✒ Lonely Beach is a traveller Shangri-la hidden on a private beach along Koh Rong's northern tip. Committed to ecofriendly living, the jungle-chic bungalows and glorious open-air dorms are breeze-cooled, and all water is dispensed via coconut-shell scoop. High season sees island-hopping trips and nightly banquets on the beach. More way-of-life than resort, Lonely Beach entices many to stay for months.

Solar-powered electricity is limited to the restaurant (evenings only), and there's no wi-fi (although Smart's 4G network is accessible). Private boat transfer from Sihanoukville is US$15 each way, or you can walk from Prek Svay village (about 45 minutes if you don't get lost). Book directly through the resort for the best prices.

Palm Beach Bungalow Resort BUNGALOW $$
(☏016 661313; www.palmbeachkohrong.com; Prek Svay; d/q from US$40/50, r with air-con from US$110; ❋ ☏) This sociable spot, popular with youthful adventure-tour groups, has a small private beach and tees up daily waterfall walks and other activities. The stilted bungalows (cold water only) are sturdy and functional, and the bar brims with life and occasional drinking games. Arrive via its private boat from Sihanoukville at 2pm (one-way/round trip US$15/25), or by *moto* (US$15 from Koh Tuch).

Sok San Beach (Long Beach)

Sok San village at the northern end of this 7km beach (p198) has developed into a mini backpacker ghetto – a bit like Koh Tuch in its early days, with cheap bungalows, cheap beer, happy snacks and banana pancakes on demand. The scene shuts down in rainy season. The rest of the beach is mostly empty, with a few midrangers near the middle, and fancy-schmancy Royal Palm Villas at the south end.

Sok San Beach Bungalows BUNGALOW $$
(☏017 777831; www.soksanbeachbungalows.com; Sok San village; bungalows from US$30; ☏) Travellers looking for a slice of old-school Koh

Rong beach life will revel in the spartan solitude of this place, which comprises 10 rickety huts with rudimentary bathrooms and an overwater restaurant serving Khmer and Western food. Note that several similarly simple bungalows nearby have attempted to steal its name; look for the one owned by Australian Julian.

Like virtually everything in Sok San village, it closes down during rainy season (June to September).

Sok San Beach Resort   RESORT $$$
(📞017 777831; www.soksanbeachresort.com; Sok San village; r US$110-200; 🆒🛜) Situated along a magnificent stretch of Sok San Beach, this boutique resort mixes stand-alone 'chalets' with hotel-style rooms. The chalets are particularly well appointed and have private terraces. It has a speedboat for island hopping and water sports. Food and drink is expensive, but Sok San village is nearby with budget-friendly bars and restaurants.

Eating

While the best food is traditionally found in the resorts – Paradise Bungalows (p199) and Nest are particularly recommended – some wonderful stand-alone dining places have opened up around the island. Most are simple affairs offering just a few tables and feet-in-the-sand dining.

Coco Hut   CAMBODIAN $
(Coconut Beach; mains US$3.50-7; ⊗7am-11pm; 🛜) The kitchen at this ordinary-looking beach bar surprises with some of the best Khmer food in the islands. The *amok* (baked

fish) is spicy and delicious, and you can't go wrong with the whole steamed red snapper. Western faves and breakfasts too. Don't overlook the drinks – bartender Sopheap's margarita was wicked good (and strong).

White Pearl Beach   THAI $
(📞096 499 0235; Long Set Beach; mains US$2.50-4; ⊗8am-11pm) Occupying a lovely patch of Long Set Beach, this is a great place to relax and watch the waves lap the shore while enjoying splendid Thai food at rock-bottom prices. They toss a few chaise lounges in the sand and serve cocktails if you want to hang out for the day.

Koh Lanta   INTERNATIONAL $
(Koh Tuch; mains US$4-5, pizzas US$9-10; ⊗24hr) Named after the famous French version of *Survivor,* which for years was filmed on Koh Rong, this restaurant and bakery offers some of the best pizzas on the island.

Moon   SOUTHEAST ASIAN $$
(Sok San village; mains US$3.50-7; ⊗8am-9pm) This unassuming local place serves up superb Khmer and Thai specialities with a heavy seafood bent, including stir-fried crab and steamed fish. The curries and salads come with plenty of zest – you've been warned.

🍷 Drinking & Nightlife

Most of the action remains in Koh Tuch village, including the famous Wednesday- and Saturday-night parties on Police Beach (p198). Additional parties are added for full moons. The hostels on Long Set Beach (p198) are self-contained party units and are

SIHANOUKVILLE FERRY TIPS

A few things to keep in mind about the ferry system between Sihanoukville and its islands.

➡ During low season, some of the advertised ferries simply don't run, so be sure to check with a person who works for the company in advance.

➡ Delays of 30 minutes to one hour – often more – are the norm.

➡ Boats tend to operate in a loop – either clockwise (Sihanoukville–Koh Rong Sanloem–Koh Rong–Sihanoukville) or (less common) counterclockwise. All companies are prone to reversing loops without notice. This can mean transfer times to and from the islands can be quite lengthy. There's not much you can do about this; just try to relax and enjoy the scenery, and be extremely conservative in your estimates of when you'll arrive anywhere.

➡ All companies ask that return tickets are stamped in advance (some say the day before, others three hours before). In high season this is particularly important, because a large number of people are transferring and seat availability often becomes an issue. In low season this is not as crucial, but sometimes the smaller ferries still fill up.

worth checking out. Sok San village has a mellow scene in high season.

★ Sky Bar
BAR

(☎081 715650; Koh Tuch; ⊙10am–last customer; ⬧) Perched way up on the hill overlooking the pier, Sky Bar is Koh Rong's most sophisticated bar, with professional cocktails, a rocking gen-X soundtrack and modern vegetarian and vegan food (raw bowls, anyone?). The views and discounted drinks make it a great happy-hour option, with the action often continuing well into the evening. The brunch is highly recommended.

Runaways
BAR

(Koh Tuch; 8am-late; ⬧) Killer drinks and groovy tunes are the hallmarks of this convivial gathering spot, popular with expats and tourists alike. Positively beautiful breakfasts, too – try the stuffed avocado or the potato omelette.

❶ Information

Bring all the cash you think you'll need with you as there are no banks or ATMs on Koh Rong. If you do run out of money, several businesses, including Koh Lanta and White Rose Guesthouse (p199), offer cash advances on credit cards for a 10% fee.

SAFE TRAVEL

Theft can be a problem on Koh Rong. Use lock-boxes if supplied in dorms, or leave valuables in your accommodation's safe.

In 2013 an American woman was murdered while hiking the jungle trail (p199) to Sok San Beach, and in 2015 there was an attempted attack on a Japanese tourist. Travellers should buddy up when walking in more isolated areas of the island, and on the beach late at night.

Koh Rong's full-tilt surge into tourism is not without problems that threaten the pristine environment that attracted travellers here in the first place. Many hastily knocked-up hostels and bars on Koh Tuch Beach don't have proper septic systems, with waste running directly into the sea, and the sand nearest the village can become strewn with trash. Apparently, business owners are working on getting septic tanks and cleaning up the beach.

❶ Getting There & Away

Fast ferries depart from one of Koh Tuch's three piers to Sihanoukville (US$15 one-way) and Koh Rong Sanloem (US$7 one-way to M'Pai Bay or Saracen Bay). The four main companies are **Cambodia Island Speed Ferry** (TBC Speed Boat; ☎069 811711; www.islandspeedferry.com; North Pier, Koh Tuch), **Speed Ferry Cambodia** (☎096

9828797; www.speedferrycambodia.com; Centre Pier, Koh Tuch), **Buva Sea** (☎016 888960; www.buvasea.com; South Pier, Koh Tuch) and **GTVC Speedboat** (☎016 331234; www.gtvcspeedboat cambodia.com; North Pier, Koh Tuch). Each runs three to six trips per day (fewer in the rainy season). There's really no telling whether a ferry will run clockwise via Sihanoukville or counterclockwise via Koh Rong (see our ferry tips). Patience is the order of the day.

There's also a daily slow boat to Sihanoukville (US$5, three hours) if you prefer a more deliberate pace or want to save a few dollars. It departs midafternoon and sometimes stops on Long Set Beach and/or Coconut Beach on the way out.

Transfer from Sihanoukville to more remote resorts and beaches on Koh Rong, such as Lonely Beach and Palm Beach, is via private boat owned by the resorts.

❶ Getting Around

BOAT

Ferry companies doing the Sihanoukville–Koh Rong Sanloem–Koh Rong loop add additional stops around Koh Rong during high season and on request in low season. Regularly served destinations include Sok San village, **Long Set Pier**, Coconut Beach and Pagoda Beach. Buva Sea and Speed Ferry Cambodia are the best bets for these. Hopping to another beach generally costs US$5.

Long-tail 'water taxis' are usually available to shuttle you from any of the above beaches back to Koh Tuch. Just head to the pier and ask around (there is usually a desk at the foot of the pier). Typically these cost US$5 to US$15 per person, depending on how far you are going, but if you're the only passenger expect to pay double. Scheduled public 'shuttles' (US$5, one or two daily, high season only) are another option to Koh Tuch from Sok San Beach or Coconut Beach.

ROAD

Koh Rong has a small network of as-yet unsealed roads, and motorbike hire is readily available, albeit at island prices (US$15 to US$20 per day). Sections of the road dissolve into mud pits in the rainy season. This doesn't seem to deter *moto* drivers, but it might deter you. Sample prices for one-way *moto* hire from Koh Tuch: US$8 to Coconut Beach, US$15 to Sok San village, US$20 to Prek Svay and US$25 to Lonely Beach.

Koh Rong Sanloem

Blessed with endless beaches and teeming jungles, Koh Rong Sanloem (កោះរ៉ុងសន្លឹម) is many people's vision of tropical bliss. It has three main settlements with three distinct personalities: Saracen Bay is the beauty queen with its graceful curve of white sand; M'Pai Bay is the social butterfly with its backpacker bars and village vibe; Sunset Beach is the wild child with its arty hostels and sunset sessions.

Unfortunately, development looms. Behind the south end of Saracen Bay, a lot the size of several football fields has been hacked out of primary forest. Meanwhile, plans have been laid for a major resort city that will take up roughly the entire northern half of the island (minus M'Pai Bay). Roads are being laid across the island, at great expense to the jungle. The hope is that any changes won't affect the island's chill vibe and culture of tasteful DIY development.

⊙ Sights & Activities

From Saracen Bay it's an easy 20-minute walk to Lazy Beach (p209) along the road that starts at Tree Bar (p210). It's a 30-minute hike (sneakers recommended) to Sunset Beach from the Central Pier (p210).

For a harder (and harder-to-find) trail, you can navigate the clear-cut forest to a **watchtower** (often mistakenly referred to as a 'lighthouse') on the island's south end. The walk takes about one hour on a trail that begins just before Dolphin Bay Resort at the extreme south of Saracen Bay (head left at the first fork, avoiding the new development). The watchtower is a prime nesting spot for sea eagles. Be aware that there are sometimes soldiers stationed at the watchtower and they may ask you for a tip (US$1 is usually fine).

Koh Rong teems with monkeys, birds and other wildlife, creating great opportunities for hiking. Several resorts rent kayaks and most can arrange snorkelling excursions, while Cambodian Diving Group, **Dive Shop** (☑ 034-933664; www.diveshopcambodia. com; Serendipity Beach Rd; ⊙7am-9pm), Ecosea Diver and Scuba Nation offer scuba trips around the island and beyond. Sunset Adventures on Sunset Beach organises all kinds of outdoor activities, including rock-climbing, freediving and guided kayak trips, plus yoga and tantra sessions.

Dive Shop Cambodia
DIVING

(☑ 097 723 2626; www.diveshopcambodia.com; Sunset Beach; 2 fun dives US$80, open-water course US$380) A PADI five-star dive centre offering the full gamut of PADI courses, as well as fun dives, out of its base at Sunset Beach. Students can avail of free dorm-room accommodation (US$7 for others). Also runs snorkelling tours. It has a small office at Saracen Bay near the middle pier.

Scuba Nation
DIVING

(☑ 012 604680; www.divecambodia.com; Saracen Bay; 2-dive package US$95, PADI Open Water Diver course US$445) A recent transplant from Sihanoukville, Scuba Nation is a PADI five-star IDC (instructor development centre) with a comfortable boat for day and liveaboard trips.

Cambodian Diving Group
DIVING

(☑ 096 224 5474; www.facebook.com/cambodian diving; M'Pai Bay; 2-dive package US$85, open-water course US$445) ⟋ This M'Pai Bay-based outfit has expert knowledge of the surrounding underwater world that only comes from years of experience diving here. Offers excellent one-day dive packages and various PADI courses. Partners with Save Cambodian Marine Life to protect the local reefs.

Save Cambodian Marine Life
VOLUNTEERING

(☑ 096 224 5474; M'Pai Bay; 1-week volunteer package US$350) ⟋ This NGO works to protect the local reefs surrounding Koh Rong Sanloem with ongoing projects including maintaining a coral nursery, organising reef clean-up dives, producing natural sunscreen and more. Volunteer packages include diving, shared accommodation and all meals.

Ecosea Diver
DIVING

(☑ 016 603400; www.ecoseadiver.com; M'Pai Bay) Another cog in the close-knit diving community of M'Pai Bay, Ecosea Diver shares a space with other dive outfits and NGO Save Cambodian Marine Life, offering everything from discovery dives (US$70) to PADI open-water courses (US$445).

Sunset Adventures
ADVENTURE SPORTS

(☑ 088 616 6484; www.facebook.com/sunset-adventures-cambodia; Sunset Beach) Tour operator based at Sunset Beach organises all kinds of outdoor activities, including rock climbing, freediving and guided kayak trips, plus yoga and tantra sessions at nearby Robinson's Bungalows.

🛏 Sleeping

Expect healthy low-season discounts of 50% or more pretty much everywhere. Most places have 24-hour electricity, the notable exception being Sunset Beach, where resorts provide part-time power through individual solar-power systems and/or generators.

Saracen Bay

This crescent-shaped, 2.5km-long sweep of white sand on the island's east coast is Koh Rong Sanloem's most popular destination – and home to the vast majority of the island's higher-end accommodation. Development threatens, but for now it remains idyllic.

Big Easy HOSTEL $
(☏ 071 960 0387; www.thebigeasycambodia.com; Saracen Bay; dm/bungalow from US$10/30; ❀ 🎧) A long-time Serendipity (Sihanoukville) fave, Big Easy has brought its formula of flashy dorms and lively bar to the white sands of Saracen Bay. The air-conditioned dorm features privacy curtains and reading lights, while the bar has regular events like quiz-night Fridays and live music. Swings in the shallow turquoise waters out front beckon passers-by.

Onederz HOSTEL $
(☏ 090 200400; www.onederz.com; Saracen Bay; dm US$10-12; ❀ 🎧) The antidote to the islands' colourful party hostels, squeaky-clean Onederz features six- and eight-bed dorms decked out in lashings of white-on-white. All beds have individual reading lamps and charging ports, plus lock-boxes, and there's a female dorm. One quibble is that the bottom bunks are basically on the floor.

★ Mad Monkey HOSTEL $$
(☏ 069 901076, 088 687 9115; www.madmonkeyhostels.com; dm US$10-11, bungalows US$50; 🎧) Part of the Mad Monkey hostel empire, this edition wins big with its secluded private cove and beaches to the north of Saracen Bay. Dorms of varying size and private bungalows are oceanfront, simple and fan-cooled, and the atmosphere is laid-back and convivial. A big, open-air bar and restaurant overlooks the sea, where people laze about in hammocks all day.

When guests do get up from their relaxation, it's usually to go on a boat trip for snorkelling or to play a beanbag-tossing game. Swimming in the secluded cove is also an activity of choice, particularly in the wee hours for couples aiming to have a go (or maybe a glow?) in the plankton.

Paradise Villas BUNGALOW $$
(☏ 093 407825; www.paradise-bungalows.com; Saracen Bay; bungalows US$50-100; ❀ 🎧) A throwback to the early days of the Southern Islands, Paradise remains a timeless testament to castaway-chic style near the far south end of Saracen Bay. Sister of Paradise Bungalows (p199) on Koh Rong, it follows similar scripts: smart, solid-wood bungalows with thick mattresses, balconies and rain showers, and a beautifully designed restaurant mixing Asian fusion with hearty European dishes.

As times change on Koh Rong Sanloem, so do times change at Paradise: about half the rooms have air-con and they have 24-hour electricity and good working wi-fi. There's kayak and SUP rental available, plus a dive centre and two speedboats.

Sara Resort RESORT $$
(☏ 097 567 8950; www.sararesort.com; Saracen Bay; d from US$75; ❀ 🎧) Occupying prime real estate near the central pier, Sara has a row of boxy bungalows with air-con and glass doors extending back from the beach. They are clean and well designed if not huge. The airy beachfront restaurant (mains US$5 to US$20) features Aussie, Thai and many other flavours, and the US$2 cocktails from 5pm to 9pm are another draw.

Green Blue Resort RESORT $$
(☏ 090 869086; www.facebook.com/greenbluebungalowresort; Saracen Bay; dm US$11-12, r without bathroooom US$30, bungalow US$90-140; ❀ 🎧) Green Blue has a delightfully homey feel, with bungalows strung with potted plants and vines, some set back from the seafront amid a well-tended garden. The restaurant serves excellent breakfasts and Turkish fare. There are two budget garden cottages and the dorm has just four beds.

Cita Resort RESORT $$$
(☏ 096 261 2418; www.facebook.com/citaresortkohrongsanloem; Saracen Bay; bungalows US$85-99; 🎧) Towards the southern end of Saracen Bay, this intimate resort has about a dozen beautifully conceived raised bungalows with upper-level bedrooms fronted by sea-view balconies, open-air bathrooms and a shaded hammock-strung lounging area below. The fantastic restaurant here dishes up fresh pasta and other Italian specialities, and there's 24-hour solar power.

Moonlight Resort RESORT $$$
(☏ 088 578 8999; www.moon-light-resort.com; Saracen Bay; r US$100-110; ❀ 🎧) Staying at this place will make you feel like one cool alien. The white, dome-shaped bungalows look

Koh Rong Sanloem

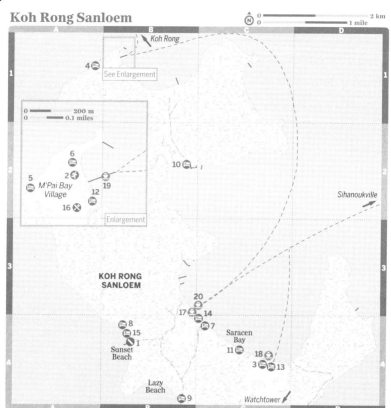

like mysterious igloos stolen from the moon, but they are sumptuous, air-conditioned and immaculate. Its Blue Moon restaurant likewise sits beneath a giant blue dome with shimmery-looking panels. There are also a couple of pools and a cocktail bar.

M'Pai Bay

This once-sleepy fishing village is attractive for backpackers with its chilled-out hostels and cool bars. Call it the next Koh Rong, only better-integrated with the village and a bit more ecofriendly (so far). There's no photogenic white sands here (the beach is a grainy yellow hue), but you can walk to good ones and there are gorgeous views from up on the hill.

Cliff HOSTEL $
(016 329508; www.facebook.com/thecliffhostel
mpaybay; M'Pai Bay; dm US$7-8, r US$30-35;
☎) The structures here – which include a

33-bed open-air dorm and a cliff-side bar and restaurant with sweeping views of the channel that separates Koh Rong Sanloem and Koh Rong – are nothing less than architectural marvels. The private rooms are compact but have plenty of rustic charm. A stairway leads down to the shore from that glorious restaurant.

Located a 10-minute walk up the hill west of the village proper, it's well worth dropping by for a drink or meal, even if you are not staying here.

My Way GUESTHOUSE $
(096 698 0160; www.mywaycambodia.com; M'Pai Bay; r with/without bathroom US$35/15; ☎) Well-managed My Way occupies a cute wooden house towards the south end of M'Pai Bay. The small en-suite rooms have dreamcatchers on the walls and stare at the ocean through sliding glass doors, while rooms at the back share a spotless bathroom with stone floor tiles. There's a good social

Koh Rong Sanloem

🟢 Activities, Courses & Tours
Cambodian Diving Group.............(see 2)
1 Dive Shop Cambodia B4
Ecosea Diver ....(see 2)
2 Save Cambodian Marine Life A2
Sunset Adventures .... (see 1)

🛏 Sleeping
Big Easy...(see 14)
3 Cita Resort C4
4 Cliff A1
5 Dragonfly Guesthouse.........................A2
6 Easy Tiger...A2
7 Green Blue Resort................................C4
8 Huba-Huba..B4
9 Lazy Beach..B4
10 Mad Monkey B2
11 Moonlight Resort..................................C4
12 My Way A2
Onederz ....(see 7)
13 Paradise Villas C4
14 Sara Resort C4
15 Sleeping Trees......................................B4
Sunboo Beach Bungalows........... (see 1)

⊗ Eating
16 Seapony Cafe A2
Titanic ....(see 14)

🍸 Drinking & Nightlife
Octopussy Beach Bar..................(see 7)
Tree Bar...(see 14)

🚌 Transport
17 Buva Sea..B3
18 Cambodia Island Speed Ferry C4
GTVC Speedboat ....(see 17)
19 M'Pai Bay Pier.......................................B2
20 Saracen Bay Central Pier....................C3
Saracen Bay South Pier .... (see 18)
Speed Ferry Cambodia ....(see 17)

vibe and wonderful French-influenced food, including brunch and daily specials.

Dragonfly Guesthouse   HOSTEL $
(☎069 493914; www.facebook.com/dragonfly guesthouserestaurant; dm/r/bungalow US$6/18/25) This chilled-out spot in M'Pai Bay operates at a languid pace, with a scenic check-in area and papasan chairs overlooking the frothy sea. Accommodation is airy and clean, and the restaurant and bar are beloved for wine and cheeseboards. It has an artsy streak, with live music, yoga sessions, art exhibitions and movie nights hosted frequently.

Easy Tiger   GUESTHOUSE $$
(☎096 915 3370; www.facebook.com/easytiger bungalows; M'Pai Bay; dm/r without bathroom

US$6/15, bungalow US$20-25) This friendly guesthouse in M'Pai Bay village has plenty of homespun appeal, thanks to its helpful owners, winning bar-restaurant and communal feel. The main building houses small private rooms and a beachfront dorm with tall, sturdy bunk beds. Out back are wooden bungalows with large verandas for those seeking more privacy, and a towering eight-bed 'tree-house' dorm.

Sunset Beach & Lazy Beach

On the back side of the island, Sunset Beach (ឆ្នេរថ្ងៃលិច; reached by walking trail or private boat) is home to just a few resorts and tent camps, where the cares of the world seem a million miles away. A 30-minute walk south through the woods is dreamy Lazy Beach, the site of a single long-running resort (although two more were being built at the time of research).

★ **Lazy Beach**   RESORT $$
(☎016 214211; www.lazybeachcambodia.com; bungalows US$75) On the southwest coast of Koh Rong Sanloem, this idyllic getaway fronts one of the most stunning beaches you'll find anywhere. The 20 bungalows have balconies and hammocks outside, and spiffy stone-floor bathrooms and double beds inside. The combined restaurant and common area is stocked with books and board games, making the resort a good fit for families.

The hotel runs its own boats from Sihanoukville at noon each day directly to the resort, though in wet season the boats generally will drop you off on the west side of the island. There's an easy walking path (about 20 minutes) from Saracen Bay, and the hotel can offer an overland shuttle service for luggage.

★ **Huba-Huba**   BUNGALOW $$
(☎088 554 5619; www.facebook.com/hubabun galow; Sunset Beach; dm US$10, tents US$20, d US$30-60, f US$90-120) Perched on secluded Sunset Beach and flanked by the jungle, this small collection of thatched-roof bungalows and glistening hardwood common spaces looks like an island fantasyland. During high season, a beach restaurant with a bar constructed from the bow of a boat serves cold beers, wine, cocktails and barbecue, and everybody goes snorkelling on a nearby reef.

Sunboo Beach
Bungalows
BUNGALOW $$

(☑017 508716; www.sunboobeachbungalows.
com; Sunset Beach; dm/d US$15/100; 🖘) This
is the more refined choice on Sunset Beach,
tempting a more well-heeled clientele with
masterful design, soothing music and a sus-
tainable bent. The common area and bar
is set under a soaring roof supported by
telephone-pole-thick bamboo rods. Light
screens lend the compact dorm a dreamy
look while the bungalows (no hot water) are
smart and inviting.

Sleeping Trees
BUNGALOW $$

(☑ 071 213 7634; www.sleeping-trees.com; Sunset
Beach; dm US$9, tree tents US$19, teepees US$30,
bungalows US$50) With unique accommoda-
tion such as tree tents and teepees sprawled
around a common area housing a restaurant, bar and pool table, this expat-owned
beach retreat will make you feel like an
incredibly fortunate castaway. There aren't
many frills, but what more do you need than
a tent strung in the trees when you're wak-
ing up on a far-flung, jungle-covered beach?

✗ Eating & Drinking

In addition to a few stand-alone restaurants
on the beach, all the resorts have attached
restaurants. Top resort kitchens include
Sara Resort (p207) and Cita Resort (p207)
at Saracen Bay, and My Way (p208) and the
Cliff (p208) in M'Pai Bay.

Koh Rong Sanloem is tame compared with
Koh Rong, but you can find some action, especially in M'Pai Bay. Mad Monkey (p207) is
full-moon party central, while there's usually
something cracking at Octopussy Beach Bar
and Tree Bar on Saracen Bay.

Titanic
SEAFOOD $

(Saracen Bay; mains US$3-6.50; ⊙8am-11pm)
This place is immensely popular for all the
right reasons – namely toes-in-the-sand
dining on delicious, excellent-value seafood.
The *amok* red curry is delicious while the
mixed seafood grill with Kampot pepper is
a steal at US$6. Come back for an English
breakfast the next morning.

Seapony Cafe
CAFE $$

(M'Pai Bay; mains US$5-6; ⊙8am-5pm Wed-Mon;
🖘🥄) Run by long-time Cambodia expat
Emma, this vegan-friendly little bakery be-
hind the beach serves Aussie cafe fare like
avocado on toast and flat whites. Bread
is baked fresh daily and it serves yummy

cakes, granola and smoothie bowls as part
of the all-day breakfast.

Tree Bar
BAR

(Saracen Bay; ⊙10am-late; 🖘) Travellers reg-
ularly perch at this locally owned tiki bar
until late into the night, playing drinking
games and sizing up who might be interest-
ed in a skinny-dip in the plankton. There's
also a sign for free Khmer lessons here.

Octopussy Beach Bar
BAR

(Saracen Bay; ⊙8am-midnight) This bamboo
beach bar under a cone-shaped, thatched
roof is centrally located on Saracen Bay
where the road to Lazy Beach begins. Shots
and cold beers, along with tackily named
cocktails, flow steadily throughout the day,
and gush into the night.

🛈 Getting There & Away

The four main ferry companies serving Saracen
Bay from Sihanoukville (US$22 return, 40 min-
utes if direct trip) are **Buva Sea** (☑ 015 888970;
www.buvasea.com; Central Pier, Saracen Bay),
Cambodia Island Speed Ferry (TBC; ☑ 093
811711; www.islandspeedferry.com; South
Pier, Saracen Bay), **GTVC Speedboat** (☑ 071
912 0000; Central Pier, Saracen Bay) and
Speed Ferry Cambodia (☑ 070 934744; www.
speedferrycambodia.com). Boats use either the
central pier or the **south pier**, so consider your
resort's proximity to the respective piers when
selecting a boat company.

Most ferries include **M'Pai Bay** on their
itineraries and also do frequent trips between
Koh Rong Sanloem and Koh Rong (US$7). Note
that unpredictable delays and cancellations are
common – see our tips (p204) for navigating the
islands' convoluted ferry system.

In addition to the fast ferries, Speed Ferry
Cambodia operates a slower cargo boat that
does the loop from Sihanoukville to the islands
(US$5, three hours to Saracen Bay). This is
a good choice if you are looking to save a few
dollars or you want to enjoy the trip at a more
deliberate pace. The approximate schedule is a
9am departure from Sihanoukville to Saracen
Bay, then an 11.30pm departure from Saracen
Bay to Koh Rong (Koh Tuch) via M'Pai Bay.

Transport to Lazy Beach and Sunset Beach
from Sihanoukville is on private boats owned
by resorts, or you can take a scheduled ferry to
Saracen Bay and walk.

🛈 Getting Around

To get between M'Pai Bay and Saracen Bay you
can take a scheduled ferry (US$7) or hire a long-
tail water taxi (US$20).

Roads linking Saracen Bay with Lazy Beach, Sunset Beach and M'Pai Bay were being built at the time of research and it may be possible to take a *moto* between these beaches by the time you read this.

Koh Sdach Archipelago

Just off the southwest tip of Botum Sakor National Park (p186), the Koh Sdach Archipelago (ប្រជុំកោះស្ដេច) is a modest grouping of 12 small islands, many of which have good snorkelling and scuba diving.

The main island, Koh Sdach (King's Island), is an authentic fishing village. It lacks beaches but is a great place to experience island life without the crowds, and from here you can hire a boat to explore the other islands, including (to the north) Koh Totang, home to a single dreamy resort. At the time of research, a trio of luxury resorts was being built south of Koh Sdach on Koh Amphil Thom and Koh Amphil Touch.

Despite a huge Chinese 'resort city' rising on the mainland opposite, the archipelago retains its character and remains refreshingly devoid of tourists. Boats to the islands leave from Kiri Sakor on the southwest edge of Botum Sakor National Park.

☉ Sights & Activities

Koh Sdach has the only village of any size in the entire archipelago and is thoroughly off the tourist trail with the small local economy based entirely around fishing.

Most island-hopping tours target **Koh Ampil**, which is a cluster of three tiny islands surrounding a spit of sand (now occupied by high-end resorts), and the long white beaches on either side of **Koh Smach**.

When conditions are right, these islands have some of the best diving in the country, with colourful, abundant corals and awe-inspiring creatures such as cuttlefish, nudibranchs, seahorses and bamboo sharks.

Octopuses Garden Diving Centre and Kuda Diver offer trips to all the best spots.

Octopuses Garden Diving Centre   DIVING
(☑086 412432; www.octopuscambodia.com; Koh Sdach; ☉half-day 2-tank dive incl lunch US$85, Open Water Diver course US$400) Run by an expat couple, this dive shop on Koh Sdach offers snorkelling and dive trips around the archipelago. Octopuses also has laid-back waterfront digs on the nature-y, northeastern tip of the island including a dorm

(US$15) and private tree-house bungalow (US$35). Meals are communal (breakfast included, dinners US$7) and the schedule is oriented around dive trips.

Kuda Divers   DIVING
(☑071 550 3222; www.kudadivers.com) In the village, a 10-minute walk north from the pier, Kuda Divers is super knowledgeable about dive sites in the area and offers fun dives (two-tank dive including equipment US$90) and PADI open-water instruction (full course US$450).

🍴 Sleeping & Eating

Koh Sdach has a few guesthouses and there's a single resort on almost-uninhabited Koh Totang.

On the back (west) side of the island are several restaurants clustered around Mean Chey Guesthouse. There are local dining spots in the main village to either side of the pier. If you are invited by a local to eat fresh fish, accept.

Mean Chey Guesthouse   GUESTHOUSE **$**
(☑011 979797; Koh Sdach; r from US$25; ❄) A short walk across the island from the pier brings you to this bustling compound, with several open-air restaurants and powder-blue concrete cottages spread out along the shoreline. The air-conditioned structures are basic but tidy and have hot water and 24-hour electricity. Additional rooms at the back near the restaurants are more susceptible to noise from the karaoke-happy restaurants.

Monorom Guesthouse   GUESTHOUSE **$$**
(☑011 666791; s US$20, d US$25-35) Koh Sdach's most comfortable digs are a five-minute walk north from the pier (walk right). The double rooms are dark but plenty comfortable and all have comfy beds, flat-screen TV, hot water and air-conditioning – rarities for Koh Sdach.

★Nomads Land   RESORT **$$$**
(☑096 317 6267; www.nomadscambodia.com; Koh Totang; bungalows s/d incl meals from US$60/90; ☉Nov-Aug) 🏖 It's hard to imagine a more relaxed place than Nomads, the greenest resort in the islands with five funky bungalows powered by solar panels and rainwater collected for drinking. It sits on a white beach on Koh Totang and is the sole accommodation on this island speck, a 15-minute ride from the mainland's Kiri Sakor village on the resort's boat.

**Doung Jai
Restaurant** CAMBODIAN $
(Koh Sdach Pier; mains US$3-6; ⊙8am-9pm)
Right on the pier, this is the best place to
eat in the village both for the food and the
breezy ambience. English is a challenge
so you'll have to be creative in express-
ing what you want, but the fried noodles
and other Khmer favourites are tasty and
the portions large.

King Café Island CAFE $
(mains US$2-5; ⊙8am-9pm) Opposite the Mo-
norom Guesthouse a short walk north of
the pier, this place slings the best coffee on
the island and – as importantly – is about
the only wi-fi hotspot. Breakfasts and light
meals available.

🛈 Getting There & Away

Speedy little outboard boats with frequent departures serve the Koh Sdach **village pier** from
Kiri Sakor village on the mainland opposite Koh
Sdach (US$2.50 per person, 10 minutes). These
same boats can be hired privately to take you to
other islands. Nomads Land resort has its own
private boat.

Share taxis serve Kiri Sakor from Koh Kong
(US$10, 2½ hours, 10am departure from Koh
Kong) and Sihanoukville. If you miss these, you
can take a private car from Koh Kong (US$60),
Sihanoukville (US$85) or Phnom Penh (US$85).

A cheaper option is to take a bus to Andoung
Tuek on NH48 and hire a *moto* to Kiri Sakor
(US$15 to US$20, 1¼ hours). Local minibuses
also serve Kiri Sakor from various points – these
can be flagged down 6km west of Andoung
Tuek at the origin of the Chinese-built highway
through Botum Sakor National Park.

Moving onward from Kiri Sakor, share taxis
or minivans depart around 7.30am to Koh Kong
and Sihanoukville. There's an express minivan
to Phnom Penh daily at 8am (US$10, five hours).
Minibuses of all stripes and rickety cargo buses
head out to NH48 throughout the day.

Domestic flights to the giant new airport in
the Dara Sakor investment zone near Kiri Sakor
could be a possibility starting in 2021.

KAMPOT PROVINCE

Kampot Province (ខេត្តកំពត) has emerged
as one of Cambodia's most alluring destinations thanks to a hard-to-beat combination
of easy-going seaside towns and lush countryside riddled with honeycombed limestone caves.

The province is renowned for producing
some of the world's finest pepper. Durian-
haters be warned: Kampot is also Cambodia's main producer of this odoriferous fruit.

Kampot

♪ 033 / POP 39,500

It's not hard to see why travellers become
entranced with Kampot (ក្រុងកំពត). This
riverside town, with streets rimmed by
dilapidated shophouse architecture, has a
dreamy quality, as if someone pressed the
snooze button a few years back and the entire town forgot to wake up. The Prek Tek
Chhouu River – more accurately an estuary –
rises and falls with the moons, serving as
both attractive backdrop and water-sports
playground for those staying in the boutique
resorts and backpacker retreats that line its
banks upstream from the town proper.

Eclipsed as a port when Sihanoukville
was founded in 1959, Kampot also makes
an excellent base for exploring Bokor National Park (p223), the neighbouring seaside
town of Kep, and the superb cave-temples
and verdant countryside of the surrounding
area. A growing expat community is contributing to new cultural developments and
more culinary variety.

⊙ Sights

Kampot is more about ambience than actual sights and the most enjoyable activity
is strolling or cycling through the central
old town district where lanes are lined
with crumbling shophouses, many built in
the mid-20th century by the town's then-
vibrant Chinese merchant population. The
best streets, a couple of which have been
well-restored in recent years, are between
the triangle delineated by the central Durian Roundabout, the post office and the old
French bridge.

Kampot Provincial Museum MUSEUM
(សារមន្ទីរខេត្តកំពត; www.kampotmuseum.org;
River Rd; US$2; ⊙8-11.30am & 2-5.30pm) This
tiny museum, inside the finely preserved
French colonial-era Old Governor's Mansion, traces the history of Kampot and the
outlying area. The artefacts, photos and text
(in Khmer, French and English) are informative and neatly displayed, including a series
of oversized panels explaining the province's
historic milestones. Rotating exhibits might
include photography exhibits on the wildlife
of Bokor National Park (p223) or paintings
by local students.

Kampot Traditional Music School
CULTURAL CENTRE

(☏017 726969; www.kcdi-cambodia.org; St 274; ☺2-6pm Mon-Fri) **FREE** During set hours, visitors are welcome to observe traditional music and dance training sessions and/or performances at this school that teaches children who are orphaned or have disabilities. Donations are very welcome. Photos are discouraged.

Tek Chhouu Rapids
RIVER

(ទឹកឈូ; Tek Chhouu Rd; US$1) Popular with locals, these modest rapids at the end of Tek Chhouu Rd northwest of Kampot are surrounded by food stalls and picnicking platforms. A *tuk tuk* here from Kampot costs around US$5. There's also a spa on the water called Tada Bokor, and it is said (by the owner) that the water has therapeutic qualities.

Thanks to the hydroelectric dams upriver (part of the US$280-million project that flooded small parts of Bokor National Park), the term 'rapids' is something of a misnomer but this is still a top spot for riverside relaxation and a chance to take in the local scene.

Old Market
HISTORIC BUILDING

(River Rd) Kampot's Old Market building, with its art-deco-style concrete facade, was constructed during the 1930s. Various shops, travel agencies and cafes rim both sides of the building.

🏃 Activities

Kampot is fast carving out a niche as a base for adventure sports. Rockclimbing and water sports on the Prek Tek Chhouu River are the main attractions, or take it down a notch with a countryside bicycle tour.

Be extremely careful swimming in the Kampong Bay River; tourists have drowned in the unpredictable currents. If you're not a strong swimmer, don't go in.

Love the River
BOATING

(☏016 627410; spaceman_g@web.de; per person US$15-19) Offers long-tail-boat charters and cruises from the Green House (p218) along the river, with stops for beach swimming and exploring a durian plantation. Captain Bjorn earns high marks for local knowledge and foresight (he brings fresh fruit and cold beer to go with the sunset).

Cruises embark in the morning between 7am and 9am, while the sunset boat leaves at 3pm. Prices vary depending on group size. Bjorn is also teaming up with Climbodia to

offer multiday countryside tours through a new company, AlterNative Cambodia.

★ Banteay Srey Project
MASSAGE

(☏012 276621; www.banteaysreyproject.org; Tek Chhouu Rd; massage from US$5; ☺8.30am-5.30pm Wed-Mon) 🍃 With an on-site women's spa and yoga studio, this social enterprise over the river empowers and generates income for local women. Daily yoga sessions on a riverfront platform are at 9am, and participants are welcome to stay and swim. Cool down with a smoothie, freshly squeezed juice or healthy meal (dishes US$2 to US$5) from its roadside Deva Vegan Cafe.

Climbodia
CLIMBING

(☏070 255210; www.climbodia.com; 34 St 724a; 2½hr discovery US$25-30, half-day US$40-50; ☺8.30am-7pm) Cambodia's first outdoor rock-climbing outfit offers highly recommended half-day and full-day programmes of climbing, abseiling and caving amid the limestone formations of Phnom Kbal Romeas, 5km south of Kampot. Cabled routes (via ferratas) have been established across some of the cliffs and they cater for both complete novices and the more experienced.

Golden Hands Massage
MASSAGE

(☏017 855200; St 724; 1hr masssage US$6-15; ☺10am-11pm) Best massage in town, according to locals, and cheap to boot. Springing for the lemongrass-scented oil is a great idea.

Kampot Dirt Bike Shop
ADVENTURE SPORTS

(☏070 240444; NH33; ☺7am-5.30pm) Two brothers run off-road day tours out of their bike-repair shop (per person US$110 to US$120). These hit La Plantation (p222) and Phnom Chhnork (p223) if you want to see some sights, or if you just want a joyride you'll find plenty of single track around.

👉 Tours

Everybody and their grandmother wants to sell you a tour in Kampot. The main day trips are to Bokor Hill Station (p223; US$13 to US$18), which also includes a sunset cruise. There are also countryside tours that usually include Phnom Chhnork (p223) cave, the nearby salt fields, a pepper farm and the Kep crab market (p229; US$12 to US$14).

Alternatively, you can hire a *remork-moto* driver and cobble together your own tour of the caves, Kep and surrounding countryside. Depending on locations, a half-/full-day tour costs about US$15/25,

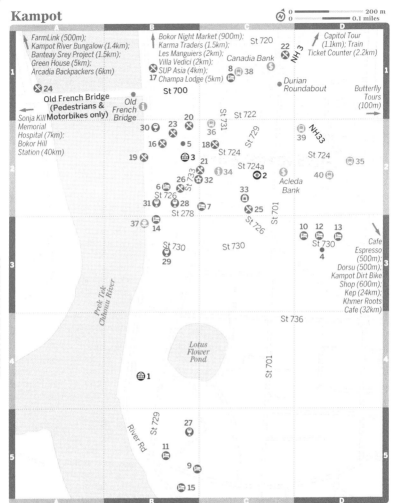

but if you want an English-speaking driver, it could cost more.

Sunset cruises (US$5 with one drink) are also extremely popular, and include stops to see fireflies, which are most visible at the new moon and around sunset.

SUP Asia
WATER SPORTS

(☏ 093 980550; www.supasia.org; 34 St 724a; 2½hr tour US$25, half-day tour US$55; ☺ 8.30am-7pm Sat-Thu Oct-Aug) SUP (stand-up paddleboarding) has come to Kampot in a big way; this company offers it as an alternative form of touring the river. Daily tours depart at

8.30am, 2.30pm and 3.30pm, taking in the riverbank sights of the local area (with a SUP lesson beforehand).

Butterfly Tours
CYCLING

(☏ 093 775592; www.butterflytours.asia; tours per person US$17-55; ☺ 7am-6pm) Take to two wheels and hit the countryside. Both cycling and motorbike tours are available through this student-run company. Destinations include pepper farms, Bokor National Park (p223) and Kampong Trach. Cycling tours emphasise interaction with local communities.

Kampot

⊙ **Sights**
1 Kampot Provincial Museum B4
2 Kampot Traditional Music School C2
3 Old Market...B2

⊕ **Activities, Courses & Tours**
4 Bison Tours...D3
Climbodia ....(see 3)
Golden Hands Massage ....(see 6)
SUP Asia...(see 3)
5 We Cycling Tour B2

⊜ **Sleeping**
6 Baraca...B2
7 Columns C2
8 Hotel Old Cinema C1
9 Mad Monkey Hostel B5
10 Magic Sponge.......................................D3
11 Makk Hotel..B5
12 Monkey Republic Kampot....................D3
13 Pepper Guesthouse D3
14 Rikitikitavi...B3
15 Two Moons..B5

⊗ **Eating**
16 Armando's Food in Progress................B2
Baraca...(see 6)
17 Ecran Noodles B1
18 Epic Arts Café C2
19 Fishmarket..B2
20 Jetzt Kampot B2
21 Kampot Seafood & Pepper..................C2

22 Night Market..C1
23 Pupe Thai Kitchen.................................B2
24 Razorback Bar BQ A1
Rikitikitavi...(see 14)
25 Rusty Keyhole II C2
Tertúlia ....(see 21)
26 Twenty Three Bistro..............................B2

⊙ **Drinking & Nightlife**
27 Flowers Home Brew & Sushi................B5
28 Infamata..B2
29 Kampot Cocktail Bar............................B3
30 Nelly's Bar B2
31 Oh Neils B2

⊙ **Entertainment**
32 Top Cat Cinema B2

⊙ **Shopping**
33 Tiny Kampot Pillows..............................C2

⊙ **Information**
34 La Plantation Office..............................C2

⊙ **Transport**
35 Bus Station D2
36 Champa Express...................................C2
37 Crab Shuttle B3
38 Giant Ibis C1
39 Kampot Express D2
40 Phnom Penh Sorya...............................D2

We Cycling Tour CYCLING
(☑096 953 3417; www.wecyclingtour.wordpress.com; St 294b; tours US$19-24) It doesn't only do cycling, but also puts together kayak tours on the Prek Tek Chhouu or *remork-moto* excursions to salt and/or pepper farms. The cycling and kayak combo tours are a big winner.

Kampot Readers FESTIVALS & EVENTS
& Writers Festival LITERATURE
(www.kampotwritersfestival.com; ☉Nov) Launched in 2015 by the KAMA (p221) arts centre, the Kampot Readers & Writers Festival brings four days of literary discussions, poetry readings, art exhibitions, concerts and creative workshops to Kampot each November.

📷 Sleeping

Inside or outside town, there is accommodation for every budget, from the US$2.50 dorm bed to the US$100-plus boutique-hotel room. The further out of town you get, the quieter the atmosphere tends to be.

Central Kampot

Options in the town proper include several cheap hostels and some gorgeous boutique properties in renovated old shophouses.

Monkey Republic Kampot HOSTEL $
(☑012 848390; www.monkeykampot.com; St 730; dm with air-con US$5-7, r with fan US$8-12; ❄☎) This 100-bed backpacker mecca in a restored villa features Kampot's nicest dorm rooms. Choose from large dorms in the main building, or new six-bed 'pods' in the neighbouring house, with individual lockers, privacy curtains and charging stations. There's an upstairs hammock lounge, while French tiles and big booths add character to the lively bar downstairs.

Baraca GUESTHOUSE $
(☑011 290434; www.baraca.org; St 726; d US$12-16; ☎) Just off the river, Baraca has bags of old-world charm, with high ceilings and original tilework floors in its four airy rooms. There's no hot water, but it's popular nonetheless, so book ahead. Great tapas

restaurant (tapas US$1.50-3, mixed plates for 2 people US$10; ⊙ 5.30-10pm Thu-Tue; 🛜🍴) and a gin bar, too.

Magic Sponge   GUESTHOUSE **$**
(📞 017 946428; www.magicspongekampot.com; St 730; dm/q/f US$5/25/30, d US$17-20; ❄️🛜) This friendly backpacker place has a rooftop dorm with impressive through-breezes, personalised fans and reading lights. Good-value private rooms are exceptionally well cared for, air-conditioned and bright. Downstairs is a movie lounge and minigolf. The lively bar-restaurant has well-regarded Indian food, live music on Wednesdays and Saturdays, and happy hour from noon to 7pm.

Pepper Guesthouse   GUESTHOUSE **$**
(📞 017 822626; guesthousepepper@yahoo.com; St 730; dm US$3, r with fan/air-con US$10/15; ❄️🛜) We're fans of this homey, locally run guesthouse in a creaky midcentury villa. Fan-only rooms have bags of character with beautiful old wood floors (room 101 is the best), while out in the front garden are two nicer bungalows with rain showers and tasteful decor. Hot water costs US$5 extra. When it rains, the parking lot becomes a lake.

Mad Monkey Hostel   HOSTEL **$**
(📞 096 872 9525; www.madmonkeyhostels. com/kampot; River Rd; dm US$6-8.50, d with/ without air-con US$24/20; ❄️@🛜🏊) Part of the Mad Monkey hostel empire, this place lures in backpackers with good-sized air-conditioned dorms and a poolside bar area that's always home to a youthful party scene. Book on its website for the best rates.

⭐**Hotel Old Cinema**   BOUTIQUE HOTEL **$$**
(📞 095 814621; www.facebook.com/pg/old cinemahotel; 27 St 700; r incl breakfast US$45-70; ❄️🛜🏊) A derelict 1930s Chinese cinema – one of Kampot's modernist architectural icons – has been lovingly restored and turned into a boutique hotel. Rooms are snug but polished and beautifully lit. Vintage prints evoke the golden age of Khmer film, while the colourful tiles in the lobby mimic the original tile work. Drop by the restaurant just to bask in the ambience.

Rikitikitavi   BOUTIQUE HOTEL **$$**
(📞 012 235102; www.rikitikitavi-kampot.com; River Rd; r incl breakfast US$53, f from US$65; ❄️🛜) One of Cambodia's best-run boutique hotels, Rikitikitavi's rooms are huge and fuse Asian-inspired decor with modern creature comforts. Ceilings are graced with stunning

beams, and palm panels and beautiful artwork adorns the walls. Plus you get swish contemporary bathrooms and mod-con amenities such as flat-screen TV, DVD player, fridge and kettle. Service is sublime.

Columns   BOUTIQUE HOTEL **$$**
(📞 092 128300; www.the-columns.com; St 728; r incl breakfast US$56-68; ❄️🛜) Set in a row of thoughtfully restored shophouses near the riverfront, this boutique hotel blends classic and modern with minimalist rooms featuring a touch of midcentury furniture, DVD player, flat-screen TV and slick modern bathrooms. Downstairs is Green's, an inviting cafe with a lovely old tile-work floor and a menu of healthy salads and shakes.

Two Moons   HOTEL **$$**
(📞 077 324889; www.twomoonshotel.com; River Rd; bungalow with fan US$34, r US$35-45, ste US$55; ➡️❄️🛜🏊) Big, bright, contemporary rooms in the main building all open onto a communal balcony, and there are some seriously jazzy top-floor 'penthouse' suites, perfect for travelling families. The sprawling garden includes an inviting pool area and good bar-restaurant. The place was fully renovated in 2019 and is looking in fine fettle.

Makk Hotel   BOUTIQUE HOTEL **$$**
(📞 089 375375; www.makkhotel.com; Riverside Rd; r incl breakfast US$50; ❄️🛜) Long on charm, this riverside hotel offers comfortable and stylish rooms and superior service; during our visit a staff member was filling a bathtub and suite with flower petals for a couple's honeymoon. Grab a drink at the bar and walk up to the roof for killer sunset views. Oh, and there are free bikes, too.

On the River

Most of the out-of-town places on the river aren't *that* far out of town – usually just a 10-minute *tuk-tuk* ride from the centre. They all have over-water pavilions or docks to facilitate swimming, and most offer some sort of kayak or other watercraft rental.

⭐**High Tide Kampot**   HOSTEL **$**
(📞 096 416 9345; www.facebook.com/hightide kampot; Tek Chhouu Rd; hammock US$1, dm with fan/air-con US$3/7, bungalow US$15; 🛜) This chill riverside spot caters to long-term backpackers who enjoy grabbing a cold one or a happy shake from the bamboo bar, then relaxing in hammocks and papasan chairs,

listening to high-fidelity reggae and trance music. Rooms are a mix of modern fan-cooled bungalows (hot water included) and neat pod-style dormitories. It hosts Saturday-night parties on its human-made beach.

Arcadia Backpackers
& Water Park   HOSTEL $
(☏097 745 5073; www.arcadiabackpackers.com; Tek Chhouu Rd; dm US$5-10, d/tr US$18/21; ☎) One of Kampot's great backpacker party scenes, riverside Arcadia organises riverboat pub crawls and offers a wide range of accommodation, from large, mixed dorms by the bar to quiet, private doubles by the water. Guests get free entry to the water park, which includes a Russian swing, a 50m water slide, a climbing wall, a diving platform and a zipline.

Those who only wish to visit the water park can do so for US$7.

Yellow Sun Hostel   HOSTEL $
(☏096 668 3214; Prek Tek Chhouu River east bank; dm US$3, garden/river hut US$14/16) With a gorgeous location way upriver and a less party-oriented crowd than other riverfront hostels, this is a place for serious unwinding. Catch rays and read a book on the overwater main pavilion, take a leisurely kayak ride, or watch fireflies at night. The super simple

A-frame bungalows are brilliantly conceived and some have private riverfrontage.

Kampot River Bungalow   BUNGALOW $
(☏011 523627, 070 370709; mamakampotriver bungalow@gmail.com; Tek Chhouu Rd; bungalows US$6; ☎) For back-to-basics living and serious relaxation this Cambodian-owned family place comes up trumps. Charismatic proprietor 'mama' cooks up mostly Khmer specialities in the river-terrace restaurant (meals from US$2). It's the spot to contemplate sunset while accommodation is in rustic palm-thatch bungalows (mattress on the floor, mosquito net and fan). Stilted bungalows have private bathroom. Book direct for the best rates.

You can also pitch your own tent for US$1.

★ Green House   BUNGALOW $$
(☏088 886 3071; www.greenhousekampot.com; Tek Chhouu Rd; bungalows US$30-40; ☎) This gorgeously conceived riverfront pad is all about tranquillity, with the best of its palm-thatch bungalows and colourful wooden cottages (with balcony) right on the river-bank. The historic teak-wood main building, which houses the restaurant, was once home to the legendary Phnom Penh bar Snowy's (aka Maxine's), transported lock,

SOUTH COAST KAMPOT

KAMPOT PEPPER

Before Cambodia's civil war, no Paris restaurant worth its salt would have been without pepper from Kampot Province, but the country's pepper farms were all but destroyed by the Khmer Rouge, who believed in growing rice, not spice.

Today, thanks to a group of eco-entrepreneurs and foodies who are passionate about pepper, Kampot-grown peppercorns, delicate and aromatic but packing a powerful punch, are making a comeback.

Kampot pepper is grown on family farms that dot Phnom Voar and nearby valleys northwest of Kompong Trach, where the unique climate and the farmers' fidelity to labour-intensive growing techniques produce particularly pungent peppercorns. In fact, Kampot pepper is so extraordinary that it's Cambodia's first-ever product to receive a 'geographical indication' (GI), just like French cheeses. Increased sales have made a huge difference for Kampot's pepper-growing families, and especially for the girls who are able to marry now that their parents can afford their dowries.

Peppercorns are picked from February to May. Black pepper is plucked from the trees when the corns are starting to turn yellow and turns black during sun-drying; red pepper is picked when the fruit is completely mature; and mild white pepper is soaked in water to remove the husks. September to February is the season for green pepper, whose sprigs have to be eaten almost immediately after harvesting – the crab-market restaurants (p229) of Kep are among the best places to experience its gentle freshness.

A packet of pepper from FarmLink (p221) boutique in Kampot, La Plantation (p222) organic pepper farm or Sothy's Pepper Farm (p225) near Kep makes an excellent souvenir or gift: the corns are lightweight and unbreakable, and if stored properly – that is, not ground! – will stay fresh for years.

stock and barrel here in 2011. No children under age 12.

The great restaurant is open from 7am to 8.45pm.

Sabay Beach   BUNGALOW $$
(☑ 031-417 9304; www.sabaybeach.com; Ordnung Chimern village; bungalow US$25-48, d US$37-42, f US$60; ☜) Those who make it all the way to Sabay Beach will be handsomely rewarded. From the palm-tree-flanked boardwalk and the dreamy bungalows to the darling open-air restaurant and the impeccable service, this unpretentious resort is one of the finest stays in the region.

Sabay also has its own swathe of sandy beach on the river, and the abundant fruit trees provide the ingredients for delicious smoothies.

Les Manguiers   RESORT $$
(☑ 092 330050; www.mangokampot.com; Prek Tek Chhouu River east bank; r with shared bathroom US$15-31, bungalows US$42-73; ☜) This rambling garden complex has canoes and bikes for rent, badminton, table tennis and a children's playground. You can jump into the river from one of four overwater gazebos. Accommodation ranges from large, bright simple rooms to stilted wooden bungalows, all with fan and cold water. Meals are served with a limited number of options at a fixed price.

Champa Lodge   BUNGALOW $$
(☑ 097 705 1399; www.champalodge.com; Kompong Kreang village; bungalows US$35-65; ☜) Set on a bend in the river amid traditional Cambodian countryside scenes, Champa is a rural hideaway with arty rooms in several traditional Khmer wooden houses, all with verandas for slothing out and admiring the bucolic views. Kayak and bike hire is available if you can drag yourself away. The restaurant-bar includes a great selection of Belgian beers.

Villa Vedici   RESORT $$
(☑ 089 290714; www.villavedici.com; Prek Tek Chhouu River east bank; r with fan US$30-55, air-con US$35-65, f US$125; ✳@☜☒) A playground for kids and adults alike offering kitesurfing, a speedboat for waterskiing and wakeboarding, plus a PlayStation on a gargantuan flat-screen in the main building's airy living room. Rooms are functional rather than frilly, but guests tend to spend most of their time lapping up the rays beside the lovely pool. Service could be more attentive.

 Eating

With everything from sushi to handmade pasta to tapas, Kampot is a culinary capital full of international influences and plenty of Khmer goodness as well. Local street-food places on Old Bridge Rd between the bridge and the Durian Roundabout are great places to grab fried noodles, soups and Khmer desserts such as sticky rice with coconut sauce.

Many of Kampot's guesthouses are worthy of a meal. Magic Sponge (p216) has good Indian food, or enjoy a meal on the water at one of the out-of-town riverside places – Green House is particularly good (try its steaks).

★ **Cafe Espresso**   CAFE $
(☑ 092 388736; NH33; mains US$4-6; ☺8am-4pm Tue-Fri, 9am-4.30pm Sat & Sun; ☜☒) It's worth the trip to this cafe on the outskirts of town. The owners are real foodies and offer a global menu that traipses from vegetarian quesadillas to Brazilian-style pork sandwiches with some especially tempting breakfast options. But it is caffeine-cravers who will really be buzzing, thanks to the regionally grown coffee blends, roasted daily on-site.

Khmer

Roots Cafe   CAMBODIAN $
(☑ 096 265 5171; www.khmerrootscafe.com; off NH33; mains US$2.50-3.50; ☺11am-5.30pm) Owner Soklim's team will help you cook your own Cambodian meal at this small, family-run cafe out on Lake Tomnop Tek Krolar (aka 'Secret Lake'), near La Plantation (p222), about 45 minutes east of Kampot via dusty back roads. Or just order à la carte and kick back and enjoy the delightfully rural surroundings amid shady trees and organic vegetable gardens.

Epic Arts Café   CAFE $
(www.epicarts.org.uk; St 724; mains US$2-4; ☺7am-4pm; ☜) ✎ A great place for breakfast, homemade cakes, infused tea and light lunches, this mellow cafe is staffed by young people who are deaf or have a disability. Profits fund arts workshops for Cambodians with disabilities and there's an upstairs shop that sells art, bags, jewellery, stuffed toys and the like.

**Pupe Thai
Kitchen**   THAI $
(☑ 097 792 2734; Tin Pan Alley; mains US$3-5.50; ☺11am-9pm Fri-Wed) Nestled amid fellow

hole-in-the wall spots in an alley off St 274, Pupe Thai brings Bangkok-quality street fare to Kampot. The Thai proprietor speaks good English and serves just a few simple dishes like *phad kapao* with egg plus heavenly fried rice.

Jetzt Kampot
BURGERS $

(☏015 572380; St 722; burgers US$5; ⊙2-10pm Mon-Sat) Easily the best burgers in Kampot, with new toppings and flavour combinations being invented each week. 'The cricket', for example, comes with cream cheese, jalapeños, spring onions and tomatoes. It also offers dorms with hot showers (US$5) and at check-in everybody gets a free draught beer.

Ecran Noodles
NOODLES $

(River Rd; dishes US$3; ⊙10.45am-8.45pm Wed-Mon) This riverfront hole-in-the-wall specialises in hand-pulled noodles and dumplings, including shrimp and seafood varieties, plus Peking duck. It's cheap and delicious, and everything is prepared right in front of you.

Night Market
MARKET $

(NH3; mains US$1.50-3; ⊙4pm-midnight) The bustling night market next to the Durian Roundabout is full of cheap food stalls where you can chow down on simple noodle and rice dishes, grilled meat and Khmer desserts such as sticky rice with coconut sauce.

★ Twenty Three Bistro
INTERNATIONAL $$

(☏088 607 9731; 23 St 726; mains US$5-10; ⊙noon-9.30pm Wed-Mon; ☎) Hot damn, there's now a twice-baked cheddar soufflé in Kampot, and this is the place that loses money making it for you. We're not sure how the owners manage it, but this seems to be haute cuisine on clearance, from expats with hefty experience in world-class restaurants and a range of European cuisines. The cocktails slay, too. Also recommended: the smoked-mackerel pâté and the sea bass, which comes in a ravishing moat of pureed cauliflower, capers, brown butter and lime.

Armando's Food in Progress
ITALIAN $$

(St 724; mains US$5-7.50; ⊙11.30am-2pm & 5.30-10pm) Ah, the joys of skilled Italian chefs washing up in provincial Cambodia to prepare gourmet Neapolitan pizzas and Italian forest-mushroom risotto, beautifully presented and washed down with an Italian red, all for less than US$10. Kampot scores another winner. At US$5, the set lunches, which can include an entire pizza, are a steal. Exciting specials and dangerous desserts.

Kampot Seafood & Pepper
INTERNATIONAL $$

(☏087 548900; St 733; US$5-10; ⊙9am-11pm) More top-notch, contemporary fusion dining has arrived in Kampot in the form of this restaurant in a beautifully refurbished old merchant house. As one might expect from the name, Kampot pepper is applied liberally to dishes as diverse as *mok cha marek chei* (sauté squid) and homemade roasted ham.

It also hosts three-hour cooking classes (per person US$20).

Rikitikitavi
INTERNATIONAL $$

(www.rikitikitavi-kampot.com; River Rd; mains US$5-8; ⊙7am-9.30pm; ☎⊿) Named after the mongoose in Rudyard Kipling's *The Jungle Book*, this riverfront terrace is all about the ambience. It's also known for its Kampot pepper chicken, burritos, slow-cooked curry and salads. Happy hour from 5pm to 7pm brings two-for-one cheer on all cocktails. This is the best place in town to kick back and enjoy a sundowner.

Fishmarket
FUSION $$

(☏012 728884; River Rd; mains US$6-15; ⊙9am-11pm) The signature place of Kampot's up-and-coming dining scene lives in a restored art-deco masterpiece on the banks of the Prek Tek Chhouu River. Plop down in the breezy open-air dining area and dig into green-tea-smoked duck, a spicy beef salad or local favourites such as peppercorn crab and the baked-fish dish *amok*.

Razorback Bar BQ
AMERICAN $$

(Old Bridge; mains US$5-7.50; ⊙7.30am-10.30pm Mon-Sat, to 10am Sun; ☎) Run by an American–Vietnamese tandem, this riverside smokehouse serves the largest, juiciest, most tender ribs in the land (Friday and Saturday evenings only), plus brisket and pulled pork. Sides like 'slaw and cornbread offer more Southern comfort, and it also serves authentic Vietnamese *pho*. Nice selection of Belgian brews and craft beer on tap.

Rusty Keyhole II
INTERNATIONAL $$

(2000 Roundabout; ribs US$5-10; ⊙8am-midnight; ☎) This popular bar-restaurant combines British pub fare and Khmer home cooking. It's best known for ribs and the Sunday roast, and is also a popular spot to watch football.

Tertúlia
PORTUGUESE $$$

(☎ 093 375085; St 733; mains US$9-15; ⊙ 5-11pm; 🐕) Tertúlia offers nothing less than a beautiful Portuguese dining experience, complete with a wine bar. Steaks and locally sourced seafood are slow cooked and delicious. Wash them down with port (US$2.50 to US$12) and top it off with a traditional dessert from south Portugal such as almond pie.

Drinking & Nightlife

There's a great variety of nightlife options for different crowds, including high-end cocktail bars, backpacker boltholes and street bars. The hostels and guesthouses on the east side of the river often have a good scene; Arcadia Backpackers (p217), Green House (p218) and High Tide (p217) are particularly recommended. The last two are known for live music.

★ Karma Traders
BAR

(☎ 016 556504; www.karmatraderskampot.com; ⊙ 8am-midnight) Reserve Tuesday nights for a visit to Karma Traders' rooftop bar, where there's live music, US$2 tacos (try the Coca-Cola pulled pork) and two-for-one drinks if you can beat the bartender in rock, paper, scissors. There's also a ping-pong room, a cinema, a pool, a slackline, a Sunday pub quiz and about a dozen rooms available (US$12 to US$16).

Infamata
BAR

(☎ 092 821700; St 726; ⊙ 6pm-1am; 🐕) With its shabby-chic interior and Botero-esque painting of a reclining lady behind the bar, Infamata is long on atmosphere and backs it up with professional cocktails, craft gin and boutique beer. Live music kicks off Thursdays and Saturdays, while high season sees the opening of the gorgeous 2nd floor. Superb fusion food rounds it out.

Kampot Cocktail Bar
COCKTAIL BAR

(☎ 088 448 1631; St 730; ⊙ 4pm-1am Mon-Sat; 🐕) A place for serious cocktail aficionados, the cocktails at KCB pack a punch and are two-for-one until 8pm. If that sounds dangerous, it is (trust us). The bartenders here have serious skills – ask about the cocktail of the day. Light bites served.

Nelly's Bar
BAR

(☎ 016 861849; River Rd; ⊙ 3pm-late) Occupying a street corner under a bougainvillea tree outside a beautiful colonial building, Nelly's is a fine place to throw back a few drinks,

with groovy tunes and a nice mix of travellers and colourful Kampot expats. The high season occasionally sees acoustic acts set up on the sidewalk. The bar is named after its house dog.

Flowers Home Brew & Sushi
CRAFT BEER

(☎ 097 707 4421; www.facebook.com/flowersnano brewery; ⊙ 3.30-8.30pm Sat & Sun; 🐕) Flowers is Kampot's hometown craft beer, with a half-dozen or so varieties that can be found in bars around town, including a lemongrass pale ale and a wheat porter. On weekend afternoons, the Japanese brewmaster taps a keg or two and hosts what are essentially open parties, with plenty of sushi (much of it not fish-related) to go around.

Oh Neils
BAR

(River Rd; ⊙ 5pm-late; 🐕) The liveliest of the little bars on the main riverfront strip in Kampot, Oh Neils has walls plastered with rock-and-roll memorabilia and a who's-who soundtrack of classic tunes from down the decades.

Entertainment

KAMA Fish Island Arts Centre
ARTS CENTRE

(Kampot Arts & Music Association; ☎ 096 255 4393; www.facebook.com/kampotarts; Fish Island; 🐕) Founded by Julien Poulson of legendary band Cambodian Space Project, this social enterprise has moved into a large new creative space on the outskirts of Kampot where Paulson's wife, Kek Soon, directs an evolving repertoire of festivals, arts classes and musical programmes. She also runs the centre's scrumptious cafe and guides cuisine and cultural tours. Rooms now available, too.

Top Cat Cinema
CINEMA

(www.facebook.com/topcatcinema; St 733; per person US$4-4.50; ⊙ 1.30pm-1am; 🐕) Film showings are by appointment on an 8m high-definition screen (for groups of at least six) or on large flat-screen TVs (for smaller groups). Movie lounges have cosy satellite chairs and powerful air-con.

Shopping

Bokor Night Market
MARKET

(River Rd; parking 1000r; ⊙ 4-10pm) With about 100 stands offering things such as jewellery, karaoke, fried ice cream, sneakers and well, everything else, this nightlife experience and shopping mecca on Kampot's market circuit has loads of potential, if not many customers. The riverside setting is pleasant and family-friendly, a stage welcomes regular concerts and the aroma of tasty street food wafts on the breeze.

Dorsu CLOTHING
(www.dorsu.org; NH33; ⊙ 8am-5pm Tue-Sun) Sharing a contemporary factory space on the outskirts of town with Cafe Espresso (p219), Dorsu sells a range of high-quality wardrobe staples, all designed and produced locally by a small team. There's also a Dorsu branch near the Old Market (p213), on St 724, that's open 10am to 7pm.

FarmLink FOOD
(🗷 033-690 2354; www.farmlink-cambodia.com; ⊙ 7.30-11.30am & 1.30-4.30pm Mon-Fri) In Kampot you can purchase pouches of peerless pepper at the FarmLink boutique, one of the pioneers of geographical-indication pepper production (p217). You can see pepper being dried in the garden out front and visitors can observe the pepper-sorting room. It's just over the New Bridge; take the first right and look for it on the left.

Tiny Kampot Pillows HANDICRAFTS, CLOTHING
(www.tinykampotpillows.com; 2000 Roundabout; ⊙ 10am-7pm) This textile shop sells, well, lots of tiny pillows made from handwoven silk, plus plenty of other accessories from clothing to bags.

ⓘ Information

Acleda Bank (St 724; ⊙ 7.30am-4pm Mon-Fri, to 11.30am Sat, ATM 24hr)

Canadia Bank (Durian Roundabout; ⊙ 8am-3.30pm Mon-Fri, to 11.30am Sat, ATM 24hr)

The free and often hilarious *Kampot Survival Guide* (www.kampotsurvivalguide.com) takes a tongue-in-cheek look at local expat life.

Tourist Information Centre (🗷 097 899 5593; lonelyguide@gmail.com; River Rd; ⊙ 7am-5pm) Led by the knowledgeable Mr Pov, Kampot's tourist office doles out free advice, sells tours and can arrange transport to area attractions such as caves, falls and Kompong Trach.

ⓘ Getting There & Away

Kampot, on NH3, is 148km southwest of Phnom Penh, 105km east of Sihanoukville and 25km northwest of Kep. Share taxis gather near the **bus station** (St 724) to whisk passengers to Phnom Penh (US$10, three hours) and Sihanoukville (US$8, four to five hours). A private taxi to Phnom Penh costs US$45 and can be booked through your guesthouse.

BOAT
An atmospheric way to get to Kep is on the **Crab Shuttle** (🗷 088 829 6644; crabshuttle@gmail. com; River Rd; ⊙ Oct-May) boat (one-way/ return US$10/15, 2½ hours), which departs at 9am and returns at 3pm for sunset views. Rabbit Island (p225; Koh Tonsay) drop-offs and pickups are possible for an extra few dollars, with a boat transfer at Kep's **Rabbit Island Pier** (NH33A).

BUS
If heading to Phnom Penh, be aware that a couple of the bus companies, including **Phnom Penh Sorya** (🗷 092 181801; NH33), go via Kep, which adds at least an hour to the trip. You're better off paying up for the more comfortable **Giant Ibis** (🗷 096 999 3333; www.giantibis. com; 7 Makara St) buses (US$10, 3½ hours, 8.30am and 2.45pm), or go with **Capitol Tour** (🗷 092 665001). Even quicker are the direct minivan services to Phnom Penh run by several companies, including **Kampot Express** (🗷 078 555123; NH33) and **Champa Express** (🗷 087 630036; St 724).

Several bus companies stop in Kep (US$3, 30 minutes) en route to Ha Tien or Phnom Penh, or you can take a *tuk tuk* (US$10, 45 minutes) or *moto* (US$6).

Guesthouses and tour agencies can arrange additional minivan transfers to Sihanoukville as well as to Koh Kong.

TRAIN
The rehabilitated train is a slow but scenic option to Phnom Penh (US$7, five hours), Takeo (US$6, three hours) and Sihanoukville (US$6, two hours). Departures are on Friday, Saturday, Sunday and Monday, at varying times; check the schedule at **www.royal-railway.com**. Kampot's **ticket counter** (🗷 078 888582; ⊙ 8am-4pm Wed-Mon) is open 8am to 4pm Wednesday to Monday; it's best to purchase tickets a few days in advance.

ⓘ Getting Around

A *moto* ride in town costs around 2000r (*tuk tuk* US$1). Sometimes the driver will ask for more if it's a holiday, you're a big group, it's raining or you take a ride longer than a few minutes.

Bicycles (US$2 per day) and motorbikes (about US$5 per day) can be rented from many guesthouses around town or from tour companies such as **Bison Tours** (🗷 012 442687; keusarun@yahoo.com; St 730; ⊙ 7am-7pm), which has the largest selection.

Around Kampot

The limestone hills east of Kampot towards Kep are littered with caves. Phnom Chhnork, surrounded by blazingly green countryside, is a real gem and can easily be visited in an afternoon along with Phnom Sorsia.

La Plantation
FARM

(✆017 842505; www.kampotpepper.com; ⊙9am-6pm) ⊘ FREE This sprawling organic pepper farm offers free guided walks in French, English and Khmer, explaining how several varieties of pepper are grown, harvested and processed. The farm also grows fruits, chillis, herbs and peanuts, and there's a restaurant and shop where you can buy pepper at steep prices. (The money helps pay for children's English classes at local schools.)

On Friday and Saturday evenings it offers dinner (US$25, advanced reservations only) on 'secret' Lake Tomnop Tek Krolar. Other activities include cooking classes and buffalo-cart rides to the lake.

A van (per person US$7 round trip) heads out to the farm from its **office** (St 274a; ⊙7am-7pm) in Kampot daily at 9am and 11.30am, returning in the afternoon. This office, which has a small pepper museum upstairs, can also help you get out there via *tuk tuk* (US$25 return with an English-speaking driver) or *moto* (US$10 to US$15).

Phnom Chhnork
CAVE

(ភ្នំឈ្នោក; US$1; ⊙7am-6pm) Phnom Chhnork is a short walk through a quilt of rice paddies from Wat Ang Sdok, where a monk collects the entry fee and a gaggle of friendly local kids offers their services as guides. From the bottom, a 203-step staircase leads up the hillside and down into a cavern as graceful as a Gothic cathedral. The view from up top is especially magical in the late afternoon, as is the walk to and from the wat.

Inside the cave you'll be greeted by a stalactite elephant, with a second elephant outlined on the flat cliff face to the right.

Tiny chirping bats live up near two natural chimneys that soar towards the blue sky, partly blocked by foliage of an impossibly green hue.

Within the **main chamber** stands a remarkable 7th-century (Funan-era) **brick temple**, dedicated to Shiva. The temple's brickwork is in superb condition thanks to the protection afforded by the cave. Poke your head inside and check out the ancient stalactite that serves as a *linga* (phallic symbol). A slippery passage, flooded in the rainy season, leads through the hill.

To get to Phnom Chhnork turn left off NH33 about 5.5km east of Kampot. Look for the sign to 'Climbodia'. From the turn-off it's 6km to the cave on a bumpy road. A return *moto* ride from Kampot costs about US$6 (*tuk tuk* US$12).

Phnom Sorsia
CAVE

(ភ្នំសសៀរ, Phnom Sia; ⊙7am-5pm) FREE Phnom Sorsia is home to several natural caves. From the parking area, a stairway leads up the hillside to a gaudy modern **temple**. From there, steps lead left up to **Rung Damrey Saa** (White Elephant Cave). A slippery, sloping staircase (where one false step will send you into the abyss) leads down and then up and then out through a hole in the other side. Exit the cave and follow the right-hand path that leads back to the temple.

Bokor Hill Station

The once-abandoned French retreat of Bokor Hill Station (កស្ថានីយ៍ភ្នំបូកគោ), inside Bokor National Park, is famed for its refreshingly cool climate and creepy derelict buildings that had their heyday during the 1920s and 1930s. On cold, foggy days it

BUSES FROM KAMPOT

DESTINATION	FARE	DURATION (HR)	FREQUENCY	COMPANY	TYPE
Bangkok	US$32	14	2 daily	Champa Express, Anny Tours (p230)	minivan
Ha Tien, Vietnam	US$8-9	2½	2 daily	Champa Express, Anny Tours	minivan
Ho Chi Minh City	US$18	12	2 daily	Champa Express, Anny Tours	minivan
Phnom Penh	US$5-10	3-4	frequent	Capitol Tour, Champa Express, Giant Ibis, Kampot Express, Phnom Penh Sorya	bus/minivan
Sihanoukville	US$5-6	4-5	several daily	Champa Express, Anny Tours	minivan

can get pretty spooky up here as mists drop visibility to nothing and the wind keens through abandoned buildings. Appropriate, then, that the foggy showdown that ends the crime thriller *City of Ghosts* (2002) was filmed here.

These days the hill station is blighted by a huge development project that includes the Thansur Bokor Highland Resort & Casino and numerous holiday villas on sale at speculative prices. There's still plenty to explore, however, including the national park and the husks of several old buildings. For a history lesson on Bokor, pop into the swish Le Bokor Palace (p224) hotel, which was brought back to life in 2018 after years of neglect.

History

In the early 1920s the French, ever eager to escape the lowland heat, established a hill station atop Phnom Bokor (1080m), known for its dramatic vistas of the coastal plain one vertical kilometre below.

The hill station was twice abandoned to the howling winds: first when Vietnamese and Khmer Issarak (Free Khmer) forces overran it in the late 1940s while fighting for independence from France, and again in 1972, when the Lon Nol regime left it to the Khmer Rouge forces that were steadily taking over the countryside. Because of its commanding position, the site was strategically important to all sides during the civil war and was one location the Vietnamese really had to fight for during their 1979 invasion. For several months, the Khmer Rouge held out in the Catholic church here while the Vietnamese shot at them from Bokor Palace, 500m away.

◉ Sights

Bokor National Park　　　　NATIONAL PARK
(ឧទ្យានជាតិប្អូកគោ, Preah Monivong National Park; motorbike/car 2000/10,000r) 🏍 The dense rainforests of this 1581-sq-km park shelter an incredible array of wildlife, including the Asiatic black bear, Malayan sun bear, clouded leopard, pileated gibbon, pigtailed macaque, slow loris and pangolin. Elephants and tigers once roamed here, but the tigers were driven out long ago and the elephants are thought to have migrated north. Trekking trips up to the hill station used to be very popular, but these days most people arrive by vehicle on new roads.

More than 300 species of bird, including several types of hornbill, also live here. Don't expect to see much terrestrial wildlife – most of the animals are nocturnal and survive by staying in more remote parts of the park. Long kept off the tourist map due to Khmer Rouge activity, Bokor today is still threatened by poaching, illegal logging and development. The summit of Phnom Bokor, once home only to the abandoned buildings of Bokor Hill Station, is now part of a multimillion-dollar tourism development, while in the southeast the Kamchay hydropower project has flooded a small section of the park.

Le Bokor Palace　　　　HISTORIC BUILDING
(www.lebokorpalace.com) Bokor's most iconic building, Le Bokor Palace opened in 1925 as a hotel before being abandoned in the 1960s. In 2018 it was brought back to life and today offers high-end accommodation and dining. Pop in for a drink and to admire the views. In the lobby is an informative timeline that runs through Bokor Hill Station's fascinating history.

Catholic Church　　　　CHURCH
FREE The squat belfry of the Romanesque Catholic church still holds aloft its cross, and fragments of glass brick cling to the corners of the nave windows; one side window holds the barest outline of a rusty crucifix. It's easy to imagine a small crowd of French colonials in formal dress assembled here for Sunday Mass. The subdividing walls inside were built by the Khmer Rouge. A bit up the hill, a sheer drop overlooks the rainforest.

Wat Sampov Pram　　　　BUDDHIST TEMPLE
(វត្តសំពៅព្រាំ) In the rare absence of fog, lichen-caked Wat Sampov Pram (Five Boats Wat) offers tremendous views over the jungle to the coastline below, including Vietnam's Phu Quoc Island. Wild monkeys like to hang out around the wat.

Popokvil Falls　　　　WATERFALL
(ទឹកធ្លាក់ពពកវិល; 2000r) From the junction at the top of the access road, take a right and head east/northeast for about 4km along a sealed road to two-tiered Popokvil Falls, which are impressive from about June to November, but dry up at other times. There's a large indoor food court near the falls if you want to grab a bite (or warm up).

🛏 Sleeping & Eating

Bokor is best visited on a day trip from Kampot. There are places to stay up on Bokor but they are very expensive (US$250 and up) and the hill station is pretty lifeless at night.

Options include fine dining at Le Bokor Palace or, at the other end of the spectrum, pizza and the like at the Popokvil Falls food court. The Thansur Bokor Highland Resort & Casino offers a Thai buffet.

ℹ️ Getting There & Away

You can either visit the hill station on an organised tour out of Kampot or rent a motorbike and travel under your own steam. The road up here is in excellent condition.

Kep

🎵 036 / POP 35,000

Founded as a seaside retreat by French colonisers in 1908 and a favoured haunt of Cambodian highrollers during the 1960s, sleepy Kep (កែប, Krong Kep, also spelled Kaeb) is drawing tourists back with seafood, sunsets and hikes in butterfly-filled Kep National Park. Its impressive range of boutique hotels squarely targets a more cultured beach crowd than the party-happy guesthouses of Kampot and the islands.

Some find Kep a bit soulless because it lacks a centre, not to mention a long sandy shoreline. Others revel in its torpid pace, content to relax at their resort, nibble on peppery crab at the famed crab market and poke around the mildewed shells of modernist villas, which still give the town a sort of postapocalyptic feel.

⊙ Sights

Scattered throughout Kep are the blackened husks of handsome mid-20th-century villas that speak of happier, more carefree times before the Khmer Rouge evacuated the town. All built according to the precepts of the modernist style, with clean lines and little adornment, they keep alive the memory of Kep's short and sweet heyday. Today many are covered in graffiti and shelter squatters (and, some say, ghosts). A few have been renovated and turned into fancy boutique hotels. Don't get your hopes up about buying one, as they were all snapped up for a song in the mid-1990s by well-connected speculators.

Besides Kep Beach, most of Kep's beaches are too shallow and rocky to make for good swimming. It is possible to swim off the beach or the jetty at the Sailing Club but the water is particularly shallow here. Better beaches can be found on Koh Tonsay (Rabbit Island).

★ **Kep National Park**   NATIONAL PARK

(ឧទ្យានជាតិកែប; 4000r) The interior of Kep peninsula is occupied by Kep National Park, where an 8km circuit, navigable by foot, mountain bike, or motorbike, begins behind Veranda Natural Resort (p228). Led Zep Cafe (p229) is responsible for the quirky yellow signs that point the way to various viewpoints, sights and trailheads. The cafe, if it's open, sells a park map for 1000r. The 'Stairway to Heaven' trail is particularly worthwhile, leading up the hill to a pagoda, a nunnery and the Sunset Rock viewpoint.

Koh Tonsay   ISLAND

(កោះទន្សាយ, Rabbit Island) If you like the rustic beachcomber lifestyle, Koh Tonsay's 250m-long main beach is for you. This is a place to while away hours or days doing little but lazing on the beach, napping, reading, sipping cocktails, eating seafood and stargazing before retiring to your threadbare bungalow and drifting off to the sound of the waves. Scheduled boats to Rabbit Island (US$8 return, 20 minutes) leave from Rabbit Island Pier (p221) at 9am and 1pm and return at 3pm or 4pm.

Kep guesthouses can arrange boat tickets or you can purchase them at the Koh Tonsay Boat Ticket Office (Rabbit Island Pier). Private boats to the island can be arranged on the spot at the ticket office and cost US$25 return for up to six people.

Rabbit Island is so named because locals say it resembles a rabbit – an example of what too much local brew can do to your imagination. The main beach, rimmed by restaurant shacks and rudimentary bungalows (US$7 to US$10 per night), is nice enough, just don't expect the sparkling white sand of Koh Rong (p197) or Koh Rong Sanloem (p205). This one is fairly narrow and might be populated by chickens or wandering cows. Still, you can swim here and it's a fine place to chill.

You can walk around the island to find more isolated beaches. The island has long been tagged for development but it appears that these plans have been put off for now.

Other islands of the Kep Archipelago include Koh Pos (Snake Island; about 30 minutes beyond Rabbit Island), which has a deserted beach and fine snorkelling but no overnight accommodation. There's also small, beachless Koh Svay (Mango Island), whose summit offers nice views. You can explore these islands for about US$75 with a private boat arranged at the pier, or Kep Adventures offers group trips.

⭐ **Sothy's Pepper Farm** FARM

(☎088 951 3505; www.mykampotpepper.asia; Phnom Vour, off NH33; ⊙9am-5pm) FREE One of the friendliest farms to visit, Sothy is passionate about his product and will gladly elaborate on the history and process behind the 'champagne of pepper (p217)'. Short tours are free and there's a wonderful gift shop on the premises if you want to bring a few packs of the good stuff back home. It's about 17km northeast of central Kep. There's also an excellent restaurant, albeit pepper ripens faster than the service!

Wat Kiri Sela BUDDHIST TEMPLE

(វត្តគិរីសិលា; US$1; ⊙7am-6pm) This Buddhist temple sits at the foot of Phnom Kompong Trach, a dramatic karst formation riddled with more than 100 caverns and passageways. From the wat, an underground passage leads to a fishbowl-like formation, surrounded by vine-draped cliffs and open to the sky. Various stalactite-laden caves shelter reclining Buddhas and miniature Buddhist shrines. The temple is in Kompong Trach, 25km northeast of Kep. Take the dirt road heading north from the centre of town for 2km.

Kep Butterfly Garden FARM

(កសិដ្ឋានមេអំបៅកែប; Jasmine Valley Trail, Kep National Park; admission incl guided tour US$2; ⊙7am-5pm) FREE This small and beautifully kept flower-filled garden is home to myriad butterflies. You can cycle or motorbike here – drive about 300m past the Rabbit Island pier, turn left at the Total station and keep going straight. There's also a hard-to-find connection path that links to the main trail in Kep National Park.

Wat Samathi BUDDHIST TEMPLE

(វត្តសមាធិ) Sitting atop a hill overlooking Kep, this tranquil wat has gorgeous views over the coast. You can take the off-shooting 'Samathi Path' from the main Kep National Park trail to get here.

Kep Beach BEACH

(ឆ្នេរកែប) This is Kep's only proper beach, although it wasn't always that way. In the prewar period, powder-white sand was trucked in from other beaches. This practice resumed in 2013 and these days the beach is looking bigger and better than ever. It's immensely popular with locals, who descend here by the busload at weekends. The eastern end of the shaded promenade along the beach is marked by Sela Cham P'dey, a statue depicting a nude fisherman's wife awaiting her husband's return.

🏃 **Activities & Tours**

Kep makes a good base for visiting Sothy's Pepper Far and La Plantation (p222), along with several delightful cave temples including Wat Kiri Sela near Kompong Trach and Phnom Chhnork (p222) and Phnom Sorsia (p222) on the road to Kampot. The best way to see the sights is to hire one of the many English-speaking *remork-moto* drivers in town (about US$25 to $US30 per day) and tailor your own countryside tour.

Kep Sailing Club WATER SPORTS

(☎078 333685; www.knaibangchatt.com/the-sailing-club; Knai Bang Chatt; ⊙8am-5pm) Open to all, the sailing club and activity centre at the hotel Knai Bang Chatt (p228) hires out sea kayaks (US$10 per hour), Hobie Cats (from US$50 per hour), paddleboards (US$10 per hour) and Optimists (US$15 per hour). Optimists are small boats for children, for whom sailing lessons are available.

Decent mountain bikes are also available at US$15 per hour, as well as kayaks and stand-up paddleboards. Among its many boat tours are a sunset cruise and a traditional fishing experience.

Kep Adventures BOATING

(☎015 892434; www.kep-adventures.com; per person full-day US$35-65, half day US$15-40, sunset US$20; ⊙Oct-May) Take to a traditional thatched-roof long-tail boat on half- or full-day tours of a few of the less-visited islands off Kep. Sunset cruises kick off at 4.30pm and include two complimentary handmade cocktails – talk about riding in style. The full-day tour includes a BBQ lunch. All tours adhere to zero-waste principles. Highly recommended.

Marine Conservation Cambodia VOLUNTEERING

(☎016 715444; www.marineconservationcambodia.org; Koh Seh) ✍ This organisation works to preserve the marine environment of the Kep Archipelago by combating the destruction illegal fishing causes to sea life. It also monitors the island group's marine life, which includes large populations of dugongs and Irrawaddy dolphins. Volunteers get hands-

Kep

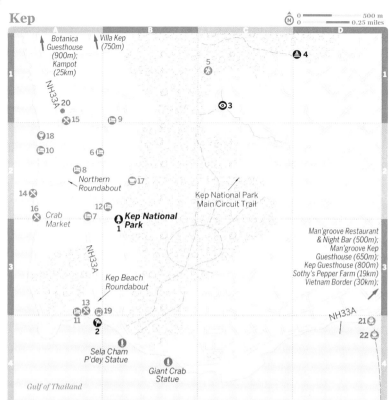

on practice, joining patrols to spot illegal fishing, as well as learning about marine conservation and helping with research.

🛏 Sleeping

Kep meanders along the shoreline for a good 5km, with resorts and guesthouses speckled along the length of the main road and perched on the dirt tracks that wander up the hills leading to Kep National Park (p224). Prices at the classiest places can feel a bit inflated, but there are plenty of good midrange options.

★**Khmer Hands Resort**   BUNGALOW $
(☑088 215 0011; www.keylightlearning.org; r US$15-25; 🛜) 🏖 Choose from sturdy, stilted, wooden bungalows and cheaper, squat, concrete huts – all with private porch – at this well-run Khmer–American venture that doubles as an English- and vocational-training school for at-risk locals. The excellent restaurant sources herbs and vege-

tables from a permaculture garden on the premises, and there's a cool gift shop under the restaurant selling pepper, handicrafts and more.

Meng Naren Guest House   BUNGALOW $
(☑070 644321; Koh Tonsay; bungalows from US$10; 🛜) Meng Naren is the biggest and most central place on the main beach of Koh Tonsay, and also has the nicest rooms, along with a breezy restaurant and happy-hour specials galore. The roomy wooden bungalows are equipped with mozzie nets, private veranda and hammocks. It organises sunset and snorkelling boat trips and a sunset beach barbecue. Electricity runs from 6.30pm until about 11pm.

Bird of Paradise   BUNGALOW $
(☑090 880413; www.birdofparadisebungalows.com; bungalows incl breakfast with fan/air-con from US$18/35; ❄🛜) Set in a relaxed, peaceful garden with adorable ducks roaming

Kep

⊙ Top Sights
1 Kep National Park B3

⊙ Sights
2 Kep Beach A4
3 Kep Butterfly Garden C1
4 Wat Samathi D1

⊖ Activities, Courses & Tours
5 Connection Path C1
  Kep Sailing Club .... (see 18)

⊟ Sleeping
6 Atmaland Resort A2
7 Bacoma A2
8 Bird of Paradise A2
9 Khmer Hands Resort B1
10 Knai Bang Chatt A2
11 Saravoan Hotel A3
   Tara Lodge .... (see 9)
12 Veranda Natural Resort B2

⊗ Eating
13 Burger Workshop A3
14 Crab Market A2
15 Deli's Kep A1
16 Kep Sur Mer A2
   La Baraka .... (see 14)
   So Kheang .... (see 14)
   Strand .... (see 10)

⊙ Drinking & Nightlife
17 Led Zep Cafe B2
18 Sailing Club A2

⊙ Information
   ABA Bank ATM .... (see 13)

⊙ Transport
19 Anny Tours A3
   Champa Express .... (see 19)
20 Diamond & Moon Moto Rental A1
   Giant Ibis .... (see 19)
21 Koh Tonsay Boat Ticket Office D4
22 Rabbit Island Pier D4

around, Bird of Paradise offers stupendous value and is well located just uphill from the main road, within walking distance of the crab market. Simple but sweet wooden bungalows, with hammocks strung from the porch, are delightfully rustic, while the aircon concrete cottages are more spacious.

Botanica Guesthouse   BUNGALOW $

(☏ 097 801 9017; www.kep-botanica.com; NH33A; r with fan/air-con US$24/32; ❄ 🛜 🏊) A little way from the action (if Kep can be said to have any action), Botanica offers exceptional value for money with attractive bungalows with contemporary bathrooms. There's a well-shaded pool, plus a pool table in the restaurant. Renovations have only improved what was already a good thing.

Bacoma   BUNGALOW $

(☏ 088 411 2424; www.bacoma.weebly.com; NH33A; r US$15-30; 🛜) Five cheap and cheerful rondavels (circular dwellings with conical thatched roofs) in the garden all have mosquito nets and fan, and share sparkling-clean shared bathrooms. There are also roomy bungalows and traditional Khmer houses with private bathroom, and the owner is a super nice guy.

Kep Guesthouse   HOSTEL $

(☏ 097 374 8080; NH33A; hammock US$3, dm US$4-5, r with fan US$9-13, with air-con & hot water US$17; ❄ 🛜) This modest hostel is Kep's nicest backpacker pad with bright, airy and

clean rooms and a dorm with a mix of single and double beds. The roof deck, with views to the ocean, is slung with hammocks in high season. The small restaurant specialises in Nepalese food.

Tara Lodge   GUESTHOUSE $$

(☏ 0966 866375; www.taralodge-kep.com; d incl breakfast US$55-65, f US$80; ❄ 🛜 🏊) The hugely friendly Tara Lodge gets a big tick for its split-level bungalows with wide verandas and all the mod cons, secreted within a verdant garden of palms and flowers, and set around a glistening pool. This is a secluded spot for some serious downtime. The upstairs terrace-restaurant serves excellent Khmer and French food and has views to Bokor. The massage pavilion is sublime.

Villa Kep   RESORT $$

(☏ 096 967 0469; www.villakep.com; r US$50-55) This Finnish-owned complex of 18 villas sprawls across the countryside on the outskirts of Kep, with a glorious pool at the centre of it all. The spacious villas are a splendid deal, albeit they are not particularly heavy on character. They come in twin configuration or with a beautiful king-sized bed. No children allowed.

Atmaland Resort   RESORT $$

(☏ 086 509021; www.atmaland.com; d/q from US$65/75, 5-bed penthouse US$125; ❄ 🛜 🏊) This family-friendly all-bungalow resort sprawls along the hillside amid a rambling mature garden with an on-site Thai and Ayurvedic vegetarian restaurant and outstanding views from the beautiful pool. It's far enough away to feel secluded, but still central enough to easily walk to Kep's crab market. Both spacious suites and standard bungalows are comfortable with attractive wicker beds and furniture.

Saravoan Hotel
BOUTIQUE HOTEL **$$**

(☑036-639 3909; saravoan_hotel@yahoo.com; Kep Beach Rd; r US$45-55; ❄️🛜🏊) Classic Kep contemporary minimalist design is the hallmark of Saravoan. The spacious rooms come with polished concrete floors, stone-wall detailing and floor-to-ceiling glass doors that open out onto arguably the best sea-view balconies in town, although they are susceptible to street noise. The terrace pool is just the place to cool off.

★Veranda Natural Resort
RESORT **$$$**

(☑012 888619; www.veranda-resort.asia; Kep Hillside Rd; r incl breakfast from US$110; ❄️🛜🏊) The unique hillside bungalows here are built of wood, bamboo and stone, and are connected by a maze of stilted walkways, making this a thoroughly memorable spot for a romantic getaway. Check out several rooms because the size and shape vary wildly. There are a couple of pools, the food is excellent and views from the restaurant pavilion are stunning.

Knai Bang Chatt
BOUTIQUE HOTEL **$$$**

(☑078 888554; www.knaibangchatt.com; r incl breakfast from US$209; ❄️@🛜🏊) Kep's original design hotel occupies a cluster of 1960s waterfront villas, with rooms out of the pages of a slick magazine. On the seafront, with only a sliver of beach but a lovely infinity pool right before the ocean. It has free yoga in the morning and in-room bathtubs, but for this price, we would've expected flawless wi-fi.

The hotel's upscale restaurant, **Strand** (☑078 333686; mains US$13-20, breakfast US$12; ⏰7am-10pm), is delicious, and its Sailing Club, a waterfront cocktail bar, is the place to be for sunset.

✕ Eating

Eating at the **crab market** (1kg crab from 50,000r) is a quintessential Kep experience. Most other restaurants in town also offer crab in some way, shape or form. Some of Kep's hotels offer fine dining. Veranda Natural Resort and Khmer Hands Resort (p226)

are a couple of the top tables, and have great views to boot.

Deli's Kep
DELI **$**

(☑088 470 7952; NH33A; sandwiches US$3.50-4; ⏰7am-7pm) This gourmet food store earns high praise for its *coppa, lomo,* saucisson and other imported meats, along with top-notch pepper (100g for US$5 to US$8), coffee and craft booze. Grab a sandwich on the way to a pepper farm, or plop down for a relaxing meal in the airy, modern space.

Burger Workshop
BURGERS **$**

(Kep Beach Rd; burgers US$3-5.50; ⏰11am-9pm) The patties here, prepared by a skilled French burger maestro, are terrific and come in beef, chicken and veggie varieties. Better yet, it doubles as a smoothie bar and has ice cream as well.

So Kheang
SEAFOOD **$$**

(crab market; mains US$4-8; ⏰7am-9pm) This tatty looking crab shack manages to have both the cheapest and the tastiest crab at the crab market. Unlike many others, it doesn't add curry to it Kampot-pepper crab, so the flavour of the pepper dominates (as it should). The one fuss is that it tends to close early, especially in low season.

Kep Sur Mer
SEAFOOD **$$**

(crab market; mains US$5-10; ⏰10.30am-10pm; 🛜) Kep Sur Mer is slightly more upscale than most others in the crab-market scene, yet is still great value. The crab cakes and crab *amok* (a baked seafood dish) are winners, and epitomise the more refined cuisine. Great drinks (half price at happy hour, 5pm to 7pm).

La Baraka
INTERNATIONAL **$$**

(☑097 461 2543; crab market; mains US$6-10; ⏰10am-2pm & 6-10pm; 🛜) A breath of fresh air from the other crab-market restaurants' identical menus, La Baraka serves a mix of European and Asian flavours with bags of seafood dishes such as sea-bass carpaccio. For non-fish-lovers there's also great pizza and pasta. The terrace, over the waves, is sunset cocktail perfection.

🍷 Drinking & Nightlife

★Sailing Club
COCKTAIL BAR

(mains US$7-12.50; ⏰10am-10pm; 🛜) With a small beach, a breezy wooden bar and a wooden jetty poking out into the sea, this is one of Cambodia's top sundowner spots. The Asian-fusion food is excellent and you can get your crab fix here, too. There's an outdoor cocktail lounge and a vastly expanded seafront terrace.

Led Zep Cafe
CAFE

(Kep National Park; ⊙hours vary) A lovely, secluded cafe and crêperie on the Kep National Park (p224) trail, a five-minute walk from the main entrance. Knocking back a chilled lime juice on the wide terrace with knock-out views overlooking the coast is the perfect pick-me-up after a hike. The crêpes are outstanding, but hours are sporadic, especially during low season.

Man'groove Restaurant & Night Bar
BAR

(⊙11am-4am) Out past the Rabbit Island pier, this is seemingly the only proper bar in Kep, with lots of beer options (including US$0.75 draughts), good cocktails and billiards. Food choices include plenty of Khmer options, fish 'n' chips and Australian steaks. The guesthouse (☎096 491 0589; off NH33A; s/d US$6/8; ☎) at the back has a few seafront bungalows.

ⓘ Information

There's no bank in Kep but there are a couple of ATMs. One is the **ABA Bank ATM** (Kep Beach Rd; ⊙24hr) near Kep Beach.

ⓘ Getting There & Around

Kep is 25km from Kampot and 41km from the Prek Chak–Xa Xia border crossing to Vietnam.

Buses stop at Kep Beach in front of a line of travel agencies and minivan offices. You can purchase tickets here or from most guesthouses.

Most buses and minivans to Phnom Penh go via Kampot, which adds an hour or so to the trip. One exception is Phnom Penh Sorya (p93) buses, which go direct to Phnom Penh. A private taxi to the capital costs US$45 to US$50. **Anny Tours** (☎096 764 6666; Kep Beach Rd; ⊙6am-9pm) and **Champa Express** (☎088 727 7277; Kep Beach Rd; ⊙6.30am-8pm) send minivans over the border to Ha Tien in Vietnam twice daily. Going the other way, the same companies serve Sihanoukville two or three times daily, with a van change in Kampot, and also serve Koh Kong with several van transfers.

For Kampot, take a *tuk tuk* (US$10, 45 minutes) or any eastbound bus or minivan. The sunset Crab Shuttle (p221) boat trip (US$10, 2½ hours, 3pm) is a nice option. There are very few *moto* drivers in town.

Motorbike rental is US$5 with **Diamond & Moon Moto Rental** (☎097 864 5062; diamondandmoon@gmail.com; scooter rental per day US$5); guesthouses and travel agencies also rent out motorbikes.

ⓘ GETTING TO VIETNAM: KEP TO HA TIEN

Getting to the border The **Prek Chak/Xa Xia border crossing** (in theory open 6am to 6pm, though it sometimes opens late and closes early) has become a popular option for linking Kampot and Kep with Ha Tien, and then onward to either the popular Vietnamese island of Phu Quoc, or to Ho Chi Minh City.

The easiest way to get to Prek Chak and on to Ha Tien, Vietnam, is to catch a minivan from Sihanoukville (US$12, five to seven hours), Kampot (US$8, two hours), or Kep (US$7, one hour). Anny Tours (p230) and Champa Express (p230) run this service with a change of vehicles at the border.

A more flexible alternative from Phnom Penh or Kampot is to take a bus to Kompong Trach, then a *moto* (about US$3) for 15km, on a good road, to the border.

In Kep, guesthouses can arrange a *moto* (US$8, 45 minutes), *tuk tuk* (US$12, one hour) or taxi (US$20, 30 minutes). Rates and times are almost double from Kampot.

At the border Vietnam grants 15-day visas on arrival for nationals of several European and Asian countries. Other nationalities, and anyone staying longer than 15 days, must purchase a visa in advance.

At Prek Chak, a *moto* driver will ask US$5 to take you to the Vietnamese border post 300m past the Cambodian one, and then all the way to Ha Tien (15 minutes, 7km). You'll save money walking across no-person's land and picking up a *moto* on the other side for US$2 to US$3.

Moving on From Ha Tien you can find onward transport to Ho Chi Minh City via the Mekong Delta route. To Phu Quoc island there are both slow and fast ferry departures until early afternoon.

BUSES FROM KEP

DESTINATION	FARE	DURATION	FREQUENCY	COMPANY	TYPE
Ha Tien	US$7-8	1½hr	4 daily	Anny Tours, Champa Express	minivan
Phnom Penh	US$5-10	3½-5hr	frequent	Champa Express, **Giant Ibis** (📞096 999 3333; www. giantibis.com; Kep Beach Rd), Phnom Penh Sorya	bus/minivan
Sihanoukville	US$7-8	5-6hr	several daily	Anny Tours, Champa Express	minivan

TAKEO

📞 032 / POP 40,000

There's not much happening at all in the languid, lakeside provincial capital of Takeo (តាកែវ), but it makes a good base from which to take a motorboat ride to the pre-Angkorian temples of Angkor Borei and Phnom Da and experience river life. Since few visitors make it out to this impoverished rural province, you'll likely have these temples, among Cambodia's most ancient and fascinating, virtually to yourself. The main attraction in Takeo town is eating freshwater lobster on the waterfront (best from August to December).

A 7th-century Chenla (pre-Angkorian) temple at Phnom Bayong and the nearby Kirivong Waterfall can be reached on day trips from Takeo, while further-flung temples in Takeo Province such as Tonlé Bati and Phnom Chisor are usually visited as day trips from Phnom Penh.

Ta Mok's House
HISTORIC BUILDING

(ផ្ទះតាម៉ុក) **FREE** A pleasant stroll via a 150m-long, railings-free bridge takes you to the house of Takeo Province's most notorious native son, Ta Mok – aka 'The Butcher' – the Khmer Rouge commander of the Southwestern Zone, where he presided over horrific atrocities. The house is now occupied by a university, but you can wander around the grounds. Ta Mok also had a residence near Anlong Veng.

🛌 Sleeping & Eating

Meas Family Homestay
HOMESTAY $

(📞011 687554, 016 781415; www.cambodian homestay.com; Angk Tasaom District; adult/child incl all meals US$20/13; 🛜) This popular and friendly family homestay has 12 rooms in a spacious compound about 7km northwest of Takeo proper, off the road to Angk Tasaom. It's a gorgeous place to ride a bike around the rice paddies, and the homestay provides complimentary wheels. Rates also include some delicious home-cooked Khmer food and cooking classes are available.

While staying here, it's also possible to volunteer to teach English at the local school.

Daunkeo Guesthouse
GUESTHOUSE $

(📞032-210303; www.daunkeo.com; St 9; r US$15-25; ❄️🛜) The smartest guesthouse in Takeo, Daunkeo is spread over three modern villas. All rooms have air-con and include satellite TV and hot-water showers, though the service leaves something to be desired and the wi-fi is unreliable. The US$25 'VIP' rooms are not a huge upgrade on the standard rooms.

Stung Takeo
CAMBODIAN $$

(📞032-665 4111; St 9; mains US$4-20; ⏰8am-9pm) Perched over the seasonal lake, Stung Takeo features a seafood-heavy menu full of traditional flavour such as squid and Kampot pepper. But the main reason to come here is for giant freshwater lobster (otherwise known as crayfish), which mature between October and December in the lake (US$45 per kilo). At other times smaller specimens are available (US$30 per kilo).

Those prices are not typos – lobster has gotten expensive in these parts, so watch your bill. The lakefront here is lined with lobster joints if you want to shop around.

Le Petit Bistro de Takeo
FRENCH $$

(📞097 991 1037; St 9; mains US$6-10; ⏰9am-9pm) Also known as Fred's French Restaurant after its affable owner, this tranquil garden restaurant is a pleasant surprise in backwater Takeo. The menu, handwritten on a chalkboard, might contain delicacies such as quiche Lorraine *or* French-style steaks, as well as French wines by the glass (US$2.75).

ℹ️ Information

Canadia Bank (NH2; ⏰8am-3.30pm Mon-Fri, to 11.30am Sat, ATM 24hr)

Takeo Tourism (📞032-931323; ⏰7.30-11.30am & 2-5pm) May be able to arrange an English-speaking guide (US$15 to US$20) to the temples.

ANGKOR BOREI & PHNOM DA

Takeo itself offers few attractions, but is a jumping-off point for visiting two fabulous sights: the archaeological museum **Angkor Borei** (សារមន្ទីរបុរាណវិទ្យាអង្គរបុរី; ☏012 201638; US$2; ⊙8am-4.30pm) and the temple-topped hills of **Phnom Da** (ប្រាសាទភ្នំដា; US$2).

Angkor Borei was known as Vyadhapura when it served as the 8th-century capital of 'water Chenla', as Takeo Province was called in Chinese annals (no doubt a reference to the extensive annual floods that still blanket much of the area). It was also an important centre during the earlier Funan period (1st to 6th centuries), when religion and culture were carried to the Mekong Delta by traders, artisans and priests from India, as the great maritime trade route between India and China passed by the Mekong Delta. The earliest datable Khmer inscription (AD 611) was discovered here and hints of this past greatness can be found in the 5.7km moated wall that still surrounds this impoverished riverine townlet.

The 45-minute outboard-boat ride to reach Angkor Borei and Phnom Da from Takeo, along Canal No 15, dug in the 1880s, is one of the best opportunities you'll have in Cambodia to see rural riverside living. There isn't accommodation or formal restaurants here, though, so you'll want to bring water and a snack from Takeo.

Hiring an outboard from Takeo's **boat dock** (St 9) costs US$35 return for up to four people. Kit (☏092 839654) is a boat driver who speaks some English if you want to reserve ahead, although rocking up is not a problem.

The canal leading out to Angkor Borei is clearly delineated in the dry season (November to May) but surrounded by flooded rice fields the rest of the year. In rainy season the water can get rough in the afternoon, so it's a good idea to head out early. When the water levels are too low you will have to travel by *moto* for the 10-minute ride between Angkor Borei and Phnom Da (US$5 return).

Angkor Borei can also be reached year-round via a circuitous land route from the north.

ℹ Getting There & Away

Takeo is on NH2, 77km south of Phnom Penh and 48km north of the Phnom Den–Tinh Bien border crossing.

At the time of research, no bus company served Takeo. To get to Phnom Penh direct, take a shared taxi (US$5 per seat, US$25 for the whole taxi) from a lot in front of the transit hub **Psar Thmei** (NH2, Central Market). For a more roundabout journey, hop on a nine-seater local *remork-moto* (seat 2000r) from Psar Thmei, a *tuk-tuk* (US$4) from Psar Thmei or the hospital, or a *moto* (US$3) wherever you spot one, and head to Angk Tasaom, the chaotic transport junction 10km northwest of Takeo on NH3. Here you can flag down both northbound buses to Phnom Penh and southbound buses to Kampot and Kep.

Private taxis will make the 45-minute trip down to Kirivong for US$20, or take a *moto* for US$10.

Trains service Takeo on Friday, Saturday, Sunday and Monday, connecting it with Phnom Penh, Kampot and Sihanoukville. Tickets cost from US$5 to US$7 and should be purchased at the **train station** (☏099 222533; http://royal-railway.com; ⊙8am-4pm Wed-Mon) a few days in advance.

Around Takeo

Affording breathtaking views of Vietnam's pancake-flat Mekong Delta, the cliff-ringed summit of **Phnom Bayong** (ភ្នំបាយ័ង; US$5) is graced by a 7th-century Chenla temple built to celebrate a victory over Funan. The *linga* (phallic symbol) originally in the inner chamber is now in Paris' Musée Guimet, but a number of flora- and fauna-themed bas-relief panels can still be seen, for example on the lintels of the three false doorways, and carved into the brickwork.

Phnom Bayong is about 3km west of the northern edge of Kirivong (Phumi Tonleab); the turn-off on NH2 is marked by a painted panel depicting the temple, 39km south of Takeo. From the turn-off, drive 2km along a sealed road, then turn left on a dirt road and proceed uphill for another kilometre or so to the parking area.

From the parking area, a twisting concrete single track leads straight up to the base of the temple. You can either walk this bit (about 30 minutes) or navigate it by motorbike

ℹ GETTING TO VIETNAM: TAKEO TO CHAU DOC

Getting to the border The remote and seldom-used **Phnom Den/Tinh Bien border crossing** (open 6am to 6pm) between Cambodia and Vietnam lies 47km southeast of Takeo town in Cambodia and offers connections to Chau Doc. Most travellers prefer the Mekong crossing at Kaam Samnor or the Prek Chak crossing near Ha Tien to the south. Take a share taxi (US$5), a chartered taxi (US$25) or a *moto* (US$15) from Takeo to the border. Entering Cambodia from Vietnam, expect to pay US$10/20 for a *moto* from the border to Kirivong/Takeo.

At the border Several nationalities can get 15-day Vietnam visas on arrival; everyone else needs to arrange one in advance. Coming into Cambodia from Vietnam, note that e-visas are not accepted for entry here.

Moving on Travellers are at the mercy of Vietnamese *xe om (moto)* drivers and taxis for the 30km journey from the border to Chau Doc. Prepare for some tough negotiations. Expect to pay US$10 to US$12.50 for a *moto,* and US$20 for a taxi.

(10 minutes) – a real thrill whether you are self-driving or on the back of a *moto* (about US$5 round trip from Kirivong). From the base of the temple, it's a 10-minute grunt straight up a crumbling, ancient staircase to the temple.

To get to Kirivong from Takeo, take a share taxi (US$3.50), a chartered taxi (US$20) or a *moto* (one-way/round trip US$10/15).

Gentle **Kirivong Waterfall** (ទឹកជ្រោះគីរីវង្ស, Chruos Phaok Waterfall) FREE is a popular bathing and picnic spot for locals just west of Kirivong. No booming cascade, but plenty of local colour and it can easily be combined with a visit to nearby Phnom Bayong. Market stalls here sell the area's most famous products: topaz and quartz, either cut like gems or carved into tiny Buddhas and nagas (mythical serpent-beings).

To get here, turn west off the NH2 at the signs for Phnom Bayong on the north edge of Kirivong. After 1km turn left onto a dirt road, continue 1.5km to the falls access road on your right, then proceed another 1km to the falls. Motorbike parking costs 1000r.

Northwestern Cambodia

POP 4.2 MILLION

Includes ➡

Kompong Chhnang....236
Pursat.............237
Battambang 241
Pailin.............254
Banteay Chhmar ...258
Prasat Preah Vihear ...264
Preah Khan of
Kompong Svay 267
Kompong Thom 269

Best Places to Eat

➡ CBT Meal at the Temple (p260)

➡ Jaan Bai (p249)

➡ La Villa (p250)

➡ Riceholic (p250)

➡ Talk2 Coffee (p258)

Best Places to Stay

➡ Bambu Hotel (p247)

➡ BeTreed Adventures (p268)

➡ Kompong Luong Homestays (p240)

➡ Sambor Village Hotel (p270)

➡ The Place (p246)

Why Go?

Looking for temples without the tourist hordes? The remote temples of Northwestern Cambodia are a world apart. While hilltop Prasat Preah Vihear is the big hitter, the other temple complexes like Preah Khan Kompong Svay (Prasat Bakan) and Sambor Prei Kuk, wrapped in vines and half-swallowed by jungle, are fabulous to explore.

In the region's heart is Tonlé Sap, teeming with fish and a birder's paradise. Boat trips from Kompong Chhnang and Krakor (near Pursat) to the floating villages that cluster along this important waterway allow you to dip your toes into life on the lake.

When forays into the region's far-flung corners are complete, the northwest has one more surprise up its sleeve. Laid-back Battambang, with its French architecture and burgeoning arts scene, is the main city here. There's a wealth of brilliant sights all within day-tripping distance of town, making it a worthy pit stop when all the hard travelling is done.

When to Go
Battambang

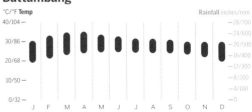

Dec–Jan Head to remote temples to explore while pleasant temperatures prevail.

Aug–Sep Rainy season in full throttle and the lush countryside is studded with palms.

Nov Best for back-country exploration, with roads neither too muddy nor too dusty.

Northwestern Cambodia Highlights

1 Battambang (p241) Chilling out amid the city's colonial-tinged charms and venturing into verdant countryside and hilltop temples.

2 Prasat Preah Vihear (p264) Soaking up the stupendous vistas from atop this dramatic mountain perch.

3 Sambor Prei Kuk (p272) Exploring the vine-entwined, pre-Angkorian brick temples of Cambodia's third Unesco World Heritage Site.

4 Kompong Luong (p239) Gliding on a paddleboat through the watery thoroughfares of this floating village, and bedding down in one of its fascinating homestays.

5 Banteay Chhmar (p258) Admiring the intricate bas-reliefs of Avalokiteshvara (a Buddhist) at this massive 12th-century temple complex.

6 Preah Khan of Kompong Svay (p267) Following a lonely road to stand in awe of this temple's mighty, jungle-encroached *gopura* (entrance pavilion).

KOMPONG CHHNANG

🎵 026 / POP 46,000

Kompong Chhnang Province (ខេត្តកំពង់ឆ្នាំង) is relatively wealthy, thanks to its proximity to the capital, fishing and agricultural industries, and abundant water resources. While it's relatively quiet in the province's sleepy capital city of Kompong Chhnang (Clay Pot Port), the bustling dock on the Tonlé Sap River is the jumping-off point for serene boat rides to two floating villages. Skimming through the watery streets in a tiny wooden paddleboat as the late-afternoon sun sends a shimmer over the river is a gorgeous way to end a day.

Outside the towns you'll find a lush landscape of yellow-green rice fields. Here, in the tiny hamlets where cows slumber beside curvaceous hay bales, the area's distinctive pottery is crafted underneath stilted homes, providing another reason to linger.

⊙ Sights

Ondong Rossey   VILLAGE

(អណ្ដូងប្រុស្សី) The quiet village of Ondong Rossey, where the area's famous red pottery is made under every stilted house, is a delightful 7km ride west of town through serene rice fields dotted with sugar palms, many with bamboo ladders running up the trunk. The unpainted pots, decorated with etched or appliqué designs, are either turned with a foot-spun wheel (for small pieces) or banged into shape with a heavy wooden spatula (for large ones).

The golden-hued mud piled up in the yards is quarried at nearby Phnom Krang Dai Meas and pounded into fine clay before being shaped and fired; only at the last stage does it acquire a pinkish hue. Pieces can be purchased at the **Pottery Development Center** in the heart of the village, although you'll get better deals buying directly from the potters at their houses.

Phnom Santuk   VIEWPOINT

(ភ្នំសន្ទុក) Phnom Santuk, a rocky hillock behind Wat Santuk, is a few kilometres south of Kompong Chhnang. The boulder-strewn summit affords fine views of the countryside, including Tonlé Sap lake, 20km to the north.

🛏 Sleeping & Eating

Sovann Phum Hotel   HOTEL $

(🎵 026-989333; sovannphumkpchotel@yahoo.com; NH5; r with fan/air-con from US$8/15, new wing incl breakfast US$35; ❄ @ 🤖 ❄) A defi-

Kompong Chhnang

🛏 Sleeping
1 Chanthea Borint Hotel............................ A3
2 Sovann Phum Hotel.............................. B3

⊗ Eating
3 Heng Chamreun Bakery......................... A1
4 Soksan Restaurant A2

nite step up from most Kompong Chhnang options in cleanliness and style, this is a popular spot for the NGO crowd. It has 30 good-sized rooms with modern bathrooms and plenty of light, plus a decent restaurant. A new wing at the back offers positively boutique-style rooms and a 1st-floor swimming pool. Book ahead.

Chanthea Borint Hotel   GUESTHOUSE $

(🎵 026-988622, 012 762988; cborint@gmail.com; Prison St; r with fan/air-con US$8/15; ❄ 🤖) Set in a shady garden, this 30-room family pad offers the most welcoming accommodation in town. The rooms are small but tidy and well cared for. The small restaurant serves breakfast only.

Soksan Restaurant   CAMBODIAN $

(NH5; mains US$2-4; ⊙6am-8pm) It may lack English signage, but there's an English

NORTHWESTERN CAMBODIA PURSAT

LOCAL KNOWLEDGE

THE KHMER ROUGE AIRPORT

The Khmer Rouge were not known as great builders, but in 1977 and 1978, slave labourers built an airfield using cement of such high quality that even today the 2440m runway and access roads look like they were paved just last week.

No one knows for sure, but it seems that **Kompong Chhnang Airport** (KZC, អាកាសយានដ្ឋានខេត្តកំពង់ឆ្នាំង), never operational under the Khmer Rouge, was intended to serve as a base for launching air attacks against Vietnam. Chinese engineers oversaw the work of tens of thousands of Cambodians suspected of disloyalty to the Khmer Rouge. Anyone unable to work was killed, often with a blow to the head delivered with a bamboo rod. In early 1979, as Vietnamese forces approached, almost the entire workforce was executed. Estimates of the number of victims, buried nearby in mass graves, range from 10,000 to 50,000.

In the late 1990s, a plan to turn the airport into a cargo hub for air-courier companies came to nought. These days, local teenagers come out here to tool around on their motorbikes, while cows graze between the taxiway and the runway. On hot days, the sun creates convincing mirages.

On an anonymous slope a few kilometres away, the Khmer Rouge dug a **cave** – said to be 3km deep – apparently for the purpose of storing weapons flown in from China. Now home to swirling bats, it can be explored with a torch (flashlight), but lacking ventilation, it gets very hot and humid.

On a hillside near a cluster of bullet-pocked cement barracks, stripped of anything of value, is a massive cement **water tank**. Inside it's a remarkable echo chamber.

The airport is about 12km west of town. Take NH5 towards Battambang for 7km and then turn left onto a concrete road.

menu at this restaurant next to Kompong Chhnang's taxi park. It specialises in fried everything and soups, or be adventurous and order the porcupinefish with omelette.

Heng Chamreun Bakery BAKERY $
(NH5; baked goods 2000-5000r; ⏱8am-9pm) Part of a renowned chain, this glistening bakery sells good sandwiches, rice cakes and other snacks ideal for the road.

ℹ Information

Acleda Bank (NH5; ⏱7.30am-4pm Mon-Fri, to 11am Sat, ATM 24hr)

Canadia Bank (NH5; ⏱8am-3.30pm Mon-Fri, to 11.30am Sat, ATM 24hr)

ℹ Getting There & Away

Kompong Chhnang is 91km north of Phnom Penh, 93km southeast of Pursat and 198km southeast of Battambang.

You can buy tickets for most leading bus companies at the **bus ticket stand** (NH5), a vendor-cart with bus-company signage in front. Buses can be flagged down at the Acleda Bank corner on NH5, but it is better to buy a ticket in advance to guarantee a seat.

Buses south to Phnom Penh (20,000r, 2½ hours), and north to Pursat (20,000r, two hours)

and Battambang (24,000r, five hours), pull through town hourly throughout the day.

The fastest way to get to Phnom Penh is by share taxi (20,000r, two hours). Vehicles wait at the central **taxi park**. Share taxis do not generally serve destinations to the northwest, such as Battambang.

ℹ Getting Around

A several-hour *remork-moto* tour taking in the pottery villages and Phnom Santuk costs around US$10. A *moto* (motorcycle taxi) should be about US$5. A *moto/remork* to the port is US$1/2 one way.

Chanthea Borint Hotel rents out bicycles (US$2 for the day).

PURSAT

🕐052 / POP 39,000
Pursat Province (ខេត្តពោធិ៍សាត់), Cambodia's fourth-largest, stretches from the remote forests of Phnom Samkos, on the Thai border, eastwards to the fishing villages and marshes of Tonlé Sap lake. Famed for its oranges, it encompasses the northern reaches of the Cardamom Mountains, linked with the town of Pursat by disreputable roads.

You know you've hit Pursat town when huge marble monument shops begin to fringe the roadside: if you're in the market for a life-size statue of a rearing horse, you're in the right place. This dusty provincial capital, known for its carvers, is no beauty, but it makes a good base for a day trip to the floating village of Kompong Luong or an expedition into the wilds of the Central Cardamoms.

◉ Sights

Bunrany Hun Sen
Development Center   ARTS CENTRE
(មជ្ឈមណ្ឌលអភិវឌ្ឍន៍ ប៊ុនរ៉ានី ហ៊ុនសែន; ☎052-951606; St 109; ⊘7-11am & 2-5pm Mon-Fri, to 11am Sat) This centre, named after the Prime Minister's wife, teaches cloth and mat weaving, sewing, marble carving and other artisanal skills to young people, and sells the items they make from a large shop on the premises. There are some real bargains here on beautiful *krama* (checked scarves) and baskets. Travellers are welcome to visit.

Koh Sampovmeas   PARK
(កោះសំពៅមាស, Golden Ship Island) This bizarre island-park, built in the shape of a ship, is Pursat's place to see and be seen around sunset. Young locals drop by for aerobics (classes from 5pm) or a game of badminton, while power-walkers pound the circuit between the manicured lawns and Khmer-style pavilions.

🛏 Sleeping & Eating

Thansour Thmey Hotel   HOTEL $
(☎012 962395; thansourthmey@gmail.com; St 102; r with fan/air-con 30,000/53,000r; ❄🛜) This place goes heavy on the Khmer woodcarvings, so if you've always wanted to sleep in an intricately carved bed, now is your chance. Rooms are tidy and the restaurant, which

serves Khmer and Chinese dishes (mains 8000r to 16,000r), is one of the best in Pursat.

Phnom Pech Hotel   HOTEL $
(☎052-951515; St 101; r with fan US$6-8, with air-con US$13-20; ❄🛜) This long-running local hotel has clean, though tired, rooms. The friendly manager is quite helpful with travel advice.

Pursat Riverside Hotel   HOTEL $$
(☎052-952168; St 101; r incl breakfast from US$25-30, deluxe r US$40-45, ste US$75-150; ❄🛜🏊) Formerly the KM Hotel, the Pursat Riverside brings another level of comfort and service to Pursat. The 146-room hotel has plush rooms hosting flat-screen TVs and beds that guarantee a contented sleep. In the extensive grounds, there are two large swimming pools, a most unexpected find for Pursat.

Reak Smey Angkor Restaurant   CAMBODIAN $
(St 101; mains 4000-8000r; ⊘6am-9pm) Hugely popular with Khmer tour groups, this family-run restaurant dishes up an extensive menu of local favourites, with plenty of noodle soups and fried-rice options. There's also a small menu of omelettes and Western breakfast plates.

ℹ Information

Staff members at Phnom Pech Hotel are relatively switched on if you need information on getting around the province, including to more remote places such as the Cardamoms.

Canadia Bank (NH5; ⊘8am-3.30pm Mon-Fri, to 11.30am Sat, ATM 24hr)

ℹ Getting There & Away

Pursat is 105km southeast of Battambang and 185km northwest of Phnom Penh along NH5.

Buses, including those of **Rith Mony** (NH5), pass through Pursat virtually all day long, shuttling southeast to Kompong Chhnang and Phnom Penh (20,000r, four hours) hourly, and

---

DON'T MISS

THE FLOATING VILLAGES OF THE TONLÉ SAP RIVER

Much less visited than other floating villages near Siem Reap, the Tonlé Sap River hamlets of **Chong Kos** (ចុងកោះ) and **Phoum Kandal** (ភូមិកណ្ដាល) are home to colourful wooden houses, with tiny terraces strung with hammocks, all built on rickety DIY pontoons.

Chong Kos is a Cambodian village and Phoum Kandal is a Vietnamese village. To fully explore the villages, hire a wooden boat (with captain) at Kompong Chhnang dock (US$10 per hour, up to three people) to paddle you through these fully buoyant towns, complete with shops, satellite TV and mobile vegetable vendors.

A two-hour boat ride will allow you to see both villages. Hiring a paddleboat offers the chance to glide within the maze of watery streets to glimpse how village life functions when everything floats.

Pursat

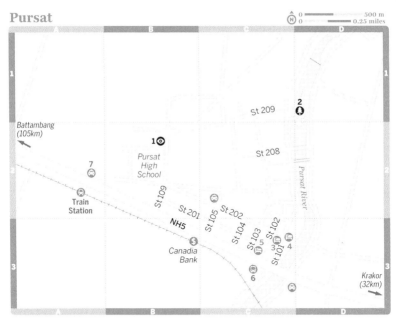

north to Battambang (15,000r, 1½ hours) hourly from around 11am onwards. **Phnom Penh Sorya** (NH5) offers direct trips to Kompong Cham (35,000r, six hours, 11.30am) and Siem Reap (32,000r, five hours, 7.15am and 2.30pm).

Share taxis serve **Phnom Penh** (24,000r, three hours) from NH5 just east of the bridge. Share taxis to **Battambang** (20,000r, 1½ hours) depart from NH5 on the western edge of town.

Pick-ups and share taxis to the remote Cardamom outpost of Osoam (40,000r, 3¼ hours) and the town of **Pramoay** (Veal Veng; 30,000r, three hours) via Kravanh (one hour) and Rovieng (two hours) leave from next to the old market.

ℹ Getting Around

Phnom Pech Hotel rents out bicycles (US$3 per day) and can try to set you up with a motorbike (US$10), which means finding a local to rent you his or hers.

Moto/remork drivers in town charge US$10/15 for a round trip to Kompong Luong.

KOMPONG LUONG

POP 10,000

Kompong Luong (កំពង់លួង) has all the amenities you might expect to find in an oversized fishing village, except that here everything floats on water. The cafes, shops, chicken coops, fish ponds, ice-making facto-

Pursat

◎ Sights
1 Bunrany Hun Sen Development
   Center B2
2 Koh Sampovmeas D1

◎ Sleeping
3 Phnom Pech Hotel C3
4 Pursat Riverside Hotel C3
5 Thansour Thmey Hotel C3

◎ Eating
Reak Smey Angkor
   Restaurant .... (see 3)

ℹ Transport
6 Phnom Penh Sorya C3
   Rith Mony .... (see 6)
7 Taxis to Battambang A2

ry, petrol station and karaoke bars arc kept from sinking by boat hulls, barrels or bunches of bamboo, as are the pagodas, the blueroofed church and the colourful houses. In the dry season, when water levels drop and the Tonlé Sap lake shrinks, the entire aquapolis is towed, boat by boat, a few kilometres north. The population of this fascinating and picturesque village is partly Vietnamese. Local children invariably delight in waving hello.

The way to explore Kompong Luong is, naturally, by boat. The official tourist rate to charter a wooden motorboat (complete with life jackets) at Kompong Luong boat landing is US$13 per hour for one to six passengers, US$20 for seven to 10, and US$2 per person for 11 or more.

The tours aren't particularly informative, as few captains speak much English, but gliding through the town and simply observing daily life makes this worthwhile. Tours pass by homes, schools, pagodas, fish shops and even a crocodile-feeding attraction for US$1 extra.

Homestay hosts can also provide boats for village exploring.

Kompong Luong has three **homestays** (per person US$4-6) available with local families, which true adventurers will appreciate. The stays, while rustic, offer a glimpse into everyday life on the water. Meals are available for US$2. You can book a homestay when you arrive at the boat landing.

As well as the homestays providing meals, there are a couple of very basic floating eateries in the village.

❶ Getting There & Around

The jumping-off point for Kompong Luong is the town of Krakor, 32km east of Pursat. From Krakor to the boat landing, where tours begin, it's 1.5km to 6km, depending on the time of year. You can get a ride on a *moto* for 2000r to 5000r.

Note that a boat ride to or from the Kompong Luong homestays will set you back US$5 (each way). If you book a tour, the boat will drop you off at the homestay for no additional charge.

NORTHERN CARDAMOM MOUNTAINS

Although the Central Cardamoms National Park (CCNP) and adjacent wildlife sanctuaries are slowly opening to ecotourism, the opportunities to explore these areas are still somewhat limited, as the ranger stations mostly exist to combat illegal logging, poaching and encroaching. Pursat is a possible gateway to the Northern Cardamoms, but most visitors going to the ecotourism centre of Osoam make their way there from the south via Koh Kong.

◉ Sights

Phnom Aural
Wildlife Sanctuary   WILDLIFE RESERVE
(ដែនជម្រកសត្វព្រៃភ្នំឧរ៉ាល់)   🏕   This 2538-sq-km sanctuary has the country's highest peak, **Phnom Aural** (1813m), and is just east of the Central Cardamoms National Park. Unfortunately the area is being destroyed from the south and the east by corrupt land speculation and rampant illegal logging, but the long-standing and reputable **DutchCo Trekking Cambodia** (☑097 679 2714; www.trekkingcambodia.com; r from US$20) 🏕 runs three-day trips to the region. Phnom Aural can be done in a day, but most do it in two or three.

Phnom Samkos
Wildlife Sanctuary   ANIMAL SANCTUARY
(ដែនជម្រកសត្វព្រៃភ្នំសំកុស)   Sandwiched between the Central Cardamoms National Park and the Thai frontier, the Phnom Samkos Wildlife Sanctuary (3338 sq km) is well and truly out in the sticks. It is threatened by timber laundering and agricultural concessions, but wildlife still abounds.

The sanctuary has Cambodia's second-highest peak, **Phnom Samkos** (1717m). Its main town is Pramoay (Veal Veng), 125km west of Pursat. This remote little outpost has three guesthouses (rooms US$5). Local *moto* drivers can take visitors to nearby ethnic-minority villages.

Osoam Cardamom
Community Centre   TOURS
(☑016 309075, 089 899895; osoamcbet@gmail.com) In the isolated settlement of Osoam, this excellent community centre organises hiking, dirt-bike (p186) and boat trips in the surrounding countryside, as well as day trips and overnights to Phnom Samkos, where elephants can be spotted. The property has seven simple, well-kept rooms (US$6) along with connections to simple guesthouses and homestays (single/double US$5/6) nearby. Electricity is limited and showers come from buckets, but this is about as close to real Cambodia as you can get..

❶ Getting There & Around

From Psar Chaa in Pursat, share taxis and pickups serve Kravanh (one hour), Rovieng (two hours) and Pramoay (three hours) year-round.

From Pramoay, the track south to Osoam is in rougher shape. It's passable by *moto* year-round, but taxis can't handle it during the height of the wet season. The road south from Osoam to Koh Kong is much better and can accommodate taxis year-round. In the dry season you can go from Pursat all the way to Koh Kong by share taxi.

You can also get to Pramoay via a dirt road (no public transport) from Samlaut in Pailin Province.

Phnom Aural Wildlife Sanctuary is best accessed from Kompong Speu, 45km west of Phnom Penh.

BATTAMBANG PROVINCE

Battambang Province (ខេត្តបាត់ដំបង; Bat Dambong) is said by proud locals to produce Cambodia's finest rice, sweetest coconuts and tastiest oranges (don't bring this up in Pursat). It has a long border with Thailand and a short stretch of the Tonlé Sap shoreline.

Battambang has passed from Cambodia to Thailand and back again several times over the past few centuries. Thailand ruled the area from 1794 to 1907 and again during WWII (1941 to 1946), when the Thais cut a deal with the Japanese and the Vichy French.

Battambang

📞 053 / POP 150,000

There's something about Battambang (បាត់ដំបង) that visitors just love. Although there's really not all that much to do in the city proper, the architecture teetering into disrepair, the riverside setting and the laid-back cafes all make up for it. It's the perfect blend of relatively urban modernity and small-town friendliness.

Outside the city's confines, meanwhile, timeless hilltop temples and bucolic villages await. Not to mention the most scenic river trip in the country, which links Battambang with Siem Reap.

That Cambodia's best-known circus (the magnificent Phare Ponleu Selpak) is here is no coincidence: the city has an enduring tradition of producing many of Cambodia's best-loved singers, actors and artists.

⊙ Sights

Much of Battambang's charm lies in its early-20th-century architecture, a mix of vernacular shophouses and French colonial construction that makes up the historic core of the city. Some of the finest colonial buildings are dotted along the waterfront (St 1), especially just south of Psar Nath (p245), itself an architectural monument, albeit a modernist one.

Battambang's Buddhist temples survived the Khmer Rouge period relatively unscathed thanks to a local commander who ignored the destructive orders from on high. Some of the best include **Wat Phiphéthear-am** (វត្តពិភិទ្ទារាម; St 4), **Wat Damrey Sor** (White Elephant Pagoda, St 127) and **Wat Kandal** (Riverside Rd).

OFF THE BEATEN TRACK

CENTRAL CARDAMOMS NATIONAL PARK

Rangers in the Central Cardamoms Protected Forest, who are supported by Conservation International (www.conservation.org), operate out of three stations in the north that are rarely visited. Even so, the rangers and military police based there play a crucial role in defending the territory, particularly at the **Kravanh ranger station** deep in the jungle south of Pursat.

The most valuable contraband at the front-line **Rovieng ranger station** is aromatic *mreah prew* (sassafras, or safrole) oil, extracted from the roots of the endangered *Cinnamomum parthenoxylon* tree. One tonne of wood produces just 30L of the oil, which has a delightful, sandalwood-like scent. Local people use it in traditional medicine, but it's safrole oil's use as the precursor in the production of the drug MDMA that has caused the most illegal logging of this tree species.

A few kilometres from Rovieng (and 53km southwest of Pursat) are the **L'Bak Kamronh Rapids**, which attract Khmers on holidays. About 25km west of Rovieng, in Pramoay Commune, the old-growth **Chhrok Preal Forest** can also be visited (though it rarely is).

To prearrange a guide, homestay or guesthouse near the Kravanh or Rovieng ranger station, try contacting forestry official **Peov Somanak** (📞 017 464663; peovsomanak@gmail.com) for advice.

Battambang

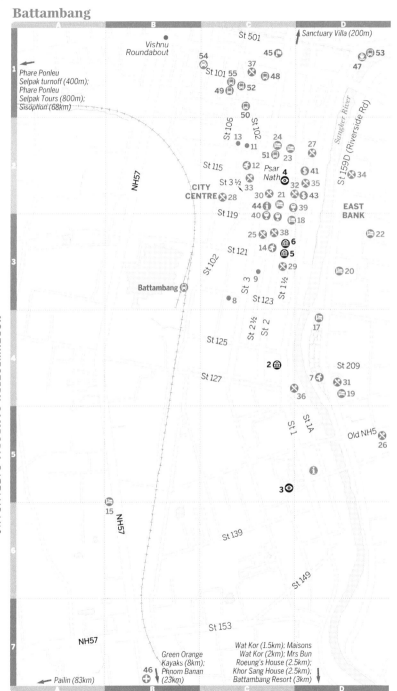

St 501

Vishnu Roundabout

54
45
53
47
St 101 55
37
48
49 52
50
St 102
St 106
13
11
24
27
51 23
St 115
12
41
Psar Nath
4
St 3½
33
32 35
CITY CENTRE 28
30 21 43
44
39
St 119
40
18
25 38
St 121
14
6
5
9
29
St 3
Battambang
8
St 123
St 1½
17
St 2½ St 2
St 125
2
St 127
7 31
36
19
St 1A
St 1
Old NH5
26
3
15
St 139
St 149
St 153

NH57

NH57

Sangker River

St 159D (Riverside Rd)

EAST BANK

22

20

Sanctuary Villa (200m)

Phare Ponleu Selpak turnoff (400m); Phare Ponleu Selpak Tours (800m); Sisophon (68km)

Green Orange Kayaks (8km); Phnom Banan (23km)

Wat Kor (1.5km); Maisons Wat Kor (2km); Mrs Bun Roeung's House (2.5km); Khor Sang House (2.5km); Battambang Resort (3km)

46

Pailin (83km)

Wat Kor Village
VILLAGE

(ភូមិវត្តគរ) About 2km south of central Battambang, the village of Wat Kor is centred around the **temple** (វត្តគរ) of the same name. It's a great place to wander, especially late in the afternoon when the opposite (east) bank of the Sangker River is bathed in amber tones by the sinking sun. Picturesque bridges span the river, the spires of Wat Kor glow bright platinum and Khmer village life is on full display.

About 1.5km beyond Wat Kor, you'll encounter the cluster of Khmer **heritage houses** that the village is known for. Built of now-rare hardwoods over a century ago and surrounded by orchard gardens, they have wide verandahs and exude the ambience of another era.

Two of the approximately 20 heritage houses in the Wat Kor area are open to visitors: **Mrs Bun Roeung's Ancient House** (ផ្ទះបុរាណអ្នកស្រី ប៊ិន រឿង; ☑ 017 818419; www.facebook.com/mrsbunshouse; suggested donation US$1) and neighbouring **Khor Sang House** (ផ្ទះបុរាណ; ☑ 092 467264; suggested donation US$1). The owner of each will give you a short tour in French or English. They have floors worn lustrous by a century of bare feet and are decorated with old furniture and family photos.

Mrs Bun Roeung's Ancient House was built in 1920 by a local lawyer. The owners have turned the rear section of the house into homestay accommodation – a unique option for architecture and history fans.

Khor Sang House was built in 1907 by the French-speaking owner's grandfather, who served as a secretary to the province's last Thai governor. The rear section dates from 1890.

Battambang Museum
MUSEUM

(សារមន្ទីរខេត្តបាត់ដំបង; ☑ 012 238320; St 1; US$3; ⊙ 8-11am & 2-5.30pm) This petite provincial museum has been given a full makeover thanks to the generous support of Friends of Khmer Culture (FOKC; www.khmerculture.net) and now has state-of-the-art lighting and detailed signage in English and Khmer. There are some beautiful Angkorian lintels and elegant statuary from all over Battambang Province, including pieces from Prasat Banan and Sneng. There is also a detailed introduction to the pre-Angkorian Neolithic period of cave-dwelling in Laang Spean Cave.

Battambang

◉ **Top Sights**
1 Romcheik 5 Artspace E3

◉ **Sights**
2 Battambang Museum............................C4
3 Governor's Residence C5
4 Psar Nath C2
5 Sangker Gallery C3
6 Tep Kao Sol C3

◉ **Activities, Courses & Tours**
7 Aerobics Classes...................................D4
8 Australian Centres for
   Development C3
9 Battambang Bike C3
10 Butterfly Tours F7
11 Coconut Lyly C2
12 Hope of Blind Seeing Hand
   Massage C2
13 Nary Kitchen C2
14 Nature Boutique Spa C3
   Soksabike.......................................(see 32)

◉ **Sleeping**
15 Au Cabaret Vert......................................B5
16 Bambu Hotel...E3
17 Classy Hotel & Spa.................................D4
18 Ganesha Family Guesthouse..................C3
19 Here Be Dragons D4
20 La Villa D3
21 Pomme C2
   Royal Hotel.....................................(see 12)
22 Sangker Villa Guest House D3
23 Seng Hout Hotel.....................................C2
24 The Place..C2

◉ **Eating**
25 About the World C3
26 Battambang BBQ & Buffet D5
27 Cafe Eden...D2
28 Cafe HOC...C2
   Chinese Noodle Dumpling .... (see 6)
   Creperie Battambang...................(see 30)
29 Flavours of India C3
30 Garage Sandwich Bar C2

31 Green Mango Café & Bakery................D4
32 Jaan Bai...C2
   Kinyei...(see 32)
33 La Casa..C2
34 La Pizza D2
   La Villa .... (see 20)
35 Lonely Tree Cafe....................................C3
36 Night Market...D2
   Riceholic.. (see 21)
37 Riverside Night Market C4
38 Vegetarian Foods Restaurant...............C1

◉ **Drinking & Nightlife**
   Here Be Dragons...........................(see 19)
39 Libations Bar C3
   Madison Pub..................................(see 14)
40 Miss Wong Battambang C2
41 Vintage Wine Bar C3

◉ **Shopping**
   Bric-à-Brac ....(see 39)
   Jewel in the Lotus .... (see 21)
   Lonely Tree Shop...........................(see 25)

ⓘ **Information**
42 Canadia Bank D2
43 Handa Medical Centre F3
44 J Trust Royal Bank.................................D2
45 Pomme Tours..C2
46 Vietnamese Consulate...........................C1
47 Yi Quoc Clinic..B7

ⓘ **Transport**
48 Angkor Express.......................................D1
49 Bayon VIP C1
50 Cambotra Express...................................C1
51 Capitol Tour..C1
   Chann Na .... (see 48)
   Gecko Moto ....(see 44)
52 Mekong Express C2
53 Phnom Penh Sorya.................................C1
54 Rith Mony..D1
55 Taxi Station...C1
56 Virak Buntham..C1

Official entry is set at US$3 per person, but the staff were only requesting a US$1 donation during our visit.

Governor's Residence   NOTABLE BUILDING
(សាលាខេត្តបាត់ដំបង; off St 139; entry by donation) The two-storey Governor's Residence, with its balconies and wooden shutters, is a handsome legacy of the early 1900s. The interior is now open to the public and has a collection of grand old furnishings, old photographs and traditional costumes inside. It was designed by an Italian architect

for the last Thai governor, who departed in 1907.

Entrance is via a small gate on St 139 on the southern side of the extensive gardens.

Cambodia Peace Gallery   MUSEUM
(ពិពណ៌សន្តិភាពកម្ពុជា; ☏ 092 455934; http://cambodiapeacegallery.org; US$5; ◷ 9am-5pm) ✐ This small museum tells the big story of Cambodia's long journey from war to peace. Exhibits are well presented in a series of buildings in the spacious compound, including some original stained-glass windows

showing different aspects of Cambodia's recent history. Other sections include some context on landmines in Cambodia and the work Cambodian peacekeepers are doing all over the world.

To get here, follow the road south to Wat Banan for about 7km.

Psar Nath MARKET

(ផ្សារណាត់; St 1; ⊙6am-late) Battambang's central market is a notable piece of art deco modernist architecture.

🏃 Activities

Heritage
Walking Trail WALKING

(www.ka-tours.org) Phnom Penh–based Khmer Architecture Tours (p65) is highly regarded for its specialist tours in and around the capital and has collaborated with Battambang Municipality to create heritage walks in Battambang's historic centre. The walks concentrate both on the French period and on the modernist architecture of the '60s. The company's website has two downloadable PDFs including a colour map and numbered highlights.

The maps are also available in the free *Faceguide* pamphlet handed out at Bric-à-Brac (p251) and a few other places around town. This is a great way to spend half a day exploring the city. Those with less time can rent a bicycle and run the combined routes in just an hour or so.

Green Orange Kayaks KAYAKING

(☑012 720386; www.facebook.com/green orangebtb; Ksach Poy; kayak trip US$15) 🖉 Kayaks can be rented from Green Orange Kayaks, part of the Friends Economic Development Association (FEDA), a local NGO that runs a community centre in Ksach Poy village, 8km south of Battambang. Self-guided kayaking trips begin at Ksach Poy's Green Orange Cafe. From there you paddle back to the city along the Sangker River. Booking ahead is recommended.

FEDA also runs a guesthouse, the Green Orange Village Bungalows (p248).

Nature Boutique Spa SPA

(☑012 251569; www.natureboutiquespa.com; St 2½; massage US$7-12, scrubs US$10, facials US$8-15; ⊙9am-9pm) One of the most sophisticated spas in Battambang. Downstairs is a shop selling keepsakes and natural beauty products. Upstairs is the serene spa, which offers a range of very affordable rubs and scrubs.

Khmer New
Generation Organization VOLUNTEERING

(☑092 790597; www.kngocambodia.org; Bospo village) 🖉 This local NGO is always looking for volunteer teachers to help out with its English-language teaching programme. Commitments of one month or longer are preferred.

Aerobics Classes HEALTH & FITNESS

(St 159D; per person 1000r; ⊙6-7am & 5-7pm) Head to Battambang's east bank to see the locals burning off the rice carbs doing aerobics. Just five minutes of working out should be enough to teach you some numbers in Khmer.

Hope of Blind Seeing
Hand Massage MASSAGE

(☑089 782663; St 115; per hour US$7; ⊙8am-10pm) 🖉 Trained blind masseurs offer soothing work-overs in an air-conditioned space.

👩‍🍳 Courses

Coconut Lyly COOKING

(☑016 399339; St 111; per person US$10) These classes are run by Chef Lyly, a graduate from Siem Reap's Paul Dubrule Cooking School. Three-hour classes (start times 9am and 3.30pm) include a visit to Psar Nath market, preparing four typical Khmer dishes (recipe book included) and then eating your handiwork afterwards. The excellent restaurant here is open from 9am to 10pm.

Nary Kitchen COOKING

(☑012 763950; www.narykitchen.com; St 111; half-day course US$10) This popular cooking class includes a visit to the local market, a four-course menu and a keepsake recipe book. Courses start at 9am and 3.30pm, lasting about three hours, plus time to eat your creations. If you're more interested in eating than cooking, Nary's restaurant is open from 8am to 10pm.

Australian Centres
for Development LANGUAGE

(☑053-677 7772; www.acdcambodia.weebly.com; St 123) 🖉 Offers well-regarded Khmer language classes, with one-to-one lessons available as well as regular weekly classes.

🖐 Tours

★ Soksabike CYCLING

(☑012 542019; www.soksabike.com; St 1½; half/full day US$27/40; ⊙departs 7.30am) 🖉 Soksabike is a social enterprise aiming to connect visitors with the Cambodian countryside and its people. The half- and full-day trips cover 25km and 40km respectively, and include stops at family-run industries such as rice-paper making and the Prahoc Factory (p253), as well as a visit to a local home. Tour prices depend on group size.

It's associated with Kinyei (p249) cafe a few doors to the north.

Butterfly Tours
CYCLING

(☏086 959569; www.butterflytours.asia; St 309; half/full day from US$17/38; ☉departs 7.30am & 1.30pm) Begun by a group of local university students, Butterfly's bicycle tours are focused on landscapes and sights or traditional life in the local area. The traditional-livelihoods tour gets rave reviews from visitors, and the company also runs tours in Kampot and Siem Reap.

Phare Ponleu Selpak Tours
CULTURAL

(☏077 554413; https://phareps.org; US$5; ☉9.30am, 10.30am, 2.30pm & 3.30pm Mon-Fri) 🏆 Guests are welcome to take a guided tour of the Phare complex (p251) during the day and observe circus, dance, music, drawing and graphic-arts classes. This is definitely US$5 well spent, and if you buy a circus ticket as well, the cost drops to US$3.

Battambang Bike
CYCLING

(☏095 578878; www.thebattambangbike.com; St 2½; tours half/full day US$18/39; ☉7am-7pm) Leads a variety of bike tours, including a half-day city tour and a half-day cycle trip to Phnom Sampeau (p253). It also runs free Sunday fun-rides and rents out both city and mountain bikes (US$2 to $5 per day). Can do bike repairs also.

🛏 Sleeping

Most of Battambang's budget options are clustered close to the central Psar Nath market, while midrange and luxury accommodation tends to be either on the east bank or out of the centre. South of town near Wat Kor village (p243) are some dreamy, away-from-it-all stays where Brangelina used to hang out when they were an item.

City Centre

⭐ The Place
HOSTEL $

(☏096 454 9158; https://theplacebtb.wixsite.com/theplace; 53 St 3; dm from US$4.25, r from US$9; ❋🛜) Battambang's first flashpacker hostel,

The Place was designed by L'Atelier Architecture & Design, who work with bamboo and other natural materials. The results are impressive with a contemporary feel in a welcoming space. Some dorms have wood-tiled walls and cubicles; others are split by a curtain. The rooftop bar is a popular spot for a sundowner.

Pomme
HOSTEL $

(☏069 233620; www.facebook.com/Pommebat tambang; 61-63 St 2½; s US$5, d & tw US$10; 🛜) A lively little backpacker pad on popular St 2½, the accommodation here is in Japanese pod-style units. They are simple partitions and very small, but they definitely count as private rooms and are good value. The bar-restaurant downstairs is a great place to grab a meal or a drink, day or night.

Seng Hout Hotel
HOTEL $

(☏012 530327; www.senghouthotel.com; St 2; r US$15-25; ❋🛜🏊) Known for on-the-ball staff who are quick to help with traveller queries, the Seng Hout has a variety of nicely decorated rooms. Some are on the smaller side, so check out a few before deciding. The open-air rooftop space is a key drawcard, and the 3rd-floor pool has great views as well.

Use of the pool is free for guests (including those from the new annexe just a few blocks away), and US$2 for outsiders.

Ganesha Family Guesthouse
GUESTHOUSE $

(☏092 135570; www.ganeshaguesthouse.com; St 1½; dm US$4.50, r US$11-24; 🛜) The best of Battambang's cheapies, Ganesha has a light-filled dorm with double-wide beds, and small private rooms with bamboo furniture and tiled bathrooms (cold water only). Downstairs is a funky cafe with a pool table.

Royal Hotel
HOTEL $

(☏016 912034; St 115; s/d with fan US$7/10, r with air-con from US$15; ❋@🛜) An old-timer on the Battambang scene, the Royal is deservedly popular. Some rooms may be faded, but the air-con rooms are decently sized and come with fridge and TV. Staff here are some of the most clued-up in town, and there's a lively bar and Jacuzzi on the rooftop.

Au Cabaret Vert
BOUTIQUE HOTEL $$

(☏053-656 2000; www.aucabaretvert.com; NH57; r incl breakfast US$35-90; ❋🛜🏊) Contemporary meets colonial at this pretty resort, a short *tuk tuk* ride southwest of the centre. Rooms are stylish and include flat-screen TV and rain shower. The swimming pool

BATTAMBANG'S EMERGING ART SCENE

Before the Khmer Rouge era, Battambang had a long history as the nation's hub for art and culture. Today, a new generation of artists is building on this heritage and Battambang is regaining its reputation as Cambodia's cultural capital. A clutch of galleries, shops and cool bars has set up in recent years – many of them on Sts 2 and 2½, creating an informal arts district right in the heart of town. Check out the local scene at the following spots:

Jewel in the Lotus (☑092 260158; 53 St 2½; ⊘8am-5pm; 🛜) This gallery features paintings, prints, vintage items, unique postcards, souvenirs, underground comics, literature, clothing and jewellery. The owner couple, Darren Swallow and Khchao Touch, know the Battambang art scene well, and Touch is a top artist in her own right.

Romcheik 5 Artspace (វិចិត្រសាលជនបទ វិចេកម៥; ☑089 373683; St 201A; US$2.50; ⊘2-7pm) This impressive space has a permanent collection upstairs displaying the edgy, contemporary works of its four founders, who in their youth were expelled from Thailand and forced to work as child labourers, before being rescued by an NGO and encouraged to express themselves through art.

Sangker Gallery (វិចិត្រសាលសង្កែ; ☑087 298086; 194 St 2; ⊘9.30am-noon & 2-6pm Mon-Fri) This little, two-storey art space hosts regular exhibitions by local artists. The gallery also runs a city art tour from 2pm to 6pm. Cost depends on the number of participants, starting at US$25 per person for two people, and the tour must be booked at least one day in advance.

Tep Kao Sol (ទេពកោសល្យ; ☑017 982992; St 2; ⊘9am-9pm) This is the gallery space of local artist Loeum Lorn, who's known for creating works out of melting coloured ice and then photographing them. It's open sporadically, so just stop by and hope for the best.

is a natural, self-cleaning pond surrounded by lush gardens, and the French-influenced food is top-notch.

Sanctuary Villa BOUTIQUE HOTEL **$$**
(☑097 216 7168; www.thesanctuaryvillabattambang.com; off St Tea Cham Rath; r incl breakfast US$50-80; ✦@🛜☀) This intimate, luxurious boutique hotel has 16 attractive villas furnished with traditional woods, tasteful silks and throw rugs, but the out-of-the-way location is not for everybody. From the White Horse roundabout on St 501 go 500m north and take a right.

East Bank

★ **Here Be Dragons** HOSTEL **$**
(☑089 264895; www.herebedragonsbattambang.com; St 159D; fan/air-con dm US$4/6, r from US$12/15; ✦🛜) A stylish fun bar, leafy front garden for relaxing and free beer on arrival make Here Be Dragons a top backpacker base. Six- and eight-bed dorms come with lock-boxes, while sunny private rooms are cheerfully decked out with brightly coloured bedding. The quiet location next to the riverside park on the east bank is a bonus.

Regular events include yoga on Tuesday and Thursday and a pub quiz on Wednesday.

★ **Bambu Hotel** HOTEL **$$**
(☑053-953900; www.bambuhotel.com; St 203; r incl breakfast US$60-90; ✦@🛜☀) Bambu's spacious rooms are designed in a Franco-Khmer motif with gorgeous tiling, stone-inlaid bathrooms and exquisite furniture. The fusion restaurant is one of the best in town and the poolside bar invites lingering. Above all else, though, it's Bambu's gracious staff that set it in a category above Battambang's other boutique offerings. Book ahead, as it's deservedly popular.

La Villa BOUTIQUE HOTEL **$$**
(☑053-730151; www.lavilla-battambang.com; St 159D; s/d/tr incl breakfast from US$65/70/75; ✦@🛜☀) For a taste of the colonial era, stay at this French-era villa renovated in vintage 1930s style. It's one of the most romantic boutique hotels in Cambodia. Gauzy mosquito nets drape over four-poster beds, original tilework graces the floors and art deco features adorn every corner, creating an old-world ambience that is hard to beat.

Sangker Villa
Guest House
BOUTIQUE HOTEL $$

(☏097 764 0017; www.sangkervilla.com; off St 203; r incl breakfast US$25-65; ✷ ☎ ☒) Sangker Villa offers the atmosphere of a boutique homestay thanks to its intimate size and is great value for money. Out back the small pool and bar provide tranquil retreats, while the bright, simply decorated rooms come with contemporary bathrooms.

Classy Hotel & Spa
HOTEL $$

(☏053-952555; www.classyhotelspa.com; St 159D; superior/deluxe/VIP r US$50/60/70; ✷ ☎ ☒) This popular monolith on the east bank of the Sangker River draws a loyal crowd thanks to its amenities, which nonguests can also enjoy. It has an excellent spa (go for a cheap, hour-long Khmer massage followed by a soak in the hot tub), a rooftop bar with stunning city views and a refreshing pool that's popular with the international crowd.

Beyond the Centre

Green Orange
Village Bungalows
GUESTHOUSE $$

(☏012 736166; www.facebook.com/green orangebtb; Ksach Poy; bungalows incl breakfast from US$20; ☎ ☒) 🍃 This smart and super clean little place is run by local NGO FEDA in the sleepy village of Ksach Poy, 8km south of Battambang. The extensive gardens include a swimming pool, and the operators offer kayaking trips on the Sangker River.

★ Maisons Wat Kor
BOUTIQUE HOTEL $$$

(☏098 555377; www.maisonswatkor.com; Wat Kor village; r incl breakfast from US$120; ✷ ☎ ☒) 🍃 About 2km south of central Battambang, Maisons Wat Kor is a secluded sanctuary of 10 rooms in traditional-style Khmer houses that once welcomed Angelina Jolie and Brad Pitt. Rooms are light-filled, spacious and come with contemporary bathrooms, and the saltwater swimming pool surrounded by lush foliage provides plenty of opportunity for chill-out time. The delightful, open-air restaurant welcomes nonguests.

Battambang Resort
RESORT $$$

(☏012 510100; www.battambangresort.com; Wat Kor village; r US$65-95; ✷ ☎ ☒) Down a dirt road from laid-back Wat Kor village (p243), Battambang Resort is a place to unwind in style. Surroundings include ponds with lily pads, tropical gardens and rice fields, while the interior common spaces feature Cambodian art and cultural artefacts and are slung with hammocks. Service is top-notch. The fine restaurant draws many ingredients from an on-site garden.

DON'T MISS

BATTAMBANG'S BAMBOO TRAIN

One of the world's unique rail journeys, Battambang's bamboo train has had many an obituary written about it over the years, but somehow it's still on the rails, despite the launch of proper passenger services on the line from Battambang to Phnom Penh and Poipet.

The **original bamboo train** (www.bambootrain.com; per person US$5; ⌚6am-6pm) used to trundle from O Dambong, a few kilometres east of Battambang's old French bridge (Wat Kor Bridge), to O Sra Lav along warped, misaligned rails and vertiginous bridges left by the French. Each bamboo train – known in Khmer as a *norry* – consists of a 3m-long wooden frame, covered lengthwise with slats made of ultralight bamboo, resting on two barbell-like bogies, connected by belts to a 6HP gasoline engine. With a pile of 10 or 15 people, or up to 3 tonnes of rice, it could cruise along at about 15km/h.

The genius of the system is that it offers a solution to the most ineluctable problem faced on any single-track line: what to do when two trains going in opposite directions meet. In the case of bamboo trains, the answer is simple: one car is quickly disassembled and set on the ground beside the tracks so that the other can pass.

This original stretch of line is up and running again, albeit with new bridges and straight tracks. Encroaching foliage has been cut back along the track, so while it is a sanitised version of the old bamboo train, it is still a fun experience.

A local investor has also created a **new track** (US$5 per person; ⌚6am-6pm) about 20km away near Prasat Banan (p254), to reconstruct the bamboo-train experience. However, it is more like a kiddies' roller-coaster ride than the original bamboo train, but it does pass through some scenic rock formations around the base of Phnom Banan. There is no need to decamp from the bamboo train on this line, as the track has passing points.

There's a free shuttle to town, but many guests prefer to just relax around the salt-water pool.

Eating

The heart of Battambang's culinary scene is its neighbouring Cambodian cooking schools, Coconut Lyly (p245) and Nary Kitchen (p245), which double as restaurants. There's a fine selection of international restaurants, in and out of town, including those at leading boutique hotels like Bambu Hotel, La Villa (p250) and Maisons Wat Kor. For street food, the original **night market** (snacks & mains 2000-8000r; ⊙4-9pm), at the northeast corner of Psar Nath, dishes up barbecued chicken, fish and pork.

City Centre

★ Lonely Tree Cafe   CAFE $
(www.thelonelytreecafe.com; St 2½; mains US$4-5.50; ⊙10am-10pm; 🛜) 🌿 Upstairs from the shop of the same name, this uber-cosy cafe serves Spanish tapas-style dishes and a few Khmer options under a soaring, bamboo-inlaid ceiling. Its mascot is an actual tree on the road to Siem Reap. Proceeds support cultural preservation and people with disabilities, among other causes.

Kinyei   CAFE $
(www.kinyei.org; 1 St 1½; coffee US$1.50-2.50, mains US$2.75-5.25; ⊙7am-4pm; 🛜) 🌿 Besides having the best coffee in town (national barista champs have been crowned here), teensy-weensy Kinyei does surprisingly good Mexican food, vegie burgers, energy salads and some of the best breakfasts in town. Aussies will appreciate the long blacks and flat whites among the coffee selection.

Garage Sandwich Bar   CAFE $
(🖉012 785507; www.facebook.com/garagebattambang; St 2½; sandwiches US$2.50; ⊙7am-6pm; 🛜) So this is a curious combination of bike-repair shop and bakery, but it works thanks to freshly baked bread and some of the best-value sandwiches in Cambodia. Choose anything from meatballs to cheese and pack a picnic for a motorbike adventure in the countryside. No rentals available, only repairs.

About the World   INTERNATIONAL $
(🖉086 920476; St 2½; mains US$2.50-4; ⊙8am-10pm Mon-Sat; 🍴) Travellers love this cosy spot for its relaxed ambience and tasty vegetarian options, including the recommended Spanish omelette and tofu burger. Those who sit indoors, where art and photography festoon the walls, do so barefoot and perched atop floor pillows. The home-brewed jackfruit rice wine (US$1) is deliciously potent.

Cafe HOC   FUSION $
(🖉012 591210; https://hopeofchildren.net; cnr Sts 106 & 117; mains US$3-4; ⊙8am-2pm & 5-10pm; 🛜) 🌿 This social enterprise has an inviting photographic menu with a compact list of Khmer and Japanese favourites, but it's best known for its all-you-can-eat Western/Khmer breakfast for just US$3. Wicker furniture and a wall-mounted chalkboard specials menu liven up the somewhat underwhelming space on a busy street corner.

The cafe supports Hope of Children, a local orphanage.

Chinese Noodle Dumpling   NOODLES $
(Lan Chov Khorko Miteanh; 🖉092 589639; 145 St 2; mains 4000-8000r; ⊙9am-9pm) The Chinese chef at this Battambang institution does bargain dumplings and serves fresh noodles a dozen or more ways, including with pork or duck soup.

Vegetarian Foods Restaurant   VEGETARIAN $
(St 102; mains 1500-3000r; ⊙6.30am-2pm; 🍴) This hole-in-the-wall eatery serves some of the most delicious vegetarian dishes in Cambodia, including rice soup, homemade soy milk and dumplings for just 1000r. Tremendous value.

Flavors of India   INDIAN $
(🖉053-731553; http://flavorsofindia.webs.com; St 121; mains US$3.50-7; ⊙9.30am-11pm; 🛜🍴) This Battambang outpost of a popular Phnom Penh Indian restaurant opened after some curry-craving expats ordered take-away all the way from the capital (290km to the southeast). Opt for the thalis (US$6 to US$8) for an excellent-value meal.

Riverside Night Market   CAMBODIAN $
(St 1; mains 4000-8000r; ⊙3pm-midnight) Locals in the mood for good-value Khmer food flock to about a dozen neon-lit eateries across the street from the Battambang Museum.

★ Jaan Bai   FUSION $$
(🖉078 263144; www.facebook.com/jaanbaicct; cnr Sts 1½ & 2; small plates US$3, mains US$4-10; ⊙11am-9pm; 🛜🍴) 🌿 Jaan Bai ('rice bowl' in Khmer) is Battambang's foodie treat, with a sleekly minimalist interior offset by beautiful French-Khmer tilework lining the

wall. The menu likewise is successfully bold. Order a few of the small plates to experience the range of flavours, or go all out with the tasting menu: seven plates plus wine for US$15 per person (minimum two people).

Jaan Bai trains and employs vulnerable youth through the Cambodian Children's Trust (www.cambodianchildrenstrust.org).

★Riceholic   JAPANESE $$
(☏087 483731; 39 St 2½; mains US$3.75-9.75; ⊙11.30am-2pm & 6-10pm, closed Tue; ☷) Run by a Japanese couple who operated pop-up kitchens in Australia, Riceholic specialises in making its own seasonings and a traditional koji (fermented sauce) from Battambang rice. The menu offers speciality ramen with a healthy tonkotsu broth made from cashew nut, plus delicious sushi and gyoza also feature on the menu.

Cafe Eden   CAFE $$
(☏053-731525; www.cafeedencambodia.com; St 1; mains US$4-7; ⊙7.30am-9pm Wed-Mon; ❋☷) 🖉 This American-run social enterprise offers a relaxed space for a hearty breakfast or an afternoon coffee. The compact lunch-and-dinner menu is Asian-fusion style, with burgers, Tex-Mex tastings, some of the best fries in town and superior jam-jar shakes, all amid blissful air-con.

At the back, its boutique sells a small range of clothing and crafts.

Creperie Battambang   FRENCH $$
(☏085 662530; 76 St 2½; crêpes US$4-7; ⊙8am-3pm & 6-10pm; ☷) Sample some delicious savoury French crêpes at this hole-in-the-wall eatery. These are Breton-style buckwheat flour pancakes and are gluten free and stuffed with goodies like cured ham and goat cheese. Sweet crêpes are also available for dessert.

La Casa   ITALIAN $$
(St 115; mains US$5-10; ⊙11am-2.30pm & 5-10pm Tue-Sun; ☷) Out of an attractive space near the bus offices, La Casa serves one of the best thin-crust pizzas in Battambang, as well as excellent pasta dishes and salads.

East Bank

Green Mango Café & Bakery   BAKERY $
(☏017 315450; www.greenmangocambodia.com; St 159D; dishes US$2.50-5; ⊙7am-8.30pm; ❋☷) Much more than just a bakery, Green Mango serves salads, sandwiches and delicious appetisers like hummus and black-bean na-

chos to complement its coffee and tea list. It has crisp air-con and wi-fi for those looking to hang out awhile.

It's a social enterprise, too, helping poor women from the countryside find work.

Battambang BBQ & Buffet   BARBECUE $
(☏096 303 3833; Old NH5; buffet 26,000r; ⊙5-10pm; ☷) Offering an all-inclusive tabletop barbecue and serve-yourself buffet, this place is unbelievably popular with local Khmers and domestic tourists. Exceptional value if you come with a hunger.

★La Villa   INTERNATIONAL $$
(☏053-730151; St 159D; mains US$5-15; ⊙11am-3pm & 6-9.30pm; ❋☷) Battambang's most atmospheric dinner option dishes up delectable Khmer, Vietnamese, French and Italian dishes, plus wines from around the world. Specialities include a tender fish fillet in lemon sauce. Sit inside under the glass atrium or bask in the colonial glow of the courtyard outside, and start with the local ice tea.

La Pizza   PIZZA $$
(☏093 607417; St 159D; pizzas US$6-10; ⊙5-10pm, closed Thu; ☷) Pizzas come in every shape and size at the popular east-bank restaurant, including by the slice (US$1.75), half size, full size and extra large. La Pizza is set in an elegant traditional wooden house with a lantern-lit garden.

🍷 Drinking & Nightlife

Here Be Dragons   BAR
(St 159D; ⊙7am-midnight; ☷) Before there was the popular Here Be Dragons hostel (p247), there was this popular bar. The watering hole hasn't forgotten its roots, and frequently rumbles till late with a mix of backpackers and expats. It offers a Wednesday pub quiz, informal ping-pong tourneys and a Saturday afternoon BBQ.

Madison Pub   BAR
(☏012 415513; St 2½; ⊙11am-late) Long-running Madison Pub may no longer occupy the strategic corner it once did, but it remains one of the best late-night bars in Battambang thanks to the convivial owner Patrice. Cheap beer, homemade rice wine and a pool table keep the crowds coming, and the kitchen turns out some fusion flavours.

Miss Wong Battambang   COCKTAIL BAR
(http://misswong.net; St 2; ⊙6pm-1am; ☷) A sophisticated Battambang outpost of one of Siem Reap's most popular cocktail bars,

Miss Wong is situated in a characterful old shophouse on St 2 and looks like a little slice of old Shanghai. Creative cocktails and Chinese dim sum are available, including lots of seasonal favourites with fresh fruit.

Vintage Wine Bar   WINE BAR
(☎086 404929; St 2½; ☺4-11pm; 🛜) Vintage is an inviting little wine bar that offers a menu of tapas-style light bites from Cambodia, Japan and the Med, including some tasting boards of cold cuts and cheeses. Happy hours run from 4pm and include wine specials like US$2 per glass and US$12 per bottle. Cheers!

Libations Bar   BAR
(☎077 531562; 112 St 2; ☺5-9pm; 🛜) Downstairs in the Bric-à-Brac hotel, this classy streetside bar caters to a relatively refined crowd with creative cocktails, craft beer, and wine and champagne by the glass. The chatty owners are a great source of information on the area. Upstairs are three arty, designed rooms.

⭐ Entertainment

★ Phare Ponleu Selpak   CIRCUS
(☎077 554413; www.phareps.org; adult/child US$14/7) Battambang's signature attraction is the internationally acclaimed circus (*cirque nouveau*) of this multi-arts centre for Cambodian children. Although it also runs shows in Siem Reap, it's worth timing your visit to Battambang to watch this amazing spectacle where it began. Shows are held two to four nights per week, depending on the season (check the website), and kick off at 7pm.

Phare, as it's known to locals, is not just a circus and is involved in lots of other projects. It trains musicians, visual artists and performing artists as well. Many of the artists you'll bump into around town lived and studied at Phare. Guests are welcome to take a guided tour (p246) of the Phare complex during the day and observe circus, dance, music, drawing and graphic-arts classes.

Tickets are sold at the door from 6pm and at many retailers around town. To get here from the Vishnu Roundabout on NH5, head west for 900m, then turn right and continue another 600m.

🔒 Shopping

Bric-à-Brac   HOMEWARES
(☎077 531549; www.bric-a-brac.asia; 112 St 2; ☺9am-9pm) This swish store, downstairs in the bijou hotel of the same name, sells handmade *passementrie* (trimmings), textiles, antiques and accessories. It also produces some of the world's finest tassels for export.

Lonely Tree Shop   ARTS & CRAFTS
(☎053-953123; 56 St 2½; ☺10am-10pm) 🖊
Fine silk bags, chunky jewellery, fashionable shirts and skirts: definitely not your run-of-the-mill charity gift shop.

ℹ️ Information

For information on what's happening in town, look out for copies of the free, biannual *Battambang Buzz* magazine, and visit the handy *Battambang Traveller* website (https://battambangtravellerposts.tumblr.com).

Informative **Pomme Tours** (☎092 955744; St 2½; ☺9am-7pm) does transport and tour bookings, rents out *motos* and sells interesting local handicrafts and clothing. A decent city map is distributed by the otherwise moribund **tourist information office** (☎012 534177; www.tourismbattambang.org; St 1; ☺7.30-11.30am & 2-5.30pm Mon-Fri).

Free wi-fi access is the norm at hotels and most cafes and restaurants.

J Trust Royal Bank (St 1; ☺8am-4pm Mon-Fri, ATM 24hr)

Canadia Bank (Psar Nath; ☺8am-3.30pm Mon-Fri, to 11.30am Sat, ATM 24hr)

Handa Medical Centre (☎095 520654; https://thehandafoundation.org/programs/medical-center; NH5; ☺emergency 24hr) Has two ambulances and usually a European doctor or two in residence.

Yi Quoc Clinic (☎012 530171, 053-953163; off NH57; ☺24hr) The best clinic in town.

Vietnamese Consulate (p351) Issues visas in a day.

ℹ️ Getting There & Away

Battambang is 290km northwest of Phnom Penh along NH5 and 80km northeast of Pailin along NH57 (formerly NH10).

BOAT

The riverboat to Siem Reap (US$20, 7am daily) squeezes through narrow waterways and passes protected wetlands, taking from five hours in the wet season to nine or more hours at the height of the dry season. Cambodia's most memorable boat trip, it's operated on alternate days by **Angkor Express** (☎012 601287) and **Chann Na** (☎012 354344), which have informal offices on the docks at the eastern end of St 501, where the boats leave from. Buy tickets in advance.

In the dry season, passengers are driven to a navigable section of the river. The best seats are away from the noisy motor. It may be possible to alight at the Prek Toal Bird Sanctuary (p134) and then be picked up there the next day for US$5 extra. Be aware that these boats, while scenic, are not always popular with local communities along the way, as the wake has caused small boats to capsize and fishing nets are regularly snagged. Many travellers also complain of overcrowding and safety issues, as there are rarely enough life jackets to go around.

BUS

Some buses now arrive and depart from Battambang's **bus station** (NH5), 2km west of the centre. Companies offer free shuttles for departing passengers, but arriving passengers will have to pay for a *remork* (US$3) into town. However, for departures from Battambang, most companies still use their company offices, which are clustered in the centre just south of the intersection of NH5 and St 4.

To Phnom Penh, if you're pinching pennies, **Capitol Tour** (☑ 012 810055; St 102) and **Rith Mony** (☑ 092 888847; St 1) generally have the lowest prices, followed by **Phnom Penh Sorya** (☑ 092 181804; St 106). For a quicker journey to the capital, many companies run express minivan services (US$8 to US$12, 4½ hours), including **Cambotra Express** (☑ 017 866286; St 106), Capitol Tour, **Bayon VIP** (☑ 070 968966; St 101), **Mekong Express** (☑ 088 576 7668; St 3) and **Virak Buntham** (☑ 017 333572; St 106).

Virak Buntham runs full-recline-sleeper night buses to Phnom Penh, but be aware that these, like all night buses to Phnom Penh, arrive at an ungodly hour.

The Mekong Express minibus is the most comfortable way to Siem Reap (US$7, 3½ hours, 8am and 2pm), while Bayon VIP runs a speedy minivan service (US$10, three hours, four daily).

Most buses to Bangkok involve a change at the border – usually to a minibus on the Thai side.

TAXI

At the **taxi station** (cnr Sts 101 & 110), share taxis to Phnom Penh (40,000r per person, 4½ hours) and Pursat (20,000r, two hours) leave from the southeast corner. Also here you'll find share taxis to Poipet (20,000r, 1¾ hours), Sisophon (16,000r, 1¼ hours) and Siem Reap (26,000r, three hours). Share taxis to Pailin (20,000r, two hours) and the Psar Pruhm–Ban Pakard (25,000r, 2½ hours) border leave from the corner of St 101 and St 4.

Prices are based on six-passenger occupancy; for the price of a whole taxi, multiply the per-passenger fare by six.

TRAIN

Very limited passenger **trains** (http://royalrailway.easybook.com) have resumed on the Battambang to Phnom Penh (US$5 per person) line with two trains per week leaving in either direction, taking around eight hours. The train departs Phnom Penh at 7.30am on Friday and Sunday and departs Battambang at 10.05am on Saturday and Monday. There are also services to Sisophon (US$3) and Poipet (US$4) at 3.10pm on Friday and Sunday. More frequent services will eventually be introduced, but there is still ongoing renovation work on some sections of the railway.

ⓘ Getting Around

English- and French-speaking *remork-moto* drivers are commonplace in Battambang, and all are eager to whisk you around on day trips. A half-day trip out of town to a single sight such as Phnom Sampeau might cost US$12, while a full-day trip taking in three sights costs US$15 to US$20, depending on your haggling skills. A *moto* costs about half that.

BUSES FROM BATTAMBANG

DESTINATION	DURATION (HR)	COST (US$)	COMPANIES	FREQUENCY
Bangkok, Thailand	9	15-16	Mekong Express, PP Sorya, Virak Buntham, Capitol	7.45am, 8.30am, 10.30am, 11.30am, noon
Ho Chi Minh City, Vietnam	10-11	26	Mekong Express	7.30am
Kompong Cham	8	9	Rith Mony	9am
Pailin	1¼	4	Rith Mony	1pm, 3pm
Phnom Penh (day)	4½-7	5-12	All companies	frequent
Phnom Penh (night)	5-6	6-15	Capitol, Mekong Express, TSS, Virak Buntham	frequent, 10pm to midnight
Poipet	2¼	4	Capitol, PP Sorya, Rith Mony, TSS	regular to 4pm
Siem Reap	3-4	4-10	Capitol, Bayon VIP, Mekong Express, PP Sorya, Rith Mony	regular to 3pm

ROADS TO WAT EK PHNOM

The rural lanes that squiggle out from Battambang are brimming with paddy-field panoramas and tiny villages where traditional crafts and produce are made. The roads leading to Wat Ek Phnom temple are particularly rewarding to explore and make for a great half-day circuit, soaking up a mix of historic sights and village life. Some highlights:

Wat Somrong Knong (វត្តសំរោងក្នុង) Built in the 19th century on the site of a pre-Angkorian temple complex, this wat was used by the Khmer Rouge as a prison, and it's believed that around 10,000 people were executed here. The complex today houses the gorgeous main pagoda and a mishmash of ancient ruins, glittery modern structures and memorials to those who perished here.

Prahoc Factory (ផ្សារប្រហុក) Here visitors can see the bustling local industry behind Cambodian *prahoc* (fermented fish paste), and the photogenic bamboo trays of fish drying in the sun along the roadside.

Pheam Ek (ពាមឯក) The industry of the village of Pheam Ek is making rice paper for spring rolls. All along the road, in family workshops, you'll see rice paste being steamed and then placed on a bamboo frame to dry in the sun.

Wat Ek Phnom (វត្តឯកភ្នំ; US$2) Hidden behind a colourful modern pagoda and a gargantuan Buddha statue is this atmospheric, partly collapsed 11th-century temple measuring 52m by 49m and surrounded by the remains of a laterite wall and an ancient *baray* (reservoir). A lintel showing the Churning of the Ocean of Milk can be seen above the eastern entrance to the central temple, whose upper flanks hold some fine bas-reliefs.

A *moto* ride in town costs around 2000r, while a *remork* ride starts from US$1.50.

Gecko Moto (089 924260; St 1; 8am-10pm) and the Royal Hotel (p246) rent out motorbikes for US$6 to US$8 per day. Bicycles can be rented at the Royal Hotel, Soksabike (p246) and Battambang Bike (p246) for about US$2 per day.

Around Battambang

The countryside around Battambang is dotted with old temples and other worthwhile sights. Heading south, Prasat Banan (p254) and Phnom Sampeau can be combined for a good half-day trip by *moto* or *remork-moto*. Moving north, a half-day excursion can take in Wat Ek Phnom, Wat Somrong Knong and a few other sites.

Combined admission to Phnom Sampeau, Prasat Banan and Wat Ek Phnom costs US$3 (if you purchase a ticket at Prasat Banan, it's valid all day long at the other two).

A detailed guidebook on many sites in the area is *Around Battambang* (US$10) by Ray Zepp, which has details on temples, wats and excursions in the Battambang and Pailin areas. Proceeds go to monks and nuns working to raise HIV/AIDS awareness and to help AIDS orphans.

Phnom Sampeau

This fabled limestone outcrop (ភ្នំសំពៅ; US$1) 12km southwest of Battambang along NH57 (towards Pailin) is known for its gorgeous views and mesmerising display of bats, which pour out of a massive cave in its cliff face. Access to the summit is via a cement road or – if you're in need of a workout – a steep staircase. The road is too steep for *remorks*. *Moto* drivers hang out near the base of the hill and can whisk you up and back for US$4.

About halfway up to the summit, a road leads under a gate and 250m up to the Killing Caves of Phnom Sampeau, now a place of pilgrimage. A staircase, flanked by greenery, leads into a cavern, where a golden reclining Buddha lies peacefully next to a glass-walled memorial filled with bones and skulls – the remains of some of the people bludgeoned to death by Khmer Rouge cadres and then thrown through the skylight above. Next to the base of the stairway is the old memorial, a rusty cage made of chicken wire and cyclone fencing and partly filled with human bones.

On the summit, several viewpoints can be discovered amid a complex of temples. As you descend from the summit's golden stupa, dating from 1964, turn left under the gate decorated with a **bas-relief** of Eiy Sei (an elderly Buddha). A deep **canyon**, its vertical sides cloaked in greenery, descends 144 steps through a natural arch to a 'lost world' of stalactites, creeping vines and bats; two Angkorian warriors stand guard.

Near the westernmost of the two antennae at the summit, two government **artillery pieces**, one with markings in Russian, the other in German, are still deployed. Near the base of the western antenna, jockey for position with other tourists on the **sunset lookout pavilion**. Looking west you'll spy Phnom Krapeu (Crocodile Mountain), a one-time Khmer Rouge stronghold.

If you visit on your own, a local guide may try to escort you around the sites and give you some history. Back down at the hill base, people gather at dusk (around 5.30pm) to witness the spectacle of a thick column of bats pouring from a cave high up on the north side of the cliff face. The display lasts a good 30 minutes as millions of bats head out in a looping line to their feeding grounds near Tonlé Sap. Note that there are lots of monkeys at this site, and you should not be flashy with your food, as angry monkeys have been known to become aggressive.

Prasat Banan

It's a 358-stone-step climb up **Phnom Banan** (ប្រាសាទភ្នំបាណន់; US$3; ⊙6am-sunset) to reach Prasat Banan, but the incredible views across surrounding countryside from the top are worth it. Udayadityavarman II, son of Suryavarman I, built Prasat Banan in the 11th century; some locals claim the five-tower layout here was the inspiration for Angkor Wat, although this seems optimistic. There are impressive carved lintels above the doorways to each of the towers

LANDMINE ALERT

Pailin and nearby parts of Battambang Province (especially the districts of Samlaut and Rotanak Mondol) are some of the most heavily landmined places in the world. De-mining sites are commonplace, sometimes quite close to the highway, and numerous amputees bear sad tribute to the horror of landmines. Stay well on the beaten track in these parts. Public roads are OK, but farm roads are risky, and venturing into Pailin's beautiful forests on foot is definitely *not* a good idea.

and bas-reliefs on the upper parts of the central tower. From the temple, a narrow stone staircase leads down the hill to three caves, which can be visited with a local guide.

Prasat Banan is 23km south of Battambang.

Prasat Phnom Banan Winery

Midway between Battambang and Prasat Banan, in an area known for its production of chilli peppers (harvested from October to January), Cambodia's only **winery** (កន្លែងផលិតស្រាភ្នំបាណន់; ☑012 665238; Bot Sala village; wine tasting US$2.50, bottles US$15-25; ⊙8am-8pm) grows Shiraz grapes to make reds. It tastes unlike most wine you've ever encountered, but is actually quite earthy and complex.

Officially recognised by Cambodia's Ministry of Industry, Mines & Energy, Banan wines belong to that exclusive club of wineries whose vintages improve significantly with the addition of ice cubes. Also made here is Banan brandy, which has a heavenly bouquet and a taste that has been compared to turpentine. Sampling takes place in an attractive garden pavilion.

The winery is 10km south of Battambang and 8km north of Prasat Banan.

Kamping Pouy

Also known as the Killing Dam, **Kamping Puoy** (កំពីងពួយ) was one of the many grandiose Khmer Rouge projects intended to recreate the sophisticated irrigation networks that helped Cambodia wax mighty under the kings of Angkor. As many as 10,000 Cambodians are thought to have perished during its construction, worked to death under the shadow of executions, malnutrition and disease.

There's little to see, but people come to picnic, and to take row boats (10,000r for two hours) out on the water.

These days, thanks to the dam, the Kamping Puoy area is one of the few parts of Cambodia to produce two rice crops a year.

Kamping Puoy is 27km west of Battambang (go via NH5 and follow the irrigation canal). It's easy to combine a visit here with a stop at Phnom Sampeau (p253).

PAILIN

☑055 / POP 36,000

Apart from shopping for gemstones and visiting a particularly colourful hilltop temple, the remote Wild West town of Pailin (ប៉ៃលិន) has little to recommend it. That said, the forested Cardamom foothills surrounding the city are beautiful. Just don't wander into them by yourself; undetonated mines are still present and caution is vital.

⊙ Sights

Phnom Khieu Waterfall   WATERFALL
(ភ្នំក្បៀវ, Blue Mountain Waterfall; motorbike/car 3000/10,000r) Phnom Khieu is the most accessible of the numerous waterfalls dropping out of the Cardamoms south of Pailin, and has water year-round. To get here, turn right off NH57 1.5km east of Wat Phnom Yat, then proceed 5km on a rough road (which gets dodgy in the rainy season). From the entrance, cross the small river via the dirt road and walk about 3km to the falls.

The area's other waterfalls are more difficult to access due to being at their most impressive during the rainy season, when the roads are often impassable. Getting to the more remote falls is risky because of the lingering presence of landmines.

Wat Phnom Yat   BUDDHIST TEMPLE
(វត្តភ្នំយ៉ាត; off NH57) From NH57, stairs lead through a garish gate up to Wat Phnom Yat, a psychedelic temple centred on an ancient *po* (sacred fig) tree. A 27m Buddha looms over the top of the staircase, while a path leads up to the colourful temple and the large golden stupas at the top of the hill.

Along the path a life-sized cement tableau shows naked sinners and their punishments: being heaved into a cauldron (the impious), de-tongued (liars) and forced to climb a spiny tree (adulterers). Medieval European triptychs don't portray a hell that is nearly so scary. The sunrises and sunsets at the top are usually nice enough to take your mind off the fire and brimstone.

Wat Khaong Kang   BUDDHIST TEMPLE
(វត្តគោងកាង) At the base of Phnom Yat hill, an impressive gate dating to 1968 leads to Wat Khaong Kang, an important centre for Buddhist teaching before the Khmer Rouge madness. The exterior wall is decorated with an especially long bas-relief of the Churning of the Ocean of Milk.

🛏 Sleeping & Eating

Pailin Ruby Guesthouse   GUESTHOUSE $
(☏ 016 477933; NH57; s with fan US$6-8, d with fan US$8-11, s with air-con US$11, d with air-con US$13-16; ❋❃) A good-value place in the centre,

Pailin

⊙ Sights
1 Wat Khaong Kang...............................B3
2 Wat Phnom Yat..................................B3

🛏 Sleeping
3 Pailin Ruby Guesthouse.....................A1

with 63 clean, spacious rooms. It's worth paying for the air-con options as they have natural light.

Bamboo Guesthouse   GUESTHOUSE $
(☏ 012 405818; r US$12-30; ❋❃❊) Bamboo is an oasis of calm on Pailin's northwestern outskirts, with 27 comfortable bungalows. The restaurant serves excellent Khmer and Thai food (mains US$4 to US$8) in outdoor pavilions, and the pool is free for guests, US$4 for outsiders. From the market head west on NH57 for 2km, turn right and proceed 800m.

★ Memoria Palace   RESORT $$
(☏ 015 430014; www.memoriapalace.com; hut US$45, bungalow US$55-80; ❋❃❊) Located 5km west of Pailin, this resort has humongous bungalows with boutique touches and great views, and a 20m-long hilltop swimming pool. There are also three fan-only,

Getting to the border The laid-back **Psar Pruhm/Ban Pakard border crossing** (6.30am to 8pm) is 102km southwest of Battambang and 18km northwest of Pailin via good sealed roads.

First get to Pailin from Battambang. In Pailin, patient travellers might get a share taxi (6000r) to the border. If nothing is going, take a *moto* (US$5) or private taxi (US$10).

At the border Formalities are straightforward and quick on both sides. Immigration officials usually quote US$35 for Cambodian tourist visas here. Ignore all offers from touts on the Thai side to help with visas.

Moving on On the Thai side, you can avoid being overcharged for transport to Chanthaburi (150B, 1½ hours, 10am, 11am, 6.30pm) by hopping on a *moto* (50B) to the nearby *sŏrngtǎaou* (pick-up truck) station. From Chanthaburi's bus station there are frequent buses to Bangkok (200B, four hours).

palm-thatch huts. The restaurant (mains US$5 to US$10) is Pailin's best, and breakfast is included. To get here, go straight where the highway bends sharply to the right 500m beyond the turn-off to Bamboo Guesthouse.

ⓘ Information

Canadia Bank (NH57; ⊙ 8am-3.30pm Mon-Fri, to 11.30am Sat, ATM 24hr)

ⓘ Getting There & Away

Hwy NH57 (sometimes still called Hwy 10), a sealed highway, originates about 6km west of Pailin and runs north to Poipet along the Thai border, making for a straightforward journey by bus, car or motorbike.

Rith Mony (NH57) has morning buses that originate in Psar Pruhm at the Thai border around 7.30am, pick up passengers in Pailin around 8am, and continue to Phnom Penh (38,000r, eight hours) via Battambang (15,000r, 1½ hours).

Share taxis to Battambang (20,000r, one hour) leave from the **taxi stand** opposite Psar Pailin on NH57.

A rough track goes from Treng District, about 25km east of Pailin, southward through the Cardamom Mountains to Koh Kong via Samlaut and Pramoay.

POIPET

♪ 054 / POP 91,000

Long the no-go part of Cambodia for tourists, notorious for its squalor, scams and sleaze, Poipet (ប៉ោយប៉ែត, pronounced 'poi-peh' in Khmer) has recently splurged on a facelift. Thanks mainly to the patronage of neighbouring Thais, whose own country bans gambling, its casino resorts – with

names like Tropicana and Grand Diamond City – are turning the town into Cambodia's little Las Vegas. However, beyond the border zone, the Poipet of times past is still very much present. The Khmers' gentle side is little in evidence, but don't worry, the rest of the country does not carry on like thi..

Poipet extends southeast from the border (the filthy O Chrou stream) for a few kilometres along NH5.

City Poipet Hotel HOTEL $
(☎ 054-967576; citypoipethotel@gmail.com; d with fan/air-con from US$8/15; ❀ ⎈) By far the nicest crash pad in Poipet, it has a whiff of style, plus decent wi-fi. It's just off the main road, about 1km southeast of the casinos.

Destiny Cafe CAFE $
(NH5; dishes US$2-3.50; ⊙ 6.30am-6.30pm; ⎈) 🖉 A fine place to hang out if you have some time to kill, with tasty Khmer and Western eats, good coffee and friendly staff. It supports an array of community projects in the local area. It's a five-minute walk southeast of Canadia Bank.

ⓘ Information

The faster you get used to making quick conversions between Cambodian riel, US dollars and Thai baht, all of which are in use here, the easier it'll be. A good rule of thumb is 4000r = US$1 = 30B.

Don't change money at the places suggested by touts, no matter how official they look. In fact, there's no need to change money at all, as baht work just fine here.

Canadia Bank (NH5; ⊙ 8am-3.30pm Mon-Fri, to 11.30am Sat, ATM 24hr) About 1km east of the border roundabout.

❶ Getting There & Away

It's worth mastering the transport tricks of this scam-ridden border to save hassle and money.

Poipet has two bus stations: the Poipet Tourist Passenger International Terminal, situated 9km east of town in the middle of nowhere, and the **main bus station**, which is at the main market, one block north of Canadia Bank off NH5. Unless you don't mind overpaying or are desperate for convenience, avoid the international tourist terminal. Unfortunately this is easier said than done, as upon exiting immigration you'll be herded towards a 'free' tourist shuttle to this terminal, where onward buses depart to Phnom Penh (US$15, eight hours), Siem Reap (US$9, 2½ hours) and Battambang (US$10, 2½ hours). Share/private taxis to Siem Reap from the international terminal cost an inflated US$12/48.

Instead, stay solo and walk or take a *moto* (2000r) for 1km along NH5 to the bus company offices near Canadia Bank, or to the main bus station nearby. Bus fares here are on average around US$5 less than at the international tourist terminal.

Unfortunately, the vast majority of buses depart in the morning (before 10.30am). If you can't get a bus, just take a share taxi – these also depart from NH5 around Canadia Bank – onward to Siem Reap (seat/whole taxi US$7.50/30), Battambang (seat/whole taxi US$7.50/30) or Phnom Penh (seat/whole taxi US$20/80). Don't take the taxis that hang out near the roundabout by the border – these charge tourists much more.

The many bus companies here include Capitol Tour, Phnom Penh Sorya, Kampuchea Angkor Express and Rith Mony. Several companies offer trips to Bangkok (US$10, five hours) until about 1pm.

All roads leading out of Poipet are sealed and in fine condition.

Very limited passenger **trains** (http://royal railway.easybook.com) have resumed from Poipet to Battambang (US$4 per person, three hours) and Phnom Penh (US$7 per person, 10

---

❶ GETTING TO THAILAND: SIEM REAP TO BANGKOK

Getting to the border By far the busiest crossing between Cambodia and Thailand, the **Poipet/Aranya Prathet border crossing** (6am to 10pm) is the route most people take when travelling between Bangkok and Siem Reap. It has earned a bad reputation over the years, with scams galore to help tourists part with their money, especially coming in from Thailand.

Frequent buses and share taxis run from Siem Reap and Battambang to Poipet. Don't get off the bus until you reach the big roundabout adjacent to the border post. Buying a ticket all the way to Bangkok can expedite things and save you the hassle of finding onward transport on the Thai side. There are now several bus companies that offer through-buses from Siem Reap to Mo Chit (p131) bus station in Bangkok.

At the border Be prepared to wait in sweltering immigration lines on both sides – waits of two or more hours are not uncommon, especially in the high season. Show up early in the morning to avoid the crowds, but be aware that rarely does anybody get across before 6.30am. You can pay a special 'VIP fee' (aka a bribe) of 200B on either side to skip the lines, but beware of scams and realise that you are contributing to longer wait times for everybody else. There is no departure tax to leave Cambodia despite what Cambodian border officials might tell you. Entering Thailand, most nationalities are issued 15-day visa waivers free of charge.

Coming in from Thailand, under no circumstances should you deal with any 'Cambodian' immigration officials who might approach you on the Thai side – this is a scam. Entering Cambodia, the official tourist visa fee is US$30, but it's common to be charged $35. If you don't mind waiting around, you can usually get the official rate if you politely hold firm. Procuring an e-visa (US$37) before travel won't save you any money but will lower your stress levels.

Moving on Minibuses wait just over the border on the Thai side to whisk you to Bangkok's Victory Monument (230B, four hours, every 30 minutes from 6.30am to 4.30pm). Or make your way 7km to Aranya Prathet by *tuk tuk* (100B) or *sǒrngtǎaou* (pick-up truck; 15B), from where there are regular buses to Bangkok's Mo Chit and Eastern stations between 5am and 3pm (229B, five to six hours). Make sure your *tuk tuk* driver takes you to the main bus station in Aranya Prathet for your 100B, not to the smaller station about 1km from the border (a common scam). The 6.40am and the 1.55pm trains (six hours) are other options to Bangkok.

hours), with two trains per week leaving in either direction, departing Poipet at 7am on Saturday and Monday. In time, there may be cross-border trains connecting Bangkok and Phnom Penh.

ℹ Getting Around

Moto drivers wait at the big roundabout adjacent to the border post to whisk you around the town proper. Expect to pay 2000r for a short ride (though they may try to charge you US$1).

SISOPHON

♪ 054 / POP 63,000

Sisophon (ស៊ីសុផុន) is strategically situated at northwest Cambodia's great crossroads, the intersection of NH5 and NH6. This dusty transit hub doesn't have much going for it, but it's the nearest town to use as a base for exploring the Angkorian temples of Banteay Chhmar. Confusingly, it's also known as Svay, Svay Sisophon, Srei Sophon and Banteay Meanchey.

NH6 (from Siem Reap and Phnom Penh) intersects NH5 (from Battambang and Phnom Penh) at the western tip of the triangular town centre.

Pyramid Hotel   HOTEL $

(♪054-668 8881; www.pyramid-hotel.com; St 2; r with air-con US$20-30; ☀ 🛜) A solid bet, the Pyramid has 44 small but spick-and-span rooms in a quiet but central location just off NH6. It also has a good rooftop restaurant.

★ Talk2 Coffee   CAFE $

(www.facebook.com/Talk2CoffeeBakery; mains US$2-4; ⏰6am-8pm; ☀ 🛜) Talk2 Coffee is the most sophisticated cafe in Sisophon. Soft lighting, old French tiles and plush furnishings make for a welcome interior. The menu includes an excellent range of coffees, teas and juices, plus great-value Cambodian

staples like *lok lak* (a traditional beef dish), fried rice and noodle soup.

ℹ Getting There & Away

Sisophon is 45km east of Poipet, 105km west of Siem Reap and 68km northwest of Battambang.

Most long-haul buses stop somewhere around the **bus station area**, spread through the centre of town. **Capitol Tour**, **Rith Mony** and **Phnom Penh Sorya** each have four or five buses per day south to Battambang (15,000r, two hours) and Phnom Penh (US$8, eight hours). Capital Tour and PP Sorya also have a couple of buses to Poipet. A few morning buses from Poipet come through en route to Siem Reap (15,000r, two hours).

Mean Chey Express (♪ 090 922111; NH6; ⏰7am-5pm) also runs comfortable minivans to Phnom Penh (US$8, 6½ hours).

From the **taxi park**, near the bus station, share taxis serve Poipet (12,000r, 40 minutes), Siem Reap (20,000r, 1½ hours), Battambang (16,000r, 1½ hours) and Phnom Penh (US$10, six hours); a private taxi to Siem Reap costs about US$25. There are also share taxis to Samraong via Kralanh for the O Smach border crossing (25,000r, three hours).

Share taxis to other northbound destinations, including Banteay Chhmar, depart from **Psar Thmei** (St 1).

There are also limited **trains** (http://royal railway.easybook.com) to Battambang (US$3, Friday and Sunday at 8.10am, two hours) and Poipet (US$3, Saturday and Monday 5.05pm, one hour).

BANTEAY CHHMAR

Beautiful, peaceful and covered in astonishingly intricate bas-reliefs, Banteay Chhmar is one of the most impressive remote temple complexes beyond the Angkor area. It was constructed by Cambodia's most prolific builder, Jayavarman VII (r 1181–1219), on the

---

ℹ GETTING TO THAILAND: SISOPHON TO SURIN

Getting to the border The remote **O Smach/Chong Chom border crossing** (6am–10pm) connects Cambodia's Oddar Meanchey Province and Thailand's Surin Province. Share taxis link Siem Reap and Sisophon with Samraong via NH68. From Samraong, take a *moto* (US$10) or a charter taxi (US$15) for the smooth drive to O Smach (30 minutes, 40km) and its frontier casino zone.

At the border The crossing itself is easy. A tourist visa to enter Cambodia will cost you US$35. Note that Cambodian e-visas cannot be used at this border. There are no Thai visas for most nationalities; travellers are just given a 30-day entry on arrival.

Moving on On the Thai side, walk to the nearby bus stop, where regular buses depart to Surin throughout the day (45B, 1½ hours, frequent from 6.10am to 5.50pm).

site of a 9th-century temple. The Global Heritage Fund (www.globalheritagefund.org) is assisting with conservation efforts here, and it is now a top candidate for Unesco World Heritage Site status.

Next to the ruins, Banteay Chhmar village is part of a worthwhile community-based tourism (CBT) scheme offering homestays, activities and guides for temple tours to assist with community development in the area. If you're looking for an opportunity to delve into Cambodian rural life and spend some quality time amid a temple complex far from the crowds, this is a great programme. All activities can be booked through the CBT Office (p260).

◉ Sights

The **Banteay Chhmar temple complex** (បន្ទាយឆ្មារ; US$5; ◷8am-6pm) consists of the impressive main temple and nine satellite temples in the immediate vicinity.

Main Temple

The recently restored main temple housed one of the largest and most impressive Buddhist monasteries of the Angkorian period, and was originally enclosed by a 9km-long wall. Now atmospherically encroached on by forest, it features several towers bearing enigmatic, Bayon-style four-faced Avalokiteshvara (a Buddhist deity), with its mysterious and iconic smile. The temple is also renowned for its 2000 sq metres of intricate carvings, which depict victorious battles and scenes from daily life.

The artistic highlights are the bas-reliefs of multi-armed images of Avalokiteshvara, unique to Banteay Chhmar, on the exterior of the southern section of the temple's western ramparts. Unfortunately, several of these were dismantled and trucked into Thailand in a brazen act of looting in 1998; only two figures – one with 22 arms, the other with 32 – remain in situ out of an original eight, but they still evoke the dazzling, intricate artistry involved in creating these carvings. The segments of the looted bas-reliefs that were intercepted by the Thais are now on display in Phnom Penh's National Museum of Cambodia (p54).

On the temple's east side, a huge bas-relief on a partly toppled wall dramatically depicts naval warfare between the Khmers (on the left) and the Chams (on the right),

with the dead (some being devoured by crocodiles) at the bottom. Further south (to the left) are scenes of land battles with infantry and elephants. There are more martial bas-reliefs along the exterior of the temple's south walls.

The once-grand entry gallery is now a jumble of fallen sandstone blocks, though elsewhere a few intersecting galleries have withstood the ravages of time, as have some almost hidden 12th-century inscriptions. Sadly, all the apsaras (nymphs) have been decapitated by looters.

Satellite Temples

The satellite temples, many hidden deep in the jungle and with Bayon-style faces of their own, are all in a ruinous state, and some are accessible only if you chop through the undergrowth. Along with **Prasat Ta Prohm** (ប្រាសាទតាព្រហ្ម) FREE, they include Prasat Samnang Tasok, Prasat Mebon, Prasat Prom Muk Buon, Prasat Yeay Choun, Prasat Pranang Ta Sok and Prasat Chen Chiem Trey. The last of these, which vaguely translates as 'Fish Farm Temple', is about 1km north of the main temple and has been all but consumed by trees. To explore these lesser-seen temples, hire a guide from the CBT Office for US$10.

Banteay Top

Banteay Top (បន្ទាយទ័ព, Fortress of the Army) FREE may be small, but its impressively tall, damaged towers are highly photogenic. Constructed around the same time as Banteay Chhmar, it may be a tribute to the army of Jayavarman VII, which confirmed Khmer dominance over the region by comprehensively defeating the Chams.

To get here from Banteay Chhmar, head towards Sisophon along NH56 for 7km, take the left-hand turn through the red ornamental gate and head east down the track for 5km.

🛏 Sleeping & Eating

CBT Homestay Program　　　HOMESTAY $
(🖉 097-516 5533, 012 435660; www.visitbanteay chhmar.org; r US$7) 🍴 Thanks to the homestay project run by the CBT (Community-Based Tourism) Office, it's possible to stay in Banteay Chhmar and three nearby hamlets. Rooms are in private homes and come with mosquito nets, fans that run when there's 24-hour electricity, and downstairs bathrooms. Part of the income goes into a community development fund. Book at least one day in advance.

If you're with a group of seven or more, book at least a month ahead.

CBT Meal at the Temple　　CAMBODIAN $
(meal per person US$4) For those interested in a particularly atmospheric meal, the CBT Office can set up lunch or dinner in the main temple at Banteay Chhmar. There's an additional charge of US$10 to US$20 for the set-up, dependent on the size of your group.

Banteay Chhmar Restaurant　　CAMBODIAN $
(🖉 031-247 5353; NH56; mains US$1-4; ⊙6am-2pm) Near the temple's eastern entrance, this rustic restaurant is the only place to dine without pre-ordering. It serves really tasty Khmer food.

🛍 Shopping

Soieries du Mékong　　ARTS & CRAFTS
(Mekong Silk Mill; www.soieriesdumekong.com; NH56; ⊙7.30am-noon & 1.30-5pm Mon-Fri) It is possible to see silk being woven and to purchase top-quality silk products destined for the French market at Soieries du Mékong, 150m south of where NH56 from Sisophon meets the moat. It's affiliated with the French NGO Enfants du Mékong (www. enfantsdumekong.com).

ℹ Information

CBT Office (Community-Based Tourism Office; 🖉 012 435660, 097-516 5533; www.visitban teaychhmar.org; NH56; ⊙8am-5pm) is the main source of local information as well as the place to book tours, activities and homestays.

ℹ Getting There & Away

Banteay Chhmar is 61km north of Sisophon and about 50km southwest of Samraong along the smoothly paved NH56. Most people visit on a long day trip from Siem Reap, which is about a two-hour drive in private transport.

From Sisophon's Psar Thmei share-taxi stand (1km north of NH6), most northbound share taxis go only as far as Thmor Pouk, although a few continue on to Banteay Chhmar (20,000r, one hour) and Samraong. A *moto* from Sisophon to Banteay Chhmar will cost US$15 to US$20 return, a taxi US$50 to US$60 return.

ANLONG VENG

🖉 065 / POP 48,000

For almost a decade this was the ultimate Khmer Rouge stronghold, home to notorious former leaders of Democratic Kampuchea, including Pol Pot, Nuon Chea, Khieu Samphan and Ta Mok. Anlong Veng (អន្លង់វែង) fell to government forces in April 1998 and about the same time Pol Pot died mysteriously nearby. Soon after, Prime Minister Hun Sen ordered that the NH67 road be bulldozed through the jungle, to ensure the population didn't have second thoughts about ending the war.

Today Anlong Veng is a bustling outpost town with little going for it beyond an association with former genocidal leaders. However, the nearby Choam–Chong Sa-Ngam border crossing connects Cambodia with an isolated part of Thailand, and for those with an interest in contemporary Cambodian history, the area's Khmer Rouge sites will have appeal. Most of the local residents, and virtually the entire political leadership and upper class, are ex–Khmer Rouge or descendants.

⊙ Sights

The main sights in Anlong Veng are locations once associated with Ta Mok (Uncle Mok, aka Brother Number Five). To his former supporters, many of whom still live in Anlong Veng, he was harsh but fair, a benevolent builder of orphanages and schools, and a leader who kept order, in stark contrast to the anarchic atmosphere that prevailed once government forces took over. But to most Cambodians, Pol Pot's military enforcer – responsible for thousands of deaths in successive purges during the terrible years of Democratic Kampuchea – was best known as 'the Butcher'. Arrested in 1999, he died in July 2006 in a Phnom Penh hospital, awaiting trial for genocide and crimes against humanity.

Ta Mok's House　　HISTORIC SITE
(ផ្ទះតាម៉ុក; US$2) On a peaceful lakeside site, Ta Mok's house is a spartan structure with a bunker in the basement, five simple wall murals downstairs (one of Angkor Wat,

DANGREK MOUNTAINS

For years the world wondered where Pol Pot and his cronies were hiding out: the answer was right here in the densely forested Dangrek Mountains, close enough to Thailand that they could flee across the border if government forces approached. North of Anlong Veng, hidden in these hills near the Thai frontier, are a number of key Khmer Rouge sites.

About 2km before the border, the road splits to avoid a house-sized boulder. A group of **statues** (រូបសំណាកសម័យខ្មែរក្រហម; NH67) hewn entirely from the boulder by the Khmer Rouge can be seen, and have been preserved as a shrine. The statues depict a woman carrying bundles of bamboo sticks on her head and two uniformed Khmer Rouge soldiers (the latter were decapitated by government forces).

Just after you arrive in the bustling border village of Choam, look for a sign for the **cremation site of Pol Pot** (កន្លែងដុតសព ប៉ុល ពុល; US$2) on the east side of NH67 (it's 50m south of and opposite the Sangam Casino entrance). Pol Pot's ashes lie under a rusted corrugated iron roof surrounded by rows of partly buried glass bottles. The Khmer Rouge leader was hastily burned here in 1998 on a pile of rubbish and old tyres – a fittingly inglorious end, some say, given the suffering he inflicted on millions of Cambodians.

Bizarre as it may sound, Pol Pot is remembered with affection by some locals, and people sometimes stop by to light incense. According to neighbours, every last bone fragment has been snatched from the ashes by visitors in search of good-luck charms. Pol Pot's spirit, like that of his deputy Ta Mok, is said to give out winning lottery numbers.

The Choam–Chong Sa-Ngam border crossing (p262) is a few hundred metres north of here, near a ramshackle **smugglers' market**. From behind the smugglers' market, a dirt road with potholes the size of parachutes – navigable only by 4WD vehicles and motorbikes (and not navigable at all in the depth of the wet season) – heads east, parallel to the Dangrek escarpment. Domestic tourists head 700m along this road to reach **Peuy Ta Mok** (ពើយតាម៉ុក, Ta Mok's Cliff) for spectacular clifftop views of Cambodia's northern plains.

About 4km east along the dirt track after Peuy Ta Mok (when the trail forks at the water-lily lake, take the left-hand track), you'll arrive at **Pol Pot's House** (ផ្ទះ ប៉ុល ពុល). Surrounded by a cinder-block wall, the jungle hideout has been comprehensively looted, though you can still see a low brick building whose courtyard hides an underground bunker. This narrow part of the track is navigable only by motorbike.

Much more difficult to get to is **Khieu Samphan's House** (ផ្ទះ ខៀវ សំផន), buried in the jungle on the bank of a stream about 5km east of Pol Pot's house.

four of Prasat Preah Vihear) and three more murals upstairs, including an idyllic wildlife scene. About the only furnishings that weren't looted are the floor tiles. To get here, head north from the bridge on NH67 for 600m, turn right (signposted for the house) and continue 200m past the so-called Tourism Information hut.

There is now a permanent photographic collection of Khmer Rouge–related images from the 1960s to 1990s, '100 Photos for Memory and Education', as part of the Anlong Veng Peace Centre initiative to heal society.

Ta Mok's Lake   LAKE

(បឹងតាម៉ុក) Swampy Ta Mok's Lake was created on Brother Number Five's orders, but the water killed all the trees; their skeletons are a fitting monument to the devastation he and his movement left behind. In the mid-

dle of the lake is a small brick structure – an outhouse, and all that remains of Pol Pot's residence in Anlong Veng.

🛏 Sleeping & Eating

Bot Uddom Guesthouse   GUESTHOUSE $
(📞011 500507; r with fan/air-con from US$7.50/15; ❄🛜) Arguably, the best option in Anlong Veng, this place offers clean rooms with massive hardwood beds. The newer annexe looks out on Ta Mok's Lake (well, swamp), and the kind owner, Tola, speaks excellent English. He can help arrange tours of the nearby sights and mountain camping trips in the dry season.

The guesthouse is a few hundred metres east of the Dove of Peace roundabout on the road to Preah Vihear.

Heng Hotel
HOTEL $$

(☏096 811 2222; henghotel2008@gmail.com; Choam Sa-Ngam; deluxe/VIP r US$18/27; ❄🛜) Live the high life up on the ridge of the Dangrek Mountains near the Thai border. This smart 36-room hotel is a cut above the local places in Anlong Veng and offers spacious rooms with all the amenities. It is well signposted in Choam Sa-Ngam.

Som O
THAI $

(NH67; mains 4000-8000r) This open-air Thai place is a hit, with excellent noodle soups, rice dishes and iced coffee. Picture menus posted above the kitchen are helpful.

ℹ️ Information

Acleda Bank (🕒7.30am-4pm Mon-Fri, to 11am Sat, ATM 24hr)

ℹ️ Getting There & Away

Anlong Veng is 124km north of Siem Reap along the nicely sealed NH67, and about 76km west of Sra Em, the turn-off for Prasat Preah Vihear.

The bus depots are on NH67, just north of the roundabout, while share taxis gather on NH67 just southwest of the roundabout.

Share taxis to Siem Reap (20,000r, 1½ hours) and Sra Em (20,000r, two hours) are most frequent in the morning. A private taxi to Sra Em costs US$30.

Rith Mony (☏092 511911; NH67) and **Liang US Express** (☏092 881175; NH67) have early-morning bus services to Phnom Penh (US$6 to US$7.50, seven hours) via Siem Reap (US$5, three hours) at 7am and 8am.

ℹ️ Getting Around

The town's focal point is the Dove of Peace Roundabout at the junction of NH67 and the new highway east to Preah Vihear. About 600m north of this monument, the NH67 crosses a bridge and continues 16km to the Thai border.

A *moto* circuit to the Thai border and back, via Ta Mok's house and grave, costs about US$8. To explore the sights along the Dangrek Mountain track as well, expect to pay around US$20 for a three-to-four-hour circuit.

PREAH VIHEAR PROVINCE

Vast, remote and hardly touched by tourism, Preah Vihear Province (ខេត្តព្រះវិហារ) is home to three of Cambodia's most impressive Angkorian legacies. Stunningly perched on a promontory high in the Dangrek Mountains, Prasat Preah Vihear became Cambodia's second Unesco World Heritage Site in 2008, sparking an armed stand-off with Thailand. Further south are the lonely, jungle-clad temples of Preah Khan, totally isolated and imbued with secret-world atmosphere. More accessible is 10th-century capital Koh Ker (p174), which is within day-tripping distance of Siem Reap.

Preah Vihear Province is genuine 'outback' Cambodia and remains desperately poor – partly because many areas were under Khmer Rouge control until 1998, and partly because until recently its transport infrastructure was in a catastrophic state. The needs of the Cambodian army in its confrontation with Thailand have expedited dramatic road upgrades in the province, making travel more straightforward, although public transport is still in short supply on some routes.

Preah Vihear City

☏064 / POP 26,000

Preah Vihear City, still commonly known by its old name, Tbeng Meanchey (ត្បែងមានជ័យ), is a sleepy provincial capital where dogs lounging in the middle of

---

ℹ️ GETTING TO THAILAND: ANLONG VENG TO PHUSING

Getting to the border The remote **Choam/Chong Sa-Ngam border crossing** (7am to 8pm) connects Anlong Veng in Oddar Meanchey Province with Thailand's Si Saket Province. A *moto* from Anlong Veng to the border crossing, 16km away, costs US$3 or US$4 (more like US$5 in the reverse direction). This road is sealed and in good condition. The crossing is right next to the smugglers' market.

At the border Formalities are straightforward, but note that if you are coming in from Thailand, e-visas are not accepted here. Cambodian visas on arrival usually cost US$35.

Moving on Once in Thailand, it should be possible to find a *sŏrngtǎaou* to Phusing, and from there a bus to Khu Khan or Si Saket. Another option is the casino buses, which leave hourly to/from Khu Khan (30 minutes) and Phusing.

LANDMINE ALERT

Until as recently as 1998, landmines were used by the Khmer Rouge to defend Prasat Preah Vihear against government forces. During the past decade, de-mining organisations made real headway in clearing the site of these enemies within. However, the advent of a border conflict with Thailand led to this area being heavily militarised once again. Both sides denied laying new landmines during the armed stand-off between Cambodia and Thailand from 2008 to 2011, but rumours persist, as several Thai and Cambodian soldiers were killed by mines in the vicinity of the temple. So do *not*, under any circumstances, stray from marked paths around Prasat Preah Vihear.

The rest of the province is heavily landmined, too, especially around Choam Ksant. Those with their own transport should travel only on roads or trails regularly used by locals.

the street are only occasionally jolted awake by passing vehicles. There's very little to see or do here, but the town is useful as a base for journeys to Prasat Preah Vihear, Preah Khan and Koh Ker (p174). Note that a closer base for Prasat Preah Vihear is Sra Em, only 30km south of the temple.

With the smooth highway running 130km east to Thala Boravit and the bridge over the Mekong to Stung Treng, Preah Vihear City and the province's remote temples are a good stop-off for travellers heading east, between the temples of Angkor and Stung Treng, Ratanakiri and Champasak Province in southern Laos.

🛏 Sleeping & Eating

★**Home Vattanak Guesthouse**   HOTEL $
(☏064-636 3000; St A14; r from US$10-20; ❄@🛜) Undoubtedly the best-value digs in Preah Vihear City, this is also a candidate for one of the best deals in the country. The 27 well-maintained rooms at this sparkling-clean hotel include wonderful beds, decent bathrooms and luxuries such as flat-screen TVs. US$10 includes air-con and hot water; US$20 gets a Jacuzzi-style tub.

Its central but quiet location, tucked down a quiet side street, is an extra bonus.

Ly Hout Guesthouse   HOTEL $
(☏012 737116; www.lyhoutguesthouse.blogspot.com; Koh Ker St; r US$15-35; ❄🛜) The smart rooms here have wooden desks and white bedspreads adorned with handsome bed-runners. Upgrade to VIP status for an ornate Khmer-carving headboard on the bed, and a fridge and kettle in your room.

Green Palace Hotel   BOUTIQUE HOTEL $$
(☏064-210757; Koh Ker St; s/d/ste incl breakfast US$35/40/50; ❄🛜) This classy hotel has raised the bar in Preah Vihear City with its glistening marble columns and crystal chandeliers in the lobby, contemporary furnishings in the oversized suites and silky bathrobes in the closets. The 7th-floor sky bar offers pastoral and mountain views for miles.

Ly Hout Coffee   CAFE $
(Koh Ker St; mains 8000-30,000r; ⏰7am-9pm; ❄🛜) This coffee shop is straight out of Phnom Penh with air-conditioning, wi-fi and a sophisticated steaming and spluttering coffee machine. Fresh French pastries are available, and the cafe shares the menu of the cavernous and somewhat soulless Ly Hout Restaurant next door.

Phnom Tbaeng Restaurant   CAMBODIAN $
(Mlou Prey St; mains 12,000-20,000r; ⏰6am-10pm) This huge glass-fronted restaurant is one of the few places in town with an English menu. Dishes include prawn soup, *tom yam* (a hot-and-sour Thai soup), noodle soups and steamed fish, as well as more adventurous options.

🛍 Shopping

Weaves of Cambodia   ARTS & CRAFTS
(☏092 346415; www.weavescambodia.com; St A22; ⏰7-11am & 1-5pm Mon-Fri, to 11am Sat) 🌿 Originally established by the Vietnam Veterans of America Foundation, Weaves of Cambodia, known locally as Chum Ka Mo, is a silk-weaving centre that provides work for landmine and polio victims, widows and orphans. Handloomed silk scarves (US$30 to US$40) and sarongs (US$70) cost half what you'll pay in Phnom Penh.

ℹ Information

Tourist Office (☏097 997 9698, 088 885 9366; Mlou Prey St; ⏰7.30-11am & 2-5pm Mon-Fri) The with-it, English-speaking Mr Thin is the man in charge here. He and his colleague Mr Heng, an

Preah Vihear City

Preah Khan St

NH64

St A8

Psar
Kompong
Pranak

St A10

Canadia
Bank

St A12

Miou Prey St

St A14

St A16

St A18

St A20

Koh Ker St

St A22

St A24

Naga
Roundabout

Koh Ker (72km);
Sra Em (82km)

Preah Khan (93km);
Kompong Thom (157km)

Chhep (40km);
Thala Boravit
(130km)

Preah Vihear City

🛏 **Sleeping**
1 Green Palace Hotel A3
2 Home Vattanak Guesthouse A2
3 Ly Hout Guesthouse A4

🍽 **Eating**
Ly Hout Coffee............................(see 3)
4 Phnom Tbaeng Restaurant................ B2

🛍 **Shopping**
5 Weaves of Cambodia........................... B3

ℹ **Transport**
6 GST Transport..................................... A2
7 TSS Transport Co A2

expert on temples, can guide you to Preah Khan
and a few lesser-known temples in the province.
Canadia Bank (☎023 868222; Koh Ker
St; ⊙8am-3.30pm Mon-Fri, to 11.30am
Sat, ATM 24hr)

ℹ Getting There & Away

Preah Vihear City is 133km north of Kompong
Thom, 82km south of Sra Em, 72km east of Koh
Ker and 185km northeast of Siem Reap. The
roads connecting it to these other destinations
are all in good shape.

GST Transport (☎088 800 8002; Koh Ker
St), **TSS Transport Co** (☎088 252 5264; Koh
Ker St) and several more companies have 7am
buses to Phnom Penh (US$5, seven hours). GST
and TSS also offer later services. All buses travel
via Kompong Thom (15,000r, two hours). For
Siem Reap, transfer in Kompong Thom.

Asia Van Transfer (p129) has daily express
minivan that passes through Preah Vihear City en
route to Stung Treng, Don Det (Laos), Ban Lung
and Kratie.

Share taxis leave from the **taxi station** (St
A10) and go to Kompong Thom (20,000r, 1½
hours), Siem Reap (25,000r, 2½ hours), Sra Em
(20,000r, one hour), Stung Treng (20,000r, one
hour) and Choam Ksant (20,000r, two hours).

Private taxis can be hired at the taxi station
to Siem Reap (US$70), Prasat Preah Vihear
(one-way/return US$60/80), and Preah Khan
(US$80 return).

Prasat Preah Vihear

Cambodia's most dramatically situated Angkorian monument, this 800m-long **temple**
(ប្រាសាទព្រះវិហារ; adult/child US$10/free;
⊙tickets 7.30am-4.30pm, temple to 5.30pm) is
perched atop an escarpment in the Dangrek
Mountains (elevation 625m), with breathtaking views of lowland Cambodia, 550m below,
stretching as far as the eye can see. In July
2008, Prasat Preah Vihear was declared Cambodia's second Unesco World Heritage Site.

Cambodia and Thailand have been spar-
ring over ownership of Prasat Preah Vihear
for centuries, with tensions flaring up most
recently from 2008 to 2011. There is still a
large military presence in and around the
temple, ostensibly for security, though it
might make some visitors uncomfortable,
and money or cigarettes are occasionally
requested by soldiers. Always check the latest security situation when in Siem Reap or
Phnom Penh, before making the long overland journey here.

History

An important place of pilgrimage for mil-
lennia, the temple was built by a succession
of seven Khmer monarchs, beginning with
Yasovarman I (r 889–910) and ending with
Suryavarman II (r 1112–1152). Like other

temple-mountains from this period, it was designed to represent Mt Meru, the sacred mountain of Buddhism and Hinduism, and was dedicated to the Hindu deity Shiva.

For generations, Prasat Preah Vihear (called Khao Phra Wiharn by the Thais) has been a source of tension between Cambodia and Thailand. This area was ruled by Thailand for several centuries, but returned to Cambodia during the French protectorate, under the treaty of 1907. In 1959 the Thai military seized the temple from Cambodia; then–Prime Minister Sihanouk took the dispute to the International Court of Justice in the Hague, gaining worldwide recognition of Cambodian sovereignty in a 1962 ruling.

The next time Prasat Preah Vihear made international news was in 1979, when the Thai military pushed more than 40,000 Cambodian refugees across the border in one of the worst cases of forced repatriation in UN history. The area was mined and many – perhaps several hundred – refugees died from injuries, starvation and disease before the occupying Vietnamese army could cut a safe passage and escort them on the long walk south to Kompong Thom.

Prasat Preah Vihear hit the headlines again in May 1998, when the Khmer Rouge regrouped here after the fall of Anlong Veng and staged a last stand that soon turned into a final surrender. The temple was heavily landmined during these final battles and de-mining was ongoing up until the outbreak of the conflict with Thailand in 2008. Re-mining seems to be the greater threat right now, with both sides accusing the other of using landmines.

In July 2011, the International Court of Justice ruled that both sides should withdraw troops from the area to establish a demilitarized zone. Then in November 2013, the ICJ confirmed its 1959 ruling that the temple belongs to Cambodia, although it declined to define the official borderline, leaving sovereignty of some lands around the temple open to dispute. The border dispute has died down in recent years and all was peaceful during the last research period, but tensions could reignite any time.

◎ Sights

The temple is laid out along a north–south processional axis with five cruciform *gopura*, decorated with exquisite carvings, separated by esplanades up to 275m long. You'll start at Gopura V at the base of the temple and gradually ascend to Gopura I at the edge of the cliff.

From the parking area, walk up the hill to toppled and crumbling **Gopura V** at the north end of the temple complex. From here, the grey-sandstone Monumental Stairway leads down to the Thai border. Back when the temple was open from the Thai side, this stairway was how most tourists entered the temple complex. Thailand claims that this part of the temple is theirs. That Gopura V appears on both the 50,000r and 2000r banknotes is an emphatic statement that Cambodia disagrees.

East of Gopura V, you'll see a set of stairs dropping off into the abyss. This is the 1800m **Eastern Stairway**. Used for centuries by pilgrims climbing up from Cambodia's northern plains, it was recently de-mined, rebuilt as a 2242-step wooden staircase and reopened.

Walking south up the slope from Gopura V, the next pavilion you get to is **Gopura IV**. On the pediment above the southern door, look for an early rendition of the Churning of the Ocean of Milk, a theme later depicted awesomely at Angkor Wat.

Keep climbing through Gopura III and II to **Gopura I**, where the galleries, with their inward-looking windows, are in a remarkably good state of repair, but the Central Sanctuary is just a pile of rubble. Outside, the cliff affords a stupendous viewpoint to Cambodia's northern plains, with the holy mountain of Phnom Kulen (487m) looming in the distance. This is a fantastic spot for a picnic.

Eco Global Museum   MUSEUM
(សារមន្ទីរធម្មជាតិសកល; Sra Em–Kor Muy Rd, Sra Em; US$3; ⊗8am-5pm) Don't be put off by the overlong name, 'Eco Global Museum Samdech Techo Hun Sen Preah Vihear', as this is actually a very informative little museum put together with the support of Unesco. Sections include an archaeology gallery, an arts gallery, an ethnographic gallery and an environment gallery. Information is well presented in English and Khmer.

🛏 Sleeping & Eating

All accommodation in the area is in Sra Em, the bustling junction town 30km south of the temple. There's plenty of basic budget accommodation about 1km west of the centre along the highway to Anlong Veng.

There are basic eateries near the entrance to the temple, just off the parking area. They

Prasat Preah Vihear

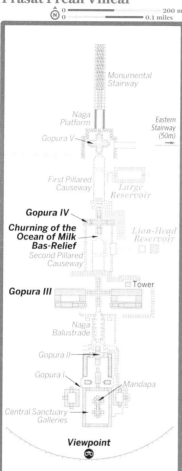

0 — 200 m
0 — 0.1 miles

Monumental Stairway

Naga Platform

Gopura V

Eastern Stairway (50m)

First Pillared Causeway

Large Reservoir

Gopura IV

Churning of the Ocean of Milk Bas-Relief

Lion-Head Reservoir

Second Pillared Causeway

Tower

Gopura III

Naga Balustrade

Gopura II

Gopura I

Mandapa

Central Sanctuary Galleries

Viewpoint

serve authentic Khmer food and a few have English menus. Choice is limited in Sra Em, though there are local eateries and BBQ shacks off the main roundabout.

Sok San Guesthouse   GUESTHOUSE $
(☏097 715 3839; Sra Em; s/d with fan US$8/10, with air-con from US$13/15; ❄️🛜) Sok San has a variety of dimly lit rooms and a restaurant with decent Thai and Cambodian food. Cheaper rooms are small and windowless. Air-con options come with mismatched furniture and windows (which look out onto the corridor). It's 1km west of Sra Em centre.

★ Preah Vihear Jaya Hotel   HOTEL $$
(☏069 217571; www.preahvihearjayahotel.com; NH 26, Sra Em; r US$25-45; ❄️🛜🏊) One of a strip of hotels on the western edge of town, Jaya stands out for its exceptional value. Spacious rooms, all set in low-rise bungalows, include a contemporary trim and large bathrooms. There is an inviting restaurant-bar at the rear of the compound and even a swimming pool.

Preah Vihear Boutique Hotel   BOUTIQUE HOTEL $$$
(☏088 346 0501; www.preahvihearhotels.com; Oknha Franna St, Sra Em; r incl breakfast US$35-100; ❄️🛜🏊) A slick boutique hotel in the unlikely setting of Sra Em, the PVBH is looking to coax higher-end templegoers from Siem Reap to stay a night. With lush bedding and a shimmering 20m outdoor pool to cool off in, it has a pretty good case. It's about 1km out of town on the road to Prasat Preah Vihear.

ℹ️ Information

Acleda Bank (⏰7.30am-3.30pm Mon-Fri, to 11.30am Sat, ATM 24hr)

ℹ️ Getting There & Away

Do not confuse Prasat Preah Vihear with Preah Vihear City (Tbeng Meanchey), which lies some 110km southeast. Most buses advertising trips to 'Preah Vihear' are headed to the city, not the temple. Prasat Preah Vihear is near Sra Em, which is 80km from Anlong Veng and 200km from Siem Reap along good paved roads.

With a private car you can get to Prasat Preah Vihear in about 2½ hours from Siem Reap. The day tour usually takes in Koh Ker and/or Beng Mealea and/or Banteay Srei en route and costs US$100 to US$150.

It makes much more sense to break up the long trip with a night in Sra Em, which is 23km from Kor Muy, where the temple information office is, and 30km from the temple proper. From Sra Em's central roundaboul, take a *moto* to Kor Muy (US$10 to US$15 return – your driver will wait for you), from where an official park-supplied *moto* will take you up to the temple (US$5 return). There is no public transport from Sra Em to Kor Muy.

From the roundabout in Sra Em, share taxis go to Siem Reap (US$10, 2½ hours), Phnom Penh (US$12.50, six hours), Preah Vihear City (US$5, one hour) and Anlong Veng (US$5, one hour). Departures to all destinations besides Siem Reap are in the morning only.

Liang US Express runs a 7.30am bus from the Sra Em roundabout to Phnom Penh (US$7.50, 10 hours) via Preah Vihear City and Kompong Thom. **Rith Mony** (☏092 511811) also has a 7.30am bus to Phnom Penh (US$10, 10 hours).

Preah Khan of Kompong Svay

For tantalising lost-world ambience, this remote **temple complex** (ប្រាសាទព្រះខាន់; US$5) about 90km south of Preah Vihear City can't be beaten. Covering almost 5 sq km, Preah Khan of Kompong Svay (not to be confused with the similarly gargantuan Preah Khan temple at Angkor) is the largest temple enclosure constructed during the Angkorian period – quite a feat when you consider the competition. Wrapped by vines and trees, and thanks to its back-of-beyond location, the site is astonishingly peaceful and you'll very likely be the only visitor.

Traditionally, Preah Khan has been the toughest of Preah Vihear Province's remote temples to reach, but upgraded provincial highways and a new dirt road to the temple have improved things dramatically. Locals say there are no landmines in the vicinity of Preah Khan, but stick to the marked paths just to be on the safe side.

Preah Khan's history is shrouded in mystery, but it was long an important religious site, and some structures here date back to the 9th century. Both Suryavarman II, builder of Angkor Wat, and Jayavarman VII lived here at various times during their lives, suggesting Preah Khan was something of a second city in the Angkorian empire. Originally dedicated to Hindu deities, Preah Khan was reconsecrated to Mahayana Buddhist worship during a monumental reconstruction in the late-12th and early-13th centuries.

As recently as the mid-1990s, the main temple was thought to be in reasonable shape, but at some point in the second half of the decade, looters arrived seeking buried statues under each *prang* (temple tower). Assaulted with pneumatic drills and mechanical diggers, the ancient temple never stood a chance, and many of the towers simply collapsed in on themselves, leaving the mess we see today. Once again, a temple that had survived so much couldn't stand the onslaught of the 20th century and its all-consuming appetite.

Among the many carvings found at Preah Khan – or recovered from looters – was the bust of Jayavarman, now in Phnom Penh's National Museum (p54). The body of the statue was discovered in the 1990s by locals who alerted authorities, making it possible for a joyous reunion of head and body in 2000.

Most locals refer to Preah Khan of Kompong Svay as Prasat Bakan; scholars officially refer to it as Bakan Svay Rolay, combining the local name for the temple and the district name.

◎ Sights

Preah Khan includes the main temple as well as several satellite temples, most notably Prasat Damrei, Prasat Preah Thkol and Prasat Preah Stung. You'll pass these on the way to the main temple. From Prasat Preah Stung at the western end of Preah Khan's

ACCESSING PRASAT PREAH VIHEAR

➡ Driving in from Sra Em, your first stop is the **information centre** (☉7am-4.30pm) in the village of Kor Muy (23km north from Sra Em). This is where you pay for entry, secure an English-speaking guide if you want one (US$15), and arrange transport via *moto* (US$5 return) or 4WD (US$25 return) up the 6.5km temple access road.

➡ Bring your passport with you when visiting Prasat Preah Vihear.

➡ The first 5km of the access road are gradual enough, but the final 1.5km is extremely steep. Nervous passengers might consider walking this last bit, especially if it's wet, but be sure to don appropriate footwear for slippery conditions. Private vehicles are allowed up this road, but you'll need a motorbike or 4WD. Parking a motorbike/car at the bottom costs 2000/3000r and at the top costs 2000/5000r.

➡ Another option is to walk up the Eastern Staircase. Look for signs to the 'Ancient Staircase' on the road from Sra Em before you get to the information centre in Kor Muy. It's around 2000 steps.

➡ It used to be possible to get to Prasat Preah Vihear from Thailand, where paved roads from Kantharalak led almost up to the Monumental Stairway. However, due to the long stand-off between Thailand and Cambodia, access from the Thai side has been forbidden since 2008. Check the situation on the ground in case things have changed.

DON'T MISS

A NIGHT IN THE TREES

If the long, bumpy journey to remote Preah Khan seems tame, consider booking the tree house at the even-more-secluded **BeTreed Adventures** (☐ 078 960420, 012 765136; http://betreed.com; Phnom Tnout, Ta Bos village; bungalows US$60, treehouse US$60; ☎) 🖋. Started in 2015 by a couple of conservation-minded expats who defected from NGOs, this place is Cambodia at its wildest. The driveway alone takes guests through four different forest ecosystems, over rickety bridges and through streams of varying depth.

Well-constructed from reclaimed wood and powered with solar panels, the digs include two comfy bungalows on stilts and a 10m-high tree house. Situated within a 42,000-hectare wildlife sanctuary, BeTreed also includes a zipline attraction that whisks guests over a massive ravine with stunning forest and mountain views, not to mention multiday hikes, one with a stop at an ancient temple. And while adventure may be in abundance here, it isn't actually the point.

baray (reservoir), an access road leads to the magnificently well-preserved eastern *gopura* of the main temple. The US$5 entry fee gains you admission to all temples.

★ Preah Khan

Main Temple   BUDDHIST TEMPLE

(ប្រាសាទព្រះខាន់, Prasat Bakan) The main temple is surrounded by a (now dry) moat similar to the one around Angkor Thom. Once through the grand gateway, the trail meanders past a *dharmasala* (pilgrim's rest house) and through another crumbling pavilion to the central temple area of half-toppled *prang* (temple towers), entangled with trees and overgrown by forest.

Despite all the damage by looters in the 1990s and more recent problems with theft, this crumbling temple, half lost to the jungle, is a remarkable site with some well-preserved bas-reliefs.

Prasat Preah Stung   BUDDHIST TEMPLE

(ប្រាសាទព្រះស្ទឹង, Prasat Muk Buon) About 2km west of Preah Khan's *baray* stands Prasat Preah Stung (known to locals as Prasat Muk Buon or Temple of the Four Faces). It's particularly memorable because its central tower (held up by bamboo scaffolding) is adorned with four enigmatic, Bayon-style faces of Avalokiteshvara.

Prasat Preah Thkol   BUDDHIST TEMPLE

(ប្រាសាទព្រះថ្កុល) On the western shore of Preah Khan's *baray* is Prasat Preah Thkol (known by locals as Mebon), an island temple similar in style to the Western Mebon at Angkor.

Prasat Damrei   BUDDHIST TEMPLE

(ប្រាសាទដំរី) Prasat Damrei (Elephant Temple) lies at the eastern end of a 3km-long *baray* and is the first temple on the Preah Khan access road. On the summit of this small pyramid temple, two of the original exquisitely carved elephants can still be seen; two others are at Phnom Penh's National Museum (p54) and the Musée Guimet in Paris.

🛏 Sleeping

For a fantastic, ecologically responsible lodging option in the area, head for BeTreed Adventures. There are also a couple of guesthouses in surrounding towns.

ℹ Information

The nearest banks are in Preah Vihear City or Kompong Thom.

ℹ Getting There & Away

Upgraded provincial highways and a dirt road to the temple mean that you can now visit Preah Khan year-round, although it's still easiest in the dry season. There's no public transport, so you'll need to drive yourself or hire a *moto* or a taxi in Preah Vihear City or Kompong Thom, or in Siem Reap for an extra-long day trip.

To get there on your own, turn west off smooth NH62 in Svay Pak, about 60km south of Preah Vihear City and 75km north of Kompong Thom. From here an all-season dirt road (substantially pitted with potholes) takes you to Ta Seng, about 30km from the highway and just 4km from the temple. These last 4km are in good shape.

Coming from Siem Reap there are other options for hardcore trail bikers. The most straightforward route is to take NH6 to Stoeng and then head north. You can also take NH6 to Kompong Kdei, head north to Khvau and then ride east on a difficult stretch of NH66 (see below).

An amazing alternative is to approach from Beng Mealea along the ancient Angkor road

(Cambodia's own Route 66 – NH66). You'll cross about 10 splendid Angkorian naga (mythical serpent-like beings) bridges, including the remarkable 77m-long Spean Ta Ong, 7km west of Khvau. The road from Beng Mealea to Khvau is now in fine condition. However, it deteriorates rapidly after Khvau. The 23km from Khvau to Ta Seng are impassable in the rainy season.

Only experienced bikers should attempt these alternative routes on rental motorbikes, as conditions range from difficult to extremely tough from every side – and you could end up lost in the middle of nowhere.

KOMPONG THOM PROVINCE

For those not wanting to rush between Phnom Penh and Siem Reap, Kompong Thom Province (ខេត្តកំពង់ធំ) makes a rewarding stopover, thanks to several intriguing sights spread across the countryside surrounding the provincial capital, Kompong Thom.

The most impressive sight is Sambor Prei Kuk, a collection of ancient, octagonal forest temples that were originally part of Isanapura, the capital of the Chenla Empire that flourished in the late 6th and 7th centuries. In 2017, the temples became Cambodia's third Unesco World Heritage Site.

Kompong Thom

♪ 062 / POP 70,000

The friendly, bustling commercial town of Kompong Thom (កំពង់ធំ) sprawls either side of the lazy curves of the Stung Sen River, which winds its way through the centre. The town is a prime launching pad for exploring nearby sights. Both the serene, tree-entwined temples of Sambor Prei Kuk (p272), named a Unesco World Heritage Site in 2017, and the colourful wats of Phnom

Santuk (p273) are easy half-day trips, while boutique accommodation and decent eating options make Kompong Thom a possible base for a long day trip to Preah Khan of Kompong Svay (p267).

◉ Sights & Activities

Sambor Village Hotel offers a variety of river cruises, including a sunset cruise and a longer journey to the boat pagodas of Trey Leak village.

Kompong Thom Museum   MUSEUM

(សារមន្ទីរខេត្តកំពង់ធំ; NH6; donations accepted; ⊙8am-5pm) [FREE] This seriously bijou museum (it's one room and a small outdoor gallery) actually packs a pretty good punch with statuary and stelae from local sites, including a fine selection of beautiful pieces from Sambor Prei Kuk (p272). It's well worth poking your head in on your way back from the site itself.

Im Sokhom Travel Agency   HISTORY

(☑012 691527; St 3; ⊙8am-5pm) Runs guided tours, including cycling trips to Sambor Prei Kuk, and can arrange transport by *moto* to Sambor Prei Kuk (US$10) or Phnom Santuk and Santuk Silk Farm (US$8).

French Governor's Residence   HISTORIC BUILDING

(ភូមិគ្រឹះអភិបាលបារាំង; Stung Sen St) About 500m west of Kompong Thom bridge is the dilapidated old French governor's residence (no entry), chiefly interesting as being next to three old mahogany trees that are home to the extraordinary sight of hundreds of large fruit bats (in Khmer, *chreoun*), with 40cm wingspans. They spend their days suspended upside-down like winged fruit, fanning themselves with their wings to keep cool. Head here around dusk to see them fly off in search of food.

NORTHWESTERN CAMBODIA KOMPONG THOM

VEAL KROUS VULTURE FEEDING STATION

In order to save three critically endangered species – the white-rumped, slender-billed and red-headed vultures – the **Wildlife Conservation Society** (www.wcs.org) set up the **Veal Krous Vulture Feeding Station** (ស្ថានីយ៍ដាក់ចំណីក្ពាត វាលគ្រូស) in the village of Dong Plet, northeast of Chaeb on the edge of the Preah Vihear Protected Forest. A cow carcass is placed in a field, and visitors waiting in a nearby bird hide watch as these incredibly rare vultures move in to devour the carrion.

Visits are offered by Siem Reap–based Sam Veasna Center (p111). Trips here involve an overnight at a WCS forest safari camp. Book at least a week ahead.

🛏 Sleeping

Arunras Hotel
& Guesthouse   HOTEL $

(☎062-961294; NH6; s/d with fan US$6/8, d with air-con US$10-15; ❄ 🛜) Dominating Kompong Thom's accommodation scene, this central establishment has 58 good-value rooms with Chinese-style decoration and on-the-ball staff. The popular restaurant downstairs dishes up tasty Khmer fare. The operators also run the 53-room Arunras Guesthouse in the same complex.

★Sambor
Village Hotel   BOUTIQUE HOTEL $$

(☎062-961391; www.samborvillage.asia; Democrat St; r/ste incl breakfast US$50/60; ❄ @ 🛜 ☃) This French-owned place brings the boutique to Kompong Thom. Spacious, bunga-low-style rooms with four-poster beds and chic bathrooms are set amid a tranquil and verdant garden with an inviting pool under the shade of a mango tree. The upstairs terrace restaurant has international cuisine and impressive hardwood flooring. Free use of mountain bikes. Located riverside, about 700m east of NH6.

Glorious Hotel & Spa   BUSINESS HOTEL $$

(☎062-210366; www.glorioushotel.asia; NH6; r US$30-55; ❄ 🛜 ☃) This chic business hotel, located on the southern outskirts of Kompong Thom, is the perfect place to clean the grit out of your nails and get a massage after a dusty *moto* journey to nearby attractions. It has an enormous pool, a relaxing spa and sparkling rooms, and staff members are warm and professional. The restaurant serves tasty Khmer and international cuisine.

WORTH A TRIP

TMATBOEY: ON THE TRAIL OF THE GIANT IBIS

Cambodia's remote northern plains, the largest remaining block of deciduous dipterocarp forest, seasonal wetlands and grasslands in Southeast Asia, have been described as Southeast Asia's answer to Africa's savannahs. Covering much of northwestern Preah Vihear Province, they are one of the last places on earth where you can see Cambodia's national bird, the critically endangered **giant ibis**.

Other rare species that can be spotted here include the woolly-necked stork, white-rumped falcon, green peafowl, Alexandrine parakeet, grey-headed fish eagle and no fewer than 16 species of woodpecker, as well as owls and other raptors. Birds are easiest to see from January to April.

In a last-ditch effort to ensure the survival of the giant ibis, protect the only confirmed breeding sites of the **white-shouldered ibis** and save the habitat of other globally endangered species, including the sarus crane and the greater adjutant, the **Wildlife Conservation Society** (www.wcs.org) set up a pioneering community-ecotourism project here.

Situated in the isolated village of **Tmatboey** inside the **Kulen Promtep Wildlife Sanctuary** (តំបន់អភិរក្សធម្មជាតិព្រៃហ្គាទេព; www.samveasna.org) 🍃, the initiative provides local villagers with education, income and a concrete incentive to do everything possible to protect the ibis. All visitors make a donation to the village conservation fund to help with maintenance and improvements to the project.

Tmatboey village lies about 5km off the smooth highway that links Preah Vihear City and Sra Em. The turn-off is 46km southeast of Sra Em and 39km northwest of Preah Vihear. The village is accessible year-round. To arrange a four-day, three-night visit contact the Siem Reap–based Sam Veasna Center (p111). Visitors sleep in wooden bungalows with bathrooms and solar hot water.

For those wanting to explore an even more remote corner of Cambodia, the Kulen Promtep Wildlife Sanctuary's newest birding site is based at the tiny outpost village of **Prey Veng**, about 60km from Tmatboey (as the giant ibis flies). Here the WCS and SVC aim to replicate the success of Tmatboey to save this habitat. Over 150 bird species have been spotted here, including the giant ibis, greater adjutant and white-winged duck.

Prey Veng also offers great opportunities for **hiking** to a hilltop Angkorian temple. Prey Veng's community-managed guesthouses provide simple accommodation.

Trips to both Tmatboey and Prey Veng can include visits to Beng Mealea, Koh Ker and Prasat Preah Vihear en route and are often combined with visits to Veal Krous Vulture Feeding Station (p269). Contact SVC for tour pricing details.

Eating

Third Place Coffee
CAFE $

(📞076 228 9430; NH6; mains US$2.40-4.80; ⏰7am-9pm; ❄🛜) Quite literally the third coffee place to open in town, it serves Bon-cafe-brewed coffee in any style you can imagine and some you cannot. The menu is a mix of breakfast favourites like noodle soup and grilled meats, plus a smattering of Western offerings. The air-con is merciful on a hot day, and bathrooms are among the best in town.

Psar Kompong Thom
CAMBODIAN $

(NH6; mains 2000-4000r; ⏰4pm-2am) Sit on a plastic chair at a neon-lit table outside Kompong Thom's main market and dig into chicken rice soup, chicken curry noodles and Khmer-style baguettes.

★ Kompong Thom
Restaurant
CAMBODIAN $$

(NH6; mains US$3-8; ⏰7am-10pm; 🛜🖉) With delightful waiters and a pocket-sized terrace overlooking the river, this restaurant is also Kompong Thom's most adventurous. Unique concoctions featuring Kampot pepper, water buffalo and stir-fried eel appear on the menu of Khmer classic.

Love Cafe & Pizza
INTERNATIONAL $$

(📞017 916219; Democrat St; mains US$2.50-4.50, pizzas US$6.50-9.50; ⏰11am-9pm Mon-Sat; 🛜) If you're in the mood for comfort food, this bamboo-walled place is a real gem. The big menu of pizzas and burgers is a winner, including some Tex-Mex moments, as is its fantastic selection of ice cream.

ℹ Information

Canadia Bank (NH6; ⏰8am-3.30pm Mon-Fri, to 11.30am Sat, ATM 24hr)

ℹ Getting There & Away

Kompong Thom is 165km north of Phnom Penh, 147km southeast of Siem Reap and 157km south of Preah Vihear City.

Dozens of buses travelling between Phnom Penh (US$5, 3½ hours) and Siem Reap (US$5, 2½ hours) pass through Kompong Thom. They drop off passengers right in front of the Arunras Hotel, which is also where you flag down a bus when you're leaving town.

Share taxis are the fastest way to Phnom Penh (25,000r, three hours) and Siem Reap (25,000r, 2½ hours). Heading north to Preah Vihear City,

Kompong Thom

Kompong Thom

◎ Sights
1 French Governor's Residence............ A3

◔ Activities, Courses & Tours
2 Im Sokhom Travel Agency.................. A3

◉ Sleeping
3 Arunras Hotel & Guesthouse.............. A3
4 Sambor Village Hotel.......................... B3

◎ Eating
5 Kompong Thom Restaurant............... A3
6 Love Cafe & Pizza................................. B3
7 Psar Kompong Thom........................... A3
8 Third Place Coffee................................ A3

share taxis cost US$5 and take two hours. Most taxi services depart from the **taxi park**, one block east of the **Tela Gas Station** on NH6; taxis to Phnom Penh depart from the Tela Gas Station.

❶ Getting Around

Im Sokhom Travel Agency (p269) rents out bicycles (US$1 per day) and motorbikes (US$5 per day).

Around Kompong Thom

Sambor Prei Kuk

Cambodia's most impressive group of pre-Angkorian monuments, **Sambor Prei Kuk** (សំបូរប្រៃគុក; www.samborpreikuk.com; US$10; ⊙6am-6pm) encompasses more than 100 mainly brick temples huddled in the forest, among them some of the oldest structures in the country. To the pride of Cambodians, the attraction recently became the country's third Unesco World Heritage Site.

Originally called Isanapura, the site served as the capital of Upper Chenla during the reign of the early 7th-century King Isanavarman, and was an important learning centre during the Angkorian era. In the early 1970s, Sambor Prei Kuk was bombed by US aircraft in support of the Lon Nol government's doomed fight against the Khmer Rouge. Some of the craters, ominously close to the temples, can still be seen. The area's last landmines were cleared in 2008.

An easy 40-minute drive from Kompong Thom, the area has a serene and soothing atmosphere, with the sandy trails between temples looping through shady forest.

❍ Sights

The main temple area consists of three complexes, each enclosed by the remains of two concentric walls. Their basic layout – a central tower surrounded by shrines, ponds and gates – may have served as an inspiration for the architects of Angkor centuries later. Many of the original statues are now in the National Museum (p54) in Phnom Penh.

It's well worth hiring a guide through community-based tourism organisation Isanbore to show you around (half/full day US$6/10). Guides are usually found hanging around the old entrance near Prasat Sambor.

Prasat Yeai Poeun   HINDU TEMPLE

(ប្រាសាទយាយព័ន្ធ, Prasat Yeay Peau) Prasat Yeai Poeun is arguably the most atmospheric of Sambor Prei Kuk's three temple groups, as it feels lost in the forest. The eastern gateway is being both held up and torn asunder by an ancient tree, the bricks interwoven

with the tree's extensive, probing roots. A truly massive tree shades the western gate.

Prasat Tor   HINDU TEMPLE

(ប្រាសាទតោ, Lion Temple) The largest of the Sambor Prei Kuk temple complexes, Prasat Tor has excellent examples of Chenla carving in the form of two large, elaborately coiffed stone lions. It also has a fine, rectangular pond, **Srah Neang Pov**.

Prasat Sambor   HINDU TEMPLE

(ប្រាសាទសំបូរ) The principal temple group, Prasat Sambor (7th and 10th centuries) is dedicated to Gambhireshvara, one of Shiva's many incarnations (the other groups are dedicated to Shiva himself). Several of Prasat Sambor's towers retain brick carvings in fairly good condition, and there is a series of large *yoni* (female fertility symbols) around the central tower.

🏃 Activities

Isanborei   COOKING

(☑017 936112; www.samborpreikuk.com) Besides running a community-based homestay program (dorm/double US$4/6), Isanborei offers cooking courses, rents out bicycles (US$2 per day) and organises ox-cart rides.

It also organises *remorks* to/from Kompong Thom.

🛏 Sleeping & Eating

Isanborei runs a great homestay programme to encourage visitors to Sambor Prei Kuk to stay another day.

You'll find plenty of restaurants (mains US$2 to US$4) serving local fare around the handicrafts market near the temple entrance.

🛍 Shopping

By the ticket office near the bridge, about 500m from the main ruins, is a giant handicrafts market with *krama*, baskets and other products made by local villagers.

❶ Information

Isanborei is a good source of local information.

❶ Getting There & Away

To get here from Kompong Thom, follow NH6 north for 5km before continuing straight on NH62 towards Preah Vihear (the road to Siem Reap veers left). After 11km turn right at the laterite sign, and continue for 14km on a sealed road to the temple entrance and parking area, which is about 500m from the Prasat Sambor temple group.

Isanborei operates a stable of *remorks* to whisk you safely to/from Kompong Thom (US$15 one way). Call for a pick-up if you're in Kompong Thom. Otherwise, a round-trip *moto* ride out here from Kompong Thom (under an hour each way) should cost US$10.

Phnom Santuk

Its forest-cloaked summit adorned with Buddha images and a series of pagodas, this holy **temple mountain** (ភ្នំសន្ទុក; US$2) 15km south of Kompong Thom is a popular site of Buddhist pilgrimage. To reach the top, huff up 809 stairs – with the upper staircase home to troops of animated macaques – or wimp out and take the paved 2.5km road. Santuk hosts an extraordinary ensemble of colourful wats and stupas, a kaleidoscopic mishmash of old and new Buddhist statuary and monuments.

Near the main white-walled pagoda is pyramid-shaped **Prasat Tuch**, which features an intricately carved sandstone exterior. Just beneath the southern side of the summit, there are a number of **reclining Buddhas**; several are modern incarnations cast in cement, while others were carved into the living rock in centuries past. Phnom Santuk has an active wat and the local monks are always interested in receiving foreign tourists.

Boulders located just below the summit afford panoramic views south towards Tonlé Sap. For travellers spending the night in Kompong Thom, Phnom Santuk is a good place from which to catch a magnificent sunset over the rice fields, although this means descending in the dark – bring a torch (flashlight).

To get here from Kompong Thom, turn left (east) off NH6 at the well-marked sign at about the 149km marker. It's around 2km from the highway to the base of the temple stairs. From Kompong Thom, a return trip by *moto* costs about US$8, and a *remork* about US$10.

Santuk Silk Farm

One of the few places in Cambodia where you can see the entire process of silk production, starting with the seven-week life cycle of the silkworm. The **farm** (កសិដ្ឋានសូត្រ សន្ទុក; ☎ 012 906604; Kakaoh village; ☉ 7am-5pm) **FREE** employs 18 locals, mostly women, as artisan weavers; you can watch them weave scarves (US$20 to US$35) and other items.

The entrance is 200m north of the Phnom Santuk entrance, on the opposite (west) side of NH6.

Prasat Kuha Nokor

This 11th-century **temple** (ប្រាសាទគុហានគរ; US$2), constructed during the reign of Suryavarman I, is in extremely good condition thanks to a lengthy renovation before the civil war. The temple is signposted from NH6 about 70km southeast of Kompong Thom and 22km north of Skuon; it's 2km from the main road. From NH6, you can get a *moto* to the temple.

NORTHWESTERN CAMBODIA AROUND KOMPONG THOM

Eastern Cambodia

POP 6.5 MILLION

Includes ➜

Kompong Cham 276
Kratie 281
Stung Treng 286
Preah Rumkel 289
Ban Lung 290
Veun Sai 296
Virachey
National Park 296
Sen Monorom 298

Best Places to Eat

➜ Bunong Kitchen (p304)

➜ Oromis Restaurant (p305)

➜ The Hangout (p305)

➜ Moustache & Nico (p280)

➜ Cafe Alee (p294)

Best Places to Stay

➜ Tree Top Ecolodge (p293)

➜ Hanchey Bamboo Resort (p279)

➜ Le Relais de Chhlong (p283)

➜ Family House Homestay (p293)

➜ Nature Lodge (p302)

Why Go?

Home to diverse landscapes and peoples, the east shatters the illusion that Cambodia is all paddy fields and sugar palms. There are plenty of those in the lowland provinces, but in the northeast they yield to the mountains of Mondulkiri and Ratanakiri Provinces, where ecotourism is playing a major role in the effort to save dwindling forests from the twin ravages of illegal logging and land concessions.

Rare forest elephants and vocal primates are found in the northeast, and endangered freshwater Irrawaddy river dolphins can be seen year-round near Kratie and Stung Treng. Thundering waterfalls, crater lakes and meandering rivers characterise the landscape, and trekking, biking, kayaking, ziplining and ethical elephant interactions are all taking off. The rolling hills and lush forests also provide a home to many indigenous communities, known collectively as Khmer Leu (Upper Khmer) or *chunchiet*.

When to Go
Kompong Cham

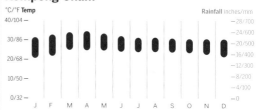

Sep–Oct Mondulkiri is particularly beautiful as blooming wildflowers colour the landscape.

Mar–Apr Low water levels make for great dolphin-watching and kayaking.

May–Jun The highlands of Ratanakiri and Mondulkiri offer an escape from the lowland heat.

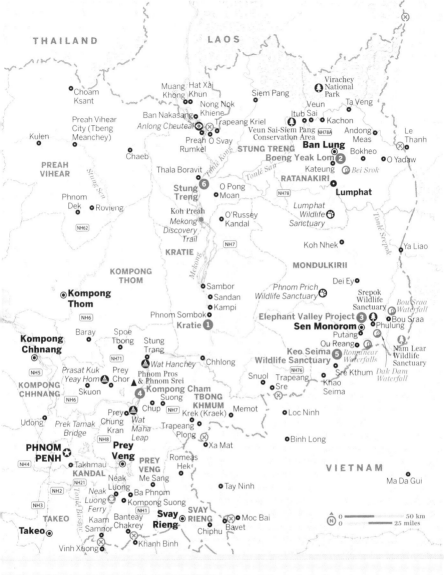

Eastern Cambodia Highlights

1 Irrawaddy dolphins
(p284) Kayaking with rare
freshwater Mekong Irrawaddy
dolphins in their river pools
near Kratie.

2 Boeng Yeak Lom
(p291) Diving into the crystal-clear
waters of this crater lake in
Ratanakiri Province.

3 Elephant Valley Project
(p299) Walking with elephants
in their element: the forests
near Sen Monorom.

4 Kompong Cham (p276)
Soaking up the charms of this
relaxing city, gateway to historic
temples, lush countryside and
friendly locals.

**5 Keo Seima Wildlife
Sanctuary** (p304) Spotting
black-shanked doucs, gibbons
and macaques in Mondulkiri's
wildlife treasure trove.

**6 Mekong Discovery
Trail** (p286) Biking down winding
riverside roads near Stung
Treng and sleeping in remote
homestays.

KOMPONG CHAM

♪ 042 / POP 118.240

Kompong Cham (កំពង់ចាម) is a clean and orderly provincial capital that bursts to life along the banks of the Mekong, where manicured gardens and well-tended walking paths draw large evening crowds. It was an important trading post during the French period, the legacy of which is evident as you wander through the streets of crumbling yet classic buildings. Nearby attractions include several Angkorian temples, as well as some atmospheric riverbank rides for cyclists and motorbikers. The town offers an accessible slice of the real Cambodia: a land of picturesque villages, pretty wats and fishing communities.

Long considered Cambodia's third city after Phnom Penh and Battambang, Kompong Cham has lately been somewhat left in the dust by the fast-growing tourist towns of Siem Reap and Sihanoukville. However, Kompong Cham remains a vibrant travel hub and acts as the stepping stone to eastern Cambodia.

⊙ Sights

There's still a fair-sized population of Cham Muslims in the area (hence the name 'Kompong Cham'). One Cham village is on the left (east) bank of the Mekong north of the old French lighthouse; its big, silver-domed mosque is clearly visible from the right bank. Another one is south of the bridge just beyond **Wat Day Doh**, a Buddhist temple that is worth a detour if visiting Koh Paen via the bamboo bridge.

Wat Hanchey   BUDDHIST TEMPLE

(វត្តហានជ័យ) This hilltop pagoda was an important centre of worship during the Chenla (pre-Angkorian) period, when, as today, it offered some of the best Mekong views in Cambodia. The foundations of several 8th-century structures, some of them destroyed by American bombs, are scattered around the compound, along with a clutch of bizarre fruit and animal statues. It's 20km north of Kompong Cham; the smooth trip out here takes about 30 minutes on a motorbike.

The highlight is a remarkable Chenla-era brick sanctuary with well-preserved inscriptions in ancient Sanskrit on the doorframe. A hole in the roof lets in a lone shaft of light. The sanctuary sits in front of a large, contemporary wat. During the Chenla empire,

this may have been an important transit stop on journeys between the ancient cities of Thala Boravit (near Stung Treng to the north) and Angkor Borei (near Takeo to the south).

Cycling out here through the pretty riverbank villages is a good way to pass half a day.

Wat Maha Leap   BUDDHIST TEMPLE

(វត្តមហាលាភ) More than a century old, sacred Wat Maha Leap is one of the last wooden pagodas left in Cambodia. Located south of town, the beautiful pagoda was only spared devastation by the Khmer Rouge because they converted it into a hospital. The wide black columns supporting the structure are complete tree trunks, resplendent in gilded patterns. The Khmer Rouge painted over the designs to match their austere philosophies, but monks later stripped the temple back to its original glory.

Many of the Khmers who were put to work in the surrounding fields perished here; 500 bodies were thrown into graves on-site, now camouflaged by a tranquil garden.

The journey to Wat Maha Leap is best done by boat from Kompong Cham. Follow the Mekong downstream for a short distance before peeling off on a sublime tributary known as Small River, which affords awesome glimpses of rural Cambodian life. A guided trip on a 40HP outboard (US$50 round trip, including stops in nearby weaving villages) gets there in less than an hour each way. Dary Sang at Lazy Mekong Daze (p280) can arrange the trip.

Small River is navigable only from July to December; at other times, travel overland. It's pretty difficult to find on your own without some knowledge of Khmer, as there are lots of small turns along the way, so hire a *moto* (motorcycle taxi; US$12 per return trip, including a stop in Prey Chung Kran weaving village; one hour each way). A *remork-moto* should cost about US$25 return. It's 20km by river and almost twice that by road.

Koh Paen   ISLAND

(កោះប៉ែន) This serene island in the Mekong River just south of town offers a slice of rural local life, with fruit and vegetable farms and traditional wooden houses. During the dry season, several sandbars – the closest thing to a beach in this part of Cambodia – appear around the island. Bicycles can be hired from some local guesthouses to explore under your own steam.

Kompong Cham

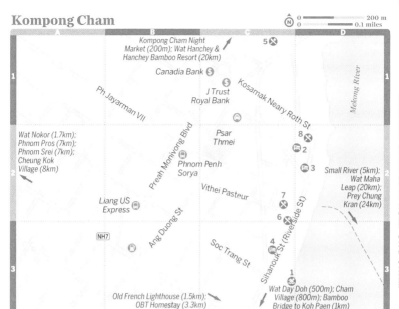

An elaborate **bamboo bridge** connects Koh Paen to the southern reaches of Kompong Cham (foreigner US$1, dry season only). The bridge is an attraction in itself, built entirely by hand each year and looking from afar like it's made of matchsticks. Sadly, its future is in doubt as a concrete bridge opened 2km south in 2018, making it functionally obsolete.

Wat Nokor Bachey   BUDDHIST TEMPLE
(វត្តនគរបាជ័យ; US$3) The original fusion temple, Wat Nokor is a modern Theravada Buddhist pagoda squeezed into the walls of a 12th-century Mahayana Buddhist shrine of sandstone and laterite. It's located down a pretty dirt road just off the highway to Phnom Penh, about 2.5km west of the centre.

It's a kitschy kind of place; many of the older building's archways have been incorporated into the new building as shrines for worship. On weekdays there are only a few monks in the complex and it's peaceful to wander among the alcoves and their hidden shrines. The entry price includes admission to Phnom Pros and Phnom Srei, both just outside town.

Old French Lighthouse   HISTORIC BUILDING
(ប៉មបាវាំងចាស) Looming over the Mekong River opposite town is an old French

Kompong Cham

⊙ Activities, Courses & Tours
1 Floating Pool C3

⊙ Sleeping
2 Daly Hotel D2
3 LBN Asian Hotel D2
4 Tmor Da Guesthouse C3

⊗ Eating
  Destiny Coffee House .... (see 6)
5 Kompong Cham Night Market C1
  Lazy Mekong Daze .... (see 4)
6 Mekong Crossing C2
7 Moustache & Nico C2
8 Smile Restaurant D2

lighthouse. For years it was an abandoned shell, but it's been renovated and features an incredibly steep and precarious staircase (more like a series of ladders). Don't attempt the climb if you're scared of heights. There are great views across the Mekong from the summit, especially at sunset.

Prey Chung Kran

Kompong Cham is famous for high-quality silk. The tiny village of Prey Chung Kran is set on the banks of the river and nearly

PHNOM PROS & PHNOM SREI

'Man Hill' and 'Woman Hill' are the subjects of local legends with many variations, one of which describes a child taken away at infancy – only to return as a powerful man who falls in love with his own mother. Disbelieving her protestations, he demands her hand in marriage. Desperate to avoid this disaster, the mother cunningly devises a deal: a competition between her team of women and his team of men to build the highest hill by dawn. If the women win, she won't have to marry him. As they toil into the night, the women build a huge fire, with flames reaching high into the sky. The men, mistaking this for sunrise, lay down their tools – and the impending marriage is foiled. Locals love to relay this tale, each adding their own details as the story unfolds. Admission to the hills is US$3 and includes entry to Wat Nokor Bachey (p277).

Phnom Srei has fine views of the countryside during the wet season and a very strokeable statue of Nandin (a sacred bull that was Shiva's mount). **Phnom Pros** is a good place for a cold drink among the inquisitive monkeys that populate the shady trees. The area between the two hills was once a killing field; a small, gilded brick stupa on the right as you walk from Man Hill to Woman Hill houses a pile of skulls.

The hills are about 7km out of town on the road to Phnom Penh. Opposite the entrance to Phnom Pros lies Cheung Kok village, home to a local ecotourism initiative, run by the NGO Amica and aimed at introducing visitors to rural life in Kompong Cham. Follow signs to the information panel, where a self-guided tour begins. You'll see a silk farm, palm-sugar plantation, *krama* weavers and more. There's also a small shop.

every household has a weaving loom. Under the cool shade provided by their stilted homes, weavers work deftly to produce *krama* that are fashionable and traditional. The most interesting thing to watch is the dyeing process, as the typical diamond-and-dot tessellations are formed at this stage. Prey Chung Kran is about 4km from Wat Maha Leap. There are additional weavers all along the road between Wat Maha Leap and Prey Chung Kran, though not nearly as many as there once were. This tradition is under threat of dying out with the older generation.

Activities

Aerobics takes place on the riverfront near the Spean Kazuna Bridge at dusk if you want to get down with the locals.

Cruises along this stretch of the Mekong used to be a key draw for Kompong Cham. Although they are increasingly rare, you can still arrange a private trip on a fishing boat to a clutch of idyllic Mekong islands upriver, where you'll encounter a slice of rustic rural life. It costs about US$25 for two to three hours. Get the timing right and turn it into a sunset cruise. Dary Sang at Lazy Mekong Daze (p280) can arrange the journey.

Cheung Kok Village　　　　ECOTOUR
(www.amica-web.org) Cheung Kok is home to a local ecotourism initiative, run by the

NGO **Amica** and aimed at introducing visitors to rural life in Kompong Cham. Follow signs to the information panel, where a self-guided tour begins. You'll see a silk farm, palm-sugar plantation, *krama* weavers and more. There's also a small shop.

It's about 7km out of town on the road to Phnom Penh.

Floating Pool　　　　SWIMMING
(off Sihanouk St; US$1; ☉7am-7pm) Bobbing above the Mekong by the Spean Kazuna Bridge is this floating river-fed pool, where you can down some beers, laze in loungers or cool off from the scorching afternoon sun.

Sleeping

Most visitors prefer to stay on the riverfront for a view over the Mekong. There are also humble homestays and atmospheric resorts further afield in the countryside.

★**Tmor Da Guesthouse**　　　　HOTEL $
(☏011 662659; Sihanouk St; r US$15-25; ❄ 🛜) This smart place is really more of a hotel than a guesthouse, offering stylish and tasteful rooms with a contemporary wood trim. The VIP units are the best riverfront deal in town. Don't be put off by the low ceiling of the mezzanine lobby, as the rooms are really very spacious once you are inside.

Daly Hotel
HOTEL $

(042-666 6637; d/tw US$15/18, ste US$35; ✳🛜) A contemporary hotel just one block from the river, the Daly is one of the best Khmer-style high-rise hotels in town. Rooms are large and bright with wall-mounted flat-screen TVs, spick-and-span bathrooms and luscious linens.

OBT Homestay
HOMESTAY $

(099 319191; obt.cambodia.booking@gmail. com; volunteer/tourist incl 2 meals US$5/10) The Organization for Basic Training accepts volunteers to teach English to local kids, but ordinary travellers looking to spend a few days going local in a Khmer village are also welcome. Tours by ox-cart, horse or boat along the Mekong are available. It's in Chiro village, on the east bank of the Mekong, a few kilometres north of the French lighthouse.

★ Hanchey Bamboo Resort
RESORT $$

(076 254 2440; www.bambooresort.org; Preaek Preah Angk; dm/bungalow US$10/63; 🛜🛏) This eye-pleasing resort built entirely from natural materials is a real stunner, perched atop a hill near Wat Hanchey (p276), 20km north of Kompong Cham. A matrix of bamboo forms the open-air restaurant and yoga studio (daily classes are included in the rates), while the 10 bungalows have thatched roofs shaped like turtle shells. There's also a block of stylish dorms.

The resort is a hospitality training centre set up by the NGO Buddhism for Social Development Action, so despite the high price point, a certain degree of patience is required.

LBN Asian Hotel
HOTEL $$

(012 999942; www.lbnasian.com; Sihanouk St; r incl breakfast US$30-110; ✳🛜) This high-rise hotel is a sign that the times they are a-changin' in Kompong Cham. The rooms are excellent value given the four-star standard and include everything from flat-screen TVs to rain showers. Nonguests can venture up to the Sky Bar on the 11th floor, which offers expansive views over the Mekong River and has some happy hour promotions..

✕ Eating

For a city of its size, the food scene here is a tad disappointing. There's little reason to stray beyond the atmospheric restaurants on the riverfront, which include a couple of international eateries and a highly regarded local restaurant.

★ Smile Restaurant
CAMBODIAN $

(www.bsda-cambodia.org; Sihanouk St; mains US$3-7; ⏱6.30am-10pm; 🛜) Run by the nonprofit Buddhism for Social Development Action (BSDA), this handsome restaurant is a huge hit with the NGO crowd for its big breakfasts and authentic Khmer cuisine, such as *char k'dau* (stir-fry with lemongrass, hot basil and peanuts) and black-pepper squid. Western dishes are on the menu as well, and it sells BSDA-made *krama* and trinkets.

Destiny Coffee House
CAFE $

(017 860775; 12 Vithei Pasteur St; mains US$3-5; ⏱7am-5pm Mon-Sat; 🛜) The international menu at this stylish and air-conditioned cafe breaks the mould with a delicious hummus platter, lip-smacking homemade cakes,

---

KRAMA CHAMELEON

The colourful chequered scarf known as the *krama* is almost universally worn by rural Khmers and is still quite popular in the cities. The scarves are made from cotton or silk, and the most famous silk *krama* come from Kompong Cham and Takeo Provinces.

Krama have a multitude of uses. They are primarily used to protect Cambodians from the sun, the dust and the wind, and it is for this reason many tourists end up investing in one during a visit. However, they are also slung around the waist as mini-sarongs, used as towels for drying the body, knotted at the neck as decorations, tied across the shoulders as baby carriers, placed upon chairs or beds as pillow covers, used to tow broken-down motorbikes and stuffed inside motorbike tyres in the event of remote punctures – the list goes on.

Krama are sold in markets throughout Cambodia and are an essential purchase for travellers using motorbikes or bicycles or taking boat services. They have become very much a symbol of Cambodia: for many Khmers, wearing one is an affirmation of their identity.

breakfast burritos, salads and wraps. For a self-proclaimed coffee house, however, it's lacking a proper espresso machine.

Lazy Mekong Daze INTERNATIONAL $
(☎011 624048; Sihanouk St; mains US$3-6; ☺6am-10pm; ☜) One of the go-to places to gather after dark thanks to a mellow atmosphere and a big-screen TV for sports and movies. The menu includes a range of Khmer, Thai and French food, plus chilli con carne and the tastiest pizzas in town. The English-speaking owner, Dary Sang, is your best bet for up-to-date tourist info.

Kompong Cham
Night Market MARKET $
(Preah Bat Ang Chan St; dishes US$1-3; ☺4-10pm) This is not a tourist night market in the conventional sense, but more a market by night for locals to browse stalls and snack out. It's a good place to sample inexpensive Cambodian food and there are plenty of drinks stalls selling fresh fruit shakes and ice-cold beers.

Mekong Crossing INTERNATIONAL $
(2 Vithei Pasteur St; mains US$2-5; ☺6.30am-10pm; ☜) Occupying a prime corner on the riverfront, this old favourite serves an OK mix of Khmer curries and Western favourites, though it shines more as a bar by night with beer on draught.

★**Moustache & Nico** FRENCH $$
(☎096 821 3005; 11 Vithei Pasteur St; mains 18,000-28,000r; ☺4pm-late, closed Mon Jun-Nov; ☜) The best Western food in Kompong Cham by leaps and bounds, with a rotating chalkboard menu of delectable homemade specialities prepared by French chef 'Moustache' and his business partner Nico. Luxuries such as pâté, Camembert cheese and cocktail olives all make cameos, while tasteful black-and-white photos grace the royal blue walls.

ℹ Information

Lazy Mekong Daze Owner Dary Sang is your best bet for up-to-date tourist info. Catch her in the off hours when she's not busy cooking pizzas.
J Trust Royal Bank (Preah Monivong Blvd; ☺8am-4pm Mon-Fri, ATM 24hr) Has an ATM.
Canadia Bank (Preah Monivong Blvd; ☺8am-3.30pm Mon-Fri, to 11.30am Sat, ATM 24hr) ATM plus cash advances on credit cards.

ℹ Getting There & Away

Phnom Penh is 120km southwest of Kompong Cham. If you are heading north to Kratie or beyond, arrange transport via the sealed road to Chhlong rather than taking a huge detour east to Snuol on NH7.

Besides buses, share taxis (20,000r) and overcrowded local minibuses (12,000r) do the dash to Phnom Penh from the **taxi park** (Preah Bat Ketmealea St) near the New Market (Psar Thmei). The trip takes two hours or more, depending on traffic in the capital. Express minivans are another option to the capital (US$6, two hours); arrange these through your guesthouse.

Morning share taxis and minibuses to Kratie (US$5, 2½ hours) and Stung Treng (US$10, 4½ hours) depart when full from the **Caltex station** (NH7) at the main roundabout. There are morning minibuses from the taxi park as well.

There are no longer any passenger boats to other towns running on the Mekong from here.

BUS

Several bus companies offer services connecting Kompong Cham to Phnom Penh, Kratie, Stung Treng and Mondulkiri, including **Phnom Penh Sorya** (☎092 181810; http://ppsorya transport.com.kh; Preah Monivong Blvd) and

BUSES FROM KOMPONG CHAM

DESTINATION	PRICE (US$)	DURATION (HR)	COMPANIES	FREQUENCY
Ban Lung	11	7	Liang US Express (van)	7.30am
Battambang	7.50	8	Liang US Express, PP Sorya	7.30am & 8.30am
Kratie via Snuol	4.50	4	PP Sorya	10am & 12.30pm
Phnom Penh	4-5	3	Liang US Express, PP Sorya	hourly till 5pm
Sen Monorom	9	6	Liang US Express (van)	8am & 1pm
Siem Reap	6.50	6	Liang US Express, PP Sorya	7.30am & 8.30am
Stung Treng	7	6	Liang US Express (van), PP Sorya	7.30am & 10am

281

GETTING TO VIETNAM: KOMPONG CHAM TO TAY NINH

Getting to the border The Trapeang Plong/Xa Mat border crossing (7am to 5pm) has become increasingly popular for those travelling between northeast Cambodia and Ho Chi Minh City. From Kompong Cham take anything heading east on NH7 towards Snuol, and get off at the roundabout in Krek (Kraek), on NH7, 55km southeast of Kompong Cham. From there, it's 20km south by *moto* (motorcycle taxi; US$5) along NH72 to snoozy Trapeang Plong.

At the border This border is a breeze: just have your Vietnamese visa ready, should you require one.

Moving on On the Vietnamese side, motorbikes and taxis go to Tay Ninh, 45km to the south – but be prepared to negotiate a lot harder than in Cambodia.

Liang US Express (088 6218585; Preah Monivong Blvd).

Getting Around

Kompong Cham has a surplus of *moto* (motorcycle taxi) and *remork-moto (tuk tuk)* drivers who speak great English and can guide you around the sights. If you sip a drink overlooking the Mekong, one of them will find you before too long. Mr Vannat is the veteran of the group and has a 4WD for hire (he also speaks French; contact him on 012 995890 or vannat_kompongcham@yahoo.com). Figure on US$10 to US$15 per day for a *moto* and US$15 to US$20 for a *remork* (slightly more if including Wat Maha Leap in your plans). Round-trip *remork* journeys to Wat Hanchey or Phnom Pros and Phnom Srei are a negotiable US$10.

Most guesthouses and restaurants on the riverfront rent motorbikes (US$5 per day) and bicycles (US$2 per day), including Lazy Mekong Daze.

KRATIE

072 / POP 35,965

A supremely mellow riverside town, Kratie (ក្រចេះ, pronounced kra-*cheh*) has an expansive riverfront and some of the best Mekong sunsets in Cambodia. It is the most popular place in the country to see Irrawaddy dolphins, which live in the Mekong River in ever-diminishing numbers. There is well-preserved French-era architecture, as Kratie was spared the wartime bombing that destroyed so many other provincial centres.

Many visitors are drawn to the rare freshwater Irrawaddy dolphins found in Kampi, about 15km north of the provincial capital, but Kratie itself is a little charmer and makes a good base from which to explore the surrounding countryside.

As a travel hub, Kratie is the natural place to break the journey when travelling overland between Phnom Penh and Ratanakiri or the 4000 Islands area in southern Laos.

⊙ Sights

The main draw here is the chance to spot the elusive Irrawaddy dolphin (p284) north of town in Kampi, as well as the scenic Mekong island of Koh Trong, located just across the river from Kratie.

Located 35km north of Kratie, Sambor is home to a turtle conservation centre and a colourful colonnaded wat.

Phnom Sombok BUDDHIST TEMPLE
(ភ្នំសំបុក; 6am-6pm) FREE This small hill with an active wat offers the best views across the Mekong on this stretch of the river. Located on the road from Kratie to Kampi, a visit here can easily be combined with a trip to see the dolphins for an extra couple of dollars.

Wat Sorsor Moi Roi BUDDHIST PAGODA
(វត្តសសរមួយរយ, Hundred Columns Temple; Sambor) FREE Wat Sorsor Moi Roi, held up by 108 columns and covered in vibrant murals, was constructed on the site of a 19th-century wooden temple, a few pillars of which are still located at the back of the compound. The **Mekong Turtle Conservation Centre** (មជ្ឈមណ្ឌលអភិរក្សអណ្ដើក- កន្ទាយមេគង្គ; 012 712071; www.facebook.com/mekongturtle; Sambor; adult/child US$4/2; 8.30am-4.30pm) is located within the temple grounds, 35km north of Kratie in the village of Sambor.

Wat Roka Kandal BUDDHIST TEMPLE
(វត្តរកាកណ្ដាល; Rue Preah Suramarit) This beautiful little temple dating from the 19th century is one of the oldest in the region. The restored interior now houses a small handicraft centre with infrequent hours. Even

Kratie

NTFP-EP (80m); Canadia Bank (130m); Pete's Pizza Pasta & Cafe (150m); Sorya Kayaking Adventures (150m); Le Tonlé Tourism Training Center (200m); Mekong Dolphin Hotel (200m); CRD Tours (200m); River Dolphin Hotel (1km); Cambodian Pride Tours (1.3km)

Kratie

🛏 Sleeping
1 Silver Dolphin Guesthouse B4

🍴 Eating
2 Jasmine Boat Restaurant A3
3 Mlub Putrea B1
4 Red Sun Falling A2
5 Tokae Restaurant B3

Relais de Chhlong. Architecture buffs might also drop in at the **House of a Hundred Pillars** (1884), about 500m north of Le Relais. According to the house's owner, the Khmer Rouge removed many of the pillars, so only 56 remain.

🏃 Activities & Tours

Riding a bike along the banks of the Mekong River is always rewarding. Other activities include kayaking and boat trips.

★Cambodian Pride Tours   TOURS
(✆ 088 836 4758; http://cambodianpridetours. com) Tours operated by experienced, Kratie-born guide Sithy, who is keen to promote real-life experiences, such as homestays and excursions supporting the local community. He organises single- and multiday trips along the Mekong Discovery Trail (p286), half-day dolphin encounters or 'local living' tours and more elaborate wildlife adventures further afield to Ratanakiri.

Sorya Kayaking Adventures   KAYAKING
(✆ 010 285656; www.soryakayaking.com; Rue Preah Suramarit; depending on numbers US$25-52) Sorya has a fleet of seven tandem kayaks and runs memorable half-day trips on the Mekong north of Kratie (October to July only) that pass through secluded sandbar beaches and areas of beautiful flooded forest. The end goal is to bring you close to the dolphins – without the engine noise.

CRDTours   TOURS
(Cambodia Rural Discovery Tours; ✆ 099 834353; http://crdtours.com; St 3; ⊙8am-noon & 2-5.30pm) 🖉 Run by the Cambodian Rural Development Team, this company focuses on sustainable tours along the Mekong Discovery Trail (p286). Homestays, volunteer opportunities and various excursions are available on the Mekong island of Koh Pdao, 20km north of Kampi. The typical price is US$38 to US$60 per day, including all meals and tours.

NTFP-EP   TOURS
(✆ 090 443322; vannarith@ntfp.org; Rue Preah Suramarit; ⊙8am-5pm Mon-Fri) The verbosely named Non-Timber Forest Products Exchange Programme (NTFP-EP) supports ecotourism projects in two Mekong communities: **Koh Pdao** (40km north of Kratie) and **Koh Samseb** (95km north of Kratie). The former is on one of the river's

if you find it closed, the shaded grounds, adjacent to some lovely traditional wooden houses, are worth a wander. It's about 2km south of Kratie on the road to Chhlong.

Chhlong   VILLAGE
(ឆ្លូង) The main attraction in this somnolent riverside town, 31km south of Kratie, is the old governor's residence, a gorgeous yellow-and-white French colonial mansion near the river. It's now a top-end boutique hotel, Le

longest islands (about 45km) and is a great base for dolphin viewing. The latter lies beside a wide basin ripe for birdwatching.

NTFP-EP is based in the WWF building. Ask for project coordinator Nob Vannarith, who can help arrange homestays, camping, cycling, fishing, birdwatching and other activities with the communities.

🛏 Sleeping

Kratie offers a good selection of guesthouses and hotels, many with river views. For something even more relaxed than Kratie, consider staying directly on the island of Koh Trong, where homestays and boutique accommodation await.

★**Le Tonlé Tourism Training Center** GUESTHOUSE $

(☏072-210505; www.letonle.org; St 3; fan r without bathroom US$9, air-con r with bathroom US$20; 🕸🏠) 🖉 The Cambodian Rural Development Team (CRDT) runs this fantastic budget guesthouse in a beautiful wooden house in the centre. With silk pillows and bed runners, agreeable art and photos, wood floors and a great hang-out area, it puts plenty of care into the design. Rooms are somewhat dark and fan-cooled, but share boutique-quality bathrooms. It doubles as a training centre for at-risk locals.

There's a great restaurant (open 6.30am to 9pm) downstairs with delicious food prepared by programme trainees. There are a few equally appealing air-conditioned rooms with private bathrooms across the street above the main CRDTours office.

Koh Trong Community Homestay I HOMESTAY $

(Koh Trong; mattress per person US$4, fan r without bathroom US$8, r with AC & bathroom US$20; 🕸) Set in an old wooden house, with dorm-style accommodation as well as proper bedrooms and fancy-pants bathrooms (that is, thrones not squats). There are two newer bungalows out back with upgraded air-con rooms. The complex is located within a pretty garden about 2km north of the island's ferry dock. Ride your bike or take a *moto* (motorcycle taxi; US$1).

River Dophin Hotel HOTEL $$

(☏072-210570; www.riverdophinhotel.com; r US$5-55; 🕸🏠🏊) Stranded somewhat inland from the riverfront action, this is nonetheless a deservedly popular place thanks to a moderate level of comfort and service (for

Kratie) and one of the town's only swimming pools (and gym!). It runs the full gamut of rooms, from fan-cooled cupboards to genuinely boutique beds. Add US$5 for breakfast. Nonguests can use the pool for US$2 per day.

Mekong Dolphin Hotel HOTEL $$

(☏072-666 6666; www.mekongdolphinhotel.com; Rue Preah Suramarit; r US$15-50; 🕸🏠) Looming large on the riverfront, this concrete high-rise is the fanciest in town, offering slick river-view rooms for US$35 and suites for your inner VIP at US$50. The cheaper rooms at the back are a huge step down in quality.

★**Le Relais de Chhlong** HISTORIC HOTEL $$$

(☏088 272 5653; www.relaisdechhlong.com; Chhlong; r incl breakfast from US$100; 🕸🏠🏊) Set in a colonnaded buttercup-yellow mansion dating to 1916, this sumptuous hotel spoils visitors with its stately furnishings, four-poster beds, silk cushions and *très chic* French restaurant. The palm-lined grounds provide ample shade, and there are rocking chairs for gazing at the Mekong. Luxuriating

---

WORTH A TRIP

KOH TRONG – AN ISLAND IN THE MEKONG

Lying just across the water from Kratie is the car-free island of Koh Trong (កោះត្រុង), an almighty 6km-long sandbar in the middle of the river. Cross here by boat and enjoy a slice of rural island life. Attractions include **two pagodas** and a **floating Vietnamese village** off the southwestern coast, as well as the chance to encounter one of the rare **Mekong mud turtles** that inhabit the western shore. The interior is where the island's famous pomelos grow.

Catch the little ferry (1000r, 10 minutes, 6am to 6pm) from the **boat dock** in Kratie. From the ferry landing on Koh Trong, a *moto* costs US$1 to the island's north tip, where most of the accommodation is. A private boat to the resorts costs about US$10 to US$15, but is only available in the rainy season. Bicycle rental is available on the island near the ferry landing for US$2, or you can do the 14km loop around the island on a *moto* (US$2.50).

DON'T MISS

DOLPHIN WATCHING AROUND KRATIE

The freshwater Irrawaddy dolphin (*trey pisaut* in Khmer) is an endangered species throughout Asia, with shrinking numbers inhabiting stretches of the Mekong in Cambodia and Laos, and isolated pockets in Bangladesh, Myanmar and Indonesian Borneo. The blue-grey cetaceans grow to 2.75m long and are recognisable by their bulging foreheads and small dorsal fins. They can live in fresh or saltwater, although they are seldom seen in the sea. For more on this rare creature, see www.worldwildlife.org/species/irrawaddy-dolphin.

Before the civil war, locals say, Cambodia was home to as many as 1000 dolphins. However, during the Pol Pot regime, many were hunted for their oils. Their numbers continued to plummet in the decades that followed, even as drastic protection measures were put in place, including a ban on fishing and commercial motorised boat traffic on much of the Mekong between Kratie and Stung Treng. But perhaps the tide is finally turning. The latest dolphin census found that, for the first time since counting began in 1997, the population actually increased in 2017 to 92, up from 80 in 2015. All of them live in deep water pools of the Mekong between Kratie and the Lao border.

The best place to see them is at Kampi, about 15km north of Kratie, on the road to Sambor. A *moto/remork* should be around US$7/10 return, depending on how long the driver has to wait. Motorboats shuttle visitors out to the middle of the river to view the dolphins at close quarters. It costs US$9 per person for one or two passengers and US$7 per person for groups of three to four (children are US$4). Encourage the boat driver to use the engine as little as possible once near the dolphins, as the noise is sure to disturb them. Sorya Kayaking Adventures (p282) runs excellent half-day trips to see the dolphins by kayak, passing through remote flooded forest and sandbars. If you prefer to stand up, Kampot-based SUP Asia (p214) runs multiday paddleboarding tours here.

It is also possible to see the river dolphins near the Lao border (p289) in Stung Treng Province.

alongside the mighty river doesn't get much better than this!

The setting in Chhlon, 31km south of Kratie, may be a little isolated, but you can book dolphin tours and cooking classes onsite or just laze by the pool until your skin crinkles.

★**Rajabori Villas**　　　BOUTIQUE HOTEL **$$$**
(☏012 770150; www.rajabori-kratie.com; Koh Trong; r incl breakfast US$65-150; 🛜🏊) A boutique lodge on the northern tip of Koh Trong island with a swimming pool and large dark-wood bungalows finished in inspired French-Khmer style. Each of the 16 rooms is uniquely designed, but all contain luxurious claw-foot tubs.This is the best accommodation in Kratie by some margin.

They will pick you up for free from the ferry pier, or a private boat from Kratie costs about US$10 to US$15 (only available in the rainy season).

🍴 Eating & Drinking

There is a good mix of Khmer and Western food on offer at Kratie restaurants, most of which are on or near the riverfront. The

south end of the *psar* (market) turns into a carnival of barbecue stands hawking meat-on-a-stick by night.

When in Kratie, keep an eye out for two famous specialities, sold on the riverfront and elsewhere: *krolan* (sticky rice, beans and coconut milk steamed inside a bamboo tube) and *nehm* (tangy raw, spiced river fish wrapped in banana leaves). The village of Thma Kreae, halfway between Kratie and Kampi, is renowned for these dishes.

Kratie is not known for nightlife, although people often linger in the riverfront restaurants until 11pm or so. Otherwise your best bet for drinking and late-night camaraderie are hostels such as **Silver Dolphin** (☏012 999810; silver.dolphinbooking@yahoo.com; 48 Rue Preah Suramarit; dm US$3, r US$5-18; ❄🛜).

★**Mlub Putrea**　　　CAMBODIAN **$**
(☏087 495070; Rue Preah Sihanouk; mains 6000-11,000r; ⏱6am-1pm & 3-9pm; 🛜) It's the fresh homemade noodles fried to perfection that have earned this no-frills spot a loyal following among visitors and locals alike. Part of the allure is also chef Nary, the petite owner with an affinity for jumbo-sized glasses.

Pete's Pizza
Pasta & Cafe INTERNATIONAL $

(☏ 010 285656; www.petescafekratie.com; Rue Preah Suramarit; dishes US$1-5; ⏰ 7am-9pm daily; 🛜) Get your home fix of pizza, pasta, toasties and salads at this internationally run riverfront cafe. The menu includes home-made bakery items such as pumpkin bread, muffins and cookies. By night it doubles as a small bar.

It's also the base for Sorya Kayaking Adventures (p282).

Tokae Restaurant CAMBODIAN $

(☏ 096 742 4445; St 10; mains US$2-5; ⏰ 6.30am-9.30pm; 🛜) Look out for Cambodia's largest *tokae* (gecko) on the wall to find this excellent little eatery. The menu offers a good mix of cheap Cambodian dishes, such as curries and *amok* (a baked fish dish), plus equally affordable Western breakfasts and comfort food. Chefs also run rooftop cooking classes (US$15), which begin with a trip across the street to the market.

Red Sun Falling INTERNATIONAL $

(Rue Preah Suramarit; mains US$2-5; ⏰ 7am-9pm; 🛜) One of the livelier spots in town, the long-running Red Sun has a relaxed cafe ambience, a good riverfront location, traveller info on the walls and a large selection of Asian and Western meals.

Jasmine Boat
Restaurant INTERNATIONAL $$

(☏ 096 331 1998; Rue Preah Suramarit; mains US$4-22; ⏰ 7am-10pm; 🛜) Occupying a prime location overlooking Kratie's busy ferry dock, this is the only place on the riverbank in town. The boat-shaped restaurant has a mixed menu of affordable Khmer specials and pricey international cuts of meat. It really shines at sunset but is a good perch any time of day.

ℹ Information

All of the recommended guesthouses are pretty switched on to travellers' needs. There is also a well-meaning (if not terribly useful) **tourist office** (☏ 088 899 2202; Rue Preah Suramarit; ⏰ 7.30-11.30am & 1.30-5.30pm Mon-Fri) on the riverfront.

Canadia Bank (Rue Preah Suramarit; ⏰ 8.30am-3.30pm Mon-Fri, to 11.30am Sat, ATM 24hr) ATM offering cash withdrawals, plus currency exchange.

ℹ Getting There & Away

Kratie is 250km northeast of Phnom Penh (via the Chhlong road) and 141km south of Stung Treng.

Phnom Penh Sorya (☏ 081 908006; http:// ppsoryatransport.com.kh; cnr St 9 & Rue Preah Suramarit) operates two buses per day to Phnom Penh (US$8, seven hours, 7.30am and 9.30am) along the slow route (via Snuol). Express minivans get to Phnom Penh in four hours via Chhlong (US$8, about six daily), and usually offer transfers onward to Sihanoukville.

Sorya has two daily buses to Siem Reap (US$11, nine hours, 7.30am and 9.30am). There's also an express minivan to Siem Reap (US$12, six hours, 7am). Share taxis (US$10) head to Phnom Penh between 6am and 8am from the **taxi park** (Rue Preah Sihanouk), with possible additional departures after lunch.

Local minibuses also serve Ban Lung from the taxi park (US$8, five hours, 8am and 1pm). Sorya has buses at 12.30pm and 2pm to Stung Treng (US$5, 2½ hours), and there's also a 7am minibus (US$6, two hours). There's a 7.30am minibus to Preah Vihear City (Tbeng Meanchey; US$15, five hours). To get to Laos, you must transfer in Stung Treng; Kratie guesthouses can arrange this.

For Sen Monorom, there are two daily minibuses (US$7, 3½ hours, 7.30am and noon). Alternatively, take a local minibus from the taxi park (US$5, four hours, two or three early-morning departures).

ℹ GETTING TO VIETNAM: KRATIE TO BINH LONG

Getting to the border The Trapeang Sre/Loc Ninh border crossing (7am to 5pm) is useful for those trying to get straight to Vietnam from Kratie or points north. First get to the bustling junction town of Snuol by bus, share taxi or minibus from Kratie, Sen Monorom or Kompong Cham. In Snuol, catch a *moto* (motorcycle taxi; US$5) for the 18km trip southeastward along smooth NH74.

At the border You'll need a prearranged visa to enter Vietnam should your nationality require it, and US$30 for a visa-on-arrival to enter Cambodia.

Moving on On the Vietnamese side, the nearest town is Binh Long, 40km to the south. Motorbikes and taxis await at the border.

ⓘ Getting Around

Most guesthouses can arrange bicycle (US$2) and motorbike (US$7) hire. An English-speaking *moto* (motorcycle taxi) will set you back US$10 to US$15 per day, and a *remork* about US$20 to US$25, depending on the destinations.

STUNG TRENG

☑ 074 / POP 35,000

Located on the Tonlé San near its confluence with the Mekong, Stung Treng (ស្ទឹងត្រែង) is a quiet town, but sees a lot of transit traffic heading north to Laos, south to Kratie, east to Ratanakiri and west to Siem Reap. Just north of the town centre, a major bridge across the San leads to the Lao border, while an important newer bridge traverses the Mekong south of town, connecting Stung Treng to Preah Vihear and Siem Reap.

Stung Treng has quite a bit of largely untapped tourist potential. The main attractions are near the Lao border, where you can boat out to a pod of Irrawaddy dolphins then kayak downstream along a pretty stretch of the Mekong dotted with flooded forest. Further north, thundering rapids cascade over the border, a spectacular sight that's a continuation of the huge Khone Falls.

◉ Sights & Activities

Dolphin-watching (p289) and kayaking trips around Preah Rumkel, near the Lao border, are the main draw. They can be arranged by tour companies out of Stung Treng.

Mekong Blue   ARTS CENTRE

(មេគង្គប្លូ; ☑ 012 622096; www.mekongblue.com; ⊙ 7.30-11.30am & 1.30-5pm Mon-Fri) Part of the Stung Treng Women's Development Centre, this silk-weaving centre on the outskirts of town specialises in exquisite silk products for sale and export. It is possible to observe the dyers and weavers, most of whom come from vulnerable or impoverished backgrounds. The centre is about 4km east of the town centre on the riverside road that continues under the bridge.

There is a small showroom on-site with a selection of silk for sale, plus a cafe. The cafe only serves cold drinks unless you book a meal in advance.

ⓖ Tours

Xplore-Cambodia   ADVENTURE

(Cambodia Mekong Trail; ☑ 088 753 3337, 011 433836; www.cambodiamekongtrail.com) Doles out brochures, booklets and advice, and tailors one- to seven-day cycling or kayak tours along the Mekong Discovery Trail. Popular one-day trips include boating to see the dolphins, hiking near Preah Rumkel, and kayaking down the Mekong. Also rents sturdy Trek mountain bikes (US$5 per day). Multiday rides are possible with a mountain bike drop-off in Kratie.

ⓛ Sleeping

Most people prefer to stay on the riverfront in Stung Treng, that is assuming they choose to spend a night here at all.

WORTH A TRIP

MEKONG DISCOVERY TRAIL

It's well worth spending a couple of days exploring the various bike rides and activities on offer along the Mekong Discovery Trail, an initiative to open up stretches of the Mekong River around Stung Treng and Kratie to community-based tourism. Once managed by the government with foreign development assistance, its trails and routes are now being kept alive by private tour companies, such as Xplore-Cambodia in Stung Treng and CRDTours (p282) and Cambodian Pride Tours (p282) in Kratie.

It's a worthy project, as it aims to offer fishing communities an alternative income, in order to protect the Irrawaddy dolphin and other rare species on this stretch of river.

There's a great booklet with routes and maps outlining excursions around Kratie and Stung Treng, but you'll be hard-pressed to secure your own copy; ask tour operators if you can photograph theirs. The routes can be tackled by bicycle or motorbike. They range in length from a few hours to several days, with optional overnights in village homestays. Routes crisscross the Mekong frequently by ferry and traverse several Mekong islands, including Koh Trong (p283).

★ 4 Rivers Hotel
HOTEL $

(✆070 507822; www.fourrivershotel.com; US$15-35; ❋@☎) Stung Treng's most appealing hotel has a surprising wine cabinet in the lobby and a sky bar on the roof overlooking the Tonlé San and Mekong River. Rooms feature a contemporary trim; it's worth paying a little extra for the river-view options.

Golden River Hotel
HOTEL $

(✆012 980678; www.goldenriverhotel.com; r US$15-35; ❋@☎) The best all-rounder in the town centre, the Golden River has 50 well-appointed rooms complete with hot-water bathrooms, fridges and TVs. Rooms at the front are a few dollars more thanks to panoramic views of the Tonlé San.

Riverside Guesthouse
GUESTHOUSE $

(✆012 257207, 097 725 7257; kimtysou@gmail.com; r with fan/air-con US$6/12; ☎) Overlooking the riverfront area, the Riverside has long been a popular travellers' hub. Rooms are basic, but then so are the prices. It's a good spot for travel information and there's a bar-restaurant downstairs. A new building 1km east of the original was also due to open.

The in-house travel agency specialises in getting people to/from Laos, Siem Reap or just about anywhere else. It also runs boat tours to the Lao border, with a trip to see the resident dolphin pod (US$100/120 for two/four people). English-speaking guides offer motorbike tours around the province.

Mekong Bird Lodge
BUNGALOW $$

(✆066 997797; mekongbird76@gmail.com; d/q US$35/70; ❋☎) This eclectic and artfully crafted complex sits on a bluff overlooking a peaceful Mekong eddy north of town. The sturdy wooden bungalows are set in lush tropical gardens and have balconies with idyllic sunset views. The place is in a perpetual state of expansion. To get here, turn left at the sign 4km north of the Tonlé San bridge.

The rustic on-site restaurant has organic food and excellent verandah views over the Mekong River. Free pick-up from Stung Treng is available for stays of two nights or more.

✗ Eating & Drinking

On the riverside promenade west of the ferry dock, a handful of street-side ven-

Stung Treng

Stung Treng

⊕ Activities, Courses & Tours
1 Xplore-Cambodia B1

⊕ Sleeping
2 Golden River Hotel B1
3 Riverside Guesthouse B1

⊗ Eating
4 Blue River A1
5 Ponika's Palace B1

⊕ Drinking & Nightlife
6 Sidewalk Cafe.....................................B2

dors peddles cold beer and noodle soup until late in the evening. Established restaurants serve mostly Khmer food, though you can find some passable international fare, too.

Blue River
CAMBODIAN $

(✆088 666 6105; mains US$4-5; ⊙10am-10pm; ☎) This floating restaurant – lit by lanterns and adorned with gnarled driftwood – is the perfect place to toss back an Angkor beer and watch the sun plunge into the Tonlé San. Food is standard Cambodian fare.

Ponika's Palace
INTERNATIONAL $

(Stung Treng Burger; ✆012 916441; mains US$2-5; ⊙6am-10pm) Need a break from *laab* salad after Laos? Burgers, pizza and English breakfasts grace the menu, along with Indian food and wonderful Khmer curries. Affable owner Ponika speaks English and cold beer is available to slake a thirst.

ⓘ **GETTING TO LAOS: TRAPEANG KRIEL TO NONG NOK KHIENE**
....

Getting to the border The remote **Trapeang Kriel/Nong Nok Khiene border** (open 6am to 5.30pm), 65km north of Stung Treng, is a popular crossing point on the Indochina overland circuit. For many years, there was a separate river crossing here, but that's no longer open. There are also no longer any through buses between Phnom Penh and Pakse. You'll need to get yourself to Stung Treng, from where there are at least two minivans per day (at 1pm and 2pm) that run across the border and onward to the 4000 Islands and Pakse. The only other option to the border is a private taxi (around US$40) or *moto* (motorcycle taxi; around US$15) from Stung Treng.

At the border Both Lao and Cambodian visas are available on arrival (remember to bring passport photos). Entering Laos, it costs US$30 to US$42 for a visa, depending on nationality, plus a US$2 fee (dubbed either an 'overtime' or a 'processing' fee, depending on when you cross) upon both entry and exit.

Entering Cambodia, the price of a visa is jacked up to US$35 from the normal US$30. The extra US$5 is called 'tea money', as the border guards have been stationed at such a remote crossing. In addition, the Cambodians sometimes charge US$1 for a cursory medical inspection upon arrival in the country, and levy a US$2 processing fee upon exit. These fees might be waived if you protest, but don't protest for too long or your vehicle may leave without you.

Moving on There's virtually zero traffic on either side of the border. If you're dropped at the border, expect to pay 150,000/50,000 kip (US$12/4) for a taxi/*săhm-lór* (Lao *tuk tuk*) heading north to Ban Nakasang (for Don Det).

Sidewalk Cafe   COFFEE
(⊙7am-9pm; �fi) Iced Americanos, free wi-fi and Alaskan air-con make this cheerful cafe by the market an inviting oasis. Also serves burgers and sandwiches.

ⓘ **Information**

Canadia Bank (⊙8.30am-3.30pm Mon-Fri, to 11.30am Sat, ATM 24hr) Has an international ATM.

Riverside Guesthouse (p287) Specialises in getting people to/from Laos, Siem Reap or just about anywhere else. Also runs boat tours to the Lao border, with a trip to see the resident dolphin pod (US$100/120 for two/four people). English-speaking guides offer motorbike tours around the province.

ⓘ **Getting There & Away**

NH7 north to the Lao border and south to Kratie is in reasonable shape these days, though it's still a bit of a bumpy ride.

Express minivans with guesthouse pick-ups as early as 4am are the quickest way to Phnom Penh (US$13, seven hours). A sleeper bus departs at 9pm (US$13, eight hours). Book through Riverside Guesthouse (p287), Xplore-Cambodia (p286) or Ponika's Palace.

Phnom Penh Sorya (☑092 504066; www. ppsoryatransport.com.kh) has a 7am bus to

Phnom Penh (US$10, nine hours) via Kratie (US$5, 2½ hours) and Kompong Cham (US$8, six hours). Additionally, local minibuses to Kratie depart regularly until 2pm from the riverfront bus lot (by the market).

There is a comfortable tourist van to Ban Lung (US$6, two hours, 8am and 1pm), with additional morning trips in cramped local minibuses from the riverfront bus lot (US$5, three hours).

The new highway west from Thala Boravit to Preah Vihear via Chhep is in great shape. **Asia Van Transfer** (☑071 844 3566, 012 505673; www.asiavantransfer.com; Riverside Guesthouse) has an express minibus to Siem Reap at 2pm daily (US$18, five hours), with a stop in Preah Vihear City (Tbeng Meanchey; US$12, three hours). **Virak Buntham** (☑092 222423; www.virakbuntham.com) runs the same route to Siem Reap at noon daily (US$12, five hours).

For Laos, minivans head over the border at around 1pm and 2pm, serving Pakse (US$15, six hours) and Don Det (US$12, three hours) respectively.

ⓘ **Getting Around**

Riverside Guesthouse (p287) and Ponika's Palace rent out motorbikes (from US$8) and bicycles (US$2). Xplore-Cambodia (p286) has sturdier mountain bikes for longer journeys (US$5).

AROUND STUNG TRENG

In addition to the homestay programme at Preah Rumkel, there are worthwhile community-based tourism initiatives, including homestays, in O'Svay, about 60km north of Stung Treng, and in Koh Preah, about 15km south of Stung Treng. Both programmes have a slew of tours and activities on offer and there may be volunteer opportunities as well. Contact CRDTours (p282) or Cambodian Pride Tours (p282) in Kratie for more information on these. Xplore-Cambodia (p286) in Stung Treng can also help organise homestay-based itineraries.

Preah Rumkel

The small village of Preah Rumkel (ព្រះរំកិល) is emerging as a hotbed of ecotourism, thanks to an established homestay programme and its proximity to the Anlong Cheuteal Irrawaddy dolphin pool near the Lao border. With dozens of islands, a rich array of birdlife, and various rapids and waterfalls cascading down from Laos, this is one of the Mekong River's wildest and most beautiful stretches, recognised by the Ramsar List of Wetlands of International Importance (www.ramsar.org).

The number of dolphins frolicking near the Anlong Cheuteal pool has unfortunately dropped to just three in recent years. The good news? Unlike at other parts of the Mekong, you're almost guaranteed to see them. While they can no longer be sighted from the shore in Preah Rumkel (they've relocated 2km upriver), there's still a US$2-per-person community charge for viewing.

Boats holding up to four people can be hired in town. Destinations include the dolphin pool (US$15), Preh Nimith (ទឹកជ្រោះព្រះនិមិត្ត; US$2) Waterfall (US$20) and the flooded forest (US$30).

Other excursions out of Preah Rumkel include a hike up a nearby mountain and a boat/hiking trip to view the rampaging Mekong rapids cascading down from Laos. The rapids are an awesome display of nature's force, especially in the wet season.

The simplest way to see all the sights is to book a tour with Xplore-Cambodia (p286) in Stung Treng. You can boat near the dolphins, hike up to Preh Nimith and then paddle downstream through the bird-rich flooded forests (all the way to Stung Treng on an overnight trip). A full-day boat, hike

and kayak excursion costs US$55 to US$85, depending on the group size.

Cambodian NGO Mlup Baitong set up Preah Rumkel's community-based homestay (☏ 096 700 7842, 071 6881597; per person US$4) programme, though it no longer maintains an office in the region. There are about 10 families participating in the programme. None of them speak English, so bookings are often easier made with Xplore-Cambodia (p286) in Stung Treng.

Meals at Preah Rumkel are available through your homestay for around US$4 per person. If you're visiting on a day trip, your tour company will arrange for villagers to prepare your lunch.

ⓘ Getting There & Away

Hire a longtail boat in O'Svay or, closer to the Laos border, Anlong Morakot, to explore the area and view the dolphins near Anlong Cheuteal. Boats cost a negotiable US$40 round trip to Preah Rumkel and the dolphin pool. Add US$10 if you want to continue upstream to the rapids. Anlong Morakot is only 4km from the border, so travellers coming in from Laos could get there in about 10 minutes on the back of a *moto* (motorcycle taxi; about US$2). Be sure to arrange onward transport to Stung Treng – either at the border or in advance through Xplore-Cambodia (p286) or Riverside Guesthouse (p287) in Stung Treng. These companies can also prearrange your *moto* and boat ride from the border to Preah Rumkel.

A taxi to Stung Treng from this area costs about US$45. A public bus departs Preah Rumkel at around 7am and returns from Stung Treng at about noon (US$5, 2½ hours).

RATANAKIRI PROVINCE

POP 195,000

Ratanakiri Province (ខេត្តរតនគិរី) is a diverse region of outstanding natural beauty that provides a remote home for a mosaic of peoples – Jarai, Tompuon, Brau and Kreung minorities, plus Lao.

Adrenaline activities abound – you can swim in clear volcanic lakes, shower under waterfalls, or trek in the vast Virachey National Park – but tourism here has been on the decline. It's a shame; the industry is the best alternative Ratanakiri has to plundering the place with gem mines, cashew orchards and rubber plantations. Hopefully someone will wake up and smell the coffee – there's plenty of that as well – before it's too late.

Ban Lung

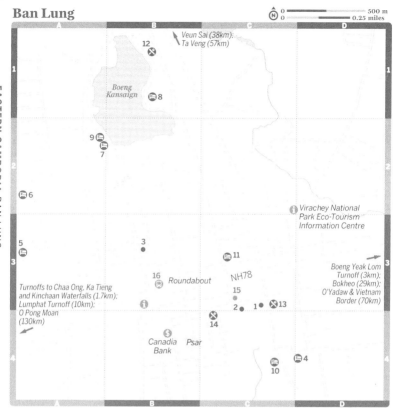

0   500 m
0   0.25 miles

Veun Sai (38km);
Ta Veng (57km)

12

Boeng
Kansaign   8

9
7

6

Virachey National
Park Eco-Tourism
Information Centre

5

3

11

16   Roundabout   NH78

Boeng Yeak Lom
Turnoff (3km);
Bokheo (29km);
O'Yadaw & Vietnam
Border (70km)

Turnoffs to Chaa Ong, Ka Tieng
and Kinchaan Waterfalls (1.7km);
Lumphat Turnoff (10km);
O Pong Moan
(130km)

15

2   1   13

14

Canadia   Psar
Bank

4

10

In the dry season, prepare to do battle with the dust of 'red-earth Ratanakiri', which will leave you with orange skin and ginger hair. The roads look like a papaya shake during the wet season. The ideal time to explore is November, just after the rains have stopped.

Ban Lung

♪ 075 / POP 45,000

Affectionately known as *dey krahorm* ('red earth') after the distinctly red ground on which it sits, Ban Lung (បានលុង) provides a popular base for a range of Ratanakiri romps. These days the roads are mostly surfaced and the bustling town lacks the backwater charm of Sen Monorom in Mondulkiri, but with attractions such as Boeng Yeak Lom just a short hop away, there is little room for complaint. Many of the people from the surrounding villages come to Ban Lung to buy and sell at the market.

◉ Sights & Activities

There are no real sights in the centre of town. The big draws on the outskirts are Boeng Yeak Lom and several waterfalls.

Overnight treks with nights spent camping or in minority villages around Ban Lung are popular, as are multiday hikes in Virachey National Park. For wildlife spotting, check out Cambodian Gibbon Ecotours (p292). Elephant rides are offered near Ka Tieng Waterfall, but are not recommended due to concerns about the animals' wellbeing. Save your elephant experience for walking with the herd at Mondulkiri's Elephant Valley Project (p299).

Keep in mind that trekking in Virachey National Park is the exclusive domain of Virachey National Park Eco-Tourism Information Centre (p296). Private tour operators also offer multiday treks, but these only go as far as the park's buffer zone. There's little forest left standing outside the park bound-

Ban Lung

⊙ **Activities, Courses & Tours**
1 DutchCo Trekking Cambodia C3
2 Highland Tours C3
   Parrot Tours .... (see 1)
3 Sona Trekking B3

🛏 **Sleeping**
4 Bee Bee's Chalets D4
5 Family House Homestay A3
6 Nature House Ecolodge A2
7 Ratanakiri Boutique Hotel.................. A2
8 Terres Rouges Lodge B1
9 Thy Ath Lodge A2
10 Tree Top Ecolodge.............................. C4
11 Yeak Loam Hotel C3

✖ **Eating**
   Cafe Alee .... (see 1)
12 Coconut Shake Restaurant B1
13 Green Carrot C3
14 Ta Nam C4

🍸 **Drinking & Nightlife**
   Banlung Reggae Bar ....(see 3)
   Crush Cafe .... (see 1)

ℹ **Transport**
15 Mr Bona Tour....................................... C3
16 Virak Buntham...................................... B3

ary, so be careful that you're not being taken for a loop – literally – around and around in the same small patch of forest.

Despite being shut out from the park, private tour companies can still design creative treks that take in minority villages and scenic spots around the province. They can also put you directly in touch with rangers if the park information centre proves unhelpful.

⭐ **Boeng Yeak Lom**   LAKE
(បឹងយក្សល្អម; US$2) At the heart of the protected area of Boeng Yeak Lom is a beautiful, emerald-hued crater lake set amid the vivid greens of the towering jungle. It is one of the most peaceful, beautiful locations Cambodia has to offer and the water is extremely clear. Several wooden piers are dotted around the perimeter, making it perfect for swimming. A small Cultural and Environmental Centre has a modest display on ethnic minorities in the province and hires out life jackets for children.

The lake is about 800m across and 50m deep, and is believed to have been formed 700,000 years ago; some believe it must have been formed by a meteor strike as the circle is so perfect. The indigenous minori-

ty people in the area have long considered Boeng Yeak Lom a sacred place and their legends talk of mysterious creatures that inhabit the waters, but don't let that put you off swimming.

The local Tompuon minority has a 25-year lease to manage the lake through to 2021, and proceeds from the entry fee go towards improving life in the nearby villages. However, developers, backed by local politicians, have long been clamouring for the sacred lands around the lake. One can only hope they are kept at bay and that Boeng Yeak Lom is preserved in all of its pristine glory.

To get to Boeng Yeak Lom from Ban Lung's central roundabout, head east towards Vietnam for 3km, turn right at the prominent minorities statue and proceed 2km or so. *Motos* (motorcycle taxis) charge about US$5 return (more if you make them wait), while *remork-motos* have been known to charge about US$10 return. It takes about an hour to reach the lake on foot from Ban Lung.

Waterfalls

Tucked amid the sprawling cashew and rubber plantations just west of Ban Lung are three waterfalls worth visiting: **Chaa Ong** (ចាអុង; 4000r), **Ka Tieng** (កាទៀង; 2000r) and **Kinchaan** (កាចាញ, Kachanh; 4000r). All are within a 20-minute *moto* (motorcycle taxi) ride of town, and visits to all three are usually included in tour companies' half- and full-day excursions. The turn-offs to all three waterfalls are 200m west of the new (though already abandoned) bus station, just beyond a Lina petrol station. Turn right (north) for Chaa-Ong, left for the other two. There's signage but it's barely visible.

You can access all three falls year-round, although they dry up from January to May and may not be worth the trip at this time. Think twice about driving yourself on a motorbike in the rainy season, as the red-clay access roads are extremely slippery when wet and you're almost guaranteed to wipe out. *Motos* (return US$6 for one waterfall, or US$10 for all three) and *remork-moto* (US$10/20 for one/three waterfalls) are a safer bet.

Lumphat & Bei Srok

The former provincial capital of Lumphat, on the banks of Tonlé Srepok, is a shadow of its former self thanks to sustained US bombing raids in the early 1970s. The Tonlé Srepok is believed to be the river depicted in the seminal antiwar film *Apocalypse Now*, in which Martin Sheen's Captain Benjamin Willard goes upriver into Cambodia in search of renegade Colonel Kurtz, played by Marlon Brando.

Bei Srok (បីស្រុក; Tuk Chrouu Bram-pul; 4000r) is a popular waterfall with seven gentle tiers. It's about 20km east of Lumphat. You can also get here on a rough road that leads south/southwest from Boeng Yeak Lom. Many Ban Lung tour companies offer Bei Srok as a day tour combined with some abandoned gem mines nearby and bomb-crater spotting around Lumphat. Access is difficult to impossible in the rainy season.

To get to Lumphat from Ban Lung, take the road to Stung Treng for 10km before heading south. The 35km journey takes about 45 minutes. Any minibus travelling between Ban Lung and Sen Monorom can drop you off here.

Tours

Day tours usually take in some combination of waterfalls, Boeng Yeak Lom, minority villages, gem mines and jungle walks. Figure on US$40 to US$50 per person per day for a couple (less for bigger groups).

Bespectacled Khieng is an indigenous Tompuon guide who runs unique one- to two-night trips in some fairly well-preserved jungle around Lumphat, with overnight stays in minority villages. His tours are cheap and he seems genuinely interested in seeing money go to Tompuon communities and guides, so tip him well. He also has an impressive hand-drawn map of Ratanakiri Province. Khieng can often be found around Boeng Yeak Lom, or you can contact him by phone on ☑097 923 0923 or email at khamphaykhieng@yahoo.com.

Several of the accommodation in town – Family House Homestay, aka Family House Tours; Tree Top Ecolodge, aka Smiling Tours; and Terres Rouges Lodge (p293), which can provide French-speaking guides – are also good at arranging guided tours and treks, as are the dedicated tour companies.

Cambodian Gibbon Ecotours   WILDLIFE
(☑097 752 9960; www.cambodiangibbons.word press.com; tours from US$100; ☺tours Nov-mid-Jun) 🔖 Spend the night in the jungle, then rise well before dawn to spend time with semi-habituated northern buff-cheeked gibbons at this community-based ecotourism project (CBET) set up by Conserva-

tion International (CI; www.conservation. org) just outside the border of Virachey National Park, north of Veun Sai. The high-season-only tours cost US$100 to US$200 per person for a one-night, two-day trip, depending on group size and which tour company you choose. Most companies in Ban Lung can arrange these trips on behalf of CI.

This species was only discovered in 2010 and the population here is believed to be one of the largest in the world at about 500 groups. Hearing their haunting dawn call and seeing them swing through the canopy is memorable. These tours also offer the opportunity to experience dense jungle, open savannah, rivers and waterfalls, and Kavet and Lao villages.

CI has an exclusive arrangement with the village near the gibbon site to run these tours within the Veun Sai–Siem Pang Conservation Area (VSSPCA). You stay at least one night in the jungle, sleeping in hammocks or in a community-based homestay. The fee includes entrance to the VSSPCA, guide, homestays and camps, and all meals. The gibbon-viewing season runs from November to mid-June – it's too wet at other times – and the visits are limited to six people at a time. For an organised tour to the area with transportation, try **Gibbon Spotting Cambodia** (☑063-966355; www.gibbon spottingcambodia.com) 🔖.

Highland Tours   ADVENTURE
(☑097 658 3841; highland.tour@yahoo.com) Kimi and Horng are husband-and-wife graduates of Le Tonlé Tourism Training Center, who have moved to the highlands to run a range of tours. These include fun day trips and a multiday tour between Veun Sai and Ta Veng that combines trekking with floating down the Tonlé San on a bamboo raft. Horng is one of the only female guides in Ratanakiri.

Sona Trekking   TREKKING
(☑097 825 0366; http://sonatrekking.com) The excitable Sona runs backpacker-oriented trips to waterfalls, minority villages, and forests on the edge of the national park. He also rents scooters (US$6) and offers ultrabasic dorm accommodation (US$2). Find him at Banlung Reggae Bar (p295).

DutchCo Trekking Cambodia   TREKKING
(☑097 679 2714; www.trekkingcambodia.com) One of the most experienced trekking oper-

LUMKUT LAKE

Lumkut (បឹងលំកុដ) is a large crater lake hemmed in by dense forest on all sides, similar to the more illustrious and accessible Boeng Yeak Lom. To get to the lake, turn south off the highway to O Yadaw about 33km east of Ban Lung. The lake is 15km south along a rough road. Access is difficult in the rainy season, so most visitors opt for the convenience of Boeng Yeak Lom.

On the way to the lake you can stop off in **Bokheo** (បរកែវ), an on-again, off-again hotspot for gem mining, 29km east of Ban Lung. Locals dig a large pit in the ground and then tunnel horizontally in their search for amethyst and zircon. The mines tend to move around so ask where to find them.

That gem mining is big business in the province is hardly surprising given that Ratanakiri means 'hill of the precious stones'. Just don't get suckered into a dream deal, as gem scams here are as old as the hills themselves.

ators in the province, run by – wait for it – a friendly Dutchman. Runs one- to five-day treks north of Veun Sai through Kavet villages and community forests, and two-day gibbon treks, among many other tours.

Parrot Tours OUTDOORS
(☏ 097 403 5884; www.trekkingincambodia.com) Parrot runs a range of overnight treks in the forests north of Itub, home to throngs of gibbons, as well as mountain biking, bamboo rafting and more. Sitha Nan is a national-park-trained guide with expert local knowledge.

🛏 Sleeping

Accommodation in Ratanakiri is terrific value, even by Cambodia standards. If the best places are booked out, several bog-standard high-rise hotels near the market have rooms in the US$10 to US$20 range, but none are worth writing home about.

⭐ Tree Top Ecolodge BUNGALOW $
(☏ 012 490333; d US$8, cottage with cold/hot water US$13/15; 🛜) 'Mr T's' place is one of the best places to stay in Cambodia's 'Wild East', with oodles of atmosphere. Rough-hewn walkways lead to huge bungalows featuring thatch roofs and hammock-strewn verandahs with verdant valley vistas. Like the bungalows, the restaurant is fashioned from hardwood and dangles over a lush ravine (it's also the only place you can get wi-fi).

Up-to-date travel advice is plentiful, especially for those who are Laos bound.

⭐ Family House Homestay HOMESTAY $
(☏ 097 481 4444; bputhea@yahoo.com; dm/d/tr US$2.50/5/7; 🛜) *Remork-moto* driver cum homestay owner Bun Puthea is one of the

friendliest, most knowledgeable people in town. Guests rave about his cheerful hilltop homestay, which has both rooms and detached bungalows spread around a colourful garden with mountain views. Sturdy wood-carved furniture, inviting hammocks and access to a kitchen make for a pleasant stay. Some rooms share bathrooms.

Bee Bee's Chalets HOMESTAY $
(☏ 088 429 2085; r/bungalow US$5/6; 🛜) This backpacker favourite has three maroon 'chalets' (in reality, simple bungalows) and two private rooms. The former are a big step up from the latter (and just US$1 more) with hammocks hanging across small porches. The hospitable owners have been known to leave a lasting impression on visitors.

Nature House Ecolodge GUESTHOUSE $
(☏ 088 204 5888; dm US$2, r US$5-7, bungalow US$10; 🛜) Hidden away in the remote northwest corner of town, this place is worth seeking out for its expansive yet inexpensive rooms. Cheaper rooms are in the main building, which includes a small restaurant, while great-value bungalows with spectacular views are in the garden.

Thy Ath Lodge HOTEL $
(☏ 017 386396; thy.ath.lodge@gmail.com; Boeng Kansaign; r US$15-25; ❄🛜) This lakeside lodge is run by a friendly family who make their guests feel very at home. Rooms are spacious and airy; options include suite-like cottages out front – an absolute steal for US$25.

⭐ Terres Rouges Lodge BOUTIQUE HOTEL $$
(☏ 012 660902; www.ratanakiri-lodge.com; Boeng Kansaign; r/ste incl breakfast from US$65/90; ❄🛜🏊) Even as the competition kicks in,

Terres Rouges remains one of the most atmospheric places to stay in provincial Cambodia. The standard rooms are small but classy, with beautiful Cambodian furniture, tribal artefacts and a long common verandah. The suites consist of spacious Balinese-style bungalows with open-plan bathrooms, set in the gorgeous garden.

If you're travelling with kids or looking for a little more comfort in Ban Lung, this option is a no-brainer. The restaurant has one of the most sophisticated menus in town.

★Ratanakiri Boutique Hotel   HOTEL $$
(☏070 565750; www.ratanakiri-boutiquehotel.com; Boeng Kansaign; standard/lake-view r US$19/25, ste US$60; ❄️🛜🏊) This smart hotel with panoramic lake views offers spry service for this remote corner of the country. With inlaid-stone bathroom walls and indigenous bed runners, the Khmer-inspired design is eye-catching, but you're mainly staying here for the combination of lake-view balconies and generous mod cons.

Yeak Loam Hotel   HOTEL $$
(☏075-974975; www.yeakloamhotel.com; r incl breakfast US$30-110; ❄️🛜🏊) Looming large over downtown Ban Lung, this stylish upmarket hotel offers 70 contemporary rooms with 40in smart TVs and inviting bathrooms. The hotel has an illuminated sky bar on the 9th floor, which draws a local crowd on weekend nights.

Ratanak Resort   BOUTIQUE HOTEL $$
(☏092 244114; www.ratanakresort.com; r incl breakfast US$39-100; ❄️🛜🏊) Located a few kilometres out of town on a bluff near Boeng Yeak Lom, Ratanak is a stylish, all-wooden resort with accommodation in upmarket bungalows. Rooms include four-poster beds with billowing drapes and useful extras for the dapper adventurer, such as a bathrobe and hairdryer. The small infinity pool here is open to nonguests for US$3.

🍴 Eating & Drinking

Ban Lung has a decent mix of Cambodian and international eateries, mostly clustered near the Parrot Tours (p293) office. Among the guesthouses, Terres Rouges Lodge has the most sophisticated menu, while Tree Top Ecolodge (p293) is also reliable.

To get down with the locals, head to the lakefront near Coconut Shake Restaurant around sunset, plop down on a mat, and order cheap beer and snacks from waterfront shacks.

★Cafe Alee   INTERNATIONAL $
(mains US$1.50-7.50; ⏱7am-9pm; 🛜🍴) 🌿 This friendly cafe has one of the more interesting menus in town, including a generous smattering of vegetarian options, a hearty lasagne and the full gamut of Khmer food. Be sure to check the exciting specials board. It often stays open later if there is drinking to be done.

It also runs a scholarship to send minority kids to college.

RESPONSIBLE TREKKING AROUND RATANAKIRI

Overnight treks in the forests of Ratanakiri are quite popular. Diehard trampers spend up to eight days sleeping in replica US Army hammocks and checking out some of the country's last virgin forest in and around Virachey National Park (p296).

Where possible, we recommend using indigenous guides for organised treks and other excursions around Ban Lung. They speak the local dialects and can secure permission to visit cemeteries (p297) that are off-limits to Khmer guides. The cemeteries are interesting for the carved effigies of the deceased that stand guard over the graves.

Unfortunately, with a few notable exceptions, the level of English among indigenous guides tends to be limited. If you need a more fluent English guide, we suggest hiring both an English-speaking Khmer guide and a minority guide, if it's within your budget.

A loose association of Tompuon guides is based at Boeng Yeak Lom (p291) – they can take you on an exclusive tour of several local Tompuon villages. They have neither a phone number nor an email so you'll just have to show up. You can observe weavers and basket-makers in action, learn about animist traditions and eat a traditional indigenous meal of bamboo-steamed fish, fresh vegetables, 'minority' rice and, of course, rice wine.

Virachey National Park also employs some indigenous guides and uses minority porters, while the tour companies we recommend can all hire indigenous guides on request.

★ Green Carrot INTERNATIONAL $

(☏071 929 3278; mains US$2-6; ⊗8am-10pm; 🛜) A great little hole-in-the-wall restaurant that turns out surprisingly sophisticated food, including healthy salads, sandwiches and wraps, plus a good range of Khmer favourites. It even does a decent burger and some very tasty pizzas. Happy hour has two-for-one cocktails from 5pm to 9pm.

Crush Cafe COFFEE

(www.facebook.com/thecrushcafe; ⊗6.30am-7pm; 🛜) Thick espressos and iced lattes, ultrafriendly English-language service and strong wi-fi make this cute little coffee shop the best in the region.

Ta Nam CAMBODIAN $

(dishes 8000-12,000r; ⊗6am-8pm; 🛜) Locals flock to this restaurant one block east of the market for wholesome Cambodian and Chinese breakfasts, including steaming bowls of noodle soup – guaranteed to give an energy boost ahead of a trek in the forest. Coffee here comes from the owner's farm 2km away. If you like it, you can buy some beans to take home.

Coconut Shake Restaurant CAMBODIAN $

(☏012 830988; Boeng Kansaign; mains 6000-16,000r; ⊗7am-9pm; 🛜) The best coconut shakes in the northeast cost just 4000r at this expansive place overlooking the lake. It has fried noodles and other Khmer fare if you're feeling peckish.

Banlung Reggae Bar BAR

(☏097 825 0366; ⊗6am-midnight) Ban Lung may be about as far as you can get from the Cambodian coast, but you'll still find a reggae bar ruling the backpacker bar scene. A tip: stick to beer. The name-brand liquors advertised are actually local substitutes.

ℹ Information

Visitors will find guesthouses or tour companies to be most useful in their quest for local knowledge.

Canadia Bank (⊗8.30am-3.30pm Mon-Fri, to 11.30am Sat, ATM 24hr) Full-service bank with an international ATM.

Tourist Office (☏075-974125; NH78; ⊗7.30-11.30am & 2-5pm Mon-Fri) Official government office with irregular opening hours and little in the way of handouts.

Virachey National Park Eco-Tourism Information Centre (☏097 730 0979, 097 333 4775; leamsou@gmail.com; ⊗8-11am & 2-5pm Mon-Fri) The place to organise trekking in Virachey National Park, though you may find more luck having a private tour company contact rangers directly (for a fee), as centre staff have limited English and are often away in the park.

🚍 Getting There & Away

Ban Lung is 510km northeast of Phnom Penh and 129km east of O Pong Moan, the junction town 19km south of Stung Treng. Highway NH78 between Ban Lung and O Pong Moan is flat, empty and fully sealed, but leave early as very little public transport departs Ban Lung in the afternoon.

A vast bus station was built on the western outskirts of town, 2.5km west of Ban Lung's main roundabout, but it now lies abandoned. Most buses depart from the market, though guesthouses and tour companies can arrange pick-ups, which is generally more convenient.

Virak Buntham (☏092 222423; www.virakbuntham.com) operates minivans to Phnom Penh (US$10 to US$14, eight to 10 hours) via Kratie and Kompong Cham. These leave at 7am, 8.30am and 12.30pm. It also has a sleeper bus at 7.30pm. Call a tour company or guesthouse to arrange an express van pick-up if coming from Phnom Penh.

Express minivans serve Stung Treng from 7.30am (US$7, two hours). Advertised trips to Laos (Don Det and Pakse) by express minivan depart at the same time and involve a van change and a few hours' wait in Stung Treng (to Don Det US$17, seven hours).

Express minivans to Siem Reap leave at 7am and 10am (US$13, seven hours). A couple of companies run minivans to Sen Monorom via the new highway (US$7, 3½ hours), with departures around 7am and noon.

Local minibuses and pick-up trucks service Lumphat (10,000r, one hour), O'Yadaw (16,000r, 1½ hours) and more remote Ratanakiri villages from the market area. Local minibuses also offer cheap transport to Kratie (25,000r) and even Phnom Penh (50,000r) for the adventurous and/or masochistic. Share taxis out of Ban Lung are rare.

🚲 Getting Around

Bicycles (US$2 to US$5) and motorbikes (US$6 to US$7) are available for hire from most guesthouses in town. **Mr Bona Tour** (☏097 994 4168; mountain bike/scooter US$5/6) is a good bet for mountain bikes and scooters. Though once common, 250cc trail bikes are increasingly hard to find, due to the cost of maintenance this far from Phnom Penh.

Motos (motorcycle taxis) hang out around the market and some drivers double as guides. Figure on US$15 to US$20 per day for a good English-speaking driver-guide. A moto to Boeng

ℹ️ GETTING TO VIETNAM: BAN LUNG TO PLEIKU

Getting to the border The O'Yadaw/Le Thanh border crossing (7am to 5pm) is 70km east of Ban Lung along smooth NH78. From Ban Lung, guesthouses advertise a 7.30am bus to Pleiku in Vietnam (US$11, five hours). The van picks you up at your guesthouse for a surcharge, which is easier than trying to arrange a ticket independently. Alternatively, take a local minibus to O'Yadaw from Ban Lung's market, and continue 25km to the border by *moto* (motorcycle taxi).

At the border Formalities are straightforward and lines nonexistent, but make sure you have a Vietnamese visa if required, as visas are not issued at the border.

Moving on Once on the Vietnamese side of the frontier, the road is nicely paved and *motos* await to take you to Duc Co (20km), where there are buses to Pleiku for onward travel to Quy Nhon and Hoi An.

Yeak Lom costs about US$5 return; to Veun Sai it's US$15 return; to any waterfall it's about US$7 or so return.

Remorks are expensive by Cambodian standards, about double what a *moto* costs.

Veun Sai

🎵 075 / POP 3285

Located on the banks of Tonlé San, Veun Sai (វិនៃស៊ី) is a cluster of Chinese, Lao and ethnic minority villages. Originally, the town was located on the north bank of the river and known as Virachey, but these days the main settlement is on the south bank. There is not a lot to see on the south side, but there are some interesting settlements on the north bank.

From the south side, cross the river on a small ferry (1000/2000r without/with a motorbike) and walk west for a couple of kilometres, passing through the Khmer village and a small minority area. Next is a wealthy Chinese village, complete with large wooden houses and inhabitants who still speak Chinese, before you finally emerge in a Lao community.

The Veun Sai area is known for its minority cemeteries, but most of them are closed to outsiders these days. The bans are at least partially the result of tourists flaunting behavioural protocols.

The closest cemetery to Veun Sai open to visitors is an ethnic Kachah cemetery in Kaoh Paek, a 45-minute boat ride upriver from Veun Sai. Expect to pay around US$20 for the boat trip from Veun Sai, or a little less than that from Kachon, 10km upriver (east) of Veun Sai. Tour companies in Ban Lung charge US$50 for an excursion here. Family House Homestay (p293), in particular, has

a good relationship with the villagers and runs informative trips.

There are clusters of food stalls on either side of the ferry dock where you can pick up basic local meals such as noodles and rice.

Veun Sai is 39km northwest of Ban Lung on an unsealed but smooth all-weather road. It is easy enough to get here under your own steam on a motorbike or with a vehicle. English-speaking guides ask US$15 or so return to take you out here on a *moto* (motorcycle taxi).

Experienced motorbike riders can ride from Veun Sai to Siem Pang (55km) in Stung Treng along a scenic trail that begins on the north side of the river.

Virachey National Park

🎵 075 / POP 1000

One of Cambodia's largest protected areas, Virachey National Park (ឧទ្យានជាតិវិរៈជ័យ; 🎵 097 333 4775; leamsou@gmail.com; ⊙ office 8-11am & 2-5pm Mon-Fri) stretches for 3325 sq km east to Vietnam, north to Laos and west to Stung Treng Province. The park has never been fully explored and is home to a number of rare mammals, including elephants, clouded leopards and sun bears. Your chances of seeing any of these creatures are slim, but you'll probably hear endangered gibbons and you might spot great hornbills, giant ibis and other rare birds.

So important is the park to the Mekong region that it was designated an Asean Heritage Park in 2003. It's only possible to visit on organised treks booked through the Virachey National Park Eco-Tourism Information Centre in Ban Lung, or arranged with park management via a private tour company. The usual gateway is Ta Veng District on the Tonlé San, about 47km north of Ban Lung on a roller coaster of a road.

Tours

Virachey has one of the more organised ecotourism programmes in Cambodia, focusing on small-scale culture, nature and adventure trekking. The programme aims to involve and benefit local minority communities. The park offers two- to eight-day treks led by English-speaking rangers. The longer your trip, the deeper you'll get into the jungle. Private operators offer tours in the park buffer zone, but are forbidden from taking tourists into the park proper. However, private tour companies can be useful in setting things up in advance with park staff, who are not always responsive.

Phnom Veal Thom
Wilderness Trek   TREKKING

(☑097 333 4775; somsophanyvnp@gmail.com; per person US$236-413) The signature trek in Virachey National Park is this six-day, five-night odyssey. The trek goes deep into the heart of the Phnom Veal Thom grasslands, an area rich in wildlife including sambar deer, gibbons, langurs, wild pigs, bears and hornbills. The price includes transport by *moto* (motorcycle taxi) to the trailhead, park admission, food, guides, porters, hammocks and boat transport.

Prices drop the larger the group. The trek starts from Ta Veng with an overnight homestay in a Brau village. Trekkers return via a different route and pass through areas of evergreen forest.

Yak Kae Waterfall Trek   TREKKING

(☑097 333 4775; somsophanyvnp@gmail.com) This leisurely three-day, two-night trek involves a homestay in an ethnic Brau village on night one and camping on night two near the Yak Kae Waterfall.

Sleeping & Eating

Most nights in the park will be spent in hammocks with mosquito-net covers. Minority village homestays are an option on some treks.

All food is carried in by guides and porters, and is included in the price of the trekking tour.

Getting There & Away

Transport by *moto* (motorcycle taxi) to the trailhead is included in the cost of your tour, or you can pay a bit extra for something more comfortable.

MONDULKIRI PROVINCE

POP 75,000

Mondulkiri Province (ខេត្តមណ្ឌលគិរី), the original 'Wild East', is a world apart from the lowlands, with not a rice paddy or palm tree in sight.

Home to the hardy Bunong people and their noble elephants, this upland area is a seductive mix of grassy hills, pine groves and rainforests of jade green. Wild animals, such as bears, leopards and especially elephants, are more numerous here than elsewhere, although sightings are usually limited to birds, monkeys and the occasional wild pig. Conservationists have established several superb ecotourism projects in the province, but are facing off against loggers, poachers, plantations and well-connected speculators.

Mondulkiri means 'Meeting of the Hills', an apt sobriquet for this land of rolling hills. It is the most sparsely populated province in the country, with just four people per square kilometre. At an average elevation of 800m, it can get quite chilly at night, so bring something warm.

Sen Monorom
🎵 073 / POP 10,000

The provincial capital of Mondulkiri, Sen Monorom (សែនមនោរម្យ) is really an over-grown village, a charming community set in the spot where the hills that give the province its name meet. In the centre of town are two lakes, leading some dreamers to call it 'the Switzerland of Cambodia'.

The area around Sen Monorom is peppered with minority villages and picturesque waterfalls, making it the ideal place to spend some time. Many of the Bunong people from nearby communities come here to trade, carrying goods in distinctive baskets on their backs. Set at 800m, when the winds blow Sen Monorom is notably cooler than the rest of Cambodia, so bring warm clothing.

⊙ Sights

Not much happens in Sen Monorom itself, but there are a few worthwhile sights within a motorbike ride or a long walk from town, including several waterfalls.

★ Bou Sraa Waterfall
WATERFALL

(ទឹកជ្រោះប៊ូស្រា; US$2.50; ⊙7am-5pm) Plunging into the dense jungle below, this is one of Cambodia's most impressive falls. Famous throughout the country, this double-drop waterfall has an upper tier of some 10m and a spectacular lower tier with a thundering 25m drop. Getting here involves a 33km, one-hour journey east of Sen Monorom on a mostly sealed road.

The sprawling **Bou Sraa Eco-Park** at the falls is home to a cultural village, craft stands and some simple eateries.

Wat Phnom Doh Kromom
BUDDHIST TEMPLE

(វត្តភ្នំដោះក្រមុំ) FREE Looming over the northeast corner of the airstrip, Wat Phnom Doh Kromom has Mondulkiri's best sunset vista, where a wooden platform lets you take in the views over Sen Monorom. Continue another 5km north to the wat for **Samot Cheur** (Ocean of Trees), a viewpoint overlooking an emerald forest to the east.

Dak Dam Waterfall
WATERFALL

(ទឹកជ្រោះដាកដាំ) FREE Dak Dam Waterfall is 25km southeast of Sen Monorom, about 2km south of the Bunong village of Dak Dam. It's very difficult to find without assistance, so it's best to take a *moto* (motorcycle taxi) or local guide; otherwise, locals are able to lead the way if you can make yourself understood.

TREAD LIGHTLY IN THE HILLS

Tourism can bring many benefits to highland communities: cross-cultural understanding, improved infrastructure, cheaper market goods, employment opportunities and tourist dollars supporting handicraft industries. However, there are also negatives, such as increased litter and pollutants, domination of the tourism business by lowland Khmers at the expense of highland minorities, and the tendency of tourists to disregard local customs and taboos.

One way to offset the negatives in a big way is to hire indigenous guides. Not only does this ensure that your tourist dollars go directly to indigenous communities, it will also enrich your own visit. Indigenous guides can greatly improve your access to the residents of highland communities, who are animists and speak Khmer only as a second language. Locals also understand taboos and traditions that might be lost on Khmer guides. Their intimate knowledge of the forests is another major asset.

Romanear Waterfall

WATERFALL

(ទឹកធ្លាក់រមនា) **FREE** Romanear is a low, wide waterfall with some convenient swimming holes, though private development threatens to change its pristine charm. Set 18km southeast of Sen Monorom, it's very difficult to find without assistance, so it's best to take a *moto* (motorcycle taxi) or local guide.

Nearby is a second waterfall, known rather originally as **Romanear II** (ទឹកធ្លាក់រមនាពីរ) **FREE**. It's by a pepper plantation near the main road between Sen Monorom and Snuol.

Monorom Falls

WATERFALL

(ទឹកធ្លាក់មនោរម្យ) **FREE** A 10m drop into a popular swimming hole, Monorom Falls is pretty if you can avoid the crowds and the attendant litter. From the west side of the airstrip, head northwest for 2.3km, turn left and proceed 1.5km. There's no legible sign at the turn-off.

Activities

Several Bunong villages around Sen Monorom make for popular excursions, although the frequently visited villages that appear on tourist maps have assimilated into modern society. In general, the further out you go, the less exposed the village.

Trips to Bunong villages can often be combined with waterfalls or ethical elephant interaction tours (eg walking with or feeding, not riding, the elephants). Each guesthouse has a preferred village to send travellers to, which is a great way to spread the wealth.

For more on Bunong culture, check out the website of the Mondulkiri Resource and Documentation Centre (www.mondulkiricentre.org), run by local NGO Mondulkiri Indigenous People Association for Development (MIPAD). MIPAD also runs the **WEHH** (☏088 613 6921; tongsamnang13@gmail.com; from US$55) 🌿 tour programme, which offers an intimate look at Bunong culture in the Dak Dam community. Itineraries include 'life on a Bunong farm', 'the handicrafts of the Bunong' and a trek into old-growth Bunong forest. Prices start from US$55 per person, subject to the size of the group.

Yoga classes (75 minutes, US$7) take place weekday mornings (and afternoons by reservation only) upstairs at the Hefalump Cafe (p305). Headline activities outside town include visiting the Elephant Valley Project and the Jahoo Gibbon Camp (p303) in Keo Seima Wildlife Sanctuary.

Mayura Zipline

ADVENTURE SPORTS

(☏011 797779, 071 888 0800; http://mondulkresort.com; Bou Sraa Waterfall; US$50; ☺9am-3.30pm) The Mayura Zipline is an adrenaline rush in the extreme, as the longest line passes right over the top of the spectacular Bou Sraa Falls. Starting on the far bank of the river, there are seven lines to navigate, plus a suspension bridge. The first four zips are warm-ups for the 300m-long high-speed flight over the waterfall.

It takes around one hour or so to navigate for smaller groups. Contact guesthouses and hotels for advance bookings or just show up at the information centre at the falls. Discounts on the price are sometimes available.

Other tours include a guided trek to the base of the lower fall (US$15).

Elephant Encounters

A backlash against riding elephants has led to a proliferation of interactive elephant experiences in Mondulkiri, with four projects offering tourists a chance to walk and interact with former working elephants in forest sanctuaries around Sen Monorom. Some are better run than others, and some ensure more of their income is ploughed into elephant welfare than others, so it pays to do some homework before signing up for an elephant encounter.

⭐**Elephant Valley Project** WILDLIFE RESERVE
(EVP; ☏099 696041; www.elephantvalleyproject.org; ☺Mon-Fri, Sun high season only) 🌿 For an original elephant experience, visit this pioneering 'walking with the herd' project, which entices local mahouts to bring their overworked or injured elephants to this 1500-hectare sanctuary. It's very popular, so make sure you book well ahead. You can visit for a day (US$95), a half-day (US$45) or overnight.

Mahouts who bring their elephants here are paid a competitive working wage to retire their elephants full-time to the forest and ecotourism. Mahouts continue to work with their elephants, feeding and caring for them and making sure they are as content as possible. The elephants, for their part, can spend their days blasting through the forest in search of food and hanging out by the river spraying mud on one another.

Visitors are not allowed to ride the elephants here. Instead, you simply walk through the forest with them and observe them in their element. In the process you learn a lot about not only elephant behaviour

Sen Monorom

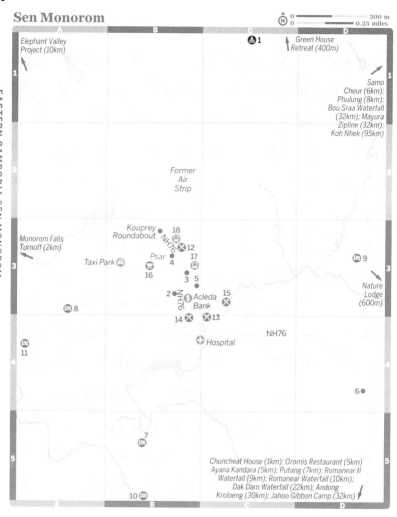

but also Bunong culture and forest ecology. Other project components include funding forestry protection for wild elephants, as well as healthcare and other support for Bunong communities in the project area in exchange for use of the forest. Most importantly, health and veterinary care are funded for all the elephants in Mondulkiri, not just those resident in the valley. The Wildlife Conservation Society lauds the EVP for helping to protect the eastern reaches of the Keo Seima Wildlife Sanctuary.

The overnight options include a stay in spacious bungalows tucked into the jungle on a ridge overlooking the valley. A two-

day package in dorm-style accommodation costs US$140, while private bungalows cost US$160. Longer stays of three days (dorm/bungalow US$270/300) and five days (US$450/500) are also available. Prices include full board. EVP does not take overnight visitors on Friday and Saturday nights and is not open to day visitors on Saturday (or Sunday in low season).

Access to the site is tightly controlled, so don't show up unannounced as there are free-range elephants wandering around. The maximum number of day-trippers allowed per group is 14.

Sen Monorom

◎ Sights
1 Wat Phnom Doh Kromom C1

◎ Activities, Courses & Tours
2 Green House B3
3 Mondulkiri Elephant & Wildlife
   Sanctuary B3
   Mondulkiri Tour Guide .... (see 3)
4 Sam Veasna Center B3
5 The Hangout Tours B3
   WEHH .... (see 4)
6 WWF D4

◎ Sleeping
7 Elephant Hill Resort B5
8 Happy Elephant A3
9 Indigenous Peoples Lodge D3
10 Mayura Hill Hotel & Resort B5
11 Tree Lodge A4

◎ Eating
12 Bamboo Cafe B3
   Bunong Kitchen .... (see 3)
13 Cinnamon Café C4
   Green House Restaurant &
   Bar .... (see 2)
   Hefalump Cafe .... (see 4)
14 Monduk...Italy B4
15 Mondulkiri Pizza C3

◎ Drinking & Nightlife
16 MK Coffee Shop B3
   The Hangout .... (see 5)

◎ Transport
17 Kim Seng Express B3
18 Rithya Express B3
   Virak Buntham .... (see 18)

If you are in Mondulkiri at the weekend, you may want to consider an alternative elephant experience, such as visiting a community-owned elephant in the village of **Putang** or **Phulung**, or one of the other experiences on offer, but we actively discourage elephant riding.

Mondulkiri Elephant
& Wildlife Sanctuary   ECOTOUR
(☑ 011 494449; www.mondulkirisanctuary.org; NH76; day visits per adult US$50, child 6-14yr US$25, under 6yr free) ◢ Established by LEAF (Local Environmental Awareness Foundation), this is a small wildlife corridor near the Otai River. Overnight trips with homestays and forest treks can be arranged. Group numbers are limited to 20 people per day. Volunteers are welcome and tours are run on both weekdays and weekends.

Trekking
Multiday forest treks run by guesthouses and tour operators are popular. Figure on about US$35 to US$50 per person per day for overnight trips, including all meals, transfer to the trailhead by *moto* (motorcycle taxi) and an English-speaking guide. Per-person prices drop for larger groups.

We recommend securing indigenous Bunong guides for these trips: they know the forests intimately and can break the ice with the locals in any Bunong villages you visit. The better guesthouse-based tour operators, such as Nature Lodge and Green House, usually employ Bunong people as porters on longer excursions, but you should request this service.

A popular day trip involves hiking 12km through the forest from the Bunong community of Putang to a waterfall in Ou Reang.

☞ Tours

Sam Veasna Center   WILDLIFE
(SVC; ☑ 063 963710, 092 554473; www.samveasna.org) ◢ SVC works with the international NGO Wildlife Conservation Society in promoting wildlife and birdwatching tours in the nearby Keo Seima Wildlife Sanctuary (p304), including rare primate spotting at the wonderful Jahoo Gibbon Camp (p303), 30km west of Sen Monorom. Mony Sang, who runs the programme, is based in Siem Reap, so it's best to book well in advance. Hefalump Cafe (p305) provides info in Sen Monorom.

The Hangout Tours   TREKKING
(☑ 088 721 9991; NH76) Specialises in wildlife-watching trips out to the Jahoo Gibbon Camp (p303) in Keo Seima Wildlife Sanctuary, priced at US$85 per person per day for groups of two or more. Also on offer are more budget-friendly romps on the edge of the sanctuary, combining forest trekking with visits to local Bunong communities.

Mondulkiri Tour Guide   TOURS
(☑ 088 593 5588; www.mondulkiritourguide.com; NH76; tours per person from US$50) Operated by experienced guide Mony Hong, who can take you deep into the bush on either a day trip or overnight visits to Ratanakiri and beyond. His office is at Monorom Pizza.

WWF   ECOTOUR
(World Wide Fund For Nature; ☑ 073-690 0096; www.panda.org; NH76) ◢ WWF has been involved in a host of ecotourism initiatives

around Mondulkiri over the years, including tours north of Sen Monorom to the Phnom Prich Wildlife Sanctuary and Srepok Wildlife Sanctuary, formerly Mondulkiri Protected Forest. These tours were suspended at the time of research, pending the appointment of new staff, but may be back on by the time you read this.

Green House TOURS
(☏ 017 905659; www.greenhouse-tour.blogspot. com; NH76) One of the longest-running tour operators in Mondulkiri, Green House organises the full range of forest treks and waterfall trips, and there are motorbikes for hire (per day US$7).

🛏 Sleeping

Hot water is a nice bonus in chilly Mondulkiri, but it usually costs a little more. Places without hot-water showers can usually provide flasks of boiling water for bathing. There is rarely need for air-conditioning in this neck of the woods. Some of the most atmospheric stays, including the Elephant Valley Project (p299) and Jahoo Gibbon Camp (p303), lie on the outskirts of town.

★**Nature Lodge** GUESTHOUSE $
(☏ 012 230272; www.naturelodgecambodia.com; s/d/f from US$10/15/30; 🖤) Sprawling across a windswept hilltop near town are 30 solid wood bungalows with private porches, hot showers and mosquito nets. Among them are *Swiss Family Robinson*–style chalets with sunken beds and anterooms. The magnificent restaurant has comfy nooks, a pool table and an enviable bar, where guests chill out and swap travel tales.

Trek-fuelling burgers and pasta are the restaurant's speciality, plus plenty of vegetarian options. An array of tours are neatly outlined on the menu, including the affiliated Mondulkiri Elephant & Wildlife Sanctuary (p301).

Indigenous Peoples Lodge BUNGALOW $
(☏ 012 471864; indigenouspeopleslodge@gmail. com; s/d/q from US$8/15/25; 🖤) Run by a Bunong family, this is a great place to stay, with a range of accommodation set in minority houses, including a traditional thatched Bunong house with an upgrade or two. The cheapest rooms involve a share bathroom, but are good value. Perks include free internet and free drop-offs in town.

Tree Lodge BUNGALOW $
(☏ 097 723 4177; www.treelodgecambodia.com; d/q/f US$7/12/15; 🖤) Sixteen bungalows of various shapes and sizes drip down a hillside at the back of the reception. Rooms have balconies and attractive open-air bathrooms, but lack any shelf space or furniture besides a bed. Hang out at the restaurant, where hammocks and tasty Khmer food await.

The young family in charge are very welcoming and can help with tour arrangements.

Happy Elephant GUESTHOUSE $
(☏ 097 616 4011; dm US$3; r US$8-15; 🖤) French-Khmer couple Vivi and Mot are your hosts with the most at this basic but atmospheric backpacker pad, which features sturdy cold-water bungalows cascading down a jungle-clad hill. They also offer tours and treks for those without a game plan.

Green House Retreat BUNGALOW $$
(☏ 017 905659; dm US$12, bungalow US$12-45; 🖤🖤) Opened in 2017, this lovely little resort on the edge of town offers a generous dorm and some stylish and spacious bungalows. There are extensive gardens, organic vegetables grown on-site and a restaurant-bar to soak up the views of the surrounding hills.

Ayana Kandara Boutique Hotel BOUTIQUE HOTEL $$
(☏ 099 763854; Road to Putang village; r US$35-50; 🖤🖤🖤) Located on a windswept hilltop about 6km south of town, this boutique resort has spectacular views of the Mondulkiri landscape. Rooms are spacious and stylish for the money and the resort includes a small swimming pool amid the manicured gardens. Given the remote location, it's best suited to those with private transport.

Chuncheat House Eco-Lodge BUNGALOW $$
(☏ 088 800 0046; r US$20-50; 🖤🖤) At this quirky lodge on the outskirts of town, the bungalows are designed in keeping with the architecture of the Bunong and other minority groups – although they are somewhat more gentrified, with en-suite bathrooms and decorative flourishes. The sweeping views are impressive and there is a small restaurant.

RESPONSIBLE ENCOUNTERS WITH ELEPHANTS

According to legend, more than one million elephants were used in the construction of Angkor Wat. In reality the numbers were closer to 6000, but elephants have long played an important role in Cambodian history. They were the tractors and tanks that gave the god-kings of Angkor the means to project their power across the region. Originally these elephants were trapped in the wild by the kingdom's indigenous communities.

This illustrious history was cut short by conflict, as captive elephants were marked as a 'legitimate war target' – they were either killed or their owners fled to neighbouring countries. Contemporary Cambodia has very few captive elephants left – just 69 at the last count (38 of which are in Mondulkiri) – and their numbers are dwindling due to overwork and old age. Most are employed in the tourism industry. With captive elephants no longer being bred, the biggest hope for the survival of their species lies with Cambodia's healthy wild population, which stands at around 500 and is protected by the country's remaining forests.

The modern-day relationship between elephants and tourism is a complex one. There are now more elephants working to carry tourists around than to haul timber or rice, so their care is dependent on the dollars that tourism generates, and once captured they cannot return to the wild. However, there is increasing evidence that riding is actually damaging to the health of the elephant. There are also ethical concerns, given that these are highly endangered wild animals.

Before you consider signing up for an elephant encounter, ask to take a closer look at the animals and their environment. There are many activities tourists take part in that can unwittingly have a negative effect on the elephants. A few things to consider:

➡ Elephants don't like being ridden, especially by anyone who is not their mahout. Most riding also involves carrying large heavy baskets and hours of exhausting work that is damaging to the animal.

➡ Only mahouts have the training to go into the water with an elephant. Tourists have been injured while swimming with elephants in Asia; elephants can lash out if forced to spend longer in the water for the tourists' experience.

➡ Keep your distance taking photos; if you're turning your back to take a selfie, stand 6m to 8m away. Note also that flash photography can spook elephants, and harsh, unnatural light can upset them.

➡ If feeding an elephant, make sure there is a barrier between you and the animal, and feed to its trunk (not its mouth). Elephants often strike out when they are frustrated by not being fed correctly or quickly enough.

➡ Mahouts have a very close relationship with their elephants, understanding the mood and when it's safe to interact; tourists shouldn't approach an elephant unsupervised.

➡ Elephants in captivity are only a small proportion of the elephant population in Cambodia. Check if some of your money is going to fund wild elephant habitat conservation.

For more on elephant welfare and tourism, check out www.elemotion.org or www.world animalprotection.org.

Compiled with assistance from Jack Highwood, Founder, Elephant Valley Project (www.elephantvalleyproject.org).

Elephant Hill Resort   HOTEL **$$**
(☏073-500 0666; http://elephant-hill-resort-kh. book.direct; r from US$80; ❋🛜❄) A good choice for families looking for a comfortable midrange option, Elephant Hill's rooms are set in spacious villas that double as suites. Each villa includes a lounge, a bedroom and an indulgent *two* bathrooms. The elaborate engravings at the restaurant are wowing, and there's a rare fitness centre, too.

⭐**Jahoo Gibbon Camp**   TENTED CAMP **$$$**
(☏community contact 088 592 8758; http://sam veasna.org; Andong Kroloeng; per person incl meals US$85-200) 🌿 At this tented camp in the Keo Seima Wildlife Sanctuary, rates

KEO SEIMA WILDLIFE SANCTUARY: MONKEY BUSINESS IN MONDULKIRI

A recent Wildlife Conservation Society (WCS) study estimated populations of 23,600 black-shanked doucs and more than 1200 southern yellow-cheeked crested gibbons in **Keo Seima Wildlife Sanctuary** (ដែនជម្រកសត្វព្រៃកែវសីមា; http://cambodia.wcs.org; Andong Kroloeng; wildlife-spotting tours per person US$85-125; 🛈) 🌿, formerly Seima Protected Forest. These are the world's largest known populations of both species. Jahoo Gibbon Camp offers the chance to trek into the wild and try to spot these primates, along with other elusive animals, thanks to an exciting project supported by the humanitarian organisation World Hope International (www.worldhope.org) in the Bunong village of Andong Kroloeng.

The Jahoo Gibbon Camp provides local villagers with an incentive to conserve the endangered primates and their habitat through providing a sustainable income. Treks wind their way through mixed evergreen forest and waterfalls, with an excellent chance of spotting the doucs and macaques along the way. Gibbons are very shy and harder to see, but thanks to recent field research by WCS and the community, the local gibbon families are more used to people than gibbons elsewhere. You'll need to be up before dawn to spot them, however, so sleeping at the camp is highly recommended.

Many other species are present in this area, including an enormous diversity of birdlife, such as the spectacular giant hornbill and peafowl. There are also chances to find the tracks and signs of more elusive species, such as bears, gaur (wild cattle) and elephants.

Registered guides, together with local Bunong guides, accompany visitors along the trails. A conservation contribution is included in the cost of the trip, which supports community development projects.

For information and booking, contact the Sam Veasna Center (p302) through the Hefalump Cafe in Sen Monorom. You can also book tours with The Hangout (p302) in Sen Monorom.

include Khmer meals and primate treks in the forest to spot rare yellow-cheeked crested gibbons and more common black-shanked doucs. Overnight tours sleeping in the camp's comfortable sheltered tents are possible through Sam Veasna Center (p301), which is good for extended stays, or The Hangout, which works for quick gibbon trips.

Humanitarian organisation World Hope International (www.worldhope.org) began working with the local Bunong community in 2019 to enhance infrastructure at the camp, with plans for more upscale lodging and facilities. Check for the latest updates at Hefalump Cafe.

★ Mayura Hill
Hotel & Resort   HOTEL $$$

(☏ 077 980980; www.mayurahillresort.com; incl breakfast r US$100-120, ste US$150; ❋ 🛜 ☲) Setting the standard for upscale accommodation in Mondulkiri, Mayura Hill is a lovely place to stay for those with the budget. The 11 villa rooms are tastefully appointed with woods and silks and the family villa includes

a bunk for the children. Facilities include a swimming pool and a five-a-side football pitch! The restaurant is the most sophisticated in town.

✖ Eating

The solid dining scene in Sen Monorom is unexpected, given the remote setting, with everything from authentic Italian pasta to Swedish meatballs and traditional Bunong soups. Many guesthouses here have restaurants, the most noteworthy of which are Nature Lodge (p302) and Mayura Hill.

★ Bunong Kitchen   CAMBODIAN $
(☏ 097 790 4244; mains US$3-4; ⏰ 6.30am-8pm; 🍴) A lovely little training restaurant for Bunong people where you can try traditional soups, such as *trav brang* (with jackfruit, pumpkin, long beans and eggplant). You'll also find locally sourced coffee and Bunong desserts including *skoo* (a boiled jungle root with honey and sugar). All dishes are vegetarian but you can add meat to them if you like.

Bamboo Cafe
INTERNATIONAL $

(http://bamboocafe.business.site; NH76; mains US$2-4; ⊙6.30am-10.30pm; 🛜🍴) This jungly, bamboo-shaded cafe has a lengthy menu running the gamut from pasta noodles to Khmer noodles and *amok* (a baked fish dish). Vegetarian options abound, as do a few vegan plates.

Cinnamon Café
BAKERY $

(dishes US$2-5; ⊙8am-8pm Mon-Sat, from noon Sun; 🛜) Taught the art of baking (and meat-balls) by some Swedish residents in Sen Monorom, this is the source of the delicious cakes that turn up in the Hefalump Cafe each day. Try spiced banana cake or pumpkin pie, or go healthy with a sandwich or salad first.

Coffee Plantation Resort
CAMBODIAN $

(☏098 777699; mains 10,000-25,000r; ⊙7am-8pm; 🛜) As the name suggests, this place is set in the grounds of an extensive coffee plantation. As well as the homegrown coffee, it offers some excellent local flavours. The *banh chev* savoury pancakes are a wholesome meal for just US$2.50, and there's delicious honey-roasted chicken.

Hefalump Cafe
CAFE $

(www.facebook.com/hefalumpcafe; NH76; cakes US$1-3; ⊙6.30am-6pm Mon-Fri, 8am-4pm Sun; 🛜) 🖉 A collaboration of various NGOs and conservation groups in town, this cafe doubles as a hospitality training centre for Bunong people. Local coffee or Lavazza, teas, cakes and healthy breakfasts make this a great spot to plan your adventures over a cuppa.

Mondulkiri Pizza
PIZZA $

(☏097 522 2219; small/large pizza US$5/10; ⊙9am-10pm; 🛜) This secluded oasis with tree swings and riverside picnic tables may be hard to find, but its big oven churns out a steady supply of stellar pizzas. Many are dispatched around town, as they deliver to your door if you're feeling lazy after a long trek. There are also three A-frame fan-cooled bungalows in the verdant garden (double/quad US$15/25).

Green House Restaurant & Bar
INTERNATIONAL $

(☏017 905659; http://greenhouse-tour.blogspot.com; NH76; mains US$2.50-5; ⊙7.30am-10pm; 🛜) As well as internet access and tour information on the menu, Green House is a long-standing staple for inexpensive Khmer and Western dishes. It also doubles as a bar by night with cheap beer and cheeky cocktails.

★Mondulk...Italy
ITALIAN $$

(☏096 674 2693; www.facebook.com/Mondulk.Italy; NH76; mains US$4.50-7; ⊙10am-1.30pm & 6-10pm Mon-Sat; 🛜) When you're craving an Aperol spritz, homemade pasta or an evening glass of wine paired with a selection of fine cheeses, you never expect you'll find such things in a remote outpost like Sen Monorom. Think again! This hole-in-the-wall Italian restaurant may not be much to look at, but the cooking and ingredients are top-notch.

★Oromis Restaurant
CAMBODIAN $$

(☏097 884 5559; US$2-10; ⊙7am-9pm; 🛜) Set amid lush gardens by the Oromis River about 5km south of town, this is a lovely place to join out-of-town Cambodians enjoying the fresh mountain air on an extended lunch session. The extensive menu includes Cambodian and Asian favourites and you can chow down in the pavilions dotted about the grounds.

🍷 Drinking & Nightlife

★The Hangout
BAR

(☏088 721 9991; ⊙7am-late) The most happening spot in town. There are bar sports including table football, occasional jam sessions and some of Sen Monorom's best Western food to complement the Khmer menu (mains US$2 to US$7). It's run by an affable Tasmanian-Khmer couple.

MK Coffee Shop
COFFEE

(www.mondulkiri-coffee.com; Market Area; ⊙7am-8pm; 🛜) Watch out Starbucks, MK Coffee is in town. It is unlikely MK Coffee will face international competition any time soon given the remoteness of Sen Monorom, but it is ready with this contemporary cafe. This is barista-brewed coffee practically from the source – it operates a coffee plantation nearby.

ℹ Information

Acleda Bank (NH76; ⊙8.30am-4pm Mon-Fri, to 11.30am Sat, ATM 24hr) Changes major currencies and has a 24-hour ATM.

The local tourist office at the Kouprey Roundabout is rarely open and barely stocks any materials. The leading guesthouses in town are much better sources of tourist information.

Hefalump Cafe (p305) This NGO-run cafe doubles as a drop-in centre for Bunong people and is the best source of information on sustainable tourism in Mondulkiri Province, including the Elephant Valley Project, the Keo Seima Wildlife Sanctuary and responsible tours to Bunong communities. It is advisable to try to book two to three days in advance to best ensure availability.

Hospital (NH76; ⊘24hr) The main hospital in Mondulkiri, but it's wiser to head to Phnom Penh in the event of something serious.

ℹ Getting There & Away

The stretch of NH76 connecting Sen Monorom to Snuol and Phnom Penh (370km) is in fantastic shape and passes through large tracts of pro-tected forest in Mondulkiri Province itself. Hard-core dirt bikers may still prefer the old French road, known as the 'King's Highway', that heads east from Keo Seima, which runs roughly parallel to NH76 and pops out near Andong Kroloeng, about 30km from Sen Monorom.

There are no longer any buses to Phnom Penh, so take an express minivan (US$10 to US$11, six hours, frequent). There are several competing companies, but local residents say Virak Bun-tham has the most spacious seating.

Kim Seng Express (☏012 790889) Up to seven minivans to Phnom Penh daily (US$10, six hours).

Rithya Express (☏092 963243; NH76) Mini-vans to Phnom Penh daily at 7am and 1pm (US$10, six hours), plus Siem Reap at 7.45am (US$18, 10 hours).

Virak Buntham Express (☏017 666955; www.virakbuntham.com) Two morning and two afternoon departures daily to Phnom Penh in 11-seater vans (US$11, six hours), as well as a sleeper bus at 10.30pm (US$11, eight hours). Also travels to Siem Reap at 7am and 6.30pm (US$18, 10 hours). Be sure to check in advance that the Siem Reap trip doesn't involve a bus change in Phnom Penh.

There is usually one morning and one afternoon express minivan to Ban Lung (US$7, three hours) and a noon express minivan to Kratie (US$7, three hours), which can be booked through your guesthouse.

Local minibuses, departing from the **taxi park**, are another way to Kratie (20,000r, four hours). Count on one morning departure at around 8am, with a possible second departure around noon.

ℹ Getting Around

English-speaking *motodups* (*moto* drivers) cost about US$15 to US$20 per day. Sample round-trip *moto* (motorcycle taxi) prices for destinations around Sen Monorom are US$12 to Bou Sraa, US$10 to Dak Dam Waterfall, US$5 to Samot Cheur and US$3 for Monorom Falls.

Most guesthouses rent out motorbikes for US$6 to US$8 per day and a few have bicycles for US$2.

Understand Cambodia

HISTORY 308

Follow the roller-coaster ride that is Cambodian history, from the heady days of the Angkorian empire to the dark days of genocidal madness.

POL POT & THE KHMER ROUGE TRIALS 325

Learn more about the leadership of the Khmer Rouge and keep abreast of the latest developments in the ongoing trial.

PEOPLE & CULTURE 328

Get the low down on Cambodia's way of life, the ethnic patchwork of its peoples, their religious beliefs and the traditional arts.

THE CAMBODIAN KITCHEN..................337

Know your noodles and plan a culinary odyssey through Cambodia with this guide to Khmer cuisine.

ENVIRONMENT.............................343

Mountains high, rivers deep, discover more about Cambodia's varied landscape, protected areas and the wild critters roaming the jungle.

History

'The good, the bad and the ugly' sums up Cambodian history. Things were good in the early years, culminating in the vast Angkor empire, unrivalled in the region during four centuries of dominance. Then the bad set in, from the 13th century, as ascendant neighbours chipped away at Cambodian territory. In the 20th century it turned downright ugly, as a brutal civil war culminated in the genocidal rule of the Khmer Rouge (1975–79), from which Cambodia is still recovering.

The Origin of the Khmers

Like many legends, the story of the origin of Cambodia is historically opaque, but it does say something about the cultural forces that brought Cambodia into existence, in particular its relationship with its great subcontinental neighbour, India. Cambodia's religious, royal and written traditions stemmed from India and began to coalesce as a cultural entity in their own right between the 1st and 5th centuries CE.

Very little is known about prehistoric Cambodia. Much of the southeast was a vast, shallow gulf that was progressively silted up by the mouths of the Mekong, leaving pancake-flat, mineral-rich land ideal for farming. Evidence of cave-dwellers has been found in the northwest of Cambodia, and carbon dating on ceramic pots found in the area shows that they were made around 4200 BCE. Examinations of bones dating to around 1500 BCE suggest that the people living in Cambodia at that time resembled the Cambodians of today. Early Chinese records report that the Cambodians were 'ugly' and 'dark' and went about naked. A healthy dose of scepticism may be required, however, when reading the reports of imperial China concerning its 'barbarian' neighbours.

The Early Cambodian Kingdoms

Cambodian might didn't begin and end with Angkor. There were a number of powerful kingdoms present in this area before the 9th century.

From the 1st century CE, the Indianisation of Cambodia occurred through trading settlements that sprang up on the coastline of what is now southern Vietnam, but was then inhabited by the Khmers. These

TIMELINE	4200 BCE	CE 100	245
	Cave-dwellers capable of making pots inhabit caves around Laang Spean; archaeological evidence suggests their vessels were similar to those still made in Cambodia today.	The religions, language and sculpture styles of India start to take root in Cambodia with the arrival of Indian traders and holy men.	The Chinese Wei emperor sends a mission to the countries of the Mekong region and is told that a barbarous but rich country called Funan exists in the Delta region.

settlements were important ports of call for boats following the trading route from the Bay of Bengal to the southern provinces of China. The largest of these nascent kingdoms was known as Funan by the Chinese, and may have existed across an area between modern Phnom Penh and the archaeological site of Oc-Eo in Kien Giang Province in southern Vietnam. Funan would have been a contemporary of Champasak in southern Laos (then known as Kuruksetra) and other lesser fiefdoms in the region.

Funan is a Chinese name and may be a transliteration of the ancient Khmer word *bnam* (mountain). Although very little is known about Funan, much has been made of its importance as an early Southeast Asian centre of power.

It is most likely that between the 1st and 8th centuries Cambodia was a collection of small states, each with its own elites who strategically intermarried and often went to war with one another. Funan was no doubt one of these states, and as a major sea port would have been pivotal in the transmission of Indian culture into the interior of Cambodia.

The little that historians do know about Funan has mostly been gleaned from Chinese sources. These report that Funan-period Cambodia (1st century to 6th century CE) embraced the worship of the Hindu deities Shiva and Vishnu and, concurrently, Buddhism. The *linga* (phallic totem) appears to have been the focus of ritual and an emblem of kingly might, a feature that was to evolve further in the Angkorian cult of the god-king. The people practised primitive irrigation, which enabled successful cultivation of rice, and traded raw commodities such as spices and precious stones with China and India.

From the 6th century, Cambodia's population gradually concentrated along the Mekong River and Tonlé Sap lake, where the majority of people remain today. The move may have been related to the development of wet-rice agriculture. Between the 6th and 8th centuries, Cambodia was a collection of competing kingdoms, ruled by autocratic kings who legitimised their rule through hierarchical caste concepts borrowed from India.

THE LEGEND OF KAUNDINYA & THE NAGA PRINCESS

Cambodia came into being, so the legend says, through the union of a princess and a foreigner. The foreigner was an Indian Brahman named Kaundinya and the princess was the daughter of a *naga* (mythical serpent-being) king who ruled over a watery land. One day, as Kaundinya sailed by, the princess paddled out in a boat to greet him. Kaundinya shot an arrow from his magic bow into her boat, causing the fearful princess to agree to marriage. In need of a dowry, her father drank up the waters of his land and presented them to Kaundinya to rule over. The new kingdom was named Kambuja.

600	802	889	924
The first inscriptions are committed to stone in Cambodia in ancient Khmer, offering historians the only contemporary accounts of the pre-Angkorian period other than from Chinese sources.	Jayavarman II proclaims independence from Java in a ceremony to anoint himself a *devaraja* (god-king) on the holy mountain of Phnom Kulen, marking the birth of the Khmer Empire of Angkor.	Yasovarman I moves the capital from the ancient city of Hariharalaya (Roluos today) to the Angkor area, 16km to the northwest, and marks the location with three temple mountains.	Usurper king Jayavarman IV transfers the capital to Koh Ker and begins a mammoth building spree, but the lack of water sees the capital move back to Angkor just 20 years later.

This era is generally referred to as the Chenla period. Like Funan, this is a Chinese term and there is little to support the idea that Chenla was a unified kingdom that held sway over all of Cambodia. Indeed, the Chinese themselves referred to 'water Chenla' and 'land Chenla'. Water Chenla was located around Angkor Borei and the temple mount of Phnom Da, near the present-day provincial capital of Takeo, and land Chenla in the upper reaches of the Mekong River and east of Tonlé Sap lake, around Sambor Prei Kuk, an essential stop on a chronological jaunt through Cambodia's history.

The Rise of the Angkorian Empire

Gradually the Cambodian region was becoming more cohesive. Before long the fractured kingdoms of Cambodia would merge to become the mighty Khmer empire.

India wasn't the only power to have a major cultural impact on Cambodia. The island of Java was also influential, colonising part of 'water Chenla' in the 8th century.

A popular place of pilgrimage for Khmers today, the sacred mountain of Phnom Kulen, northeast of Angkor, is home to an inscription that tells of Jayavarman II (r 802–50) proclaiming himself a 'universal monarch', or *devaraja* (god-king) in 802. It is believed that he may have resided in the Buddhist Shailendras' court in Java as a young man and was inspired by the great Javanese temples of Borobudur and Prambanan near present-day Yogyakarta. Upon his return to Cambodia, he instigated an uprising against Javanese control over the southern lands of Cambodia. Jayavarman II then set out to bring the country under his control through alliances and conquests, becoming the first monarch to rule most of what we call Cambodia today.

Jayavarman II was the first of a long succession of kings who presided over the rise and fall of the greatest empire mainland Southeast Asia has ever seen, one that was to bequeath the stunning legacy of Angkor. The key to the meteoric rise of Angkor was a mastery of water and an elaborate hydraulic system that allowed the ancient Khmers to tame the elements. The first records of the massive irrigation works that supported the population of Angkor date to the reign of Indravarman I (r 877–89), who built the *baray* (reservoir) of Indratataka. His rule also marks the flourishing of Angkorian art, with the building of temples in the Roluos area, notably Bakong.

By the turn of the 11th century, the kingdom of Angkor was losing control of its territories. Suryavarman I (r 1002–49), a usurper, moved into the power vacuum and, like Jayavarman II two centuries before, reunified the kingdom through war and alliances, stretching the frontiers of the empire. A pattern was beginning to emerge, which was repeated throughout the Angkorian period: dislocation and turmoil, followed by reunification and further expansion under a powerful king. Architecturally, the most productive periods occurred after times of turmoil, indi-

1002	1112	1152	1177
Suryavarman I comes to power and expands the extent of the kingdom by annexing the Buddhist kingdom of Louvo (known as Lopburi in modern-day Thailand). He also increases trade links with the outside world.	Suryavarman II commences the construction of Angkor Wat, the mother of all temples, dedicated to Vishnu and designed as his funerary temple.	Suryavarman II is killed in a disastrous campaign against the Dai Viet (Vietnamese), provoking this rising northern neighbour and sparking centuries of conflict between the two countries.	The Chams launch a surprise attack on Angkor by sailing up Tonlé Sap lake. They defeat the powerful Khmers and occupy the capital for four years.

cating that newly incumbent monarchs felt the need to celebrate, even legitimise, their rule with massive building projects.

By 1066, Angkor was again riven by conflict, becoming the focus of rival bids for power. It was not until the accession of Suryavarman II (r 1112–52) that the kingdom was again unified. Suryavarman II embarked on another phase of expansion, waging costly wars in Vietnam and the region of central Vietnam known as Champa. He is immortalised as the king who, in his devotion to the Hindu deity Vishnu, commissioned the majestic temple of Angkor Wat. For an insight into events in this epoch, see the bas-reliefs on the southwest corridor of Angkor Wat, which depict Suryavarman II's reign.

Suryavarman II had brought Champa to heel and reduced it to vassal status, but the Chams struck back in 1177 with a naval expedition up the Mekong and into Tonlé Sap lake. They took the city of Angkor by surprise and put King Dharanindravarman II to death. The following year a cousin of Suryavarman II rallied the Khmer troops and defeated the Chams in yet another naval battle. The new leader was crowned Jayavarman VII in 1181.

Jayavarman VII

A devout follower of Mahayana Buddhism, Jayavarman VII (r 1181–1219) built the city of Angkor Thom and many other massive monuments. Indeed, many of the temples visited around Angkor today were constructed during Jayavarman VII's reign. However, Jayavarman VII is a figure of many contradictions. The bas-reliefs of the Bayon depict him presiding over battles of terrible ferocity, while statues of the king depict a meditative, otherworldly aspect. His programme of temple construction and other public works was carried out in great haste, no doubt bringing enormous hardship to the labourers who provided the muscle, and thus accelerating the decline of the empire. He was partly driven by a desire to legitimise his rule, as there may have been other contenders closer to the royal bloodline, and partly by the need to introduce a new religion to a population predominantly Hindu in faith. However, in many ways he was also Cambodia's first progressive leader, proclaiming the population equal, abolishing castes and embarking on a programme of school, hospital and road building.

Decline & Fall of Angkor

Angkor was the epicentre of an incredible empire that held sway over much of the Mekong region, but like all empires, the sun was to eventually set. A number of scholars have argued that decline was already on the horizon at the time Angkor Wat was built, when the Angkorian empire was at the height of its remarkable productivity. There are indications

Cambodia's Funan-period trading port of Oc-Eo, now located in Vietnam's Mekong Delta, was a major commercial crossroads between Asia and Europe, and archaeologists there have unearthed Roman coins and Persian pottery.

1181	1219	1253	1296
The Chams are vanquished as Jayavarman VII, the greatest king of Angkor and builder of Angkor Thom, takes the throne, changing the state religion to Mahayana Buddhism.	Jayavarman VII dies aged in his 90s, and the empire of Angkor slowly declines due to a choking irrigation network, religious conflict and the rise of powerful neighbours.	The Mongols of Kublai Khan sack the Thai kingdom of Nanchao in Yunnan, sparking an exodus southwards, which brings Thais into direct conflict with the weakening Khmer empire.	Chinese emissary Chou Ta Kuan spends one year living at Angkor and writes The Customs of Cambodia, the only contemporary account of life in the great Khmer capital.

Cambodia's turbulent past is uncovered in a series of articles, oral histories and photos on an excellent website called 'Beauty and Darkness: Cambodia in Modern History'. Find it at www. mekong.net/cambodia.

that the irrigation network was overworked and slowly starting to silt up due to the massive deforestation that had taken place in the heavily populated areas to the north and east of Angkor. This was exacerbated by prolonged periods of drought in the 14th century, which was more recently discovered through the advanced analysis of dendrochronology, or the study of tree rings, in the Angkor area.

Massive construction projects such as Angkor Wat and Angkor Thom no doubt put an enormous strain on the royal coffers and on thousands of slaves and common people who subsidised them in hard labour and taxes. Following the reign of Jayavarman VII, temple construction effectively ground to a halt, in large part because Jayavarman VII's public works had quarried local sandstone into oblivion and left the population exhausted.

Another challenge for the later kings was religious conflict and internecine rivalries. The state religion changed back and forth several times during the twilight years of the empire, and kings spent more time engaged in iconoclasm, defacing the temples of their predecessors, than building monuments to their own achievements. From time to time this boiled over into civil war.

Angkor was losing control over the peripheries of its empire. At the same time, the Thais were ascendant, having migrated south from Yunnan, China, to escape Kublai Khan and his Mongol hordes. The Thais, first from Sukothai, later Ayuthaya, grew in strength and made repeated incursions into Angkor before finally sacking the city in 1431 and making off with thousands of intellectuals, artisans and dancers from the royal court. During this period, perhaps drawn by the opportunities for sea trade with China and fearful of the increasingly bellicose Thais, the Khmer elite began to migrate to the Phnom Penh area. The capital shifted several times over the centuries but eventually settled in present-day Phnom Penh.

From 1500 until the arrival of the French in 1863, Cambodia was ruled by a series of weak kings beset by dynastic rivalries. In the face of such intrigue, they sought the protection – granted, of course, at a price – of either Thailand or Vietnam. In the 17th century, the Nguyen lords of southern Vietnam came to the rescue of the Cambodian king in return for settlement rights in the Mekong Delta region. The Khmers still refer to this region as Kampuchea Krom (Lower Cambodia), even though it is well and truly populated by the Vietnamese today.

In the west, the Thais controlled the provinces of Battambang and Siem Reap from 1794 and held influence over the Cambodian royal family. Indeed, one king was crowned in Bangkok and placed on the throne at Udong with the help of the Thai army. That Cambodia survived through the 18th century as a distinct entity is due to the preoccupations of its

1353	1431	1516	1594
Lao prince Chao Fa Ngum ends his Angkor exile and is sponsored by his Khmer father-in-law on an expedition to conquer the new Thai kingdoms, declaring himself leader of Lan Xang (Land of a Million Elephants).	The Thais sack Angkor definitively, carting off most of the royal court to Ayuthaya, including nobles, priests, dancers and artisans.	King Ang Chan I ascends the throne, defeats the Thais in a ballle that gives modern-day Siem Reap its name and 'rediscovers' the great walled city of Angkor Thom on a hunting expedition.	The temporary Cambodian capital of Lovek falls when, legend says, the Siamese fire a cannon of silver coins into its bamboo defences. Soldiers cut down the bamboo to retrieve the silver, leaving the city exposed.

neighbours: while the Thais were expending their energy and resources fighting the Burmese, the Vietnamese were wholly absorbed by internal strife. The pattern continued for more than two centuries, the carcass of Cambodia pulled back and forth between two powerful tigers.

The French in Cambodia

The era of yo-yoing between Thai and Vietnamese masters came to a close in 1863, when French gunboats intimidated King Norodom I (r 1860–1904) into signing a treaty of protectorate. Ironically, it really was a protectorate, as Cambodia was in danger of going the way of Champa and vanishing from the map. French control of Cambodia developed as a sideshow to its interests in Vietnam, uncannily similar to the American experience a century later, and initially involved little direct interference in Cambodia's affairs. The French presence also helped keep Norodom on the throne despite the ambitions of his rebellious half-brothers.

By the 1870s, French officials in Cambodia began pressing for greater control over internal affairs. In 1884 Norodom was forced into signing a treaty that turned his country into a virtual colony, sparking a two-year rebellion that constituted the only major uprising in Cambodia before WWII. The rebellion only ended when the king was persuaded to call upon the rebel fighters to lay down their weapons in exchange for a return to the status quo.

During the following decades, senior Cambodian officials opened the door to direct French control over the day-to-day administration of the country, as they saw certain advantages in acquiescing to French power. The French maintained Norodom's court in splendour unseen since the heyday of Angkor, helping to enhance the symbolic position of the monarchy. In 1907 the French were able to pressure Thailand into returning the northwest provinces of Battambang, Siem Reap and Preah Vihear in return for concessions of Lao territory to the Thais. This meant Angkor came under Cambodian control for the first time in more than a century.

King Norodom I was succeeded by King Sisowath (r 1904–27), who was succeeded by King Monivong (r 1927–41). Upon King Monivong's death, the French governor-general of Japanese-occupied Indochina, Admiral Jean Decoux, placed 19-year-old Prince Norodom Sihanouk on the Cambodian throne. The French authorities assumed young Sihanouk would be pliable, but this proved to be a major miscalculation.

During WWII, Japanese forces occupied much of Asia, and Cambodia was no exception. However, with many in France collaborating with the occupying Germans, the Japanese were happy to let their new Vichy France allies control affairs in Cambodia. The price was conceding to Thailand (a Japanese ally of sorts) much of Battambang and Siem Reap Provinces once again, areas that weren't returned until 1947. However,

Chinese emissary Chou Ta Kuan lived in Angkor for a year in 1296, and his observations have been republished as *The Customs of Cambodia* (2000), a fascinating insight into life during the height of the empire.

1772	1834	1863	1884
Cambodia is caught between the powerful Vietnamese and Siamese, and the latter burn Phnom Penh to the ground, another chapter in the story of inflamed tensions, which persist today.	The Vietnamese take control of much of Cambodia during the reign of Emperor Minh Mang and begin a slow revolution to 'teach the barbarians their customs'.	The French force King Norodom I into signing a treaty of protectorate, which prevents Cambodia being wiped off the map and thus begins 90 years of French rule.	Rebellion against French rule in Cambodia erupts in response to a treaty giving French administrators wide-ranging powers. The treaty is signed under the watch of French gunboats in the Mekong River.

after the fall of Paris in 1944 and with French policy in disarray, the Japanese were forced to take direct control of the territory by early 1945.

After WWII, the French returned, making Cambodia an autonomous state within the French Union, but retaining de facto control. The immediate postwar years were marked by strife among the country's various political factions, a situation made more unstable by the Franco-Vietminh War then raging in Vietnam and Laos, which spilled over into Cambodia. The Vietnamese, as they were also to do 20 years later in the war against Lon Nol and the Americans, trained and fought with bands of Khmer Issarak (Free Khmer) against the French authorities.

The Sihanouk Years

The postindependence period was one of peace and prosperity. It was Cambodia's golden era, a time of creativity and optimism. Phnom Penh grew in size and stature, the temples of Angkor were the leading tourist destination in Southeast Asia and Sihanouk played host to a succession of influential leaders from across the globe. However, dark clouds were circling, as the American war in Vietnam became a black hole, sucking in neighbouring countries.

In late 1952 King Sihanouk dissolved the fledgling parliament, declared martial law and embarked on his 'royal crusade', a travelling campaign to drum up international support for his country's independence. Independence was proclaimed on 9 November 1953 and recognised by the Geneva Conference of May 1954, which ended French control of Indochina. In 1955, Sihanouk abdicated, afraid of being marginalised amid the pomp of royal ceremony. The 'royal crusader' became 'citizen Sihanouk'. He vowed never again to return to the throne. Meanwhile his father became king. It was a masterstroke that offered Sihanouk both royal authority and supreme political power. His newly established party, Sangkum Reastr Niyum (People's Socialist Community), won every seat in parliament in the September 1955 elections and Sihanouk was to dominate Cambodian politics for the next 15 years.

Although he feared the Vietnamese communists, Sihanouk considered South Vietnam and Thailand – both allies of the mistrusted USA – the greatest threats to Cambodia's security, even survival. In an attempt to fend off these many dangers, he declared Cambodia neutral and refused to accept further US aid, which had accounted for a substantial chunk of the country's military budget. He also nationalised many industries, including the rice trade, which angered many Chinese-Cambodians. In 1965 Sihanouk, convinced that the USA had been plotting against him and his family, broke diplomatic relations with Washington and veered towards the North Vietnamese and China. In addition, he agreed to let the communists use Cambodian territory in their battle against South

One of the definitive guides to Angkor is *A Guide to the Angkor Monuments* by Maurice Glaize, first published in the 1940s and now out of print. Download it free at www.theangkorguide.com.

1907	1941	1942	1947
French authorities successfully negotiate the return of the northwest provinces of Siem Reap, Battambang and Preah Vihear, which have been under Thai control since 1794.	A young King Sihanouk ascends the throne aged just 19 years old, beginning an incredible political career that will span about 70 years.	Japanese forces occupy Cambodia, leaving the administration in the hands of Vichy France officials, but fanning the flames of independence as the war draws to a close.	The provinces of Battambang, Siem Reap and Sisophon, seized by the Thais during the Japanese occupation, are returned to Cambodia.

Vietnam and the USA. Sihanouk was taking sides, a dangerous position in a volatile region.

These moves and his socialist economic policies alienated conservative elements in Cambodian society, including the army brass and the urban elite. At the same time, left-wing Cambodians, many of them educated abroad, deeply resented his domestic policies, which stifled political debate. Compounding Sihanouk's problems was the fact that all classes were fed up with the pervasive corruption in government ranks, some of it uncomfortably close to the royal family. Although most peasants revered Sihanouk as a semidivine figure, in 1967 a rural-based rebellion broke out in Samlot, Battambang, leading him to conclude that the greatest threat to his regime came from the left. Bowing to pressure from the army, he implemented a policy of harsh repression against left-wingers.

By 1969 the conflict between the army and leftist rebels had become more serious, as the Vietnamese sought sanctuary deeper in Cambodia. Sihanouk's political position had also decidedly deteriorated – due in no small part to his obsession with filmmaking, which was leading him to neglect affairs of state. In March 1970, while Sihanouk was on a trip to France, General Lon Nol and Prince Sisowath Sirik Matak, Sihanouk's cousin, deposed him as chief of state, apparently with tacit US consent. Sihanouk took up residence in Beijing, where he set up a government-in-exile in alliance with an indigenous Cambodian revolutionary movement that Sihanouk had nicknamed 'les Khmers Rouges'. This was a definitive moment in contemporary Cambodian history, as the Khmer Rouge exploited its partnership with Sihanouk to draw new recruits into its small organisation. Talk to many former Khmer Rouge fighters and they'll say that they 'went to the hills' (a euphemism for joining the Khmer Rouge) to fight for their king and knew nothing of Mao or Marxism.

Descent into Civil War

The lines were drawn for a bloody era of civil war. Sihanouk was condemned to death in absentia, a divisive move on the part of the new government that effectively ruled out any hint of compromise for the next five years. Lon Nol gave communist Vietnamese forces an ultimatum to withdraw their units within one week, which amounted to a declaration of war, as the Vietnamese did not want to return to the homeland to face the Americans.

On 30 April 1970, US and South Vietnamese forces invaded Cambodia in an effort to flush out thousands of Viet Cong and North Vietnamese troops who were using Cambodian bases in their war to overthrow the South Vietnamese government. As a result of the invasion, the Vietnamese communists withdrew deeper into Cambodia, further destabilising

The commercial metropolis that is now Ho Chi Minh City (Saigon) in Vietnam was, in 1600, a small Cambodian village called Prey Nokor.

1953	1955	1962	1963
Sihanouk's royal crusade for independence succeeds and Cambodia goes it alone without the French on 9 November, ushering in a new era of optimism.	King Sihanouk abdicates the throne to enter a career in politics; he founds the Sangkum Reastr Niyum (People's Socialist Community) party and wins the election with ease.	The International Court rules in favour of Cambodia in the long-running dispute over the dramatic mountain temple of Preah Vihear, perched on the Dangkrek Mountains on the border with Thailand.	Pol Pot and Ieng Sary flee from Phnom Penh to the jungles of Ratanakiri. With training from the Vietnamese, they launch a guerrilla war against Sihanouk's government.

the Lon Nol government. Cambodia's tiny army never stood a chance and within the space of a few months, Vietnamese forces and their Khmer Rouge allies overran almost half the country. The ultimate humiliation came in July 1970 when the Vietnamese occupied the temples of Angkor.

In 1969 the USA launched Operation Menu, the secret bombing of suspected communist base camps in Cambodia. For the next four years, until bombing was halted by the US Congress in August 1973, huge areas of the eastern half of the country were carpet-bombed by US B-52s, killing what is believed to be many thousands of civilians and turning hundreds of thousands more into refugees. Undoubtedly, the bombing campaign helped the Khmer Rouge in their recruitment drive, as more and more peasants were losing family members to the aerial assaults. While the final, heaviest bombing in the first half of 1973 may have saved Phnom Penh from a premature fall, its ferocity also helped to harden the attitude of many Khmer Rouge cadres and may have contributed to the later brutality that characterised their rule.

Savage fighting engulfed the country, bringing misery to millions of Cambodians; many fled rural areas for the relative safety of Phnom Penh and provincial capitals. Between 1970 and 1975, several hundred thousand people died in the fighting. During these years, the Khmer Rouge came to play a dominant role in trying to overthrow the Lon Nol regime, strengthened by the support of the Vietnamese, although the Khmer Rouge leadership would vehemently deny this from 1975 onwards.

The leadership of the Khmer Rouge, including Paris-educated Pol Pot and Ieng Sary, had fled into the countryside in the 1960s to escape the summary justice then being meted out to suspected leftists by Sihanouk's security forces. They consolidated control over the movement and began to move against opponents before they took Phnom Penh. Many of the Vietnamese-trained Cambodian communists who had been based in Hanoi since the 1954 Geneva Accords returned down the Ho Chi Minh Trail to join their 'allies' in the Khmer Rouge in 1973. Many were dead by 1975, executed on the orders of the anti-Vietnamese Pol Pot faction. Likewise, many moderate Sihanouk supporters, who had joined the Khmer Rouge as a show of loyalty to their fallen leader rather than a show of ideology to the radicals, were victims of purges before the regime took power. This set a precedent for internal purges and mass executions that were to eventually bring the downfall of the Khmer Rouge.

It didn't take long for the Lon Nol government to become very unpopular as a result of unprecedented greed and corruption in its ranks. As the US bankrolled the war, government and military personnel found lucrative means to make a fortune, such as inventing 'phantom soldiers' and pocketing their pay, or selling weapons to the enemy. Lon Nol was widely perceived as an ineffectual leader, obsessed by superstition, for-

The French did very little to encourage education in Cambodia, and by the end of WWII, after 70 years of colonial rule, there were no universities and only one high school in the whole country.

1964	1969	1970	1971
After the US-sponsored coup against President Diem in South Vietnam, Sihanouk veers left, breaking diplomatic ties with the USA and nationalising the rice trade, antagonising the ethnic Chinese business community.	US President Nixon authorises the secret bombing of Cambodia, which starts with the carpet bombing of border zones, but spreads to the whole country, continuing until 1973 and killing up to 250,000 Cambodians.	Marking the start of a five-year civil war, Sihanouk throws in his lot with the Khmer Rouge after being overthrown by his cousin Prince Sirik Matak and military commander Lon Nol, and sentenced to death in absentia.	Lon Nol, leader of the Khmer Republic, launches the disastrous Chenla offensive against Vietnamese communists and their Khmer Rouge allies in Cambodia. He suffers a stroke, but struggles on as leader until 1975.

tune tellers and mystical crusades. This perception increased with his stroke in March 1971 and for the next four years his grip on reality seemed to weaken as his brother Lon Non's power grew.

Despite massive US military and economic aid, Lon Nol never succeeded in gaining the initiative against the Khmer Rouge. Large parts of the countryside fell to the rebels and many provincial capitals were cut off from Phnom Penh. Lon Nol fled the country in early April 1975, leaving Sirik Matak, who refused evacuation to the end, in charge. 'I cannot alas leave in such a cowardly fashion...I have committed only one mistake, that of believing in you, the Americans' were the words Sirik Matak poignantly penned to US ambassador John Gunther Dean. On 17 April 1975 – two weeks before the fall of Saigon (now Ho Chi Minh City) – Phnom Penh surrendered to the Khmer Rouge.

The Khmer Rouge Revolution

Upon taking Phnom Penh, the Khmer Rouge implemented one of the most radical and brutal restructurings of a society ever attempted; its goal was a pure revolution, untainted by those that had gone before, to transform Cambodia into a peasant-dominated agrarian cooperative. Within days of the Khmer Rouge coming to power, the entire population of Phnom Penh and provincial towns, including the sick, elderly and infirm, was forced to march into the countryside and work as slaves for 12 to 15 hours a day. Disobedience of any sort often brought immediate execution. The advent of Khmer Rouge rule was proclaimed Year Zero. Currency was abolished and postal services ground to a halt. The country cut itself off from the outside world.

In the eyes of Pol Pot, the Khmer Rouge was not a unified movement, but a series of factions that needed to be cleansed. This process had already begun with attacks on Vietnamese-trained Khmer Rouge and Sihanouk's supporters, but Pol Pot's initial fury upon seizing power was directed against the former regime. All the senior government and military figures who had been associated with Lon Nol were executed within days of the takeover. Then the centre shifted its attention to the outer regions, which had been separated into geographic zones. The loyalist Southwestern Zone forces, under the control of one-legged general Ta Mok, were sent into region after region to 'purify' the population, a process that saw thousands perish.

The cleansing reached grotesque heights in the final and bloodiest purge against the powerful and independent Eastern Zone. Generally considered more moderate than other Khmer Rouge factions, the Eastern Zone was ideologically, as well as geographically, closer to Vietnam. The Pol Pot faction consolidated the rest of the country before moving against the east from 1977 onwards. Hundreds of leaders were executed

For more on the incredible life and times of Norodom Sihanouk, read the biography *Prince of Light, Prince of Darkness* (1994) by Milton Osborne.

1973	1975	1977	1979
Sihanouk and his wife Monique travel down the Ho Chi Minh Trail to visit Khmer Rouge allies at the holy mountain of Phnom Kulen near Angkor, a propaganda victory for Pol Pot.	The Khmer Rouge march into Phnom Penh on 17 April and turn the clocks back to Year Zero, evacuating the capital and turning the whole nation into a prison without walls.	The Pol Pot faction of the Khmer Rouge launches its bloodiest purge against the Eastern Zone of the country, sparking a civil war along the banks of the Mekong and drawing the Vietnamese into the battle.	Vietnamese forces liberate Cambodia from Khmer Rouge rule on 7 January, just two weeks after launching the invasion, and install a friendly regime in Phnom Penh.

before open rebellion broke out, sparking a civil war in the east. Many Eastern Zone leaders fled to Vietnam, forming the nucleus of the government installed by the Vietnamese in January 1979. The people were defenceless and distrusted – 'Cambodian bodies with Vietnamese minds' or 'duck's arses with chicken's heads' – and were deported to the northwest with new, blue *krama* (scarves). Had it not been for the Vietnamese invasion, all would have perished, as the blue *krama* was a secret party sign indicating an eastern enemy of the revolution.

It is still not known exactly how many Cambodians died at the hands of the Khmer Rouge during the three years, eight months and 20 days of its rule. The Vietnamese claimed three million deaths, while foreign experts long considered the number closer to one million. Yale University researchers undertaking ongoing investigations estimated that the figure was close to two million.

Hundreds of thousands of people were executed by the Khmer Rouge leadership, while hundreds of thousands more died of famine and disease. Meals consisted of little more than watery rice porridge twice a day, but were meant to sustain men, women and children through a back-breaking day in the fields. Disease stalked the work camps, malaria and dysentery striking down whole families; death was a relief for many from the horrors of life. Some zones were better than others, some leaders fairer than others, but life for the majority was one of unending misery and suffering in this 'prison without walls'.

As the centre eliminated more and more moderates, Angkar (the organisation) became the only family people needed and those who did not agree were sought out and crushed. The Khmer Rouge detached the Cambodian people from all they held dear: their families, their food, their fields and their faith. Even the peasants who had supported the revolution could no longer blindly follow such insanity. Nobody cared for the Khmer Rouge by 1978, but nobody had an ounce of strength to do anything about it...except the Vietnamese.

Enter the Vietnamese

Relations between Cambodia and Vietnam have historically been tense, as the Vietnamese have slowly but steadily expanded southwards, encroaching on Cambodian territory. Despite the fact the two communist parties had fought together as brothers in arms, old tensions soon came to the fore.

From 1976 to 1978, the Khmer Rouge instigated a series of border clashes with Vietnam, and claimed the Mekong Delta, once part of the Khmer empire. Incursions into Vietnamese border provinces left hundreds of Vietnamese civilians dead. On 25 December 1978 Vietnam launched a full-scale invasion of Cambodia, toppling the Pol Pot government two

During the 1960s, Cambodia was an oasis of peace while wars raged in neighbouring Vietnam and Laos. By 1970 that had all changed. For the full story, read *Sideshow: Kissinger, Nixon and the Destruction of Cambodia*, by William Shawcross (1979).

1980	1982	1984	1985
Cambodia is gripped by a terrible famine, as the dislocation of the previous few years means that no rice has been planted or harvested, and worldwide 'Save Kampuchea' appeals are launched.	Sihanouk is pressured to join the Khmer Rouge as head of the Coalition Government of Democratic Kampuchea (CGDK), a new military front against the Vietnamese-backed government in Phnom Penh.	The Vietnamese embark on a major offensive in the west of Cambodia and the Khmer Rouge and its allies are forced to retreat to refugee camps and bases inside Thailand.	There is a changing of the guard at the top and Hun Sen becomes Prime Minister of Cambodia, a title he still holds today with the Cambodian People's Party (CPP).

weeks later. As Vietnamese tanks neared Phnom Penh, the Khmer Rouge fled westward with as many civilians as it could seize, taking refuge in the jungles and mountains along the Thai border.

The Vietnamese installed a new government led by several former Khmer Rouge officers, including current Prime Minister Hun Sen, who had defected to Vietnam in 1977. The Khmer Rouge's patrons, the Chinese communists, launched a massive reprisal raid across Vietnam's northernmost border in early 1979 in an attempt to buy their allies time. It failed and after 17 days the Chinese withdrew, their fingers badly burnt

SIHANOUK: THE LAST OF THE GOD-KINGS

Norodom Sihanouk was a towering presence in the topsy-turvy world of Cambodian politics. A larger-than-life character of many enthusiasms and shifting political positions, amatory exploits dominated his early life. Later he became the prince who stage-managed the close of French colonialism, led Cambodia during its golden years, was imprisoned by the Khmer Rouge and, from privileged exile, finally returned triumphant as king. He was many things to many people, but he proved himself a survivor.

Sihanouk, born in 1922, was not an obvious contender for the throne, as he was from the Norodom branch of the royal family. He was crowned in 1941, at just 19, with his education incomplete. In 1955 Sihanouk abdicated and turned his attention to politics, his party winning every seat in parliament that year. By the mid-1960s Sihanouk had been calling the shots in Cambodia for a decade.

The conventional wisdom was that 'Sihanouk is Cambodia', his leadership the key to national success. However, as the country was inexorably drawn into the American war in Vietnam and government troops battled with a leftist insurgency in the countryside, Sihanouk was increasingly seen as a liability.

On 18 March 1970, the National Assembly voted to remove Sihanouk from office. He went into exile in Beijing and joined the communists. Following the Khmer Rouge victory on 17 April 1975, Sihanouk returned to Cambodia as head of the new state of Democratic Kampuchea. He resigned after less than a year and was confined to the Royal Palace as a prisoner of the Khmer Rouge. He remained there until early 1979 when, on the eve of the Vietnamese invasion, he was flown back to Beijing.

Sihanouk never quite gave up wanting to be everything for Cambodia: international statesman, general, president, film director and man of the people. On 24 September 1993, after 38 years in politics, he settled once more for the role of king. On 7 October 2004 he once again abdicated, and his son King Sihamoni ascended the throne.

Norodom Sihanouk died on 15 October 2012 in Beijing and his body was flown back to Cambodia a few days later. More than one million Cambodians lined the streets from the airport to the Royal Palace and his body was laid in state for 100 days before an elaborate state funeral. However, Sihanouk's place in history is assured, the last in a long line of Angkor's god-kings.

1989	1991	1993	1994
As the effects of Mikhail Gorbachev's perestroika (restructuring) begin to impact on communist allies, Vietnam feels the pinch and announces the withdrawal of its forces from Cambodia.	The Paris Peace Accords are signed, in which all parties, including the Khmer Rouge, agree to participate in free and fair elections supervised by the UN.	The pro-Sihanouk royalist party Funcinpec, under the leadership of Prince Ranariddh, wins the popular vote, but the communist CPP threatens secession in the east to muscle its way into government.	The Khmer Rouge targets foreign tourists in Cambodia, kidnapping and killing groups travelling by taxi and train to the South Coast, reinforcing Cambodia's overseas image as a dangerous country.

by their Vietnamese enemies. The Vietnamese then staged a show trial in Cambodia in which Pol Pot and Ieng Sary were condemned to death in absentia for their genocidal acts.

A traumatised population took to the road in search of surviving family members. Millions had been uprooted and had to walk hundreds of kilometres across the country. Rice stocks were decimated, the harvest left to wither and little rice planted, sowing the seeds for a widespread famine in 1979 and 1980.

As the conflict in Cambodia raged, Sihanouk agreed in 1982, under pressure from China, to head a military and political front opposed to the Phnom Penh government. The Sihanouk-led resistance coalition brought together – on paper, at least – Funcinpec (the French acronym for the National United Front for an Independent, Neutral, Peaceful and Cooperative Cambodia), which comprised a royalist group loyal to Sihanouk; the Khmer People's National Liberation Front, a noncommunist grouping under former prime minister Son Sann; and the Khmer Rouge, officially known as the Party of Democratic Kampuchea and by far the most powerful of the three. The crimes of the Khmer Rouge were swept aside to ensure a compromise that suited the realpolitik of the day.

Lon Nol's military press attaché was known for his colourful, even imaginative, media briefings that painted a rosy picture of the increasingly desperate situation on the ground. With a name like Major Am Rong, few could take him seriously.

For much of the 1980s Cambodia remained closed to the Western world, save for the presence of some humanitarian aid groups. Government policy was effectively under the control of the Vietnamese, so Cambodia found itself very much in the Eastern-bloc camp. The economy was in tatters for most of this period, as Cambodia, like Vietnam, suffered from the effects of a US-sponsored embargo.

In 1984, the Vietnamese overran all the major rebel camps inside Cambodia, forcing the Khmer Rouge and its allies to retreat into Thailand. From this time the Khmer Rouge and its allies engaged in guerrilla warfare aimed at demoralising its opponents. Tactics used by the Khmer Rouge included shelling government-controlled garrison towns, planting thousands of mines in rural areas, attacking road transport, blowing up bridges, kidnapping village chiefs and targeting civilians. The Khmer Rouge also forced thousands of men, women and children living in the refugee camps it controlled to work as porters, ferrying ammunition and other supplies into Cambodia across heavily mined sections of the border.

The Vietnamese, for their part, laid the world's longest minefield, known as K-5 and stretching from the Gulf of Thailand to the Lao border, in an attempt to seal out the guerrillas. They also sent Cambodians into the forests to cut down trees on remote sections of road to prevent ambushes. Thousands died of disease and from injuries sustained from landmines. The Khmer Rouge was no longer in power, but for many the 1980s were almost as tough as the 1970s – it was one long struggle to survive.

1995	1996	1997	1998
Prince Norodom Sirivudh is arrested and exiled for allegedly plotting to kill Prime Minister Hun Sen, removing another potential rival from the scene.	British deminer Christopher Howes, working in Cambodia with the Mines Advisory Group (MAG), is kidnapped by the Khmer Rouge and later killed, together with his interpreter Houn Hourth.	Second Prime Minister Hun Sen overthrows First Prime Minister Norodom Ranariddh in a military coup, referred to as 'the events of 1997' in Cambodia.	Pol Pot dies on 15 April as Anlong Veng falls to government forces, and many observers ponder whether the timing is coincidental.

The Politics of Disaster Relief

The Cambodian famine became a new front in the Cold War, as Washington and Moscow jostled for influence from afar. As hundreds of thousands of Cambodians fled to Thailand, a massive international famine relief effort, sponsored by the UN, was launched. The international community wanted to deliver aid across a land bridge at Poipet, while the new Vietnamese-backed Phnom Penh government wanted all supplies to come through the capital via Kompong Som (Sihanoukville) or the Mekong River. Both sides had their reasons – the new government did not want aid to fall into the hands of its Khmer Rouge enemies, while the international community didn't believe the new government had the infrastructure to distribute the aid – and both fears were right.

During the US bombing campaign, more bombs were dropped on Cambodia than were used by all sides during WWII.

Some agencies distributed the slow way through Phnom Penh, and others set up camps in Thailand. The camps became a magnet for half of Cambodia, as many Khmers still feared the return of the Khmer Rouge or were seeking a new life overseas. The Thai military convinced the international community to distribute all aid through its channels and used this as a cloak to rebuild the shattered Khmer Rouge forces as an effective resistance against the Vietnamese. Thailand demanded that, as a condition for allowing international food aid for Cambodia to pass through its territory, food had to be supplied to the Khmer Rouge forces encamped in the Thai border region as well. Along with weaponry supplied by China, this international assistance was essential in enabling the Khmer Rouge to rebuild its military strength and fight on for another two decades.

The UN Comes to Town

The arrival of Mikhail Gorbachev in the Kremlin saw the Cold War draw to a close. It was the furthest-flung Soviet allies who were cut adrift first, leaving Vietnam internationally isolated and economically crippled. In September 1989, Vietnam announced the withdrawal of all its troops from Cambodia. With the Vietnamese gone, the opposition coalition, still dominated by the Khmer Rouge, launched a series of offensives, forcing the now-vulnerable government to the negotiating table.

To the End of Hell: One Woman's Struggle to Survive Cambodia's Khmer Rouge is the incredible memoir of Denise Affonço, one of the only foreigners to live through the Khmer Rouge revolution, due to her marriage to a senior intellectual in the movement.

Diplomatic efforts to end the civil war began to bear fruit in September 1990, when a peace plan was accepted by both the Phnom Penh government and the three factions of the resistance coalition. According to the plan, the Supreme National Council (SNC), a coalition of all factions, would be formed under the presidency of Sihanouk. Meanwhile, the UN Transitional Authority in Cambodia (Untac) would supervise the administration of the country for two years, with the goal of free and fair elections.

1999	2000	2002	2003
Cambodia finally joins Asean after a two-year delay, taking its place among the family of Southeast Asian nations, which welcome the country back onto the world stage.	The Cambodian Freedom Fighters (CFF) launch an 'assault' on Phnom Penh. Backed by Cambodian-American dissidents, the attackers are lightly armed, poorly trained and politically inexperienced.	Cambodia holds its first ever local elections at commune level, a tentative step towards dismantling the old communist system of control and bringing grass-roots democracy to the country.	The CPP wins the election, but political infighting prevents the formation of the new government for almost a year until the old coalition with Funcinpec is revived.

Untac undoubtedly achieved some successes, but for all of these, it is the failures that were to cost Cambodia dearly in the 'democratic' era. Untac was successful in pushing through many international human-rights covenants; it opened the door to a significant number of nongovernmental organisations (NGOs); and, most importantly, on 25 May 1993, elections were held with an 89.6% turnout. However, the results were far from decisive. Funcinpec, led by Prince Norodom Ranariddh, took 58 seats in the National Assembly, while the Cambodian People's Party (CPP), which represented the previous communist government, took 51 seats. The CPP had lost the election, but senior leaders threatened a secession of the eastern provinces of the country. As a result, Cambodia ended up with two prime ministers: Norodom Ranariddh as first prime minister, and Hun Sen as second prime minister.

Even today, Untac is heralded as one of the UN's success stories. Another perspective is that it was an ill-conceived and poorly executed peace because so many of the powers involved in brokering the deal had their own agendas to advance. To many Cambodians who had survived the 1970s, it was unthinkable that the Khmer Rouge would be allowed to play a part in the electoral process after presiding over a genocide.

The UN's disarmament programme took weapons away from rural militias who for so long provided the backbone of the government's provincial defence network against the Khmer Rouge and this left communities throughout the country vulnerable to attack. Meanwhile the Khmer Rouge used the veil of legitimacy conferred upon it by the peace process to reestablish a guerrilla network throughout Cambodia. By 1994, when it was finally outlawed by the government, the Khmer Rouge was arguably a greater threat to the stability of Cambodia than at any time since 1979.

Untac's main goals had been to 'restore and maintain peace' and 'promote national reconciliation', and in the short term it achieved neither. It did oversee free and fair elections, but these were later annulled by the actions of Cambodia's politicians. Little was done during the UN period to try to dismantle the communist apparatus of state set up by the CPP, a well-oiled machine that continues to ensure that former communists control the civil service, judiciary, army and police today.

Only a handful of foreigners were allowed to visit Cambodia during the Khmer Rouge period of Democratic Kampuchea. US journalist Elizabeth Becker was one who travelled there in late 1978; her book *When the War Was Over* (1986) tells her story.

The Slow Birth of Peace

When the Vietnamese toppled the Pol Pot government in 1979, the Khmer Rouge disappeared into the jungle. The guerrillas eventually boycotted the 1993 elections and later rejected peace talks aimed at establishing a ceasefire. In 1994, the Khmer Rouge resorted to a new tactic of targeting tourists, with horrendous results for a number of foreigners in Cambodia. During 1994, three people were taken from a taxi on the road to

2004	2005	2006	2007
In a move that catches observers by surprise, King Sihanouk abdicates the throne and is succeeded by his son King Sihamoni, a popular choice as Sihamoni has steered clear of politics.	Cambodia joins the WTO, opening its markets to free trade, but many commentators feel it could be counterproductive, as the economy is so small and there is no more protection for domestic producers.	Lawsuits and counter lawsuits see political leaders moving from conflict to courtroom in the new Cambodia. The revolving doors stop with opposition leader Sam Rainsy back in the country and Prince Ranariddh out.	Royalist party Funcinpec continues to implode in the face of conflict, intrigue and defections, with democrats joining Sam Rainsy, loyalists joining the new Norodom Ranariddh Party and others joining the CPP.

Sihanoukville and subsequently shot. A few months later another three foreigners were seized from a train bound for Sihanoukville and in the ransom drama that followed they were executed as the army closed in.

The government changed course during the mid-1990s, opting for more carrot and less stick in a bid to end the war. The breakthrough came in 1996 when Ieng Sary, Brother Number Three in the Khmer Rouge hierarchy and foreign minister during its rule, was denounced by Pol Pot for corruption. He subsequently led a mass defection of fighters and their dependants from the Pailin area, and this effectively sealed the fate of the remaining Khmer Rouge. Pailin, rich in gems and timber, had long been the economic crutch that kept the Khmer Rouge hobbling along. The severing of this income, coupled with the fact that government forces now had only one front on which to concentrate their resources, suggested the days of civil war were numbered.

By 1997, cracks were appearing in the coalition and the fledgling democracy once again found itself under siege. But it was the Khmer Rouge that again grabbed the headlines. Pol Pot ordered the execution of Son Sen, defence minister during the Khmer Rouge regime, and many of his family members. This provoked a putsch within the Khmer Rouge leadership, and the one-legged hardliner general Ta Mok seized control, putting Pol Pot on 'trial'. Rumours flew about Phnom Penh that Pol Pot would be brought there to face international justice, but events dramatically shifted back to the capital.

A lengthy courting period ensued in which both Funcinpec and the CPP attempted to win the trust of the remaining Khmer Rouge hardliners in northern Cambodia. Ranariddh was close to forging a deal with the jungle fighters and was keen to get it sewn up before Cambodia's accession to Asean, as nothing would provide a better entry fanfare than the ending of Cambodia's long civil war. He was outflanked and subsequently outgunned by Second Prime Minister Hun Sen. On 5 July 1997, fighting again erupted on the streets of Phnom Penh as troops loyal to the CPP clashed with those loyal to Funcinpec. The heaviest exchanges were around the airport and key government buildings, but before long the dust had settled and the CPP once again controlled Cambodia. Euphemistically known as 'the events of 1997' in Cambodia, much of the international community condemned the violence as a coup.

As 1998 began, the CPP announced an all-out offensive against its enemies in the north. By April it was closing in on the Khmer Rouge strongholds of Anlong Veng and Preah Vihear, and amid this heavy fighting Pol Pot evaded justice by dying a natural death on 15 April in the captivity of his former Khmer Rouge comrades. The fall of Anlong Veng in April was followed by the fall of Preah Vihear in May, and the surviving big three,

HISTORY THE SLOW BIRTH OF PEACE

The Killing Fields (1985) is the definitive film on the Khmer Rouge period in Cambodia. It tells the story of American journalist Sydney Schanberg and his Cambodian assistant Dith Pran during and after the war.

2009	2010	2011	2013
Comrade Duch, aka Kaing Guek Eav, commandant of the notorious S-21 prison, goes on trial for crimes committed during the Khmer Rouge regime.	As the annual Bon Om Tuk (Water Festival) draws to a close on 22 November, more than 350 people die as revellers swarm across a narrow bridge in huge numbers.	The simmering border conflict over the ancient temple of Preah Vihear spills over into actual fighting between Cambodia and Thailand. A ceasefire is negotiated by Asean chair Indonesia.	In Cambodia's fifth postwar election the united opposition Cambodia National Rescue Party (CNRP) wins 55 seats in the National Assembly. CNRP cites voting irregularities but the CPP ignores calls for an investigation.

Ta Mok, Khieu Samphan and Nuon Chea, were forced to flee into the jungle near the Thai border with their remaining troops.

The 1998 election result reinforced the reality that the CPP was now the dominant force in the Cambodian political system and on 25 December Hun Sen received the Christmas present he had been waiting for: Khieu Samphan and Nuon Chea were defecting to the government side. The international community began to pile on the pressure for the establishment of some sort of war-crimes tribunal to try the remaining Khmer Rouge leadership. After lengthy negotiations, agreement was finally reached on the composition of a court to try the surviving leaders of the Khmer Rouge. The CPP was suspicious of a UN-administered trial as the UN had sided with the Khmer Rouge–dominated coalition against the government in Phnom Penh, and the ruling party wanted a major say in who was to be tried and for what. The UN for its part doubted that the judiciary in Cambodia was sophisticated or impartial enough to fairly oversee such a major trial. A compromise solution – a mixed tribunal of three international and four Cambodian judges requiring a super majority of two plus three for a verdict – was eventually agreed upon.

Will Democracy Prevail?

In 2002 Cambodia's first-ever local elections were held to select village- and commune-level representatives, an important step in bringing grassroots democracy to the country. Despite national elections since 1993, the CPP continued to monopolise political power at local and regional levels and only with commune elections would this grip be loosened. The national elections of July 2003 saw a shift in the balance of power, as the CPP consolidated its grip on Cambodia and the Sam Rainsy–led Cambodia National Rescue Party (CNRP) overtook Funcinpec as the second party. This trend continued into the 2008 election when the CPP's majority grew. However, the 2013 election saw a massive reversal in the trend as the opposition managed to stay united through the election campaign. The return of CNRP leader Sam Rainsy from self-imposed exile saw his party come close to victory over the CPP. However, in the subsequent years, the CPP has been cracking down hard on the opposition, which was officially dissolved in late 2017. Whether this is a 'descent into outright dictatorship' – to quote a final edition headline of newspaper *Cambodia Daily* before it was shut down by the government – remains to be seen. The CPP used COVID-19 as an excuse to delay a politically-charged trial for current opposition leader Kem Sokha. Meanwhile, the economic devastation wrought by the pandemic diverted attention away from politics to more everyday struggles as the nation's economy contracted in 2020 for the first time in more than two decades.

The Documentation Center of Cambodia is an organisation established to document the crimes of the Khmer Rouge as a record for future generations. Its excellent website has a wealth of information about Cambodia's darkest hour. Take your time to visit www.dccam.org.

2016	2017	2018	2021
Opposition leader Sam Rainsy once again chooses exile ahead of imprisonment as the CPP press defamation charges and he is formally barred from returning to the country in October.	The CPP loses almost one third of its seats to the CNRP in nationwide commune elections. Party leader Kem Sokha is placed under de facto house arrest shortly after, and in November the Supreme Court dissolves the CNRP.	With the opposition neutralised, the CPP scores a landslide victory in National Assembly elections, taking all 125 seats.	After largely escaping the worst of the COVID-19 pandemic in 2020, Cambodia sees its first big wave of cases right as it launches a slow vaccination campaign.

Pol Pot & the Khmer Rouge Trials

The Khmer Rouge controlled Cambodia for three years, eight months and 20 days, a period etched into the consciousness of the Khmer people. The Vietnamese ousted the Khmer Rouge on 7 January 1979, but Cambodia's civil war continued for another two decades until 1999. More than 20 years after the Khmer Rouge regime's collapse, the Extraordinary Chambers in the Courts of Cambodia (ECCC) commenced trials to bring those responsible for the deaths of about two million Cambodians to justice.

The Khmer Rouge Tribunal

Case 001

Case 001, the trial of Kaing Guek Eav, aka Comrade Duch, began in 2009. Duch was seen as a key figure as he provided the link between the regime and its crimes in his role as head of S-21 prison. Duch was sentenced to 35 years in 2010, but this was reduced to just 19 years in lieu of time already served and his cooperation with the investigating team. For many Cambodians this was a slap in the face, as Duch had already admitted overall responsibility for the deaths of about 17,000 people. Convert this into simple numbers and it equates to about 10 hours of prison time per victim. However, an appeal verdict announced on 3 February 2012 extended the sentence to life imprisonment.

To learn more about the origins of the Khmer Rouge and the Democratic Kampuchea regime, read *How Pol Pot Came to Power* (1985) and *The Pol Pot Regime* (1996), both written by Yale University academic Ben Kiernan.

Case 002

Case 002 began in November 2011, involving the most senior surviving leaders of the Democratic Kampuchea (DK) era: Brother Number Two Nuon Chea, former DK head of state Khieu Samphan, and former DK Foreign Minister Ieng Sary and his wife, former DK Minister of Social Affairs Ieng Thirith. Ieng Sary died on 14 March 2013 and Ieng Thirith was ruled unfit to stand trial due to the onset of dementia (she later died as well). Both Nuon Chea and Khieu Samphan received two separate life sentences – the first for crimes against humanity in August 2014, and a second for genocide in November 2018. Both parties appealed the latter conviction. Nuon Chea died in August 2019, putting his appeal in limbo. The ECCC was due to rule on Khieu Samphan's appeal in late 2020.

Pol Pot travelled up the Ho Chi Minh Trail to visit Beijing in 1966, at the height of the Cultural Revolution there. He was obviously inspired by what he saw, as the Khmer Rouge went even further than the Red Guards in severing links with the past.

Cases 003 & 004

Case 003 was lodged in 2009 against head of the DK navy, Meas Muth, and head of the DK air force, Sou Met. The latter died in 2013, but in 2015 the ECCC named additional suspects under Case 004: Im Chaem, a regional commander accused of murder, extermination and enslavement in the DK's Northwestern Zone; her co-commander, Yim Tith; and top DK Central Zone official Ao An, accused of genocide against the Cham minority. The cases took years to develop amid fierce opposition from the Cambodian government, which wanted to draw a line under proceedings with the completion of Case 002. In 2015 the accused were finally charged, but one by one the indictments collapsed as the Cambodian co-investigating judge on the ECCC panel refused to bring charges. As of late 2019 Prime Minister Hun Sen continued to openly oppose the cases and observers saw little hope of the accused ever being put on trial.

Cost

More than US$300 million has been spent to date, against a backdrop of allegations of corruption and mismanagement on the Cambodian side. Some Cambodians feel the trial will send an important political message about accountability that may resonate with some of the Cambodian leadership today. However, others argue that the trial is a major waste of money, given the overwhelming evidence against surviving senior leaders, and that a truth and reconciliation commission may have provided more compelling answers for Cambodians who want to understand what motivated the average Khmer Rouge cadre.

Brother Number One (2011) is a feature-length documentary that follows New Zealand rower Rob Hamill on a personal journey to discover who was responsible for the murder of his brother Kerry Hamill in S-21 prison in 1978.

Pol Pot & His Comrades

Pol Pot: Brother Number One

Pol Pot is a name that sends shivers down the spines of Cambodians and foreigners alike. It is Pol Pot who is most associated with the bloody madness of the regime he led between 1975 and 1979, and his policies heaped misery, suffering and death on millions of Cambodians.

Pol Pot was born Saloth Sar in a small village near Kompong Thom in 1925. As a young man he won a scholarship to study in Paris, where he came into contact with the Cercle Marxiste and communist thought, which he later transformed into a politics of extreme Maoism.

In 1963, Sihanouk's repressive policies sent Saloth Sar and his comrades fleeing to the jungles of Ratanakiri. It was from this moment that Saloth Sar began to call himself Pol Pot. Once the Khmer Rouge was allied with Sihanouk, following his overthrow by Lon Nol in 1970 and subsequent exile in Beijing, its support soared and the faces of the leadership became familiar. However, Pol Pot remained a shadowy figure, leaving public duties to Khieu Samphan and Ieng Sary.

When the Khmer Rouge marched into Phnom Penh on 17 April 1975, few people could have anticipated the hell that was to follow. Pol Pot and his clique were the architects of one of the most radical and brutal revolutions in the history of humankind. It was Year Zero and Cambodia was on a self-destructive course to sever all ties with the past.

Enemies of the People (2009) follows Cambodian journalist and genocide survivor Thet Sambath as he wins the confidence of Brother Number Two in the Khmer Rouge, Nuon Chea, eventually coaxing him to give new testimony on his role in the genocidal regime.

Pol Pot was not to emerge as the public face of the revolution until the end of 1976, after he returned from a trip to see his mentors in Beijing. He granted almost no interviews to foreign media and was seen only on propaganda movies produced by government TV. Such was his aura and reputation that, by the last year of the regime, a cult of personality was developing around him.

After being ousted by the Vietnamese, Pol Pot spent much of the 1980s living in Thailand and was able to rebuild his shattered forces and once again threaten Cambodia. His enigma increased as the international media speculated on his real fate. His demise was reported so often that when he finally died on 15 April 1998, many Cambodians refused to believe it until they had seen footage of his body. Even then, many were sceptical and rumours continue to circulate about exactly how he met his end. Officially, he was said to have died from a heart attack, but a full autopsy was not carried out before his body was cremated on a pyre of burning tyres.

Nuon Chea: Brother Number Two

Long considered one of the main ideologues and architects of the Khmer Rouge revolution, Nuon Chea studied law at Bangkok's Thammasat University before joining the Thai Communist Party. He was appointed Deputy Secretary of the Communist Party of Kampuchea upon its secretive founding in 1960 and remained Pol Pot's second in command throughout the regime's rule, with overall responsibility for internal security. He was sentenced to life imprisonment for crimes against humanity in 2014, a verdict that was upheld on appeal in November 2016. He was subsequently convicted for genocide in 2018 before passing away in 2019 at the age of 93.

Ieng Sary: Brother Number Three

One of Pol Pot's closest confidants, Ieng Sary fled to the jungles of Ratanakiri in 1963, where he and Pol Pot both underwent intensive guerrilla training in the company of North Vietnamese communist forces. Ieng Sary was one of the public faces of the Khmer Rouge and became foreign minister of Democratic Kampuchea. Until his death in 2013, he maintained that he was not involved in the planning or execution of the genocide. However, he did invite many intellectuals, diplomats and exiles to return to Cambodia from 1975, the majority of whom were subsequently tortured and executed in S-21 prison. He helped hasten the demise of the Khmer Rouge as a guerrilla force with his defection to the government side in 1996 and was given an amnesty for his earlier crimes.

Khieu Samphan: Brother Number Nine

Khieu Samphan studied economics in Paris and some of his theories on self-reliance were credited with inspiring Khmer Rouge economic policies. During the Sihanouk years of the 1960s, Khieu Samphan spent several years working with the Sangkum government and putting his more moderate theories to the test. During a crackdown on leftists in 1967, he fled to the jungle to join Pol Pot and Ieng Sary. During the Democratic Kampuchea period, he was made head of state from 1976 to 1979. Along with Nuon Chea, he was sentenced twice to life imprisonment by the ECCC as part of Case 002 – in 2014 and again in 2018. The second sentence, for genocide, remains under appeal.

Comrade Duch: Commandant of S-21

Born Kaing Guek Eav in Kompong Thom in 1942, Duch initially worked as a teacher before joining the Khmer Rouge in 1967. Based in the Cardamom Mountains during the civil war of 1970–75, he was given responsibility for security and political prisons in his region, where he refined his interrogation techniques. Following the Khmer Rouge takeover, he was moved to S-21 prison and was responsible for the interrogation and execution of thousands of prisoners. He fled Phnom Penh as Vietnamese forces surrounded the city, and his whereabouts were unknown until he was discovered living in Battambang Province by British photojournalist Nic Dunlop. The first to stand trial and be sentenced in Case 001, Comrade Duch cooperated through the judicial process. He was sentenced to life imprisonment in early 2012.

The Future

With the collapse of Cases 003 and 004, the ECCC is nearing the end of its mandate in Cambodia. While many have criticised the tribunal for achieving just three convictions since it was established in 1997, others laud the court for providing a measure of closure for victims and their families, especially through the landmark genocide convictions of Brothers Two and Nine in 2018. Keep up to date with the latest developments in the trial by visiting the official website of the Cambodia Tribunal Monitor (www.cambodiatribunal.org) and the official ECCC site (www.eccc.gov.kh/en).

Pick up a copy of *When Clouds Fell From the Sky* (2015) by Robert Carmichael, a book that tells the story of a Cambodian diplomat's disappearance on his return to Cambodia in 1977 and his family's search for justice more than 30 years later.

Khieu Samphan tries to exonerate himself in his 2004 publication, *Cambodia's Recent History and the Reasons Behind the Decisions I Made*.

The Khmer Rouge period is politically sensitive in Cambodia, due in part to the connections the current leadership has with the communist movement – so much so that the history of the genocide was not taught in high schools until 2009.

People & Culture

A tumultuous history, an incredible heritage of architecture, sculpture and dance, a modern arts scene, and a fascinating mosaic of people and faiths all go towards making Cambodia's rich national character. Visitors have ample opportunity to drink it all in, from the stunning Temples of Angkor – the ultimate embodiment of Khmer artistic prowess – to cultural revival programmes like Phare Cambodian Circus in Battambang or Cambodia Living Arts in Phnom Penh.

The National Psyche

Since the glory days of the Angkorian empire, the Cambodian people have been on the losing side of many a battle – their country all too often a minnow amid the circling sharks – and popular attitudes have been shaped by this history. At first glance, Cambodia appears to be a nation of shiny, happy people, but look deeper and it is a country of evident contradictions. Light and dark, rich and poor, love and hate, life and death – all are visible on a journey through the kingdom. Most telling of all is the evidence of the nation's glorious past set against the more recent tragedy of its present.

Angkor is everywhere: on the flag, the national beer, cigarettes, hotels and guesthouses – anything and everything. It's a symbol of nationhood and fierce pride – no matter how ugly things got in the bad old days, the Cambodians built Angkor Wat and it doesn't get bigger than that.

Contrast this with the abyss into which the nation was sucked during the years of the Khmer Rouge. 'Pol Pot' is a dirty word in Cambodia due to the death and suffering he inflicted on the country.

As for Cambodian attitudes towards their regional neighbours, these are complex. Thais aren't always popular, as some Cambodians feel they fail to acknowledge their cultural debt to Cambodia and generally look down on their less affluent neighbour. Cambodian attitudes towards the Vietnamese are more ambivalent. There is a certain level of mistrust, as many feel the Vietnamese aspire to colonise their country. (Many Khmers still call the lost Mekong Delta 'Kampuchea Krom', meaning 'Lower Cambodia'.) However, this mistrust is balanced with a grudging respect for

Jayavarman VII was a Mahayana Buddhist who directed his faith towards improving the lot of his people, with the construction of hospitals, universities, roads and shelters.

THE POPULATION OF CAMBODIA

Cambodia's second postwar population census was carried out in 2008 and put the country's population at about 13.5 million. The current population is estimated at around 16 million and, with a rapid growth rate of about 2% per year, it's predicted to reach 20 million by 2025.

Phnom Penh is the largest city, with a population of about two million. Other major population centres include the boom towns of Siem Reap, Sihanoukville, Battambang and Poipet.

The much-discussed imbalance of men to women due to years of conflict is not as serious as it was in 1980, but it's still significant: there are about 95 males to every 100 females, up from 86.1 to 100 in 1980. There is, however, a marked imbalance in age groups: more than 40% of the population is under the age of 16.

CAMBODIAN GREETINGS

Cambodians traditionally greet each other with the *sompiah*, which involves pressing the hands together in prayer and bowing, similar to the *wai* in Thailand. The higher the hands and the lower the bow, the more respect is conveyed – important to remember when meeting officials or the elderly. In recent times this custom has been partly replaced by the handshake but, although men tend to shake hands with each other, women usually use the traditional greeting with both men and women. It is considered acceptable (or perhaps excusable) for foreigners to shake hands with Cambodians of both sexes.

the Vietnamese role in Cambodia's 'liberation' from the Khmer Rouge in 1979. But when liberation became occupation in the 1980s, the relationship soured once more.

The Cambodian Way of Life

For many older Cambodians, life is centred on family, faith and food, an existence that has stayed the same for centuries. Family is more than the traditional nuclear family, it's the extended family of third cousins and obscure aunts – as long as there is a bloodline, there is a bond. Families stick together, solve problems collectively, listen to the wisdom of the elders and pool resources. The extended family comes together during times of trouble and times of joy, celebrating festivals and successes, mourning deaths and disappointments. Whether the Cambodian house is big or small, there will be a lot of people living inside.

For the majority of the population still living in the countryside, these constants carry on as they always have: several generations sharing the same roof, the same rice and the same religion. But during the dark decades of the 1970s and 1980s, this routine was ripped apart by war and ideology, as the peasants were dragged into a bloody civil war and later forced into slavery. The Khmer Rouge organisation Angkar took over as the moral and social beacon in the lives of the people. Families were forced apart, children turned against parents, brothers against sisters. The bond of trust was broken and is only slowly being rebuilt today.

For the younger generation, brought up in a postconflict, postcommunist period of relative freedom, it's a different story – arguably thanks to their steady diet of MTV and steamy soaps. Cambodia is experiencing its very own '60s swing, as the younger generation stands ready for a different lifestyle to the one their parents had to swallow. This creates plenty of friction in the cities, as rebellious teens dress as they like, date whomever they wish and hit the town until all hours. More recently this generational conflict has spilled over into politics as the Facebook generation helped deliver some shock results that saw the grip on power of the governing Cambodian People's Party (CPP) weaken after the 2013 elections (the CPP has since strengthened its grip anew).

Cambodia is set for major demographic shifts in the next couple of decades. Currently, just 25% of the population lives in urban areas, which contrasts starkly with the country's more developed neighbours. Increasing numbers of young people are likely to migrate to the cities in search of opportunity, forever changing the face of Cambodian society. However, for now at least, Cambodian society remains much more traditional than that of Thailand and Vietnam, and visitors need to keep this in mind.

Lowland Khmers are being encouraged to migrate to Cambodia's northeast where there is plenty of available land. But this is home to the country's minority peoples, who have no indigenous concepts of property rights or land ownership, so this may see their culture marginalised in coming years.

Multiculturalism

According to official statistics, more than 90% of the people who live in Cambodia are ethnic Khmers, making the country the most ethnically homogeneous in Southeast Asia. However, unofficially, the figure is

KHMER KROM

The Khmer Krom people of southern Vietnam are ethnic Khmers separated from Cambodia by historical deals and Vietnamese encroachment on what was once Cambodian territory. Nobody is sure just how many of them there are and estimates vary from one million to seven million, depending on who is doing the counting.

The history of Vietnamese expansion into Khmer territory has long been a staple of Khmer textbooks. King Chey Chetha II of Cambodia, in keeping with the wishes of his Vietnamese queen, first allowed Vietnamese to settle in the Cambodian town of Prey Nokor in 1623. It was obviously the thin end of the wedge, as Prey Nokor is now better known as Ho Chi Minh City (Saigon).

The Vietnamese government has pursued a policy of forced assimilation since independence, which has involved ethnic Khmers taking Vietnamese names and studying in Vietnamese. According to the Khmer Kampuchea Federation (KKF), the Khmer Krom continue to suffer persecution, including lack of access to health services, religious discrimination and outright racism. Several monks have been defrocked for nonviolent protests in recent years and the Cambodian government has even assisted in deporting some agitators, according to Human Rights Watch.

Many Khmer Krom would like to see Cambodia act as a mediator in the quest for greater autonomy and ethnic representation in Vietnam, but the Cambodian government takes a softly, softly approach towards its more powerful neighbour, perhaps born of the historic ties between the two political dynasties.

For more about the ongoing struggles of the Khmer Krom, visit www.khmerkrom.org.

probably smaller due to a large influx of Chinese and Vietnamese in the past century. Other ethnic minorities include Cham, Lao and the indigenous peoples of the rural highlands.

Ethnic Khmers

The Khmers have inhabited Cambodia since the beginning of recorded regional history (around the 2nd century), many centuries before Thais and Vietnamese migrated to the region. Over the centuries, the Khmers have mixed with other groups residing in Cambodia, including Javanese and Malays (8th century), Thais (10th to 15th centuries), Vietnamese (from the early 17th century) and Chinese (since the 18th century).

Ethnic Vietnamese

The Vietnamese are one of the largest non-Khmer ethnic groups in Cambodia. According to government figures, Cambodia is host to around 100,000 Vietnamese, though unofficial observers claim the real figure may be somewhere between half a million and one million. The Vietnamese play a big part in the fishing and construction industries in Cambodia. There is still some distrust between the Cambodians and the Vietnamese, though, even of the Vietnamese who have been living in Cambodia for generations.

Even the destructive Khmer Rouge paid homage to the mighty Angkor Wat on its flag, with three towers of the temple in yellow, set against a blood-red background.

Ethnic Chinese

The government claims there are around 50,000 ethnic Chinese in Cambodia; however, informed observers estimate half a million to one million in urban areas. Many Chinese Cambodians have lived in Cambodia for generations and have adopted the Khmer culture, language and identity. Until 1975, the ethnic Chinese controlled the economic life of Cambodia and in recent years they have reemerged as a powerful economic force, mainly due to increased investment by overseas Chinese.

Ethnic Cham

Cambodia's Cham Muslims (known locally as the Khmer Islam) officially number around 200,000. Unofficial counts put the figure higher at around 500,000. The Cham live in villages on the banks of the Mekong, Tonlé Sap and other rivers, with the heaviest concentrations in the provinces of Kompong Cham, Kompong Speu and Kompong Chhnang. They suffered vicious persecution between 1975 and 1979, when a large part of their community was targeted. Many Cham mosques that were destroyed under the Khmer Rouge have since been rebuilt.

Ethno-Linguistic Minorities

Cambodia's diverse Khmer Leu (Upper Khmer) or *chunchiet* (ethnic minorities), who live in the country's mountainous regions, probably number around 100,000.

The majority of these groups live in the northeast of Cambodia, in the provinces of Ratanakiri, Mondulkiri, Stung Treng and Kratie. The largest group is the Tompuon (many other spellings are also used), who number nearly 20,000. Other groups include the Bunong, Kreung, Kavet, Brau and Jarai.

The hill tribes of Cambodia have long been isolated from mainstream Khmer society, and there is little in the way of mutual understanding. They practise shifting cultivation, rarely staying in one place for long. Finding a new location for a village requires a village elder to mediate with the spirit world. Very few of the minorities retain the sort of colourful traditional costumes found in Thailand, Laos and Vietnam.

Look out for Chinese and Vietnamese cemeteries dotting the rice fields of provinces to the south and east of Phnom Penh. Khmers do not bury their dead, but practise cremation, and the ashes may be interred in a stupa in the grounds of a wat.

Religion

Buddhism

Buddhism arrived in Cambodia with Hinduism but only became the official religion from the 13th and 14th centuries. Most Cambodians today practise Theravada Buddhism. Between 1975 and 1979 many of Cambodia's Buddhist monks were murdered by the Khmer Rouge and nearly all the country's wats (more than 3000) were damaged or destroyed. In the late 1980s, Buddhism once again became the state religion and today young monks are a common sight throughout the country. Many wats have been rebuilt or rehabilitated and money-raising drives for this work can be seen on roadsides across the country.

The ultimate goal of Theravada Buddhism is nirvana – 'extinction' of all desire and suffering to reach the final stage of reincarnation. By feeding monks, giving donations to temples and performing regular worship at the local wat, Buddhists hope to improve their lot, acquiring enough merit to reduce their number of rebirths.

Every Buddhist male is expected to become a monk for a short period in his life, optimally between the time he finishes school and starts a career or marries. Men or boys under 20 years of age may enter the *sangha* (monastic order) as novices. Nowadays men may spend as little as 15 days to accrue merit as monks.

The famous Hindu epic the *Ramayana* is known as the *Reamker* in Cambodia. Reyum Publishing issued a beautifully illustrated book, *The Reamker* (1999), telling the story.

Hinduism

Hinduism flourished alongside Buddhism from the 1st century AD until the 14th century. During the pre-Angkorian period, Hinduism was represented by the worship of Harihara (Shiva and Vishnu embodied in a single deity). During the time of Angkor, Shiva was the deity most in favour with the royal family, although in the 12th century he was superseded by Vishnu. Today some elements of Hinduism are still incorporated into important ceremonies involving birth, marriage and death.

Animism

Both Hinduism and Buddhism were gradually absorbed from beyond the borders of Cambodia, fusing with the animist beliefs already present among the Khmers before Indianisation. Local beliefs didn't disappear but were incorporated into the new religions to form something uniquely Cambodian. The concept of Neak Ta has its foundations in animist beliefs regarding sacred soil and the sacred spirit around us. Neak Ta can be viewed as a mother-earth concept, an energy force uniting a community with its earth and water. It can be represented in many forms, from stone or wood to termite hills – anything that symbolises both a link between the people and the fertility of their land. The sometimes phallic representation of Neak Ta helps explain the popularity of Hinduism and the worship of the *lingam* (phallic symbol).

The purest form of animism is practised among the minority people known as Khmer Leu. Some have converted to Buddhism, but the majority continue to worship spirits of the earth and skies and their forefathers.

Islam

Cambodia's Muslims are descendants of Chams, who migrated from what is now central Vietnam after the final defeat of the kingdom of Champa by the Vietnamese in 1471. Like Buddhists in Cambodia, the Cham Muslims call the faithful to prayer by banging a drum, rather than with the call of the muezzin.

Christianity

Christianity has made limited headway into Cambodia compared with neighbouring Vietnam. There were a number of churches in Cambodia before the war, but many of these were systematically destroyed by the Khmer Rouge, including Notre Dame Cathedral in Phnom Penh. Christianity made a comeback of sorts throughout the refugee camps on the Thai border in the 1980s, as a number of food-for-faith-type charities set up shop dispensing religion with every meal. Many Cambodians changed their public faith for survival, before converting back to Buddhism on their departure from the camps, earning the moniker 'rice Christians'.

The Arts

The Khmer Rouge's assault on the arts was a terrible blow to Cambodian culture. Indeed, for a number of years the consensus among Khmers was that their culture had been irrevocably lost. The Khmer Rouge not only did away with living bearers of Khmer culture but also destroyed cultural artefacts, statues, musical instruments, books and anything else that served as a reminder of a past it was trying to efface. The temples of Angkor were spared as a symbol of Khmer glory and empire, but little else survived. Despite this, Cambodia is witnessing a resurgence of traditional arts and a growing interest in experimentation in modern arts and cross-cultural fusion.

Architecture

Khmer architecture reached its peak during the Angkorian era (9th to 14th centuries). Some of the finest examples of architecture from this period are Angkor Wat and the structures of Angkor Thom.

Today, most rural Cambodian houses are built on high wood pilings (if the family can afford it) and have thatched roofs, walls made of palm mats and floors of woven bamboo strips resting on bamboo joists. The shady space underneath is used for storage and for people to relax at midday. Wealthier families have houses with wooden walls and tiled roofs, but the basic design remains the same.

The French left their mark in Cambodia in the form of some handsome villas and government buildings built in neoclassical style, Romanesque pillars and all. Some of the best architectural examples are in Phnom Penh, but most of the provincial capitals have at least one or two examples of architecture from the colonial period. Battambang and Kampot are two of the best-preserved colonial-era towns, with handsome rows of shophouses and the classic governors' residences.

During the 1950s and 1960s, Cambodia's so-called golden era, a group of young Khmer architects shaped the capital of Cambodia in their own image, experimenting with what is now called New Khmer Architecture. Vann Molyvann (1926–2017) was the most famous proponent of this school of architecture, designing a number of prominent Phnom Penh landmarks such as the Olympic Stadium (p57), the Chatomuk Theatre (p88) and Independence Monument (p57). The beach resort of Kep was remodelled at this time, as the emergent Cambodian middle class flocked to the beach, and there are some fantastic if dilapidated examples of New Khmer Architecture around the small town. Boutique hotels Knai Bang Chatt (p228) and Villa Romonea in Kep are both restored examples from this period.

To discover examples of New Khmer Architecture, visit the website of Khmer Architecture Tours (www.ka-tours.org) or sign up for one of its walking tours of Phnom Penh or Battambang. The website includes downloadable printouts for DIY tours of each city.

For more on the life and work of late national architect Vann Molyvann, check out the documentary *The Man Who Built Cambodia* (2014).

Cinema

Back in the 1960s, the Cambodian film industry was booming. Between 1960 and 1975, more than 300 films were made, some of which were exported all around Asia, including numerous films by then head-of-state Norodom Sihanouk. However, the advent of Khmer Rouge rule saw the film industry disappear overnight and it didn't recover for more than a quarter of a century.

The film industry in Cambodia was given a new lease of life in 2000 with the release of *Pos Keng Kong* (The Giant Snake). A remake of a 1960s Cambodian classic, it tells the story of a powerful young girl born from a rural relationship between a woman and a snake king. It's an interesting love story, albeit with dodgy special effects, and achieved massive box-office success around the region.

The success of *Pos Keng Kong* heralded a minirevival in the Cambodian film industry and local directors now turn out several films a year. However, many of these are amateurish horror films of dubious artistic value.

At least one overseas Cambodian director has enjoyed major success in recent years: Rithy Panh. His film *The Missing Picture,* which used clay figurines to tell his personal story of survival under the Khmer Rouge, was nominated for an Academy Award for Best Foreign Language Film in 2014.

SIHANOUK & THE SILVER SCREEN

Between 1965 and 1969 Sihanouk (former king and head of state of Cambodia) wrote, directed and produced nine feature films, a figure that would put the average workaholic Hollywood director to shame. Sihanouk took the business of making films very seriously, and family and officials were called upon to play their part: the minister of foreign affairs acted as the male lead in Sihanouk's first feature, *Apsara* (1965), and his daughter, Princess Bopha Devi, the female lead. When, in the same movie, a show of military hardware was required, the air force was brought into action.

Sihanouk often took on the leading role himself. Notable performances saw him as a spirit of the forest and as a victorious general. Perhaps it was no surprise, given the king's apparent addiction to the world of celluloid dreams, that Cambodia should challenge Cannes with its Phnom Penh International Film Festival. The festival was held twice, in 1968 and 1969. Also, perhaps unsurprisingly, Sihanouk won the grand prize on both occasions. He continued to make movies in later life and made around 30 films during his remarkable career.

His success goes back to 1995, when *People of the Rice Fields* was nominated for the Palme d'Or at the Cannes Film Festival. His other films include *One Night after the War* (1997), the story of a young Khmer kickboxer falling for a bar girl in Phnom Penh; and the award-winning *S-21: The Khmer Rouge Killing Machine* (2003), a powerful documentary in which survivors from Tuol Sleng are brought back to confront their guards.

The definitive film about Cambodia is *The Killing Fields* (1985), directed by Roland Joffé, which tells the story of American journalist Sydney Schanberg and his Cambodian assistant Dith Pran. Most of the footage was actually shot in Thailand, as it was filmed in 1984 when Cambodia was effectively closed to the West.

Quite a number of international films have been shot in Cambodia since the turn of the millennium, including *Tomb Raider* (2001), *City of Ghosts* (2002) and *Two Brothers* (2004), all worth seeking out for their beautiful Cambodian backdrops. Angelina Jolie returned to Cambodia in 2015–16 to film *First They Killed My Father,* a full-length feature film based on the book by Luong Ung, available on Netflix since September 2017.

For more on Cambodian films and cinema, pick up a copy of *Kon: The Cinema of Cambodia* (2010), published by the Department of Media and Communication at the Royal University of Cambodia. Also look out for the Cambodia International Film Festival (www.cambodia-iff.com), held in Phnom Penh every year.

The Last Reel (2014; www. thelastreel.info) is an award-winning film from Cambodia that explores the impact of Cambodia's dark past on the next generation. Michael Moore awarded it his Grand Founder's Prize at the 2016 Traverse City Film Festival.

Dance

More than any of the other traditional arts, Cambodia's royal ballet is a tangible link with the glory of Angkor. Its traditions stretch long into the past, when the dance of the *apsara* (heavenly nymph) was performed for the divine king. Early in his reign, King Sihanouk released the traditional harem of royal *apsaras* that came with the crown.

Dance fared particularly badly during the Pol Pot years. Very few dancers and teachers survived. In 1981, with a handful of teachers, the University of Fine Arts was reopened and the training of dance students resumed.

Much of Cambodian royal dance resembles that of India and Thailand (the same stylised hand movements, the same sequined, lamé costumes and the same opulent stupa-like headwear), as the Thais incorporated techniques from the Khmers after sacking Angkor in the 15th century. Although royal dance was traditionally an all-female affair (with the exception of the role of the monkey), more male dancers are now featured. Known as *robam preah reachtrop* ('dance of royal wealth') in Khmer, the most popular classical dances are the Apsara dance and the Wishing dance.

Rithy Panh's The Missing Picture (2013) became the first Cambodian film to be shortlisted for 'Best Foreign Language Film' at the 2014 Oscars.

Folk dance is another popular element of dance performances that are regularly staged for visitors in Phnom Penh and Siem Reap. Folk dances draw on rural lifestyle and cultural traditions for their inspiration. One of the most popular folk dances is *robam kom araek,* the 'bamboo stick dance', involving bamboo poles and some nimble footwork. Also popular are fishing and harvest-themed dances that include plenty of flirtatious interaction between male and female performers.

Other celebrated dances are only performed at certain festivals or at certain times of the year. The *trot* is very popular at Khmer New Year to ward off evil spirits from the home or business. A dancer in a deer costume runs through the property pursued by a hunter and is eventually slain.

Chinese New Year (*Tet* to the Vietnamese in Cambodia) sees elaborate lion dances performed all over Phnom Penh and other major cities in Cambodia.

Contemporary dances include the popular *rom vong* or circle dance, which is likely to have originated in neighbouring Laos. Dancers move around in a circle taking three steps forward and two steps back. Hip-

SPORT IN CAMBODIA

The national sport of Cambodia is *pradal serey* (Cambodian kickboxing). It's similar to kickboxing in Thailand (don't make the mistake of calling it 'Thai boxing' over here, though) and there are regular weekend bouts on CTN and TV5. It's also possible to go to the TV arenas and watch the fights live.

Football is another national obsession, although the Cambodian team is a real minnow, even by Asian standards. Many Cambodians follow the English Premier League religiously and regularly bet on games.

The French game of pétanque, also called boules, is also very popular here and the Cambodian team has won several medals in regional games.

hop and breakdancing is fast gaining popularity among urban youngsters and is regularly performed at outdoor events.

Music

The bas-reliefs on some of the monuments in the Angkor region depict musicians and *apsaras* holding instruments similar to the traditional Khmer instruments of today, demonstrating that Cambodia has a long musical tradition all of its own.

Customarily, music was an accompaniment to a ritual or performance that had religious significance. Musicologists have identified six types of Cambodian musical ensemble, each used in different settings. The most traditional of these is the *areak ka,* an ensemble that performs at weddings. The instruments of the *areak ka* include a *tro khmae* (three-stringed fiddle), a *khsae muoy* (single-stringed bowed instrument) and *skor areak* (drums), among others. *Ahpea pipea* is another type of wedding music that accompanies the witnessing of the marriage and *pin peat* is the music that is heard at ballet performances and shadow-puppet displays.

Much of Cambodia's golden-era music from the prewar period was lost during the Pol Pot years. The Khmer Rouge targeted singers, and the great Sinn Sisamouth, Ros Sereysothea and Pen Ron, Cambodia's most famous songwriters and performers, all disappeared in the early days of the regime.

After the war, many Khmers settled in the USA, where a lively Khmer pop industry developed. Influenced by US music and later exported back to Cambodia, it has been enormously popular. Cambodians are now returning to the homeland raised on a diet of rap in the US or France, and lots of artists are breaking through, such as the KlapYaHandz collective started by Sok 'Cream' Visal.

There's also a burgeoning local pop industry, many of whose stars perform at outdoor concerts in Phnom Penh. It's easy to join in the fun by visiting one of the innumerable karaoke bars around the country. Preap Sovath is the Robbie Williams of Cambodia and if you flick through the Cambodian channels for more than five minutes chances are he will be performing. Meas Soksophea is the most popular female singer, with a big voice, but it's a changing industry and new stars are waiting in the wings.

Dengue Fever is the ultimate fusion band, rapidly gaining a name for itself beyond the USA and Cambodia. Cambodian singer Chhom Nimol fronts five American prog rockers who dabble in psychedelic sounds. In a similar vein, Phnom Penh–based band Cambodian Space Project rode the formula to considerable international acclaim with velvet-voiced female lead, Kak Channthy, backed by talented expat instrumentalists. Channthy died tragically in a vehicular accident in Phnom Penh in 2018.

One form of music unique to Cambodia is *chapaye,* a sort of Cambodian blues sung to the accompaniment of a two-stringed wooden

Check out www.tinytoones.org for info about a hip-hop cooperative seeking to inspire Cambodian youth to adopt a healthier lifestyle free of drugs and exposure to HIV. Keep an eye out for its performances around Phnom Penh.

instrument, similar in sound to a bass guitar played without an amplifier. There are a few old masters, such as Kong Nay (the Ray Charles of Cambodia), left alive, but *chapaye* is still often shown on late-night Cambodian TV before transmission ends. Kong Nay has toured internationally in countries such as Australia and the US, and has even appeared with Peter Gabriel at the WOMAD music festival in the UK.

For more on Cambodian music, pick up a copy of *Dontrey: The Music of Cambodia* (2011), published by the Department of Media and Communication at the Royal University of Cambodia. There is also an excellent rockumentary feature called *Don't Think I've Forgotten,* which is about Cambodia's lost rock-and-roll era; watch it at www.dtifcambodia.com.

Amrita Performing Arts (www. amritaperforming arts.org) has worked on a number of ground-breaking dance and theatre projects in Cambodia, including collaborations with French and Japanese performers.

Sculpture

The Khmer empire of the Angkor period produced some of the most exquisite carved sculptures found anywhere on earth. Even in the pre-Angkorian era, the periods generally referred to as Funan and Chenla, the people of Cambodia were producing masterfully sensuous sculpture that was more than just a copy of the Indian forms on which it was modelled. Some scholars maintain that the Cambodian forms are unrivalled, even in India itself.

The earliest surviving Cambodian sculptures date from the 6th century AD. Most depict Vishnu with four or eight arms. A large eight-armed Vishnu from this period is displayed at the National Museum (p54) in Phnom Penh.

Also on display at the National Museum is a statue of Harihara from the end of the 7th century, a divinity who combines aspects of both Vishnu and Shiva but looks more than a little Egyptian with his pencil moustache and long, thin nose – a reminder that Indian sculpture drew from the Greeks, who in turn were influenced by the Pharaohs.

Innovations of the early Angkorian era include freestanding sculpture that dispenses with the stone aureole that in earlier works supported the multiple arms of Hindu deities. The faces assume an air of tranquillity, and the overall effect is less animated.

The Banteay Srei style of the late 10th century is commonly regarded as a high point in the evolution of Southeast Asian art. The National Museum has a splendid piece from this period: a sandstone statue of Shiva holding Uma, his wife, on his knee. Sadly, Uma's head was stolen some time during Cambodia's turbulent years. The Baphuon style of the 11th century was inspired to a certain extent by the sculpture of Banteay Srei, producing some of the finest works to have survived today.

Cambodia's great musical tradition was almost lost during the Khmer Rouge years, but the Cambodian Master Performers Program is dedicated to reviving it. Visit its website at www. cambodian masters.org.

The statuary of the Angkor Wat period is felt to be conservative and stilted, lacking the grace of earlier work. The genius of this period manifests itself more clearly in the immense architecture and incredible bas-reliefs of Angkor Wat itself.

The final high point in Angkorian sculpture is the Bayon period from the end of the 12th century to the beginning of the 13th century. In the National Museum, look for the superb representation of Jayavarman VII, an image that projects both great power and sublime tranquillity.

As the state religion swung back and forth between Mahayana Buddhism and Hinduism during the turbulent 13th and 14th centuries, Buddha images and bodhisattvas were carved only to be hacked out by militant Hindus on their return to power. By the 15th century stone was generally replaced by polychromatic wood as the material of choice for Buddha statues. A beautiful gallery of post-16th-century Buddhas from around Angkor is on display at the National Museum.

Cambodian sculptors are rediscovering their skills now that there is a ready market among visitors for reproduction stone carvings of famous statues and busts from the time of Angkor.

The Cambodian Kitchen

Unlike the culinary colossi that are its neighbours Thailand and Vietnam, Cambodia is not that well known in international food circles. But Cambodian cuisine is also quite special, with a great variety of national dishes, some drawing on the cuisine of its neighbours, but all with a unique Cambodian twist. You are bound to find something that takes your fancy, whether your tastes run to spring rolls or curry.

Staples & Specialities

No matter what part of the world you come from, if you travel much in Cambodia, you are going to encounter food that is unusual, strange, maybe even immoral, or just plain weird. The fiercely omnivorous Cambodians find nothing strange in eating insects, algae, offal or fish bladders. They will dine on a duck foetus, brew up some brains or snack on some spiders. They will peel live frogs to grill on a barbecue or down wine infused with snake to increase their virility.

To the Khmers there is nothing 'strange' about anything that will sustain the body. To them a food is either wholesome or it isn't; it's nutritious or it isn't; it tastes good or it doesn't. And that's all they worry about. They'll try anything once, even a burger.

Rice, Fish & Soup

Cambodia's abundant waterways provide the fish that is fermented into *prahoc* (fermented fish paste), which forms the backbone of Khmer cuisine. Built around this are the flavours that give the cuisine its kick: the secret roots, the welcome herbs and the aromatic tubers. Together they give the salads, snacks, soups and stews a special aroma and taste that smacks of Cambodia.

Rice from Cambodia's lush fields is the principal staple, enshrined in the Khmer word for 'eating' or 'to eat', *nyam bai* – literally 'eat rice'. Many a Cambodian, particularly drivers, will run out of steam if they run out of rice. It doesn't matter that the same carbohydrates are available in other foods, it is rice and rice alone that counts. Bat-

Teuk trey (fish sauce), one of the most popular condiments in Cambodian cooking, cannot be taken on international flights, in line with regulations on carrying strong-smelling or corrosive substances.

WE DARE YOU: TOP FIVE

Crickets Anyone for cricket? Deep-fried, crunchy and seasoned.

Duck foetus Unborn duck, feathers and all.

Durian Nasally obnoxious spiky fruit, banned on flights.

Prahoc Crushed, salted and fermented fish paste, almost a biological weapon.

Spiders Just like it sounds, deep-fried tarantulas.

tambang Province is Cambodia's rice bowl and produces the country's finest yield.

For the taste of Cambodia in a bowl, try the local *kyteow*, a rice-noodle soup that will keep you going all day. This full, balanced meal will cost you just 5000r in markets and about US$2 in local restaurants. Don't like noodles? Then try the *bobor* (rice porridge), a national institution, for breakfast, lunch and dinner, and best sampled with some fresh fish and a splash of ginger.

A Cambodian meal almost always includes a *samlor* (traditional soup), which will appear at the same time as the other courses. *Samlor machou bunlay* (hot and sour fish soup with pineapple and spices) is popular.

Freshwater fish forms a huge part of the Cambodian diet thanks to the natural phenomenon that is the Tonlé Sap lake. The fish come in every shape and size, from the giant Mekong catfish to teeny-tiny whitebait, which are great beer snacks when deep-fried. *Trey ahng* (grilled fish) is a Cambodian speciality (*ahng* means 'grilled' and can be applied to many dishes). Traditionally, the fish is eaten as pieces wrapped in lettuce or spinach leaves and then dipped into *teuk trey,* a fish sauce that is a close relative to Vietnam's *nuoc mam*, but with the addition of ground peanuts.

As well as eating the notorious tarantulas of Skuon, Cambodians also like to eat crickets, beetles, larvae and ants. Some scientists have suggested insect farms as a way to solve food problems of the future. This time, Cambodia might be ahead of the curve.

Salads

Cambodian salad dishes are popular and delicious, although they're quite different from the Western idea of a cold salad. *Phlea sait kow* is a beef-and-vegetable salad flavoured with coriander, mint and lemongrass. These three herbs find their way into many Cambodian dishes.

Desserts & Fruits

Desserts can be sampled cheaply at night markets around the country. One sweet snack to look out for is the ice-cream sandwich. Popular with the kids, it involves putting a slab of homemade ice cream into a piece of sponge or bread.

Cambodia is blessed with many tropical fruits and sampling these is an integral part of a visit to the country. All the common fruits can be found in abundance, including *chek* (banana), *menoa* (pineapple) and *duong* (coconut). Among the larger fruit, *khnau* (jackfruit) is very common, often weighing more than 20kg. The *tourain* (durian) usually needs no introduction, as you can smell it from a mile off; the exterior is green with sharp spikes, while inside is a milky, soft interior regarded by the Chinese as an aphrodisiac.

The fruits most popular with visitors include the *mongkut* (mangosteen) and *sao mao* (rambutan). The small mangosteen has a purple skin that contains white segments with a divine flavour, while the rambutan has an interior like a lychee and an exterior covered in soft red and green spikes.

BOTTOMS UP

When Cambodians propose a toast, they usually stipulate what percentage must be downed. If they are feeling generous, it might be just *ha-sip pea-roi* (50%), but more often than not it is *moi roi pea-roi* (100%). This is why they love ice in their beer, as they can pace themselves over the course of the night. Many a *barang* (foreigner) has ended up face down on the table at a Cambodian wedding when trying to outdrink the Khmers without the aid of ice.

Best of all, although common throughout the world, is the *svay* (mango). The Cambodian mango season is from March to May. Other varieties of mango are available year-round, but it's the hot-season ones that are a taste sensation.

Drinks

Beer

It's never a challenge to find a beer in Cambodia and even the most remote village usually has a stall selling a few cans. Angkor is the national beer, produced in vast quantities in a big brewery down in Sihanoukville. It costs around US$2 to US$3 for a 660mL bottle in most restaurants and bars. Draught Angkor is available for around US$0.75 to US$1.50 in the main tourist centres. Other popular local brands include Cambodia Beer, aiming to topple Angkor as the beer of choice, and provincial favourite Gold Crown.

A beer brand from neighbouring Laos, Beerlao, is very drinkable and is also one of the cheapest ales available. Tiger Beer is produced locally and is a popular draught in the capital. Some Khmer restaurants have a bevy of 'beer girls', each promoting a particular beer brand. They are always friendly and will leave you alone if you prefer not to drink.

Craft beer is taking off in Phnom Penh and there are now nearly a dozen microbreweries in the city. Try Himawari, Cerevisia Craft Brewery aka Botanico (p84), or Riel Brewing (p84).

A word of caution for beer seekers in Cambodia: while the country is awash with good brews, there's a shortage of refrigeration in the countryside. Copy the locals and learn how to say, '*Som teuk koh*' (ice, please).

Wine & Spirits

Local wine in Cambodia generally means rice wine, which is popular with the minority peoples of the northeast. Some rice wines are fermented for months and are super strong, while other brews are fresher and taste more like a demented cocktail. Either way, if you are invited to join a session in a minority village, it's rude to decline. Other local wines include light sugar-palm wine and ginger wine.

In Phnom Penh and Siem Reap, foreign wines and spirits are sold in supermarkets at bargain prices, given how far they have to travel. Wines from Australia, Europe and South America start at about US$5, while the famous names of the spirit world cost between US$7 and US$15. Craft spirits made locally with Cambodian ingredients, including Seekers (p84) gin and Samai (p84) rum, have a higher price tag. Both distilleries are located in Phnom Penh and offer tours.

Tea & Coffee

Chinese-style *tai* (tea) is a bit of a national institution, and in most Khmer and Chinese restaurants a pot will automatically appear for no extra charge as soon as you sit down. *Kaa fey* (coffee) is sold in most restaurants. It is either black or *café au lait*, served with dollops of condensed milk. Slick air-conditioned coffee shops are now common across Cambodia and offer the full range of Americanos and lattes, which can be hot or iced and are typically quite strong.

Water & Soft Drinks

Drinking tap water *must* be avoided, especially in the provinces, as it is rarely purified and may lead to stomach complaints. Locally produced mineral water starts at 1000r per bottle at shops and stalls. Better still, bring your own reusable bottle and refill it at designated shops, restau-

Some Cambodian nightclubs allow guests to rent premium bottles of spirits, such as Johnnie Walker Blue Label, to display on the table – a way of maintaining face despite the fact it's actually Johnnie Walker Red Label in the glass.

The local brew for country folk is sugar-palm wine, distilled daily direct from the trees and fairly potent after it has settled. Sold in bamboo containers off the back of bicycles, it's tasty and cheap, although only suitable for those with a cast-iron stomach.

rants and hotels across Cambodia. **Refill Not Landfill** (www.refillthe world.com) is a great resource that can direct you to refill stations.

Although tap water should be avoided, it is generally OK to have ice in your drinks. Throughout Cambodia, *teuk koh* (ice) is produced with treated water at local ice factories, a legacy of the French.

All the well-known soft drinks are available in Cambodia. Bottled drinks are about 1000r, while canned drinks cost about 2000r, more again in restaurants or bars.

Teuk kalohk are popular throughout Cambodia. They are a little like fruit smoothies and a great way to wash down a meal.

Dining Out

Whatever your tastes, some eatery in Cambodia is sure to help out, be it the humble peddler, a market stall, a local diner or a slick restaurant.

It's easy to sample inexpensive Khmer cuisine throughout the country, mostly at local markets and cheap restaurants. For more refined Khmer dining, the best restaurants are in Phnom Penh and Siem Reap, where there is also the choice of excellent Thai, Vietnamese, Chinese, Indian, French and Mediterranean cooking. Chinese and Vietnamese food is available in towns across the country, due to the large urban populations of both of these ethnic groups.

There are often no set hours for places to eat, but, as a general rule of thumb, street stalls are open from very early in the morning until early evening, although some stalls specialise in the night shift. Most restaurants are open all day, while some of the fancier places only open for lunch (usually 11am to 2.30pm) and dinner (usually 5pm to 10pm).

Eating Options

Cambodia has a great range of dining options in the cities, but the choice dries up in remote areas. Booking ahead is only occasionally necessary in Phnom Penh or Siem Reap during peak season.

Restaurants These range from local hole-in-the-wall spots to sophisticated bistros. Most cuisines are covered in the cities, but it's mainly Cambodian, Chinese and Vietnamese elsewhere.

Cafes Perhaps a legacy of the French, Cambodia has a healthy coffee culture. The best cafes are found in Phnom Penh and Siem Reap.

Markets Most major markets have food stalls, which are an inexpensive place to sample the local cuisine.

Dining Out with Kids

Both Phnom Penh and Siem Reap have child-friendly eateries, although most restaurants in Cambodia are pretty friendly towards children. Some international restaurants have a children's menu available. High chairs are generally only found at international restaurants and fast-food outlets. Baby-changing facilities are almost nonexistent in Cambodian restaurants.

Street Snacks

Street food is an important part of everyday Cambodian life. Like many Southeast Asians, Cambodians are inveterate snackers. They can be found at impromptu stalls at any time of the day or night, delving into a range of unidentified frying objects. Drop into the markets for an even greater range of dishes and the chance of a comfortable seat. It's a cheap, cheerful and cool way to get up close and personal with Khmer cuisine.

For the scoop on countryside cooking in Cambodia, pick up *From Spiders to Waterlilies* (2009), a cookbook produced by Romdeng (p76) restaurant in Phnom Penh.

Friends (p76) is one of the best-known restaurants in Phnom Penh, turning out a fine array of tapas, shakes and specials to help street children in the capital. Its cookbook *The Best of Friends* is a visual feast showcasing its best recipes.

COOKING COURSES

If you are really taken with Cambodian cuisine, it's possible to learn some tricks of the trade by signing up for a cooking course. This is a great way to introduce your Cambodian experience to your friends – no one wants to sit through a slide show of photos, but offer them a mouth-watering meal and they will all come running. There are courses available in Phnom Penh, Siem Reap, Battambang, Kampot and Kratie, and more are popping up all the time.

Here's a list of five top street snacks to look out for:

Banh chev Rice pancake stuffed with yummy herbs, bean sprouts and a meat or fish staple.

Bobor Rice porridge, like congee in China, popular with dried fish and egg or zip it up with chilli and black pepper.

Chek chien Deep-fried bananas; these are a popular street snack at any time of day.

Loat Small white noodles that almost look like bean sprouts; they taste delicious fried up with beef.

Nam ben choc Thin rice noodles served with a red chicken curry or a fish-based broth.

In the Cambodian Kitchen

Enter the Cambodian kitchen and you will learn that fine food comes from simplicity. Essentials consist of a strong flame, clean water, basic cutting utensils, a mortar and pestle, and a well-blackened pot or two.

Cambodians eat three meals a day. Breakfast is either *kyteow* or *bobor*. Baguettes are available at any time of day or night, and go down well with a cup of coffee.

Lunch starts early, around 11am. Traditionally, lunch is taken with the family, but in towns and cities many workers now eat at local restaurants or markets.

Dinner is the time for family bonding. Dishes are arranged around the central rice bowl and diners each have a small eating bowl. The procedure is uncomplicated: spoon some rice into your bowl, and lay 'something else' on top of it.

When ordering multiple courses from a restaurant menu, don't worry – don't even think – about the proper succession of courses. All dishes are placed in the centre of the table as soon as they are ready. Diners then help themselves to whatever appeals to them, regardless of who ordered what.

Before it became a member of the World Trade Organization (WTO), copyright protection was almost unknown in Cambodia. During that period, there was a host of copycat fast-food restaurants, including Khmer Fried Chicken, Pizza Hot and Burger Queen, all now sadly defunct.

Table Etiquette

Sit at the table with your bowl on a small plate, chopsticks or fork and spoon at the ready. Some Cambodians prefer chopsticks, some prefer fork and spoon, but both are usually available. Each place setting will include a small bowl, usually located at the top right-hand side, for the dipping sauces.

When serving yourself from the central bowls, use the communal serving spoon so as not to dip your chopsticks or spoon into the food. To begin eating, just pick up your bowl, bring it close to your mouth and spoon in the food.

Some dos and don'ts:

➡ *Do* wait for your host to sit first.

➡ *Don't* turn down food placed in your bowl by your host.

➟ *Do* learn to use chopsticks.

➟ *Don't* leave chopsticks in a V-shape in the bowl, a symbol of death.

➟ *Do* tip about 5% to 10% in restaurants, as wages are low.

➟ *Don't* tip if there is already a service charge on the bill.

➟ *Do* drink every time someone offers a toast.

➟ *Don't* pass out face down on the table if the toasting goes on all night.

Vegetarians & Vegans

Few Cambodians understand the concept of strict vegetarianism and many will say something is vegetarian to please the customer when in fact it is not. If you are not a strict vegetarian and can deal with fish sauces and the like, you should have few problems ordering meals. Those who eat fish can sample Khmer cooking at its best. Most international eateries feature a few vegetarian menu options, while in the major tourist centres there are now some fantastic vegetarian and vegan restaurants.

In Khmer and Chinese restaurants, stir-fried vegetable dishes are readily available, as are vegetarian fried-rice dishes. However, it is unlikely these 'vegetarian' dishes have been cooked in separate woks from other fish- and meat-based dishes. Indian restaurants in the popular tourist centres can cook up genuine vegetarian food, as they usually understand the vegetarian principle better than the *prahoc*-loving Khmers.

One of the most popular street snacks in Cambodia is the unborn duck foetus. The white duck eggs contain a little duckling, feathers and all. Don't order *kaun pong tier* if you want to avoid this.

Environment

Cambodia's landscape ranges from the highs of the Cardamom Mountains to the lows of the Tonlé Sap basin, and includes some critically endangered species clinging on in the protected areas and national parks. However, these species and their habitat are under threat from illegal logging, agricultural plantations and hydroelectric dams. Cambodia faces a challenge to balance the economy and its need for electricity against the desire to develop sustainable ecotourism.

The Land

Cambodia's borders as we know them today are the result of a classic historical squeeze. As the Vietnamese moved south into the Mekong Delta and the Thais pushed west towards Angkor, Cambodia's territory, which in Angkorian times stretched from southern Burma to Saigon and north into Laos, began to shrink. Only the arrival of the French prevented Cambodia from going the way of the Chams, who became a people without a state. In that sense, French colonialism created a protectorate that actually protected.

Modern-day Cambodia covers 181,035 sq km, making it a little more than half the size of Vietnam or about the same size as England and Wales combined. To the west and northwest it borders Thailand, to the northeast Laos, to the east Vietnam and to the south is the Gulf of Thailand.

Cambodia's two dominant geographical features are the mighty Mekong River and a vast lake, the Tonlé Sap. At Phnom Penh the Mekong splits into three channels: the Tonlé Sap River, which flows into, and out of, the Tonlé Sap lake; the Upper River (usually called simply the Mekong or, in Vietnamese, Tien Giang); and the Lower River (the Tonlé Bassac, or Hau Giang in Vietnamese). The rich sediment deposited during the Mekong's annual wet-season flooding has made central Cambodia incredibly fertile. This low-lying alluvial plain is where the vast majority of Cambodians live – fishing and farming in harmony with the rhythms of the monsoon.

In Cambodia's southwest quadrant, much of the landmass is covered by mountains: the Cardamom Mountains (Chuor Phnom Kravanh), covering parts of the provinces of Koh Kong, Battambang, Pursat and Pailin, which are now opening up to ecotourism; and, southeast of there, the Elephant Mountains (Chuor Phnom Damrei), situated in the provinces of Kompong Speu, Koh Kong and Kampot.

Cambodia's 435km coastline is a big draw for visitors on the lookout for isolated tropical beaches. There are islands aplenty off the coast of Sihanoukville, Kep and Koh Kong.

Along Cambodia's northern border with Thailand, the plains collide with a striking sandstone escarpment more than 300km long that towers up to 550m above the lowlands: the Dangkrek Mountains (Chuor Phnom Dangkrek). One of the best places to get a sense of this area is Prasat Preah Vihear.

In the northeastern corner of the country, the plains give way to the Eastern Highlands, a remote region of densely forested mountains that

Cambodia's highest mountain, at 1813m, is Phnom Aural on the border of Pursat and Kampong Speu Provinces.

extends east into Vietnam's Central Highlands and north into Laos. The wild provinces of Ratanakiri and Mondulkiri provide a home for many minority (hill-tribe) peoples and are taking off as an ecotourism hotspot.

Wildlife

Cambodia's forest ecosystems were in excellent shape until the 1990s. The years of war took their toll on some species, but others thrived in the remote jungles of the southwest and northeast. Ironically, peace brought increased threats as loggers felled huge areas of primary forest and the illicit trade in wildlife targeted endangered species. Due to years of in-accessibility, scientists have only relatively recently managed to research and catalogue the country's plant and animal life.

The Tonlé Sap provides a huge percentage of Cambodians' protein intake, 70% of which comes from fish. The volume of water in the Tonlé Sap can expand by up to a factor of 70 during the wet season.

Animals

Cambodia is home to more than 200 species of mammal, including elephants, Asiatic black bears ('moon bears') and sun bears, leopards and wild oxen. Some of the biggest characters, however, are the smaller creatures, including the binturong (nicknamed the bearcat), the pileated gibbon – the world's largest populations live in the Cardamoms and the Keo Seima Wildlife Sanctuary (p304) in Mondulkiri – the pangolin and the slow loris, which hangs out in trees all day. The country also has a great variety of butterflies.

Most of Cambodia's fauna is extremely hard to spot in the wild. The easiest way to see a healthy selection is to visit the Phnom Tamao Wildlife Rescue Centre (p100) near Phnom Penh, which provides a home for rescued animals and includes all the major species.

A whopping 720 bird species find Cambodia a congenial home, thanks in large part to its year-round water resources. Relatively common birds include ducks, rails, cranes, herons, egrets, cormorants, pelicans, storks

TONLÉ SAP – HEARTBEAT OF CAMBODIA

The Tonlé Sap, the largest freshwater lake in Southeast Asia, is an incredible natural phenomenon that provides fish and irrigation waters for half the population of Cambodia. It is also home to 90,000 people, many of them ethnic Vietnamese, who live in 170 floating villages.

Linking the lake with the Mekong at Phnom Penh is a 100km-long channel known as the Tonlé Sap River. From June to early October, wet-season rains rapidly raise the level of the Mekong, backing up the Tonlé Sap River and causing it to flow northwestward into the Tonlé Sap lake. During this period, the lake surface increases in size by a factor of four or five, from 2500 sq km to 3000 sq km up to 10,000 sq km to 16,000 sq km, and its depth increases from an average of about 2m to more than 10m. An unbelievable 20% of the Mekong's wet-season flow is absorbed by the Tonlé Sap. In October, as the water level of the Mekong begins to fall, the Tonlé Sap River reverses direction, draining the waters of the lake back into the Mekong.

This extraordinary process makes the Tonlé Sap an ideal habitat for birds, snakes and turtles, as well as one of the world's richest sources of freshwater fish: the flooded forests make for fertile spawning grounds, while the dry season creates ideal conditions for fishing. Experts believe that fish migrations from the lake help to restock fisheries as far north as China.

This unique ecosystem was declared a Unesco Biosphere Reserve in 2001, but this may not be enough to protect it from the twin threats of upstream dams and rampant deforestation. Dams have been in operation on the Chinese section of the Mekong, known locally as the Lancang, for years. Now the massive new Xayaboury Dam in Laos, which began producing electricity in 2019, has become the first major dam to be put into operation on the Middle or Lower Mekong. Ten additional dams are planned for the river south of China.

and parakeets, with migratory shorebirds, such as waders, plovers and terns, around the South Coast estuaries. Serious twitchers should consider a visit to Prek Toal Bird Sanctuary (p134); Ang Trapeng Thmor Reserve, home to the extremely rare sarus crane, depicted on the bas-reliefs at Angkor; or the Tmatboey Ibis Project (p270), where the critically endangered giant ibis, Cambodia's national bird, can be seen. For details on birdwatching in Cambodia, check out the Siem Reap–based Sam Veasna Center (p111).

Cambodia is home to about 240 species of reptile, including at least 17 known species of venomous snake such as the Malayan pit viper, cobra and krait. While data is scarce, snake bites are thought to kill dozens of Cambodians every year and to be responsible for a similar number of amputations to landmines. Educate yourself on preventing and treating snake bites at www.snakebiteinitiative.org.

Endangered Species

Unfortunately, it is getting mighty close to checkout time for a number of species in Cambodia. The kouprey (wild ox), declared Cambodia's national animal by King Sihanouk back in the 1960s, is classified as 'Critically Endangered (Possibly Extinct)' by the IUCN Red List, as none have been spotted in at least 30 years.

Other animals under serious threat in Cambodia include the Asian elephant, banteng, gaur, Asian golden cat, black gibbon, clouded leopard, fishing cat, marbled cat, sun bear, pangolin, giant ibis and Siamese crocodile. Tigers have been declared functionally extinct in Cambodia – the last confirmed sighting was in 2007 – although conservation group Wildlife Alliance and the Cambodian government are working on an ambitious plan to reintroduce tigers to the Cardamom Rainforest Landscape.

Cambodia has some of the last remaining freshwater Irrawaddy dolphins (*trey pisaut* in Khmer), instantly identifiable thanks to their bulging forehead and short beak. Viewing them at Kampi, near Kratie, is a popular activity. Irawaddy dolphins can also be spotted in estuaries along the South Coast, including in Peam Krasaop Wildlife Sanctuary and Ream National Park.

In terms of fish biodiversity, the Mekong is second only to the Amazon, but dam projects threaten migratory species. The Mekong giant catfish, which can weigh up to 300kg, is critically endangered due to habitat loss and overfishing.

The following environmental groups – staffed in Cambodia mainly by Khmers – are playing leading roles in protecting Cambodia's wildlife.

Birdlife International (www.birdlife.org)

Conservation International (www.conservation.org)

Fauna & Flora International (www.fauna-flora.org)

Wildlife Alliance (WildAid; www.wildlifealliance.org)

Wildlife Conservation Society (www.wcs.org)

WWF (www.worldwildlife.org)

Plants

No one knows how many plant species are present in Cambodia because no comprehensive survey has ever been conducted, but it's estimated that the country is home to 15,000 species, at least a third of them endemic.

In the southwest, rainforests grow to heights of 50m or more on the rainy southern slopes of the mountains, with montane (pine) forests in cooler climes above 800m and mangrove forests fringing the coast. In the northern mountains there are broadleaved evergreen forests, with trees soaring 30m above a thick undergrowth of vines, bamboos, palms

One of the main causes of snakebites in Cambodia, the Malayan pit viper is known as the 'living landmine' because of its tendency to lie motionless and hidden.

Best estimates are that there are 250 to 500 wild elephants in Cambodia, mainly concentrated in Mondulkiri Province and the Cardamom Mountains.

and assorted woody and herbaceous ground plants. The northern plains support dry dipterocarp forests, while around the Tonlé Sap there are flooded (seasonally inundated) forests. The Eastern Highlands are covered with deciduous forests and grassland. Forested upland areas support many varieties of orchid.

The sugar palm, often seen towering over rice fields, provides fronds to make roofs and walls for houses, and fruit that's used to produce medicine, wine and vinegar. Sugar palms grow taller over the years, but their barkless trunks don't get any thicker, hence they retain shrapnel marks from every battle that has ever raged around them.

National Parks

The *khting vor* (spiral-horned ox), so rare that no one had ever seen a live specimen, was considered critically endangered until DNA analysis of its distinctive horns showed that the creature had never existed – the 'horns' belonged to ordinary cattle and buffalo!

In the late 1960s Cambodia had six national parks, together covering 22,000 sq km (around 12% of the country). The long civil war effectively destroyed this system and it wasn't reintroduced until 1993, when a royal decree designated 23 areas as national parks, wildlife sanctuaries, protected landscapes and multiple-use areas. Several more protected forests have been added to the list in the last 15 years, bringing the area of protected land in Cambodia to over 75,000 sq km, or around 41% of the country.

This is fantastic news in principle, but in practice the authorities don't always protect these areas in any way other than drawing a line on a map. The government has enough trouble finding funds to pay the rangers who patrol the most popular parks, let alone to recruit staff for the remote sanctuaries, though in recent years a number of international NGOs have been helping to train and fund teams of enforcement rangers.

Created in 2016, Southern Cardamom National Park (p185), at 4104 sq km, is now the largest protected area in Cambodia. It is part of the vast, magnificent Cardamom Rainforest Landscape (p186), which encompasses 11 contiguous protected areas covering more than 20,000 sq km in the country's southwest.

Outside the Cardamoms, the largest protected area is the Mondulkiri Protected Forest (3721 sq km), which is contiguous with Yok Don National Park in Vietnam. It is followed by yet another protected area newly designated in 2016, the Prey Lang Wildlife Sanctuary (3600 sq km), which covers bits of four provinces in the north of the country.

Environmental Issues

Doing Your Bit

Every visitor to Cambodia can make at least a small contribution to the country's ecological sustainability.

CAMBODIA'S MOST IMPORTANT NATIONAL PARKS

PARK	SIZE	FEATURES	ACTIVITIES	BEST TIME TO VISIT
Bokor	1581 sq km	hotel-casino, ghost town, views, waterfalls	trekking, cycling, wildlife watching	Nov-May
Kirirom	350 sq km	waterfalls, vistas, pine forests	hiking, mountain biking, wildlife watching	Nov-Jun
Keo Seima Wildlife Sanctuary	3000 sq km	waterfalls, gibbons, elephants	trekking, wildlife watching	Nov-May
Southern Cardamom National Park	4104 sq km	rivers, waterfalls, jungle, elephants	hiking, cycling, wildlife watching	Nov-Jun
Virachey National Park	3325 sq km	unexplored jungle, waterfalls	trekking, adventure, wildlife watching	Nov-Apr

➡ Dispose of your rubbish responsibly.

➡ Drink fresh coconuts, in their natural packaging, rather than soft drinks in throwaway cans and bottles.

➡ Buy a 'Refill Not Landfill' water bottle in Siem Reap and use it in your travels.

➡ Choose trekking guides who respect both the ecosystem and the people who live in it.

➡ Avoid eating wild meat, such as bat, deer and shark fin.

➡ Don't touch live coral when snorkelling or diving, and don't buy coral souvenirs.

➡ If you see wild animals being killed, traded or eaten, take down details of what and where, and contact the **Wildlife Alliance** (🖉rescue hotline 012 500094; www.wildlifealliance.org/cambodia), an NGO that helps manage the government's Wildlife Rapid Rescue Team. Rescued animals are either released or taken to the Phnom Tamao Wildlife Rescue Centre (p100).

Logging

The greatest threat to Cambodia's globally important ecosystems is logging for charcoal and timber and to clear land for cash-crop plantations. During the Vietnamese occupation, troops stripped away swaths of forest to prevent Khmer Rouge ambushes along highways. The devastation increased in the 1990s, when the shift to a capitalist market economy led to an asset-stripping bonanza by well-connected businesspeople.

International demand for timber is huge and, as neighbouring countries such as Thailand and Vietnam began to enforce much tougher logging regulations, foreign logging companies flocked to Cambodia. At the height of the country's logging epidemic in the late 1990s, just under 39% of its total surface area had been allocated as concessions, amounting to almost all Cambodia's forest land except national parks and protected areas.

Under pressure from donors and international institutions, all logging contracts were effectively frozen in 2002, pending further negotiations with the government. However, this only served to increase illegal logging. According to Global Forest Watch (GFW; www.globalforestwatch. org), Cambodia experienced the highest rate of tree-cover loss in the world – a 14.4% increase in its rate of forest loss per year – between 2001 and 2014, well outpacing notorious deforesters Brazil and Indonesia. The peak year for deforestation was 2010, when Cambodia lost a total of 2379 sq km of tree cover.

To put it in perspective, in 1973 about 42% of the country was covered in dense forest. By 2014 only about 11% remained, according to GFW. Much of the devastation was perpetrated in the supposedly protected forests in northwestern and eastern Cambodia, including in what is now known as the Prey Lang Wildlife Sanctuary. Here the government granted 'economic land concessions' to businesses to establish plantations of cash crops such as rubber, mango, cashew and jackfruit, or agro-forestry groves of acacia and eucalyptus to supply woodchips for the paper industry.

In 2012 Cambodia issued a moratorium on new economic land concessions. However, the damage had already been done. In 2018 the government dissolved two protected areas – the 750 sq km Snuol Wildlife Sanctuary in Kratie Province and the 400 sq km Roneam Daun Sam Wildlife Sanctuary in Battambang Province – simply because there was nothing left to protect. Meanwhile the decimation continues in the Prey Lang Wildlife Sanctuary. According to the Prey Lang Community Network (PLCN), a grassroots volunteer group, the equivalent of 21 football fields per day were disappearing in the sanctuary as recently as 2018.

ENVIRONMENT ENVIRONMENTAL ISSUES

At least eight forest defenders have been killed in Cambodia since 2007, including three in one incident in 2018. A film about the life of popular environmental activist Chhut Vuthy, gunned down in 2012, is banned in Cambodia.

Cambodia became the first Southeast Asian country to establish a national park when it created a protected area in 1925 to preserve the forests around the temples of Angkor.

What does it all mean? One effect has been the destruction of livelihood for indigenous communities that relied on the forests. From an ecological perspective, deforestation has contributed to worsening floods along the Mekong in the short run, but the long-term implications could be much worse. Without trees to cloak the hills, rains will inevitably carry away large amounts of topsoil during future monsoons and in time this will have a serious effect on Tonlé Sap.

Pollution

Phnom Penh's air isn't as bad as Bangkok's, but as vehicles multiply it's getting worse. In provincial towns and villages, the smoke from garbage fires can ruin your dinner or lead to breathing difficulties and dry coughs.

Detritus of all sorts, especially plastic bags and bottles, can be seen in distressing quantities on beaches, around waterfalls, along roads and carpeting towns, villages and hamlets.

Cambodia has extremely primitive sanitation systems in urban areas, and nonexistent sanitary facilities in rural areas, with only a tiny percentage of the population having access to proper facilities. These conditions breed and spread disease: epidemics of diarrhoea are not uncommon and it is the number-one killer of young children in Cambodia.

Damming the Mekong

The Mekong rises in Tibet and flows for 4800km before continuing through southern Vietnam into the South China Sea. This includes almost 500km in Cambodia, where it can be up to 5km wide. With energy needs spiralling upwards throughout the region, it is very tempting for developing countries like Cambodia and its upstream neighbours to build hydroelectric dams on the Mekong and its tributaries.

Environmentalists fear that damming the mainstream Mekong may be nothing short of catastrophic for the flow patterns of the river, the migratory patterns of fish, the survival of the freshwater Irrawaddy dolphin and the very life of the Tonlé Sap. Plans currently under consideration include the Sambor Dam, a massive 3300MW project 35km north of Kratie. Work is also under way on the Don Sahong (Siphandone) Dam, just north of the Cambodia–Laos border.

Also of concern is the potential impact of dams on the annual monsoon flooding of the Mekong, which deposits nutrient-rich silt across vast tracts of land used for agriculture. A drop of just 1m in wet-season water levels in the Tonlé Sap would result in the flood area decreasing by around 2000 sq km, with potentially disastrous consequences for Cambodia's farmers.

Ominously, water levels in the Mekong and Tonlé Sap fell to historic lows in 2019. Experts pinned this primarily on abnormally low monsoon rainfall levels, but suspect that the 100 dams now in operation on the mainstream Mekong or its tributaries were likely a contributing factor as well.

Sand Extraction

Sand dredging in the estuaries of Koh Kong Province, including inside the protected Peam Krasaop Wildlife Sanctuary (p179), has had a detrimental effect on delicate mangrove ecosystems and the sea life that depends on them. Sand dredging has also had a devastating effect on coastal communities like Koh Sralau, which was the subject of the short film *A Lost World* (2016) by Kalyanee Mam.

Almost 500,000 cu metres of illegally cut timber were smuggled from Cambodia to Vietnam between 2016 and 2018, according to the Environmental Investigation Agency (www.eia-international.org), a UK-based NGO.

Despite responsibility for nearly 20% of the Mekong River's waters, China is not a member of the Mekong River Commission (MRC; www.mrcmekong.org), which is ostensibly committed to the sustainable development of the mighty river.

Survival Guide

DIRECTORY A–Z ... 350

Accessible Travel 350

Embassies
& Consulates. 350

Electricity 351

Food 351

Insurance...............351

Internet Access. 351

Language Courses.......351

Legal Matters 352

LGBTQI+ Travellers...... 352

Maps.................. 352

Money................. 353

Opening Hours 354

Photography 354

Post................... 354

Public Holidays......... 354

Safe Travel............. 354

Telephone 356

Time 356

Toilets................. 356

Tourist
Information 356

Visas.................. 356

Volunteering 357

Women Travellers.......357

Work 358

TRANSPORT 359

GETTING THERE
& AWAY 359

Entering the Country.... 359

Air 359

Land 360

Sea 362

GETTING AROUND......362

Air 362

Bicycle 362

Boat 362

Bus 363

Car & Motorcycle 363

Local Transport......... 364

Train 365

HEALTH 366

LANGUAGE 370

Directory A–Z

Accessible Travel

Broken pavements, pot-holed roads and stairs as steep as ladders at Angkor ensure that for most people with mobility impairments, Cambodia is not going to be an easy country in which to travel. Few buildings have been designed with people with a disability in mind, although new projects, such as the international airports at Phnom Penh and Siem Reap, and top-end hotels, include wheelchair-accessible ramps and toilets. Transport in the provinces is usually very overcrowded, but taxi hire from point to point is an affordable option.

On the positive side, the Cambodian people are usually very helpful towards all foreigners, and local labour is cheap if you need someone to accompany you at all times. Most guesthouses and small hotels have ground-floor rooms that are reasonably easy to access.

The biggest headache also happens to be the main attraction: the temples of Angkor. Causeways are une-ven, obstacles common and staircases daunting, even for able-bodied people. It is likely to be some years before things improve, although some ramping has been introduced at major temples.

Wheelchair travellers will need to undertake a lot of research before visiting Cambodia. Your best bet for advice about travelling in the country would be to contact the relevant organisation for your particular disability.

Download Lonely Planet's free Accessible Travel guides from http://lptravel.to/AccessibleTravel.

Embassies & Consulates

Many countries have embassies in Phnom Penh, though some travellers will find that their nearest embassy is in Bangkok.

In genuine emergencies assistance may be available, but only if all other channels have been exhausted. If you have all your money and documents stolen, the embassy can assist with getting a new passport, but a loan for onward travel is out of the question.

Australian Embassy (Map p62; ☑023-213470; www.cambodia.embassy.gov.au; 16 National Assembly St, Phnom Penh; ⏲8.30am-noon & 1.30-5pm Mon-Fri)

Chinese Embassy (Map p50; ☑012 901937; http://kh.china-embassy.org/eng; 156 Mao Tse Toung Blvd, Phnom Penh; ⏲visas 8.30-11.30am Mon-Fri)

French Embassy (Map p52; ☑023-260010; http://kh.ambafrance.org; 1 Monivong Blvd, Phnom Penh; ⏲8.30-11.30am Mon-Fri)

German Embassy (Map p62; ☑023-216193; http://phnom-penh.diplo.de; 76-78 St 214, Phnom Penh; ⏲8.30-11.30am Mon, Wed & Fri)

Indian Embassy (Map p62; ☑023-210912; http://embindpp.gov.in; 50 St 214, Phnom Penh; ⏲9am-5.30pm Mon-Fri)

Indonesian Embassy (Map p52; ☑023-217934; http://kemlu.go id/phnompenh/en; 1 St 466, Phnom Penh; ⏲8am-noon & 2-4pm Mon-Fri)

Japanese Embassy (Map p52; ☑023-217161; www.kh.emb-japan.go.jp; 194 Norodom Blvd, Phnom Penh; ⏲8am-noon & 1.30-5.15pm Mon-Fri)

Lao Embassy (Map p82; ☑023-99/931; 15-17 Mao Tse Toung Blvd, Phnom Penh; ⏲8.30-11.30am & 2-4.30pm Mon-Fri)

BOOK YOUR STAY ONLINE

For more accommodation reviews by Lonely Planet authors, check out http://lonelyplanet.com/cambodia. You'll find independent reviews, as well as recommendations on the best places to stay.

Malaysian Embassy (☎023-216177; www.kln.gov.my; 220 Norodom Blvd, Phnom Penh; ⊙8am-noon & 1.30-4.30pm Mon-Fri)

Myanmar Embassy (Map p52; ☎023-223761; 181 Norodom Blvd, Phnom Penh; ⊙8.30am-12.30pm & 2-4.30pm Mon-Fri)

Philippine Embassy (Map p52; ☎023-333303; http://phnompenhpe.dfa.gov.ph; 182 Norodom Blvd, Phnom Penh; ⊙8am-5pm Mon-Fri)

Singaporean Embassy (Map p62; ☎023-210862; www.mfa.gov.sg/phnompenh; 129 Norodom Blvd, Phnom Penh; ⊙8am-12.30pm & 2-5pm Mon-Fri)

Thai Embassy (Map p52; ☎023-726306; www.thaiembassy.org/phnompenh; 196 Norodom Blvd, Phnom Penh; ⊙8.30-11am & 3-4.30pm Mon-Fri)

UK Embassy (Map p52; ☎061 300011; www.gov.uk/world/cambodia; 27-29 St 75, Phnom Penh; ⊙8.15am-noon & 1-4.45pm Mon-Fri)

US Embassy (Map p68; ☎023-728000; http://kh.usembassy.gov; 1 St 96, Phnom Penh; ⊙by appointment)

Vietnamese Embassy (Map p82; ☎097 7492430; 436 Monivong Blvd, Phnom Penh; ⊙8-11.30am & 1-4pm Mon-Fri) Also has consulates in **Battambang** (Map p242; ☎053-952894, 097 332 1188; St 3; ⊙8.30-11am & 2-5pm Mon-Fri), issuing visas in a day; and **Sihanoukville** (Map p190; ☎034-934039; 310 Ekareach St; ⊙8am-noon & 2-4pm Mon-Sat), also with speedy visa processing.

Electricity

Type A
120V/60Hz

Type C
220V/50Hz

Food

See the Cambodian Kitchen section on p337 for more on Cambodian cuisine.

Insurance

Health insurance is essential. Make sure your policy covers emergency evacuation: limited medical facilities mean evacuation by air to Bangkok in the event of serious injury or illness.

Worldwide travel insurance is available at www.lonelyplanet.com/travel-insurance. You can buy, extend and claim online anytime – even if you're already on the road.

Internet Access

Wi-fi is pretty much ubiquitous in cafes and guesthouses across the country and is almost always free. Fast 4G access via local SIM cards is available for as little as US$1 for 4 gigabytes. 4G coverage through one or more providers is excellent in all but the most remote areas. Internet cafes are still an option in most cities. Charges range from 1500r to US$2 per hour.

Language Courses

The only language courses available in Cambodia at present are in Khmer and are aimed at expat residents of Phnom Penh rather than travellers. Try the Institute of Foreign Languages at the **Royal University of Phnom Penh** (Map p50; ☎023-885419; www.rupp.edu.kh/ifl; Russian Confederation Blvd). Also check out the noticeboards at popular guesthouses, restaurants and bars, where one-hour lessons are often advertised by private tutors.

TIPPING TIPS

In many Cambodian restaurants, change will be returned in some sort of bill holder. If you leave the change there it will often be taken by the restaurant proprietor. If you want to make sure the tip goes to the staff who have served you, leave the tip on the table or give it to the individuals directly. In some places, there may be a communal tip box that is shared by staff.

PRACTICALITIES

Newspapers The *Phnom Penh Post* (www.phnompenh post.com) offers the best balance of Cambodian and international news, including business and sport. Other good English-language newspapers and magazines have closed in recent years, either due to political pressure or for business reasons. A variety of international magazines and newspapers is also widely available in Phnom Penh and Siem Reap.

Radio BBC World Service broadcasts on 100.00FM in Phnom Penh. Cambodian radio stations are mainly government-controlled and specialise in phone-ins and product placements.

Smoking All hotels and most guesthouses offer non-smoking rooms these days. Smoking was officially banned in some public places such as cafes, restaurants and bars in 2016, but in practice its enforcement seems down to the individual businesses.

TV Cambodia has a dozen or so local Khmer-language channels, but most of them support the ruling CPP and churn out a mixture of karaoke videos, soap operas and ministers going about their business. Most midrange hotels have cable TV with access to between 20 and 120 channels, including some obscure regional channels, international movie channels, and the big global news and sports channels such as BBC and FOX Sports.

Video Cambodia uses the PAL and NTSC video systems.

Weights & Measures Cambodians use the metric system for everything except precious metals and gems, where they prefer Chinese units of measurement.

Legal Matters

While guesthouses in backpacker zones such as the southern islands openly advertise 'happy' (ie weed-laced) snacks and shakes, marijuana is not actually legal in Cambodia. Marijuana is traditionally used in some Khmer dishes, so there is plenty of it around, but if you are a smoker, be discreet.

If you insist on partaking, avoid purchasing from *remork-moto (tuk tuk)* drivers or other street dealers as they could be setting you up. There have been several busts of foreigner-owned bars and restaurants in Phnom Penh and Siem Reap in recent years where ganja was smoked.

Attitudes are considerably less relaxed about other narcotic substances and there have been high-profile arrests of foreigners for possession of harder drugs than marijuana. Be particularly careful with anything labelled 'cocaine' in Cambodia. Most of what is sold as coke, particularly in Phnom Penh, is actually pure heroin and far stronger than what may be found elsewhere. Several foreigners have died from snorting the stuff.

Also think twice about buying any pills from a 'friendly' street dealer, as they may turn out to be tranquillisers and you'll wake up as a robbery victim.

LGBTQI+ Travellers

The LGBTQI+ scene in Cambodia is certainly not as wild as that in Thailand, but both Phnom Penh and Siem Reap have plenty of gay-friendly establishments. Siem Reap in particular has a well-developed, if low-key, gay scene centred around its guesthouses.

As Theravada Buddhists, Cambodians are quite tolerant of homosexuality, although this applies more to foreigners than to Cambodians, who can be reluctant to come out of the closet. As with heterosexual couples, passionate public displays of affection are considered a basic no-no.

Checking into hotels across Cambodia, there is little consideration over how travelling foreigners are related. However, it is prudent not to announce your sexuality.

Recommended websites when planning a trip include the following:

Cambodia Gay (www.cambodia-gay.com) Promoting the LBTQI+ community in Cambodia.

Utopia (www.utopia-asia.com) Gay travel information and contacts, including some local gay terminology.

Maps

The best all-rounder for Cambodia is the Gecko *Cambodia Road Map*. At 1:750,000 scale, it has lots of detail and accurate place names. Other popular foldout maps include Nelles *Cambodia, Laos and Vietnam Map* at 1:1,500,000, although the detail is limited, and the Periplus *Cambodia Travel Map* at 1:1,000,000, with city maps of Phnom Penh and Siem Reap.

Lots of free maps, subsidised by advertising, are available in Phnom Penh and Siem Reap at leading hotels, guesthouses, restaurants and bars.

Money

Cambodia's currency is the riel, abbreviated in our listings to a lower-case 'r' written after the sum. Cambodia's second currency (some would say its first) is the US dollar, which is accepted everywhere and by everyone, though small amounts of change may arrive in riel. Businesses may quote prices in US dollars or riel, but in towns bordering on Thailand in the north and west it is sometimes Thai baht (B).

If three currencies seems a little excessive, perhaps it's because the Cambodians are making up for lost time: during the Pol Pot era, the country had *no* currency. The Khmer Rouge abolished money and blew up the National Bank building in Phnom Penh.

The Cambodian riel comes in notes of the following denominations: 100r, 200r, 500r, 1000r, 2000r, 5000r, 10,000r, 20,000r, 50,000r and 100,000r.

Dollar bills with a small tear are unlikely to be accepted by Cambodians, so it's worth scrutinising the change you are given to make sure you don't have bad bills. There are also fake US dollar bills in circulation in Cambodia, so check any larger denominations such as US$50 and US$100 bills carefully before accepting them.

ATMs

There are credit-card-compatible ATMs (Visa, MasterCard, JCB, Cirrus) in most major cities. There are also ATMs at the Cham Yeam, Poipet and Bavet borders if arriving by land from Thailand or Vietnam. There are no ATMs on the southern islands.

Machines usually give you the option of withdrawing in US dollars or riel. Single withdrawals of up to US$500 at a time are usually possible, providing your account can handle it. Stay alert when using ATMs late at night.

Canadia Bank and ABA Bank have the most extensive network, including ATMs at petrol stations, and popular hotels, restaurants and shops. Acleda Bank has the widest network of branches in the country, including all provincial capitals, but their ATMs generally only take Visa-affiliated cards. Most ATM withdrawals incur a charge of US$4 to US$5.

Cash

The US dollar remains king in Cambodia. Armed with enough cash, you won't need to visit a bank at all because it is possible to change small amounts of dollars for riel at hotels, restaurants and markets. It is always handy to have about US$10 worth of riel kicking around, as it is good for *motos* (unmarked motorcycle taxis), *remork-motos (tuk tuks)* and markets. Pay for something cheap in US dollars and the change comes in riel.

The only other currency that can be useful is Thai baht, mainly in the west of the country. Prices in towns such as Koh Kong, Poipet and Sisophon are often quoted in baht, and even in Battambang it is common.

In the interests of making life as simple as possible when travelling overland, organise a supply of US dollars before arriving in Cambodia. Cash in other major currencies can be changed at banks or markets in major cities. However, most banks tend to offer a poor rate for any nondollar transaction so it can be better to use money changers, which are found in and around every major market.

Western Union and MoneyGram are both represented in Cambodia for fast, if more expensive, money transfers. Western Union is represented by Acleda Bank, and MoneyGram by Canadia Bank.

Credit Cards

Top-end hotels, airline offices and upmarket boutiques and restaurants generally accept most major credit cards (Visa, MasterCard, JCB and sometimes American Express), but many pass the charges straight on to the customer, meaning an extra 2% to 3% on the bill.

Cash advances on credit cards are available in Phnom Penh, Siem Reap, Sihanoukville, Kampot, Battambang, Kompong Cham and other major towns, and cash advance is the only way to get cash on the southern islands. Most banks advertise a minimum charge of US$5.

Several travel agents and hotels in Phnom Penh and Siem Reap can arrange cash advances for about 5% commission; this can be particularly useful if you get caught short at the weekend.

Tipping

In a country as poor as Cambodia, tips can go a long way.

SHOPPING

High-quality handmade crafts, including silk clothing and accessories, stone and wood carvings, and silver, are widely available, especially in Siem Reap, Phnom Penh and towns with particular handicraft specialities. Hill tribes in Mondulkiri and Ratanakiri produce hand-woven cotton in small quantities. Phnom Penh and Siem Reap are homes to shops and organisations that contribute to reviving traditional crafts and supporting people who are disadvantaged or disabled.

FESTIVAL WARNING

In the run-up to major festivals such as P'chum Ben or Chaul Chnam Khmer, there is a palpable increase in the number of robberies, particularly in Phnom Penh. Cambodians need money to buy gifts for relatives or to pay off debts, and for some individuals theft is the quickest way to get this money. Be more vigilant at night at these times. Guard your smartphone vigilantly and don't take valuables out with you unnecessarily.

Hotels 2000r to US$1 per bag plus a small tip for the cleaner at fancier hotels.

Remorks and moto drivers Not expected for short trips.

Restaurants A few thousand riel, up to 5% or 10% at fancier restaurants.

Temples Drop a few thousand riel in the contribution box, especially if a monk has shown you around.

SERVICE CHARGE

Many of the upmarket hotels levy a 10% service charge, but this doesn't always make it to the staff. It is also included in some high-end restaurant bills.

Opening Hours

Everything shuts down during the major holidays of Chaul Chnam Khmer (Khmer New Year), P'chum Ben (Festival of the Dead) and Chaul Chnam Chen (Chinese New Year).

Banks 8am–3.30pm Monday to Friday, Saturday mornings

Bars 5pm–late

Government offices 7.30am–11.30am and 2pm–5pm Monday to Friday

Local markets 6.30am–5.30pm

Museums Hours vary, but usually open seven days a week

Restaurants International restaurants 7am–10pm or meal times; local restaurants 6.30am–9pm

Shops 8am–6pm, later in tourist centres

Photography

Be polite about photographing people: don't push cameras into their faces, and show respect for monks and people at prayer. In general, the Khmers are remarkably courteous people and if you ask nicely, they'll agree to have their photograph taken. The same goes for filming, although in rural areas you will often find children desperate to get in front of the lens and excited at seeing themselves played back on screen. Some people will expect money in return for their photo being snapped; be sure to establish this before clicking away.

While there are no official restrictions on taking photographs at border crossings or military bases, use discretion and your own best judgement. If the officials are unfriendly, then they probably won't appreciate you snapping away.

Lonely Planet's *Guide to Travel Photography* is full of helpful tips for photography while on the road.

Post

The postal service is hit and miss from Cambodia; send anything valuable by courier or from another country. Ensure postcards and letters are franked before they vanish from your sight.

Letters and parcels sent further afield than Asia can take up to two or three weeks to reach their destination. Use a courier to speed things up; **EMS** (www.ems.post/en/global-network/ems-operators/ems-cambodia) has branches at every major post office in the country. DHL and Fed Ex are present in major cities such as Phnom Penh, Siem Reap and Sihanoukville.

Public Holidays

Banks, ministries and embassies close down during public holidays and festivals, so plan ahead if visiting Cambodia during these times. Cambodians also roll over holidays if they fall on a weekend and take a day or two extra during major festivals. Add to this the fact that they take a holiday for international days here and there, and it soon becomes apparent that Cambodia has more public holidays than almost any other nation on earth!

International New Year's Day 1 January

Victory over the Genocide 7 January

International Women's Day 8 March

International Workers' Day 1 May

International Children's Day 8 May

King's Birthday 13–15 May

King's Mother's Birthday 18 June

Constitution Day 24 September

Commemoration Day 15 October

Independence Day 9 November

International Human Rights Day 10 December

Safe Travel

➡ The most common crime is bag or mobile-phone snatching, often perpetrated by thieves riding in tandem on motorcycles.

➡ Remember the golden rule: stick to marked paths in remote areas (due to the possible presence of landmines).

➡ *Phnom Penh Post* (www.phnompenhpost.com) is a good source for breaking news, so check its website before you hit the road to check the political pulse and catch up with any recent events on the ground such as demonstrations.

➡ Take care with some of the electrical wiring in guesthouses around the country, as it can be pretty amateurish.

Crime & Violence

Incidents of bag snatching in Phnom Penh and Siem Reap are common and the motorbike thieves don't let go, dragging passengers off bicycles or *motos* and endangering lives. Smartphones are a particular target, so avoid using your smartphone in public, especially at night, as you'll be susceptible to drive-by thieves.

Walking or riding alone late at night is not ideal, certainly not in rural areas. There have been several incidents of lone females being assaulted in isolated forests or rural areas, usually after dark.

Should anyone be unlucky enough to be robbed, it is important to note that the Cambodian police are the best that money can buy! Any help, such as a police report, is going to cost you. The going rate depends on the size of the claim, but anywhere from US$5 to US$50 is possible.

Violence against foreigners is extremely rare, but it pays to take care in crowded bars or nightclubs in Phnom Penh. If you get into a standoff with rich young Khmers in a bar or club, swallow your pride and back down. Many carry guns and have an entourage of bodyguards.

Mines, Mortars & Bombs

Never touch any rockets, artillery shells, mortars, mines, bombs or other war material you may come across. The most heavily mined part of the country is along the Thai border area, but mines are a problem in much of Cambodia. In short: *do not stray from well-marked paths under any circumstances*. If you are planning any walks, even in safer areas such as the remote northeast, it is imperative you take a guide as there may still be unexploded ordnance (UXO) from the American bombing campaign of the early 1970s.

Scams

Most scams are fairly harmless, involving a bit of commission here and there for taxi, *remorks* or *moto* drivers, particularly in Siem Reap.

There have been one or two reports of police set-ups in Phnom Penh, involving planted drugs. This seems to be very rare, but if you fall victim to the ploy, it may be best to pay them off before more police get involved at the local station, as the price will only rise when there are more mouths to feed.

There is quite a lot of fake medication floating about the region. Safeguard yourself by only buying prescription drugs from reliable pharmacies or clinics.

Beware the Filipino blackjack scam: don't get involved in any gambling with seemingly friendly Filipinos unless you want to part with plenty of cash.

Beggars in places such as Phnom Penh and Siem Reap may ask for milk powder for an infant in arms. Some foreigners succumb to the urge to help, but the beggars usually request the most expensive milk formula available and return it to the shop to split the proceeds after the handover.

Dangerous Drugs

Watch out for *yaba*, the 'crazy' drug from Thailand, known rather ominously in Cambodia as *yama* (the Hindu god of death). Known as ice or crystal meth elsewhere, it's not just any old diet pill from the pharmacist but homemade methamphetamines produced in labs in Cambodia and the region beyond. The pills are often laced with toxic substances, such as mercury, lithium or whatever else the maker can find. *Yama* is a dirty drug and more addictive than users would like to admit, provoking powerful hallucinations, sleep deprivation

GOVERNMENT TRAVEL ADVICE

Government travel advisories tend to err on the side of caution, so take their warnings with a pinch of salt.

Australian Department of Foreign Affairs (www.smartraveller.gov.au)

Canadian Government (www.voyage.gc.ca)

German Foreign Office (www.auswaertiges-amt.de)

Japanese Ministry of Foreign Affairs (www.anzen.mofa.go.jp)

Netherlands Government (www.minbuza.nl)

New Zealand Ministry of For UK Foreign Office (www.gov.uk/foreign-travel-advice/cambodia)

US Department of State (www.travel.state.gov/content/passports/en/country/cambodia.html)

and psychosis. Steer clear of the stuff unless you plan on an indefinite extension to your trip.

Telephone

A wealth of domestic mobile providers means dirt-cheap prices for local cellular services. Calls and texts are free within the same network, and just a few cents per minute/message to other networks.

Dialling

To place a long-distance domestic call from a mobile (cell) number or a landline, or to dial a mobile number, dial zero, the area code (or mobile prefix) and the number. Leave out the zero and the area code if you are making a local call. Drop the zero from the mobile prefix or regional (city) code when dialling into Cambodia from another country.

Mobile Phones

Your home provider will charge you a fortune for roaming in Cambodia, so pick up a local SIM card as soon as you arrive. If you arrive by air, you'll find booths for all Cambodian mobile-phone providers just outside the airport exit. They stay open late and have English-speaking staff to sort you out. Around US$3 yields a generous bundle of calls and texts and several gigabytes of data. Be prepared to show your passport.

Time

Cambodia is in the Indochina time zone, which means GMT/UTC plus seven hours. Thus, noon in Phnom Penh is midnight the previous day in New York, 5am in London, 1pm in Hong Kong and 3pm in Sydney, depending on daylight saving hours in those cities. There is no daylight saving time.

Toilets

Cambodian toilets are mostly of the sit-down 'throne' variety. The occasional squat toilet turns up here and there, particularly in the most budget of budget guesthouses in the provinces or out the back of provincial restaurants.

The issue of toilets and what to do with used toilet paper is a cause for concern. Generally, if there's a wastepaper basket next to the toilet, that is where the toilet paper goes, as many sewerage systems cannot handle toilet paper. Toilet paper is seldom provided in the toilets at bus stations or in other public buildings, so keep a stash with you at all times.

Many Western toilets also have a hose spray in the bathroom, aptly named the 'bum gun' by some. Think of this as a flexible bidet, used for cleaning and ablutions as well as hosing down the loo.

Public toilets are rare, the only ones in the country being along Phnom Penh's riverfront and some beautiful wooden structures dotted about the temples of Angkor. The charge is usually 500r for a public toilet, although they are free at Angkor on presentation of a temple pass. Most local restaurants have some sort of toilet.

Should you find nature calling in remote border areas, don't let modesty drive you into the bushes: *there may be landmines not far from the road or track*. Stay on the roadside and do the deed, or grin and bear it until the next town.

Tourist Information

Cambodia has only a handful of tourist offices, and those encountered by the independent traveller in Phnom Penh and Siem Reap are generally of limited help.

However, in the provinces the staff are sometimes happy to see visitors, if the office happens to be open. These offices generally have little in the way of brochures or handouts though. Generally speaking, fellow travellers, guesthouses, hotels and free local magazines are more useful than tourist offices. The official tourism website for Cambodia is www.tourismcambodia.org.

Visas

A one-month tourist visa costs US$30 on arrival, while tourist e-visas cost US$37 and easily extendable business visas cost US$35.

Further Information

Most visitors to Cambodia require a one-month tourist visa (US$30). Most nationalities receive this on arrival at Phnom Penh, Siem Reap or Sihanoukville airports, and at land borders, but citizens of Afghanistan, Algeria, Bangladesh, Iran, Iraq, Nigeria, Pakistan, Saudi Arabia, Sri Lanka and Sudan need to make advance arrangements.

It is also possible to arrange a visa through Cambodian embassies overseas or an online e-visa (US$30, plus a US$7 processing fee) through the Ministry of Foreign Affairs (www.evisa.gov.kh). They cost more than a regular tourist visa-on-arrival but are mildly more convenient and do not take up an entire page in your passport.

E-visas are accepted at all three international airports and at four land borders: Poipet/Aranya Prathet and Cham Yeam/Hat Lek (both Thailand); Bavet/Moc Bai (Vietnam); and Trapaeng Kriel/Dong Kalaw (Laos).

Passport holders from Asean member countries do not require a visa to visit Cambodia.

Those seeking work in Cambodia should opt for a business visa-on-arrival (US$35) as it is easily extended for longer periods, including multiple entries and exits. A tourist visa can be extended only once and only for one month, and does not allow for re-entry.

Travellers are sometimes overcharged when crossing at land borders with Thailand, as immigration officials demand payment in baht and round up the figure considerably. Overcharging is also an issue at the Laos border, but not usually at Vietnam borders. Arranging a visa in advance can help avoid overcharging.

Overstaying a visa currently costs US$5 a day.

For visitors continuing to Vietnam, one-month single-entry visas cost US$55 and take two days in Phnom Penh, or just one day via the Vietnamese consulate in Sihanoukville. Most visitors to Laos can obtain a visa on arrival (US$30 to US$42) and most visitors heading to Thailand do not need a visa.

Visa Extensions

Visa extensions are issued by the large immigration office located directly across the road from Phnom Penh International Airport.

Extensions are easy to arrange, taking just a couple of days. It costs US$45 for one month (for both tourist and business visas), US$75 for three months, US$155 for six months and US$285 for one year (the latter three prices relate to business visas only). It's pretty straightforward to extend business visas ad infinitum. Travel agencies in Phnom Penh can help with arrangements for a small fee.

Volunteering

For volunteering with a difference, Cambodia hosts a huge number of NGOs, some of which do require volunteers from time to time. We recommend that travellers avoid volunteering with orphanages.

The **Cooperation Committee for Cambodia** (CCC; Map p82; ✆023-214152; www.ccc-cambodia.org; 9-11 St 476) in Phnom Penh has a handy list of all NGOs, both Cambodian and international, and is extremely helpful.

Siem Reap–based organisation **ConCERT** (www.concertcambodia.org) has a 'responsible volunteering' section on its website that offers advice on preparing for a stint as a volunteer. Also in Siem Reap, **Journeys Within Our Community** (www.jwoc.info), which empowers low-income Cambodians to become community leaders, has some long-term volunteer opportunities.

Another avenue is professional volunteering through an organisation back home that offers one- or two-year placements in Cambodia. One of the largest organisations is **Voluntary Service Overseas** (www.vsointernational.org) in the UK, but other countries also have their own organisations, including **Australian Volunteers International** (www.avi.org.au) and New Zealand's **Volunteer Service**

Abroad (www.vsa.org.nz). The UN also operates its own volunteer program; details are available at www.unv.org. Other general volunteer sites with links all over the place include www.voluntourism.org and www.goabroad.com/volunteer-abroad.

Backpacker-oriented guesthouses, restaurants and bars are often looking for young Western faces to help out in all kinds of ways, especially during the high season (roughly November to April). The best resource for these opportunities in Cambodia is **Workaway** (www.workaway.info).

Women Travellers

Women will generally find Cambodia a hassle-free place to travel. Foreign women are unlikely to be targeted by local men, and will probably find Khmer men to be courteous and polite, although some of the guys in the guesthouse industry can be a little flirtatious from time to time. At the same time it pays to be careful. As

THE PERILS OF ORPHAN TOURISM

'Orphan tourism' has brought unscrupulous elements into the world for Cambodian children.

Save the Children says that it is often a myth that children in orphanages have no parents. Many are there because their parents simply can't afford to feed, clothe and educate them'. Only about one-quarter of Cambodian children in institutions are thought to be genuine orphans.

Many orphanages in Cambodia are scams where children are at risk of abuse and neglect. To be sure, there are legitimate, well-meaning orphanages in Cambodia. But a growing body of evidence, backed by Unicef, Save the Children and Friends International, suggests that even well-run orphanages do more harm than good. Genuine orphans are better off remaining in their hometowns with community- or family-based networks.

You should avoid visiting, donating to, or volunteering in Cambodian orphanages. Learn more at www.thinkchildsafe.org/thinkbeforevisiting before you inadvertently contribute to the problem.

is the case in many places, walking or riding a bike alone late at night can be risky.

Khmer women dress fairly conservatively, in general preferring long-sleeved shirts and long trousers or skirts. In the countryside, it is quite rare for most Khmer women to wear singlet tops or very short skirts or shorts. So when travellers do, people tend to stare. If you're planning on bathing in a village or river, a sarong is essential.

Tampons and sanitary napkins are widely available in the major cities and provincial capitals, but if you are heading into very remote areas for a few days, it is worth having your own supply.

Work

Jobs are available throughout Cambodia, but apart from teaching English or helping out in guesthouses, bars or restaurants, most are for professionals and are arranged in advance. There is a lot of teaching work available for English-language speakers and salary is directly linked to experience. Anyone with an English-language teaching certificate can earn considerably more than those with no qualifications.

For information about work opportunities with NGOs, call into Phnom Penh's **Cooperation Committee for Cambodia** (CCC; Map p82; ☏023-214152; www.ccc-cambodia.org; 9-11 St 476), which has a noticeboard for positions vacant. If you are thinking of applying for work with NGOs, you should bring copies of your education certificates and work references. However, most of the jobs available are likely to be on a voluntary basis, as most recruiting for specialised positions is done in home countries or through international organisations.

Other places to look for work include the classifieds section of the *Phnom Penh Post* and on noticeboards at guesthouses and restaurants in Phnom Penh.

Transport

GETTING THERE & AWAY

Lots of independent travellers enter or exit the country via the numerous land borders shared with Thailand, Vietnam and Laos. There is also the option to cross via the Mekong River between Vietnam and Cambodia. Flights, cars and tours can be booked online at lonelyplanet.com/bookings.

Entering the Country

Cambodia has three international gateways for arrival by air – Phnom Penh, Siem Reap and Sihanoukville – and a healthy selection of land borders with neighbouring Thailand, Vietnam and Laos. Formalities at Cambodia's international airports are generally smooth. Crossing at land borders is relatively easy, but immigration officers may try to wangle some extra cash, either for

the visa or via some other scam. Photos are no longer required for visas on arrival at airports, although some land crossings still require them and charge US$2 to US$3 if you do not have one.

Passport

➡ Six-month passport validity required to enter the country.

➡ Cambodian visas take up an entire passport page unless you are entering on a tourist e-visa, which takes up about a quarter-page.

Air

Airports & Airlines

Phnom Penh International Airport (PNH; ☎023-862800; http://pnh.cambodia-airports. aero) is the gateway to the Cambodian capital, while **Siem Reap International Airport** (Map p102; ☎063-962400; www.cambodia-airports.com) serves visitors to the temples of Angkor. Both

airports have a good range of services, including restaurants, bars, shops and ATMs. **Sihanoukville International Airport** (☎012-333524; https://kos.cambodia-airports. aero; off Hwy 4) serves a dozen or so Chinese cities plus Bangkok, Ho Chi Minh City and Kuala Lumpur.

Flights to Cambodia are expanding, but most connect only as far as regional capitals. **Cambodia Angkor Air** (☎023-212564; www.cambodiaangkorair.com) is the national airline and offers a handful of international flight connections to destinations around the region, including Beijing, Danang, Guangzhou and Ho Chi Minh City.

Thai Airways (www.thaiair.com) and **Bangkok Airways** (www.bangkokair.com) offer the most daily international flights connections, all via Bangkok. **Emirates** (www.emirates.com) flies daily to Dubai via Bangkok.

Air Asia (www.airasia.com) has daily flights from

CLIMATE CHANGE & TRAVEL

Every form of transport that relies on carbon-based fuel generates CO_2, the main cause of human-induced climate change. Modern travel is dependent on aeroplanes, which might use less fuel per kilometre per person than most cars but travel much greater distances. The altitude at which aircraft emit gases (including CO_2) and particles also contributes to their climate change impact. Many websites offer 'carbon calculators' that allow people to estimate the carbon emissions generated by their journey and, for those who wish to do so, to offset the impact of the greenhouse gases emitted with contributions to portfolios of climate-friendly initiatives throughout the world. Lonely Planet offsets the carbon footprint of all staff and author travel.

DEPARTURE TAX

International departure tax of US$25 is included in the ticket price at the point of purchase so there is no need for cash dollars when you leave the country.

Phnom Penh and Siem Reap to Bangkok, while **Jetstar** (www.jetstar.com) connects the same two cities to Singapore. AirAsia also serves Sihanoukville from Bangkok. Other airlines connecting Bangkok to Phnom Penh and/or Siem Reap are domestic budget carriers **Lanmei Airlines** (☏023-981363; www.lanmeiairlines.com) and **JC International Airlines** (☏023-989707; www.jcairline.com), and Thai budget carrier **Thai Smile** (www.thaismile air.com).

From Phnom Penh JC International adds three weekly flights to Yangon and serves Bangkok and Macau. **Vietjet Air** (www.vietjetair.com) has a few useful routes, such as Siem Reap to Hanoi. Lanmei Airlines serves Bangkok and Hong Kong from Phnom Penh, and a host of Chinese cites from both Phnom Penh and Siem Reap.

Vietnam Airlines (www.vietnamairlines.com) has several useful connections, including from both Phnom Penh and Siem Reap to Ho Chi Minh City, as well from Phnom Penh to Vientiane and Siem Reap to Luang Prabang, Danang and Hanoi. **Philippine Airlines** (www.philippineairlines.com) has four or five weekly flights to Phnom Penh from Manila.

Other regional centres with multiple daily direct flights to Cambodia include Hong Kong, Kuala Lumpur, Seoul and Taipei.

Land

Border Crossings

Cambodia shares one border crossing with Laos, five crossings with Thailand and seven with Vietnam. Cambodian visas are now available at all the land crossings with Laos, Thailand and Vietnam.

Visas (p356) on arrival are available in Laos, while most nationalities enjoy 15 to 30 days visa-free access to Thailand. Vietnam grants visas on arrival only to limited nationalities, so check your passport status before heading to the border. Most borders are open during the core hours of 7am to 5pm. However, some of the most popular crossings are open later in the evening and other more remote crossings close for lunch.

There are few legal money-changing facilities at the more remote border crossings, so be sure to have

POPULAR LAND CROSSINGS

LAOS

For Laos, the Trapeang Kriel/Nong Nok Khiene crossing connects Stung Treng in Cambodia with Don Det in Laos.

THAILAND

BORDER CROSSING	CAMBODIAN TOWN	CONNECTING TOWN
Poipet/Aranya Prathet (p257)	Siem Reap	Bangkok
Cham Yeam/Hat Lek (p182)	Koh Kong City	Trat
O Smach/Chong Chom (p258)	Samraong	Surin
Psar Pruhm/Ban Pakard (p256)	Pailin	Chanthaburi
Choam/Chong Sa-Ngam (p262)	Anlong Veng	Phusing

VIETNAM

BORDER CROSSING	CAMBODIAN TOWN	CONNECTING TOWN
Bavet/Moc Bai (p92)	Phnom Penh	Ho Chi Minh City
Kaam Samnor/Vinh Xuong (p93)	Phnom Penh	Chau Doc
Prek Chak/Xa Xia (p229)	Kep, Kampot	Ha Tien, Phu Quoc
Phnom Den/Tinh Bien (p232)	Takeo	Chau Doc
O'Yadaw/Le Thanh (p296)	Ban Lung	Pleiku
Trapeang Plong/Xa Mat (p281)	Kompong Cham	Tay Ninh
Trapeang Sre/Loc Ninh (p285)	Kratie	Binh Long

Cambodia Border Crossings

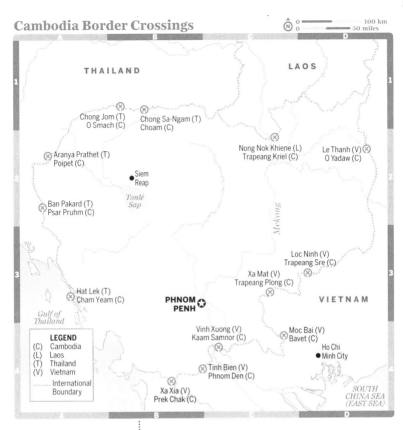

some small-denomination US dollars handy.

Tourist visas are available at all crossings for US$30, but Cambodian immigration officers at the land border crossings, especially with Thailand and Laos, have a reputation for petty extortion. Travellers are occasionally asked for a small 'immigration fee' of some kind or some sort of bogus health certificate costing US$1. More serious scams include overcharging for visas by demanding payment in Thai baht and forcing tourists to change US dollars into riel at a poor rate. Hold your breath, stand your ground, and don't let this experience flavour your impression of Cambodians overall.

Before making a long-distance trip, be aware of border closing times, visa regulations and any transport scams. Border details change regularly, so ask around or check the Lonely Planet Thorn Tree (lonelyplanet.com/thorntree).

LAOS

Cambodia and Laos share a remote frontier that includes some of the wildest areas of both countries. There is only one border crossing (p288) open to foreigners.

THAILAND

Cambodia and Thailand share an 805km border and there are now five legal international border crossings, and many more options for locals.

VIETNAM

Cambodia and Vietnam share a long frontier with a bevy of border crossings. Foreigners are currently permitted to cross at seven places. Cambodian visas are now available at all crossings, but for entry to Vietnam 15- to 30-day visa-free entry is available on arrival for citizens of 24 nations, including all Asean countries, Japan, South Korea, Scandinavian countries, France, Germany, Italy, Spain and the UK.

Bus

Plenty of companies advertise cross-border bus trips to/from Laos, Vietnam and especially Thailand. While these will generally get you to where you are going, they almost always involve a change of bus at the border, which can be time-consuming if the bus on the other side of the border is late.

Car & Motorcycle

Car drivers and motorcycle riders will need registration papers, insurance documents and an International Driving Licence (although not officially recognised) to bring vehicles into Cambodia. It is complicated to bring in a car but relatively straightforward to bring in a motorcycle, as long as you have a *carnet de passage* (vehicle passport). This acts as a temporary import-duty waiver and should save a lot of hassles when dealing with Cambodian customs.

Sea

There are currently no official sea borders between Cambodia and its neighbours, although Sihanoukville is an international port and Asian cruise ships regularly dock there. There have been plans in place for years to set up an international port near Kampot for sea connections to Phu Quoc Island in Vietnam.

GETTING AROUND

Air

Airlines in Cambodia

Domestic flights offer a great way to avoid Cambodia's often miserable roads, as the country's three functioning airports are all well connected to each other these days. With the exception of the Phnom Penh–Sihanoukville route, flights are very cheap. Airlines tend to come and go, with most of the newer ones existing to serve the booming Chinese market.

Cambodia Airways (☏096 852 5555; www.cambodia-airways. com) Connects Siem Reap with Phnom Penh and Sihanoukville.

Cambodia Angkor Air (☏023-212564; www.cambodia angkorair.com) Offers multiple daily flights between Phnom Penh and Siem Reap, and Siem Reap and Sihanoukville.

JC International Airlines (☏023-989707; www.jcairline. com) Daily discounted flights between Phnom Penh and Siem Reap.

Lanmei Airlines (☏023-981363; www.lanmeiairlines. com) New budget airline links Phnom Penh and Siem Reap, and links both cities to Sihanoukville.

Sky Angkor Airlines (☏063-967300; www.skyangkorair. com) Has several weekly flights between Siem Reap and Sihanoukville.

Helicopter

There are two private helicopter companies offering scenic flights over the temples of Angkor and charter flights for high-flyers.

Helicopters Cambodia (☏012 814500; www.helicopters cambodia.com) Has offices in Phnom Penh and Siem Reap, and is affiliated with Helicopters New Zealand.

Helistar (Map p134; ☏088 888 0016; www.helistarcambodia. com; Airport Rd) A reliable helicopter company with offices in both Phnom Penh and Siem Reap.

Bicycle

Cambodia is a great country for experienced cyclists to explore. A mountain bike is the recommended set of wheels thanks to the notorious state of the roads. Most roads have a flat unpaved trail along the side, which is useful for cyclists.

Much of Cambodia is pancake flat or only moderately hilly. Safety, however, is a considerable concern on the newer surfaced roads, as local traffic travels at high speed. Bicycles can be transported around the country in the back of pickups or on the roof of minibuses.

Guesthouses and hotels in Cambodia rent out bicycles for US$1 to US$2 per day, or US$7 to US$15 for an imported brand such as Giant or Trek.

Top bikes, safety equipment and authentic spare parts are now readily available in Phnom Penh at very reasonable prices.

PEPY Tours (www.pepy tours.com) ☏ is a bicycle and volunteer tour company offering adventures throughout Cambodia. PEPY promotes 'adventurous living, responsible giving' and puts funds back into community education and other projects.

Boat

Cambodia's 1900km of navigable waterways are not as important as they once were for the average tourist, given major road improvements. North of Phnom Penh, the Mekong is easily navigable as far as Kratie, but there are no longer regular passenger services on these routes, as buses have taken all the business. There are scenic boat services between Siem Reap and Battambang, and the Tonlé Sap lake is also navigable year-round, although only by smaller boats between March and July.

Traditionally the most popular boat services with foreigners are those that run between Phnom Penh and Siem Reap. The express services do the trip in as little as five hours. The first couple of hours out of Phnom Penh along the Tonlé Sap River are scenic, but it becomes less interesting when the river morphs into the Tonlé Sap lake, which is like a vast sea, offering little scenery. It's more popular (and much cheaper) to take a bus on the paved road instead.

The small boat between Siem Reap and Battambang is more rewarding, as the river scenery is truly memorable, but it can take as long as a whole day with delays.

Bus

The range of road transport is extensive. On sealed roads, the large air-conditioned buses and speedy express minivans are the most popular choices. Elsewhere in the country, a shared taxi or local minibus is the way to go.

All major cities are now well linked by bus to Phnom Penh along sealed roads, but if you're travelling from one end of the country to the other you may have to change buses in Phnom Penh or another hub.

While it doesn't cover all bus companies, **bookmebus** (www.bookmebus.com) is a reliable bus-ticket booking site, including for more obscure routes (Sen Monorom to Siem Reap, anyone?) and cross-border trips.

Buses are reasonably safe but accidents can happen on Cambodia's dicey roads, and there have been several big accidents involving buses or express minivans where tourists were killed.

Express minivans, which usually take the form of modern Ford Transits or Toyota Hiaces, operate a one-seat/one-passenger policy and are reasonably comfortable, but they are sometimes driven by maniacs, so check the reviews.

Older local minibuses serve most provincial routes but are not widely used by Western visitors. They are very cheap but painfully slow and often uncomfortably overcrowded, with people spilling out the back and kids vomiting everywhere; still, they don't lack local charm.

Car & Motorcycle

Car and motorcycle rental are comparatively cheap in Cambodia and many visitors rent a car or bike for greater flexibility to visit out-of-the-way places and to stop when they choose. Almost all car rental in Cambodia includes

ROAD SAFETY

Many more people are now killed and injured each month in traffic accidents than by landmines. While this is partly down to landmine awareness efforts and ongoing clearance programs, it is also due to a huge increase in the number of vehicles on the roads and drivers travelling at dangerous speeds. Be extremely vigilant when travelling under your own steam and take care crossing the roads on the high-speed national highways. It's best not to travel on the roads at night due to a higher prevalence of accidents at this time. This especially applies to bikers, as several foreigners are killed each year in motorbike accidents.

Cambodia has some of the best roads (read worst roads) in the world for dirt biking, particularly in the provinces of Preah Vihear, Mondulkiri, Ratanakiri and the Cardamom Mountains. Only experienced off-road bikers should take to these roads with a dirt bike. There are several specialised dirt-bike touring companies in Cambodia.

Novice riders should stick to riding smaller semi-automatic mopeds. Drive with due care and attention, as medical facilities and ambulances are less than adequate beyond Phnom Penh, Siem Reap and Battambang. If you have never ridden a motorcycle before, Cambodia is not the ideal place to start, but once out of the city it does get easier. If you're a beginner, make sure you are under the supervision of someone who knows how to ride.

a driver, although self-drive rentals are also available in Phnom Penh.

Driving Licences

According to official rules, to drive a car you need a Cambodian licence, but the law is seldom applied. Local travel agents and some motorbike renters can arrange a Cambodian licence in less than a week for around US$35.

When it comes to renting motorcycles, it's a case of no licence required. If you can drive the bike out of the shop, you can drive it anywhere, or so the logic goes.

Fuel & Spare Parts

Fuel is relatively expensive in Cambodia compared with other staples. Fuel prices are generally much higher in central Phnom Penh and Siem Reap (4000r to 5000r, or US$1 to US$1.25, per litre) than elsewhere because of high rents. Highway petrol stations in the provinces are a good bet for cheap fuel (as

low as 3000r per litre for gasoline, or 2200r per litre for diesel).

Fuel is readily available throughout the country. Even the most isolated communities usually have someone selling petrol out of Fanta or Johnnie Walker bottles. Some sellers mix this fuel with kerosene to make a quick profit, so use it sparingly, in emergencies only.

When it comes to spare parts, Cambodia is flooded with Chinese, Japanese and Korean motorcycles, so it's easy to get parts for Hondas, Yamahas or Suzukis, but finding a part for a specialist make is another matter. The same goes for cars. Spares for Japanese cars are easy to come by, but if you are driving something obscure, bring substantial spares.

Hire
CAR

Car hire is generally only available with a driver and is most useful for sightseeing around

Phnom Penh and Angkor, and for conveniently travelling between cities. Some tourists with a healthy budget also arrange cars or 4WDs with drivers for touring the provinces. Hiring a car with a driver is about US$40 to US$50 for a day in and around Cambodia's towns. Heading into the provinces it rises to US$60 or more, plus petrol, depending on the destination. Hiring 4WDs will cost around US$60 to US$120 a day, depending on the model and the distance travelled. Self-drive car rentals are available in Phnom Penh, but think twice about driving yourself due to chaotic road conditions and personal liability in the case of an accident.

MOTORCYCLE

It is possible to explore Cambodia by motorbike. Anyone planning a longer ride should try out the bike around town for a day or so first to make sure it is in good health.

Motorcycles are available for hire in Phnom Penh and other provincial capitals and tourist towns. In Siem Reap motorcycle rental is still technically forbidden, but of late authorities are taking a relaxed view and a growing number of places now hire out motorbikes to tourists.

A 100cc motorbike usually rents for US$4 to US$6 per day (US$15 to US$20 on the islands). Costs are around US$15 to US$25 for a 250cc dirt bike.

Insurance

If you are travelling in a tourist vehicle with a driver, then the car is usually insured. When it comes to motorcycles, many rental bikes are not insured and you will have to sign a contract agreeing to a valuation for the bike if it is stolen. Make sure you have a strong lock and always leave the bike in guarded parking where available.

Do not even consider hiring a motorcycle if you are daft enough to be travelling in Cambodia without medical insurance.

Road Conditions & Hazards

Whether travelling or living in Cambodia, it is easy to lull yourself into a false sense of security and assume that down every rural road is yet another friendly village. However, even with the demise of the Khmer Rouge, odd incidents of banditry and robbery do occur in rural areas. There have also been some nasty bike-jackings in Sihanoukville. When travelling in your own vehicle, and particularly by motorcycle in rural areas, make certain you check the latest security information in communities along the way.

Be particularly careful about children on the road, as you'll sometimes find kids hanging out in the middle of a major highway. Livestock on the road is also a menace; hit a cow and you'll both be pizza.

Other general security suggestions for those travelling by motorcycle:

➡ Try to get hold of a good-quality helmet.

➡ Carry a basic repair kit, including some tyre levers, a puncture-repair kit and a pump.

➡ Always carry a rope for towing.

➡ In remote areas always carry several litres of water.

➡ Travel in small groups, not alone, and stay close together.

➡ Don't be cheap with the petrol, as running out of fuel in a rural area could jeopardise your health.

➡ Do not smoke marijuana or drink alcohol and drive.

➡ Keep your eyes firmly fixed on the road; Cambodian potholes eat people for fun.

Road Rules

If there are road rules in Cambodia it is doubtful that anyone is following them. Size matters and the biggest vehicle wins by default. The best advice if you drive a car or ride a motorcycle in Cambodia is to take nothing for granted.

In Cambodia traffic drives on the right. There are some traffic lights at junctions in Phnom Penh, Siem Reap and Sihanoukville, but where there are no lights, most traffic turns left into the oncoming traffic, edging along the wrong side of the road until a gap becomes apparent. For the uninitiated it looks like a disaster waiting to happen, but Cambodians are quite used to the system. Foreigners should stop at crossings and develop a habit of constant vigilance. Never assume that other drivers will stop at red lights; these are considered optional by most Cambodians, especially at night.

Phnom Penh is the one place where, amid all the chaos, traffic police take issue with Westerners breaking even the most trivial road rules. Make sure you don't turn left at a 'no left turn' sign or travel with your headlights on during the day (although, strangely, it doesn't seem to be illegal for Cambodians to travel without headlights at night). Laws requiring that bikes have mirrors and that drivers (not passengers, even children) wear helmets are being enforced around the country by traffic police eager to levy fines. Foreigners are popular targets.

Local Transport

Bus

Phnom Penh has several public city bus routes that are proving popular with local students, but are not yet widely used by visitors. Elsewhere there are no public bus networks.

Cyclo

As in Vietnam and Laos, the cyclo (bicycle rickshaw or pedicab) is a cheap way to get around urban areas. In Phnom Penh cyclo drivers can either be flagged down on main roads or found waiting around markets and major hotels. It is necessary to bargain the fare if taking a *cyclo* from outside an expensive hotel or popular restaurant or bar. Fares range from US$1 to US$3. There are few *cyclos* in the provinces, and in Phnom Penh the *cyclo* has almost been driven to extinction by the *moto* (motorcycle taxi).

Moto

Motos, also known as *motodups* (meaning *moto* driver), are small motorcycle taxis. They are a quick way of making short hops around towns and cities. Prices range from 2000r to US$1.50 or more, depending on the distance and the town; expect to pay more at night. In the past it was rare for prices to be agreed in advance, but with the increase in visitor numbers, a lot of drivers have got into the habit of overcharging. It's probably best to negotiate up front, particularly in the major tourist centres, outside fancy hotels or at night.

Remork-Moto & Auto-Rickshaw

The *remork-moto* (*remork*) is a large trailer hitched to a motorcycle and pretty much operates as a low-tech local bus with oh-so-natural air-conditioning. They are used throughout rural Cambodia to transport people and goods, and are often seen on the edge of towns ready to ferry farmers back to the countryside.

Most popular tourist destinations, including Phnom Penh, Siem Reap and the South Coast, have their very own tourist versions of the *remork*, with a canopied trailer hitched to the back of the motorbike for two people in comfort or as many as you can pile on at night. These are

a great way to explore temples, as you get the breeze of the bike but some protection from the elements.

In recent years a sizable fleet of Indian-made auto-rickshaws – similar to the Indian rickshaw or the Thai *tuk tuk* – has invaded Cambodia's urban landscape. They are zippier than their *remork* cousins, but much more compact – opt for a *remork* if you are more than two or three passengers and/or have a lot of luggage.

Remorks and auto-rickshaws are interchangeably known as *tuk tuks*, and can be ordered in larger provincial capitals via ride-hailing apps **Grab** (www.grab.com) and/or **PassApp** (www.passapptaxis.com) at prices much lower than you're likely to get on the street.

Rotei Ses

Rotei means 'cart' or 'carriage' and *ses* is 'horse', but the term is used for any cart pulled by an animal. Cambodia's original 4WD, ox-carts, usually pulled by water buffalo or cows, are a common form of transport in remote parts of the country, as only they can get through thick mud in the height of the wet season. Some local community-tourism initiatives now include cart rides.

Share Taxi

In these days of improving roads, share taxis are losing ground to express minivans. When using share taxis, it is an advantage to travel in numbers, as you can buy spare seats to make the journey more comfortable. Double the price for the front seat and quadruple it for the entire back row. It is important to remember that there aren't necessarily fixed prices on

every route, so you have to negotiate. For major destinations they can be hired individually, or you can pay for a seat and wait for other passengers to turn up. Guesthouses are also very helpful when it comes to arranging share taxis, albeit at a price.

Taxi

Taxi hire in towns and cities is getting easier, but there are still very few metered taxis, with just a handful of operators in Phnom Penh. Guesthouses, hotels and travel agents can arrange cars for sightseeing in and around towns. Ride-hailing apps have entered the market. In the provinces they are generally used to hail *remorks* but in the main cities can be used for small or large cars.

Train

Mothballed for years, Cambodia's rail system has been rehabilitated in recent years and limited passenger services resumed in 2016 through national carrier **Royal Railways** (☑078 888583; www.royal-railway.com). Currently there are two lines. The southern line links Phnom Penh with Sihanoukville via Kampot and Takeo, with departures on weekend mornings. The northern line – built before WWII and reopened in 2018 – runs from Phnom Penh to Poipet on the Thai border on Friday and Sunday mornings via Pursat and Battambang. Plans call for plugging the Cambodian line into the Trans-Asian Railway network, which will link Singapore and China, but connecting Phnom Penh with Ho Chi Minh City via a Mekong bridge will take a few years yet.

Health

General health is more of a concern in Cambodia than most other parts of Southeast Asia, due to a lack of international-standard medical-treatment facilities, a prevalence of tropical diseases and poor sanitation. Once you venture into rural areas you are very much on your own, although most provincial capitals have a reasonable clinic these days.

If you feel particularly unwell, try to see a doctor rather than visit a hospital; hospitals in rural areas are pretty primitive and diagnosis can be hit and miss. If you fall seriously ill in Cambodia you should head to Phnom Penh or Siem Reap, as these are the only places in the country with decent emergency treatment. Pharmacies in the larger towns are remarkably well stocked and you don't need a prescription to get your hands on anything from antibiotics to antimalarials. Prices are also very reasonable, but do check the expiry date, as some medicines may have expired.

While the potential dangers can seem quite unnerving, in reality few travellers experience anything more than an upset stomach. Don't let these warnings make you paranoid.

BEFORE YOU GO

Health Insurance

Do not visit Cambodia without medical insurance. Hospitals are extremely basic in the provinces and even in Phnom Penh the facilities are not necessarily what you may be used to at home. Anyone who has a serious injury or illness while in Cambodia may require emergency evacuation to Bangkok. With an insurance policy costing no more than the equivalent of a bottle of beer a day, this evacuation is free. Without an insurance policy, it will cost between US$10,000 and US$20,000.

Medical Checklist

Following is a list of items to consider including in a medical kit.

➡ aspirin or paracetamol – for pain or fever

➡ antihistamine – for allergies, or to ease the itch from insect bites or stings

➡ cold and flu tablets, throat lozenges and nasal decongestant

➡ multivitamins – especially for long trips, when dietary vitamin intake may be inadequate

➡ loperamide or diphenoxylate – 'blockers' for diarrhoea

➡ rehydration mixture – to prevent dehydration, which may occur during bouts of diarrhoea

➡ insect repellent, sunscreen, lip balm and eye drops

➡ calamine lotion or aloe vera – to ease irritation from sunburn

➡ antifungal cream or powder – for fungal skin infections and thrush

➡ antiseptic (such as povidone-iodine) – for cuts and grazes

➡ bandages, plasters and other wound dressings

➡ water-purification tablets or iodine

➡ sterile kit (sealed medical kit containing syringes and needles) – highly recommended, as Cambodia has potential medical-hygiene issues

CONTACT LENSES

People wearing contact lenses should be aware that Cambodia is an extremely dusty country and this can cause much irritation when travelling. It is generally bearable in cars, but when travelling by motorcycle or pickup, it is most definitely not. Pack a pair of glasses.

IN CAMBODIA

Availability & Cost of Healthcare

The best clinics and hospitals in Cambodia are found in Phnom Penh and Siem Reap. A consultation usually costs in the region of US$20 to US$50, plus medicine. Elsewhere, facilities are more basic, although a private clinic is usually preferable to a government hospital. For serious injuries, seek treatment in Bangkok.

Infectious Diseases

Dengue Fever

This viral disease is transmitted by mosquitoes. There is only a small risk to travellers, except during epidemics, which usually occur during and just after the wet season.

Unlike the malaria mosquito, the *Aedes aegypti* mosquito, which transmits the dengue virus, is most active during the day and is found mainly in urban areas.

Signs and symptoms of dengue fever include a sudden onset of high fever, headache, joint and muscle pains (hence its old name, 'breakbone fever'), plus nausea and vomiting. A rash of small red spots appears three to four days after the onset of fever.

Seek medical attention if you think you may be infected. A blood test can diagnose infection, but there is no specific treatment for the disease. Aspirin should be avoided, as it increases the risk of haemorrhaging, but plenty of rest is advised.

There is no vaccine against dengue fever. The best prevention is to avoid mosquito bites at all times.

Fungal Infections

Fungal infections occur more commonly in hot weather and are usually on the scalp,

between the toes (athlete's foot) or fingers, in the groin and on the body (ringworm). Ringworm, a fungal infection, not a worm, is contracted from infected animals or other people. Moisture encourages these infections.

To prevent fungal infections wear loose, comfortable clothes, avoid artificial fibres, wash frequently and dry yourself carefully.

Hepatitis

Hepatitis is a general term for inflammation of the liver. Several different viruses cause hepatitis, and they differ in the way that they are transmitted. The symptoms are similar in all forms of the illness, and include fever, chills, headache, fatigue, feelings of weakness, and aches and pains, followed by loss of appetite, nausea, vomiting, abdominal pain, dark urine, light-coloured faeces, jaundiced (yellow) skin and yellowing of the whites of the eyes.

Hepatitis A and E are both transmitted by ingesting contaminated food or water. Seek medical advice, but there is not much you can do apart from resting, drinking lots of fluids, eating lightly and avoiding fatty foods.

There are almost 300 million chronic carriers of hepatitis B in the world. It is spread through contact with infected blood, blood products or body fluids; for example, through sexual contact, unsterilised needles, blood transfusions or contact with blood via small breaks in the skin. Hepatitis C and D are spread in the same way as hepatitis B and can also lead to long-term complications.

HIV & AIDS

Infection with the human immunodeficiency virus (HIV) may lead to acquired immune deficiency syndrome (AIDS), which is a fatal disease. Any exposure to blood, blood products or body fluids may put the individual at risk.

The disease is often transmitted through sexual contact or dirty needles, so vaccinations, acupuncture, tattooing and body piercing can be potentially as dangerous as intravenous drug use.

Intestinal Worms

These parasites are most common in rural Cambodia. The various worms have different ways of infecting people. Some may be ingested in food such as under cooked meat (eg tapeworms) and some enter through your skin (eg hookworms). Consider having a stool test when you return home to check for worms and to determine the appropriate treatment.

Malaria

This serious and potentially fatal disease is spread by mosquitoes. If you are travelling in endemic areas it is extremely important to avoid mosquito bites and to take tablets to prevent the disease developing if you become infected. There is no malaria in Phnom Penh, Siem Reap and most other major urban areas in Cambodia, so visitors on short trips to the most popular places do not need to take medication. Malaria is most prevalent along remote areas of the Thai border and on some offshore islands. Malaria self-test kits are widely available in Cambodia, but are not that reliable.

Symptoms of malaria include fever, chills and sweating, headache, aching joints, diarrhoea and stomach pains, usually preceded by a vague feeling of ill health. Seek medical help immediately if malaria is suspected, as, without treatment, the disease can rapidly become more serious or even fatal.

Sexually Transmitted Infections (STIs)

Gonorrhoea, herpes and syphilis are among these infections. Sores, blisters or a rash around the genitals and discharges or pain when urinating are common symptoms. With some STIs, such as wart virus or chlamydia, symptoms may be less marked or not observed at all, especially in women. Reliable condoms are widely available throughout urban areas of Cambodia.

Typhoid

Typhoid fever is a dangerous gut infection caused by contaminated water and food. Medical help must be sought.

In its initial stages sufferers may feel they have a bad cold or flu on the way, as early symptoms are a headache, body aches and a fever that rises a little each day until it is around 40°C (104°F) or higher. There may also be vomiting, abdominal pain, diarrhoea or constipation.

In the second week, the high fever continues and a few pink spots may appear on the body; trembling, delirium, weakness, weight loss and dehydration may occur.

Traveller's Diarrhoea

Simple things like a change of water, food or climate can all cause a mild bout of diarrhoea, but a few rushed toilet trips with no other symptoms are not indicative of a major problem. Almost everyone gets a mild bout of the runs on a longer visit to Cambodia.

Dehydration is the main danger with diarrhoea, particularly in children or the elderly as it can occur quite quickly. Under all circumstances *fluid replacement* is the most important thing to remember. Stick to a bland diet as you recover. Commercially available oral rehydration salts are very useful; add them to boiled or bottled water.

Gut-paralysing drugs such as Lomotil or Imodium can be used to bring relief from the symptoms of diarrhoea, although they do not actually cure the problem. Only use these drugs if you do not have access to toilets and *must* travel.

Environmental Hazards

Food

There is an adage that says, 'If you can cook it, boil it or peel it you can eat it...otherwise forget it'. This is slightly extreme, but many travellers have found it is better to be safe than sorry. Vegetables and fruit should be washed with purified water or peeled where possible. Beware of ice cream that is sold in the street (or anywhere), as it might have melted and refrozen. Shellfish such as mussels, oysters and clams should be avoided, as should undercooked meat, particularly in the form of mince.

Heat Exhaustion

Dehydration and salt deficiency can cause heat exhaustion. Take time to acclimatise to high temperatures, drink sufficient liquids and do not do anything too physically demanding.

Salt deficiency is characterised by fatigue, lethargy, headaches, giddiness and muscle cramps; salt tablets may help, but adding extra salt to your food is better.

Heatstroke can occur if the body's heat-regulating mechanism breaks down, causing the body temperature to rise to dangerous levels. Long, continuous periods of exposure to high temperatures and insufficient fluids can leave you vulnerable to heatstroke.

Insect Bites & Stings

Bedbugs live in various places, but particularly in dirty

RECOMMENDED VACCINATIONS

Plan ahead for vaccinations, as some require more than one injection over a period of time, while others should not be given in combination.

Record all vaccinations on an International Certificate of Vaccination, available from your doctor. It is a good idea to carry this as proof of your vaccinations when travelling in Cambodia.

Recommended vaccinations for a trip to Cambodia are listed here, but it is imperative that you discuss your needs with your doctor.

Diphtheria and tetanus Vaccinations for these two diseases are usually combined.

Hepatitis A This vaccine provides long-term immunity after an initial injection and a booster at six to 12 months. The hepatitis A vaccine is also available in a combined form with the hepatitis B vaccine – three injections over a six-month period are required.

Hepatitis B Vaccination involves three injections, with a booster at 12 months.

Polio A booster every 10 years maintains immunity.

Tuberculosis Vaccination against TB (BCG vaccine) is recommended for children and young adults who will be living in Cambodia for three months or more.

Typhoid Vaccination against typhoid may be required if you are travelling for more than a few weeks in Cambodia.

mattresses and bedding, and are evidenced by spots of blood on bedclothes or on the wall. Bedbugs leave itchy bites in neat rows. Calamine lotion or Stingose spray may help.

All lice cause itching and discomfort. They make themselves at home in your hair (head lice), your clothing (body lice) or in your pubic hair (crabs). You catch lice through direct contact with infected people or by sharing combs, clothing and the like. Powder or shampoo treatment will kill the lice, and infected clothing should be washed in very hot, soapy water and left to dry in the sun.

Leeches may be present in damp rainforest conditions; they attach themselves to your skin to suck your blood. Trekkers often get them on their legs or in their boots. Salt or a lighted cigarette end will make them fall off.

Sandflies inhabit beaches (usually the more remote ones) across Southeast Asia. They have a nasty bite that is extremely itchy and can easily become infected. Use an antihistamine to quell

TAP WATER

The number-one rule is *be careful of water and ice,* although both are usually factory produced, a legacy of the French. If you don't know for certain that the water is safe, assume the worst. Reputable brands of bottled water or soft drinks are usually fine, but you can't safely drink tap water. Only use water from containers with a serrated seal. Tea and coffee are generally fine, as they're made with boiled water.

the itching, and, if you have to itch, use the palm of your hand and not your nails or infection may follow.

Prickly Heat

Prickly heat is an itchy rash caused by excessive perspiration trapped under the skin. It usually strikes people who have just arrived in a hot climate. Keeping cool, bathing often, drying the skin, using a mild talcum or prickly heat powder, or finding air-conditioning may help.

Snakes

To minimise the chances of being bitten by a snake, always wear boots, socks and long trousers when walking

through undergrowth where snakes may be present.

Traditional Medicine

Traditional medicine or *thnam boran* is very popular in rural Cambodia. There are *kru Khmer* (traditional medicine men) in most districts of the country and some locals trust them more than modern doctors and hospitals. Working with tree bark, roots, herbs and plants, they boil up brews to supposedly cure all ills. However, when it comes to serious conditions such as snake bites, their treatments can be counterproductive.

Language

The Khmer language is spoken by approximately nine million people in Cambodia, and is understood by many in neighbouring countries. Although Khmer as spoken in Phnom Penh is generally intelligible to Khmers nationwide, there are several distinct dialects in other parts of the country. Most notably, inhabitants of Takeo Province tend to modify or slur hard consonant/vowel combinations, especially those with 'r'. For example, *bram* (five) becomes *pe-am*, *sraa* (alcohol) becomes *se-aa*, and *baraang* (French for foreigner) becomes *be-ang*. In Siem Reap there's a Lao-sounding lilt to the local speech – some vowels are modified, eg *poan* (thousand) becomes *peuan*, and *kh'sia* (pipe) becomes *kh'seua*.

Though English is fast becoming Cambodia's second language, the Khmer population still clings to the Francophone pronunciation of the Roman alphabet and most foreign words. This is helpful to remember when spelling Western words and names aloud – 'ay-bee-see' becomes 'ah-bey-sey' and so on.

The pronunciation guides in this chapter are designed for basic communication rather than linguistic perfection. Read them as if they were English, and you shouldn't have problems being understood. Some consonant combinations are separated with an apostrophe for ease of pronunciation, eg 'j-r' in j'rook (pig) and 'ch-ng' in ch'ngain

WANT MORE?

For in-depth language information and handy phrases, check out Lonely Planet's *Southeast Asia Phrasebook*. You'll find it at **shop.lonelyplanet.com**, or you can buy Lonely Planet's iPhone phrasebooks at the Apple App Store.

(delicious). Also note that k is pronounced as the 'g' in 'go'; kh as the 'k' in 'kind'; p as the final 'p' in 'puppy'; ph as the 'p' in 'pond'; r as in 'rum' (hard and rolling); t as the 't' in 'stand'; and th as the 't' in 'two'.

Vowels and vowel combinations with an h at the end are pronounced with a puff of air at the end. Vowels are pronounced as follows:

a and ah shorter and harder than aa
aa as the 'a' in 'father'
ae as the 'a' in 'cat'
ai as in 'aisle'
am as the 'um' in 'glum'
av like a nasal ao (without the 'v')
aw as the 'aw' in 'jaw'
awh as the 'aw' in 'jaw' (short and hard)
ay as ai (slightly nasal)
e as in 'they'
eh as the 'a' in 'date' (short and hard)
eu like 'oo' (with flat lips)
euh as eu (short and hard)
euv like a nasal eu (without the 'v')
ey as in 'prey'
i as in 'kit'
ia as the 'ee' in 'beer' (without the 'r')
ih as the 'ee' in 'teeth' (short and hard)
ii as the 'ee' in 'feet'
o as the 'ow' in 'cow'
œ as 'er' in 'her' (more open)
oh as the 'o' in 'hose' (short and hard)
ohm as the 'ome' in 'home'
ow as in 'glow'
u as the 'u' in 'flute' (short and hard)
ua as the 'ou' in 'tour'
uah as ua (short and hard)
uh as the 'u' in 'but'
uu as the 'oo' in 'zoo'

BASICS

The Khmer language reflects the social standing of the speaker and the subject through personal pronouns and 'politeness words'. These range from the simple *baat* for men and *jaa* for women, placed at the end of a sentence and meaning 'yes' or 'I agree', to the very formal and archaic *Reachasahp* or 'royal language', a separate vocabulary reserved for addressing the king and very high officials. Many of the pronouns are determined on the basis of the subject's age and gender in relation to the speaker.

Foreigners are not expected to know all of these forms. The easiest and most general personal pronoun is *niak* (you), which may be used in most situations, for either gender. Men of your age or older can be called *lowk* (Mister). Women of your age or older can be called *bawng srei* (older sister) or, for more formal situations, *lowk srei* (Madam). *Bawng* is an informal, neutral pronoun for men or women who are (or appear to be) older than you. For the third person (he/she/they), male or female, singular or plural, the respectful form is *koat* and the common form is *ke*.

Hello.	ជម្រាបសួរ	johm riab sua
Goodbye.	លាសិនហើយ	lia suhn hao-y
Excuse me./ Sorry.	សូមទោស	sohm toh
Please.	សូម	sohm
Thank you.	អរគុណ	aw kohn
You're welcome.	អត់អីទេ/ សូមអញ្ជើញ	awt ei te/ sohm onh-jernh
Yes.	បាទ/ចាស	baat/jaa (m/f)
No.	ទេ	te

How are you?
អ្នកសុខសប្បាយទេ? niak sohk sabaay te

I'm fine.
ខ្ញុំសុខសប្បាយ kh'nyohm sohk sabaay

What's your name?
អ្នកឈ្មោះអ្វី? niak ch'muah ei

My name is ...
ខ្ញុំឈ្មោះ... kh'nyohm ch'muah ...

Does anyone speak English?
ទីនេះមានអ្នកចេះ tii nih mian niak jeh
ភាសាអង់គ្លេសទេ? phiasaa awngle te

I don't understand.
ខ្ញុំមិនយល់ទេ/ kh'nyohm muhn yuhl te/
ខ្ញុំស្ដាប់មិនបាន kh'nyohm s'dap muhn baan te

ACCOMMODATION

Where's a hotel?
អ្នកតើលនៅឯណា? ohtail neuv ai naa

I'd like a room ...	ខ្ញុំសុំបន្ទប់...	kh'nyohm sohm bantohp ...
for one person	សម្រាប់ មួយនាក់	samruhp muy niak
for two people	សម្រាប់ ពីរនាក់	samruhp pii niak
with a bathroom	ដែលមាន បន្ទប់ទឹក	dail mian bantohp tuhk
with a fan	ដែលមាន កង្ហារ	dail mian kawnghahl
with a window	ដែលមាន បង្អួច	dail mian bawng uoch

How much is it per day?
តម្លៃមួយថ្ងៃ damlay muy th'ngay
ប៉ុន្មាន? ponmaan

DIRECTIONS

Where is a/the ...?
...នៅឯណា? ... neuv ai naa

How can I get to ...?
ផ្លូវណាទៅ...? phleuv naa teuv ...

Go straight ahead.
ទៅត្រង់ teuv trawng

Turn left.
បត់ឆ្វេង bawt ch'weng

Turn right.
បត់ស្ដាំ bawt s'dam

at the corner
នៅកាច់ជ្រុង neuv kait j'rohng

behind
នៅខាងក្រោយ neuv khaang krao-y

in front of
នៅខាងមុខ neuv khaang mohk

next to
នៅជាប់ neuv joab

opposite
នៅទល់មុខ neuv tohl mohk

EATING & DRINKING

Where's a ...?	...នៅឯណា?	... neuv ai naa
food stall	កន្លែងលក់ម្ហូប	kuhnlaing loak m'howp
market	ផ្សារ	psar
restaurant	ភោជនីយដ្ឋាន	resturawn

Do you have a menu in English?

មានម៉ឺនុយជា ភាសាអង់គ្លេសទេ?	mien menui jea piasaa awnglay te

What's the speciality here?

ទីនេះមានម្ហូប អ្វីពិសេសទេ?	tii nih mien m'howp ei piseh te

I'm vegetarian.

ខ្ញុំតមសាច់	kh'nyohm tawm sait

I'm allergic to (peanuts).

កុំដាក់ (សណ្តែកដី)	kohm dak (sandaik dei)

Not too spicy, please.

សូមកុំធ្វើហឹរពេក	sohm kohm twœ huhl pek

This is delicious.

អានេះឆ្ងាញ់ណាស់	nih ch'ngain nah

The bill, please.

សូមគិតលុយ	sohm kuht lui

Fruit & Vegetables

apple	ផ្លែប៉ោម	phla i powm
banana	ចេក	chek
coconut	ដូង	duong
custard apple	ទៀប	tiep
dragonfruit	ផ្លែស្រការនាគ	phlai srakaa neak
durian	ធូរេន	tourain
grapes	ទំពាំងបាយជូរ	tompeang baai juu
guava	ត្របែក	trawbaik
jackfruit	ខ្នុរ	khnau
lemon	ក្រូចឆ្មារ	krow-it ch'maa
longan	ម៉ៀន	mien
lychee	ផ្លែគូលេន	phlai kuulain
mandarin	ក្រូចខ្ជិច	krow-it khwait
mango	ស្វាយ	svay
mangosteen	មង្ឃុត	mongkut

orange	ក្រូចពោធិ៍សាត់	kroch pow saat
papaya	ល្ហុង	l'howng
pineapple	ម្នាស់	menoa
pomelo	ក្រូចថ្លុង	kroch th'lohng
rambutan	សាវម៉ាវ	sao mao
starfruit	ស្ពឺ	speu
vegetables	បន្លែ	buhn lai
watermelon	ឪឡឹក	euv luhk

Meat & Fish

beef	សាច់គោ	sach kow
chicken	សាច់មាន់	sach moan
crab	ក្តាម	k'daam
eel	អន្ទង់	ahntohng
fish	ត្រី	trey
frog	កង្កែប	kawng kaip
lobster	បង្កង	bawng kawng
pork	សាច់ជ្រូក	sach j'ruuk
shrimp	បង្គា	bawngkia
snail	ខ្យង	kh'jawng
squid	មឹក	meuk

Other

bread	នំប៉័ង	nohm paang
butter	បឺរ	bœ
chilli	ម្ទេស	m'teh
curry	ការី	karii
fish sauce	ទឹកត្រី	teuk trey
fried	ចៀន/ឆា	jien/chaa
garlic	ខ្ទឹមស	kh'tuhm saw
ginger	ខ្ញី	kh'nyei
grilled	អាំង	ahng
ice	ទឹកកក	teuk koh
lemongrass	ស្លឹកគ្រៃ	sluhk krey
noodles (egg/rice)	មី/គុយទាវ	mii/kyteow
pepper	ម្រេច	m'rait

rice	បាយ	bai
salt	អំបិល	uhmbuhl
soup	ស៊ុប	sup
soy sauce	ទឹកស៊ីអ៊ីវ	teuk sii iw
spring rolls (fresh/fried)	ណែម/ឆាយ៉	naim/chaa yaw
steamed	ចំហុយ	jamhoi
sugar	ស្ករ	skaw

Drinks

beer	ប៊ីយ៉ែរ	bii-yœ
coffee	កាហ្វេ	kaa fey
lemon juice	ទឹកក្រូច ឆ្មា	teuk kroch ch'maa
orange juice	ទឹកក្រូច ពោធិ៍សាត់	teuk kroch pow sat
tea	តែ	tai
water	ទឹក	teuk

EMERGENCIES

Help!
ជួយខ្ញុំផង!   juay kh'nyohm phawng

Call the police!
ជួយហៅប៉ូលិសមក!   juay hav police mok

Call a doctor!
ជួយហៅ   juay hav
ត្រូវពេទ្យមក!   kruu paet mok

I've been robbed.
ខ្ញុំត្រូវចោរប្លន់   kh'nyohm treuv jao plawn

I'm ill.
ខ្ញុំឈឺ   kh'nyohm cheu

I'm allergic to (antibiotics).
ខ្ញុំមិនត្រូវជាតុ   kh'nyohm muhn treuv thiat
(អង់ទីប៊ីយ៉ូទិក)   (awntiibiowtik)

Where are the toilets?
បង្គន់នៅឯណា?   bawngkohn neuv ai naa

SHOPPING & SERVICES

I want to see the ...
ខ្ញុំចង់ទៅមើល...   kh'nyohm jawng teuv mœl ...

What time does it open?
វាបើកម៉ោងប៉ុន្មាន?   wia baok maong pohnmaan

What time does it close?
វាបិទម៉ោងប៉ុន្មាន?   wia buht maong pohnmaan

I'm looking for the ...   ខ្ញុំរក...   kh'nyohm rohk ...

bank   ធនាគារ   th'niakia
post office   ប្រៃសណីយ៍   praisuhnii
public telephone   ទូរស័ព្ទ សាធារណៈ   turasahp saathiaranah
temple   វត្ត   wawt

How much is it?
នេះថ្លៃប៉ុន្មាន?   nih th'lay pohnmaan

That's too much.
ថ្លៃពេក   th'lay pek

No more than ...
មិនលើសពី...   muhn lœh pii ...

What's your best price?
អ្នកដាច់ប៉ុន្មាន?   niak dach pohnmaan

I want to change US dollars.
ខ្ញុំចង់ដូរ   kh'nyohm jawng dow
ដុល្លារអាមេរិក   dolaa amerik

What is the exchange rate for US dollars?
មួយដុល្លារ   muy dolaa
ដូរបានប៉ុន្មាន?   dow baan pohnmaan

TIME & DATES

What time is it?
ឥឡូវនេះម៉ោងប៉ុន្មាន?   eileuv nih maong pohnmaan

in the morning	ពេលព្រឹក	pel pruhk
in the afternoon	ពេលរសៀល	pel r'sial
in the evening	ពេលល្ងាច	pel l'ngiach
at night	ពេលយប់	pel yohp
yesterday	ម្សិលមិញ	m'suhl mein
today	ថ្ងៃនេះ	th'ngay nih
tomorrow	ថ្ងៃស្អែក	th'ngay s'aik

Monday	ថ្ងៃចន្ទ	th'ngay jahn
Tuesday	ថ្ងៃអង្គារ	th'ngay ahngkia
Wednesday	ថ្ងៃពុធ	th'ngay poht
Thursday	ថ្ងៃព្រហស្បតិ៍	th'ngay prohoah
Friday	ថ្ងៃសុក្រ	th'ngay sohk
Saturday	ថ្ងៃសៅរ៍	th'ngay sav
Sunday	ថ្ងៃអាទិត្យ	th'ngay aatuht

TRANSPORT

Where's the ...?	...នៅឯណា?	... neuv ai naa
airport	វាលយន្ត	wial yohn
	ហោះ	hawh
bus stop	ចំណត	jamnawt
	ឡានឈ្នួល	laan ch'nual
train station	ស្ថានីយ	s'thaanii
	រថភ្លើង	roht plœng

When does the ... leave?	...ចេញម៉ោង	... jeinh maong
	ប៉ុន្មាន?	pohnmaan
boat	ទូក	duk
bus	ឡានឈ្នួល	laan ch'nual
train	រថភ្លើង	roht plœng
plane	យន្តហោះ	yohn hawh

What time does the last bus leave?

ឡានឈ្នួលចុងក្រោយ ចេញទៅម៉ោងប៉ុន្មាន? — laan ch'nual johng krao-y jein teuv maong pohnmaan

I want to get off (here).

ខ្ញុំចង់ចុះ(ទីនេះ) — kh'nyohm jawng joh (tii nih)

How much is it to ...?

ទៅ...ថ្លៃប៉ុន្មាន? — teuv ... th'lay pohnmaan

Please take me to (this address).

សូមជូនខ្ញុំទៅ (អាសយដ្ឋាននេះ) — sohm juun kh' nyohm teuv (aasayathaan nih)

Here is fine, thank you.

ឈប់នៅទីនេះក៏បាន — chohp neuv tii nih kaw baan

Numbers

Khmers count in increments of five – after reaching the number five (bram), the cycle begins again with the addition of one, ie 'five-one' (bram muy), 'five-two' (bram pii) and so on to 10, which begins a new cycle. For example, 18 has three parts: 10, five and three.

There's also a colloquial form of counting that reverses the word order for numbers between 10 and 20 and separates the two words with duhn: pii duhn dawp for 12, bei duhn dawp for 13 and so on. This form is often used in markets, so listen keenly.

1	មួយ	muy
2	ពីរ	pii
3	បី	bei
4	បួន	buan
5	ប្រាំ	bram
6	ប្រាំមួយ	bram muy
7	ប្រាំពីរ	bram pii
8	ប្រាំបី	bram bei
9	ប្រាំបួន	bram buan
10	ដប់	dawp
11	ដប់មួយ	dawp muy
12	ដប់ពីរ	dawp pii
16	ដប់ប្រាំមួយ	dawp bram muy
20	ម្ភៃ	m'phei
21	ម្ភៃមួយ	m'phei muy
30	សាបសិប	saamsuhp
40	សែសិប	saisuhp
100	មួយរយ	muy roy
1000	មួយពាន់	muy poan
1,000,000	មួយលាន	muy lian

1st	ទីមួយ	tii muy
2nd	ទីពីរ	tii pii
3rd	ទីបី	tii bei
4th	ទីបួន	tii buan
10th	ទីដប់	tii dawp

GLOSSARY

apsara – heavenly nymph or angelic dancer, often represented in Khmer sculpture

Asean – Association of Southeast Asian Nations

Avalokiteshvara – Bodhisattva of Compassion and the inspiration for Jayavarman VII's Angkor Thom

baray – reservoir

boeng – lake

Chenla – pre-Angkorian period, 6th to 8th centuries

chunchiet – ethnic minorities

CNRP – Cambodia National Rescue Party

CPP – Cambodian People's Party

cyclo – pedicab; bicycle rickshaw

devaraja – cult of the god-king, established by Jayavarman II, in which the monarch has universal power

devadas – goddesses

EFEO – École Française d'Extrême Orient

essai – wise man or traditional medicine man

Funan – pre-Angkorian period, 1st to 5th centuries

Funcinpec – National United Front for an Independent, Neutral, Peaceful and Cooperative Cambodia; royalist political party

garuda – mythical half-man, half-bird creature

gopura – entrance pavilion in traditional Hindu architecture

Hun Sen – Cambodia's prime minister (1985–present)

Jayavarman II – the king (r 802–50) who established the cult of the god-king, kicking off a period of amazing architectural productivity that resulted in the extraordinary temples of Angkor

Jayavarman VII – the king (r 1181–1219) who drove the Chams out of Cambodia before embarking on an ambitious

construction program, including the walled city of Angkor Thom

Kampuchea – the name Cambodians use for their country; to non-Khmers, it is associated with the bloody rule of the Khmer Rouge, which insisted that the outside world adopt for Cambodia the name Democratic Kampuchea from 1975 to 1979

Khmer – a person of Cambodian descent; the language of Cambodia

Khmer Krom – ethnic Khmers living in Vietnam

Khmer Rouge – a revolutionary organisation that seized power in 1975 and implemented a brutal social restructuring, resulting in the suffering and death of millions of Cambodians during its four-year rule

krama – scarf

linga – phallic symbols

Mahayana – literally, 'Great Vehicle'; a school of Buddhism (also known as the Northern School) that built upon and extended the early Buddhist teachings; see also Theravada

moto – small motorcycle with driver; a common form of transport in Cambodia

naga – mythical serpent, often multiheaded; a symbol used extensively in Angkorian architecture

nandi – sacred ox, vehicle of Shiva

NGO – nongovernmental organisation

NH – national highway

Norodom Ranariddh, Prince – son of King Sihanouk and former leader of Funcinpec

Norodom Sihanouk, King – former king, head of state, film director and a towering figure in modern-day Cambodia

Pali – ancient Indian language that, along with Sanskrit, is the root of modern Khmer

phnom – mountain or hill

Pol Pot – the former leader of the Khmer Rouge; responsible for the suffering and deaths of

millions of Cambodians; previously known as Saloth Sar

prasat – stone or brick hall with religious or royal significance

preah – sacred

psar – market

Ramayana – an epic Sanskrit poem composed around 300 BC featuring the mythical Ramachandra, the incarnation of the god Vishnu

remork-moto – trailer pulled by a motorcycle; often shortened to *remork*

rom vong – Cambodian circle dancing

Sangkum Reastr Niyum – People's Socialist Community; a national movement, led by King Sihanouk, that ruled the country during the 1950s and 1960s

Sanskrit – ancient Hindu language that, along with Pali, is the root of modern Khmer language

stung – river

Suryavarman II – the king (r 1112–52) responsible for building Angkor Wat and for expanding and unifying the Khmer empire

Theravada – a school of Buddhism (also known as the Southern School or Hinayana) found in Myanmar (Burma), Thailand, Laos and Cambodia; this school confined itself to the early Buddhist teachings; see also Mahayana

tonlé – large river

UNDP – UN Development Programme

Unesco – UN Educational Scientific and Cultural Organization

Untac – UN Transitional Authority in Cambodia

vihara – temple sanctuary

WHO – World Health Organization

Year Zero – 1975; the year the Khmer Rouge seized power

yoni – female fertility symbol

Behind the Scenes

SEND US YOUR FEEDBACK

We love to hear from travellers – your comments keep us on our toes and help make our books better. Our well-travelled team reads every word on what you loved or loathed about this book. Although we cannot reply individually to your submissions, we always guarantee that your feedback goes straight to the appropriate authors, in time for the next edition. Each person who sends us information is thanked in the next edition – the most useful submissions are rewarded with a selection of digital PDF chapters.

Visit **lonelyplanet.com/contact** to submit your updates and suggestions or to ask for help. Our award-winning website also features inspirational travel stories, news and discussions.

Note: We may edit, reproduce and incorporate your comments in Lonely Planet products such as guidebooks, websites and digital products, so let us know if you don't want your comments reproduced or your name acknowledged. For a copy of our privacy policy visit lonelyplanet.com/privacy.

OUR READERS

Many thanks to the travellers who used the last edition and wrote to us with helpful hints, useful advice and interesting anecdotes:

Eulalia Anglada, Toby Clipson, Suzanne Cox, Sam Emons, Alejandro Gámez, Quentin Given, Frances Howard, Alison Lea, Man-Chi Liu, Charlotte Pinder, Lenka Pivonkova, Caroline Rowland, Hanna Specht, Diane Strong, Has van Vlokhoven, Verena Wimmer

WRITER THANKS

Nick Ray

A huge and heartfelt thanks to the people of Cambodia, whose warmth, strength and spirit have made it such a fascinating place to visit over the years. Biggest thanks are reserved for my lovely wife, Kulikar Sotho, and our children, Julian and Belle, as without their support and encouragement my adventures would not be possible. Thanks also to mum and dad for giving me a taste for travel from a young age. Thanks to fellow travellers and residents, friends and contacts in Cambodia who have helped shaped my knowledge and experience in this country. There is no room to thank everyone, but you all know who you are, as we meet for anything from beers to eco-tourism conferences and film festivals with alarming regularity. Thanks also to my co-authors Greg Bloom and Mark Johanson for going the distance to ensure this is a worthy new edition. Finally, thanks to the Lonely Planet team who have worked on this title. The author may be the public face, but a huge amount of work goes into making this a better book behind the scenes.

Mark Johanson

Arkun (thank you) Theara Hout, Dary Sang, Virginia Brumby, Bun Puthea and Sithy Hengchan for all of your tips, help and wisdom either before or during my travels in Cambodia. A big *gracias* to my partner Felipe for enduring my long absences from home. Thanks to my parents for instilling in me a curiosity for the unknown and an insatiable thirst for travel. Also, thanks to my fellow writers Nick Ray and Greg Bloom for their invaluable insights.

Greg Bloom

The biggest thanks goes to my team on the home front: to Windi for doing more than holding down the fort, for taking care of the little 'uns while I was away and during the deadline crunch. And of course to Anna, Callie and Rocco for the smiles and comic relief. On the road, thanks to fellow writer Nick for the tips and bar-research support in Kampot. And to Joel for the yarns and Katey for the intel.

ACKNOWLEDGEMENTS

Climate map data adapted from Peel MC, Finlayson BL & McMahon TA (2007) 'Updated World Map of the Köppen-Geiger Climate Classification', *Hydrology and Earth System Sciences*, 11, 1633–44.

Cover photograph: Angkor Wat, Michael Nolan/ Getty Images©

Illustration p144-5 by Michael Weldon

THIS BOOK

This 12th edition of Lonely Planet's *Cambodia* guidebook was curated by Nick Ray, and researched and written by Nick, Greg Bloom and Mark Johanson. The 11th edition was written by Nick Ray and Ashley Harrell, and the 10th was written by Nick Ray and Jessica Lee. This guidebook was produced by the following:

Destination Editor
James Smart

Senior Product Editors Kate Chapman, Sandie Kestell, Kathryn Rowan

Regional Senior Cartographer Diana von Holdt

Product Editors Paul Harding, Ross Taylor

Book Designers Lauren Egan, Clara Monitto

Assisting Editors
Janet Austin, James Bainbridge, Michelle Coxall, Kellie Langdon, Gabrielle Stefanos, Simon Williamson

Assisting Cartographer
Julie Dodkins

Script Checker Oeu Vearyda

Cover Researcher
Brendan Dempsey-Spencer

Thanks to Will Allen, Joel Cotterell, Laura Crawford, Karen Henderson, Kate James

Index

A

accessible travel 350
accommodation 16, 24-5, *see also individual locations*
  booking 350
  language 371
activities 36-41, *see also individual activities*
aerobics 60
AIDS 367
air travel 359-60, 362
Angkor kings 146, *see also individual kings*
Angkor National Museum 105
Angkor temples & structures 137-76, **140-1, 2, 9, 21, 144**
  accommodation 137, 147, 168-9, 176
  admission fees 149
  Angkor Thom 156-61, **156, 30-1, 145**
  Angkor Wat 9, 150-6, **152, 155, 28-9, 144**
  architecture 146-7
  Bakong 167-8
  Banteay Kdei 163
  Banteay Samré 173
  Banteay Srei 169-70
  Baphuon 159
  Bayon 9, 156-9, **158, 9, 144**
  Beng Mealea 170-1, **170**
  Chau Say Tevoda 164
  Chau Srei Vibol 173
  code of conduct 138
  crowds 148
  Eastern Mebon 166
  food 137, 155, 168-9, 176
  history 138-46

Map Pages **000**
Photo Pages **000**

itineraries 144-5, 147-9, **144-5**
  Kleangs 161
  Koh Ker 174-6, **175**
  Lolei 168
  Phimeanakas 161
  Phnom Bakheng 163-4, **164**
  Phnom Bok 173-4
  Phnom Chisor 101
  Phnom Krom 174
  Prasat Bram 176
  Prasat Krahom 176
  Prasat Kravan 167
  Prasat Leung 176
  Prasat Suor Prat 161-2
  Pre Rup 166-7
  Preah Khan 165-6, **165, 145**
  Preah Ko 168, **145**
  Preah Neak Poan 166, **167**
  Preah Palilay 161
  Preah Pithu 161
  Roluos temples 167-9
  Royal Enclosure 161
  shopping 168
  Spean Thmor 164-5
  Sra Srang 163, **145**
  symbols 151
  Ta Keo 164
  Ta Nei 164
  Ta Prohm 162-3, **162**
  Ta Som 166
  Terrace of the Leper King 159
  Terrace of Elephants 159-61
  Thommanon 164
  tours 149
  travel seasons 147
  travel within 149-50
  walking tours 160, **160**
  websites 149
  Western Baray 174
  Western Mebon 174
Angkor Zipline 154, **40**

Angkorian Empire 310-11
animals 344-5, *see also individual species*, wildlife watching
animism 332
Anlong Veng 260-2
Apopo Visitor Centre 105
apsaras 153
architecture 61, 332-3
area codes 19
art galleries, *see* museums & galleries
Artisans Angkor 15, 90, 105, **15**
arts 332-6, *see also architecture, dance, sculpture*
ATMs 353
auto-rickshaw travel 365

B

Bakong 167-8
bamboo train 248
Ban Lung 13, 290-6, **290**
Banteay Chhmar 9, 258-60, **9**
Banteay Samré 173
Banteay Srei 169-70
Banteay Srei District 131-4
Baphuon 159
bargaining 21
Bassac Lane 88
bathrooms 356
Battambang 14, 241-53, **242-3, 14**
  accommodation 246-9
  activities 245
  courses 245
  drinking 250-1
  entertainment 251
  nightlife 250-1
  shopping 251
  sights 241-5
  tours 245-6
  travel to/from 251-2
  travel within 252

Battambang Province 241-54
Bayon 9, 156-9, **158, 9, 144**
bears 100-1
beaches 10, **10-11**
  Coconut Beach 198
  Kep Beach 225
  Koh Tuch Beach 198
  Koh Yor Beach 180
  Lazy Beach 209
  Long Beach 196
  Long Set Beach 198
  Ochheuteal Beach 189-90
  Otres Beach 189
  Police Beach 198
  Ream Beach 195
  Saracen Bay 207
  Serendipity Beach 191
  Sok San Beach 198
beer 84, 339, *see also breweries*
Bei Srok 292
Beng Mealea 170-1, **170**
bicycle travel, *see* cycling, mountain biking
birdwatching
  Ang Trapaeng Thmor Reserve 136
  Kulen Promtep Wildlife Sanctuary 270
  Prek Toal Bird Sanctuary 134-5
  Ream National Park 195
  Siem Reap 111
bites 345, 368-9
blood donations 56
boat travel 204, 362
boat trips 37, *see also kayaking*
  Chi Phat 188
  Kampot 213, 214
  Kep 225-6
  Koh Kong 181
  Koh Rong 198-9
  Phnom Penh 60
Boeng Yeak Lom 13, 291-2, **13**
Bokheo 293

Bokor Hill Station 222-4, **32**
Bokor National Park 223
books 331
  cooking 342
  history 312, 313, 314, 317, 321, 322, 325, 327
border crossings 360-2, **361**
  Laos 288
  Thailand 131, 182, 256, 257, 258, 262
  Vietnam 92, 93, 229, 232, 281, 285, 296
Botum Sakor National Park 187
Bou Sraa Waterfall 298
boxing, see kickboxing
breweries 17, 84, see also beer
  Botanico 84
  Flowers Home Brew & Sushi 220
  Hops Brewery 84
  Kingdom Brewery 67
  Riel Brewing Taproom 84
Buddhism 331
budget 19
bus travel 363, 364
bushwalking, see hiking
business hours 19, 354
butterflies 131
  Banteay Srei Buttefly Centre 131
  Kep Butterfly Garden 225

C
Cambodian Cultural Village 109
Cambodian Living Arts 67, **58**
car travel 363-4
Cardamom Mountains 13, 240-1, **13**
Cardamom Rainforest Landscape 186
caves 222
cell phones 18, 356
cemetery etiquette 297
Central Cardamoms National Park 241
Chaa Ong 291
Cham people 331
Chambok 101-2
Channthy, Kak 89
Chau Say Tevoda 164
Chau Srei Vibol 173
Chhlong 282
Chi Phat 187-9
child abuse 66

children, travel with 42-4, 108, 340
Chinese people 330
Choeung Ek 55-6
Chong Kneas 135-6
Chong Kos 238
Christianity 332
chunchiet cemeteries 297
cinema, see films
civil war 316-18
circuses 124, 251
climate 18, 26-7
climate change 359
coffee 339
consulates 350-1
cooking courses 341
  Battambang 245
  Phnom Penh 66
  Sambor Prei Kuk 272
  Siem Reap 110-11
costs 19
courses, see cooking courses, language courses, martial arts courses
COVID-19 3, 22
credit cards 353
culture 328-36
currency 18, 353-4
cycling 37-8, 362
  Battambang 245
  Kampot 214
  Mekong Discovery Trail 286
  Phnom Pehn 64
  Siem Reap 112
cyclo travel 364-5

D
Dak Dam Waterfall 298
dams 348
dance 124, 334-5, **58**
dangers, see safety
Dangrek Mountains 261
dengue fever 367
departure tax 360
diarrhoea 368
dirt biking 38, 213
disabilities, travellers with 350
distilleries 23
  Samai Distillery 84
  Seekers Independent Spirits 84
diving & snorkelling 38-9
  Koh Rong 199, **36**
  Koh Rong Sanloem 206
  Koh Sdach Archipelago 211

Southern Islands 203
dolphins, Irrawaddy 14, 23, 345, 348, 284, 289, **14**
drinks 85-8, 339-40
  cocktails 17, **17**
  coffee 339
  craft beer 17, 84, 339
  language 373
  wine 254, 339
driving, see car travel

E
Eastern Cambodia 46, 274-306, **275**
  accommodation 274
  food 274
  highlights 275
  travel seasons 274
Eastern Mebon 166
eating, see food
economy 22
electricity 351
elephant encounters 299-301, 303, **12-13**
embassies 350-1
emergencies 19
  language 373
environmental issues 22, 346-8
  climate change 359
  endangered species 345
etiquette 21, 138, 341-2
events see festivals & events
exchange rates 19

F
Factory Phnom Penh 22, 56
famine relief 321
farms
  Angkor Silk Farm 108
  Kep Butterfly Garden 225
  La Plantation 222
  Santuk Silk Farm 273
  Sothy's Pepper Farm 225
ferry travel 204, see also boat travel
festivals & events 26-7, see also individual locations
  Bon Om Tuk 27
  Chinese New Year 26
  Khmer New Year 26
  P'chum Ben 27
films 23, 323, 326, 333-4
fishing 199

floating villages
  Chong Kneas 135-6
  Chong Kos 238
  Me Chrey 135
  Phoum Kandal 238
food 337-9, see also individual locations
  amok fish curry 16, **16**
  crab 16, **16**
  etiquette 341-2
  Kampot pepper 16, 217, **16**
  Khmer barbecue 79
  language 372-3
  prahoc 253
  street food 79, 340-1
  tours 112
football 335
Funan 309
Funcinpec 320, 322, 323
fungal infections 367

G
galleries, see museums & galleries
gardens, see parks & gardens
gay travellers 23, 352
genocide 54-5, 318-19, 325
geography 343-4
gibbons 292
golf 65, 109-10
greetings 329

H
health 366-9
heat exhaustion 368
hepatitis 367
highlights 6-7, **6-7**
hiking 39-40
  Ban Lung 292
  Cardamom Mountains 240
  Chi Phat 188
  Koh Rong 199
  Ratanakiri 294
  Sen Monorom 301
  Virachey National Park 297
Hinduism 331
history 308-24
  Angkorian Empire 310-11
  books 312, 313, 314, 317, 321, 322, 325, 327
  civil war 315-17
  French in Cambodia 313-14
  Khmer Rouge 317-18
  Sihanouk years 314-15

history *continued*
  Temples of Angkor
    138-46
  Vietnamese enter 318-20
HIV 367
holidays 354
homestays 24
horse riding 109
hostels 24
hotels 24
Hun Sen 319, 323

I

Ieng Sary 327
immigration 359
Indravarman I 138
insurance 351
internet access 351
internet resources 19, 23, 44
Islam 332
itineraries 28-35, **28**, **30**,
  33, **34-5**

J

Jayavarman II 310
Jayavarman VII 139-42, 311

K

Ka Tieng 291
Kaing Guek Eav 327
Kamping Puoy 254
Kampot 14, 23, 212-21,
  214, **14**
  accommodation 215-18
  activities 213-14
  drinking 220-1
  entertainment 220
  food 218-20
  nightlife 220
  shopping 220-1
  sights 212-13
  tourist information 221
  tours 213-14
  travel to/from 221
  travel within 221
Kampot Province 212-30
Kaundinya 309
kayaking 38-9, *see also*
  boat trips
  Battambang 245
  Koh Rong 198-9
  Koh Rong Sanloem 206
  Kratie 282
  Me Chrey 135

Map Pages **000**
Photo Pages **000**

Kbal Chhay Cascades 189
Kbal Spean 172-3
Keo Seima Wildlife
  Sanctuary 12, 304
Kep 224-9, **226**
Kep National Park 224
Khieu Samphan 327
Khmer Krom people 330
Khmer language 370-5
Khmer people 330
Khmer Rouge 317-18, 325-7
Khnar Po 136
kickboxing 335
Killing Fields of Choeung
  Ek 55-6
Kinchaan 291
Kirirom National Park 101
Kirivong Waterfall 232
Kleangs 161
Koh Dach 97-8
Koh Ker 174-6, **175**
Koh Kong City 179-84, **180**
Koh Kong Conservation
  Corridor 13, 184-9
Koh Kong Island 180
Koh Paen 276-7
Koh Pos 224
Koh Rong 11, 197-205, **200**,
  11, **32-3**, **36**
Koh Rong Sanloem 11, 205-
  11, **208**, **10-11**
Koh Sdach Archipelago 11,
  211-12, **11**
Koh Svay 224
Koh Ta Kiev 196-7
Koh Thmei 197
Koh Trong 283
Kompong Cham 276-81,
  277
Kompong Chhnang 236-7,
  236
Kompong Khleang 134
Kompong Luong 239-40
Kompong Pluk 135
Kompong Thom 269-72,
  271
Kompong Thom Province
  269-73
krama 279
Kratie 4, 14, 281-6, **282**,
  4-5, **14**

L

landmines 176, 263, 355
language 21, 370-5
  courses 67, 245, 351
Lara Croft: Tomb Raider
  163
legal matters 352

LGBTQI+ travellers 23, 352
linga 172
logging 347-8
Lolei 168
Lon Nol 316, 317
Lumkut 293
Lumphat 291

M

Mahendraparvata 171
malaria 367
maps 352
markets
  Angkor Night Market 125
  Bokor Night Market 220
  crab market (Kep)
    16, 228
  Made in Cambodia
    Market 127
  Night Market (Kampot)
    219
  Night Market (Phnom
    Penh) 89
  Old Market (Kampot) 213
  Phnom Penh 79, **2**
  Psar Chaa 118, 125, **115**
  Psar Leu 182
  Psar Nath 245
  Psar Thmei 15, 56
  Road 60 Night Market
    121
  Russian Market 15, 83-5,
    87, 89, **82**, **16**
  smugglers' market 261
martial arts 111
  courses 679
massages 65-6, 213, 245
Me Chrey 135
measures 352
media 92, 352
meditation 99
Mekong Discovery Trail 286
Mekong River 4, 348, **4-5**
mobile phones 18, 356
Mondulkiri Province 12,
  297-306, **12-13**
money 18, 19, 353-4
monkeys 304, **38**
Monorom Falls 299
moto travel 365
motorcycle travel 38,
  363-4
  dirt biking 38
  quad biking 40, 110
  Siem Reap 112
mountain biking, *see also*
  cycling
  Chi Phat 188
  Phnom Penh 64

museums & galleries, 23
  Angkor Borei 231
  Angkor Conservation 165
  Angkor National
    Museum 105
  Battambang Museum
    243-4
  Cambodia Landmine
    Museum 131
  Cambodia Peace Gallery
    244-5
  CMAC Peace Museum of
    Mine Action 168
  Eco Global Museum 265
  HUMAN Gallery 247
  Jewel in the Lotus 247
  Kampot Provincial
    Museum 212
  Kbach Arts 56
  Kompong Thom Museum
    269
  National Museum of
    Cambodia 54, **58**
  Romcheik 5 Artspace
    247
  Sangker Gallery 247
  Tep Kao Sol 247
  Tuol Sleng Genocide
    Museum 54-5, **59**
  War Museum 105
music 335-6

N

National Library
  (Phnom Penh) 60
National Museum of
  Cambodia 54, **58**
national parks & nature
  reserves 13-14, 346, *see*
  also wildlife sanctuaries
  & reserves
  Bokor National Park 223
  Botum Sakor National
    Park 187
  Cardamom Rainforest
    Landscape 186
  Central Cardamoms
    National Park 241
  Kep National Park 224
  Kirirom National Park
    101
  Ream National Park 195
  Southern Cardamom
    National Park 185-7
  Virachey National Park
    13, 296-7
newspapers 352
nightlife 85-8
Norodom Sihanouk 314-15,
  319, 333

Northwestern Cambodia
46, 233-73, **234-5**
accommodation 233
climate 233
food 233
highlights 234
travel seasons 233
Nuon Chea 326-7

O
Ondong Rossey 236
opening hours 19, 354
orphan tourism 357

P
paedophilia 66
Pailin 254-6, **255**
palaces
Royal Palace
(Phnom Penh) 53, **53**,
30-1, 59
pangolins 184
parks & gardens, see also
national parks & nature
reserves
Koh Sampovmeas 238
Senteurs d'Angkor
Botanic Garden 108
passports 359
pepper 16, 217, **16**
Phare Ponleu Selpak 251
Phare the Cambodian
Circus 124
Phimeanakas 161
Phnom Bakheng 163-4,
164
Phnom Bayong 231
Phnom Bok 173-4
Phnom Chisor 101
Phnom Da 231
Phnom Khieu Waterfall 255
Phnom Krom 174
Phnom Kulen 171-2, **41**
Phnom Penh 45, 48-98,
49, 50-1, 62-3, 68-9,
82, 2, 17, 31 ,58-9
accommodation 48, 70-5
activities 60-6
climate 48
courses 66-7
drinking 17, 84, 85-8, **17**
emergencies 91
entertainment 88-9
festivals & events 70
food 48, 75-85
highlights 49
history 49-52
internet access 91

markets 89
medical services 92
nightlife 17, 85-8, **17**
safety 57, 91
shopping 89-91
sights 52-60
tourist information 93
tours 67-70
travel seasons 48
travel to/from 93-6
travel within 96-7
walking tours 61, **61**
Phnom Pros 278
Phnom Sampeau 253-4
Phnom Santuk 273
Phnom Sombok 281
Phnom Srei 278
Phnom Tamao Wildlife
Rescue Centre 100-1
Phnom Udong 98-9
photography 354
Phoum Kandal 238
planning
budgeting 19
calendar of events 26-7
Cambodia basics 18-19
Cambodia's regions 45-6
children, travel with
42-4, 108, 340
first-time visitors 20-1
internet resources 19, 23
itineraries 28-35
repeat visitors 22-3
travel seasons 18, 26-7
plants 345-6
Poipet 256-8
Pol Pot 261, 317, 323,
325, 326
Pol Pot's House 261
politics 22, 324
pollution 348
Popokvil Falls 223
population 23, 328
postal services 354
pradal serey 335
prahoc 337
Prasat Banan 254
Prasat Bram 176
Prasat Krahom 176
Prasat Kravan 167
Prasat Kuha Nokor 273
Prasat Bram 176
Prasat Krahom 176
Prasat Kravan 167
Prasat Preah Vihear 9,
264-6, **266**, **9**
Prasat Suor Prat 161-2
Pre Rup 166-7

Preah Khan 165-6, **165**,
145
Preah Khan of Kompong
Svay 267-9
Preah Ko 168
Preah Neak Poan 166,
167, 145
Preah Palilay 161
Preah Pithu 161
Preah Rumkel 289
Preah Vihear City 262-4,
264
Preah Vihear Province 262-9
Prek Toal Bird Sanctuary
134-5
Prey Chung Kran 277-8
Prey Veng 270
Psar Thmei 15
public holidays 354
Pursat 237-9, **239**

Q
quad biking 40, 110

R
radio 352
Ramayana Mural 54, **59**
Ratanakiri Province 13,
289-97
Ream National Park 195
religion 331-2
remork-moto travel 365
rock climbing 213
Roluos temples 167-9
Romanear Waterfall 299
rotei travel 365
Royal Palace (Phnom
Penh) 53, **53**, **30-1, 59**
running 60
Russian Market 15, 83-5,
87, 89, **82, 16**

S
safe travel 354-6
landmines 176, 263, 355
Phnom Penh 57, 91
Siem Reap 126
Sam Rainsy 324
Sambor Prei Kuk 272
sand dredging 348
sculpture 336
Sen Monorom 298-306,
300
share taxis 365
shopping 15, 353, 15,
see also individual
locations, markets
language 373

Siem Reap 23, 45, 103-31,
104, 106, 110, 114, 132
accommodation 103,
112-17
activities 109-10
children, travel with 108
climate 103
courses 110-11
drinking 122-4
emergencies 126
entertainment 124-5
food 16, 22, 103, 117-22
highlights 104
history 104 5
internet access 126
medical services 126
nightlife 122-4
safety 126
shopping 125-6, 127
sights 105-9
tourist information 126
tours 111-12
travel seasons 103
travel to/from 128-9
travel within 129-30
Sihanouk, King Norodom
314-15, 319, 333
Sihanoukville 189-95, **190**
silk farms 108, 273
Silver Pagoda (Phnom
Penh) 53-4
Sisophon 258
smoking 352
snorkelling, see diving &
snorkelling
South Coast 46, 177-232,
178
accommodation 177
climate 177
food 177
highlights 178
travel seasons 177
travel to/from 179
Southern Cardamom
National Park 185-7
Southern Islands 22-3,
196-212
spas 65-6, 110, 245
spirits 339
sport 335
stand-up paddleboarding
38-9, 214
Stung Treng 286-8, **287**
Suryavarman I 139
Suryavarman II 139
swifts 181
swimming 64-5, 109, 278

INDEX T-Z

T

Ta Mok's House 230, 260
Ta Nei 164
Ta Prohm 162-3, **162**, **8**, **145**
Ta Som 166
Takeo 230-2
tap water 339-40, 369
Tatai River 13, 184-5, **13**, **25**
Tatai Waterfall 184-5
taxes 360
taxis 365
tea 339
Tek Chhouu Rapids 213
telephone services 356
temples, see also Angkor temples & structures
  Banteay Chhmar 9, 258-60, **9**
  Phnom Da 231
  Phnom Sombok 281
  Prasat Preah Vihear 9, 264-6, **266**, **9**
  Preah Ang Chek Preah Ang Chorm 105-8
  Preah Khan of Kompong Svay 267-9
  Silver Pagoda (Phnom Penh) 53-4
Wat Athvea 108
Wat Bo 108
Wat Dam Nak 109
Wat Ek Phnom 253
Wat Hanchey 276-306
Wat Khaong Kang 255
Wat Kiri Sela 225
Wat Kor Village 243
Wat Leu 189
Wat Maha Leap 276
Wat Neang Kok 180-1
Wat Nokor Bachey 277
Wat Ounalom 57
Wat Phnom 56-7
Wat Phnom Doh Kromom 298
Wat Phnom Yat 255
Wat Preah Inkosei 108

Wat Roka Kandal 281
Wat Samathi 225
Wat Sampov Pram 223
Wat Somrong Knon 223
Wat Sorsor Moi Roi 281
Wat Thmei 109
Yeay Peau 100
Terrace of the Leper King 159
teuk trey 337
Thommanon 164
time 356
tipping 21, 352, 353
Tmatboey 270
toilets 356
Tonlé Bati 99-100
Tonlé Sap 344
tourist information 356
tours, see individual locations
train travel 365
travel to/from Cambodia 359-62
travel within Cambodia 362-5
trekking, see hiking
Tuol Sleng Genocide Museum 54-5, **59**
TV 352
typhoid 368

U

Udong 98-9

V

vacations 354
vaccinations 368
Vamana 166
vegans 342
vegetarians 342
Veun Sai 296
video 352
Vietnamese people 330
Virachey National Park 13, 296-7
visas 18, 356-7
volunteering 357
vultures 269

W

walking, see hiking
walking tours
  Angkor Thom 160, **160**
  Phnom Penh 61, **61**
Wat Kor Village 243
water 339-40, 369
waterfalls
  Ban Lung 291
  Bei Srok 292
  Bou Sraa Waterfall 298
  Chaa Ong 291
  Chambok 101
  Dak Dam Waterfall 298
  Ka Tieng 291
  Kbal Chhay Cascades 189
  Kbal Spean 172
  Kinchaan 291
  Kirivong 232
  Monorom Falls 299
  Phnom Khieu 255
  Phnom Kulen 171-2, 41
  Popokvil Falls 223
  Preah Rumkel 289
  Romanear Waterfall 299
  Tatai Waterfall 184-5
  Yak Kae Waterfall 297
weather 18, 26-7
weights 352
Western Baray 174
Western Mebon 174
wildlife
  dolphins, Irrawaddy 14, 23, 345, 348, 284, 289, **14**
  elephants 12, 299-301, **12-13**
wildlife sanctuaries & reserves
  Angkor Centre for Conservation of Biodiversity 131
  Ang Trapaeng Thmor Reserve 136
  Banteay Srei Butterfly Centre 131
  Crocodile Protection Sanctuary 185-6

Elephant Valley Project 12, 299-301, **12-13**
Keo Seima Wildlife Sanctuary 12, 304
Kulen Promtep Wildlife Sanctuary 270
Mondulkiri Elephant & Wildlife Sanctuary 301
Peam Krasaop Wildlife Sanctuary 179
Phnom Aural Wildlife Sanctuary 240
Phnom Samkos Wildlife Sanctuary 240
Phnom Tamao Wildlife Rescue Centre 100-1
Prek Toal Bird Sanctuary 134-5
wildlife watching 40, see also birdwatching
  Cambodian Gibbon Ecotours 292
  dolphins 284
  gibbons 301, 304
  Veal Krous Vulture Feeding Station 269
  Wildlife Alliance 100
  Wildlife Alliance Release Station Tours 188
wine 339
wineries 254
women travellers 357-8
work 358

Y

Yasovarman I 138
Yeak Lom Lake 13, 291-2, **13**
yoga 66, 109

Z

ziplining 40
  Angkor 154, **40**
  Koh Rong 199
  Mayura Zipline 299

Map Legend

Sights

- Beach
- Bird Sanctuary
- Buddhist
- Castle/Palace
- Christian
- Confucian
- Hindu
- Islamic
- Jain
- Jewish
- Monument
- Museum/Gallery/Historic Building
- Ruin
- Shinto
- Sikh
- Taoist
- Winery/Vineyard
- Zoo/Wildlife Sanctuary
- Other Sight

Activities, Courses & Tours

- Bodysurfing
- Diving
- Canoeing/Kayaking
- Course/Tour
- Sento Hot Baths/Onsen
- Skiing
- Snorkelling
- Surfing
- Swimming/Pool
- Walking
- Windsurfing
- Other Activity

Sleeping

- Sleeping
- Camping
- Hut/Shelter

Eating

- Eating

Drinking & Nightlife

- Drinking & Nightlife
- Cafe

Entertainment

- Entertainment

Shopping

- Shopping

Information

- Bank
- Embassy/Consulate
- Hospital/Medical
- Internet
- Police
- Post Office
- Telephone
- Toilet
- Tourist Information
- Other Information

Geographic

- Beach
- Gate
- Hut/Shelter
- Lighthouse
- Lookout
- Mountain/Volcano
- Oasis
- Park
- Pass
- Picnic Area
- Waterfall

Population

- Capital (National)
- Capital (State/Province)
- City/Large Town
- Town/Village

Transport

- Airport
- Border crossing
- Bus
- Cable car/Funicular
- Cycling
- Ferry
- Metro/MRT/MTR station
- Monorail
- Parking
- Petrol station
- Skytrain/Subway station
- Taxi
- Train station/Railway
- Tram
- Underground station
- Other Transport

Routes

- Tollway
- Freeway
- Primary
- Secondary
- Tertiary
- Lane
- Unsealed road
- Road under construction
- Plaza/Mall
- Steps
- Tunnel
- Pedestrian overpass
- Walking Tour
- Walking Tour detour
- Path/Walking Trail

Boundaries

- International
- State/Province
- Disputed
- Regional/Suburb
- Marine Park
- Cliff
- Wall

Hydrography

- River, Creek
- Intermittent River
- Canal
- Water
- Dry/Salt/Intermittent Lake
- Reef

Areas

- Airport/Runway
- Beach/Desert
- Cemetery (Christian)
- Cemetery (Other)
- Glacier
- Mudflat
- Park/Forest
- Sight (Building)
- Sportsground
- Swamp/Mangrove

Note: Not all symbols displayed above appear on the maps in this book

OUR STORY

A beat-up old car, a few dollars in the pocket and a sense of adventure. In 1972 that's all Tony and Maureen Wheeler needed for the trip of a lifetime – across Europe and Asia overland to Australia. It took several months, and at the end – broke but inspired – they sat at their kitchen table writing and stapling together their first travel guide, *Across Asia on the Cheap*. Within a week they'd sold 1500 copies. Lonely Planet was born.

Today, Lonely Planet has offices in the US, Ireland and China, with a network of over 2000 contributors in every corner of the globe. We share Tony's belief that 'a great guidebook should do three things: inform, educate and amuse'.

OUR WRITERS

Nick Ray

Siem Reap, Temples of Angkor, Northwestern Cambodia A Londoner of sorts, Nick comes from Watford, the sort of town that makes you want to travel. He currently lives in Phnom Penh and has written countless guidebooks on the countries of the Mekong region, including contributing to Lonely Planet's *Laos*, *Myanmar* and *Vietnam* books. When not writing, he is often out exploring the remote parts of the region as a location scout or line producer for the world of television and film, including anything from *Tomb Raider* to *Top Gear*. Cambodia is one of his favourite places on earth and he was excited to get back to some remote corners of the far north once more. Nick also wrote the Plan section.

Greg Bloom

South Coast Born in California and raised in the northeast United States, Greg is a freelance writer, editor, tour guide and travel planner based out of Manila and El Nido, Philippines. He got his first taste of international life at the age of 12 when he lived in Chile for a half year with his dad. He graduated from university with a degree in international development, but it was journalism that would ultimately lure him overseas. Greg began his writing career in the late '90s in Ukraine, working as a journalist and later editor-in-chief of the *Kyiv Post*, an English-language weekly. He has contributed to some 50 Lonely Planet titles, mostly in Eastern Europe and Asia. In addition to writing, Greg organises customised adventure tours in north Palawan (Philippines). Accounts of his Lonely Planet trips over the years are at www.mytripjournal.com/bloomblogs. Greg also wrote the Understand and Survival sections.

Mark Johansen

Phnom Penh, Eastern Cambodia Mark Johanson grew up in Virginia, USA, and has called five different countries home over the past decade while circling the globe reporting for British newspapers (*The Guardian*), American magazines (*Men's Journal*) and global media outlets (CNN, BBC). When not on the road, you'll find him gazing at the Andes from his current home in Santiago, Chile. Follow his adventures at www.markjohanson.com. Mark also wrote the Cambodian Kitchen chapter of the Understand section.

Published by Lonely Planet Global Limited
CRN 554153
12th edition – December 2021
ISBN 978 1 78701 670 5
© Lonely Planet 2021   Photographs © as indicated 2021
10 9 8 7 6 5 4 3 2 1
Printed in Singapore